Soil Fertility and Fertilizers

Contents

CHAPTER 13 *Agricultural Productivity and Environmental Quality* 447

Index 503

Preface

Soil Fertility and Fertilizers: An Introduction to Nutrient Management, seventh edition, was first published in 1956 under the title *Soil Fertility and Fertilizers.* Although this seventh edition has been substantially revised to reflect rapidly advancing knowledge and technologies in plant nutrition and nutrient management, the outstanding contributions of Dr. Samuel L. Tisdale (1918–1989) and Dr. Werner L. Nelson (1914–1992) will always be remembered and appreciated.

The importance of soil fertility and plant nutrition to the health and survival of all life cannot be overstated. As human populations continue to increase, human disturbance of the Earth's ecosystem to produce food and fiber will place greater demand on soils to supply essential nutrients. Therefore, it is essential that we increase our understanding of the chemical, biological, and physical properties and relationships in the soil-plant-atmosphere continuum that control nutrient availability.

The soil's native ability to supply sufficient nutrients has decreased with higher plant productivity levels associated with increased human demand for food. One of the greatest challenges of our generation will be to develop and implement soil-, crop-, and nutrient-management technologies that enhance plant productivity and the quality of the soil, water, and air. If we do not improve and/or sustain the productive capacity of our fragile soils, we cannot continue to support the food and fiber demand of our growing population.

To the Student

The goal of this book is to impart to the student a thorough understanding of plant nutrition, soil fertility, and nutrient management so that she or he can (1) describe the influence of soil biological, physical, and chemical properties and interactions on nutrient availability to crops; (2) identify plant nutrition–soil fertility problems and recommend proper corrective action; and (3) identify soil- and nutrient-management practices that maximize productivity and profitability while maintaining or enhancing the productive capacity of the soil and quality of the environment.

The specific objectives are to (1) describe how plants take up or absorb plant nutrients and how the soil system supplies these nutrients; (2) identify and describe plant-nutrient deficiency symptoms and methods used to quantify nutrient problems; (3) describe how soil organic matter, cation exchange capacity, soil pH, parent material, climate, and human activities affect nutrient availability; (4) evaluate nutrient and soil amendment materials on the basis of content, use, and effects on the soil and the crop; (5) quantify, using basic chemical principles, application rates of nutrients and amendments needed to correct plant nutrition problems in the field; (6) describe nutrient response patterns, nutrient-use efficiency, and the economics involved in nutrient use; and (7) describe and evaluate soil and nutrient management practices that either impair or sustain soil productivity and environmental quality.

To the Teacher

Motivate your students to learn by showing them how the knowledge and skills gained through the study of soil fertility will be essential for success in their careers. Use teaching methodologies that enhance their critical thinking and problem-solving skills. In addition to understanding the qualitative soil fertility and plant-nutrition relationships, students must know how to quantitatively evaluate nutrient availability and nutrient management. Environmental protection demands that nutrients be added in quantities and by methods that maximize crop productivity and recovery of the added nutrients.

Since some of the examples used in this text may not be representative of your specific region, frequently integrate additional field examples from your region to illustrate the qualitative and quantitative principles. Strongly reinforce the reality that production agriculture, sustainability, and environmental quality are compatible provided soil-, crop-, and nutrient-management technologies are used properly. Develop in your students the desire and discipline to expand beyond this text through reading and self-learning. Demand of your students what will be demanded of them after they graduate—to think, communicate, cooperate, and solve problems from an interdisciplinary perspective.

We hope your students find the text a valuable resource throughout their careers. Please feel free to provide suggestions for enhancing the effectiveness of the text as a teaching and learning aid.

John L. Havlin
James D. Beaton

CHAPTER 1

Introduction

Humans historically depended on hunting and gathering of food to sustain life. As populations grew, organized agricultural systems were needed to ensure food security (Table 1-1). Since cultures have not developed at the same rate, all of the systems shown in Table 1-1 currently exist in the world. As a result, famine has been a reality in much of the underdeveloped regions that exhibit the highest population growth rates and rely on inefficient and unproductive farming methods. In contrast, developed countries utilizing modern agricultural technologies are generally self-sufficient in food production and provide the majority of food exports to underdeveloped and developing nations.

The incidence of famine, or risk of death due to food shortage, substantially decreased over the last few years (Fig. 1-1). Unfortunately, these data do not include people severely undernourished or exhibiting various levels of nutrient deficiencies, currently estimated to be about 600 million people (Table 1-2). The number of people at risk of famine and undernourishment in Africa and Asia will likely increase over the next 50 years, although the percentage of the total population at risk will decrease. In contrast, substantial improvements in food security are projected for Latin America and Southeast Asia. Despite improvements in food security in some regions, by 2060, 640 million people, or 9% of the population in developing countries, will be at risk of famine or undernourishment.

The importance of increasing agricultural productivity to secure sufficient food for a growing population is obvious. The world's population has doubled over the last 40 years to 6 billion people, with over 9 billion projected by 2060 (Fig. 1-2). About 95% of the projected increase in population will occur in developing countries, primarily in Asia and Africa. Currently, total food production is increasing faster than world population, and the number of undernourished is declining (Fig. 1-3). By 2060 increases in global food production are projected to be 100 to 300% of 1980 levels (Table 1-3). Are sufficient land resources available to expand agriculture production to meet the food demands expected in 2060? In developing countries, for example, 3.6 billion people have access to 16 billion acres, or 0.22 persons per acre (Table 1-4). Depending on input levels, this land area could support between 6 and 33 billion people. Therefore, sufficient land area exists to meet potential food demands; however, critical non-agricultural land uses (wildlife habitat, forests, municipal, industrial, etc.) will reduce available land area for cultivation. Estimates of only 20 to 30% additional new land being brought under production illustrate the dependence on increasing productivity per unit land area. Advances in agricultural

Table 1-1 **Capability of Agricultural Systems to Produce Food and Support Population**

Agricultural System	*Cultural Stage or Time*	*Cereal Yield (t/ac)*	*World Population (millions)*	*Acres per Person*
Hunting and gathering	Paleolithic		7	
Shifting agriculture	Neolithic (10,000 years ago)	0.45	35	98.8
Medieval rotation	A.D. 500–1450	0.45	900	3.7
Livestock farming	Late 1700s	0.89	1,800	1.7
Modern agriculture	Twentieth century	1.78	4,200	0.7
	Twenty-first century	2.67	12,000	0.2

SOURCE: McCloud, 1975, *Agron J.*, 67:1.

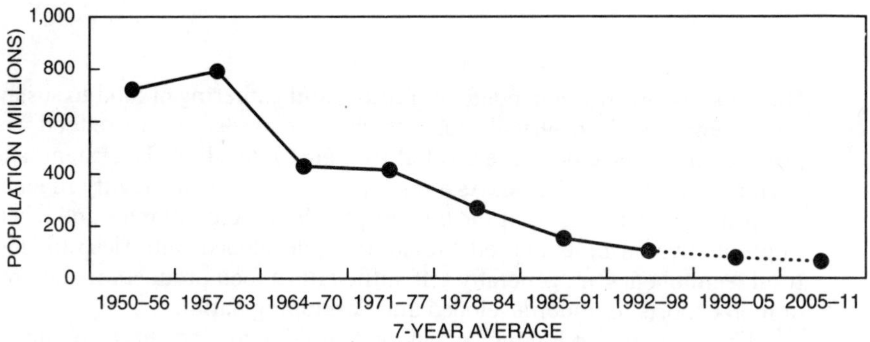

Figure 1-1 **Average world population at risk of death due to famine.** ***(Data adapted from Chen and Kates, 1994, FAO, 2001.)***

Table 1-2 **Population at Risk of Undernourishment in Underdeveloped or Developing Regions***

Region	*1980*	*2000*	*2020*	*2040*	*2060*
			Millions		
Africa	120 (26)	185 (22)	292 (21)	367 (19)	415 (18)
Latin America	36 (10)	40 (8)	39 (6)	33 (4)	24 (3)
South and Southeast Asia	321 (25)	330 (17)	330 (13)	232 (8)	130 (4)
West Asia	27 (18)	41 (16)	55 (14)	64 (12)	72 (11)
Total	504 (23)	596 (17)	716 (14)	696 (11)	641 (9)

*Numbers in parentheses are percentages of population.

SOURCE: USDA—Economic Research Service, 1996, AER-740.

production technologies must occur to enhance productivity per unit of land and ensure food security.

In the United States, the amount of farmland has remained relatively stable at approximately 1 billion acres, with about 500 million acres in cropland and pasture. Although the number of farms and producers has decreased dramatically, with a concomitant

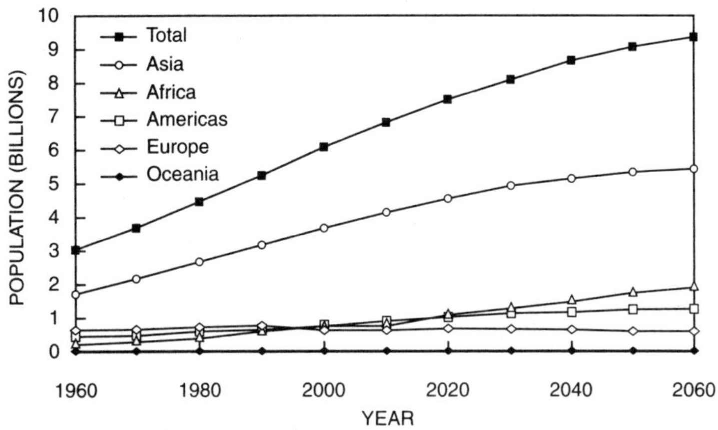

Figure 1-2 Increase in world population from 1960 to 2060. *(GeoHive, 2003, http://www.geohive.com/ index.php.)*

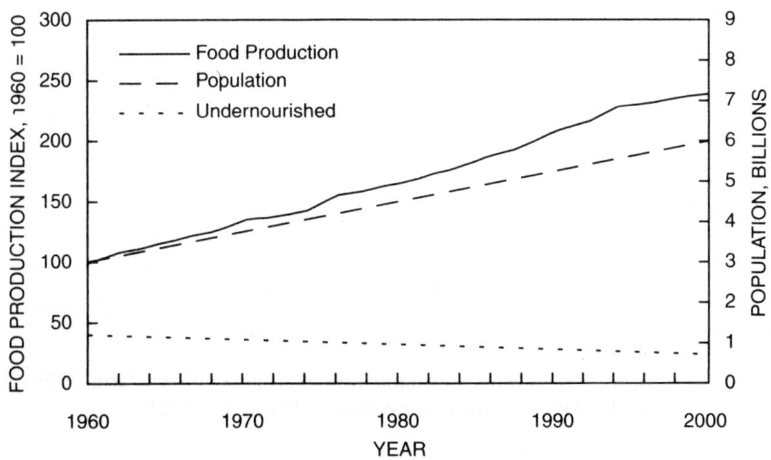

Figure 1-3 **Growth in world population and food production compared to the population of undernourished.** ***(USDA–ERS, 2003, AER 823.)***

Table 1-3 Projected Global Production of Food Commodities Through 2060

Commodity	*1980*	*2000*	*2020*	*2040*	*2060*
	*Million Tons**				
Wheat	441	603	742	861	958
Rice	249	368	480	586	659
Coarse grains	741	1,022	1,289	1,506	1,669
Animal products	82	108	138	164	184
Dairy	470	613	750	877	997
Protein feed	36	52	64	76	85
Total	2019	2,766	3,463	4,070	4,552

*Wheat, rice, and coarse grain in million tons; animal products in million tons carcass weight; dairy products in million tons whole milk equivalent; protein feed in million tons protein equivalent.
SOURCE: USDA—ERS, 1996, AER-740.

Table 1-4 Population Supporting Capacities in Developing Countries in 2000

Location	Total Land Area	Population	Current Population Supporting Capacity	Potential Population Supporting Capacity Low Inputs	Potential Population Supporting Capacity High Inputs
	Million Acres	*Millions*	*Persons per Acre*		
Africa	7,109	780	0.11	0.35	1.81
Southwest Asia	1,672	265	0.16	0.18	0.19
South America	4,372	393	0.09	0.32	2.83
Central America	672	215	0.32	0.43	1.93
Southeast Asia	2,218	1,937	0.87	1.11	2.86
Total	16,043	3,590	0.22	0.35	2.07

SOURCE: Compiled by Economic Research Service (1996).

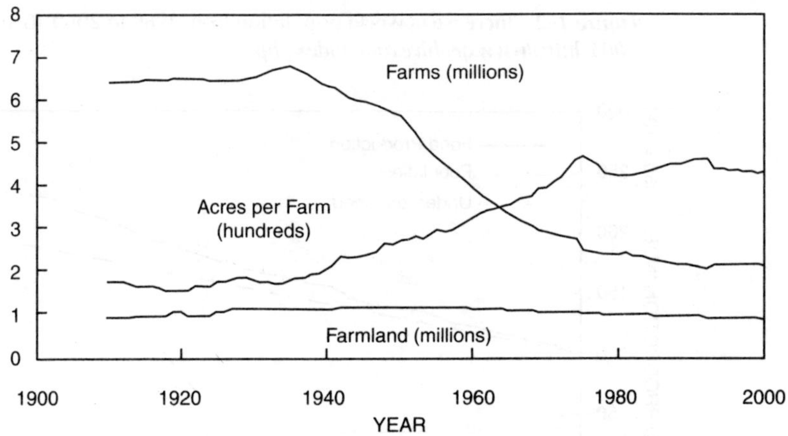

Figure 1-4 Farms, farmland, and average acres per farm, 1900–2002. *(USDA–ERS, Census of Agriculture, 1954, 1992, 2002.)*

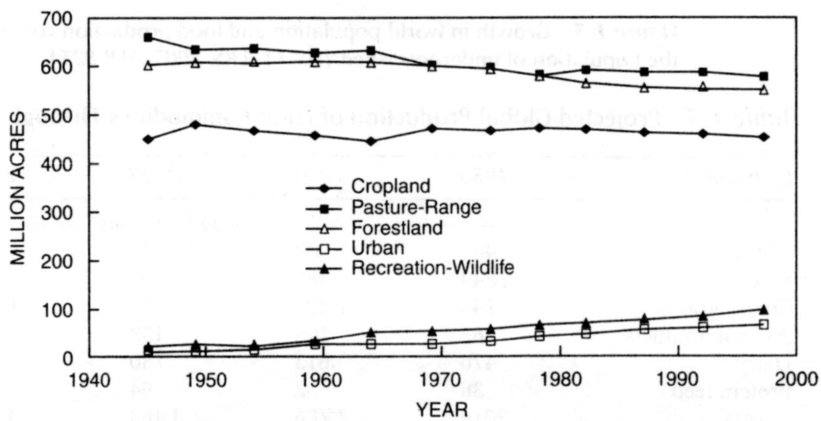

Figure 1-5 Major land uses in the United States. *(USDA–ERS, 2003, Ag Handbook No. AH722.)*

increase in farm size, the total land area used for food and fiber production will not likely increase (Figs. 1-4 and 1-5). Currently the United States produces 23, 32, and 51% of the world's wheat, coarse grains, and soybeans, accounting for 33, 65, and 30% of the world trade, respectively. The United States currently supplies about 50% of the world food aid in cereal grains. Therefore, substantial increases in productivity per acre will be needed if the United States is to remain a major food exporter, which is essential to assure world food security.

Historically in the United States, crop yields have increased greatly over the last half-century (Fig. 1-6). This remarkable achievement is directly related to the development and adoption of agricultural technology over the last 60 years (Fig. 1-7). The principal factors contributing to higher crop yields include development of improved varieties

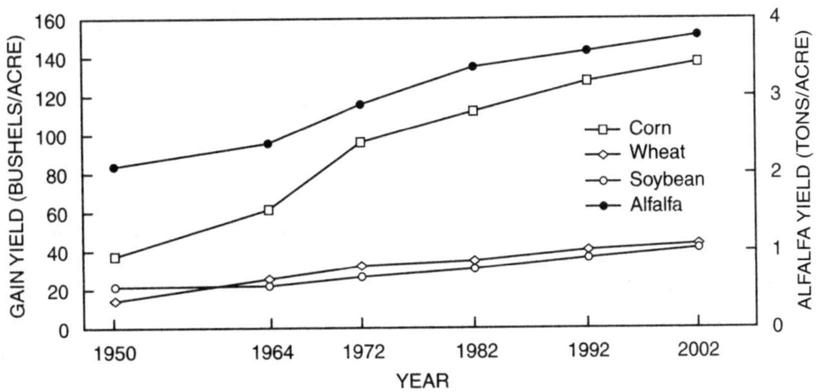

Figure 1-6 Average yields of major crops in the United States, 1950–2002. *(USDA–ERS.)*

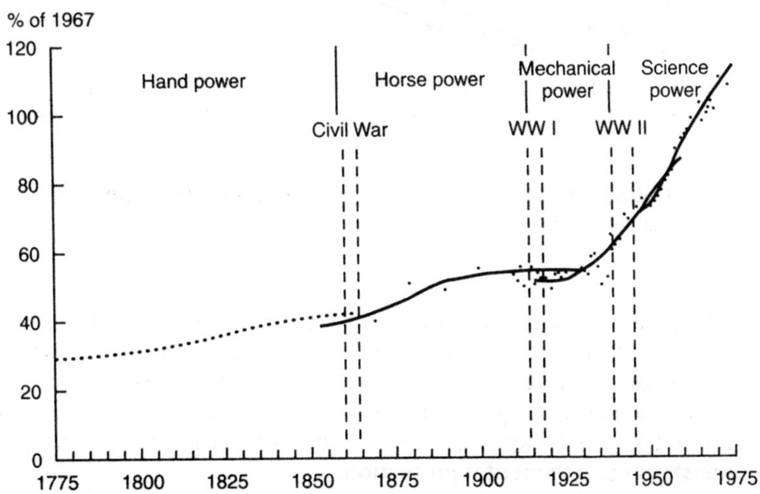

Figure 1-7 U.S. agricultural productivity growth during the past 200 years. *(Farrell, 1981,* Productivity in U.S. Agriculture, *ESS Report No. AGESS810422, USDA.)*

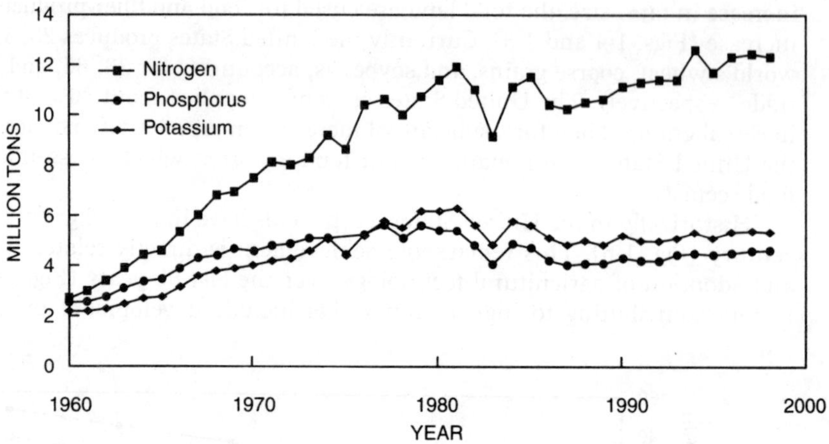

Figure 1-8 **U.S. commercial fertilizer use, 1960–1998. *(USDA–ERS, 2003,* Ag Handbook No. AH722.*)***

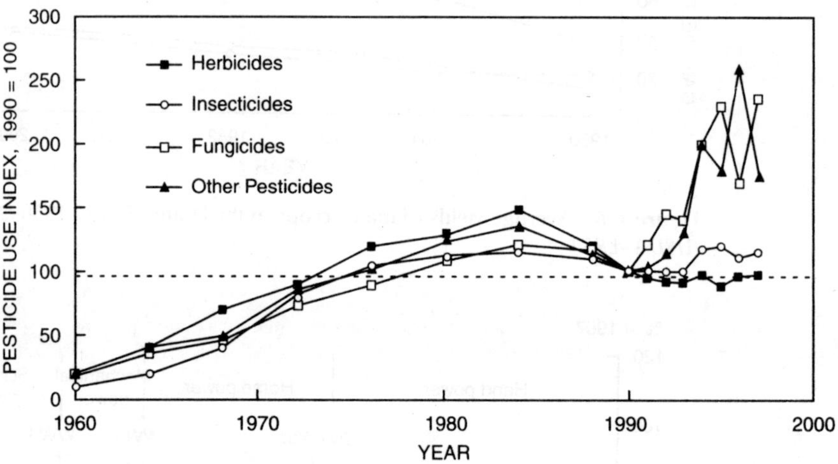

Figure 1-9 **Total pesticide use on major crops, 1960–1997. *(USDA–ERS, 2003,* Statistical Bulletin No. 969.*)***

and hybrids, nutrient and pest management, soil and water conservation, and cultural practices. Development and use of fertilizer and pesticides is directly related to increased crop productivity in the United States (Figs. 1-8 and 1-9). Since 1980, concerns for environmental quality have resulted in the development and adoption of improved input management technologies that have stabilized nutrient and pesticide use and provided important environmental protection.

Producer adoption of many agronomic technologies developed since 1950 has increased crop productivity (Table 1-5). These data demonstrate that the technologies contributing most to the increase in average corn yields from 32 to 100 bushels per acre (bu/a) were nitrogen fertilization, breeding/ genetics, weed control, and other cultural practices. In contrast, decreased

Table 1-5 **Corn Yield Increases with Changing Production Practices in Minnesota, 1930–1979**

Cultural Practice or Yield Limiting Factor	*Contribution to 1979 Yield* *bu/a*	*kg/ha*	*% Net Gain/Loss*
Pre-1930 Yield Levels	*32.1*	*2,012*	—
Sources of Productivity Gains/Losses			
Hybrids			
Double crosses	5.9	371	9
Three-way crosses	0.5	28	1
Single crosses	3.7	235	6
Genetic gain	29.1	1,825	43
Fertilizer N	31.9	2,003	47
Plant population	14.4	905	21
Herbicides	15.5	975	23
Row spacing	2.8	173	4
Planting date	5.8	364	8
Drilling vs. hill drop	5.1	322	8
Fall plowing	3.6	224	5
Rotations			
Soybeans	7.7	484	11
Alfalfa/clovers	-2.2	-136	-3
Sweet clover	-5.1	-318	-7
Interference effect	-4.6	-291	-7
Manure	-10.1	-633	-15
Organic matter	-9.1	-571	-13
Insects			
Corn borer	-3.5	-220	-5
Corn rootworm	-2.3	-145	-3
Soil erosion	-6.5	-345	-8
Unidentified negative factors	-15.5	-975	-23
Net gain	*68.1*	*4,275*	—
1977–1979 Yield Level	*100.2*	*6,287*	—

SOURCE: Cardwell, 1982, *Agron J.*, 74:984.

use of manure and declining organic matter (OM) contributed to yield loss. Evaluation of the yield gains and losses shows that if losses had not occurred, yields would have been 158 bu/a instead of 100 bu/a. Elimination of fertilizer would decrease yields 40 to 90%, depending on the crop, soil, and climatic region. If fertilizer were not used, about 30 to 40% more land would be needed. Therefore, growers must take advantage of technologies that increase productivity, as well as those that minimize productivity loss, and encroachment on high-risk marginal lands.

Yield Limiting Factors

Obtaining the maximum production potential of a particular crop depends on the growing season environment and the skill of the producer to identify and eliminate or minimize factors that reduce yield potential. More than 50 factors affect crop growth and yield potential (Table 1-6).

Table 1-6 Factors Affecting Crop Yield Potential

Climate Factors	*Soil Factors*	*Crop Factors*
Precipitation	Organic matter	Crop species/variety
Quantity	Texture	Planting date
Distribution	Structure	Seeding rate and geometry
Air temperature	Cation exchange capacity	Row spacing
Relative humidity	Base saturation	Seed quality
Light	Slope and topography	Evapotranspiration
Quantity	Soil temperature	Water availability
Intensity	Soil management factors	Nutrition
Duration	Tillage	Pests
Altitude/latitude	Drainage	Insects
Wind	Others	Diseases
Velocity	Depth (root zone)	Weeds
Distribution		Harvest efficiency
CO_2 concentration		

Although the producer cannot control many of the climate factors, most of the soil and crop factors can and must be managed to maximize productivity.

For maximum yield potential, plants must utilize a high percentage of the available solar energy. Based on available solar energy, the maximum potential yield for most crops far exceeds current yield levels. For example, maximum potential yields are nearly 600, 250, and 300 bushels per acre of corn, soybean, and wheat, respectively. Worldwide, the dominant stresses reducing crop yield potential are related to plant available water, temperature, and nutrient availability (Table 1-7). Environment and nutrient-related stresses occur on about 55% and 20% of the land area, respectively.

For high yields, controllable and uncontrollable factors must operate in unison, because many of them are interrelated. Most factors influencing yield potential interact with each other to either increase or decrease plant growth and/or yield (Chapter 11). The challenge

Table 1-7 Primary Soil-Related Stresses That Reduce Crop Yield Potential

	Million Sq. Miles	*% of Total*
Continuous moisture stress	14.1	27.9
Continuous low temperatures	8.4	16.7
Seasonal moisture stress	4.0	7.9
Low nutrient-holding capacity	3.0	6.0
Shallow soils	2.9	5.6
Excessive nutrient leaching	1.7	3.4
High aluminum (soil acidity)	1.6	3.1
Low moisture and nutrient status	1.4	2.7
Low water-holding capacity	1.3	2.6
Other stresses	10.5	20.8
Few constraints	1.6	3.1
Total	50.5	99.8

SOURCE: USDA—ERS, 2003, Ag Economic Report No. 823.

of a producer is to accurately identify all yield-limiting factors and eliminate or minimize the influence of those that can be managed. The importance of this principle was identified in the efforts of 19th-century-scientists Justus von Leibig and Carl Sprengel. The *Law of the Minimum* is as follows:

> Every field contains a maximum of one or more and a minimum of one or more nutrients. With this minimum, be it lime, potash, phosphoric acid, magnesia, or any other nutrient, the yields stand in direct relation. It is the factor that governs and controls . . . yields. Should this minimum be lime . . . yield . . . will remain and be no greater even though the amount of potash, silica, phosphoric acid, etc . . . be increased a hundred fold.

All successful agricultural producers use this important principle, either knowingly or unknowingly. For example, a producer may have planted the correct variety at the optimum time and population and may have applied all of the optimum nutrients using the most efficient methods, but still might not attain maximum yield potential because plant available water was the most limiting factor (Fig. 1-10). Thus, until the producer minimizes water as a limiting factor to yield potential, yield response to management of any other factor(s) will be substantially less than if plant available water were nonlimiting. Figure 1-11 graphically illustrates the Law of the Minimum.

Sufficient nutrient availability is required to realize maximum yield potential. Before thoroughly discussing the complex chemical, biological, and physical factors of soil that influence the supply of nutrients to plants, as well as nutrient management strategies to optimize crop productivity, a brief review of the nutrients required for plant growth is necessary.

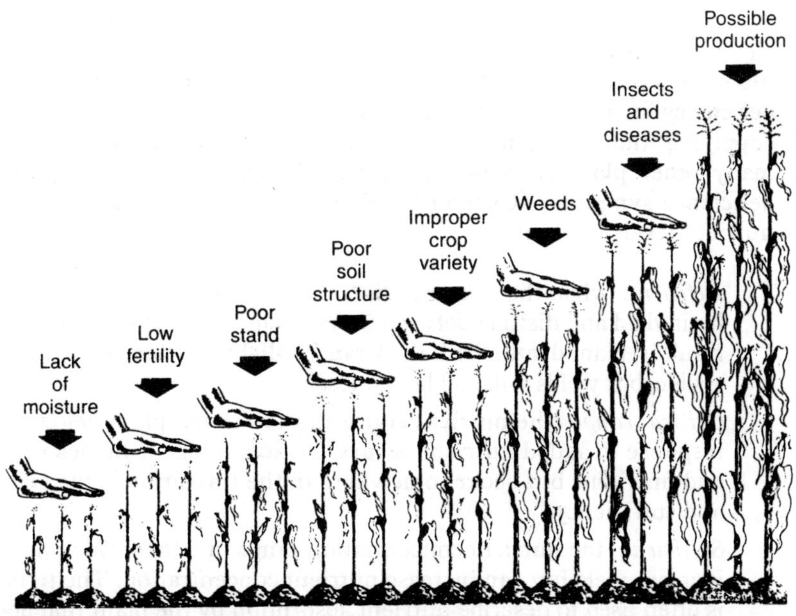

Figure 1-10 **Leibig's Law of the Minimum states that the most limiting factor determines yield potential. Producers should minimize or eliminate the most limiting factor first, then the second most limiting factor, and so forth. Only in this manner can maximum yield potential be achieved *(Source: Potash and Phosphate Institute)*.**

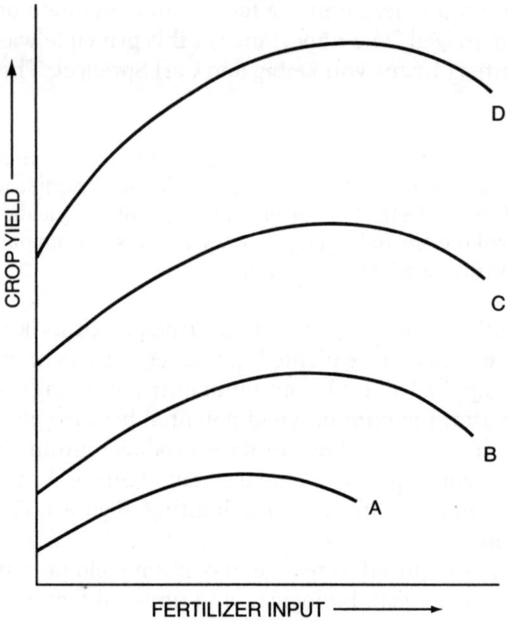

Figure 1-11 **Yield response to nitrogen (N) fertilizer with water, phosphorus (P), and seeding rate limiting yield potential (A); with only P and seeding rate limiting yield potential (B); with only seeding rate limiting yield potential (C); and with no manageable factors limiting yield potential (D).**

Elements in Plant Nutrition

A mineral element is considered essential to plant growth and development if the element is involved in plant metabolic functions and the plant cannot complete its life cycle without the element. Usually the plant exhibits a visual symptom indicating a deficiency in a specific nutrient, which normally can be corrected or prevented by supplying that nutrient. Visual nutrient deficiency symptoms can be caused by many other plant stresses; therefore, caution should be exercised when diagnosing deficiency symptoms (Chapter 9). The following terms are commonly used to describe nutrient levels in plants:

Deficient: when the concentration of an essential element is low enough to severely limit yield and distinct deficiency symptoms are visible. Extreme deficiencies can result in plant death. With moderate or slight deficiencies, symptoms may not be visible, but yields will still be reduced.

Critical range: the nutrient concentration in the plant below which a yield response to added nutrient occurs. Critical levels or ranges vary among plants and nutrients but occur somewhere in the transition between nutrient deficiency and sufficiency.

Sufficient: the nutrient concentration range in which added nutrient will not increase yield but can increase nutrient concentration. The term *luxury consumption* is often used to describe nutrient absorption by the plant that does not influence yield.

Excessive or toxic: when the concentration of essential or other elements is high enough to reduce plant growth and yield. Excessive nutrient concentration can cause an imbalance in other essential nutrients, which can also reduce yield.

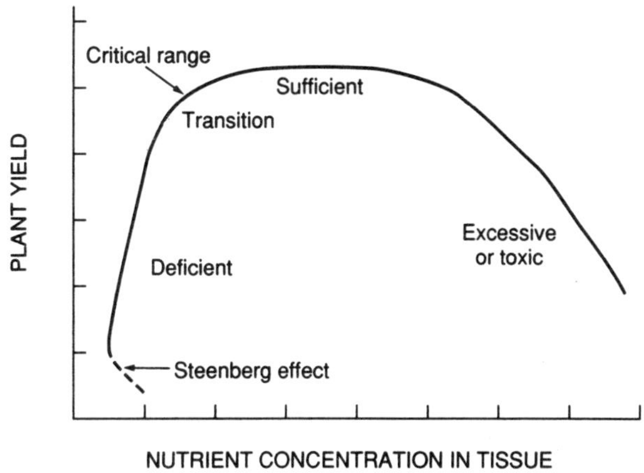

Figure 1-12 **Relationship between essential plant nutrient concentration and plant growth or yield. As nutrient concentration increases toward the critical level, plant yield increases. Above the critical level the plant contains sufficient levels for normal growth and can continue to absorb nutrients without increasing yield (luxury consumption). Excessive absorption of a nutrient or element can be toxic to the plant and reduce yield or cause plant death.**

In Figure 1-12, yield is severely affected when a nutrient is deficient, and when the nutrient deficiency is corrected, growth increases more rapidly than nutrient concentration. Under severe deficiency, rapid increases in yield with added nutrient can cause a small decrease in nutrient concentration. This is called the Steenberg effect (Fig. 1-12) and results from dilution of the nutrient in the plant by rapid plant growth. When the concentration reaches the critical range, plant yield is generally maximized. Nutrient sufficiency occurs over a wide concentration range, where yield is unaffected. Increases in nutrient concentration above the critical range indicate that the plant is absorbing nutrients above that needed for maximum yield, commonly called *luxury consumption*. Elements absorbed in excessive quantities can reduce plant yield directly through toxicity or indirectly by reducing concentrations of other nutrients below their critical ranges.

Seventeen elements are considered essential to plant growth (Table 1-8). Carbon (C), hydrogen (H), and oxygen (O) are not considered mineral nutrients but are the most abundant elements in plants. The photosynthetic process in green leaves converts CO_2 and H_2O into simple carbohydrates from which amino acids, sugars, proteins, nucleic acid, and other organic compounds are synthesized. Despite recent increases, the supply of CO_2 is relatively constant. The supply of H_2O rarely limits photosynthesis directly but does so indirectly through the various effects resulting from moisture stress.

The remaining 14 essential elements are classified as macronutrients and micronutrients, and the classification is based on their relative abundance in plants (Table 1-8). The macronutrients are nitrogen (N), phosphorus (P), potassium (K), sulfur (S), calcium (Ca), and magnesium (Mg). Compared with the macronutrients, the concentrations of the eight micronutrients—iron (Fe), zinc (Zn), manganese (Mn), copper (Cu), boron (B), chloride (Cl), molybdenum (Mo), and nickel (Ni)—are very small. Four additional elements—sodium (Na), cobalt (Co), vanadium (Va), and silicon (Si)—have been established as essential micronutrients in some plants. Micronutrients are often referred to as minor elements, but this label does not mean that they are less important than macronutrients. Micronutrient deficiency or toxicity can reduce plant yield just as macronutrient deficiency or toxicity does.

Although aluminum (Al) is not an essential plant nutrient, Al in plants can be high when soils contain relatively large amounts of Al (Chapter 3). In fact, plants absorb many nonessential elements, and more than 60 elements have been identified in plant materials. When plant material is burned, the remaining plant ash contains all of the essential and nonessential mineral elements except C, H, O, N, and S, which are volatilized as gases.

Table 1-8 **Relative and Average Plant Nutrient Concentrations**

Nutrient		*Concentration in Plants**		
Name	*Symbol*	*Relative*	*Average*	*Classification*
Hydrogen	H	60,000,000	6 %	
Oxygen	O	30,000,000	45 %	
Carbon	C	30,000,000	45 %	
Nitrogen	N	1,000,000	1.5 %	
Potassium	K	400,000	1.0 %	Macronutrients
Phosphorus	P	30,000	0.2 %	
Calcium	Ca	200,000	0.5 %	
Magnesium	Mg	100,000	0.2 %	
Sulfur	S	30,000	0.2 %	
Chloride	Cl	3,000	100 ppm (0.01 %)	
Iron	Fe	2,000	100 ppm	
Boron	B	2,000	20 ppm	
Manganese	Mn	1,000	50 ppm	Micronutrients
Zinc	Zn	300	20 ppm	
Copper	Cu	100	6 ppm	
Molybdenum	Mo	1	0.1 ppm	
Nickel	Ni	0.1	0.01 ppm	

*Concentration expressed on a dry matter weight basis.

Plant nutrient content is affected by many factors including soil, climate, crop variety, and management. Because many biological and chemical reactions occur with nutrients in soils, plants do not absorb all of the nutrients applied, regardless of nutrient source. Proper management can maximize the proportion of applied nutrient absorbed by the plant (Chapter 10). As plants absorb nutrients from the soil, complete their life cycle, and die, the nutrients in the plant residue are returned to the soil. These plant nutrients are subject to the same biological and chemical reactions as nutrients applied as fertilizer and waste materials. Although this cycle varies considerably among nutrients, understanding nutrient dynamics in the soil-plant-atmosphere system is essential to successful nutrient management.

The remaining chapters will detail our current knowledge of soil fertility and nutrient management. Use of this knowledge to identify nutrient availability problems and provide economically and environmentally sound nutrient-management recommendations will be essential to a world with a secure supply of safe nutritious food, fiber, and other agricultural commodities.

Study Questions

1. Assess the risk of famine in the world over the next fifty years. What will the world population be in 2050?
2. Crop yields have increased more in the last fifty years than in the two hundred years before 1950. What factors are related to the increased yields since 1950?
3. Using Tables 1-2 and 1-3, plot the total food production and total number of people at risk of hunger projected over the next sixty years. What can you conclude?

4. Using Figure 1-5, identify which land uses have increased at the expense of forests and rangelands.
5. In Table 1-7, prioritize the climate, soil, and crop factors limiting crop yield potential from most to least effect on reducing yield. Which of these factors can be managed?
6. Define the Law of the Minimum and provide an example.
7. List the essential nutrients required in plants.
8. Crop yields have been increasing with time because of advances in tillage, varieties, pest control, fertilization, and so on. What factor(s) will *ultimately* limit further yield increases?
9. List three factors that would cause the difference between the response curves in Figure 1-11.
10. Among the environmental factors limiting crop response to nutrients, which is probably the most easily and inexpensively changed?

Selected References

Epstein, E. 1972. *Mineral nutrition of plants: Principles and perspectives.* New York: John Wiley & Sons.

Mengel, K., and E. A. Kirkby. 1987. *Principles of plant nutrition.* Bern, Switzerland: International Potash Institute.

Römheld, V., and H. Marscher. 1991. Function of micronutrients in plants. In J. J. Mortredt et al. (Eds.), *Micronutrients in agriculture. No. 4.* Madison, Wis.: Soil Science Society of America.

Russel, D. A., and G. G. Williams. 1977. History of chemical fertilizer development. *SSSAJ.* 41: 260–65.

Viets, F. G. 1977. A perspective on two centuries of progress in soil fertility and plant nutrition. *SSSAJ.* 41: 242–49.

CHAPTER 2

Basic Soil-Plant Relationships

The interaction of numerous physical, chemical, and biological properties in soils controls plant nutrient availability. Understanding these processes and how they are influenced by environmental conditions during the growing season enables us to optimize nutrient availability and plant productivity. The purpose of this chapter is to provide a review of basic chemical reactions in soils, ion movement in soil solution, and ion uptake by plants.

Nutrient supply to plant roots is a very dynamic process (Fig. 2-1). Plants nutrients (cations and anions) are *absorbed* from the soil solution and release small quantities of ions (H^+, OH^-, and HCO_3^-) back to the solution (reactions 1 and 2). As plants absorb nutrients, the nutrient concentration in the soil solution decreases. As a result, several chemical and biological reactions occur to *buffer* or resupply the soil solution. The specific reaction that occurs depends on the specific cation or anion. Ions *adsorbed* to the surface of soil minerals *desorb* from these surfaces to resupply the soil solution (reaction 3). Ion exchange (*adsorption* and *desorption*) in soil is an important chemical reaction to plant nutrient availability. Soils also contain minerals that can *dissolve* to resupply the soil solution (reaction 6). Addition of nutrients or ions through fertilization or other inputs increases ion concentration in the soil solution. Although some of the added ions remain in solution, some are *adsorbed* to mineral surfaces (reaction 4) or *precipitated* as solid minerals (reaction 5).

As soil microorganisms degrade plant residues they can absorb ions from the soil solution into their tissues (reaction 7). When microbes or other organisms die, they release nutrients back to the soil solution (reaction 8). Microbial reactions are important to plant nutrient availability as well as other properties related to soil productivity. Microbial activity is dependent on adequate energy supply from organic C (i.e., crop residues), inorganic ion availability, and numerous environmental conditions. Plant roots and soil organisms utilize O_2 and respire CO_2 through metabolic activity (reactions 9 and 10). As a result, CO_2 concentration in the soil air is greater than in the atmosphere. Diffusion of gases in soils decreases dramatically with increasing soil water content.

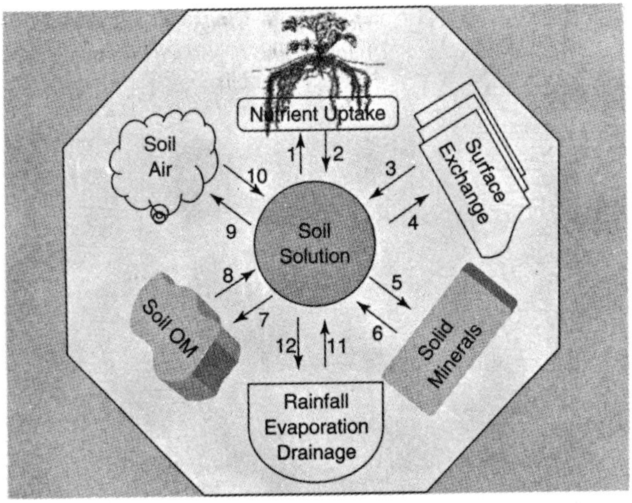

Figure 2-1 **Diagram of the various soil components that influence plant nutrient concentration in the soil solution.**

Numerous environmental factors and human activities can influence ion concentration in soil solution, which interacts with the mineral and biological processes in soils (reactions 11 and 12). For example, adding P fertilizer to soil initially increases the $H_2PO_4^-$ concentration in soil solution. With time, the $H_2PO_4^-$ concentration will decrease with plant uptake (reaction 1), $H_2PO_4^-$ adsorption on mineral surfaces (reaction 4), and P mineral precipitation (reaction 5).

All of these processes and reactions are important to plant nutrient availability; however, depending on the specific nutrient, some processes are more important than others. For example, microbial processes are more important to N and S availability than mineral surface exchange reactions, whereas the opposite is true for K, Ca, and Mg. These chemical and biological processes are complex, and only their general description and importance to plant nutrient availability are presented.

Ion Exchange in Soils

Cation and anion exchange in soils occurs on surfaces of clay minerals, inorganic compounds, organic matter (OM), and roots (Fig. 2-2). Ion exchange is a reversible process by which a cation or anion adsorbed on the surface is exchanged with another cation or anion in the liquid phase. Cation exchange is generally considered to be more important, since the *cation exchange capacity* (CEC) is much larger than the *anion exchange capacity* (AEC) of most agricultural soils. Ion exchange reactions in soils are very important to plant nutrient availability and retention in soil. Thus, it is essential that we understand the origin of the surface charge on soil minerals and OM.

Cation Exchange

Solid materials in soils comprise about 50% of the volume, with the remaining volume occupied by water and air. The solid portion comprises both inorganic minerals and

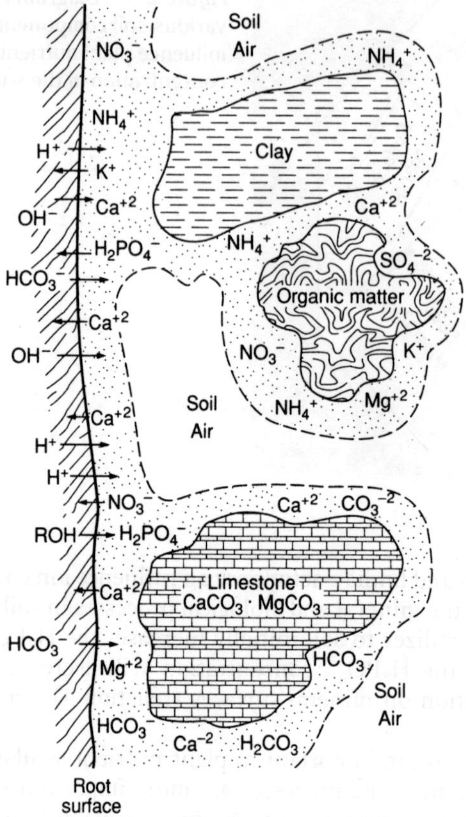

Figure 2-2 **Diagram of the mineral and organic exchange surfaces in soils.**

OM in various stages of decay and humification. The inorganic fraction consists of sand, silt, and clay particles. The clay fraction primarily consists of aluminosilicate minerals comprised of sheets of layers of silica (Si) tetrahedra and aluminum (Al) octahedra (Fig. 2-3). The structure of a Si tetrahedra is one Si^{+4} cation bonded to four O^{-2} anions, whereas the Al octahedra is one Al^{+3} cation bonded to six OH^{-} anions. The long sheets or layers of tetrahedra and octahedra are bonded together to form the aluminosilicate or clay minerals.

The clay minerals exist in 1:1, 2:1, and 2:1:1 forms (Fig. 2-4 and Fig. 2-5). Kaolinite is the most common 1:1 clay and is composed of one Si sheet and one Al sheet (Fig. 2-4). The 2:1 clays are composed of an Al octahedral layer between two Si tetrahedral layers. Examples of 2:1 clays are mica, montmorillonite, and vermiculite (Fig. 2-5). Chlorites are 2:1:1 aluminosilicates commonly found in soils. This clay mineral consists of an interlayer Al (acid soils) or Mg (basic soils) hydroxide sheet in addition to the 2:1 structure referred to previously.

Clay minerals exhibit negative (CEC) and positive (AEC) surface charge. The major source of negative charge arises from replacement of either the tetrahedral Si^{+4} or octahedral Al^{+3} cations with cations of lower charge. Cation replacement in minerals is called *isomorphic substitution* and occurs predominately in the 2:1 minerals, with very

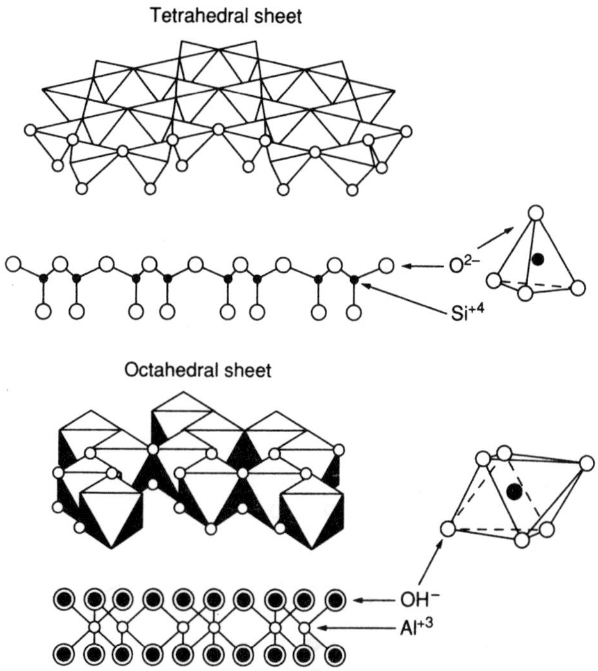

Figure 2-3 **Chemical structure of Si tetrahedra, Al octahedra, and the tetrahedral and octahedral sheets. *(Adapted from Sposito, 1989,* The Chemistry of Soils, *Oxford University Press.)***

little substitution in the 1:1 minerals. Isomorphic substitution occurs during the formation of these minerals and is largely unaffected by present environmental conditions.

In mica, substitution of Al^{+3} for one out of every four Si^{+4} cations in the tetrahedral layer results in an increase of one negative (−) charge. In montmorillonite, Mg^{+2} or Fe^{+2} replaces some of the octahedral Al^{+3}, again resulting in an increase of one charge for each substitution. Compare the unsubstituted 2:1 pyrophyllite mineral in Figure 2-4 with the isomorphic substitution in the 2:1 mica and montmorillonite minerals in Figure 2-5. In the 2:1 vermiculite, isomorphic substitution occurs in both the octahedral and tetrahedral layers.

The location of the isomorphic substitution (tetrahedral, octahedral, or both) imparts specific properties to the clay minerals that affect the quantity of (−) surface charge or CEC (Table 2-1). For example, isomorphic substitution in the tetrahedral layer locates the negative charge closer to the mineral surface compared with octahedral substitution. The high (−) surface charge combined with the unique geometry of the tetrahedral layers allows K^+ cations to neutralize the (−) charge between two 2:1 layers (Fig. 2-5). The resulting mica mineral exhibits a lower c-spacing, and the mineral is considered "collapsed," with very little of the (−) surface charge available to attract cations. Thus, mica has a lower CEC than montmorillonite because the interlayer surfaces are not exposed (Table 2-1).

The (−) charge associated with isomorphic substitution is uniformly distributed over the surface of the clay minerals and is considered a *permanent charge* and unaffected by solution pH (Fig. 2-6). Another source of charge is associated with *edge charge* of the clay minerals (Fig. 2-7). The quantity of negative (−) or positive (+) charge on the edges depends on soil solution pH. The edge charge is called a *pH-dependent charge*. Under low pH the edge is (+) charged because of the excess H^+ ions associated with the exposed

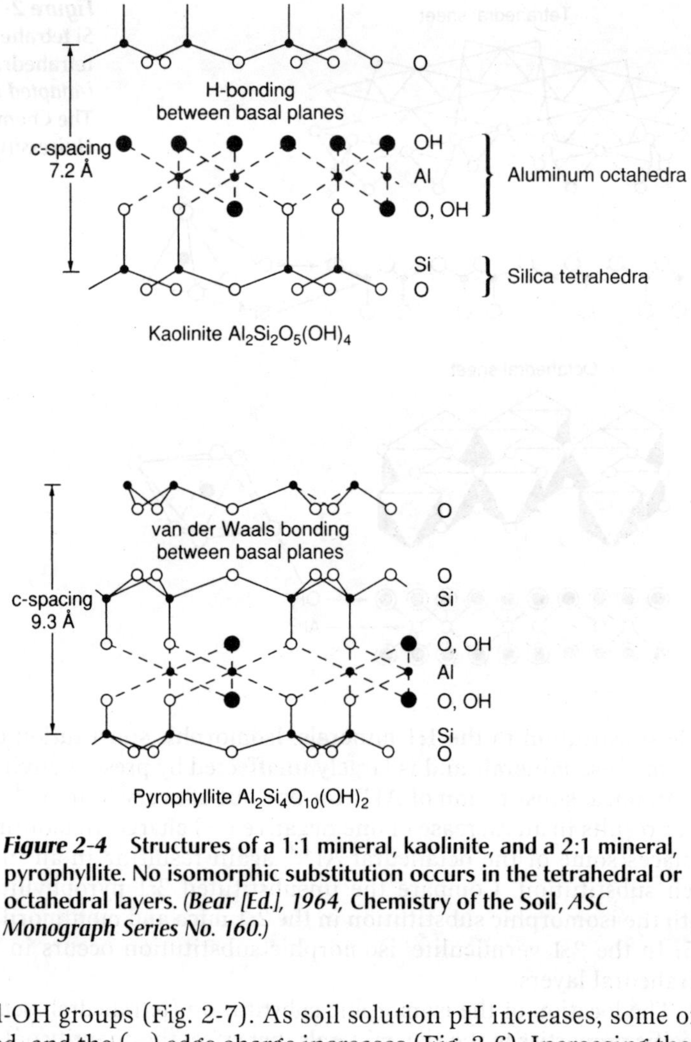

Figure 2-4 **Structures of a 1:1 mineral, kaolinite, and a 2:1 mineral, pyrophyllite. No isomorphic substitution occurs in the tetrahedral or octahedral layers.** ***(Bear [Ed.], 1964,*** **Chemistry of the Soil,** ***ASC Monograph Series No. 160.)***

Si-OH and Al-OH groups (Fig. 2-7). As soil solution pH increases, some of the H^+ ions are neutralized, and the (−) edge charge increases (Fig. 2-6). Increasing the pH above pH 7.0 results in a nearly complete removal of H^+ ions on the Si-OH and Al-OH groups, which maximizes the (−) edge charge. Only about 5 to 10% of the (−) charge on 2:1 clays is pH dependent, whereas 50% or more of the charge developed on 1:1 clay minerals is pH dependent.

Another source of pH-dependent charge is associated with soil OM (Fig. 2-8). Most of the (−) charge originates from the dissociation of H^+ from carboxylic acid and phenolic acid groups. As pH increases, some of these H^+ ions are neutralized, increasing the (−) surface charge.

Quantifying CEC and AEC

CEC is one of the most important soil chemical properties influencing nutrient availability and retention in soil. Soil CEC represents the total quantity of (−) surface charge on minerals and OM available to attract cations in solution. CEC is expressed as milliequivalents

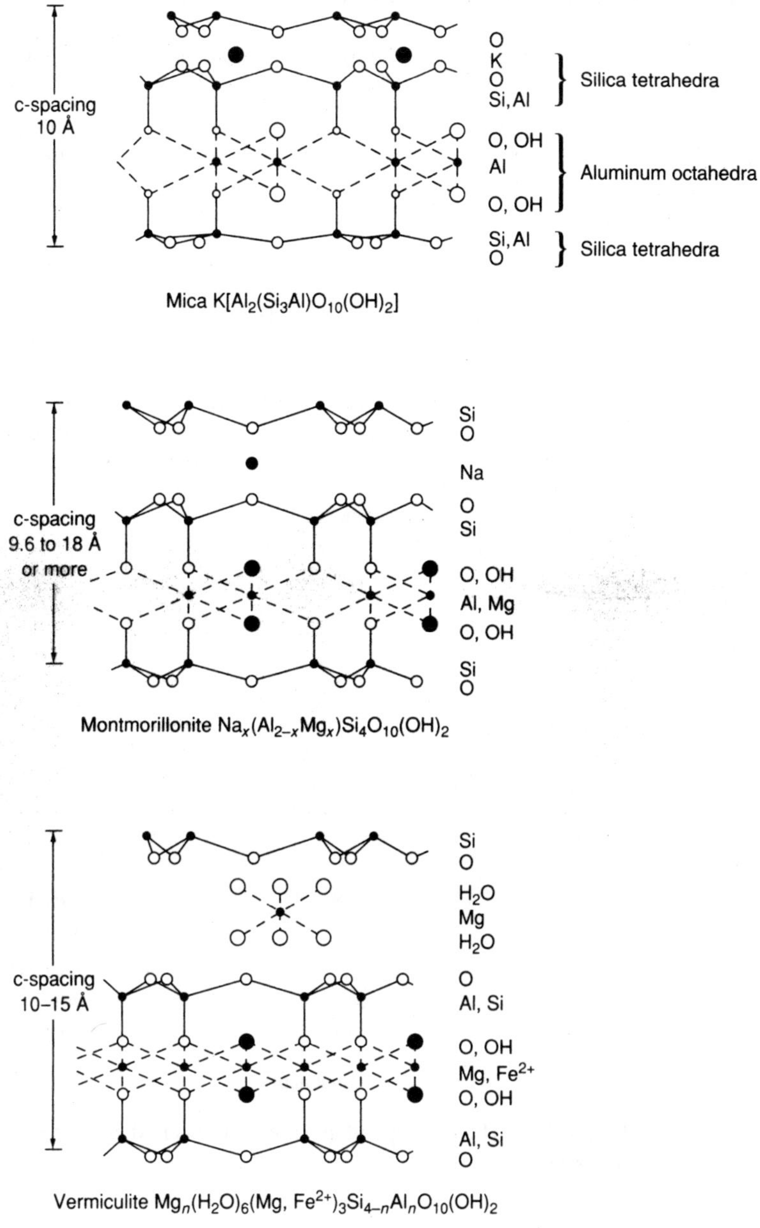

Figure 2-5 **Structures of mica, montmorillonite, and vermiculite, all 2:1 minerals. Isomorphic substitution occurs in the tetrahedral and octahedral layers.** ***(Bear [Ed.], 1964,*** **Chemistry of the Soil,** ***ACS Monograph Series No. 160.)***

Table 2-1 **Common Aluminosilicate Minerals in Soils**

Clay Mineral	*Layer Type*	*Layer Charge*	*c-Spacing (A)*	*CEC (meq/100 g)*	*pH-Dependent Charge*
Kaolinite	1:1	0	7.2	1–10	High
Mica (Illite)	2:1	1.0	10	20–40	Low
Vermiculite	2:1	0.8	10–15	120–150	Low
Montmorillonite	2:1	0.4	Variable	80–120	Low
Intergrade*	2:1:1	1.0	14	20–40	High
Organic matter				100–300	High

*Intergrade is a 2:1:1 mineral with a Mg or Al hydroxide interlayer.

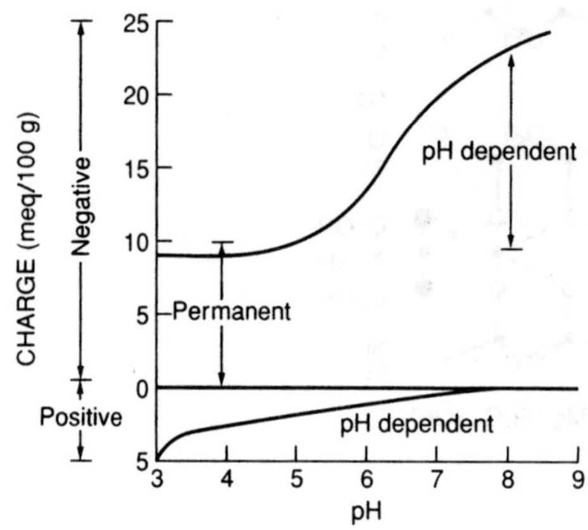

Figure 2-6 **Permanent and pH-dependent charge associated with clay minerals.**

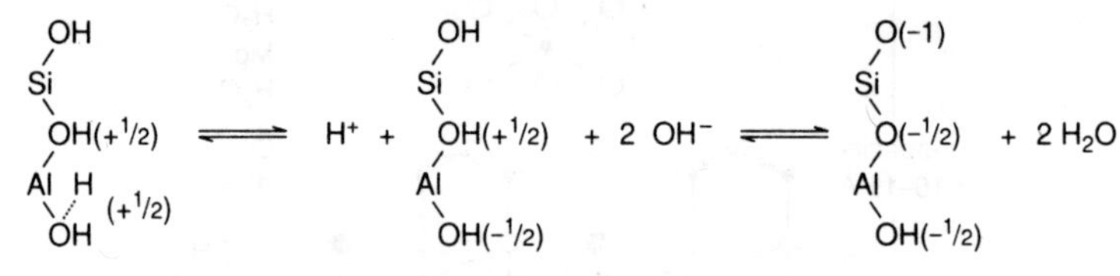

Figure 2-7 **The pH-dependent charge associated with broken edges of kaolinite.**

of (−) charge per 100 g of oven-dried soil (meq/100 g).[1] The meq unit is used instead of mass because CEC represents both the meq/100 g of (−) charge and the total meq/100 g of cations adsorbed to the CEC. Since the specific cations associated with CEC will vary, it is more meaningful to simply quantify the total charge involved.

[1]The SI unit system is used by the scientific community. Thus, meq/100 g becomes cmol/kg in SI units, representing the centimoles (cmol) of charge per kilogram of soil. The conversion is 1 meq/100 g soil = 1 cmol/kg. We use meq/100 g in this text because most soil-testing laboratories in the United States use meq/100 g for CEC measurement.

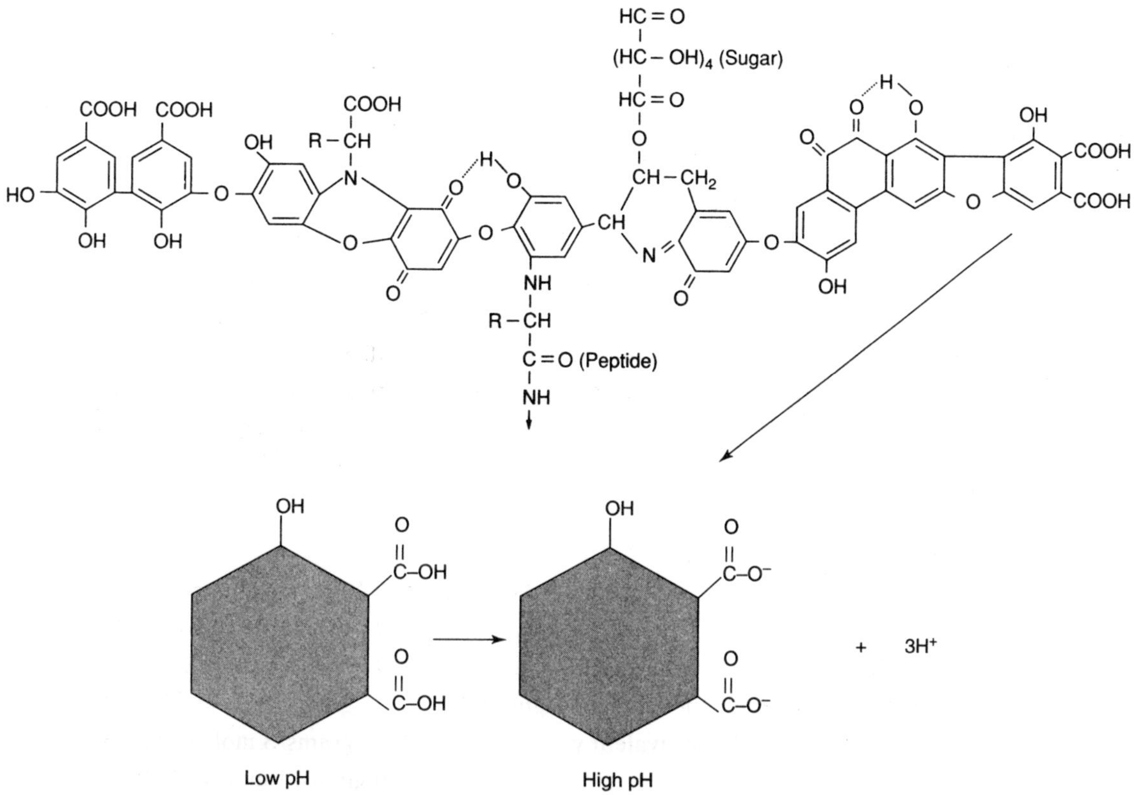

Figure 2-8 **Suggested structure for humic acid in soil. The COOH and OH groups are the pH-dependent sites, where increasing pH increases (−) sites or CEC and decreasing pH increases (+) sites or AEC.**

The definitions of equivalents and equivalent weight are as follows:

- Atomic weight: mass (grams) of 6×10^{23} atoms of the substance. One mole (m) of substance is 6×10^{23} atoms, molecules, ions, compounds, and so on; therefore, units of atomic weight are grams per mole (g/m). A mole exactly represents 6×10^{23} atoms, ions, compounds, and so on, just like the word *dozen* exactly represents 12!
- Equivalent weight: mass (grams) of a substance (e.g., cation, anion, or compound) that will react with 1 gram of H^+, or 1 mole (6×10^{23}) of charges; therefore, units of equivalent weight are grams per equivalent (g/eq).

The definitions of atomic weight and equivalent weight are very similar:

$$\textit{atomic weight} = \text{grams}/6 \times 10^{23} \text{ ions or molecules}$$

$$\textit{equivalent weight} = \text{grams}/6 \times 10^{23}\ (-) \text{ or } (+) \text{ charges} = \text{g/mole charge} = \text{g/eq}$$

In reactions, the atomic weight and equivalent weight are related. For example, consider a soil that contains 1 mole of K^+ cations:

$$\begin{aligned} 1 \text{ mole } K^+ \text{ ions} &= 6 \times 10^{23}\ K^+ \text{ ions} \\ &= 6 \times 10^{23} \text{ or 1 mole } (+) \text{ charges} \end{aligned}$$

$$\begin{aligned}\text{From the periodic table the atomic weight of } K^+ &= 39 \text{ grams/mole } K^+ \text{ ions}\\ \text{Therefore, the equivalent weight of } K^+ &= 39 \text{ grams/mole } (+) \text{ charge or}\\ &= 39 \text{ grams/equivalent}\end{aligned}$$

Since the number of ions and charges are equal for K^+, the atomic weight = equivalent weight.

For a *divalent* ion:

$$\begin{aligned}1 \text{ mole } Ca^{+2} \text{ ions} &= 6 \times 10^{23}\ Ca^{+2} \text{ ions}\\ &= 2 \times (6 \times 10^{23})(+) \text{ charges}\\ &= 2 \text{ mole } (+) \text{ charges}\\ \text{From the periodic table the atomic weight of } Ca^{+2} &= 40 \text{ grams/mole of } Ca^{+2} \text{ ions}\\ \text{Therefore, the equivalent weight of } Ca^{+2} &= 40 \text{ grams/2 mole } (+) \text{ charge or}\\ &= 20 \text{ grams/1 mole } (+) \text{ charge}\\ &= 20 \text{ grams/equivalent}\end{aligned}$$

For a *trivalent* ion:

$$\begin{aligned}1 \text{ mole } Al^{+23} \text{ ions} &= 6 \times 10^{23}\ Al^{+3} \text{ ions}\\ &= 3 \times (6 \times 10^{23})(+) \text{ charges}\\ &= 3 \text{ mole } (+) \text{ charges}\\ \text{From the periodic table the atomic weight of } Al^{+3} &= 27 \text{ grams/mole of } Al^{+3} \text{ ions}\\ \text{Therefore, the equivalent weight of } Al^{+3} &= 27 \text{ grams/3 mole } (+) \text{ charge or}\\ &= 9 \text{ grams/1 mole } (+) \text{ charge}\\ &= 9 \text{ grams/equivalent}\end{aligned}$$

The use of equivalent weight in soil fertility is a convenient way to quantify cations and anions involved in exchange reactions (see Fig. 2-2). If K^+ replaces Ca^{+2} on the exchange surface, then it will take 2 moles of K^+ to replace or exchange 1 mole of Ca^{+2} [2 (+) charges exchanges with 2 (+) charges]. If Ca^{+2} replaces Al^{+3}, then 3 moles Ca^{+2} replaces 2 moles Al^{+3} [6 (+) charges exchanges with 6 (+) charges]. Therefore, 1 mole of (+) charge replaces 1 mole of (+) charges regardless of which ions are involved or:

$$1 \text{ equivalent of A} = 1 \text{ equivalent of B}$$

where A and B are ions or compounds involved in the reaction.

The equivalent weight of a compound is determined by knowing the reaction involved. For example:

$$CaCO_3 + 2H^+ \leftrightarrows Ca^{+2} + CO_2 + H_2O$$

The equivalent weight of calcium carbonate ($CaCO_3$) is determined from the periodic table by: 1 molecular weight of $CaCO_3$ (100 g/m) neutralizes or reacts with 2 moles $2H^+$; remember 1 mole H^+ = 1 equivalent H^+ (1 mole ions = 1 mole charge for univalent ions) thus,

$$\frac{100 \text{ g } CaCO_3}{2 \text{ moles } H^+} = \frac{50 \text{ g } CaCO_3}{1 \text{ mole } H^+} = \frac{50 \text{ g } CaCO_3}{\text{Eq}}$$

The CEC of a soil is strongly affected by the nature and amount of clay minerals and OM present in the soil (Table 2-1). Soils with predominately 2:1 minerals have higher CEC than soils with predominately 1:1 minerals. Soils with high clay and OM contents have a higher CEC than sandy, low OM soils. Typical CEC values for different soil textures are as follows:

Sands (light colored)	3 to 5 meq/100 g
Sands (dark colored)	10 to 20
Loams	10 to 15
Silt loams	15 to 25
Clay and clay loams	20 to 50
Organic soils	50 to 100

The example below shows the importance of content and type of clay mineral and OM on soil CEC.

EXAMPLE

A soil has 27% clay (1/3 each of kaolinite, montmorillonite, vermiculite) and 4% OM. Calculate the CEC in meq/100 g of this soil.

kaolinite	→	10 meq/100 g × 9%	=	0.9
montmorillonite	→	100 meq/100 g × 9%	=	9.0
vermiculite	→	140 meq/100 g × 9%	=	12.6
OM	→	200 meq/100 g × 4%	=	8.0
		Soil CEC	=	30.5 meq/100 g

In practice, substantial technical expertise is required to quantify specific clay mineral content in soils and, thus, these analyses are not routinely performed. The previous example is for illustrative purposes only. Except for Al^{+3}, most of the exchangeable cations are plant nutrients (Table 2-2). In acidic soils the principal cations are Al^{+3}, H^+, Ca^{+2}, Mg^{+2}, and K^+; while in neutral and basic soils the predominant cations are Ca^{+2}, Mg^{+2}, K^+, and Na^+. Cations are adsorbed to the CEC with different adsorption strengths, influencing the ease with which cations can be replaced or exchanged with other cations. For most minerals, the strength of cation adsorption, or *lyotropic series*, is

$$Al^{+3} > H^+ > Ca^{+2} > Mg^{+2} > K^+ = NH_4{}^+ > Na^+.$$

The properties of the cations determine the strength of adsorption or ease of desorption. First, the strength of adsorption is directly proportional to the charge on the cations (> charge > adsorption strength). The H^+ ion is unique because of its very small size and high charge density; thus, its adsorption strength is between Al^{+3} and Ca^{+2}. Second, the adsorption strength for cations with similar charge is determined by the size or radii of the hydrated cation (Table 2-2). As the size of the hydrated cation increases, the distance between the cation and the clay surface increases. Larger hydrated cations cannot get as close to the exchange surface as smaller cations, resulting in decreased strength of adsorption.

Table 2-2 Cation and Anions Associated with Surface Exchange in Soils

Ion	*Atomic Weight (g/mole)*	*Equivalent* Weight (g/eq)*	*Nonhydrated*	*Ionic Radii Hydrated*
			nm	
Cations				
Al^{+3}	27	9	0.051	
H^+	1	1		
Ca^{+2}	40	20	0.099	0.96
Mg^{+2}	24	12	0.066	1.08
K^+	39	39	0.133	0.53
NH_4^+	18	18	0.143	0.56
Na^+	23	23	0.097	0.79
Anions				
$H_2PO_4^-$	97	97		
SO_4^{-2}	96	48		
NO_3^-	62	62		
Cl^-	35	35		
OH^-	17	17		

*g/eq or mg/meq.

Determination of CEC

A conventional method of CEC measurement is to extract a soil sample with neutral 1 N ammonium acetate (NH_4OAc). All of the exchangeable cations are replaced by NH_4^+, and the CEC becomes saturated with NH_4^+. If this NH_4^+ saturated soil is extracted with a solution of a different salt, such as $BaCl_2$, the Ba^{+2} will replace NH_4^+. If the soil-$BaCl_2$ suspension is filtered, the filtrate will contain NH_4^+ that was previously adsorbed to the CEC. The quantity of NH_4^+ in the leachate is a measure of the CEC (see diagram on top of page 25).

For example, suppose that the concentration of NH_4^+ in the filtrate was 270 ppm (20 g of soil extracted with 200 ml of KCl solution). The CEC is calculated as follows:

$$\begin{aligned} 270 \text{ ppm } NH_4^+ &= 270 \text{ mg } NH_4^+/l \\ (270 \text{ mg } NH_4^+/l) \times (0.2\, l/20 \text{ g soil}) &= 2.7 \text{ mg } NH_4^+/\text{g soil} \\ (2.7 \text{ mg } NH_4^+/\text{g soil})/(18 \text{ mg } NH_4^+/\text{meq}) &= 0.15 \text{ meq CEC/g soil} \\ 0.15 \text{ meq CEC/g soil} \times 100/100 &= 15 \text{ meq/100 g soil} \\ \text{CEC} &= 15 \text{ meq/100 g soil} \end{aligned}$$

The equivalent weight of NH_4^+ is given in Table 2-2.

Base Saturation

One of the important properties of a soil is its base saturation (%BS), which is defined as the percentage of total CEC occupied by Ca^{+2}, Mg^{+2}, K^+, and Na^+. In the following diagram, the cations on the exchange are both acids (Al^{+3}, H^+) and bases (Ca^{+2}, Mg^{+2},

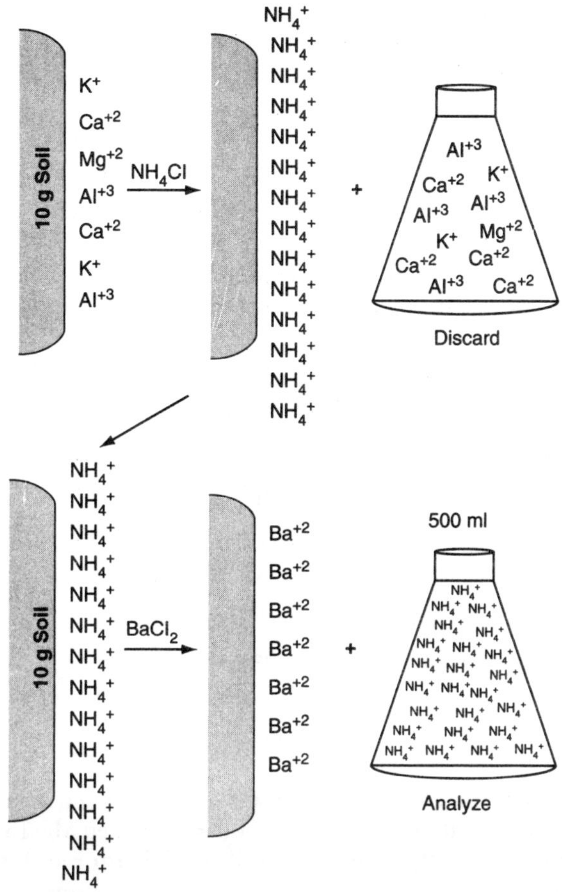

K$^+$). In this example, Na$^+$ is not included in the bases because most soils with appreciable exchangeable acidity usually contain negligible exchangeable Na$^+$. There are 12 (+) charges as bases and 12 (+) charges as acids, or 50% BS (12/24 × 100).

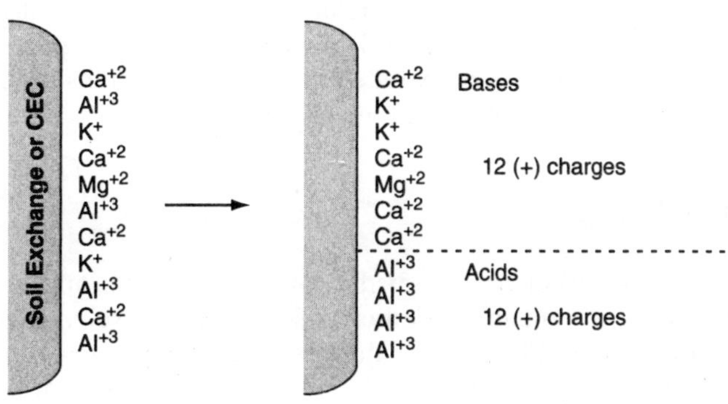

To further illustrate, suppose that the following ions were measured in the 200-ml NH_4OAc extract obtained from leaching the 20 g of soil in the *previous CEC example*, where CEC = 15 meq/100 g soil.

$$Ca^{+2} = 100 \text{ ppm}$$
$$Mg^{+2} = 30 \text{ ppm}$$
$$K^{+} = 78 \text{ ppm}$$

The equivalent weights of the cations are found in Table 2-2. The following calculations are used to express the cation concentrations in CEC units and determine %BS.

$$\begin{aligned}
Ca^{+2} = 150 \text{ ppm} &= 150 \text{ mg/l} \times (0.2 \text{ l}/20 \text{ g soil})/(20 \text{ mg/meq}) \times 100/100 \\
&= 7.5 \text{ meq } Ca^{+2}/100 \text{ g soil} \\
Mg^{+2} = 30 \text{ ppm} &= 30 \text{ mg/l} \times (0.2 \text{ l}/20 \text{ g soil})/(12 \text{ mg/meq}) \times 100/100 \\
&= 2.5 \text{ meq } Mg^{+2}/100 \text{ g soil} \\
K^{+} = 78 \text{ ppm} &= 78 \text{ mg/l} \times (0.2 \text{ l}/20 \text{ g soil})/(39 \text{ mg/meq}) \times 100/100 \\
&= 2 \text{ meq } K^{+}/100 \text{ g} \\
\text{Total} &= 12 \text{ meq bases}/100 \text{ g} \\
\text{Base saturation } \% &= (\text{total bases/CEC}) \times 100 \\
&= [(12 \text{ meq}/100 \text{ g})/(15 \text{ meq}/100 \text{ g})] \times 100 \\
&= 80\% \text{ BS}
\end{aligned}$$

The saturation with any cation may be calculated in a similar fashion. For example, from the preceding data, %Mg saturation = (2.5 meq Mg/15 meq CEC) × 100 = 16.7%Mg.

Generally, %BS of uncultivated soils is higher for arid- than for humid-region soils. In humid regions, the %BS of soils formed from limestones or basic igneous rocks is greater than that of soils formed from sandstones or acidic igneous rocks.

The availability of Ca^{+2}, Mg^{+2}, and K^{+} to plants increases with increasing BS%. For example, a soil with 80% BS would provide cations to growing plants far more easily than the same soil with 40% BS. The relation between %BS and cation availability is modified by the nature of the soil colloids. As a rule, soils with large amounts of OM or 1:1 clays can supply nutrient cations to plants at a much lower %BS than soils high in 2:1 clays.

Base saturation increases with increasing soil pH (Fig. 2-9). In this example, pH 5.5 equals about 50% BS and pH 7.0 equals 90% BS. Although the shape of the curve varies slightly among different soils, the relationship can be helpful in evaluating lime requirements for acidic soils (see Chapter 3). Increasing pH has a greater affect on increasing CEC in the OM fraction in soil compared to the mineral fractions (Fig. 2-10). Thus, the influence of pH on CEC is greatest in soils high in OM.

Anion Exchange

Anions in soil solution are adsorbed to (+)-charged sites on clay mineral surfaces and OM. The (+) charge responsible for anion adsorption and exchange occurs on the mineral edges (Fig. 2-7) and OM (Fig. 2-8). Anion exchange may also occur with OH groups on the hydroxyl surface of kaolinite. Displacement of OH ions from hydrous Fe and Al oxides is

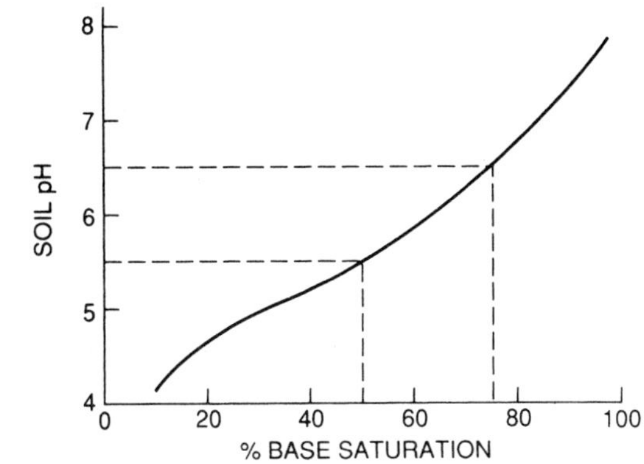

Figure 2-9 **General relationship between soil pH and base saturation.**

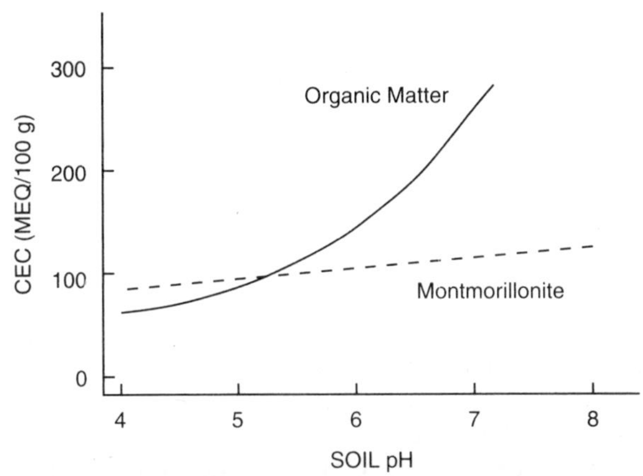

Figure 2-10 **Influence of pH on CEC in pure OM and montmorillonite clay mineral.**

considered to be an important mechanism for anion exchange, particularly in highly weathered soils of the tropics and subtropics.

AEC increases as soil pH decreases (Fig. 2-6). Further, AEC is much greater in acid soils high in 1:1 clays and those containing Fe and Al oxides than it is in soils with predominately 2:1 clays. Montmorillonitic minerals usually have an AEC of less than 5 meq/100 g, whereas kaolinites can have an AEC as high as 40 meq/100 g at pH 4.7. Anions such as Cl^- and NO_3^- may be adsorbed, although not to the extent of $H_2PO_4^-$ and SO_4^{-2}. The order of adsorption strength is $H_2PO_4^- > SO_4^{-2} > NO_3^- > Cl^-$. In most soils $H_2PO_4^-$ is the primary anion adsorbed, although some acidic soils also adsorb significant quantities of SO_4^{-2}. The mechanisms for $H_2PO_4^-$ adsorption in soils are much more complex than the simple electrostatic attraction as with SO_4^{-2}, NO_3^-, and Cl^-. The $H_2PO_4^-$ can be adsorbed by Al and Fe oxide minerals through reactions that result in chemical bonds that are nonelectrostatic (Fig. 2-11).

Buffering Capacity

Plant nutrient availability depends on the concentration of nutrients in solution but, more importantly, on the capacity of the soil to maintain the concentration. The *buffer capacity* (BC) represents the ability of the soil to resupply an ion to the soil solution. The BC involves

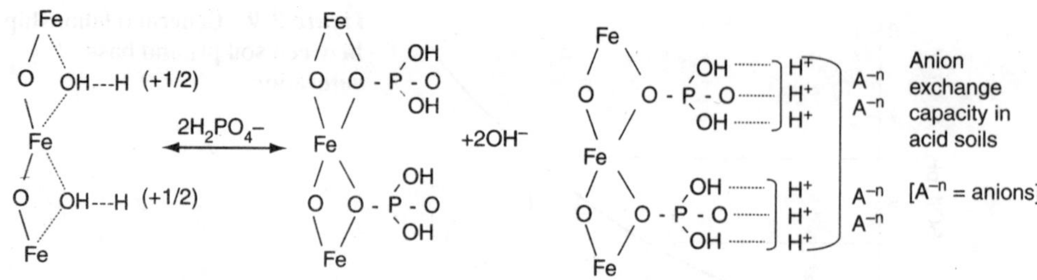

Figure 2-11 **Chemical adsorption of phosphate ($H_2PO_4^-$) to iron hydroxide [$Fe(OH)_3$] minerals in soils and how anion exchange may be exhibited in acid soils.**

all of the solid components in the soil system; thus, cations and anions must exist in soils as solid compounds, adsorbed to exchange sites, and in soil OM (Fig. 2-1). For example, when H^+ in solution is neutralized by liming, H^+ will desorb from the exchange sites. The solution pH is thus buffered by exchangeable H^+ and will not increase until significant quantities of exchangeable H^+ have been neutralized. Similarly, as plant roots absorb or remove nutrients such as K^+, exchangeable K^+ is desorbed to resupply solution K^+. With some nutrients, such as $H_2PO_4^-$, solid P minerals dissolve to resupply or buffer the solution $H_2PO_4^-$ concentration.

Soil BC can be described by the ratio of the concentrations of absorbed (ΔQ) and solution (ΔI) ions: Figure 2-12 illustrates the quantity (Q) and intensity (I) relationships between two soils. Soil A has a higher BC than soil B, as indicated by the steeper slope (ΔQ/ΔI). Thus, increasing the concentration of adsorbed ions increases the solution concentration in soil B much more than that in soil A, indicating that $BC_A > BC_B$. Alternatively, decreasing the solution concentration by plant uptake decreases the quantity of ion in solution much less in soil A than in soil B.

The BC in soil increases with increasing CEC, OM, and other solid constituents in the soil. For example, the BC of montmorillonitic, high-OM soils is greater than that of kaolinitic, low-OM soils. Since CEC increases with increasing clay content, fine-textured

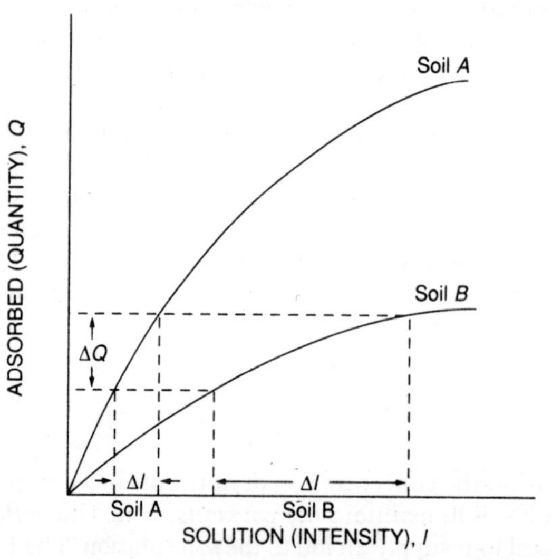

Figure 2-12 **Relationship between quantity of adsorbed nutrient and concentration of the nutrient in solution (intensity). BC (ΔQ/ΔI) of soil A is greater than that of soil B.**

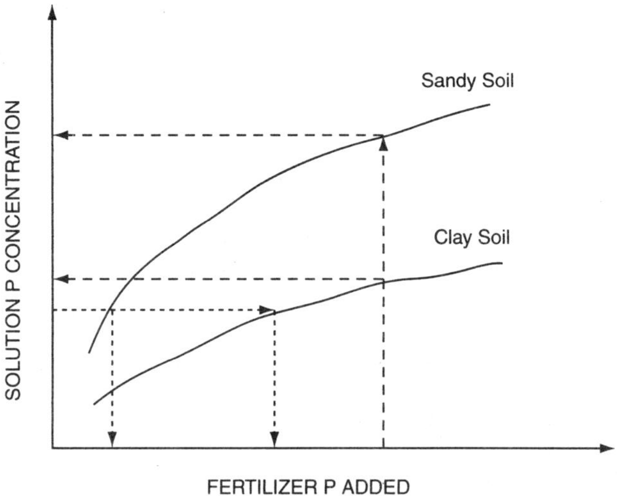

Figure 2-13 Graphical representation of the influence of BC on changes in solution P concentration with addition of fertilizer P. To maintain the same solution P concentration in both soils, fertilizer P rate would be greater in the clay soil than the sandy soil (-------). If the same rate of fertilizer P is added to both soils (– – – – – – –), the resulting solution $H_2PO_4^-$ concentration will be greater in the sandy soil than in the clay soil because the $BC_{clay} > BC_{sand}$.

soils will exhibit higher BC than coarse-textured soils. If exchangeable K^+ decreases (e.g., as a result of plant uptake), the capacity of the soil to buffer solution K^+ is reduced. The nutrient will likely become deficient, and K^+ fertilizer will be needed to increase exchangeable K^+ and correct the K^+ deficiency. Addition of P fertilizer will increase adsorbed $H_2PO_4^-$, while some $H_2PO_4^-$ will also precipitate as solid P compounds that contribute to the BC of P in soils. Thus, it is apparent that BC is a very important soil property that strongly influences nutrient availability. Figure 2-13 further illustrates the BC relationships in soils. If the same rate of fertilizer P is added to both soils, the resulting solution $H_2PO_4^-$ concentration will be greater in the sandy soil than in the clay soil because the $BC_{clay} > BC_{sand}$. Alteratively, if we wanted to establish the same solution P concentration in both soils, then more fertilizer P would be needed in the clay soil compared to the sandy soil, again because $BC_{clay} > BC_{sand}$.

Root Cation Exchange Capacity

Plant roots exhibit a CEC ranging from 10 to 30 meq/100 g in monocotyledons (grasses) and 40 to 100 meq/100 g in dicotyledons (broadleaves, legumes) (Table 2-3). The exchange properties of roots are attributable mainly to carboxyl groups (COOH), similar to the exchange sites on humus (Fig. 2-8), and account for 70 to 90% of root CEC.

Legumes and other plant species with high root CEC tend to absorb divalent cations preferentially over monovalent cations, whereas the reverse occurs with grasses. These root

Table 2-3 **CEC of Roots**

Species	*CEC meq/100 g Dry Root*
Wheat	23
Corn	29
Bean	54
Tomato	62

CEC properties help to explain why, in grass-legume pastures on soils containing less than adequate K^+, the grass survives but the legume disappears. The grasses absorb K^+ more effectively than legumes.

Mineral Solubility in Soils

The solubility of a mineral refers to the concentration of the elements or ions in solution supported or maintained by the specific mineral. For example, when $CaSO_4 \cdot 2H_2O$ (gypsum) is added to water it dissolves:

$$CaSO_4 \cdot 2H_2O \leftrightarrows Ca^{+2} + SO_4^{-2} + 2H_2O$$

The product of the two ions Ca^{+2} and SO_4^{-2} is called the solubility product, or Ksp, where

$$Ksp = (Ca^{+2})\ (SO_4^{-2})$$

The Ksp is a constant, such that when the product of the ion concentrations is < Ksp the mineral will dissolve and when the product of the ion concentrations is > Ksp then the mineral will precipitate.

When $CaSO_4 \cdot 2H_2O$ is added to water it begins to dissolve and the reaction initially proceeds only to the right as the concentration of Ca^{+2} and SO_4^{-2} increases. Eventually as more $CaSO_4 \cdot 2H_2O$ dissolves, the back reaction will start to occur and an *equilibrium* between the forward (*dissolution*) and back (*precipitation*) reactions is established. When this occurs, the solution is *saturated*. If more water is added, Ca^{+2} and SO_4^{-2} in solution are diluted or their concentration decreases. When this occurs the product of the concentrations is < Ksp, causing more $CaSO_4 \cdot 2H_2O$ to dissolve. If enough water is added to dissolve *all* of the solid, then equilibrium ceases to exist and the solution is *unsaturated*. Similarly, if water is removed (i.e., evaporation), then more $CaSO_4 \cdot 2H_2O$ will precipitate because the product of the concentrations is > Ksp. Likewise in this example, if $MgSO_4$ were added, the resulting SO_4^{-2} concentration would increase *causing* more $CaSO_4 \cdot 2H_2O$ to precipitate since the product of the concentrations $(Ca^{+2})\ (SO_4^{-2})$ > Ksp.

There are many minerals in soils that influence the concentrations of ions and plant nutrients in soil solution. For example in acid soils, $FePO_4 \cdot 2H_2O$ is a common mineral that influences P availability.

$$FePO_4 \cdot 2H_2O + 2H^+ \leftrightarrows Fe^{+3} + H_2PO_4^- + 2H_2O$$

The Ksp for this reaction is:

$$Ksp = \frac{(Fe^{+3})(H_2PO_4^-)}{(H^+)^2}$$

As the soil solution concentration of $H_2PO_4^-$ decreases with plant uptake, the product of the ion concentrations is now < Ksp, so the $FePO_4 \cdot 2H_2O$ mineral dissolves to resupply or buffer solution $H_2PO_4^-$. Alternatively, if $H_2PO_4^-$ is added through fertilizers or manures, the $H_2PO_4^-$ concentration in solution increases causing $FePO_4 \cdot 2H_2O$ to precipitate (product of the concentrations > Ksp). The reaction also shows that the solubility is dependent on pH, which was not the case with $CaSO_4 \cdot 2H_2O$. With $FePO_4 \cdot 2H_2O$, increasing pH (decreasing H^+ concentration) causes Fe^{+3} and $H_2PO_4^-$ to decrease as $FePO_4 \cdot 2H_2O$ precipitates. Recall that Ksp is a constant, so if the denominator decreases the numerator must also decrease. Solubility relationships are particularly important for plant availability of P and many of the micronutrients. As evident in Figure 2-1, solubility reactions are essential to buffering solution concentration of many plant nutrients.

Supply of Nutrients from OM

Microbial activity and the cycling of nutrients through soil OM substantially impacts plant nutrient availability. The soil solution concentration of N, S, P, and several micronutrients are intimately related to the organic fraction in soils.

In virgin (uncultivated) soil the OM content is determined by soil texture, topography, and climatic conditions that predominately influence the quantity of CO_2 fixed by plants (total plant biomass) and recycled to the soil. Generally, OM content is higher in cooler than in warmer climates and, with similar annual temperature and vegetation, increases with an increase in effective precipitation. These differences are related to reduced potential for OM oxidation with cooler temperatures and increased biomass production with increased rainfall. Soil OM content is greater in fine-textured than in coarse-textured soils and is related to increased biomass production in finer-textured soils because of improved soil-water storage and reduced OM oxidation potential. Soil OM contents are higher under grassland vegetation than under forest cover. These relations are generally true for well-drained soil conditions. Under poor drainage, aerobic decomposition is impeded and organic residues build up to high levels, regardless of temperature or soil texture. In general, soils with higher OM content will be more productive. The influence of soil and crop management on soil OM and its relationship to soil and crop productivity is discussed in Chapter 13.

Soil OM comprises organic materials in all stages of decomposition. The conceptual relationship between crop residues and their degradation through autotrophic and heterotrophic microbial processes that ultimately form relatively stable soil humus is shown in Figure 2-14. The size of these components depends on climate, soil type, and soil and crop management, all of which influence the quantity of crop residues produced and returned to the soil. Fresh plant or other organic residues are subject to fairly rapid decomposition. The relatively small heterotrophic biomass (1 to 8% of total soil OM) represents soil microorganisms and fauna responsible for the majority of organic-inorganic transformations that influence nutrient availability. Soil humus, the largest component of soil OM, is relatively resistant to microbial degradation; however, it is essential for maintaining optimum soil physical conditions important for plant growth, water-holding capacity, nutrient availability , and many other properties important to soil productivity (see Chapter 13; Table 13-4). The primary microbial processes involved in fresh residue and humus turnover or cycling in soils are *mineralization* and *immobilization*.

$$\begin{array}{c}\text{Organic}\\\text{Complexed}\\\text{Nutrients}\end{array} \underset{\textit{immobilization}}{\overset{\textit{mineralization}}{\rightleftarrows}} \begin{array}{c}\text{Inorganic}\\\text{Nutrients in}\\\text{Solution}\end{array}$$

These reactions, combined with other physical, chemical, and environmental factors, are important in OM stability and in plant nutrient availability (Fig. 2-1). As plant and other organic residues are returned to the soil, many different types of soil microorganisms degrade

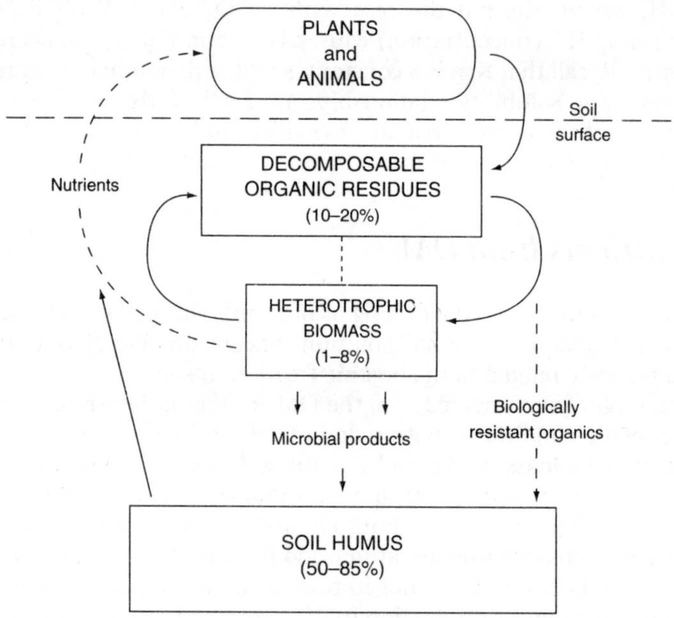

Figure 2-14 **Conceptual model of the degradation of plant residues to stable soil humus. Relative sizes of the microbial and organic biomass components are shown.** *(Doran and Smith, 1987,* SSSA Spec. Publ. 19, *p. 55.)*

these residues to a family of relatively stable organic compounds called *humus* (Fig. 2-8). In the degradation process, organically complexed ions in the residue can be *mineralized* or converted from organic to inorganic forms of the particultuar nutrient (i.e., N, S, P). If there are insufficient nutrients in the residue to meet the microbial demand, then inorganic ions in the soil solution will be *immobilized* into the microbial tissues. The microbial cycle of *mineralization* and *immobilization* occurs over a wide range in environmental conditions, but activity is maximized at about the same relative moisture and temperature conditions optimum for plant growth. These microbial transformations important to nutrient availability will be covered in more detail in Chapter 4.

Movement of Ions from Soils to Roots

Ion absorption by plant roots requires contact between the ion and the root surface. There are generally three ways in which nutrients reach the root surface: (1) root interception, (2) mass flow, and (3) diffusion. The relative importance of these mechanisms in supplying nutrients to plant roots is shown in Table 2-4.

Root Interception

Root interception represents exchange of ions through physical contact between the root and mineral surfaces (Fig. 2-15). Ion absorption by root interception is enhanced by increasing the quantity of absorbing roots in a given volume of soil. As roots develop and exploit

Table 2-4 **Significance of Root Interception, Mass Flow, and Diffusion in Ion Transport to Corn Roots**

Nutrient	*Nutrient Required for 200 bu/a of Corn*	*Percentage Supplied by*		
		Root Interception	*Mass Flow*	*Diffusion*
N	225	1	99	0
P	45	2	4	94
K	200	2	20	78
Ca	50	120	440	0
Mg	55	27	280	0
S	25	4	94	2
Cu	0.12	8	400	0
Zn	0.40	25	30	45
B	0.25	8	350	0
Fe	2.5	8	40	52
Mn	10.40	25	130	0
Mo	0.012	8	200	0

Note: The contribution of diffusion was estimated by the difference between total nutrient needs and the amounts supplied by interception and mass flow.

more soil, soil solution and soil surfaces retaining adsorbed ions are exposed to the increasing root mass. Ions such as H^+ adsorbed to the surface of root hairs may exchange with ions held on the surface of clays and OM because of the intimate contact between roots and soil particles. The ions held by electrostatic forces at these sites oscillate within a certain volume (Fig. 2-15). When the oscillation volumes of two ions overlap, ion exchange occurs. In this way, Ca^{+2} on a clay surface could then presumably be absorbed by the root and utilized by the plant.

The quantity of nutrients that can come in direct contact with plant roots is the amount in a volume of soil equal to the volume of roots. Roots usually occupy 1% or less of the soil; however, roots growing through soil pores with higher-than-average nutrient content could contact a maximum of 3% of the available soil nutrients.

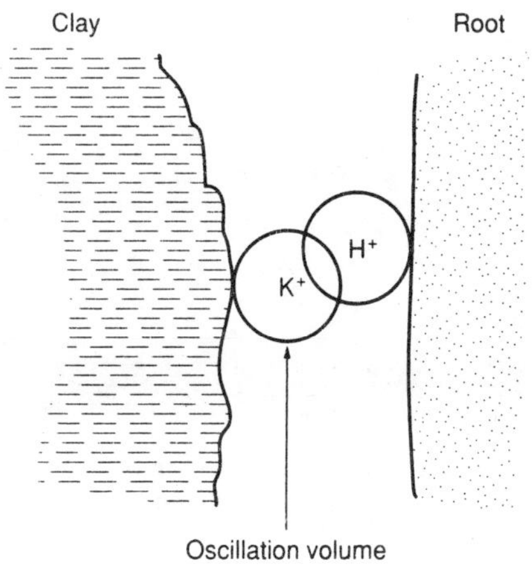

Figure 2-15 **Conceptual model for root interception or contact exchange of nutrients between ions on soil and root exchange sites. Overlapping oscillation volumes cause exchange of H^+ on the root with K^+ on the clay mineral surface.**

Root interception of nutrients can be enhanced by mycorrhiza, a symbiotic association between fungi and plant roots. The beneficial effect of mycorrhiza is greatest when plants are growing in infertile soils. The extent of mycorrhizal infection is also enhanced under conditions of slightly acidic soil pH, low P, adequate N, and low soil temperatures. The hyphal threads of mycorrhizal fungi act as extensions of plant root systems, resulting in greater soil contact. (See Figure 10-10 for a diagrammatic representation of a mycorrhizal-infected root.) The two major groups of mycorrhizas are ectomycorrhizas and endomycorrhizas. The ectomycorrhizas occur mainly in the tree species of the temperate zones but can also be found in semiarid zones. The endomycorrhizas are more widespread. The roots of most agronomic crops have vesicular arbuscular mycorrhiza. The fungus grows into the cortex. Inside the plant cells, small structures known as arbuscules, considered to be the site of transfer of nutrients from fungi to host plants, are formed. The positive effect of inoculation of English oaks with ectomycorrhizas is shown in Figure 2-16.

Increased nutrient absorption is due to the larger nutrient-absorbing surface provided by the fungi, which can be up to 10 times that of uninfected roots. Fungal hyphae can extend up to 8 cm into the soil surrounding the roots, thus increasing absorption of nutrients. Enhanced P uptake is the primary cause of improved plant growth from mycorrhiza, which results in improved uptake of other elements (Table 2-5).

Figure 2-16 Differential growth responses of sixteen-week-old English oaks *(Quercus robur L.)* inoculated (left) with *Pisolithus tinctorius* (Pers.) Coker and Couch, an ectomycorrhizal former, and uninoculated (right). *(Garrett, School of Forestry, Fisheries, and Wildlife, University of Missouri, Columbia, Mo.)*

Table 2-5 **Effect of Inoculation of Endomycorrhiza and P on Nutrient Content in Corn Shoots**

	Content in Shoots (μg)			
	No P		*25 ppm P Added*	
Element	*No Mycorrhiza*	*Mycorrhiza*	*No Mycorrhiza*	*Mycorrhiza*
P	750	1,340	2,970	5,910
K	6,000	9,700	17,500	19,900
Ca	1,200	1,600	2,700	3,500
Mg	430	630	990	1,750
Zn	28	95	48	169
Cu	7	14	12	30
Mn	72	101	159	238
Fe	80	147	161	277

SOURCE: Lambert et al., 1979, *J. Soil Sci.* 43:976.

Mass Flow

Mass flow occurs when ions in soil solution are transported to the root as a result of transpirational water uptake by the plant, water evaporation at the soil surface, and percolation of water in the soil profile. Transport of ions in the soil solution to root surfaces by mass flow is an important factor in supplying nutrients to plants (Table 2-4).

The quantity of nutrients reaching roots by mass flow is determined by the rate of water flow or the water consumption of plants and the average nutrient concentrations in the soil water. Mass flow can also supply an excess of Ca^{+2}, Mg^{+2}, several micronutrients, and most of the soluble nutrients, such as NO_3^-, Cl^-, and SO_4^{-2} (Table 2-4). As soil moisture is reduced (increased soil moisture tension), water transport to the root surface decreases. Mass flow is reduced at low temperatures because the transpirational demands of plants and water evaporation at the soil surface decreases at low soil temperatures.

Diffusion

Diffusion occurs when an ion moves from an area of high concentration to one of low concentration. As roots absorb nutrients from the surrounding soil solution, the nutrient concentration at the root surface decreases compared with the "bulk" soil solution concentration (Fig. 2-17). Therefore, a nutrient concentration gradient is established that causes ions to diffuse toward the root. A high plant requirement for a nutrient results in a large concentration gradient, favoring a high rate of ion diffusion from the soil solution to the root surface. Most of the P and K move to the root by diffusion (Table 2-4). Ion diffusion in soils can be quantified by the following equation (Fick's law) that helps us understand the factors that influence diffusion in soil:

$$\frac{dC}{dt} = De \cdot A \cdot \frac{dC}{dX}$$

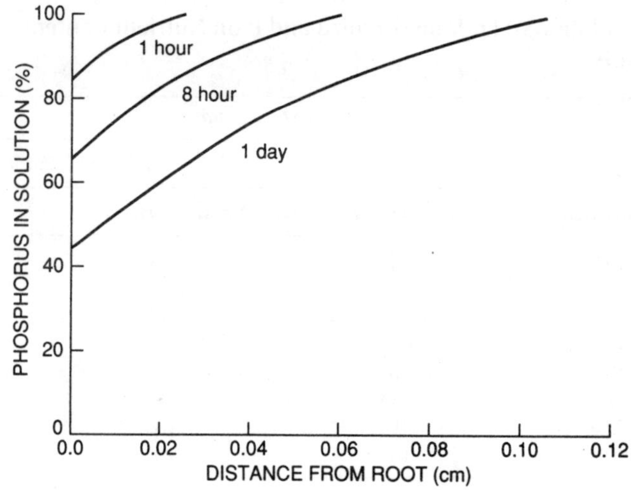

Figure 2-17 **The influence of P uptake on the distribution of P in the soil solution as a function of distance from the root surface.**

where dC/dt = rate of diffusion (change in concentration C with time)
dC/dX = concentration gradient (change in concentration with distance)
De = effective diffusion coefficient
A = cross-sectional area through which the ions diffuse

The diffusion equation shows that the rate of nutrient diffusion (dC/dt) is directly proportional to the concentration gradient (dC/dX). As the difference in nutrient concentration between the root surface and the bulk solution increases, the rate of nutrient diffusion increases. Also, increasing the cross-sectional area for diffusion increases dC/dt. The diffusion rate is proportional to the diffusion coefficient, D*e*, which controls how far nutrients can diffuse to the root. For a given spacing between roots, D*e* determines the fraction of nutrients in the soil that can reach the roots during a specific period of plant growth. D*e* is described as follows:

$$De = Dw \cdot \theta \cdot \frac{1}{T} \cdot \frac{1}{b}$$

where Dw = diffusion coefficient in water
θ = volumetric soil water content
T = tortuosity factor
b = soil buffer capacity (BC)

This relationship shows that as soil moisture content (θ) increases, D*e* increases, which results in an increase in diffusion rate, dC/dt. As moisture content decreases, moisture films around soil particles become thinner and ion diffusion through these films becomes more *tortuous*. Transport of nutrients to the root surface is most effective at a soil moisture content corresponding to field capacity. Therefore, raising θ reduces tortuosity, or the diffusion path length, which in turn increases dC/dt. Tortuosity (T) is also related to soil texture. Nutrients diffusing in fine-textured soils experience a more tortuous path to the root surface. As T increases with increasing clay content, 1/T decreases, which reduces the D*e* and thus dC/dt. Also, ions diffusing through soil moisture in clay soils are much more likely to be attracted to adsorption sites in a clay than in a sandy soil.

The diffusion coefficient in soil (D*e*) is directly related to the diffusion coefficient for the same nutrient in water (D*w*). Inherent in the D*w* term is a temperature factor such that increasing temperature increases D*w*, D*e*, and then dC/dt. The D*e* is inversely related to *b*. Increasing BC of the soil decreases D*e*, which decreases dC/dt. Compared to a soil with a high BC, a low-BC soil would likely have higher nutrient concentration in solution resulting in a higher D*e*, and higher potential dC/dt. Increasing the solution ion concentration also increases the diffusion gradient, dC/dX, which contributes to increased dC/dt.

Ion uptake by roots, which is responsible for creating and maintaining the diffusion gradient, is strongly influenced by temperature. Within the range of about 10 to 30°C, an increase of 10°C usually causes the rate of ion absorption to go up by a factor of two or more. Nutrient diffusion is slow under most soil conditions and occurs over very short distances in the vicinity of the root surface. Typical diffusion distances are 1 cm for N, 0.2 cm for K, and 0.02 cm for P. The mean distance between corn roots in the top 15 cm of soil is about 0.7 cm, indicating that some nutrients would need to diffuse half of this distance, or 0.35 cm, before they would be in a position to be absorbed by the plant root.

Roots do not absorb all nutrients at the same rate, causing certain ions to accumulate at the root surface, especially during periods of rapid absorption of water. This situation results in back diffusion, where the concentration gradient is away from the root surface and back toward the soil solution. Nutrient diffusion away from the root is much less common than diffusion toward the root; however, higher concentrations of some nutrients in the rhizosphere can affect the uptake of other nutrients.

The importance of diffusion and mass flow in supplying ions to the root surface depends on the ability of the solid phase of the soil to replenish or buffer the soil solution. Ion concentrations are influenced by the types of clay minerals in the soil and the distribution of cation and anions on the CEC or AEC. For example, the ease of replacement of Ca^{+2} from colloids by plant uptake varies in this order: peat > kaolinite > illite > montmorillonite. An 80% Ca-saturated 2:1 clay provides the same percentage of Ca^{+2} release as a 35% Ca-saturated kaolinite or a 25% Ca-saturated peat.

Mass flow and diffusion processes are also important in nutrient management. Soils that exhibit low diffusion rates because of high BC, low soil moisture, or high clay content may require application of immobile nutrients near the roots to maximize nutrient availability and plant uptake.

Ion Absorption by Plants

The uptake and transport of water and ions have been studied for many decades. Although recent advances in biotechnology have enhanced our understanding of these processes, only a basic description is provided in this text.

Plant uptake of ions from the soil solution can be described by *passive* and *active* processes, where ions passively move to a "boundary" through which ions are actively transported to organs in plant cells that metabolize the nutrient ions. Solution composition or ion concentrations outside and inside of the boundary are controlled by different processes, each essential to plant nutrition and growth.

Water and Ion Uptake by Roots

A considerable fraction of the total volume of the root is accessible for the passive absorption of ions. Water and ion uptake occurs at the root hairs and the rest of the root epidermis (Fig. 2-18). The apparent free space or *apoplast* is the intercellular spaces of the epidermal and cortical cells. The apoplast allows transport of water and ions in root tissue regions that do not require transport across an impermeable membrane. Water uptake from the soil into the apoplast occurs through *capillary action* and *osmosis*. Capillary action results when the intercellular space is smaller than the water-filled space in the soil, thus the matrix potential in the cortex is more negative than in the surrounding soil, and water will move to areas of lower water potential. Osmosis is the transport of water from an area of low to high solute concentration.

The *casparian bands* in the endodermis function as an impermeable barrier, which allows the endodermis to select and regulate ion absorption. Water transport through the apoplastic pathway into the xylem vessels occurs primarily in young tissues where casparian bands are not fully developed (Fig. 2-18). In older tissues, the casparian band prevents water and ion transport directly into the xylem. Thus, water and ions entering the cell or cytoplasm must be transported across the plasma membrane (Fig. 2-19). Once inside the cell, water and ion transport can occur through the symplastic pathway through cellular connections or plasmadesma (Fig. 2-19).

The concentration of ions in the apparent free space is normally less than the bulk solution concentration; therefore, diffusion occurs in response to the resulting high to low concentration gradient. Interior surfaces of cells in the cortex are negatively charged, attracting cations. Cation exchange readily occurs along the extracellular surfaces and explains why cation uptake usually exceeds anion uptake. To maintain electrical neutrality, the root cells release H^+, decreasing soil solution pH near the root surface. Diffusion and ion exchange are passive processes because uptake into the apoplast is controlled by ion concentration (diffusion) and electrical (ion exchange) gradients. These processes are nonselective and do not require energy produced from metabolic reaction within the cell.

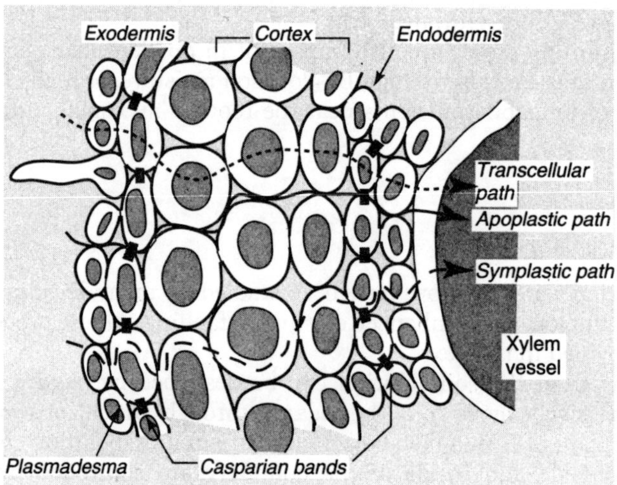

Figure 2-18 **Cross section of a plant root. Site of passive uptake is the apparent free space, which is outside of the casparian strip in the cortex.**

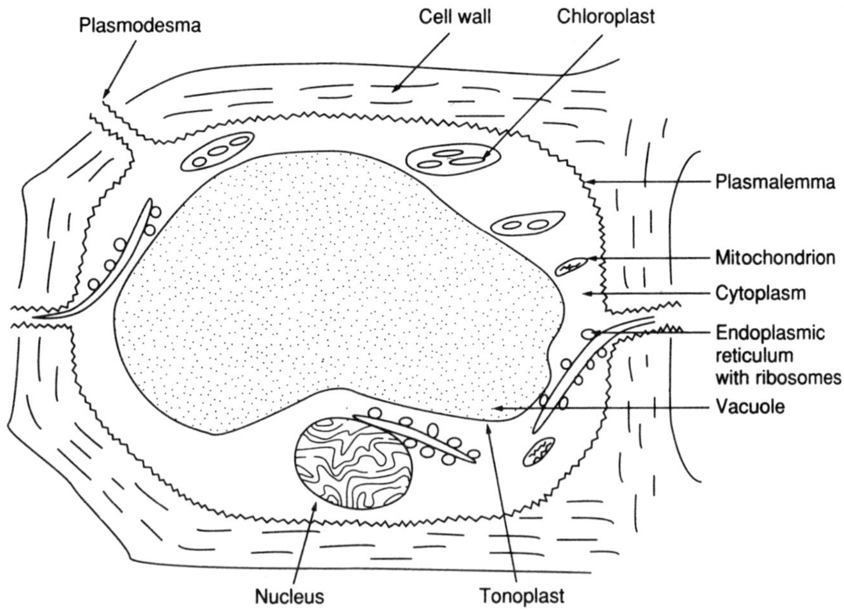

Figure 2-19 **Diagram of a plant cell. Active ion uptake occurs at the plasmalemma.** *(Mengel and Kirkby, 1987,* **Principles of Plant Nutrition,** *IPI.)*

Passive and Active Ion Uptake by Cells

In a plant cell, the plasma membrane (plasmalemma) and tonoplast are selectively permeable barriers consisting primarily of phospholipids and proteins that regulate transport of water, ions, and metabolites into the cell and vacuole, respectively (Fig. 2-19). Plasma membranes are permeable to O_2, CO_2, and some neutral compounds; are slightly permeable to water; and are nearly impermeable to inorganic ions and small-molecular-weight organic compounds (i.e. sucrose, amino acids, etc.). Proteins are required to transport H^+, inorganic ions, and organic solutes across the plasma membrane and the tonoplast at rates sufficient to meet the needs of the cell. To maintain a relatively constant internal environment, membrane permeability properties ensure that ions and molecules such as glucose, amino acids, and lipids readily enter the cell, metabolic intermediates remain in the cell, and unneeded compounds leave the cell.

Whether a molecule or ion is transported actively or passively across a membrane (casparian band, plasma membrane, or tonoplast) depends on the concentration and charge of the ion or molecule, which in combination represent the electrochemical driving force. Ions and molecules diffuse from areas of high to low concentrations. Thus, diffusion does not require the plant to expend energy. In contrast, for ions diffusing against the concentration gradient, energy is required. Thus, passive transport across the plasma membrane, for example, occurs with the electrochemical potential and active transport occurs against the electrochemical potential, a process that requires the cell to expend energy.

As a result, ion concentration on either side of the plasma membrane and tonoplast are different. The H^+ concentration can be a thousandfold higher (lower pH) in the apoplast and vacuole than in the cytoplasm (~ pH 7), but Ca^{+2} concentration gradients can vary over an even wider range (Ca^{2+} concentration is ~100 nM in the cytoplasm). K^+ concentration

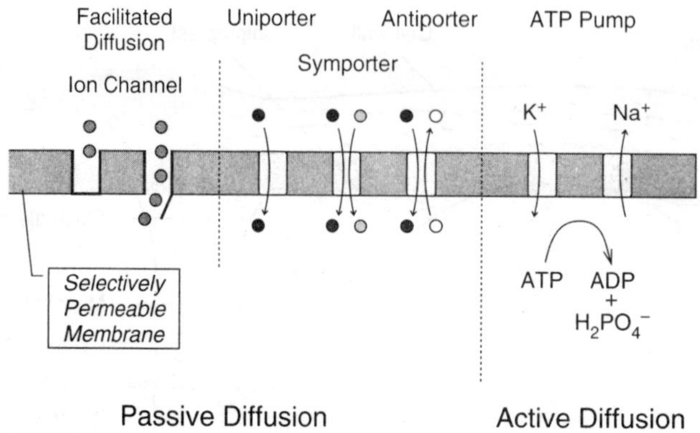

Figure 2-20 Generalized diagram of passive and active transport processes that include protein channels and other facilitated diffusion transport mechanism, as well as ATP pump mechanism to transport ions and molecules against a concentration gradient.

is much higher in the cytoplasm than in the apoplast. These concentration gradients are maintained by the combined actions of passive and active transport mechanisms, discussed next (Fig. 2-20). At ~ pH 7 proteins in the cytoplasm are negatively charged. These and other charge imbalances result in the establishment of an electric potential gradient at the plasma membrane. This potential creates a strong electric field that provides the energy for ion transport against concentration gradients, and the opening and closing of channels through the selectively permeable membranes (voltage-gated channels).

Passive Transport *Simple diffusion* through membranes occurs with small, nonpolar molecules (i.e., O_2, CO_2). For small, polar species (i.e., H_2O, ions, amino acids), specific proteins in the membrane facilitate the diffusion down the electrochemical gradient. This mechanism is refered to as *facilitated diffusion*.These proteins form channels, which can open and close, and through which ions or H_2O molecules pass in single file at very rapid rates (Fig. 2-20). For example, water movement across the tonoplast and plasma membrane is determined by osmotic pressure gradients and by passive transport through channel proteins called *aquaporins* that act as "water channels" to facilitate water transport across membranes. Aquaporins account for 5 to 10% of the total protein in a membrane. A K^+ and NH_4^+ transport channel has been suggested that is lined with (–) charges, where K^+ moves across the membrane because of the net negative charge inside the cell. In addition, Na^+ can also enter the cell by facilitated diffusion since the concentration inside is less than that outside the cell; however, Na^+ transport outside the cell requires an active transport mechanism, since it is against the electrochemical gradient.

Another mechanism involves *transporters* or *cotransporters* responsible for the transport of ions and molecules across membranes (Fig. 2-20). Transporter proteins, in contrast to channel proteins, bind only one or a few substrate molecules at a time. After binding a molecule or ion, the transporter undergoes a structural change specific to a specific ion or molecule. As a result the transport rate across a membrane is slower than that associated with channel proteins. Three types of transporters have been identified. *Uniporters* transport one molecule (i.e. glucose, amino acids) at a time down a concentration gradient. In contrast, *antiporters* and *symporters* catalyze movement of one type of ion or molecule against its concentration gradient coupled to movement of a different ion or molecule down its concentration gradient (Fig. 2-20). Therefore, the energy for *antiporter* and *symporter* transport originates from the electric potential and/or chemical gradient of a secondary ion or molecule, which is often H^+. The high H^+ concentration in the apoplast provides the energy for symporter transport of NO_3^- and other anions. Examples of antiporter transport

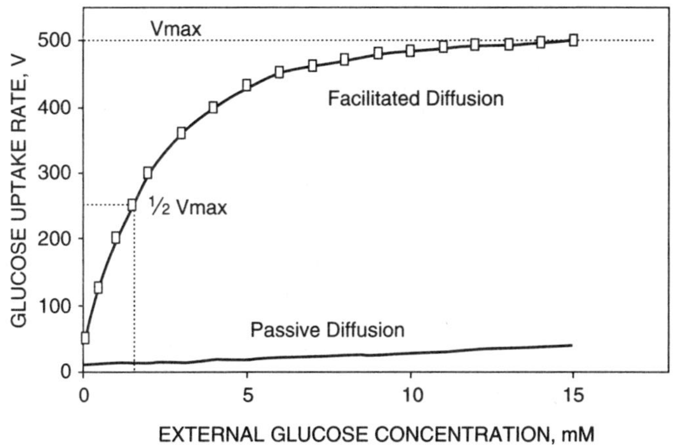

Figure 2-21 **Comparison between simple diffusion and facilitated transport on the rate of glucose transport across a membrane.**

are $H^+ - Na^+$ and $H^+ - Ca^{+2}$ transport into the vacuole. Evidence of facilitated transport is shown in Figure 2-21, where the rate of glucose uptake is substantially greater than that observed with simple diffusion along a concentration gradient.

Active Transport Larger, more-charged molecules have greater difficulty in moving across a membrane, requiring active transport mechanisms (i.e., sugars, amino acids, DNA, ATP, ions, phosphate, proteins, etc.). Active transport across a selectively permeable membrane occurs through ATP-powered pumps that transport ions against their concentration gradients (Fig. 2-20). This mechanism utilizes energy released by hydrolysis of ATP. In plant cells, H^+-ATP pumps transfer H^+ across the plasma membrane or tonoplast to acidify the cytoplasm or vacuole, respectively. The $Na^+ - K^+$ ATP pump transports K^+ into the cell and Na^+ out of the cell, which maintains a high cytoplasm K^+ concentration essential for maintaining the electrical potential gradient across the plasma membrane. The Ca^{+2} ATP pump transports Ca^{2+} out of the cytoplasm, which maintains Ca^{+2} concentration lower than in extracellular areas, which is essential for establishing a high concentration gradient that provides the energy for facilitated Ca^{+2} diffusion into the cell.

Study Questions

1. Define *cation exchange capacity* (CEC). What units are commonly used to express CEC?
2. Identify the origin of CEC in mineral soil colloids and factors that influence CEC.
3. Explain the influence of the following on CEC in soils:
   a. increasing pH from 6.0 to 7.5
   b. increasing weathering intensity (over the long term)
   c. adding bases such as Ca^{+2} or Mg^{+2}
4. Which clay minerals would likely be present in a weathered acid soil?

5. Why are 2:1 clay minerals more common in soils of the Midwest or Great Plains regions of North America?
6. As soils age from thousands of years of weathering, some soil properties change. List two of these properties and how these changes might effect soil productivity.
7. What are the two sources of negative charge in clay minerals?
8. What is meant by *buffer capacity* (BC)? What soil properties determine the soil BC?
9. Thirty lb P/a is added to two soils. The resulting solution P concentration in soil A is 4 times lower than soil B, although plant uptake in soil A is greater than soil B. What is causing the differences in these soil and plant P observations?
10. What is the *lyotropic series* for cations and anions? Does this explain nutrient mobility in soils and availability to plants? What is the basis for the lyotropic series for cations?
11. In addition to clay minerals, what other soil constituents contribute to total CEC?
12. How does CEC buffer nutrient concentration in soil solution?
13. Why does anion adsorption appear to be of little importance in most agricultural soils? Why are AECs of ultisols usually greater than those of mollisols?
14. With what type of soil would the ammonium aceptate method provide a good estimate of CEC? On what types would it provide a poor estimate? Explain why.
15. What are active and passive absorption of elements by root cells? How are the inner and outer space of cells involved? What is the proposed mechanism that describes active absorption?
16. You are addressing a group of farmers and business managers who understand crop production but are not familiar with the technical aspects of plant nutrition and soil fertility. You have to explain the nature of cation exchange and why it is important to crop production. How would you proceed? After the speech, someone asks why Cl^- and NO_3^- will leach from soils but $H_2PO_4^-$, which also has a negative charge, will not. What is your answer?
17. What is root interception?
18. Mass flow can potentially move enough Ca and Mg to the plant root to meet the nutritional needs. Which anions would most likely move with them and why?
19. Describe the relative importance of root interception, diffusion, and mass flow in nutrient transport to plant roots? What is the effect of soil texture on these mechanisms? Why?
20. What soil factors influence diffusion of nutrient ions to roots? Describe and explain a practical way of improving the diffusion of nutrients?
21. Briefly describe the influence of the following on ion diffusion in soils.
    a. temperature
    b. soil moisture
    c. soil texture
    d. buffer capacity
    e. specific ion (i.e. one ion vs. another)
22. A *solution* contains 20 ppm Ca^{+2}. Express the Ca^{+2} concentration in the following terms:
    a. grams Ca^{+2} in 1,000,000 ml water (ml = milliliter = 0.001 liter)
    b. grams Ca^{+2} in 100 ml water

   c. % Ca^{+2} in the 100 ml water
   d. mg Ca^{+2}/kg water [mg = milligram = 0.001 gram = 0.000001 kilogram (kg)]
   e. Molarity (M or moles Ca^{+2}/liter)

23. A *solution* contains 0.1 M KOH. Calculate the K^+ concentration in the following terms:
   a. g K^+/1
   b. mg K^+/ml
   c. mg K^+/kg
   d. ppm K^+
   e. % K^+

24. A *soil* contains 1,000 ppm Ca^{+2} (surface 6 inches). Express the Ca^{+2} concentration in the following terms.
   a. grams Ca^{+2}/1,000,000 g soil
   b. grams Ca^{+2}/100 g soil
   c. % Ca^{+2}
   d. mg Ca^{+2}/kg soil
   e. lbs Ca^{+2}/afs (afs = acre furrow slice or 1 acre area 6 inches deep)

25. A *soil* was sampled to a depth of 6 inches. The sample was analyzed for several cations with the following results: Ca^{+2} = 453 ppm; Mg^{+2} = 82 ppm; K^+ = 227 ppm; Na^+ = 28 ppm.
   a. Calculate the lbs/afs for each nutrient.
   b. Calculate the % content for each nutrient.
   c. Calculate the mg/kg for each nutrient.

26. A *solution* contains the following: Ca^{+2} = 1000 ppm; Mg^{+2} = 480 ppm; K^+ = 400 ppm; Na^+ = 460 ppm.
   a. Calculate the M (mole/liter) for each nutrient.
   b. Calculate the % concentration for each nutrient.
   c. Calculate the mg/kg for each nutrient.

27. There are 6×10^{23} ions of Ca^{+2} in 1 mole.
   a. How much does this many Ca^{+2} ions weigh?
   b. How many individual charges are there in this many Ca^{+2} ions?
   c. How much does 6×10^{23} charges of Ca^{+2} weigh?

28. There are 6×10^{23} ions of Al^{+3} in 1 mole.
   a. How much does this many Al^{+3} ions weigh?
   b. How many individual charges are there in this many Al^{+3} ions?
   c. How much does 6×10^{23} charges of Al^{+3} weigh?

29. One equivalent is 6×10^{23} charges of an ion (or 1 mole of charges).
   a. How much does one equivalent of Ca^{+2} weigh?
   b. How much does one equivalent of Al^{+3} weigh?

30. A solution contains 30 ppm Ca^{+2}. How many mg Ca^{+2} are in 500 ml of the solution?

31. A soil contains 800 ppm Ca^{+2}. Calculate the lbs Ca^{+2}/afs and the meq Ca^{+2}/100g soil.

32. A soil contains 0.5% Ca^{+2}. Calculate the lbs Ca^{+2}/afs and the meq Ca^{+2}/100g soil.

33. A soil is 40% acid saturated. Ten g soil are titrated with 25 mL 0.05 N base. Calculate the CEC.

34. Twenty g soil were extracted with NH_4OAc and the extract diluted to 1 liter. The solution was analyzed for cation content and contained: 38 ppm Ca^{+2}; 9 ppm Mg^{+2}; 7 ppm K^+; 4 ppm Na^+. Estimate the CEC. If the measured CEC were 20 meq/100g, calculate the BS%.

Selected References

Bohn, H. L., B. L. McNeal, and G. A. O'Connor. 1979. *Soil chemistry.* New York: John Wiley & Sons.

Epstein, E. 1972. *Mineral nutrition of plants: Principles and perspectives.* New York: John Wiley & Sons.

Mengel, K., and E. A. Kirkby. 1987. *Principles of plant nutrition.* Bern, Switzerland: International Potash Institute.

Rendig, V. V., and H. M. Taylor. 1989. *Principles of soil–plant relationships.* New York: McGraw-Hill.

Tan, K. H. 1982. *Principles of soil chemistry.* New York: Marcel Dekker.

CHAPTER 3

Soil Acidity and Alkalinity

General Concepts

In water, an acid is a molecule that donates H^+ to some other molecule. Conversely, a base is a molecule that accepts H^+. An acid, when mixed with water, ionizes into H^+ and the accompanying anions, as represented by the dissociation of acetic acid (CH_3COOH) or hydrochloric acid (HCl):

$$CH_3COOH \leftrightarrows CH_3COO^- + H^+$$
$$HCl \leftrightarrows Cl^- + H^+$$

As a strong acid, when HCl is added to water, 100% dissociates into $Cl^- + H^+$. Only 1% H^+ dissociation occurs in a weak acid such as CH_3COOH. The H^+ concentration in solution, or active acidity, increases with the strength of the acid. The undissociated acid is considered potential acidity. The total acidity of a solution is the sum of the active and potential acid concentrations. For example, suppose that the active and potential acidity are 0.099 M and 0.001 M[*], respectively. The total acid concentration is 0.100 M, and since the H^+ activity is nearly equal to the total acidity, this would be a strong acid. With weak acids, the H^+ activity is much less than the potential acidity. For example, a 0.1 M weak acid that is 1% dissociated means that the H^+ activity is $0.1 \text{ M} \times 0.01 = 0.001$ M.

Pure water undergoes slight dissociation:

$$H_2O \leftrightarrows H^+ + OH^-$$

The H^+ actually attaches to another H_2O molecule to give:

$$H_2O + H^+ \leftrightarrows H_3O^+$$

Since both H^+ and OH^- are produced, H_2O is a weak acid and weak base. The H^+ (or H_3O^+) and OH^- concentrations in pure H_2O, not in equilibrium with atmospheric CO_2, are

[*] M = molarity (moles/liter)

10^{-7} M. The product of H^+ and OH^- concentration, shown in the following equation, is the dissociation constant for water, or Kw.

$$[H^+] \times [OH^-] = [10^{-7} M] \times [10^{-7} M] = 10^{-14} = K_w$$

In equilibrium with atmospheric CO_2, the pH of H_2O is ~ 5.7 because of the following reaction:

$$H_2O + CO_2 \leftrightarrows H^+ + HCO_3^-$$

This is the reason why rainfall is a natural source of soil acidity.

Adding an acid to H_2O will increase $[H^+]$, but $[OH^-]$ would decrease because K_w is a constant 10^{-14}. For example, in a 0.1 M HCl solution, the $[H^+]$ is 10^{-1} M; thus the $[OH^-] = 10^{-13}$ M by:

$$K_w = [H^+] \times [OH^-] = 10^{-14}$$
$$[10^{-1} M] \times [OH^-] = 10^{-14}$$
$$[OH^-] = 10^{-13}$$

The H^+ concentration in solution can be conveniently expressed using pH and is defined as follows:

$$pH = \log \frac{1}{[H^+]} = -\log[H^+]$$

Thus, a solution with $[H^+] = 10^{-5}$ M has a pH of 5.0. Each unit increase in pH represents a tenfold decrease in $[H^+]$ or increase in $[OH^-]$ (Table 3-1).

Table 3-1 **Relationship Between pH and H^+ and OH^- Concentration**

	Concentration (M)	
pH	*H^+*	*OH^-*
1	10^{-1}	10^{-13}
2	10^{-2}	10^{-12}
3	10^{-3}	10^{-11}
4	10^{-4}	10^{-10}
5	10^{-5}	10^{-9}
6	10^{-6}	10^{-8}
7	10^{-7}	10^{-7}
8	10^{-8}	10^{-6}
9	10^{-9}	10^{-5}
10	10^{-10}	10^{-4}
11	10^{-11}	10^{-3}
12	10^{-12}	10^{-2}
13	10^{-13}	10^{-1}
14	10^{-14}	10^{-0}

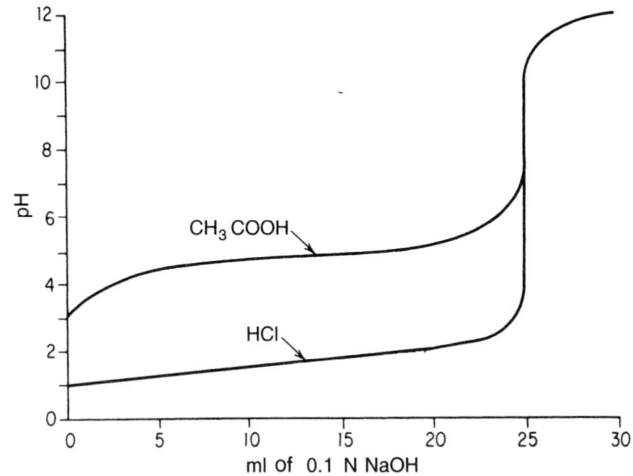

Figure 3-1 Titration of 0.10 N CH_3COOH and 0.10 N HCl with 0.1 N NaOH.

Solutions with pH < 7 are acidic, those with pH > 7 are basic, and those with pH = 7 are neutral. The pH represents the H^+ concentration in solution and does not measure the undissociated or *potential* acidity. For example, the pH of completely dissociated 0.1 M HCl is 1.0, while the pH of 0.1 M CH_3COOH, a weak acid, is 3.0. Similarly, the pH of 0.1 M NaOH, a strong base, is 13.0, while the pH of 0.1 M NH_4OH, a weak base, is 11.0.

When acids and bases are combined, both are neutralized, forming a salt and water:

$$HCl + NaOH \leftrightarrows Na^+ + Cl^- + H_2O$$

$$HCl \rightarrow H^+ \; Cl^- \qquad NaOH \rightarrow Na^+ \; OH^- \qquad (H^+ + OH^- \rightarrow H_2O)$$

If a quantity of acid is *titrated* with a base and the pH of the solution is determined at intervals during the titration, a curve is obtained by plotting pH against the amounts of base added (Fig. 3-1). Titration curves for strong and weak acids differ markedly. The neutralization reaction of HCl with NaOH is given in the previous equation, and that of CH_3COOH with NaOH is

$$CH_3COOH + NaOH \leftrightarrows CH_3COO^- + Na^+ + H_2O$$

$$CH_3COOH \rightarrow CH_3COO^- \; H^+ \qquad NaOH \rightarrow Na^+ \; OH^- \qquad (H^+ + OH^- \rightarrow H_2O)$$

Buffers

A pH buffer maintains the solution pH within a narrow range when small amounts of acid or base are added. Buffering defines the resistance to a change in pH (see Chapter 2). An example of a buffer system is CH_3COOH and CH_3COONa:

$$CH_3COOH \leftrightarrows H^+ + CH_3COO^-$$
$$CH_3COONa \leftrightarrows Na^+ + CH_3COO^-$$

For example, a solution containing 1 M CH_3COOH and 1 M CH_3COONa has a pH of 4.6, compared with pH 2 for CH_3COOH alone. Adding the highly dissociated CH_3COONa to CH_3COOH increases the CH_3COO^- concentration, which shifts the equilibrium to form CH_3COOH. The pH remains at 4.6 even with a tenfold dilution with H_2O; however, dilution of 1 M CH_3COOH would raise the pH to 3.0. Thus, adding CH_3COONa to CH_3COOH buffers the solution pH.

If 10 ml of 1 M HCl is added to the CH_3COOH / CH_3COONa buffer solution, the pH will decrease to only 4.5, because the additional H^+ will shift the $CH_3COOH \leftrightharpoons H^+ + CH_3COO^-$ equilibrium to the left and the decreased CH_3COO^- will be replaced by the CH_3COO^- supplied from the dissociation of CH_3COONa (equilibrium shift to the right in $CH_3COONa \leftrightharpoons Na^+ + CH_3COO^-$).

Conversely, if 10 ml of 1 M NaOH is added, the OH^- neutralizes H^+ to form water. Because of the large supply of undissociated CH_3COOH, the equilibrium shifts to the right, resupplying H^+; thus, the pH increases to only 4.7.

Soils behave like buffered weak acids, with the CEC of humus and clay minerals providing the buffer for soil solution pH.

Soil Acidity

About 25 to 30% of the world's soils are acidic and represent some of the most important food-producing regions (Fig. 3-2). In the United States most of the acidic soils occur in the east and northwest regions, where annual precipitation exceeds 24 in.

Sources of Soil Acidity

Precipitation As discussed earlier, H_2O in equilibrium with atmospheric CO_2 has a pH ~5.7 resulting from:

$$H_2O + CO_2 \leftrightharpoons H_2CO_3 \leftrightharpoons H^+ + HCO_3^-$$

The precipitation pH varies with region, with lower pH in the eastern U.S. regions and other areas of intense industrial activity as a result of greater pollutant-loading into the atmosphere (Fig. 3-3). Primary pollutants are SO_2, NH_3, and various NO_x gases that include *nitric oxide* (NO), *nitrogen dioxide* (NO_2), and *nitrous oxide* (N_2O). The global sources of NO_X gases include fossil fuel combustion (40%), biomass combustion (22%), lightning (15%), soil microbial activity (15%), and chemical oxidation of NH_3 (8%).

About 50% of the global SO_2 emission is anthropogenic, primarily related to burning coal to produce electricity and other industrial emissions (i.e., steel manufacturing, etc.). The remaining 50% of SO_2 emissions is due to natural processes including ocean biogenic production (20%), volcanoes (10%), soil, plant, and animal emissions (10%), wind-raised dust (6%), coastal zone and wetland biogenic sources (2%), and biomass burning (2%).

The emission of NH_3 varies depending on region. In North America and Europe, 65 to 75% is due to livestock production (including manure application to soils), 10 to 15% from fertilizer application, and the remainder from industrial sources.

Ultimately, the oxidation and hydrolysis reactions of these gases in the atmosphere (reactions with O_2 and H_2O) is the production of NH_4^+ and H^+. The emission of NH_3 is not acid-forming since it combines with H_2O by:

$$NH_3 + H_2O \leftrightharpoons NH_4^+ + OH^-$$

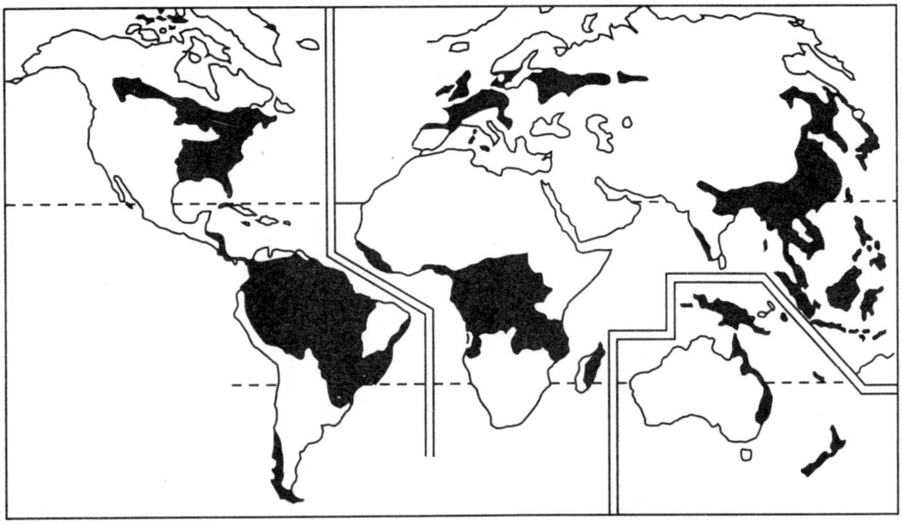

(a)

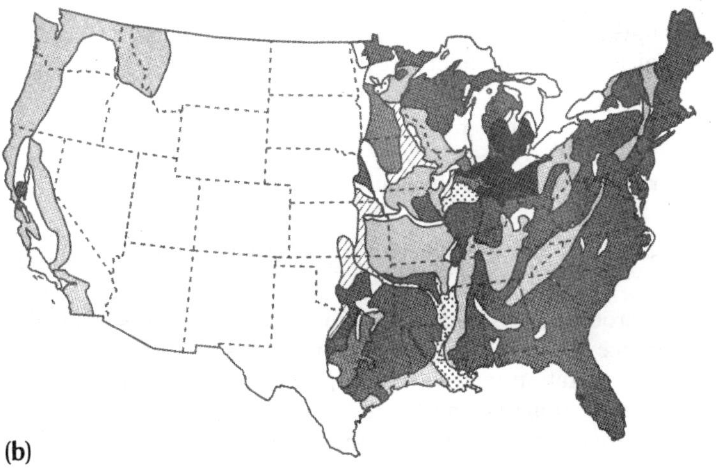

(b)

- Area of soils dominantly very rich in lime
- Area having mixed pattern of soils of high and medium lime (or available calcium) content
- Areas where soils are acidic, but lime or calcium in other available forms is within reach of deep-rooted plants
- Areas of acidic soils, poor in lime and other available forms of calcium
- Area where soils and parent materials are dominantly fairly rich in lime, though surface soil is somewhat acidic in places
- Area having mixed pattern of soils of medium and low lime content
- Areas having mixed pattern of high, medium, and low lime content

Figure 3-2 **Major regions in the world (a) and the United States (b) with predominantly acidic soils.**

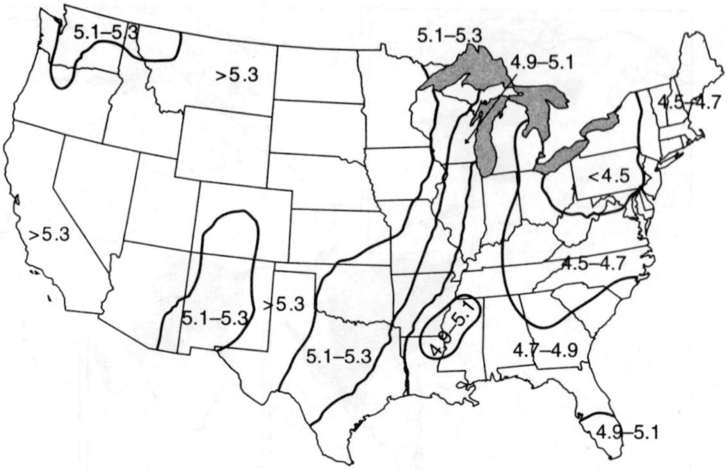

Figure 3-3 **Distribution of precipitation pH in the U.S.** ***(2002 data from the National Atmospheric Deposition Program.)***

The base (OH^-) produced neutralizes some of the acids produced from NO_X and SO_2 emission. However, once in the soil, microorganisms convert NH_4^+ to NO_3^-, producing H^+ by:

$$NH_4^+ + 2O_2 \leftrightarrows NO_3^- + H_2O + 2H^+$$

When SO_2 enters the atmosphere the acid-producing reaction is:

$$SO_2 + {}^1/_2O_2 + H_2O \leftrightarrows SO_4^{-2} + 2H^+$$

Soil OM As microorganisms decompose soil OM, they release CO_2 that quickly reacts with H_2O to produce H^+ and HCO_3^- (see previous discussion). Decomposition of organic residues and root respiration increases CO_2 in soil air to about ten times atmospheric CO_2; thus, acidity produced from CO_2 in soil air is greater than that produced in the atmosphere. In addition, microorganisms produce organic acids by:

$$\text{Organic C} \rightarrow \text{R-COOH} \rightarrow \text{R-COO}^- + H^+$$

The type of residue added influences the quantity of acid produced. For example, residue in a conifer forest produces more acid than in soils under deciduous forest or grasslands. Also, soil OM contains reactive carboxylic and phenolic groups that behave as weak acids releasing H^+ (Figure 2–8). Soil OM content varies with the environment, vegetation, and soil; thus, its contribution to soil acidity varies accordingly. In peat and muck soils and in mineral soils containing large amounts of OM, organic acids contribute significantly to soil acidity.

Nutrient Transformations and Uptake Transformations of nutrients in soil can be both acid-producing and acid-consuming (Table 3-2). Inspection of N and S transformations shows little net effect on soil pH. Leaching of NO_3^- and SO_4^{-2} results in a decrease in pH as the basic cations would also leach.

Table 3-2 Selected Nutrient Transformations and Nutrient Uptake in Soils That Influence Soil pH

Process	*Reaction*	*pH Effect**
Nitrogen		*mole* H^+/*mole* N *or* S
Mineralization	$R\text{-}NH_2 + H^+ + H_2O \rightleftarrows R\text{-}OH + NH_4^+$	−1
Denitrification	$2NO_3^- + 2H^+ \rightleftarrows N_2 + 2\frac{1}{2}O_2 + H_2O$	−1
Urea hydrolysis	$(NH_2)_2CO + 3H_2O \rightleftarrows 2NH_4^+ + 2OH^- + CO_2$	−1
NO_3^- uptake	$NO_3^- + 8H^+ + 8e^- \rightleftarrows NH_2 + 2H_2O + OH^-$	−1
Immobilization	$NH_4^+ + R\text{-}OH \rightleftarrows R\text{-}NH_2 + H^+ + H_2O$	+1
Nitrification	$NH_4^+ + 2O_2 \rightleftarrows NO_3^- + H_2O + 2H^+$	+2
Volatilization	$NH_4^+ + OH^- \rightleftarrows NH_3 + H_2O$	+1
NH_4^+ uptake	$NH_4^+ + R\text{-}OH \rightleftarrows R\text{-}NH_2 + H^+ + H_2O$	+1
Sulfur		
Mineralization	$R\text{-}S + 1\frac{1}{2}O_2 + H_2O \rightleftarrows SO_4^{-2} + 2H^+$	+2
SO_4^{-2} uptake	$SO_4^{-2} + 8H^+ + 8e^- \rightleftarrows SH_2 + 2H_2O + 2OH^-$	−2

*Negative number represents increase in pH; positive number represents decrease in pH.

Plants alter the soil pH through imbalances in cation/anion uptake. As cations are absorbed by plant roots, electrical neutrality is maintained through uptake of an anion or extrusion of a H^+. When anions are absorbed, uptake of cations or extrusion of OH^- or HCO_3^- occurs to maintain electrical neutrality. When cation exceeds anion uptake, excess H^+ is released into the rhizophere, while OH^- / HCO_3^- is released when anion exceeds cation uptake. Generally, most plants take up more cations than anions, resulting in soil acidification. For example in legumes, cation uptake anion uptake because legumes provide a majority of N through N_2-fixation. Alternatively, rhizosphere pH will increase slightly with plants relying entirely on NO_3^-, which does not commonly occur (Fig. 3-4). The net effect of non-leguminous plants on rhizosphere pH depends on the proportional supply of NH_4^+ and NO_3^-.

Leaching Water transported below the root zone carries dissolved or soluble ions and compounds. The most soluble anions are NO_3^-, Cl^-, and HCO_3^-, while the most soluble cations are Na^+, K^+, Ca^{+2}, and Mg^{+2}. Electrical neutrality of the soil solution must be maintained, thus, as anions leach, basic cations also leach reducing precent base saturation (%BS) and pH. As NO_3^- is produced from nitrification of NH_4^+ from plant residues, manures, soil OM,

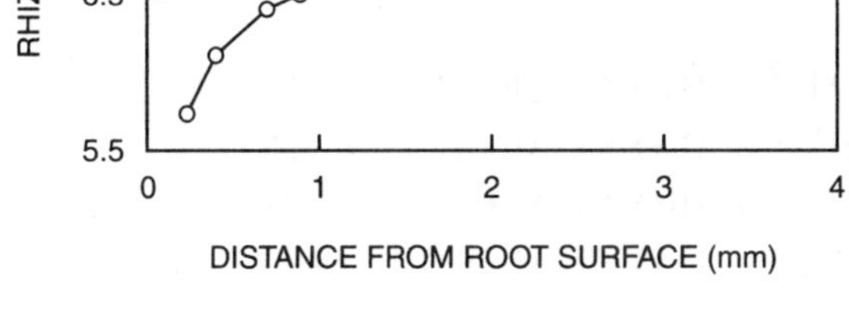

Figure 3-4 Influence of NH_4^+ (○) and NO_3^- (□) uptake in ryegrass on rhizosphere pH. *(Adapted from Gahoonia et al., 1992,* Plant Soil *140: 241–248.)*

or N fertilizers, no net H^+ would be produced if all the NO_3^- were absorbed by plants (Table 3-2). Unfortunately, crop recovery of NO_3^- is not complete and some NO_3^- leaching occurs in nearly every cropping situation. Nitrate leaching is also greater under legume pastures compared to unfertilized grass pastures. Similar differences in soil acidity have been observed between deciduous and leguminous forest systems.

The net effect of crop growth on soil acidity depends on plant species, the proportion of NH_4^+ and NO_3^- uptake, total biomass production (or yield), quantity of plant material harvested, and quantity of NO_3^- leached. Higher legume or nonlegume (fertilized with NH_4^+) biomass production results in greater soil acidity. Soil acidity would be lower with grain harvest compared to grain plus residues. Increasing the quantity of biomass left in the field increases acidity produced through microbial degradation. Soils and environments exhibiting greater leaching potential will be more acidifying.

Clay Minerals, Al and Fe Oxides, Soil OM The dissociation of H^+ from edges of clay minerals, Al and Fe oxides, and soil OM surfaces contributes to soil acidity and pH buffering. The edges of clay minerals such as kaolinite (1:1) and montmorillonite (2:1) can buffer soil pH (Fig. 2-7). The pH buffering capacity associated with carboxylic acid groups in soil OM is illustrated in Figure 2-8. The pH buffering capacity associated with Al and Fe oxides behaves similarly, as follows:

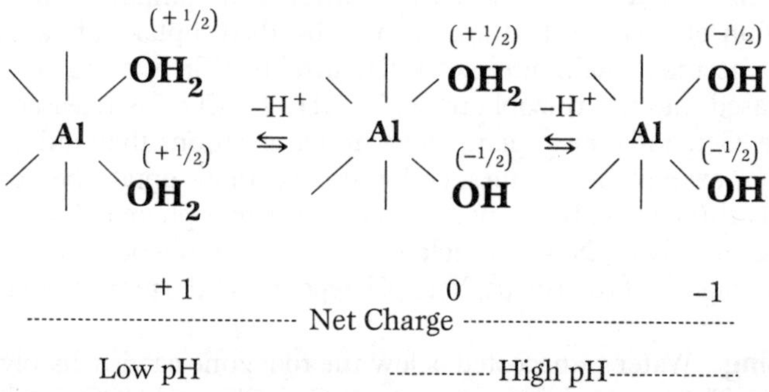

As pH decreases, adsorbed H^+ increases, which increases the surface (+) charge or AEC. Soils with high clay, Al/Fe oxide, and/or soil OM contents exhibit greater pH buffer capacity than sandy and/or low OM soils.

Al and Fe Hydrolysis As soil pH decreases, the concentration of Al^{+3} in soil solution increases because of dissolution of $Al(OH)_3$ according to:

$$Al(OH)_3 + 3H^+ \leftrightharpoons Al^{+3} + 3H_2O$$

The equilibrium reaction shows that as pH decreases (increasing H^+), the equilibrium shifts to the right where $Al(OH)_3$ dissolves to produce Al^{+3}, which can then be adsorbed to the CEC. Depending on pH, Al^{+3} will hydrolyze according to:

$$Al^{+3} + H_2O \leftrightharpoons Al(OH)^{+2} + H^+$$
$$Al(OH)^{+2} + H_2O \leftrightharpoons Al(OH)_2^{+} + H^+$$
$$Al(OH)_2^{+} + H_2O \leftrightharpoons Al(OH)_3^{0} + H^+$$
$$Al(OH)_3^{0} + H_2O \leftrightharpoons Al(OH)_4^{-} + H^+$$

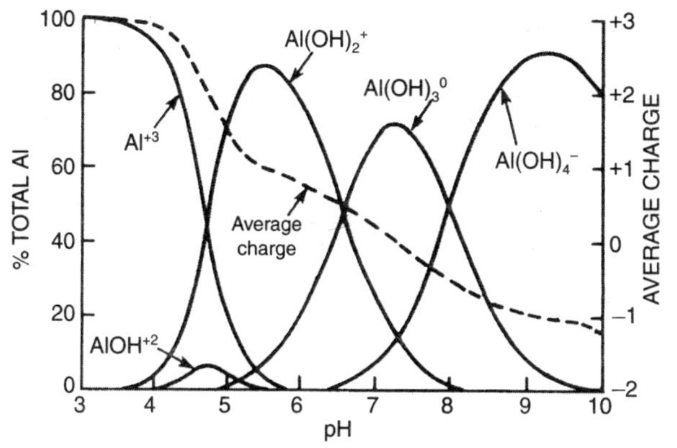

Figure 3-5 **Relationship between pH and the distribution and average charge of soluble Al species.**

Each successive step occurs at a higher pH. Figure 3-5 illustrates the range in pH wherein the various Al hydrolysis species predominate. At low pH, more of the Al hydrolysis species are (+) charged, which enables greater Al adsorption to CEC.

Hydrolysis of Al^{+3} generates H^+ and lowers pH, unless there is a source of OH^- to neutralize H^+.

If a base is added (i.e., $CaCO_3$), H^+ will be neutralized first. With continued addition of base, Al^{+3} hydrolyzes, with the production of H^+. In this way, Al^{+3} hydrolysis buffers the increase in solution pH. Soil pH will not increase until sufficient base is added to decrease soluble Al^{+3}. It should be noted that $Al(OH)_3$ will precipitate at pH 6.5, decreasing Al^{+3} in solution and increasing pH.

Fe hydrolysis is similar to that of Al.

$$Fe^{+3} + H_2O \leftrightarrows Fe(OH)^{+2} + H^+$$
$$Fe(OH)^{+2} + H_2O \leftrightarrows Fe(OH)_2{}^+ + H^+$$
$$Fe(OH)_2{}^+ + H_2O \leftrightarrows Fe(OH)_3{}^0 + H^+$$
$$Fe(OH)_3{}^0 + H_2O \leftrightarrows Fe(OH)_4{}^- + H^+$$

Although this reaction is more acidic than Al hydrolysis, the acidity is buffered by Al hydrolysis reactions. Thus, Fe hydrolysis has little effect on soil pH until most of the soil Al has reacted. Al and Fe hydroxides occur as amorphous or crystalline colloids, coating the clay and other mineral surfaces. They are also held between the lattices of expanding clay minerals, preventing collapse of these lattices as water is removed during drying.

Soluble Salts Acidic, neutral, or basic salts in the soil solution originate from mineral weathering, OM decomposition, or addition as fertilizers and manures. The cations of these salts will displace adsorbed Al^{+3} in acidic soils and thus decrease soil solution pH as the Al^{+3} hydrolyzes. Divalent cations have a greater effect on lowering soil pH than monovalent metal cations (see the lyotropic series in Chapter 2).

Band-applied fertilizer will result in a high soluble-salt concentration in the affected soil zone, which will decrease pH through Al^{+3} hydrolysis. With high rates of band-applied fertilizer in soils with pH $<$ 5.0 to 5.5, the increased soluble Al^{+3} can be detrimental to plant growth.

Fertilizers Fertilizer materials vary in their soil reaction pH. Nitrate sources carrying a basic cation are less acid-forming than $NH_4{}^+$ sources. Compared with P fertilizers, those

Table 3-3 Soil Acidity Produced by N and S Fertilizers

Fertilizer Source	*Soil Reaction*	*mole H^+/ mole N+S*	*$CaCO_3$ Equiv.**
Anhydrous ammonia	$NH_3 + 2O_2 \rightarrow H^+ + NO_3^- + H_2O$	1	3.6
Urea	$(NH_2)_2CO + 4O_2 \rightarrow 2NO_3^- + 2H^+ + CO_2 + H_2O$	1	3.6
Ammonium nitrate	$NH_4NO_3 + 2O_2 \rightarrow 2NO_3^- + 2H^+ + H_2O$	1	3.6
Ammonium sulfate	$(NH_4)_2SO_4 + 4O_2 \rightarrow 2NO_3^- + 4H^+ + SO_4^{-2} + H_2O$	2	7.2
Monoammonium phosphate	$NH_4H_2PO_4 + O_2 \rightarrow 2NO_3^- + 2H^+ + H_2PO_4^- + H_2O$	2	7.2
Diammonium phosphate	$(NH_4)_2HPO_4 + O_2 \rightarrow 2NO_3^- + 3H^+ + H_2PO_4^- + H_2O$	1.5	5.4
Elemental S	$2S + 3O_2 + 2H_2O \rightleftarrows 2SO_4^{-2} + 4H^+$	2	7.2
Ammonium thiosulfate	$(NH_4)_2S_2O_3 + 6O_2 \rightarrow 2SO_4^{-2} + 2NO_3^- + 6H^+ + H_2O$	1.5	5.4

*$CaCO_3$ equivalent → lbs $CaCO_3$ required per lbs N applied to neutralize acidity in the fertilizer.
SOURCE: Adams, 1984, *Soil Acidity and Liming*, No. 12, p. 234, ASA.

containing or forming NH_4^+ exhibit greater effect on soil pH (Table 3-3). The acidity produced is greater when S and P sources are combined with NH_4^+ than with N only sources. Phosphoric acid released from dissolving P fertilizers such as triple superphosphate and monoammonium phosphate can temporarily acidify localized zones at the site of application. The former material will reduce pH to as low as 1.5, whereas the latter will decrease pH to approximately 3.5; however, the quantity of H^+ produced is very small and has little long-term effect on bulk soil pH. Diammonium phosphate will initially raise soil pH to about 8, unless the initial soil pH is greater than the pH of the fertilizer (see Chapter 5). Acidity produced by the nitrification of the NH_4^+ will offset this initial pH increase.

Table 3-3 shows the theoretical quantity of $CaCO_3$ needed to neutralize the acidity produced per unit of N or S fertilizer applied. For example with $(NH_4)_2SO_4$, 7.2 lbs $CaCO_3$ are needed to neutralize the H^+ produced per lb of N applied. The method used to determine the $CaCO_3$ equivalent for $(NH_4)_2SO_4$ is as follows:

4 moles of H^+ produced/2 mole N applied

or,

4 equivalent weights of H^+ produced/2 equivalent weights of N

thus,

4 equivalent weights of $CaCO_3$ are needed to neutralize 4 equivalent weights of H^+ produced / 2 equivalent weights of N

$$\frac{4 \times 50 \text{ g } CaCO_3/\text{eq}}{2 \times 14 \text{ g N/eq}} = \frac{7.2 \text{ lb } CaCO_3}{\text{lb N}}$$

The theoretical $CaCO_3$ equivalents are usually an overestimate of the $CaCO_3$ required to neutralize the acidity produced from application of fertilizers. As previously discussed, root absorption of fertilizer anions (NO_3^-, SO_4^{-2}, or $H_2PO_4^-$) would neutralize some of the acidity produced from nitrification of NH_4^+ or oxidation of S (Table 3-3). When anion uptake effects are considered, the $CaCO_3$ equivalent is often reduced by 50%, which may be too extreme considering the acidity produced with NH_4^+ uptake.

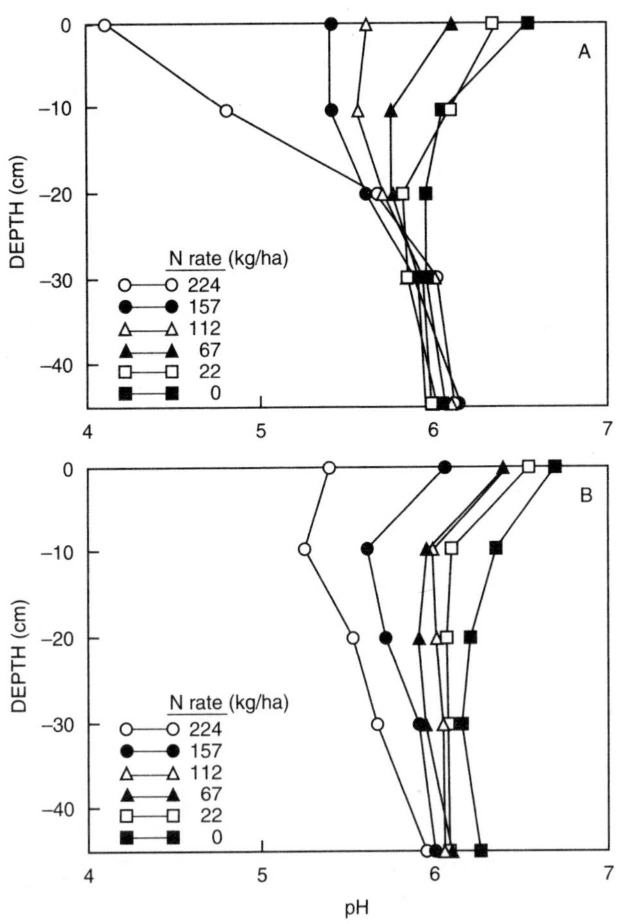

Figure 3-6 **Soil pH decreases dramatically with increasing N rate and years of application. Soil fertilized annually since 1946 (A) and fertilized annually from 1946 to 1965 (no N applied since 1965). Soils were sampled in 1985.** ***(Schwab et al., 1990,*** **SSSAJ,** ***53:1412–1417.)***

Long-Term Effects

The extent and rate of soil pH decline will vary among soils and management. A problem might develop in 5 years on a sandy soil or 10 years on a silt loam soil, but might take 15 years or more on a clay loam. Soil acidity is an increasing problem in certain areas where lime use has been decreasing. In long-term studies in Kansas, surface soil pH decreased more than 2 pH units (6.5 to 4.1 pH) with forty years of 200 lb N/a applied annually as NH_4NO_3 to bromegrass (Fig. 3-6). With only 20 years of N fertilization, surface soil pH decreased only 1 pH unit (6.5 to 5.5 pH).

The Soil as a Buffer

Soil behaves like a weak acid that will buffer pH. In acid soils adsorbed Al^{+3} will be in equilibrium with Al^{+3} in soil solution, which hydrolyzes to produce H^+, depending on solution pH. If H^+ is neutralized by a base (i.e., $CaCO_3$), solution Al^{+3} precipitates as $Al(OH)_3$, causing exchangeable Al^{+3} to desorb to resupply solution Al^{+3}. Thus, soil pH remains the same or is buffered. As more base is added, the preceding reaction continues, with more adsorbed

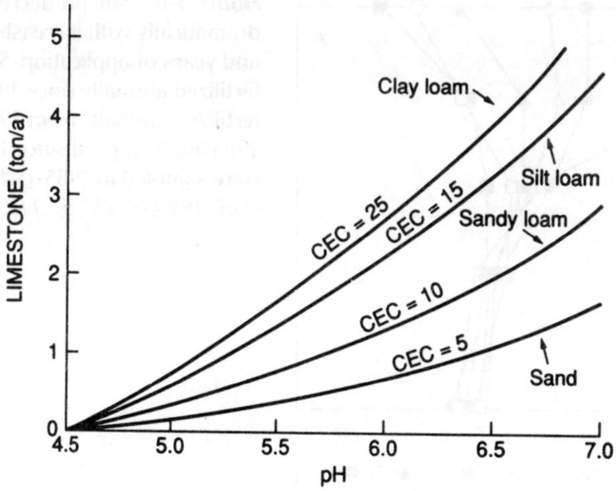

Figure 3-7 **Approximate limestone (tons/a) required to raise surface soil pH (7-inch depth) of soil of four textural classes with typical CEC (meq/100 g soil).**

Al^{+3} neutralized and replaced on the CEC with the cation of the added base. As a result, soil pH gradually increases.

The reverse of the preceding reaction also occurs. As acid is continually added, OH^- in the soil solution is neutralized. Gradually, the $Al(OH)_3$ dissolves, to resupply OH^-, which increases Al^{+3} in solution and subsequently on the CEC. As the reaction continues, soil pH continuously but slowly decreases as the Al^{+3} replaces adsorbed basic cations.

The quantity of clay minerals and OM in a soil determine the extent of buffering in soils. Soils containing large amounts of clay and OM are highly buffered and require larger amounts of lime to increase the pH than soils with a lower BC. Sandy soils with small amounts of clay and OM are poorly buffered and require only small amounts of lime to effect a given change in pH. Soils containing mostly 1:1 clays (Ultisols and Oxisols) are generally less buffered than soils with principally 2:1 clay minerals (Alfisols and Mollisols). For example, the lime requirement increases with increasing clay content and CEC (Fig. 3-7).

Determination of Active and Potential Acidity in Soils

Active Acidity

Active acidity represents the H^+ and Al^{+3} concentration in the soil solution. Currently, the most accurate and widely used method involves measuring pH in a saturated paste or a more diluted soil-water mixture with a pH meter and glass electrode. Soil pH is a useful indicator of the presence of exchangeable Al^{+3} and H^+. Exchangeable H^+ is present at pH < 4, while exchangeable Al^{+3} occurs predominantly at pH <5.5.

Increasing the dilution of the soil from saturation to 1:1 to 1:10 soil:water ratio increases the measured pH compared with the pH of a saturated paste. To minimize differences in solution ion concentration between soils, some laboratories dilute the soil with 0.01 M $CaCl_2$ instead of water. Adding Ca^{+2} decreases the pH compared with soil diluted with water. Changes in measured pH with dilution and added salt are generally small, ranging between 0.1 and 0.5 pH unit.

Potential Acidity

Potential acidity represents the H^+ and Al^{+3} on the CEC. Soil pH measurements are excellent indicators of soil acidity, but do not measure potential acidity. Quantifying potential soil acidity requires titrating the soil with a base, which can be used to determine the lime requirement or quantity of $CaCO_3$ needed to increase the pH to a desired level. Thus, the lime requirement of a soil is related not only to soil pH, but also to its BC or CEC (Fig. 3-7). High-clay and/or high-OM soils have higher BCs and lime requirements, whereas coarse-textured soils low in clay and OM have lower BCs and lime requirements. An example liming calculation for two soils with CEC = 20 meq/100 g and 10 meq/100g is shown in the following:

Clay soil →

$$\begin{aligned} \text{CEC} &= 20 \text{ meq/100 g} \\ \text{Initial pH} &= 5.0 \ \ (50\% \text{ BS from Fig 2-9}) \\ \text{Desired pH} &= 6.5 \ \ (80\% \text{ BS from Fig 2-9}) \end{aligned}$$

Need to increase %BS from 50 → 80% or neutralize 30% of CEC occupied by acids; thus

$$(0.30)\,\frac{20 \text{ meq CEC}}{100 \text{ g Soil}} = \frac{6.0 \text{ meq acids}}{100 \text{ g Soil}} = \frac{6.0 \text{ meq CaCO}_3}{100 \text{ g Soil}}$$

Therefore, the quantity of pure $CaCO_3$ needed is

$$\frac{6.0 \text{ meq CaCO}_3}{100 \text{ g Soil}} \times \frac{50 \text{ mg CaCO}_3}{\text{meq}} = \frac{300 \text{ mg CaCO}_3}{100 \text{ g Soil}}$$

Thus,

$$\frac{300 \text{ mg CaCO}_3}{100 \text{ g Soil}} \times \frac{1 \text{ g}}{1000 \text{ mg}} = \frac{0.30 \text{ g CaCO}_3}{100 \text{ g Soil}} = \frac{0.30 \text{ lb CaCO}_3}{100 \text{ lb Soil}}$$

$$\frac{0.30 \text{ lb CaCO}_3}{100 \text{ lb Soil}} \times \frac{2 \times 10^4}{2 \times 10^4} = \frac{6{,}000 \text{ lb CaCO}_3}{2 \times 10^6 \text{ lb Soil}} = \frac{6{,}000 \text{ lb CaCO}_3}{\text{afs}}$$

Assuming the same initial and final pH and %BS, the $CaCO_3$ required for a sandy loam soil (CEC = 10 meq/100 g) would be only 3,000 lb $CaCO_3$/afs.

Determining Lime Requirement

The lime requirement of a soil can be determined by several different methods. Titrating a soil with a base [i.e., $Ca(OH)_2$] will increase soil pH (Fig. 3-8). After equilibration, pH is determined and the pH values are plotted against meq of base added. From these data it is simple to determine the amount of lime to be added. For example, increasing pH from 4.5

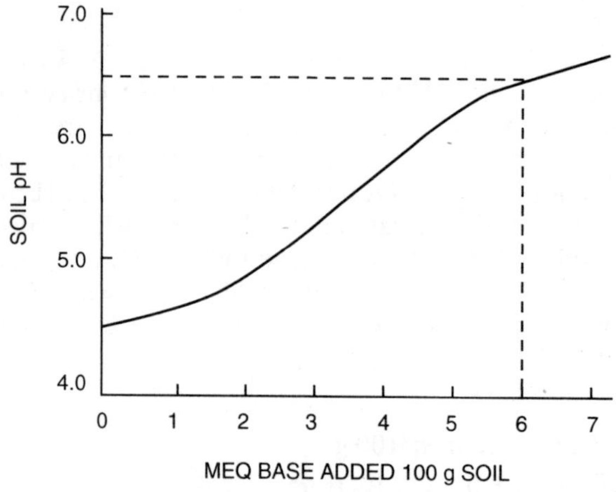

Figure 3-8 **Example titration to determine lime requirement of an acid sandy loam soil. Initial soil pH is 4.5. Increasing addition of base (meq/100 g soil) increases soil pH.**

to 6.5 requires adding 6.0 meq base/100 g soil (Fig. 3-8). Thus, the quantity of $CaCO_3$ needed to increase pH to 6.5 would be:

$$\frac{6.0 \text{ meq CaCO}_3}{100 \text{ g Soil}} \times \frac{50 \text{ mg CaCO}_3}{\text{meq}} = \frac{300 \text{ mg CaCO}_3}{100 \text{ g Soil}}$$

The conversion to lbs $CaCO_3$/afs was illustrated previously = 6,000 lbs $CaCO_3$/afs.

The common methods to estimate lime requirement are based on the change in pH of a buffered solution added to a soil. When a buffer solution (usually ≥ 7.3 pH) is added to an acid soil, the buffer pH is depressed in proportion to the original soil pH and its BC. A large drop in buffer pH would indicate a low pH soil with a large reserve or potential acidity, and a high lime requirement. Field and laboratory calibration of the decrease in buffer pH, the amount of lime required to increase pH to the desired level (i.e., the lime requirement), can be determined.

The Shoemaker, McLean, and Pratt (SMP) single-buffer method for measuring the lime requirement of acidic soils has been widely adopted by U.S. soil-testing laboratories. The SMP method is commonly used for soils with relatively high lime requirements (≥ 2 tons/ac), pH < 5.8, OM < 10%, and appreciable quantities of soluble Al^{+3}. The SMP method used on soils with low lime requirements will frequently result in overliming.

Using Al toxicity to plants as a basis for lime recommendations has also been used. The Mehlich buffer method works similarly to the SMP buffer; however, the quantity of exchangeable acidity (primarily Al^{+3}) is determined. The lime requirement is established to reduce exchangeable Al^{+3} to zero (100% BS). The Mehlich buffer method is predominately used in highly weathered and leached soils.

Neutralizing Soil Acidity

Liming Reactions in Soil

Liming reactions begin with the neutralization of H^+ in the soil solution by adding a base (usually OH^- or HCO_3^-) originating from the lime material. For example, $CaCO_3$ behaves as follows:

$$CaCO_3 + 2H^+ \leftrightarrows Ca^{+2} + CO_2 + H_2O$$

The fast reaction of $2H^+ + CO_3^{-2} \rightarrow CO_2 + H_2O$ neutralizes H^+ in soil solution. Exchangeable H^+ desorbs from the CEC to buffer the decreasing H^+ in solution. Two H^+ on the CEC are replaced by one Ca^{+2}. In this way, both soil pH and %BS increase (Fig. 2-9).

Since the majority of exchangeable acidity occurs as exchangeable Al^{+3}, the neutralization reaction can be represented by:

Step 1 Exchange $2Al^{+3}$ on the CEC with $3Ca^{+2}$ from the $CaCO_3$

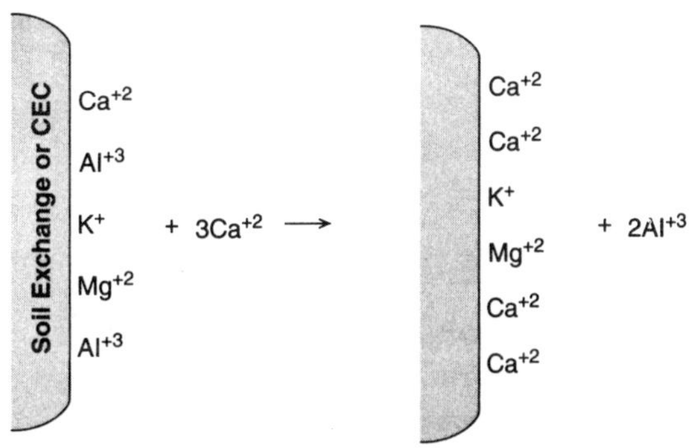

Step 2 Al^{+3} in solution hydrolyzes (reacts with water) to produce $6H^+$; the $Al(OH)_3$ precipitates out of solution

$$2Al^{+3} + 6H_2O \leftrightarrows 2Al(OH)_3 + 6H^+$$

Step 3 the CO_3^{-2} (from $CaCO_3$) neutralizes the H^+ produced from Step 2

$$3CO_3^{-2} + 6H^+ \leftrightarrows 3CO_2 + 3H_2O$$

Overall Reaction

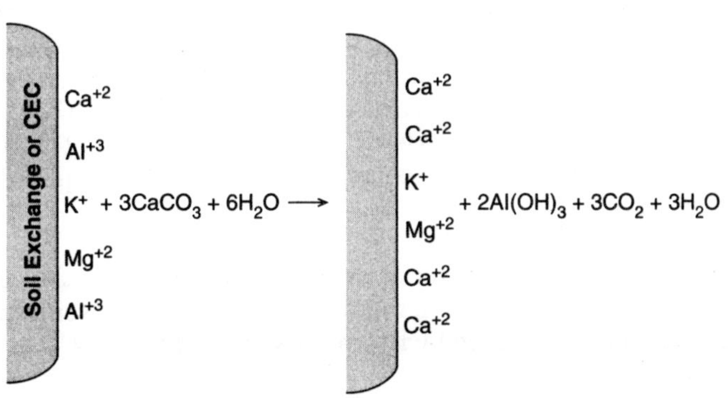

The rate of the reaction is directly related to the rate at which the H^+ ions are neutralized in solution. As long as sufficient $CaCO_3$ is available, H^+ will be converted to H_2O. The continued removal of H^+ from the soil solution will ultimately result in the precipitation of

Table 3-4 Properties of Common Lime Materials

Lime Material	Molecular Wt.	Equivalent Wt.	CCE*	Ca Content
	g/mole	g/equiv.	%	%
CaO	56	28	179	71
$Ca(OH)_2$	74	36	135	54
$CaMg(CO_3)_2$	184	46	109	22 (13% Mg)
$CaCO_3$	100	50	100	40
$CaSiO_3$	116	58	86	46

*CCE → calcium carbonate equivalent represents the neutralizing value of the material compared to pure $CaCO_3$. For example, $Ca(OH)_2$ neutralizes 35% more acid than the same weight of $CaCO_3$.

Al^{+3} as $Al(OH)_3$ and replacement on the CEC with Ca^{+2}. Thus, as soil pH increases, %BS also increases (Fig. 2-9).

Liming Materials

The common lime materials are Ca and Mg oxides, hydroxides, carbonates, and silicates (Table 3-4). The accompanying anion must neutralize H^+ in solution and hence Al^{+3} in solution and on the CEC.

Gypsum ($CaSO_4 \cdot 2H_2O$) and other neutral salts cannot neutralize H^+, as shown by:

$$CaSO_4 \cdot 2H_2O + 2H^+ \leftrightarrows Ca^{+2} + 2H^+ + SO_4^{-2} + 2H_2O$$

In fact, neutral salts lower soil pH. In the previous example, Ca^{+2} replaces adsorbed Al^{+3} that increases solution Al^{+3} and decreases pH. This is especially true with band-applied salts where the localized fertilized zone pH is depressed. Although gypsum will not neutralize soil pH, increasing Ca^{+2} in solution may enhance growth if Ca^{+2} is marginally deficient. Also, formation of $AlSO_4^0$ reduces Al^{+3} in solution and subsequent potential Al toxicity. Other neutral salts that are not liming materials include $MgSO_4 \cdot 7H_2O$, KCl, $CaCl_2$, and $MgCl_2$. NaOH could be considered a liming material except for addition of Na on the CEC is not recommended (discussed in the following section).

Calcium Oxide Calcium oxide (CaO) is the only material to which the term *lime* may be correctly applied. Also known as unslaked lime, burned lime, or quicklime, CaO is a white powder, shipped in paper bags because of its caustic properties. It is manufactured by roasting $CaCO_3$ in a furnace, driving off CO_2. CaO is the most effective of all liming materials with a *calcium carbonate equivalent* (CCE) of 179%, compared with pure $CaCO_3$ (Table 3-4). When unusually rapid results are required, either CaO or $Ca(OH)_2$ should be used.

Calcium Hydroxide Calcium hydroxide [$Ca(OH)_2$], or slaked lime, hydrated lime, or builders' lime, is a white powder and difficult to handle. Neutralization of acid occurs rapidly. Slaked lime is prepared by hydrating CaO and has a CCE of 136% (Table 3-4).

Calcium and Calcium-Magnesium Carbonates Calcium carbonate ($CaCO_3$), or calcite, and calcium-magnesium carbonate [$CaMg(CO_3)_2$], or dolomite, are common liming materials. Limestone is most often mined by open-pit methods. The quality of crystalline limestones

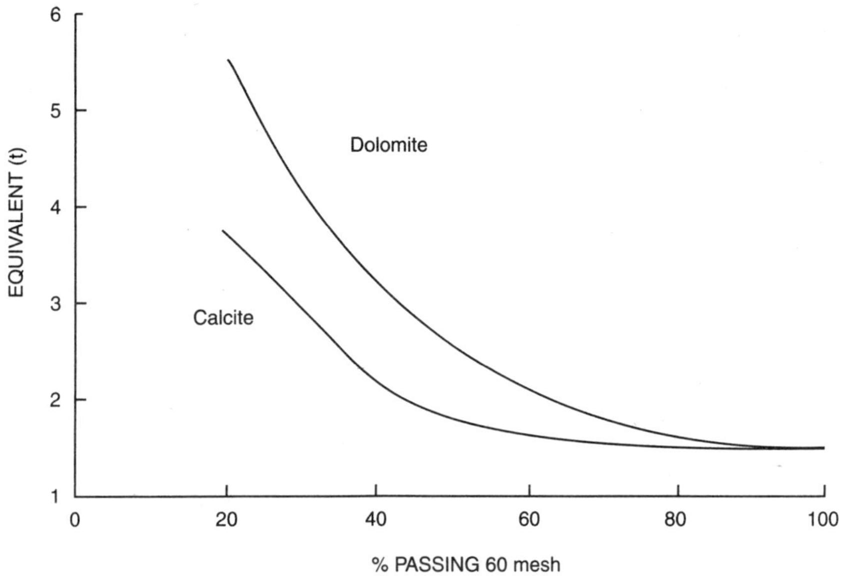

Figure 3-9 **The effect of limestone fineness on the relative effectiveness of calcitic and dolomitic limestones for increasing crop yield.**

depends on clay content and other impurities. The CCE varies from 65 to 105%. The CCE of pure $CaCO_3$ is theoretically established at 100%, while CCE of pure dolomite is 109%. The CCE of most agricultural lime is 80 to 95%. Although dolomite has a slightly higher CCE than calcite, dolomite has a lower solubility and thus will dissolve more slowly. For dolomite to be as effective as calcite at the same application rate, dolomite should be ground twice as fine or react twice as long (Fig. 3-9).

Marl Marls are soft, unconsolidated deposits of $CaCO_3$ frequently mixed with earthen impurities and usually quite moist. Marl deposits are generally thin, recovered by dragline or power shovel after the overburden has been removed. The fresh material is stockpiled and allowed to dry before being applied to the land. Marl is almost always low in Mg, and its CCE ranges from 70 to 90%, depending on clay content.

Calcium Silicates Calcium metasilicate from natural deposits in North America has a CCE of 86. $CaSiO_3$ also occurs in slag by-products of iron manufacturing. In the blast-furnace reduction of Fe ore, $CaCO_3$ loses CO_2 and forms CaO, which combines with molten Si to produce a slag that is either air or water cooled. The CCE of slags ranges from 60 to 90%, and usually contain appreciable amounts of Mg and P, depending on the source of Fe ore and manufacturing process.

Miscellaneous Liming Materials Other materials used as liming agents in areas close to their source include fly ash from coal-burning power-generating plants, sludge from water treatment plants, lime or flue dust from cement manufacturing, pulp mill lime, carbide lime, acetylene lime, packinghouse lime, and so on. These by-products contain varying amounts of Ca and Mg.

Calcium Carbonate Equivalent of Liming Materials

The value of a liming material depends on the quantity of acid that a unit weight of lime will neutralize, which is related to the composition and purity. Pure $CaCO_3$ is the standard against which other liming materials are measured, and its neutralizing value is considered to be 100%. The calcium carbonate equivalent (CCE) is defined as the acid-neutralizing capacity of a liming material expressed as a weight percentage of $CaCO_3$. Consider the following reactions:

$$CaCO_3 + 2H^+ \leftrightarrows Ca^{+2} + CO_2 + H_2O$$
$$Ca(OH)_2 + 2H^+ \leftrightarrows Ca^{+2} + 2H_2O$$

In each reaction, 1 mole of CO_3^{-2} will neutralize 2 moles of H^+. The molecular weight of $CaCO_3$ is 100 g/mole, whereas that of $Ca(OH)_2$ is only 74 g/mole; thus, 74 g of $Ca(OH)_2$ will neutralize the same amount of acid as 100 g of $CaCO_3$. Therefore, the neutralizing value, or CCE, of equal weights of the two materials is calculated by:

$$\frac{100 \text{ g/mole}}{74 \text{ g/mole}} \times 100 = 135\% \text{ CCE}$$

Therefore, $Ca(OH)_2$ will neutralize 1.35 times as much acid as the same weight of $CaCO_3$; hence its CCE is 135%. The same procedure is used to calculate the neutralizing value of other liming materials (Table 3-4). Dolomite is unique, in that there are 2 CO_3^{-2} in each $CaMg(CO_3)_2$ so $\frac{1}{2}$ the molecular weight is used to determined CCE.

Lime material composition can also be expressed by Ca and/or Mg content of the pure mineral (Table 3-4). For example, pure $CaCO_3$ contains 40% Ca calculated by the ratio of molecular weights:

$$\frac{40 \text{ g Ca/mole}}{100 \text{ g } CaCO_3\text{/mole}} \times 100 = 40\% \text{ Ca}$$

Fineness of Limestone

The effectiveness of agricultural limestones also depends on the particle size distribution or *fineness*, because the reaction rate depends on the surface area in contact with the soil. CaO and $Ca(OH)_2$ are powders with the smallest particle size, but limestones need to be crushed to reduce particle size. When crushed limestone is thoroughly incorporated into the soil, the reaction rate will increase with increasing fineness (Fig. 3-10). Decreasing the particle size fraction of a liming material decreases the lime rate required to raise soil pH, or decreases the effectiveness of a given lime rate (Fig. 3-11). In this example, a 100-mesh lime material (100% efficient) requires only 0.5 ton/a to increase soil pH to 7.0, whereas a 50-mesh lime material (40% efficient) requires 1 ton/a. When applied at the same lime rate, increasing the proportion of finer particles improves crop productivity because of increased neutralization of soil acids (Fig. 3-12).

Because limestone cost increases with fineness, materials that require minimum grinding, yet contain enough fine material to change pH rapidly, are preferred. Agricultural limestones contain both coarse and fine materials.

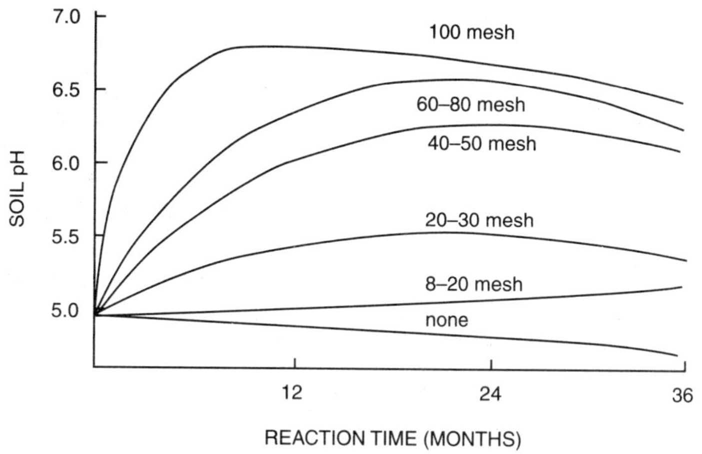

Figure 3-10 Typical effect of lime particle size on soil pH over three years.

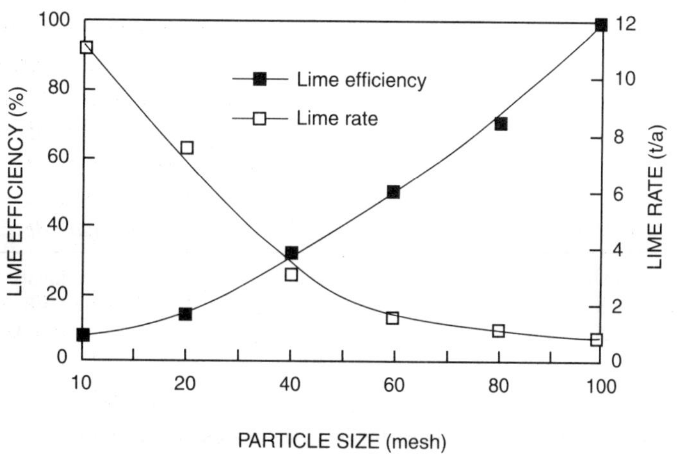

Figure 3-11 **Relative lime efficiency of different size fractions of limestone in raising soil pH to 7.0. Greater lime rates are needed for coarser lime material to raise soil pH to the same level as a finer material.**

Fineness is quantified by measuring the distribution of particle sizes in a given limestone sample. Particle size distribution or fineness represents the particles passing through or retained on a specific sieve size. Sieve size is the number of openings per inch (mesh). A 60-mesh sieve has 60 openings per inch. A particle passing 60-mesh sieve would have a diameter <0.0098 inch (<0.25 mm). Most agricultural lime contains a range of particle sizes from very fine, dust-size particles to coarse, sand-size particles. The standards for particle size distribution vary between states (Table 3-5). The fineness factor is the sum of the percentages of each size fraction multiplied by the appropriate efficiency factor (Table 3-6).

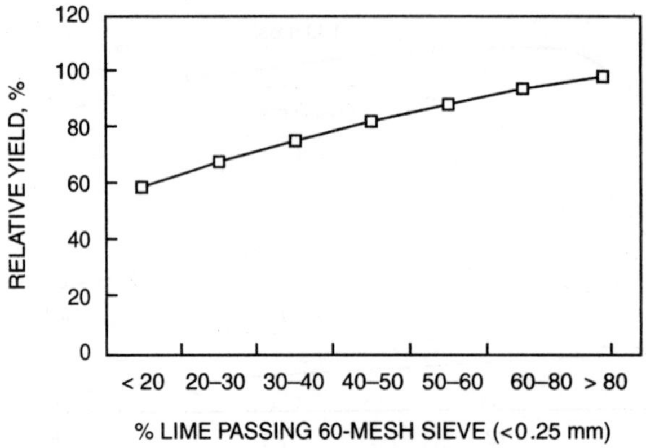

Figure 3-12 **Effect of increasing proportion of finer particles on relative crop yield. Data are averages of lime responses on six different crops over 6 to 8 years.** ***(Adapted from Barber, 1984,*** **Soil Acidity and Liming,** ***Agron No. 12, ASA.)***

Table 3-5 **Fineness Factors for Agricultural Limestone in the United States and Canada**

United States		*Canada*	
Particle Size	*Efficiency Factor*	*Particle Size*	*Efficiency Factor*
mesh	%	sieve no.	%
>8	0	>10	0
8–60	0.5	10–60	0.4
<60	1.0	<60	1.0
*Texas**		*Missouri**	
Particle Size	*Efficiency Factor*	*Particle Size*	*Efficiency Factor*
mesh	%	mesh	%
>8	0	>8	0
8–20	0.2	8–40	0.25
20–60	0.6	40–60	0.6
<60	1.0	>60	1.0

*Several examples are included to illustrate variation in standards between states.

Overall Lime Quality

The effective calcium carbonate (ECC) rating of a limestone is the product of the CCE and fineness factor. Manufacturers guarantee the CCE and fineness of any lime product sold. Table 3-6 illustrates the calculation of ECC. Thus, if 4,000 lbs $CaCO_3$/a were recommended, it would take 4,000 lbs/a ÷ 0.743 = 5,384 lbs/a of material "A" and 4,000 lbs/a ÷ 0.528 = 7,576 lbs/a of material "B" to increase soil pH to the same level.

For the same degree of fineness, the material that costs the least per unit of CCE should be used. For example, assume that a calcitic limestone (CCE = 95%) and a dolomitic limestone (CCE = 105%), both with the same fineness, are available. Both cost $35/ton applied. Based on CCE, the calcitic limestone will cost 105/95 × 35, or $38.68/ton, compared with dolomite at $35.00/ton. In addition, the dolomite supplies Mg, which can be deficient in some humid-region soils.

Table 3-6 Fineness Effects on Effective Calcium Carbonate (ECC) Content of Two Lime Sources

	Lime Material "A"	*Lime Material "B"*
Calcium Carbonate Equivalent (CCE)	90	60
Fineness (% passing or retained on the seive)		
> 8 mesh	5	2
8–60 mesh	25	20
< 60 mesh	70	78
Fineness Factor Calculation (Table 3-5)		
> 8 mesh × 0 efficiency	5 × 0 = 0	2 × 0 = 0
8–60 mesh × 0.5 efficiency	25 × 0.5 = 12.5	20 × 0.5 = 10
< 60 mesh × 1.0 efficiency	70 × 1.0 = 70	78 × 1.0 = 78
Total Fineness Factor (FF = sum of 3 individual factors)	70 + 12.5 = 82.5	78 + 10 = 88
Effective Calcium Carbonate (ECC) = CCE × FF	0.90 × 82.5 = 74.3	0.60 × 88 = 52.8

Use of Lime in Agriculture

Direct Benefits

The soil pH range for optimum production varies widely among crops (Fig. 3-13). On Alfisols and Mollisols, liming to pH 6.5 to 6.8 is optimum for most crops except forage legumes (alfalfa, sweetclover) where liming to pH 6.8 to 7.0 is recommended. Liming Ultisols and Oxisols to > pH 6.5 can reduce P and micronutrient availability. Liming organic soils to > pH 5.0 is not practical because of the large quantities of lime required to increase pH or %BS, as shown by this example:

Organic soil →

$$\begin{aligned} \text{CEC} &= 60\text{ meq}/100\text{ g} \\ \text{Initial pH} &= 4.0\ (25\%\text{BS}) \\ \text{Desired pH} &= 6.0\ (75\%\text{BS}) \end{aligned}$$

Need to increase %BS from 25 to 75% or neutralize 50% of CEC occupied by acids; thus

$$(0.50)\frac{60\text{ meq CEC}}{100\text{ g Soil}} = \frac{30\text{ meq acids}}{100\text{ g Soil}} = \frac{30\text{ meq CaCO}_3}{100\text{ g Soil}}$$

Therefore, the quantity of pure $CaCO_3$ needed is

$$\frac{30\text{ meq CaCO}_3}{100\text{ g Soil}} \times \frac{50\text{ mg CaCO}_3}{\text{meq}} = \frac{1{,}500\text{ mg CaCO}_3}{100\text{ g Soil}}$$

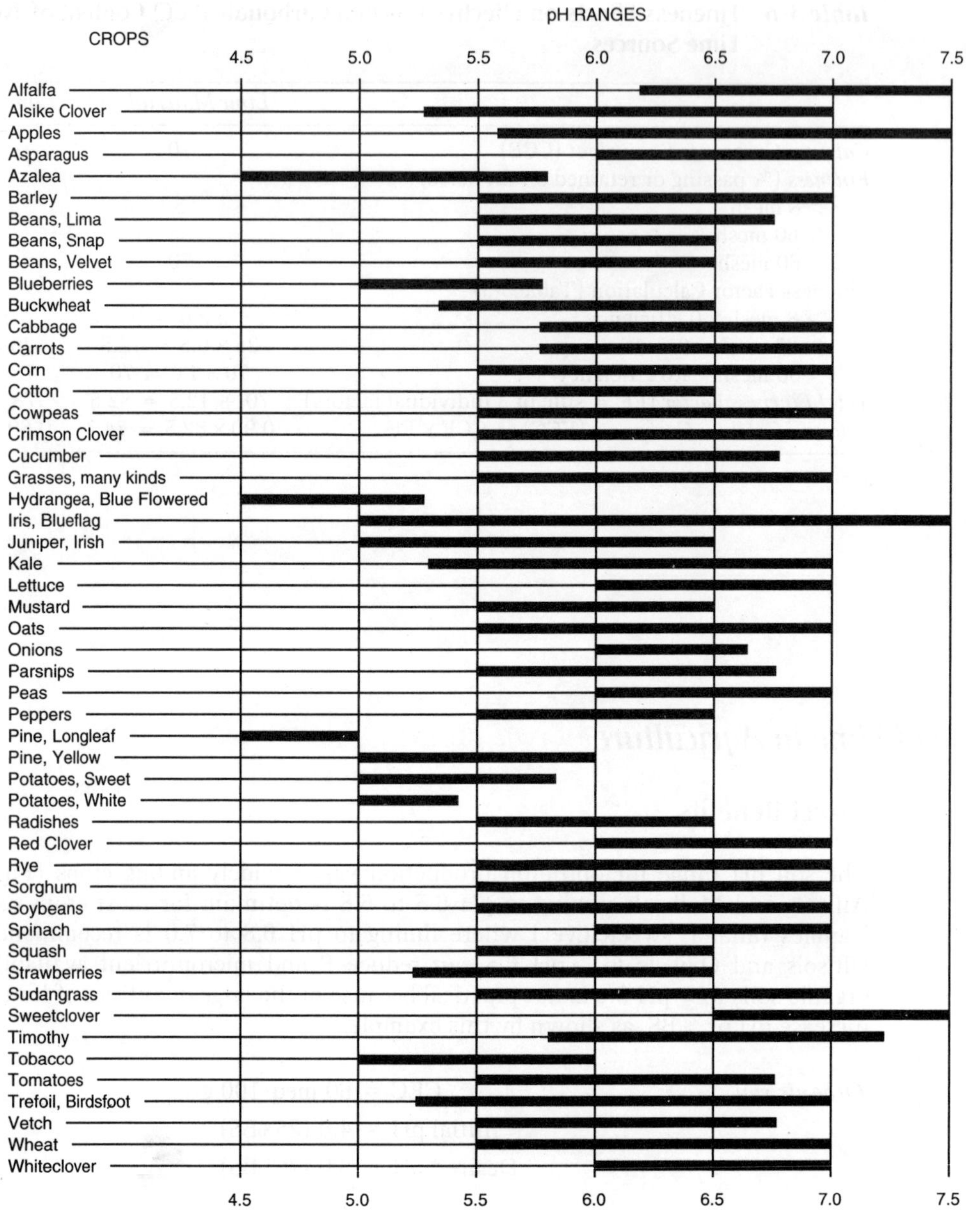

Figure 3-13 **Range in soil pH for optimum growth of selected crops.**

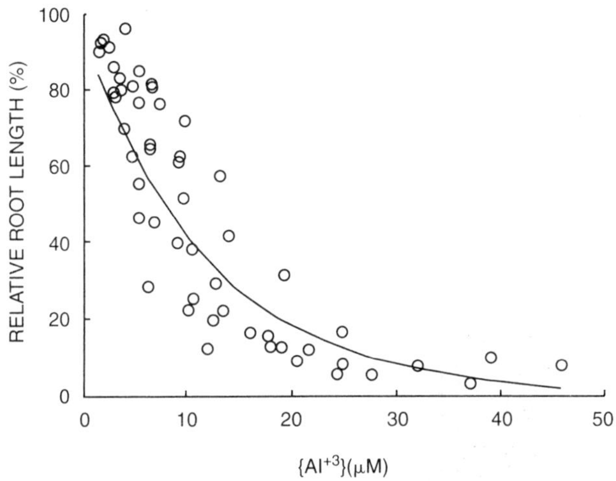

Figure 3-14 Relative taproot length of soybean as a function of Al^{+3} in solution. Taproot lengths were measured after four days of growth and compared with root elongation in zero Al^{-3} treatments.

Thus,

$$\frac{1{,}500 \text{ mg } CaCO_3}{100 \text{ g Soil}} \times \frac{1 \text{ g}}{1{,}000 \text{ mg}} = \frac{1.5 \text{ } CaCO_3}{100 \text{ g Soil}} = \frac{1.5 \text{ lb } CaCO_3}{100 \text{ lb Soil}}$$

$$\frac{1.5 \text{ lb } CaCO_3}{100 \text{ lb Soil}} \times \frac{2 \times 10^4}{2 \times 10^4} = \frac{30{,}000 \text{ lb } CaCO_3}{2 \times 10^6 \text{ lb Soil}}$$

$$= \frac{30{,}000 \text{ lb } CaCO_3}{\text{afs}} = 15 \text{ tons } CaCO_3/\text{a}$$

Al^{+3} Toxicity Al^{+3} toxicity is probably the major growth-limiting factor in many acidic soils, particularly at pH <5.0 to 5.5. The toxic effects of excessive Al^{+3} on root growth can seriously influence plant growth and yield. Figure 3-14 shows how increasing Al^{+3} in soil solution decreases root length. Excess Al^{+3} interferes with cell division in plant roots; inhibits nodule initiation; fixes P in less available forms in soils; decreases root respiration; interferes with enzymes governing the deposition of sugars in cell walls; increases cell wall rigidity; and interferes with the uptake, transport, and use of nutrients and water by plants. At $\leq$pH 4.5, H^+ toxicity damages root membranes and restricts growth of many beneficial bacteria. The greatest single direct benefit of liming many acidic soils is the reduction in the solubility of Al^{+3}.

In most soils, lime sufficient to raise pH to about 5.5 to 5.7 reduces exchangeable Al^{+3} to $<10\%$ of the CEC ($>90\%$BS) and eliminates Al^{+3} toxicity problems (Fig. 3-15). When lime is added to acid soils, exchangeable and solution Al^{+3} is reduced by precipitation as $Al(OH)_3$, which increases yield potential (Table 3-7). Figure 3-16 illustrates the influence of increasing soil pH on exhangeable Al^{+3}, Al^{+3} concentration in leaves, and crop productivity. Increasing Al^{+3} in solution also restricts plant uptake of Ca and Mg (Fig. 3-17).

Crops and varieties of the same crop differ widely in their susceptibility to Al^{+3} toxicity, thus, Al^{+3} tolerance is genetically controlled (Table 3-8). Different varieties of soybeans, wheat, and barley vary widely in their tolerance to Al^{+3} (Fig. 3-18). Some grasses are quite Al^{+3} tolerant. Al^{+3} toxicity may not always be economically correctable with conventional liming practices. Planting more Al^{+3}-tolerent species or varieties can reduce the lime requirement. Future advances in the use of biotechnology and

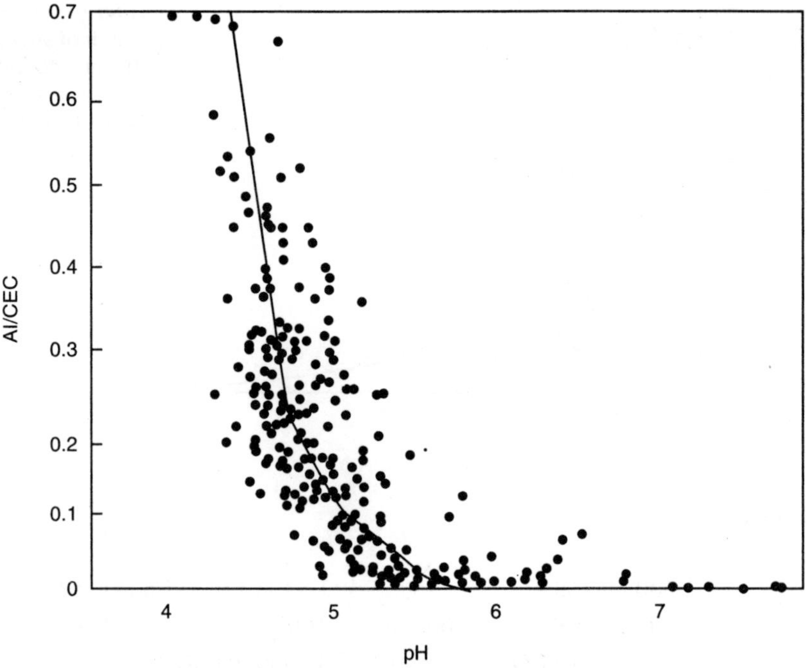

Figure 3-15 **As soil pH increases, Al^{+3} saturation decreases. In most soils, little or no effect of Al^{+3} toxicity on plant growth is observed above pH 5.0 to 5.5.**

related genetic modification techniques shows great potential for improving Al^{+3} tolerance in crops.

One short-term management strategy for reducing Al^{+3} toxicity to seedlings is band application of fertilizer P (Table 3-9). These data show that band application of P at wheat planting dramatically reduces Al^{+3} toxicity and increases wheat yield.

Although difficult to distinguish from Al^{+3} toxicity, Mn^{+2} toxicity also increases with decreasing pH (Chapter 8). Generally Mn^{+2} toxicity can be observed at pH 5.0 to 5.5, while Al^{+3} and Mn^{+2} toxicity can be observed at <pH 5.0. Mn^{+2} toxicity has been observed in rapeseed, alfalfa, barley, soybean, and potato.

Table 3-7 **Lime Effects on Wheat Yields, Soil pH, and Exchangeable and Solution Al^{+3}**

Lime Rate	*Wheat Yield*	*Soil pH*	*Al^{+3}*
lb ECC/a	*bu/a*		*ppm*
0	14	4.6	102
3,000	37	5.1	26
6,000	38	5.9	0
12,000	37	6.4	0

SOURCE: Whitney and Lamond, 1993, *Liming Acid Soils,* Kansas State Univ. Coop. Ext. MF-1065.
Note: 1986 to 1989 average yield data, soil pH, and Al^{+3} measured in 1989, initial soil pH 4.7.

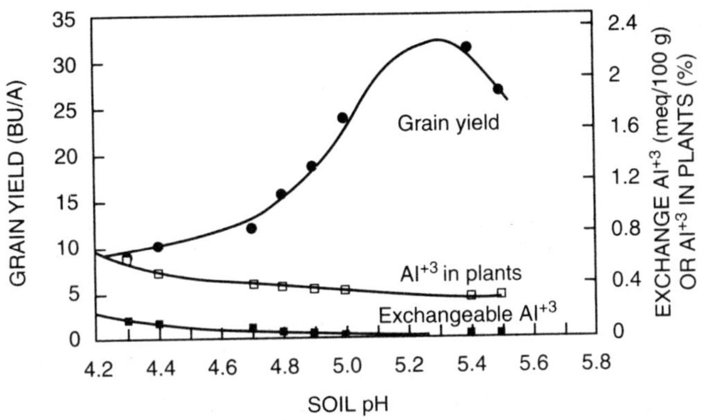

Figure 3-16 Effect of increasing soil pH on wheat grain yield, Al^{+3} on the CEC, and Al^{+3} in wheat leaves *(Patiram et al., 1990.* J. Ind. Soil Sci. *38: 719–722.)*

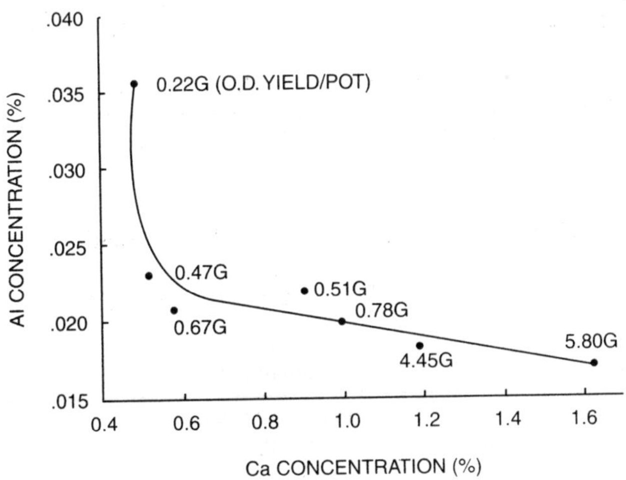

Figure 3-17 Relationship between Al and Ca concentration in cotton tops from nonleached subsoil. *(Soileau et al., 1969,* SSSA Proc., *33:919.)*

Table 3-8 Aluminum Tolerance of Selected Crops

Highly Sensitive	*Sensitive*	*Tolerant*	*Highly Tolerant*
Alfalfa	Canola	Ryegrass	Orchard grass*
Annual medics	Barley	Tall fescue	Rhodes grass
Red clover	Wheat*	White clover	Lovegrass
	Buffel grass	Orchard grass*	Paspalum
	Lesedeza	Wheat*	Oats
	Cotton	Subterranean clover	Triticale
	Soybean	Lupins	Yellow serradella
	Sorghum	Dallsigrass	Cereal rye
	Peanuts	Corn	Bermuda grass
		Rice	Bahia grass

*Some crops are listed twice because Al tolerance depends on variety.

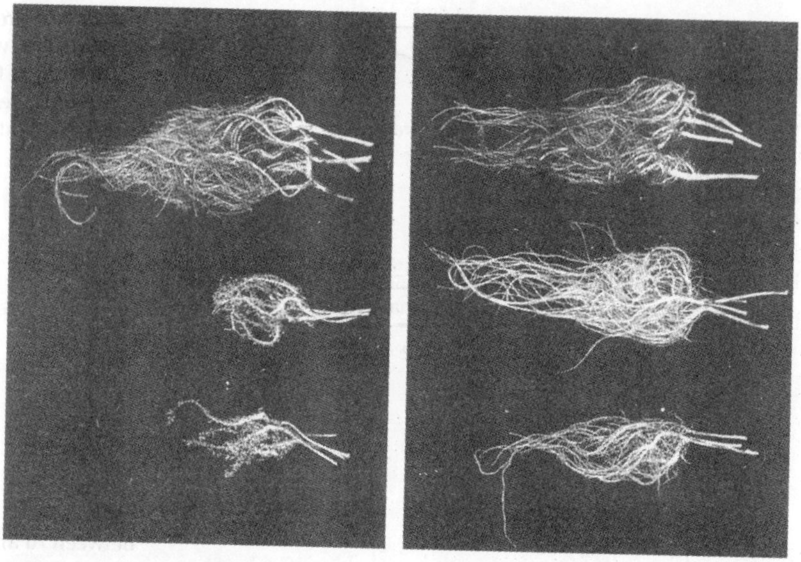

Figure 3-18 Differential effects of Al^{+3} on root growth of Perry (top) and Chief (bottom) soybean varieties grown in solution containing 2 ppm Ca. Left to right: 0, 8, 12 ppm Al^{+3} added. *(Foy et al., 1969,* Agron. J., *61:505.)*

Table 3-9 Lime, P, and Variety Effects on Two-Year Average Wheat Yields

		Method of Application and P_2O_5 Rate (lbs/a)		
Variety	*Lime Rate*	*0*	*40 Broadcast*	*40 Subsurface Band*
	lb ECC/a		*Wheat yield (bu/a)*	
Karl	0	38	42	54
	3,750	51	51	57
	7,500	49	49	55
2163	0	49	53	56
	3,750	58	57	60
	7,500	58	54	61

SOURCE: R. Laymond, Kansas State Univ.

Indirect Benefits

Nutrient Availability In low pH, high Al and Fe oxide soils, P precipitates as insoluble Fe/Al-P compounds (Chapter 5). Liming acidic soils will precipitate Al^{+3} as $Al(OH)_3$ and Fe^{+3} as $Fe(OH)_3$, thus increasing plant available P (Table 3-10). Alternatively, liming soils to pH 6.8 to 7.0 can reduce P availability because of the precipitation of Ca or Mg phosphates. A liming program should be planned so that the pH can be kept between 5.5 and 6.8 if maximum benefit is to be derived from applied P.

With the exception of Mo, micronutrient availability decreases with increasing pH (Chapter 8). This can be detrimental because of the toxic nature of many micronutrients

Table 3-10 Potential Plant Nutrition Problems Associated with Soil Acidity

Nutrient Problem	*Soil pH and Other Conditions*	*Effect of Lime Amendments*
Al and Mn toxixity	usually pH <5.0–5.5, depends on crop and variety	Exchangeable Al and solution Al and Mn decrease with increasing pH
H^+ toxicity	pH <4.0, Al / Mn toxicity commonly occurs first; observed mostly in solution culture	Decrease solution and exchangeable H^+
Ca deficiency	Low CEC, pH <4.5–4.8, tropical, highy weathered soils	Increase exchangeable Ca
Mg deficiency	pH <5.5, low CEC or %BS	Increase exchangeable Mg with dolomitic lime
Mo deficiency	pH <5.0	Increase solution Mo
N deficiency	pH <5.0–5.5, decreased nitrification and mineralization; low OM	Increase heterotrophic microbial activity; add residues and other organic materials as OM decomposition increases pH
P deficiency	pH <5.0; highly weathered soils dominant in Al / Fe oxides	Decrease exchangeable Al and AEC; increase %BS and CEC; increase solubility of Al-P and Fe-P minerals
K deficiency	pH <5.0, low CEC, low %BS, highly leached soils with high exchangeable Al	Decrease exchangeable Al, increase %BS

even at relatively low solution concentrations. Adequate lime addition reduces solution concentration of many micronutrients, and soil pH values of 5.6 to 6.0 are usually sufficient to minimize toxicity while maintaining adequate micronutrient availability.

Mo availability increases with liming, and deficiencies are infrequent at ≥pH 7.0. Because of the effect on availability of other micronutrients, liming to pH 7.0 is not normally recommended for most crops in humid areas.

Most of the organisms that nitrify NH_4^+ to NO_3^- require Ca; therefore, nitrification is enhanced by liming to a pH of 5.5 to 6.5 (Chapter 4). Decomposition of plant residues and breakdown of soil OM are also faster in this pH range. The effect of liming on mineralization and nitrification is shown in Table 3-11. Application of lime just before incubation almost doubled the mineralization of organic N. However, lime added 1 or 2 years before sampling had little or no effect on release of mineral N in two of the soils. Although adding lime at the start of the incubation increased nitrification, earlier lime applications had an even greater effect.

Symbiotic and nonsymbiotic N_2 fixation is favored by adequate liming (Chapter 4). Activity of *Rhizobium* is restricted by soil pH < 6.0; thus, liming will increase legume growth because of increased N_2 fixation. With nonsymbiotic N_2-fixing organisms, N_2 fixation increases in adequately limed soils, which increases the decomposition of crop residues.

Soil Physical Conditions Structure of fine-textured soils may be improved by liming, as a result of increased soil OM content and enhanced flocculation of Ca-saturated clays. Favorable effects of lime on soil structure include reduced soil crusting, better emergence

Table 3-11 Influence of Liming on Mineralization and Nitrification in Three Acid Soils*

Soil	*Treatment*	*Organic N Mineralized*	*Nitrification*
		ppm	%
Site 1 (pH 5.5, 0.20% soil N)	No lime	36	8
	Limed at start of incubation	61	66
	Limed 2 years before in the field	33	94
Site 2 (pH 5.4, 0.13% soil N)	No lime	40	7
	Limed at start of incubation	72	64
	Limed 2 years before in the field	44	93
Site 3 (pH 5.7, 0.83% soil N)	No lime	90	28
	Limed at start of incubation	177	83
	Limed 2 years before in the field	134	94

* Soils incubated for 4 weeks after lime addition. Lime applied in the field 2 years before sampling and incubation.
SOURCE: Nyborg and Hoyt, 1978, *Can. J. Soil Sci.*, 58:331.

of small-seeded crops, and lower power requirements for tillage operations. However, the overliming of Oxisols and Ultisols can result in the deterioration of soil structure, with a decrease in water percolation. Ca also improves the physical conditions of sodic soils. Increased salt concentration due to $CaCO_3$ dissolution is responsible for preventing clay dispersion and decreases in hydraulic conductivity.

Plant Diseases Reducing soil acidity by liming may have a significant role in the control of certain plant pathogens. Clubroot is a disease of cole crops that reduces yields and causes the infected roots to enlarge and become distorted. Lime does not directly affect the clubroot organism, but at soil pH > 7.0 germination of clubroot spores is inhibited (Table 3-12). Alternatively, liming increases the incidence of diseases such as scab in root crops. Severity of take-all infection in wheat, with resultant reductions in yield, is increased by liming soils to near neutral pH.

Table 3-12 Effect of Liming on Clubroot Disease in Cauliflower

	Lime Applied in 1978			*Lime Applied in 1979*		
Lime Rate, ton/a	*Marketable Yield, %*	*Clubroot Rating**	*pH at Harvest*	*Marketable Yield, %*	*Clubroot Rating**	*pH at Harvest*
0	48	3.3	5.6	28	3.8	5.7
2.5	73	1.8	6.6	39	3.8	6.4
5.0	81	1.1	6.9	63	3.4	6.7
10.0	86	0.2	7.1	74	2.5	7.2

*Clubroot rating = Σ [# roots at a rating × rating] / total # roots. Rating: 0, no visible clubroot; 1, fewer than 10 galls on the lateral roots; 2, more than 10 galls on the lateral roots, taproot free of clubroot; 3, galls on taproot; 4, severe clubbing on all roots.
SOURCE: Waring, 1980, Proc. 22nd Annu. Lower Mainland Hort. Improvement Assoc. Growers' Short Course, pp. 95–96.

Application of Liming Materials

Tillage Systems

For high limes rates, broadcasting one-half the lime, followed by disking and/or plowing, and then broadcasting the other half and disking, is effective in mixing lime thoughout the 0- to 6-in. depth. Lime recommendations are generally made on the basis of a 6-in. soil depth. With deeper tillage, lime recommendations should be increased. In Kansas, for example, recommended lime rates are adjusted according to expected depth of incorporation (Table 3-13). Thus, less lime is applied for incorporation to 3-in. depth compared with 7-in. depth.

Neutralization of subsoil acidity through deep incorporation of surface-applied lime is possible with large tillage equipment. The effect of incorporation depth of surface-applied lime on cotton growth showed that the amount and depth of cotton rooting were increased by mixing lime to a depth of 18 in. (Fig. 3-19). Mixing lime even deeper, to depths of 24 in., may be needed to maximize crop productivity (Fig. 3-20).

Surface lime applications without some mixing in the soil are not immediately effective in increasing soil pH below the surface 0- to 2-in. depth. In several studies it was observed that 10 or more years were required for surface-applied lime without incorporation to raise

Table 3-13 **Adjustment Factor for Depth of Incorporation Lime**

Incorporation Depth (in.)	*Adjustment Factor*
3	0.43
5	0.71
7	1.00
9	1.29
11	1.57

SOURCE: P. Witney, Kansas State Univ.

Figure 3-19 **Amount and depth of cotton rooting as affected by depth of lime incorporation. From left to right: unlimed; limed 0 to 6 in.; limed 0 to 8 in.** *(Doss et al., 1979,* Agron. J., *71:541.)*

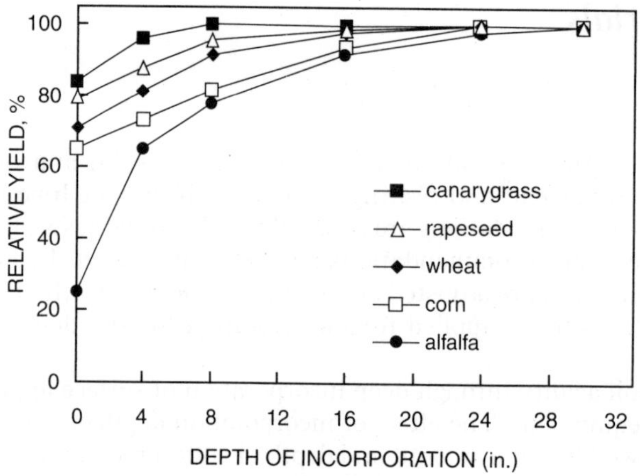

Figure 3-20 **Effect of depth of lime incorporation on relative crop yield.** *(Adapted from Bouldin, 1979,* Cornell Int. Agr. Bull. *74, Cornell Univ., and Pinkerton and Simpson, 1986,* Aust. J. Exper. Agric., *26: 107–113.)*

Table 3-14 **Effect of Surface Soil pH Levels on Subsoil pH**

Soil Depth (in.)	*pH at Various Depths with Increasing Surface Soil pH*			
0–7	4.9	5.5	6.0	6.5
7–14	4.9	5.2	5.9	6.7
14–21	4.7	4.8	5.2	5.4

SOURCE: Ohio Agronomy Guide, 1985, Cooperative Extension Service, Ohio State Univ.

the soil pH at a depth of 6 in. Keeping surface soils at a higher pH over time is one option to increase subsoil pH (Table 3-14).

No-Tillage Systems

With no-till cropping systems, surface soil pH can decrease substantially in a few years because of the acidity produced by surface-applied N fertilizers and decomposition of crop residues (Table 3-15). If the increased acidity is concentrated in the soil surface, surface liming applications are effective. With low pH subsoils, limestone should be incorporated to the desired depth before initiating a no-tillage system. If subsoil pH is adequate, maintenance of both surface and subsoil pH can be accomplished with surface lime applications. In no-tillage

Table 3-15 **Soil pH After 7 Years of Continuous Under Conventional and No-Tillage**

N Rate	*Soil Depth*	*Conventional Tillage*		*No Tillage*	
lbs/a	*Inches*	*Limed*	*Unlimed*	*Limed*	*Unlimed*
150	0–2	5.3	4.9	5.5	4.3
	2–6	5.9	5.1	5.3	4.8
	6–12	6.0	5.5	5.8	5.5
300	0–2	5.9	5.2	5.9	4.8
	2–6	6.3	5.6	5.9	5.5
	6–12	6.2	5.7	6.0	5.9

SOURCE: Blevins et al., 1978, *Agron. J.*, 40:322.

systems, surface-applied lime every three years can be as effective in maintaining surface and subsoil pH as annual lime applications. Where incorporation is not possible, surface application of limestone to acid soils is effective even though the immediate effect occurs only near the soil surface.

Time and Frequency of Liming Applications

For rotations with legumes and other crops with higher optimum pH ranges (Fig. 3-13), lime should be applied 3 to 6 months before seeding. Sufficient time for acid neutralization is particularly important on low pH soils. Applied too close to planting, lime may not have adequate time to react. For example, if clover follows fall-seeded wheat, lime is best applied prior to wheat planting. The caustic forms of lime [CaO and $Ca(OH)_2$] should be spread well before planting to prevent injury to germinating seeds.

Lime application frequency generally depends on soil texture, N source and rate, crop removal, precipitation patterns, and lime rate. On sandy soils, more applications are preferable, whereas on fine-textured soils, larger amounts may be applied less often. Finely divided lime reacts more quickly, but its effect is maintained over a shorter period than coarse materials.

The only reliable method to determine reliming needs is through soil testing. Samples should be taken at least every 3 years, unless production problems potentially related to soil acidity persist.

Equipment

Dry lime applied by the supplier or the producer is the most common method. The spinner truck spreader that distributes lime in a semicircle from the rear of the truck is common in agricultural and turf crops (Fig. 3-21).

Suspending lime in water, or *fluid lime*, is another approach to lime application. Mixing equipment used for conventional suspension fertilizers can be readily utilized to produce fluid lime. Very finely ground lime (100% passing a 100-mesh sieve and 80 to 90% passing a 200-mesh sieve) with 50% H_2O, along with a suspending agent such as attapulgite clay, is applied with a fluid fertilizer applicator (Fig. 3-21). Because of the material fineness and fluid application, acid neutralization is rapid and the lime distribution pattern is more uniform than dry lime application. Several disadvantages associated with fluid lime are (1) only a small amount can be applied at any one time ($\leq$1,000 lb ECC/a), and (2) fluid lime costs two to four times more than dry lime.

Regardless of the method employed, care should be taken to ensure uniform application. Nonuniform distribution can result in excesses and deficiencies in different parts of the same field and corresponding nonuniform crop growth.

Calcareous Soils

General Description

Calcareous soils contain measurable quantities of native $CaCO_3$. Calcareous surface soils commonly occur in semiarid and arid regions where annual precipitation is less than 20 in. (Fig. 3-22). As precipitation increases from semiarid to humid regions, depth to $CaCO_3$

Figure 3-21 Examples of commercial equipment to apply dry (top) and fluid lime (bottom).

increases (Fig 3-23). Generally, when annual precipitation exceeds 30 to 40 in., no free lime or $CaCO_3$ is present in the rooting zone.

Calcareous soils typically have soil pH ≥ 7.2. The pH of a soil containing $CaCO_3$ in equilibrium with atmospheric CO_2 is 8.5; however, the tenfold higher CO_2 content decreases pH to 7.2 to 7.5. Calcareous soils with pH ≥ 7.6 are influenced by high salt and/or Na content.

Acidifying Calcareous Soil

Acidification may be needed for crops with a low optimum pH range (Fig. 3-13) grown on calcareous soils. To decrease soil pH, the $CaCO_3$ would have to be dissolved or neutralized by adding acid or acid-forming materials. In most field crop situations, reducing soil pH by neutralizing $CaCO_3$ is not practical. For example, the quantity of elemental S° needed to neutralize a soil with only 2% $CaCO_3$ (0- to 6-in. depth) is estimated by:

2% $CaCO_3$ content in 6-in. surface soil depth
(acre furrow slice [afs] or 2×10^6 lb soil/a)

$$2\%\ CaCO_3 = \frac{2\text{ g }CaCO_3}{100\text{ g Soil}} = \frac{2{,}000\text{ mg }CaCO_3}{100\text{ g Soil}}$$

$$\frac{2000\text{ mg }CaCO_3}{100\text{ g Soil}} \times \frac{1\text{ meq}}{50\text{ mg }CaCO_3} = \frac{40\text{ meq }CaCO_3}{100\text{ g Soil}}$$

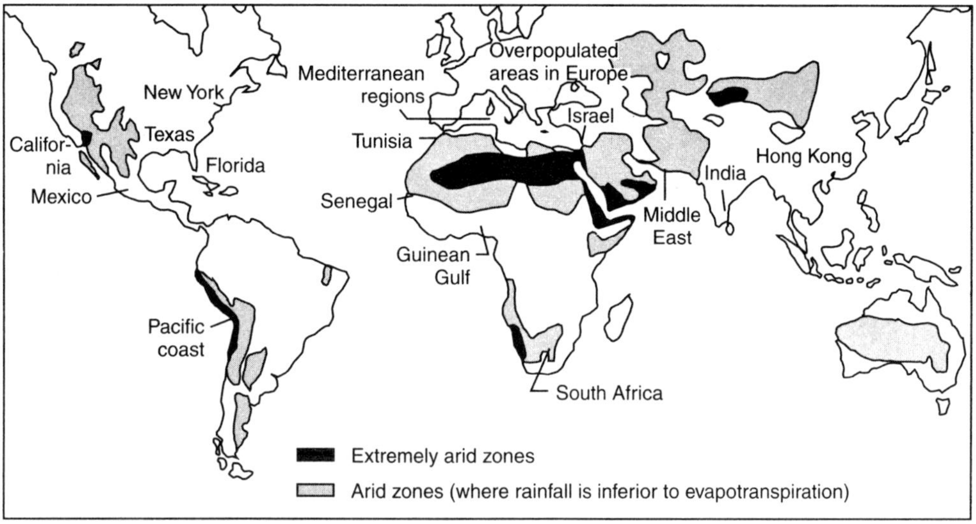

(a)

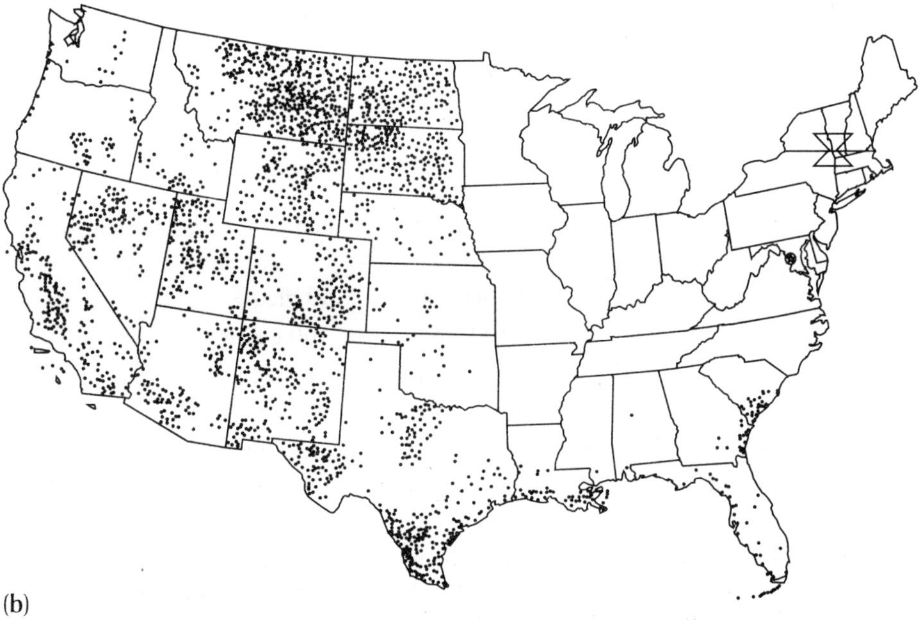

(b)

Figure 3-22 Extent of arid and semiarid regions in the world (a) and the areas in the United States (b) where soil salinity limits yield potential. *(USDA-NRCS, 1992.)*

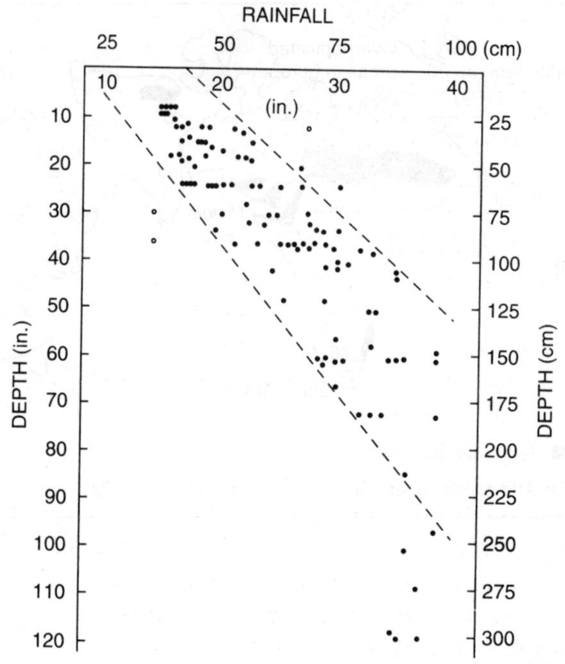

Figure 3-23 **As rainfall increases from one region to another, the depth to measurable $CaCO_3$ content increases. Thus, in arid and semiarid regions, $CaCO_3$ is present in the surface soil.**

Thus, if there are 40 meq $CaCO_3$, then 40 meq of acid is required to neutralize the $CaCO_3$.

$$\frac{40 \text{ meq CaCO}_3}{100 \text{ g Soil}} = \frac{40 \text{ meq S°}}{100 \text{ g Soil}}$$

$$\frac{40 \text{ meq S°}}{100 \text{ g Soil}} \times \frac{16 \text{ mg S°}}{\text{meq}} = \frac{640 \text{ mg S°}}{100 \text{ g Soil}}$$

$$\frac{0.64 \text{ g S°}}{100 \text{ g Soil}} \times \frac{2 \times 10^4}{2 \times 10^4} = \frac{12{,}800 \text{ g S°}}{2 \times 10^6 \text{ g Soil}} = \frac{12{,}800 \text{ lb S°}}{2 \times 10^6 \text{ lb Soil}} = 6.4 \text{ tons S°/afs}$$

Once neutralized, soil pH would likely be about the same as before neutralization because the CEC would still be nearly 100% saturated with basic cations (100%BS). To ultimately lower soil pH below 7, additional S° would be needed to produce H^+ and Al^{+3}, which would in turn reduce the %BS necessary to lower soil pH. The additional quantity of S° can be estimated similarly to the pH-BS calculations shown earlier.

In some regions where the surface soil is slightly acidic, land leveling to facilitate irrigation and for other purposes can expose calcareous subsoils that are unfavorable for optimum plant growth. Problems of high soil pH are not confined to arid and semiarid areas. Acidifying paddy soil has increased rice yields, which is often related to increased availability of micronutrients. Farmers in humid regions may overlime or dust from limestone-graveled roads may blow onto field borders, causing localized and excessively high pH. In other areas, moderately acidic soils may need further acidification for optimum production of potatoes, blueberries, cranberries, azaleas, rhododendrons, camellias, or conifer seedlings. The chemistry of soil acidification is the reverse of liming acid soils, and several acidic or acid-forming materials can be used.

Elemental S° Elemental S° is an effective soil acidulent. When S° is applied, the soil reaction is:

$$2S + 3O_2 + 2H_2O \leftrightarrows 2SO_4^{-2} + 4H^+$$

For every mole of S° applied and oxidized, 2 moles of H^+ are produced, which decreases soil pH. The oxidation of S° is accomplished through activity which microbial may be slow, particularly in cold and dry alkaline soils with no history of S° application. Finely ground S° should be broadcast and incorporated several weeks or months before planting to assure complete reaction.

Under some conditions, it may be advisable to acidulate a zone near the plant roots to increase water penetration or P and micronutrient availability. Both of these conditions frequently need to be corrected on saline-alkaline soils. Elemental S° can be applied in bands as either granular S° or S° suspensions. When S° is band applied, lower rates are required than broadcast S° (Chapter 7).

Sulfuric Acid Sulfuric acid (H_2SO_4) has been used for reclaiming Na- or B-affected soils, increasing availability of P and micronutrients, reducing NH_3 volatilization potential, increasing water penetration, controlling certain weeds and soilborne pathogens, and enhancing the establishment of range grasses. The favorable influence of H_2SO_4 and other acidifying treatments on sorghum (Fig. 3-24) and rice yield (Table 3-16) is partially related to increased nutrient availability.

H_2SO_4 can be added directly to the soil, but it requires the use of special acid-resistant equipment and clothing. It can be dribbled on the surface or applied with a knife applicator (Chapter 10). It can also be applied in ditch irrigation water. H_2SO_4 has the advantage of reacting instantaneously with the soil.

Aluminum Sulfate Aluminum sulfate [$Al_2(SO_4)_3$] is used by floriculturists for acidulating soil for production of azaleas, camellias, and similar acid-tolerant ornamentals, although it

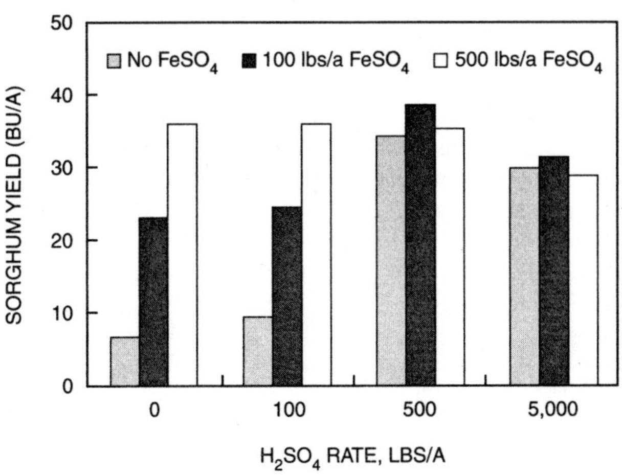

Figure 3-24 **Effects of H_2SO_4 and $FeSO_4$ on grain sorghum yields on a calcareous soil. Reducing soil pH with H_2SO_4 increases Fe availability to similar levels as adding $FeSO_4$.** ***(Mather, 1985,*** **Fertilizer Technology and Use,** ***Chap. 11. Soil Sci. Soc. Am.)***

Table 3-16 **Effect of Soil Acidifiers on the Yield of Two Varieties of Rice**

Soil Amendment	*Bluebonnet 50*	*IR661*
	bu/a	
Control	40	87
Gypsum	43	96
S	48	100
H_2SO_4	55	104

SOURCE: Reproduced with permission of CSIRO PUBLISHING, Melbourne Australia, from the *Australian Journal of Experimental Agriculture and Animal Husbandry* vol. 20:725 (Chapman, 1980) http://www.publish.csiro.au/journals/ajea

is not commonly used in agriculture. When $Al_2(SO_4)_3$ is added to water, it hydrolyzes to produce an acid solution:

$$Al_2(SO_4)_3 + 6H_2O \leftrightarrows 2Al(OH)_3 + 6H^+ + 3SO_4^{-2}$$

Iron sulfate ($FeSO_4$) is applied to soils for acidification and as an Fe source will behave similarly to $Al_2(SO_4)_3$.

Ammonium Polysulfide Liquid ammonium polysulfide (NH_4S_x) is used to lower soil pH and to increase water penetration in irrigated saline-alkaline soils. It can be applied in a band 3 or 4 in. to the side of the seed or metered into ditch irrigation systems. Band application is more effective in correcting micronutrient deficiencies than application through irrigation water. The polysulfide decomposes into ammonium sulfide and colloidal S^o when applied. The S^o and S^{-2} are oxidized to H_2SO_4. Potassium polysulfide was developed for similar purposes.

Acidification in Fertilizer Bands Because of the high BC for pH of calcareous soils, it is usually too expensive to use enough acidifying material for complete neutralization of $CaCO_3$. It is unnecessary to neutralize the entire soil mass because soil zones more favorable for root growth and nutrient uptake can be created by confining the acid-forming materials to bands and other localized placement. Band-applied ammonium thiosulfate and ammonium polyphosphate fertilizers can acidify soil in and near the band, which can increase micronutrient availability (Fig. 3-25).

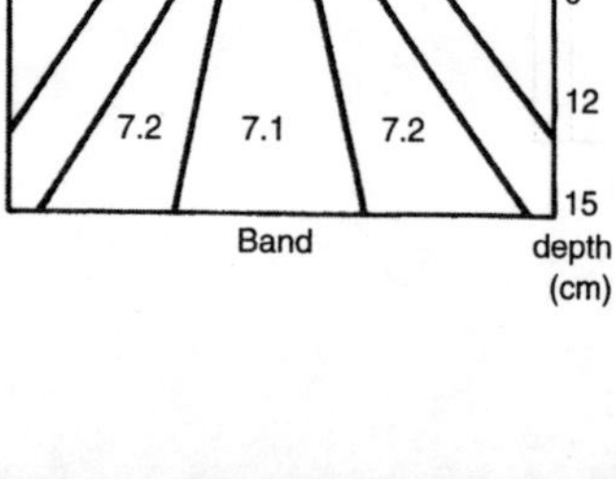

Figure 3-25 **Application of a P-S fertilizer solution lowers soil pH in the vicinity of a fertilizer band (X denotes point of application).** ***(Leiker, M.Sc. thesis, Kansas State Univ., 1970.)***

Saline, Sodic, and Saline-Sodic Soils

In arid and semiarid regions, runoff water and groundwater collected in depressions evaporates and the salts in the water accumulate. Water also moves upward from artesian sources and shallow water tables. Due to prevailing high evaporative conditions, H_2O evaporates, leaving salts at the soil surface to form saline, sodic, or saline-sodic soils. These soils are widespread in semiarid and arid regions, where the rainfall is not sufficient for adequate leaching, usually less than 20 in./yr (Fig. 3-22). Approximately 10% (13 billion acres) of global land area is affected by salt. Of cultivated soils, about 20% are saline and 35% are sodic. Salt marshes of the temperate zones, mangrove swamps of the subtropics and tropics, and interior salt marshes adjacent to salt lakes are areas where such soils are found.

Rapid extension of irrigated lands over the last four decades has increased salinity of cultivated soils. Large areas of the Indian subcontinent have been rendered unproductive by salt accumulation and poor water management. Salinity is a major problem in wetland rice.

Salt buildup is an existing or potential danger on almost all of the irrigated land in semiarid and arid regions of the United States, and salinity on nonirrigated cropland and rangeland in these regions is increasing. Accumulated salts contain the cations Na^+, K^+, Ca^{+2}, and Mg^{+2}, and the anions Cl^-, SO_4^{-2}, HCO_3^-, and CO_3^{-2}. They can be weathered from minerals and accumulate in areas where the precipitation is too low to provide leaching.

Na is particularly detrimental, because of both its toxic effect on plants and effect on soil structure. When a high percentage of the CEC is occupied by Na^+, soil aggregates disperse, reducing natural aggregation and soil structure. These soils become impermeable to water, develop hard surface crusts, and may keep a water layer, or "slick spot," on the surface longer than low Na^+ soils. For example, data from several Vertisols and Oxisols in Australia show that as exchangeable Na^+ increases, the percentage of dispersed clay increases (Fig. 3-26), resulting in substantial decreases in hydraulic conductivity (or greater impermeability to water).

Dispersion problems occur at different exchangeable Na^+ contents. Fine-textured soils with montmorillonitic clays disperse when about 15% of the CEC is Na^+ saturated. On

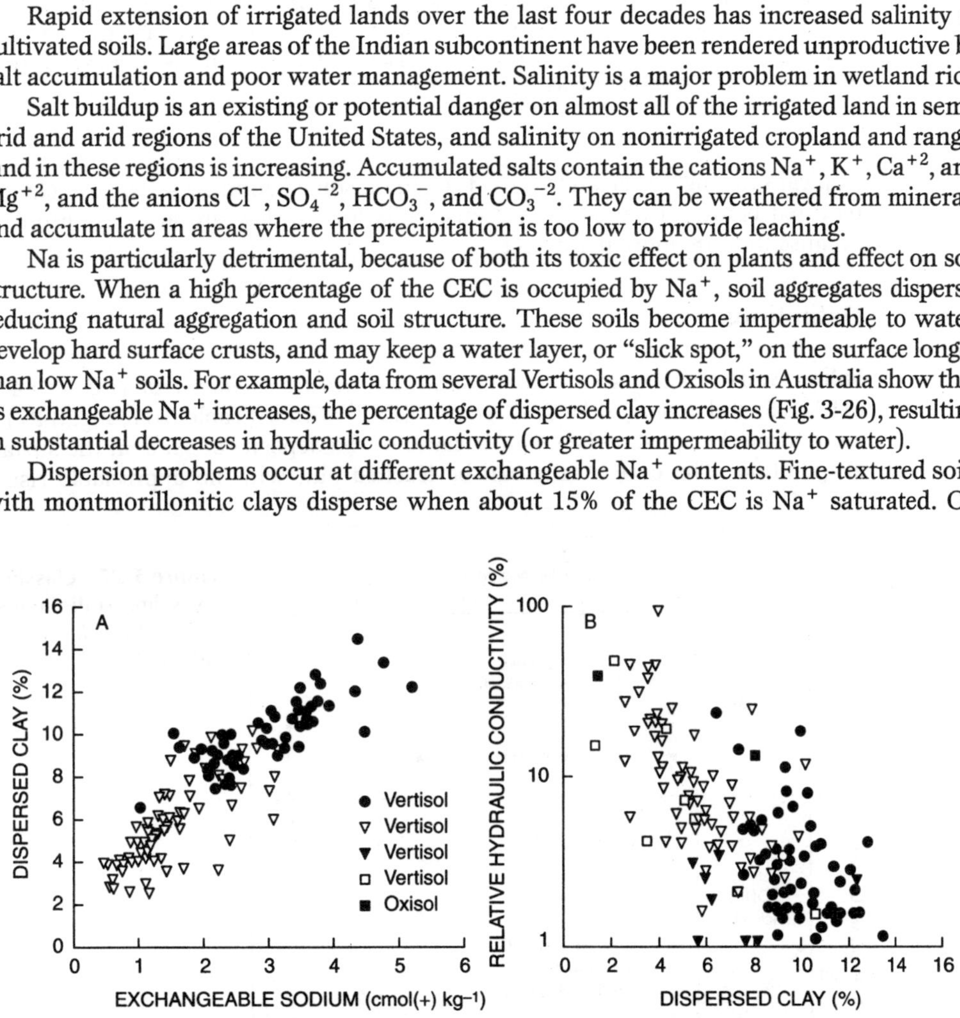

Figure 3-26 **Increasing exchangeable Na content increases the amount of clay dispersed (A) and decreases the hydraulic conductivity (B). Data represent Vertisols and Oxisols in Australia.** *(Reproduced with permission of CSIRO PUBLISHING, Melbourne Australia, from the* Australian Journal of Soil Research *vol. 31:683–750 (Sumner, 1993) http://www.publish.csiro.au/journals/ajsr)*

Table 3-17 **Classification and Properties of Salt-Affected Soils**

Classification	EC_{se} *(mmho/cm)* *	*Soil pH*	*ESP %*	*Physical Condition*
Saline	>4.0	<8.5	<15	Normal
Sodic	<4.0	>8.5	>15	Poor
Saline-sodic	>4.0	<8.5	>15	Normal

*EC_{se} represents the electrical conductivity of the saturated extract. Distilled H_2O is added to a soil sample to exactly fill the pore space. After equilibration, the soil water is removed through vacumn filtration. An electrode is inserted into the saturated soil extract and the electrical conductivity is measured. A high EC_{se} means a high salt concentration (more ions in solution conducts more current). Low salt concentration would result in a low EC_{se} reading. The unit mmho/cm comes from the unit of electrical resitance (ohm), such that conductivity, or the opposite of resistance, is given the unit "mho". An "mmho" is 0.001 × mho. The "cm" unit in mmho/cm comes from the separation distance between the (−) and (+) charged surfaces of the electrode that senses EC_{se}. Also, mmho/cm = ds/m in SI units.

tropical soils high in Fe and Al oxides and on some kaolinitic soils, 40% Na^+ saturation is required before dispersion is serious. Soils low in clay are also less prone to problems because they are more permeable.

Definitions

Saline Soils Saline soils have a *saturated extract conductivity* (EC_{se}) >4 mmhos/cm, pH <8.5, and *exchangeable* Na^+ *percent* (ESP) <15% (Table 3-17; Fig. 3-27). Saline soils were formerly called *white alkali* because of the deposits of salts on the surface following evaporation. The excess salts can be leached out, with no appreciable rise in pH. The

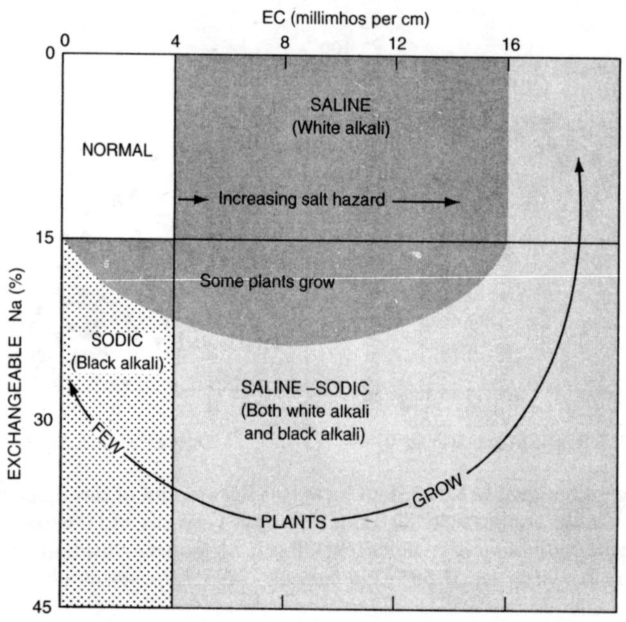

Figure 3-27 **Classification system for saline, sodic, and saline-sodic soils. *(U.S. Salinity Lab,* Handbook 60, *1954.)***

concentration of soluble salts is sufficient to interfere with plant growth, although salt tolerance varies with plant species.

Sodic Soils Sodic soils occur when ESP >15%, $EC_{se} < 4$ mmhos/cm, and pH > 8.5 (Table 3-17). They were formerly called *black alkali* because of the dissolved OM deposited on the surface along with the salts. In sodic soils, excess Na^+ disperses soil colloids and creates nutritional disorders in most plants.

Saline-Sodic Saline-sodic soils have both $EC_{se} > 4$ mmhos/cm to qualify as saline and high exchangeable Na^+ (>15% ESP) to qualify as sodic; however, soil pH is usually <8.5. In contrast to saline soils, when the salts are leached out, the exchangeable Na^+ hydrolyzes and the pH increases, which results in a sodic soil.

Relationships

Several interrelated parameters are commonly used to quantify salt and Na^+ affected soils. By measuring EC_{se} of a soil, the total quantity of salts in the soil solution can be estimated as follows:

$$EC_{se} \times 10 = \text{total soluble cations (meq/l)}$$

Also,

$$\text{Total dissolved salts (ppm or mg/L)} = 640 \times EC_{se} \text{ (mmhos/cm)}$$

If the soluble cations are measured in the saturated extract, the sodium adsorption ratio (SAR) can be calculated as follows:

$$SAR = \frac{Na^+}{\sqrt{\dfrac{(Ca^{+2} + Mg^{+2})}{2}}} \qquad \text{(all units in meq/L)}$$

SAR values exceeding 13 are indicative of sodicity problems. Because of the equilibrium relationships between solution and exchangeable cations in soils, the SAR should be related to the quantity of Na^+ on the CEC, which is expressed as the *exchangeable* Na^+ *ratio* (ESR). The ESR is defined as follows:

$$ESR = \frac{\text{Exchangeable } Na^+}{\text{Exchangeable } (Ca^{+2} + Mg^{+2})} \qquad \text{(all units in meq/100 g soil)}$$

Figure 3-28 illustrates the relationship between solution and exchangeable cations in salt-affected soils. This relationship can be used to estimate the ESR if the quantity of exchangeable cations has not been measured. The following equation represents the linear relationship shown in Figure 3-28.

$$ESR = 0.015 \text{ (SAR)}$$

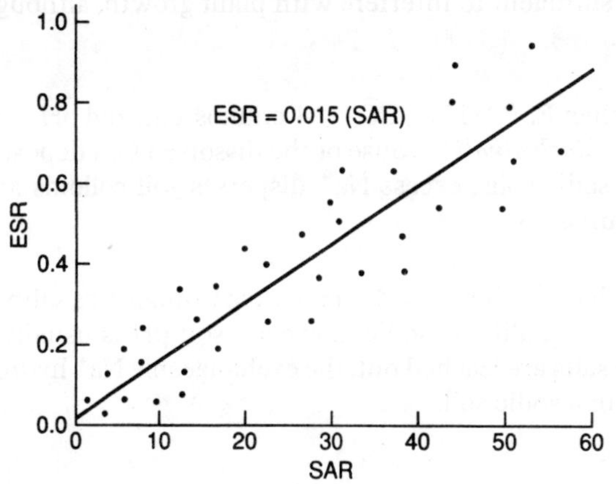

Figure 3-28 **Relationship between ESR and SAR in salt-affected soils.**

Subsequently, ESR is related to the exchangeable Na^+ percentage (ESP) previously used to classify Na^+ affected soils (Table 3-17) and is given by

$$\text{ESP} = \frac{\text{Exchangeable Na}^+}{\text{CEC}} \times 100 \qquad \text{(all units in meq/100 g soil)}$$

$$\text{ESP} = \frac{100\ \text{ESR}}{1 + \text{ESR}}$$

These parameters and interrelationships are valuable in characterizing the solution and exchange chemistry of salt- and Na^+-affected soils. The following example illustrates how these relationships can be used. Additional examples are provided in the instructors' manual.

A soil analysis revealed that the saturated extract contained 20 meq Ca^{+2}/L; 10 meq Mg^{+2}/L; and 100 meq Na^+/L. The EC_{se} = 2.2 mmho/cm; soil pH = 8.6; and CEC = 25 meq/100 g. Evaluate this soil for potential salinity or sodicity problems.

$$\text{SAR} = \frac{100}{\sqrt{\dfrac{(20 + 10)}{2}}} = 25.8$$

$$\text{ESR} = 0.015\,(25.8) = 0.39$$

$$\text{ESP} = \frac{100(0.39)}{1 + 0.39} = 28\%$$

Since the ECse <4 mmho/cm and the ESP >15%, this soil would be classified as sodic. Gypsum application would likely be recommended to reduce the ESP (see p. 92 for example calculation).

Effects on Plant Growth

Soil salinity limits plant growth by (1) a water imbalance in the plant (physiological drought), (2) ion imbalances that result in increased energy consumption (carbohydrate respiration) to maintain metabolic processes, and (3) toxicity from Na^+ and Cl^-. The high

Table 3-18 Sensitivity of Several Crops to Leaf Burn Caused by Cl^- in Sprinkler Irrigation

Tolerant	*Semitolerant*	*Sensitive*	*Very Sensitive*
Cotton	Barley	Alfalfa	Potato
Sugar beet	Corn	Sesame	Tomato
Sunflower	Safflower	Soybeans	Fruit crops
	Sorghum		Citrus fruits

SOURCE: Meas et al., 1982, *Irrigation Science*.

osmotic pressure in the soil solution causes a correspondingly low soil water potential and, when in contact with a plant cell, the solute moves toward the soil solution and the cell collapses (called plasmolysis). Salt-affected plants may exhibit stunted growth and have darker green leaf color. In woody species, excessive soil salinity may cause substantial leaf burn. Saline irrigation water can also result in leaf burn, depending on the crop (Table 3-18). As soil salinity increases above threshold levels (Table 3-19), plant growth rate decreases. Top growth is usually affected more than root growth.

High Na^+ is toxic to plants roots, especially during drought conditions when the Na^+ concentration in the soil solutions increases and enhances dehydration of root tissue. Under sodic conditions, Na^+ can replace Ca^{+2} in cell membranes, increasing membrane permeability and transport of ions. Many plants, especially grasses, accumulate Na^+ in leaves, resulting in necrosis of leaf tips and edges.

Although Cl^- is an essential micronutrient, excess Cl^- in soil solution or in irrigation water can reduce productivity in sensitve crops. Woody plants are more sensitive to Cl^- than nonwoody species. For most crops, the salinity tolerance provides an approximate guideline for Na^+ and Cl^- toxicity (Table 3-19).

Toxicity to excessive B occurs in some arid region soils. B accumulates in leaf tissues causing necrosis. Removing grass clippings can help remove some B from the system. Most turf grasses are B tolerant, whereas many fruit and vegetable crops are sensitive (Chapter 10).

Although in most situations yield decrease is related to total salt concentration in the soil solution, excess soil salinity may induce nutrient imbalances (deficiencies or toxicities). For example, excessive SO_4^{-2} and low Ca^{+2} and/or Mg^{+2} can occur in saline soils, causing internal browning in lettuce, blossom-end rot in tomato and pepper, and blackheart in celery. Plants differ greatly in their tolerance to soil salinity (Table 3-19). For example, old alfalfa is more tolerant than young alfalfa. Barley and cotton have considerable salt tolerance, but high salt will affect vegetative more than reproductive growth. Cultivar or variety differences also exist. For example, soybean varieties differ in Cl^- exclusion (Table 3-20). Effective excluders of Na^+ and Cl^- may still exhibit low yield because of salt-related water stress. Tolerant crops that do not exclude Na^+ have a capacity to maintain a high K^+/Na^+ ratio in the growing tissue. Conventional breeding and genetic engineering methods are being used to improve adaptation and tolerance to saline environments.

Quantifying Salt Tolerance

Plant tolerance to soil salinity is expressed as the yield decrease with a given amount of soluble salts compared with yield under nonsaline conditions. Threshold salinity levels have been established for most crops and represent the minimum salinity level (EC_{se}) above which salinity limits growth and/or yield (Table 3-19). These values represent general guidelines, since many interactions among plant, soil, water, and environmental factors influence salt tolerance. Above

Table 3-19 Salt Tolerance of Selected Crops

Crop	*Threshold EC_{se} (mmhos/cm)*	*% Yield Decrease/ Unit EC_{se} Increase*	*EC_{se} at 50 % Yield Loss*	*Salt Tolerance Rating**
Alfalfa	2.0	7.3	8.8	MS
Almond	1.5	18	4.3	S
Apple	1.0	15	4.3	S
Apricot	1.6	23	3.8	S
Avocado	1.0	24	3.1	S
Barley (forage)	6.0	7.0	13.1	MT
Barley (grain)	8.0	5.0	18.0	T
Bean	1.0	19	3.6	S
Beet (garden)	4.0	9.0	9.6	MT
Bent grass	—	—	—	MS
Bermuda grass	6.9	6.4	14.7	T
Blackberry	1.5	22	3.8	S
Boysenberry	1.5	22	3.8	S
Broad bean	1.6	9.6	6.8	MS
Broccoli	2.8	9.1	8.3	MT
Bromegrass	—	—	—	MT
Cabbage	1.8	9.7	7.0	MS
Canary grass (reed)	—	—	—	MS
Carrot	1.0	14	4.6	S
Clover (berseem)	1.5	5.8	10.1	MT
Clover (red, ladino, alsike)	1.5	12	5.7	MS
Corn (forage)	1.8	7.4	8.6	MS
Corn (grain, sweet)	1.7	12	5.9	MS
Cotton	7.7	5.2	17.3	T
Cowpea	1.3	14	4.9	MS
Cucumber	2.5	13	6.3	MS
Date	4.0	3.6	17.9	T
Fescue (tall)	3.9	5.3	13.3	MT
Flax	1.7	12	5.9	MS
Grape	1.5	9.5	6.8	MS
Grapefruit	1.8	16	4.9	S
Hardinggrass	4.6	7.6	11.2	MT
Lemon	1.0	—	—	S
Lettuce	1.3	13	5.1	MS
Lovegrass	2.0	8.5	7.9	MS
Meadow foxtail	1.5	9.7	6.7	MS
Onion	1.2	16	4.3	S
Orange	1.7	16	4.8	S
Orchard grass	1.5	6.2	9.6	MT
Peach	3.2	19	5.8	S
Peanut	3.2	29	4.9	MS
Pepper	1.5	14	5.1	MS
Plum	1.5	18	4.3	S
Potato (sweet)	1.5	11	6.0	MS
Potato (white)	1.7	12	5.9	MS
Radish	1.2	13	5.0	MS
Rice (paddy)	3.0	12	7.2	MS
Ryegrass (perennial)	5.6	7.6	12.2	MT

Table 3-19 (continued)

Crop	Threshold EC_{se} (mmhos/cm)	% Yield Decrease/ Unit EC_{se} Increase	EC_{se} at 50% Yield Loss	Salt Tolerance Rating*
Sorghum	4.8	8.0	11.1	MT
Soybean	5.0	20	7.5	MT
Spinach	2.0	7.6	8.6	MS
Strawberry	1.0	33	2.5	S
Sudan Grass	2.8	4.3	14.4	MT
Sugar Beet	7.0	5.9	15.5	T
Sugarcane	1.7	5.9	10.2	MS
Tomato	2.5	9.9	7.6	MS
Trefoil (big)	2.3	19	4.9	MS
Trefoil (birdsfoot)	5.0	10	10.0	MT
Vetch (common)	3.0	11	7.5	MS
Wheat	6.0	7.1	13.0	MT
Wheat Grass (crested)	3.5	4.0	16.0	MT
Wheat Grass (fairway)	7.5	6.9	14.7	T
Wheat Grass (tall)	7.5	4.2	19.4	T
Wild Rye (beardless)	2.7	6.0	11.0	MT

*S, sensitive; MS, moderately sensitive; MT, moderately tolerant; T, tolerant.

Table 3-20 Leaf-Scorch Ratings, Yield, and Cl^- Concentration in Leaves and Seeds of Five Susceptible and Ten Tolerant Soybean Cultures

			Concentration of Cl^-	
	Leaf Scorch*	Yield	Leaves	Seed
		bu/a	%	ppm
Cl susceptible	3.4	15	1.67	682
Cl tolerant	1.0	24	0.09	111

*1 = none, 5 = severe.
SOURCE: Parker et al., 1986.

the threshold EC_{se} level, plant growth generally decreases linearly with increasing salinity. Figure 3-29 illustrates this relationship. Thus, relative yield loss (Y) at any given EC_{se} level can be calculated for any crop from the values in Table 3-19 for threshold levels (A) and the percentage yield decrease per unit increase in EC_{se} level (B) above the threshold by the following:

$$Y = 100 - b(EC_{se} - A)$$

For example, alfalfa yield decreases about 7.3% per unit increase in EC_{se} above the 2.0 mmho/cm EC_{se} threshold (Table 3-19). Thus, if a soil analysis showed 4.0 mmho/cm EC_{se}, then the estimated relative alfalfa yield would be:

$$Y = 100 - 7.3(4.0 - 2.0) = 85.4\%$$

Using these linear relationships, plants can be categorized into groups based on sensitivity or tolerance to soil salinity (Fig. 3-30). These ratings are only relative but can be used to estimate yield depression at specific soil salinity levels.

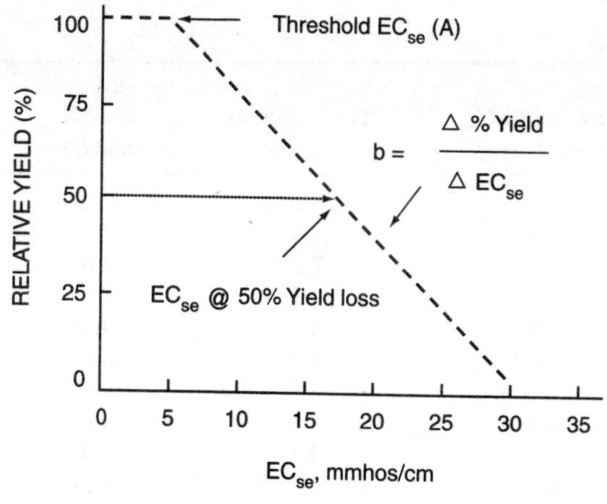

Figure 3-29 **Graphical representation of salt tolerance threshold (A) and yield loss associated with increasing EC_{se}. The slope "b" represents the % yield loss per unit increase in EC_{se}.**

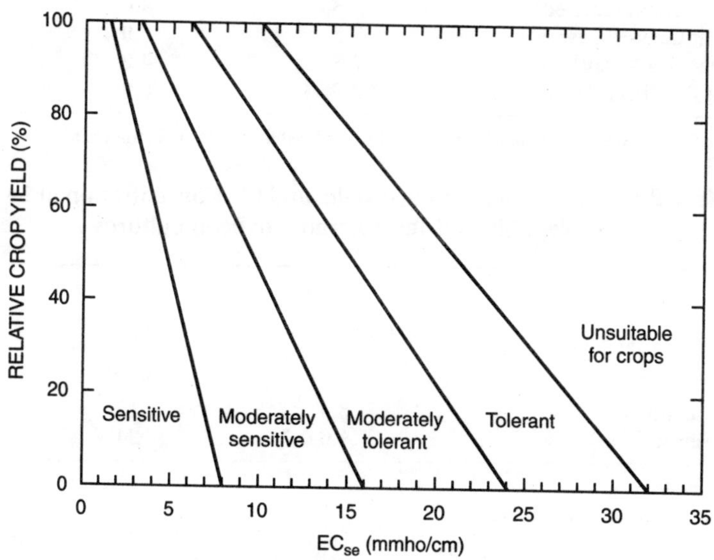

Figure 3-30 **Divisions for classifying crop tolerance to salinity.**

Factors Affecting Salt Tolerance

Plant Factors For some plants soil salinity influences growth at all growth stages, but for many crops sensitivity varies with the growth stage. For example, several grain crops (e.g., rice, wheat, corn, and barley) are relatively salt tolerant at germination and maturity but are very sensitive during early seedling and, in some cases, vegetative growth stages. In contrast, sugarbeet, safflower, soybean, and many bean crops (including soybean) are sensitive during germination. This effect depends on variety, especially with soybean. The amount of growth reduction and/or yield loss often depends on the variety, particularly with many grasses and some legume crops. Differences in salt tolerance have also been observed between different vine and fruit tree rootstocks. Fruit tree and some vine crops are particularly sensitive to Cl^- toxicity; however, salt-tolerant varieties exhibit reduced Cl^- accumulation in the roots and/or Cl translocation from roots to above-ground tissues. Most grasses used in the turf industry are relatively salt tolerant (Table 3-19).

Soil Factors In general, crops grown on nutrient-deficient soils are more salt tolerant than the same crops grown in soils with sufficient nutrients. Lower growth rates and lower water demand are likely causes for the increased tolerance to soil salinity. In these cases nutrient deficiency is the most limiting factor to maximum yield potential; thus, nutrient additions would increase plant growth and yield potential and subsequently decrease salt tolerance. Because saline and sodic soils have pH > 7.0, micronutrient deficiencies can be more common (Chapter 8). Overfertilization with N can decrease salt tolerance in some crops because of increased vegetative growth and water demand. At recommended rates, little or no effect on soil salinity or salt tolerance is observed with either inorganic or organic nutrient addition. Continued overapplication of manure, as well as N and K fertilizers, can increase soil salinity, especially in poorly drained, irrigated soils. Overapplication with band-applied fertilizers containing relatively high concentrations of N and K can cause salt damage to germinating seeds and seedlings (Chapter 10).

Proper irrigation management is essential to reducing soil salinity effects on plant growth and yield. Total salt concentration in the soil solution is the highest when the water content has been reduced by evapotranspiration. With irrigation, soil solution salts are diluted and EC_{se} decreases. If soil salinity increases above threshold levels (Fig. 3-30) during dry periods, more frequent irrigation will be required to prevent water and salinity stress and, thus, negative effects on plant growth and yield. Also, the percentage of plant available water decreases with increasing salinity (higher osmotic potential), requiring more frequent irrigation. Excessive irrigation reduces aeration, especially in poorly drained soils, and can reduce salt tolerance in some plants. Under furrow irrigation conditions, excess water leaches into the furrow area; however, soil water movement from the bottom of the furrow to the midrow area deposits salts as water evaporates from the soil surface. Salt-sensitive crops must be planted to the side of the midrow to minimize salt injury to germinating seeds and seedlings (Fig. 3-31). Much lower water rates are used in trickle irrigation compared with furrow irrigation, resulting in greater salt accumulation and potential for yield losses.

Environmental Factors Under hot, dry conditions, most crops are less salt tolerant than under cool, humid conditions because of greatly increased evapotranspiration demand. These climatic effects of temperature and humidity on salt tolerance are particularly important with the most salt-sensitive crops (Table 3-19).

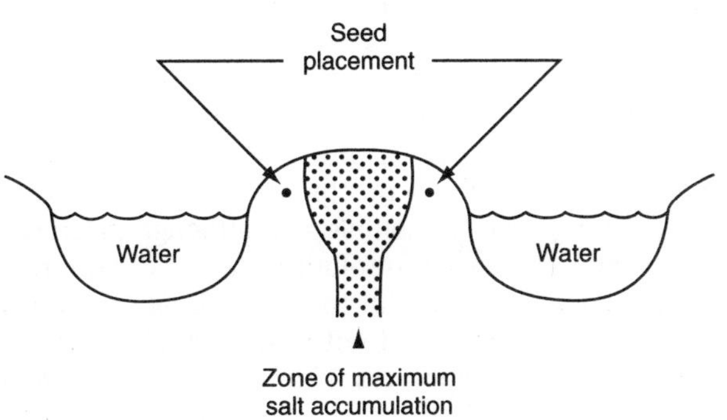

Figure 3-31 **In furrow-irrigated cropping systems, salts accumulate near the center of the bed. Seeds should be planted on the side of the beds to avoid salinity problems.** ***(Ludwick et al., 1978, Colorado State Univ. Coop. Ext. No. 504.)***

Managing Saline and Sodic Soils for Crop Production

Saline soils are relatively easy to reclaim if adequate amounts of low-salt irrigation waters are available and internal and surface drainage are feasible. Salts must be leached below the root zone and out of contact with subsequent irrigation water.

The quantity of irrigation water needed to leach the salts out of the root zone, or the leaching requirement (LR), can be estimated by the following relationship:

$$LR = \frac{EC_{iw}}{5(EC_{se}) - EC_{iw}}$$

where

$$LR = \text{leaching requirement}$$
$$EC_{se} = \text{threshold } EC_{se} \text{ for a given crop}$$
$$EC_{iw} = \text{EC of irrigation water}$$

For example, Kentucky bluegrass threshold $EC_{se} = 3.0$. If the $EC_{iw} = 1.5$., then the LR is:

$$LR = \frac{1.5}{5(3) - 2} = 0.115$$

LR represents the additional water (LR = 11.5%) needed to leach out salts over that needed to saturate the profile. Although this relationship provides an estimate of the water volume needed to reduce the salts in the soil, more sophisticated calculations are generally used to precisely estimate the amount of leaching water needed. The amount of leaching water required depends on (1) the desired EC_{se}, which depends on the salt tolerance of the intended crop; (2) irrigation water quality (EC_{iw}); (3) rooting or leaching depth; and (4) soil water-holding capacity.

As seen in the LR calculation, the quality of the irrigation water used to leach salts below the root zone is an important factor in managing soil salinity. The EC and SAR of the available water must be determined before application. Based on these values, the quality of the water can be evaluated (Fig. 3-32). As the EC and SAR of the irrigation water increase, greater precautions should be taken in using it to leach salts below the root zone.

In soils with a high water table, drain installation may be required before leaching. If there is a dense calcareous or gypsiferous layer or the soil is impervious, deep chiseling or plowing may be needed to improve infiltration. When only rainfall or limited irrigation is available, surface organic mulches will reduce evaporation and increase drainage.

Managing the soil to minimize salt accumulation is essential, especially in semiarid and arid regions. Maintaining the soil near field capacity with frequent watering dilutes salts. Light leaching before planting or light irrigation after planting moves salts below the planting and early rooting zone. If water is available, periodic leaching when crops are not growing will move salts out of the root zone. Much of the salt may precipitate as $CaSO_4 \cdot 2H_2O$ and $CaCO_3$ or $MgCO_3$ during dry periods and will not react as soluble salt, although precipitation of Ca and Mg will increase the proportion of Na^+ present in solution (see SAR definition).

Managing soils for improved drainage is essential for controlling soil salinity. When ridge-tillage systems are used, the salt moves upward with capillary H_2O and is deposited on the center of the ridges where the water evaporates. Planting on the shoulders or edge of the ridges helps to avoid problems associated with excess salts (Fig. 3-31).

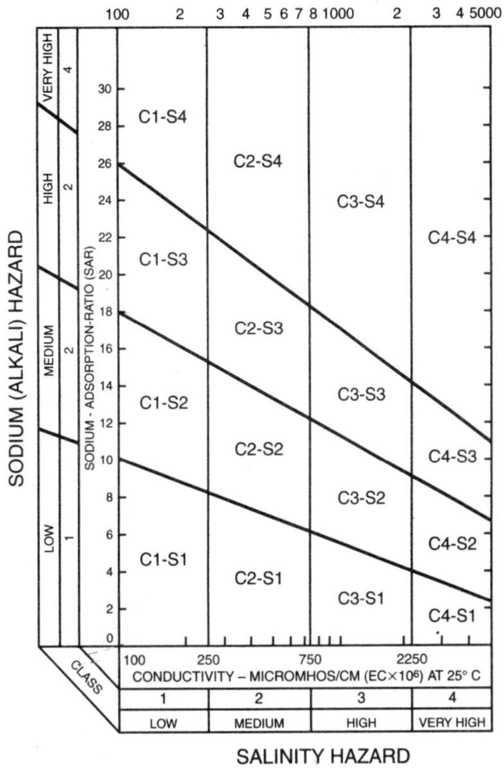

1. Salinity classification	2. Sodium classification
C1 - Low-salinity water can be used for irrigation with most crops on most soils, with little likelihood that a salinity problem will develop. Some leaching is required, but this occurs under normal irrigation practices except in soils of extremely low permeability.	S1 - Low-sodium water can be used for irrigation on almost all soils with little danger of the development of a sodium problem. However, sodium-sensitive crops, such as stone-fruit trees and avocados, may accumulate injurious amounts of sodium in the leaves.
C2 - Medium-salinity water can be used if a moderate amount of leaching occurs. Plants with moderate salt tolerance can be grown in most instances without special practices for salinity control.	S2 - Medium-sodium water may present a moderate sodium problem in fine-textured (clay) soils unless there is gypsum in the soil. This water can be used on coarse-textured (sandy) or organic soils that take water well.
C3 - High-salinity water cannot be used on soil with restricted drainage. Even with adequate drainage, special management for salinity control may be required, and plants with good salt tolerance should be selected.	S3 - High-sodium water may produce troublesome sodium problems in most soils and will require special management, good drainage, high leaching, and additions of organic matter. If there is plenty of gypsum in the soil a serious problem may not develop for some time. If gypsum is not present, it or some similar material may have to be added.
C4 - Very-high-salinity water is not suitable for irrigation under ordinary conditions but may be used occasionally under very special circumstances. The soil must be permeable, drainage must be adequate, irrigation water must be applied in excess to provide considerable leaching, and very-salt-tolerant crops should be selected.	S4 - Very-high-sodium water is generally unsatisfactory for irrigation except at low- or medium-salinity levels, where the use of gypsum or some other amendment makes it possible to use such water.

Figure 3-32 **Diagram for the classification of irrigation waters.** *(U.S. Salinity Laboratory,* Handbook 60, *1954.)*

In sodic and saline-sodic soils, exchangeable Na^+ and/or EC_{se} must be reduced, which can be difficult because the soil clay may be dispersed, preventing infiltration. Exchange of Na^+ is most often accomplished with Ca^{+2} by adding the appropriate rate of gypsum ($CaSO_4 \cdot 2H_2O$). The reaction is:

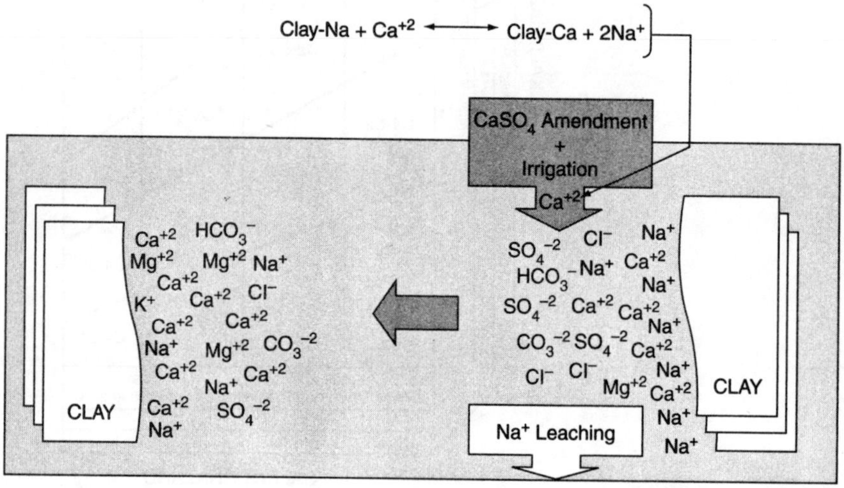

Estimating the quantity of $CaSO_4 \cdot 2H_2O$ required is similar to the calculation for estimating the $CaCO_3$ required to increase pH. For example, a soil with CEC = 20 meq/100 g contains 15% ESP, and we need to reduce the ESP to 5%; thus, 15% − 5% = 10% reduction in ESP.

Thus,

$$0.10 \times \frac{20 \text{ meq CEC}}{100 \text{ g Soil}} = \frac{2 \text{ meq Na}^+}{100 \text{ g Soil}} = \frac{2 \text{ meq CaSO}_4 \cdot 2\text{H}_2\text{O}}{100 \text{ g Soil}}$$

$$\frac{2 \text{ meq CaSO}_4 \cdot 2\text{H}_2\text{O}}{100 \text{ g Soil}} \times \frac{86 \text{ mg CaSO}_4 \cdot 2\text{H}_2\text{O}}{\text{meq}} = \frac{172 \text{ mg CaSO}_4 \cdot 2\text{H}_2\text{O}}{100 \text{ g Soil}}$$

$$\frac{172 \text{ mg CaSO}_4 \cdot 2\text{H}_2\text{O}}{100 \text{ g Soil}} \times \frac{1 \text{ g}}{1{,}000 \text{ mg}} = \frac{0.172 \text{ g}}{100 \text{ g}} = \frac{0.172 \text{ lb}}{100 \text{ lb}}$$

$$\times \frac{2 \times 10^4}{2 \times 10^4} = \frac{3{,}440 \text{ lb CaSO}_4 \cdot 2\text{H}_2\text{O}}{\text{afs}}$$

If it were desired to reduce exchangeable Na^+ in 0- to 12-in. depth instead of 0- to 6-in. depth (afs) then the $CaSO_4 \cdot 2H_2O$ rate would be doubled (6,880 lbs/a-ft). The recommended gypsum would be broadcast-applied followed by slow irrigation to dissolve the $CaSO_4 \cdot 2H_2O$ and move the Ca^{+2} into the target soil depth. The Na-Ca exchange and leaching process can take several weeks or months.

In calcareous soils, the soil already has an available source of Ca^{+2} in $CaCO_3$. Thus, the amendment could be an acid or acid-forming material to dissolve the $CaCO_3$ to produce Ca^{+2} that would then replace exchangeable Na^+ according to:

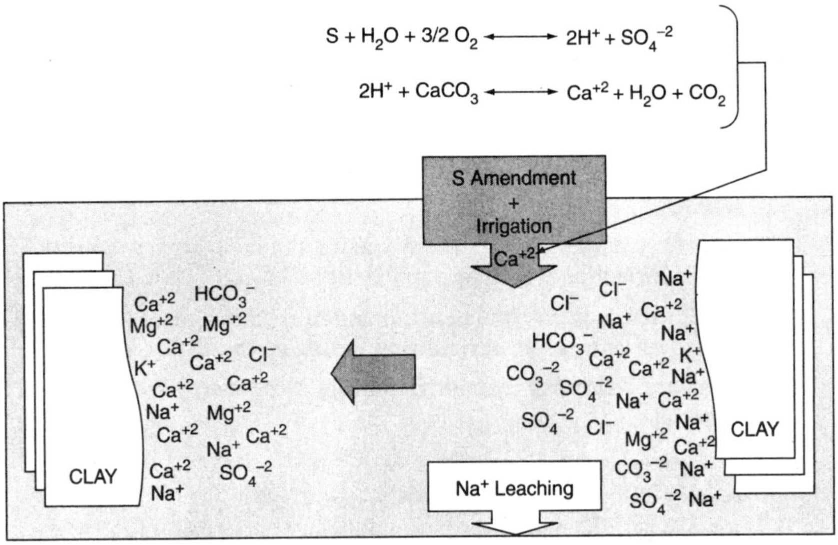

In the previous example, assume the soil also contained 2% $CaCO_3$. Thus, a reduction of 2 meq exchangeable Na^+/100 g soil is still required; however, elemental S will be added that will oxidize to produce $2H^+$, which will dissolve exactly 2 meq $CaCO_3$/100 g soil to produce 2 meq Ca^{+2}/100 g soil. The calculation for S rate is:

$$\frac{2 \text{ meq Na}^+}{100 \text{ g Soil}} = \frac{2 \text{ meq S}}{100 \text{ g Soil}}$$

$$\frac{2 \text{ meq S}}{100 \text{ g Soil}} \times \frac{16 \text{ mg S}}{\text{meq}} = \frac{32 \text{ mg S}}{100 \text{ g Soil}}$$

$$\frac{32 \text{ mg S}}{100 \text{ g Soil}} \times \frac{1 \text{ g}}{1{,}000 \text{ mg}} = \frac{0.032 \text{ g}}{100 \text{ g}} = \frac{0.032 \text{ lb}}{100 \text{ lb}} \times \frac{2 \times 10^4}{2 \times 10^4} = \frac{640 \text{ lb S}}{\text{afs}}$$

Since the oxidation of S is a microbially mediated reaction, additional time is required for the amendment process to be completed. In some situations, the remediation of sodic soils can take several months, often taking the field out of production until the remediation process is completed.

Study Questions

1. What is an acid? A solution has a pH value of 6.0. What is the H^+ activity?
2. How are acids neutralized? What are the principal sources of soil acidity?
3. Distinguish between active and potential acidity. Which of these two forms is measured when a pH determination is made?
4. Solution A has a pH of 3.0. Solution B has a pH of 6.0. The active acidity of solution A is how many times greater than that of solution B?
5. How is soil pH affected by fertilizer applications? Provide several example reactions.
6. Define lime requirement. The term *agricultural* lime usually refers to what material?

7. How does soil BC influence the lime requirement of soil?

8. How is the lime requirement of a soil determined?

9. Write the chemical reactions that occur when lime is added to an acid soil.

10. Can $CaSO_4$ be used as a liming agent? Write the neutralization reaction.

11. Define *neutralizing value* or *calcium carbonate equivalent* (CCE). What is the CCE of Na_2CO_3?

12. You analyze limestone and find that it has a neutralizing value of 85%. How many tons of this limestone would be equivalent to 3 tons of pure $CaCO_3$?

13. In addition to purity and neutralizing value, what other property of limestone is important to its value as an agricultural liming material?

14. Using the following reactions, indicate if the material can be used as a suitable liming material.

a. clay-$2H^+ + CaSO_4$ = clay-$Ca^+ + 2H^+ + SO_4^{-2}$

b. clay-$2H^+ + 2KOH$ = clay-$2K^+ + 2H_2O$

c. clay-$2H^+ + Mg(HCO_3)_2$ = clay-$Mg^{+2} + CO_2 + H_2O$

d. clay-$2H^+ + 2KCl$ = clay-$2K^+ + 2HCl$

e. clay-$2H^+ + Na_2CO_3$ = clay-$2Na^+ + CO_2 + H_2O$

15. Adding lime will increase %BS of an acid soil. A grower indicates that adding gypsum will do the same thing at half the cost. What would you advise this grower?

16. A soil has a pH of 5.5 and a CEC of 20 meq/100 g (60% BS). Fifty g of soil were titrated with 50 ml of 0.12 N KOH to pH 6.8. Calculate the final %BS and the lime recommendation (lbs/afs).

17. We want to raise the soil pH from 5.5 to 7.0. The CEC is 30 meq/100 g. Using Figure 2-9, calculate the lbs/afs of $CaCO_3$.

18. A grower received a lime recommendation of 8 tons/afs of 80% ECC lime material. His soil test results showed pH = 5.5 and CEC = 26 meq/100 g. The grower thought that this recommendation was too high. How much would the soil pH increase if the grower only applied 4 tons/afs of the lime material? (Use Figure 2-9.)

19. A golf course superintendent wants to plant fescue in two fairways that have drastically different soil properties.

Fairway 1—silt loam texture; soil pH = 5.7; %BS = 58%; CEC = 15 meq/100 g

Fairway 2—clay loam texture; soil pH = 6.0; %BS = 60%; CEC = 40 meq/100 g

a. Calculate the $CaCO_3$ (lbs/afs) required to neutralize soil acidity in Fairway 1 to pH 6.8 and %BS of 90%.

b. Calculate the $CaCO_3$ (lbs/afs) required to neutralize soil acidity in Fairway 2 to pH 6.8 and %BS of 90%.

20. A soil had an initial pH of 5.5 and a CEC = 25 meq/100 g. After the producer applied the lime the pH increased to 6.5. How much lime did she apply? (Use Figure 2-9 and assume all the lime reacted.)

21. A soil has the following properties: Clay content = 50%; CEC = 40 meq/100 g; pH 5.2; %Ca saturation = 40; %Mg saturation = 6; %K saturation = 8; %Na saturation = 0. The lab recommended 3 tons/afs of $CaCO_3$. Is this a good recommendation? If not, what would you recommend? Show all calculations.

22. A grower received a lime recommendation of 4 tons $CaCO_3$/afs. The only material available is dolomite or $CaMg(CO_3)_2$. The dolomite has a CCE of 90% and 54% passes a 60-mesh screen, 25% passes an 8-mesh screen, while the remainder will not pass the 8-mesh screen.

a. Calculate the ECC of this dolomite.

b. How many lbs dolomite/afs does he need to apply?

23. Titration of a 50 g soil sample with 10 ml of 0.25 N NaOH raises soil pH from 5.3 to 6.5. How many lbs/afs of the following materials would be required?

a. Pure $CaCO_3$

b. Pure $CaMg(CO_3)_2$

c. Lime material with CCE of 85% and the following screen analysis.

mesh size	% of material
<60	50
8–60	25
>8	25

24. Are benefits derived from deep mixing of lime in soil? Can long-term liming of surface soil influence subsoil acidity?

25. You have lost the liming recommendations sent to you by the soil laboratory, but you do recall that 3 tons/a were recommended for field B. Because the pH is the same in both fields, you apply 3 tons to field A as well. Have you acted wisely? Why or why not?

26. 25 ml of 1.0 N H_2SO_4 was added to 5 g of calcareous soil. All of the lime was neutralized. The excess acid was titrated with 40 ml of 0.5 N NaOH. Calculate the lime content (%).

27. Answer the following questions for the soil data listed below.

	Exchangeable Cations (ppm Soil)	Cations in Saturated Extract (ppm Solution)
Ca	1,600	180
Mg	600	20
Na	1,000	900
K	600	5

CEC (me/100 g) = 17 pH (sat'd paste) = 8.6

$CaCO_3$ (%) = 2 EC_{se} (mmho/cm) = 4.5

a. Calculate CEC and compare with measured CEC. Suggest a reason why the two values may be different.

b. Calculate SAR and estimate SAR from the exchangeable cation data.

c. Calculate and estimate ESR and ESP.

28. Explain how S acidulates a soil.

29. What are the main cations in saline, sodic, and saline/sodic soils? Explain how sodic soils become impermeable.

30. Write the chemical reactions when S is added as an amendment to reduce exchangeable Na.

31. Explain why $CaSO_4$ is effective in reclaiming saline soils.

32. A soil has the following properties: pH 8.6; ESP = 18%; CEC = 25 me/100 g; $CaCO_3$ = 2%.

a. Calculate the SAR.

b. A lab recommended adding 4,300 lbs gypsum/afs. Calculate the final ESP if the grower followed the recommendation.

c. If the grower added S instead of gypsum, calculate the final $CaCO_3$ content.

33. A laboratory analysis showed the following results:

CEC = 28 meq/100 g	solution Ca = 6 meq/1
$CaCO_3$ = 0.2%	solution Mg = 2 meq/1
soil pH = 8.6	solution Na = 36 meq/1
EC = 5.2 mmhos/cm	

a. Calculate SAR, ESR, and ESP.

b. Calculate the S (lbs/afs) required to neutralize all the lime.

c. Calculate the gypsum (lbs/afs) required to reduce ESP to 5%.

34. A golf course manager complained that when he irrigated the fairways the water would not infiltrate very readily. Soil samples were collected and the soil solution (saturated extract) contained:

1,600 ppm Ca^{+2} 960 ppm Ca^{+2} 2,760 ppm Na^{+}

The CEC was 35 meq/100 g soil and the lab recommended lowering the ESP to 5% to improve infiltration.

a. Calculate the gypsum required to lower ESP to 5% (lbs/a-ft).

b. How much S (lb/a-ft would be required to lower the ESP to 5%?

c. The soil contained 0.2% lime. Was there enough lime present to supply enough Ca^{+2} to lower ESP to 5%?

Selected References

Adams, F. (Ed.). 1984. *Soil acidity and liming.* Madison, Wis.: Soil Science Society of America.

Alley, M. M., and L. W. Zelazny. 1987. Soil acidity: Soil pH and lime needs. In J. R. Brown (Ed.), *Soil testing: Sampling, correlation, calibration, and interpretation.* Madison, Wis. Special Publication No. 21. Soil Science Society of America.

Bresler, E., B. L. McNeal, and D. L. Carter. 1982. *Saline and sodic soils.* New York: Springer-Verlag.

Follett, R. H., L. S. Murphy, and R. L. Donahue. 1981. *Fertilizers and soil amendments.* Englewood Cliffs, N.J.: Prentice-Hall.

Kamprath, E. J., and C. D. Fox. 1985. Lime-fertilizer-plant interactions in acid soils. In O. P. Englestad (Ed.), *Fertilizer technology and use.* Madison, Wis.: Soil Science Society of America.

McLean, E. O. 1973. Testing soils for pH and lime requirement. In L. M. Walsh and J. D. Beaton (Eds.), *Soil testing and plant analysis.* Madison, Wis.: Soil Science Society of America.

CHAPTER 4

Nitrogen

The N Cycle

Nitrogen (N) is the most frequently deficient nutrient in most nonlegume cropping systems. Many inorganic and organic sources are available to supply N to crops. The quantities of N_2 fixed by legumes can be sufficient for their growth. Understanding the chemistry and biology of soil N is essential for maximizing productivity while reducing the impacts of N inputs on the environment.

The ultimate source of all N used by plants is N_2, which constitutes 78% of the earth's atmosphere. Unfortunately, higher plants cannot metabolize N_2 directly into protein. N_2 must first be converted to plant available N by:

- microorganisms that live symbiotically on legume roots,
- free-living or nonsymbiotic soil microorganisms,
- atmospheric electrical discharges forming N oxides, or
- the manufacture of synthetic N fertilizers.

The large reservoir of atmospheric N_2 is in equilibrium with all fixed forms of N in soil, seawater, and living and nonliving organisms (Table 4-1). About 262,000 mt N/ha (117,000 tons N/ac) are present in the atmosphere. As N_2 is fixed by these different processes, numerous microbial and chemical processes release N_2 back to the atmosphere. Cycling of N in the soil-plant-atmosphere system involves many transformations between inorganic and organic forms (Fig. 4-1). The N cycle can be divided into N inputs or gains, N outputs or losses, and N cycling within the soil, where N is neither gained nor lost (Table 4-2). Except for industrial and combustion fixation, all of these N transformations occur naturally; however, humans influence many of these N processes. The purpose of this chapter is to describe the chemical and microbial cycling of N and how humans influence or manage these transformations to optimize N availability to plants.

Table 4-1 **Approximate Distribution of N Throughout the Soil-Plant/Animal-Atmosphere System**

N Source	*Metric Tons*	*% of Total*
Atmosphere	3.9×10^{15}	99.3840
Sea (various)	2.4×10^{13}	0.6116
Soil (nonliving)	1.5×10^{11}	0.0038
Plants	1.5×10^{10}	0.00038
Microbes in soil	6×10^{9}	0.00015
Animals (land)	2×10^{8}	0.000005
People	1×10^{7}	0.00000025

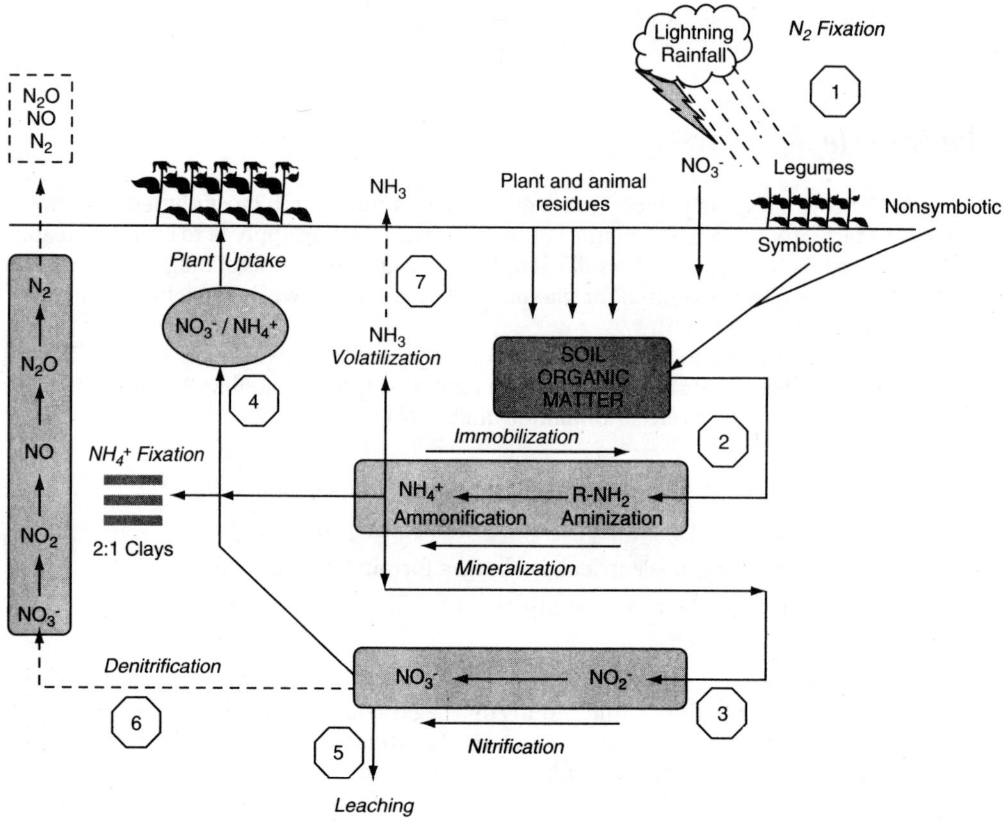

Figure 4-1 The N cycle. In step 1, N in plant and animal residues and N derived from the atmosphere through electrical, combustion, and industrial processes (N_2 is combined with H_2 or O_2) is added to the soil. In step 2, organic N in the residues is mineralized to NH_4^+ by soil organisms. Plant roots absorb a portion of the NH_4^+. In step 3, much of the NH_4^+ is converted to (NO_3^-) by nitrifying bacteria in a process called nitrification. In step 4, NO_3^- and NH_4^+ are taken up by plant roots and used to produce the protein in crops that are eaten by humans or fed to livestock. In step 5, some NO_3^- is lost to groundwater or drainage systems as a result of downward movement through the soil in percolating water. In step 6, some NO_3^- is converted by denitrifying bacteria into N_2 and nitrogen oxides (N_2O and NO) that escape into the atmosphere, completing the cycle. In step 7, some NH_4^+ can be converted to NH_3 through a process called volatilization.

Table 4-2 **N Inputs, Outputs (Losses), and Cycling in the Soil-Plant-Atmosphere System***

N Inputs or Gains	*N Outputs or Losses*	*No Net N Gain or Loss (Cycling)*
Fixation	Plant uptake	Immobilization
Biological	Denitrification	Mineralization
Industrial	Volatilization	Nitrification
Electrical	Leaching	
Combustion	NH_4^+ fixation†	
Animal manure		
Crop residue		

*Some N inputs, outputs, and cycling components can be influenced by management but generally are not managed.
†Some fixed NH_4^+ can be released (input).

Functions and Forms of N in Plants

Forms

Plants contain 1 to 6% N by weight and absorb N as both nitrate (NO_3^-) and ammonium (NH_4^+) (Fig. 4-1). In moist, warm, well-aerated soils, soil solution NO_3^- is generally greater than NH_4^+. Both move to plant roots by mass flow and diffusion.

The rate of NO_3^- uptake is usually high, causing an increase in rhizosphere pH. When plants absorb high levels of NO_3^-, there is an increase in anion (HCO_3^-, OH^-, organic anions) transport out of cells and an increase in cation absorption (Ca^{+2}, Mg^{+2}, K^+). Plants metabolize NO_3^- to NH_4^+ to amino acids and to proteins. NO_3^- reduction is an energy-requiring process that uses 2 nitrate reductase (NADH) molecules for each NO_3^- reduced in protein synthesis. Thus, NH_4^+ is the preferred N source since energy is conserved compared to NO_3^- (one less step in the reduction process). Plants supplied with NH_4^+ may have increased carbohydrate and protein levels compared with NO_3^-.

Plant uptake of NH_4^+ proceeds best at neutral pH values and is depressed by increasing acidity. Absorption of NH_4^+ reduces Ca^{+2}, Mg^{+2}, and K^+ uptake while increasing $H_2PO_4^-$, SO_4^{-2}, and Cl^- absorption. Rhizosphere pH decreases with NH_4^+ uptake, caused by H^+ exuded by the root to maintain electroneutrality or charge balance inside the plant. Differences in 2 pH units have been observed for NH_4^+ versus NO_3^- uptake. This acidification can affect both nutrient availability and biological activity in the vicinity of roots.

NH_4^+ tolerance limits are narrow. High levels of NH_4^+ can retard growth and restrict K^+ uptake. In contrast, plants can accumulate and tolerate comparatively high NO_3^- levels in tissues.

Preference of plants for either NH_4^+ or NO_3^- is determined by plant age and type, environment, and other factors. Cereals, corn, sugar beets, pineapple, rice, and ryegrass use either form of N. Kale, celery, bush beans, and squash grow best when provided with some NO_3^-. Some plants, such as blueberries, Chenopodium album, and certain rice cultivars, cannot tolerate NO_3^-. Solanaceous crops, such as tobacco, tomato, and potato, prefer a high NO_3^-/NH_4^+ ratio.

Plant growth is often improved when the plants are nourished with both NO_3^- and NH_4^+ compared with NO_3^- or NH_4^+ alone. Mixtures are beneficial at certain growth stages for some genotypes of corn, sorghum, soybeans, wheat, and barley. Increased nonlegume

Table 4-3 Responses of Corn Hybrids Supplied with Differing N Sources

Year	*Hybrid*	*N Source*	*Grain Yield*	*Kernel Number*	*Kernel Weight*
			(g/plant)	(no./plant)	(mg/kernel)
1986	B73 × LH51	All NO_3	254	688	369
		NO_3/NH_4	275	764	361
	FS 854	All NO_3	277	818	339
		NO_3/NH_4	315	1,000	315
1987	B73 × LH51	All NO_3	154	540	285
		NO_3/NH_4	193	691	279
	B73 × LH38	All NO_3	161	603	267
		NO_3/NH_4	180	742	243
	CB59G × LH38	All NO_3	137	475	288
		NO_3/NH_4	154	545	283
	LH74 × LH51	All NO_3	181	592	306
		NO_3/NH_4	199	607	328

SOURCE: Below and Gentry, 1988, *Better Crops*, 72(2).

yields with NH_4^+ nutrition are associated with greater tillering. Corn yields increased from 8 to 25% with $NH_4^+ + NO_3^-$, compared with yields with NO_3^- alone, which was related to increased numbers of kernels/plant and not to heavier kernels (Table 4-3). These data illustrate that genotypes differ in their physiological response to NH_4^+. Recent research results demonstrated that NH_4^+ application postsilking or during grain fill was required to maximize corn yields and that a 50:50 NH_4^+ to NO_3^- ratio was optimum.

$NH_4^+ + NO_3^-$ nutrition is a major factor influencing the occurrence and severity of plant diseases. Some diseases are more severe when solution $NH_4^+ < NO_3^-$; others are more severe when NO_3^- predominates. Two processes may be involved. One is the direct effect of N form on pathogenic activity, the other is the influence of NO_3^- or NH_4^+ on organisms capable of altering the availability of micronutrient cations. For example, a high NO_3^- supply stimulates certain bacteria, which lowers the availability of Mn to wheat. The effect of N form on rhizosphere soil pH is partially responsible for differences observed in disease incidence and severity.

Functions

Before NO_3^- can be used in the plant, it must be reduced to NH_4^+ or NH_3. Nitrate reduction involves 2 enzyme-catalyzed reactions that occur in roots and/or leaves, depending on the plant species. Both reactions occur in series so that toxic nitrite (NO_2^-) does not accumulate.

	Reduction Reaction	*Enzyme*	*Reaction Site*
Step 1	$NO_3^- \rightarrow NO_2^-$	Nitrate reductase	Cytoplasm
Step 2	$NO_2^- \rightarrow NH_3$	Nitrite reductase	Chloroplast

The NH_3 produced is assimilated into amino acids that are subsequently combined into proteins and nucleic acids. Proteins provide the framework for chloroplasts, mitochondria, and other structures in which most biochemical reactions occur. The type of protein formed is controlled by a specific genetic code found in nucleic acids, which determines the quantity and arrangement of amino acids in each protein. One of these nucleic acids, deoxyribonucleic acid (DNA), present in the nucleus and mitochondria of the cell, duplicates the genetic information in the chromosomes of the parent cell to the daughter cell. Ribonucleic acid (RNA), present in the nucleus and cytoplasm of the cell, executes the instructions coded within DNA molecules. Most enzymes controlling these metabolic processes are also proteins and are continually metabolized and resynthesized.

In addition to the formation of proteins, N is an integral part of chlorophyll, which converts light into chemical energy needed for photosynthesis. The basic chlorophyll structure is the porphyrin ring, composed of 4 pyrrole rings, each containing 1 N and 4 C atoms (Fig. 4-2). A single Mg atom is bonded in the center of each porphyrin ring.

An adequate supply of N is associated with high photosynthetic activity, vigorous vegetative growth, and a dark green color. An excess of N in relation to other nutrients, such as P, K, and S, can delay crop maturity. Stimulation of heavy vegetative growth early in the growing season can be a disadvantage in regions where soil moisture limits plant growth. Early-season depletion of soil moisture without adequate replenishment before the grain-filling period can depress yields. If N is used properly in conjunction with other needed inputs, it can speed the maturity of crops and reduce the energy required to dry grain to 15.5% moisture or permit earlier harvest (Table 4-4).

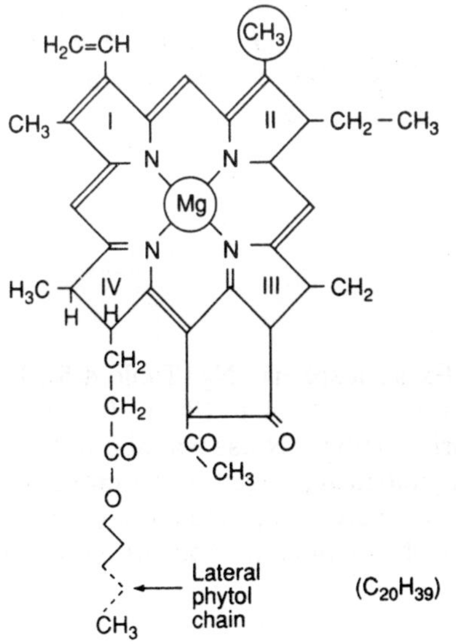

Figure 4-2 **A simplified representation of a chlorophyll molecule.**

Table 4-4 **Effect of N on Corn Grain Yield and Moisture Content**

N (lb/a)	*Yield (bu/a)*	*Grain Moisture (%)*
0	66	36.1
60	101	30.0
120	135	27.9
180	158	26.9
240	167	28.2
300	168	27.2

SOURCE: Ohio State Univ., 1979, 17th Annu. Agron. Demonstration, *Farm Sci. Rev.*

The supply of N influences carbohydrate utilization. When N supplies are low, carbohydrates will be deposited in vegetative cells, causing them to thicken. When N supplies are adequate and conditions are favorable for growth, proteins are formed from the manufactured carbohydrates. With less carbohydrate deposited in the vegetative portion, more protoplasm is formed, and, because protoplasm is highly hydrated, a more succulent plant results. Excessive succulence in cotton weakens the fiber, and with grain crops, lodging may occur, particularly with a low K supply or with varieties not adapted to high levels of N. In some cases, excessive succulence enhances susceptibility to diseases or insects. Crops such as wheat and rice have been modified for growth at higher densities and at higher levels of N fertilization. Shorter plant height and improved lodging resistance have been bred into plants, which respond in yield to much higher rates of N.

Visual Deficiency Symptoms

When plants are N deficient, leaves appear yellow. The loss of protein N from chloroplasts in older leaves produces the yellowing, or chlorosis, indicative of N deficiency. Chlorosis usually appears first on the lower leaves, the upper leaves remaining green; under severe N deficiency, lower leaves turn brown and die. This necrosis begins at the leaf tip and progresses along the midrib until the entire leaf is dead (see color plates inside book cover).

The tendency of newer growth to remain green as the lower leaves yellow or die indicates the mobility of N in the plant. When the roots are unable to absorb sufficient N, protein in the older plant parts is converted to soluble N, translocated to the active meristematic tissues, and reused in the synthesis of new protein.

Symbiotic N_2 Fixation

Biological N_2 Fixation

Many organisms have the unique ability to fix atmospheric N_2 (Table 4-5). Estimates of total annual biological N_2 fixation worldwide range from 130 to 180 $\times 10^6$ metric tons, with about 50% fixed by *Rhizobia*. In contrast, world fertilizer N use was about 80 $\times 10^6$ metric tons in 2001. In the United States, reliance on biological N_2 fixation for crop production has declined dramatically since the 1950s because of increased production and use of low-cost synthetic N fertilizers (Fig. 4-3). About 20% of N supplied to crops in the United States is from legumes and crop residues (Table 4-6).

N_2 Fixation by Legumes

When legume root growth begins, special N_2-fixing bacteria in soil invade root hairs and multiply. Legume roots respond by forming tumor-like structures called *nodules* on the root surface (Fig. 4-4). The specialized bacteria called *Rhizobia* inside the nodule absorb N_2 from soil air and convert it to NH_4^+ (Fig.4-5). Rhizobia use the enzyme nitrogenase and energy from the transformation of ATP to ADP to break the strong triple bond ($N \equiv N$) in N_2. Plants provide the energy (sugars, carbohydrates, ATP) for the bacteria to fix N_2 and provides NH_4^+ for production of proteins by the host plant. The *symbiotic* relationship between legume host plant and nodule bacteria is mutually beneficial. Most of the fixed N_2 is utilized by the host plant, although some may be excreted from the nodule into the soil and used by other nearby plants, or released as nodules decompose after the plant dies.

Table 4-5 **Economically Important Microorganisms Involved in Biological N Fixation**

Organisms	*General Properties*	*Agricultural Importance*
Azotobacter	Aerobic; free fixers; live in soil, water, rhizosphere (area surrounding the roots), leaf surfaces	Minor benefit to agriculture; found in vascular tissue of sugarcane, with abundant sucrose as a possible energy source for N_2 fixation
Azospirillum	Microaerobic; free fixers; or found in association with roots of grasses	Inoculation benefits some nonlegume crops, shown to increase root hair development
Rhizobium	Fix N in legume-Rhizobium symbiosis	Legume crops are benefited by inoculation with proper strains
Actinomycetes, Frankia	Fix N in symbiosis with nonlegume wood trees—alder, Myrica, Casuarina	Potentially important in reforestation, wood production
Blue-green algae, Anabaena	Contain chlorophyll, as in higher plants; aquatic and terrestrial	Enhance rice in paddy soils; *Azolla* (a water fern)—*Anabaena-Azolla* symbiosis; used as green manure

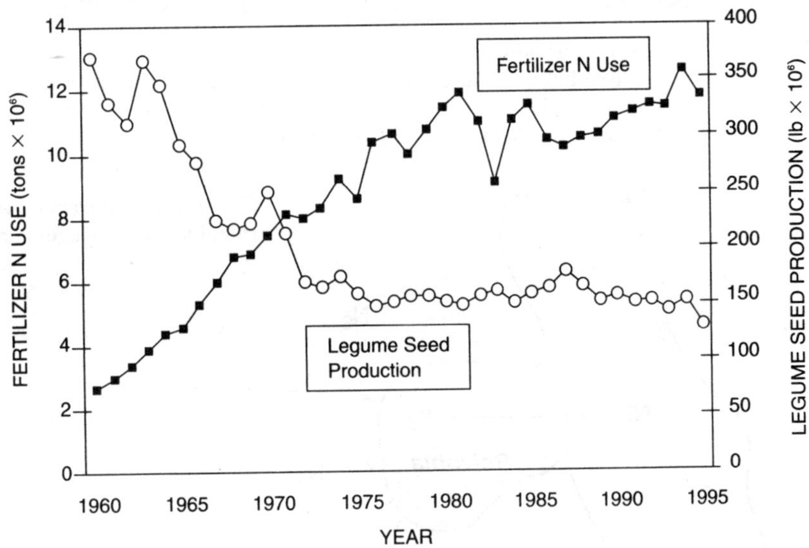

Figure 4-3 **Inverse relationship between N fertilizer use and legume seed production in the United States.**

Table 4-6 **Estimated Percentage of Total N Added to U.S. Cropland by Various Sources**

N Source	*Total Amount (million tons)*	*% of Total*
Commercial N	8.55	57
Legumes, crop residues	3.74	25
Animal manures	2.14	14
Other sources	0.52	04

SOURCE: USDA, 1992.

Figure 4-4 Example of nodules on soybean (a) showing differences in nodulation between varieties, alfalfa (b) showing non-inoculated (left) and inoculated (right) with proper *Rhizobia* bacteria. *(Courtesy D. Israel (soybean) and J. Burns, D. Chamblee, and J. Green (alfalfa), NC State University.)*

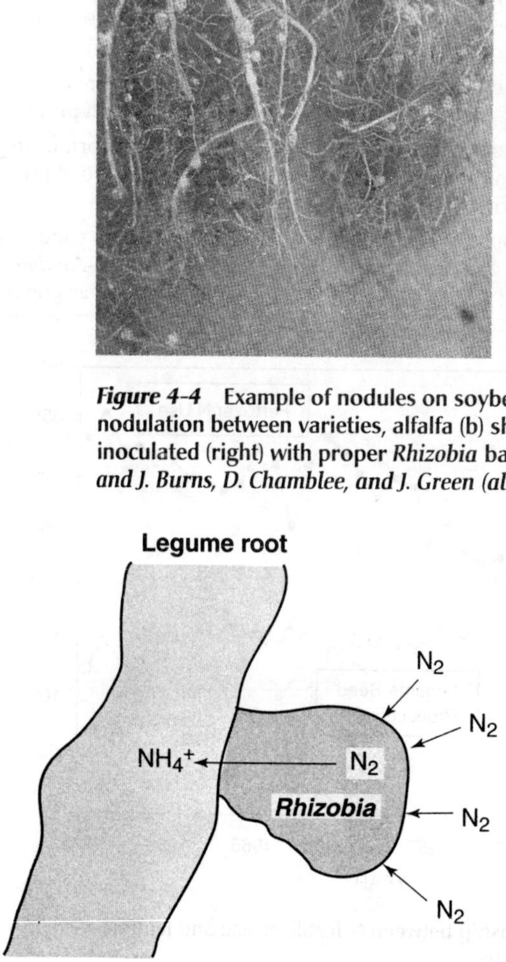

Figure 4-5 Conversion of N_2 to NH_4^+ by rhizobia inside a legume root nodule.

$$N_2 + 16\,ATP + 2H^+ \xrightarrow{\text{nitrogenase}} 2NH_4^+ + 16\,ADP + H_2$$

Numerous rhizobium species exist, each requiring a specific host legume plant. For example, symbiotic bacteria with soybean will not fix N_2 with alfalfa. Inoculation of the legume seed with the correct inoculum is recommended the first time a field is planted to a new legume species. For example, 40% increases in N_2 fixation by alfalfa have been obtained by carefully matching cultivars and strains of inoculum.

Some soils have high populations of native *Rhizobia* specific for the intended legume. If crop N requirement is provided by the native *Rhizobia*, inoculation may not increase yield.

Sufficient native *Rhizobia* occur when legume crops are frequently grown in the same fields or with previous legume inoculations. Producers generally inoculate legumes at planting regardless of the presence of native *Rhizobia* because the economic risk of poor production is far greater than the cost of the inoculum. Inoculation assures the producer an adequate population of *Rhizobia* for the crop.

The presence of nodules on legume roots does not necessarily indicate N_2 fixation by active *Rhizobia*. Mature effective alfalfa nodules tend to be large, elongated (2 to 4 by 4 to 8 mm), often clustered on the primary roots, and have pink to red centers. The red color is due to leghemoglobin, which indicates that *Rhizobia* are actively fixing N_2. Ineffective nodules are small ($<$ 2 mm in diameter), usually numerous, and scattered over the entire root system. In some cases, they are very large ($>$ 8 mm in diameter), few in number, and have white or pale-green centers.

Quantity of N_2 Fixed

Generally, nodule bacteria fix 25 to 80% of the total legume N (Table 4-7). N_2 fixation by most perennial legumes ranges from 100 to 200 lbs/a/yr, although under optimum conditions N fixation can reach two to three times these values. Short-season annual legumes often fix between 50 and 100 lbs N/a/yr. Table 4-8 shows that N_2 fixation represented two-thirds of total N uptake in the first year of alfalfa production.

Table 4-7 **N_2 Fixed by Legumes in Temperate Climates**

	N fixed (lb/a/yr)	
Legume	*Range*	*Typical*
Alfalfa	50–300	200
Beans	20–80	40
Black gram	80–140	100
Chickpeas	20–100	50
Clovers (general)	50–300	150
Cluster beans	30–200	60
Cowpeas	60–120	90
Crimson clover	30–180	125
Fava beans	50–200	130
Green gram	30–60	40
Hairy vetch	50–200	100
Kudzu	20–150	110
Ladino clover	60–240	180
Lentils	40–130	60
Lespedezas (annual)	30–120	85
Peanuts	20–200	60
Peas	30–180	70
Red clover	70–160	115
Soybeans	40–260	100
Sweet clover	20–160	20
Trefoil	30–150	105
Vetch	80–140	80
White clover	30–150	100
Winter peas	10–80	50

Table 4-8 **N Budget for First Year Alfalfa Illustrating Symbiotically Fixed and Soil N in Plant Parts**

	Harvest		
N Budget Component	*First (July 12)*	*Second (Aug. 30)*	*Third (Oct. 20)*
	kg/ha		
Forage yield	3503	3054	1156
Total plant N	118	127	59
Total N_2 fixed	57	102	34
Herbage	52	74	22
Roots and crown	5	28	12
N from soil	61	25	25
Herbage	54	18	16
Roots and crown	7	7	9

SOURCE: Heichel and Barnes, 1981, *Crop Sci*, 21:330–35.

The amount of N_2 fixed by *Rhizobia* varies with the yield level; the effectiveness of inoculation; the N obtained from the soil, either from decomposition of OM or from residual N; and environmental conditions. A high-yielding legume crop such as soybeans, alfalfa, or clover contains large amounts of N (Table 4-9).

Soybeans remove about 1.5 lbs N/bu from the soil and fix 40% or more of the total N in the plant. However, on sandy, low OM soils, soybeans may fix 80% or more. In many environments, the quantity of N removed by soybean grain at harvest exceeds the quantity of N_2 fixed (Table 4-10). For example, when only 40% of the grain N was due to N_2 fixation, soil N exported in the grain exceeded N fixed in the grain, and thus soil N was depleted (274 lbs/a of N). In contrast, when 90% of the N was fixed, soil N was increased (122 lbs/a of N).

Factors Affecting N_2 Fixation

Soil pH Soil acidity can restrict the survival and growth of *Rhizobia* in soil and severely affect nodulation and N_2-fixation processes (Fig. 4-6). Generally at pH < 5.5 to 6.0, Al^{+3}, Mn^{+2}, and H^+ toxicity accompanied by low Ca^{+2} and $H_2PO_4^-$, can severely reduce rhizobial infection, root growth, and legume productivity. Significant differences in sensitivity

Table 4-9 **Variation of N_2 Fixation with Legume Species, Productivity, and Soil N Content**

Species	*Total N_2 Fixed (%)*	*Dry Matter Yield (lb/a)*
Hay and pasture legumes		
*Alfalfa**	63	6,809
*Red clover**	65	6,230
*Birdsfoot trefoil**	40	4,880
Grain legumes		
Soybean†	76	2,494
Soybean††	52	7,837

*3.7% soil OM and 12 ppm soil NO_3-N concentration (0- to 6-in. depth).
†1.8% soil OM and 12 ppm soil NO_3-N concentration (0- to 8-in. depth).
††4.8% soil OM and 31 ppm soil NO_3-N concentration (0- to 8-in. depth).
SOURCE: Heichel et al., 1981, *Crop Sci.*, 21:330–35.

Table 4-10 **Soybean N Budget Illustrating the Allocation of Soil and Fixed N_2 Among Plant Components, and the Return of N to the Soil with 40 and 90% of Plant N from Fixation**

			Fixed N Content		*Soil N Export in Grain*		*Fixed N Return in Residue*		*N Loss (−) or Gain (+)*	
Crop Component	*Dry Matter*	*Total N Content*	*40%*	*90%*	*40%*	*90%*	*40%*	*90%*	*40%*	*90%*
	lb/ac									
Grain	2,100	151	61	136	90	15	—	—	—	—
Residue*	3,424	40	16	37	—	—	16	37	—	—
Total plant	5,524	191	77	173	—	—	—	—	274	122

*Pod walls, leaves, stems, roots, and nodules; incomplete grain harvest would increase this value.
SOURCE: Heichel and Barnes, 1984, ASA Spec. Publ. 46, pp. 46–59.

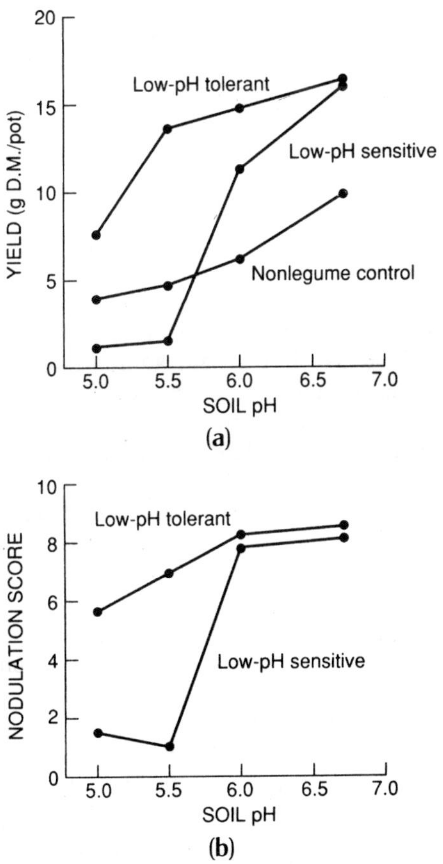

Figure 4-6 **Forage yields (a) and nodulation scores (b) of alfalfa inoculated with low-pH-tolerant and low-pH-sensitive strains of *Rhizobium meliloti*. Barley was the nonlegume control. *(Rice, 1989,* Can. J. Plant Sci. *62:943.)***

between rhizobia to soil acidity exists. Soil pH < 6.0 drastically reduces *rhizobium meliloti* population, degree of nodulation, and alfalfa yield, whereas soil pH 5.0 to 7.0 has little effect on *rhizobium trifoli* associated with red clover.

Liming acid soils increases alfalfa growth dependent on *rhizobium meliloti*. For locations where lime may not be readily available, high levels of inoculum and rolling inoculated

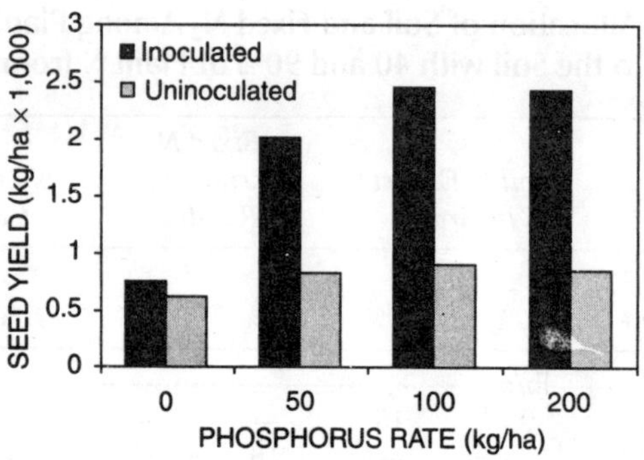

Figure 4-7 **Soybean yield as influenced by P availability and inoculation.** *(Singleton et al., 1990,* **Applied BNF Technology: A Practical Guide for Extension Specialists,** *NifTAL, Paia, HI.)*

seeds in a slurry of pulverized lime can improve inoculation and alfalfa production, provided Al^{+3} and Mn^{+2} are below toxic levels. Another approach is to select and use acid-tolerant rhizobia (Fig. 4-6).

Mineral Nutrient Status In acid soils, Ca^{+2} and $H_2PO_4^-$ deficiencies can limit rhizobial growth and reduce host plant productivity (Fig. 4-7). N_2 fixation requires more Mo than the host plant because Mo is a component of nitrogenase; thus, Mo deficiency is the most important micronutrient deficiency affecting this process. Initiation and development of nodules can also be affected by Co, B, Fe, and Cu deficiencies. Differences exist in the sensitivity of various rhizobial strains to nutrient stress.

As with any plant, legumes prefer mineral N because it requires less energy for the plant to take up N directly from the soil than to fix N_2. If soil N is sufficient to meet crop growth potential, then inoculation is not needed. Maximum N_2 fixation occurs only when available soil N is at a minimum. Excess NO_3^- in the soil can reduce nitrogenase activity, reducing N_2 fixation. The reduction in N_2 fixation is related to the competition for photosynthate between NO_3^--reduction and N_2-fixation reactions. Table 4-9 shows that legumes grown on soils low in profile NO_3^- obtain more N by fixation compared with legumes grown on high-N soils.

Sometimes a small amount of N fertilizer at planting time ensures that young legume seedlings have adequate N until the rhizobia become established on the roots. Early spring N application can be beneficial for legume crops where rhizobial activity is restricted by cold, wet conditions. N_2 fixation by common bean is low and usually unreliable, and N fertilization is recommended.

Photosynthesis and Climate A high rate of photosynthate production is strongly related to increased N_2 fixation by rhizobia. Factors that reduce the rate of photosynthesis will reduce N_2 fixation. These factors include reduced light intensity, moisture stress, and low temperature.

Legume Management In general, any management practice that results in reduced legume stands or yield will reduce the quantity of N_2 fixed by legumes. These factors include water and nutrient stress, excessive weed and insect pressure, and improper harvest management. Harvest practices vary greatly with location, but excessive cutting frequency, premature harvest, and delayed harvest, especially in the fall, can reduce legume stands and the quantity of N fixed.

Fixation by Leguminous Trees and Shrubs N_2 fixation by leguminous trees is important to the ecology of tropical and subtropical forests and to agroforestry systems in developing countries. Numerous leguminous tree species fix appreciable amounts of N_2. Well-known examples in the United States are mimosa, acacia, and black locust. Three woody leguminous species—Gliricidia sepium, Leucaena leucocephala, and Sesbania biospinosa—are used as green manure crops in rice-based cropping systems.

Some widely distributed nonleguminous plants also fix N_2 by a mechanism similar to legume and rhizobial symbiosis. Certain members of the following plant families are known to bear root nodules and to fix N_2: Betulaceae, Elaegnaceae, Myricaceae, Coriariaceae, Rhamnaceae, and Casurinaceae. Alder and ceanothus, two species commonly found in the Douglas fir forest region of the Pacific Northwest, can potentially contribute substantial N to the ecosystem. Frankia, an actinomycete, is responsible for N_2 fixation by these nonleguminous woody plants (Table 4-5).

Legume N Availability to Nonlegume Crops

Yields of nonlegume crops are often increased when they are grown following legumes. For example, when corn follows soybean, the N required for optimum yield is less than that required for corn after corn (Fig. 4-8). Although the difference has been attributed to

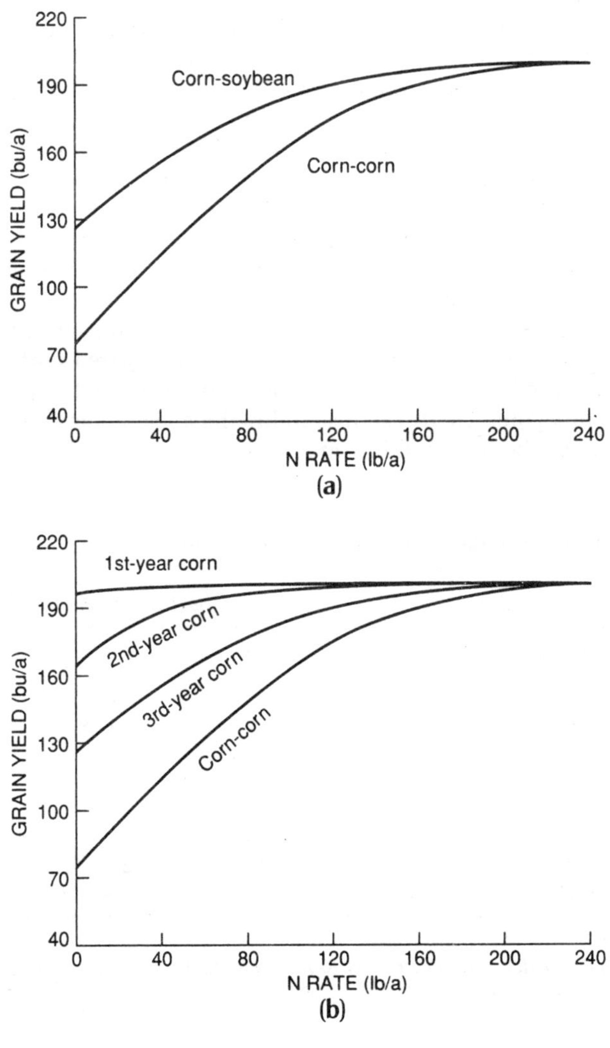

Figure 4-8 **Generalized corn response to N fertilization when corn follows an annual legume (a) or a perennial legume (b) compared with continuous corn.**

increased N availability from the previous legume crop, rotation benefits are not limited to legume rotations in that some of the benefits can be related to increased soil N availability, reduced soilborne diseases, and improved soil physical properties (Chapter 13).

When a perennial legume such as alfalfa is used in rotation, the response of corn to applied N varies with time (Fig. 4-8). Little or no response of corn to N fertilization is observed in the first year; however, the amount of N required for optimum crop production increases with time as the legume N reserves are depleted. N availability in the legume cropping system depends on the quantity of N_2 fixed, the amount and type of legume residue returned, and soil and environmental conditions influencing residue decomposition and N mineralization. Legume N incorporated into the soil from first-year alfalfa varies between 35 and 300 kg/ha. Vigorous high N_2 fixing, alfalfa stands can usually supply all or most of the N to a nonlegume crop in the first year. Several studies suggest that the N credit commonly attributed to legumes in rotation is overestimated. These contrasting results can probably be explained by soil, climate, and legume management effects.

Crop utilization of N in green manure crops is also highly variable. Legume residue N availability during the first subsequent cropping year ranges between 20 and 50%. Table 4-11 shows that barley grown for 5 years after legumes contained 30 to 80 lbs of N and yielded 60 to 70 bua more than unfertilized (N) barley not following legumes. The beneficial effects of legumes were most pronounced in the first years after incorporating legume residues, although residual N availability continued even after 5 years.

The yield benefit of rotations with some legumes may not always be related to the legume N supply. Figure 4-9 illustrates that corn-yield response to fertilizer N was similar following soybean or wheat. The rotation response compared with continuous corn is commonly referred to as a *rotation effect* and will be discussed in the next section.

With forage legumes, only part of the N_2 fixed is returned to the soil because most of the forage is harvested. Forages grown for green manure or as winter cover crops likely return more fixed N_2 to the soil, depending on species, yield, and management. For example, legume N availability can be greater in a one-cut system compared with a three-cut system because of the increased amount of N incorporated with less frequent harvests (Fig. 4-9). Whether the nonlegume yield response following a legume is due to N or to a rotation effect, the benefit can be observed for several years.

Table 4-11 **Yield and N Uptake of Barley Grown After Legumes**

	Barley Yield (bu/a)			*Barley N Uptake (lb/a)*		
	No Legume	*Alfalfa**	*Red Clover**	*No Legume*	*Alfalfa**	*Red Clover**
1970	66	41	70	59	44	68
1971	27	51	51	26	63.8	22
1972	26	50	40	26	55	42
1973	32	52	48	26	46	33
1974	27	35	37	208	29	24
1975	22	31	26	—	—	—
Total	20	26	272	158	238	189
Mean	34	43	45	—	—	—

*Grown in 1968 and 1969.

SOURCE: Leitch, 1976, *Alfalfa Production in the Peace River Region,* Alberta Agriculture and Agriculture Canada Research Station, Beaverlodge, Alberta.

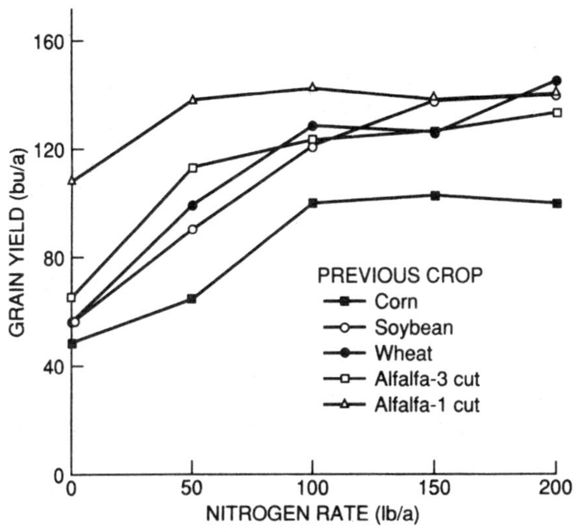

Figure 4-9 **Corn grain yields as influenced by previous crop and fertilizer N.** *(Heichel, 1987, Role of Legumes in Conservation Tillage Systems,* **Soil Cons. Serv. Am.,** *p. 33.)*

Optimum utilization of legume N by a nonlegume grain crop requires that mineralization of legume N occur over the same time as crop N uptake. Legume N mineralization by soil microbes is controlled predominately by environment. The quantity of crop N uptake also varies during the season. Thus, for maximum utilization of legume N by the nonlegume crop, N uptake must be in *synchrony* with N mineralization. For example, the N uptake period for winter wheat is considerably earlier than for corn (Fig. 4-10). The hypothetical distribution of N mineralization shows that corn N uptake is more synchronous with N mineralization than is winter wheat. Therefore, compared with corn, winter wheat may not utilize much legume N and, when mineralization occurs, the inorganic N is subject to leaching and other losses. Therefore, efficient management of legume N requires careful crop selection.

Legumes grown with forage grasses generally supply N for both crops. Table 4-12 shows that about 70% of the grass N originated from the legume. Legume N availability to a

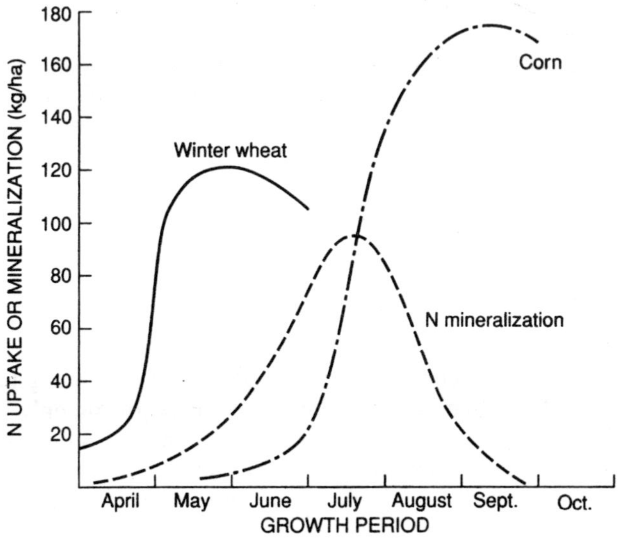

Figure 4-10 **Synchrony of soil N mineralization and crop N uptake in corn and winter wheat.**

Table 4-12 N Transfer from Legumes to Grass

	*N in Grass from Legume (%)**		
Community	*Harvest 1*	*Harvest 2*	*Harvest 3*
Grass–alfalfa†	64	68	68
Grass–trefoil†	68	66	79

*Percentage of grass N received from legume via N transfer.
†Legume/grass ratio was 2:3 for the reed canary grass–alfalfa and 3:2 for reed canary grass–trefoil.
SOURCE: Brophy et al., 1987, *Crop Sci.*, 27:372–80.

companion crop is not well understood. Small amounts of amino acids and other organic N compounds may be excreted by the legume roots. Microbial decomposition of the sloughed-off root and nodule tissue may also contribute N to the crop growing with legumes. Under some conditions, the quantity of fixed N_2 and/or legume N availability is not sufficient, and N fertilization is required for optimum production of both nonlegume and legume crops.

Legume Rotations

The primary reason for including legumes in a rotation is to supply N, but with development and availability of relatively inexpensive fertilizer N, most agricultural production does not involve legume N (Fig. 4-3). In a livestock farming system, the main purpose of legumes is to supply large amounts of high-quality forage, whether hay or pasture. Legumes are generally of superior quality, with higher protein and mineral concentrations compared with N-fertilized grasses.

Management decisions regarding the use of legumes or fertilizer N are based on the highest net return on investment. Like other input costs, the fertilizer N cost increases with time because of increased manufacturing and transportation costs. As a consequence, interest in legumes to substitute partially for the fertilizer N requirements of nonlegume crops has increased. In some developing countries, commercial N may not be available or is too expensive. Therefore, cropping systems that include legumes are essential to supply some of the N needed for nonlegumes.

In spite of the advantages of legume rotations, it may not always be economical and thus varies greatly between regions (Table 4-13). For example, producers may not have a use or market for forage legumes. Higher water use and lower drought tolerance in some legumes is a disadvantage in semiarid areas.

Nonsymbiotic N_2 Fixation

Soil Microorganisms

Nonsymbiotic N_2 fixation in soils occurs with certain strains of free-living bacteria and blue-green algae (Table 4-5). Blue-green algae are autotrophic, requiring only light, water, N_2, CO_2, and essential nutrients. These algae are more common in flooded than in well-drained soils. Because they need light, they contribute only small quantities of N in upland agricultural soils after crop canopy closure. In desert or semiarid regions, blue-green algae or lichens containing them become active following occasional rains and fix considerable

Table 4-13 Examples of Regional Use of Legumes in Cropping or Conservation Tillage Systems

Region	*Legume Species*	*Cropping or Tillage System*
Southeast	Crimson clover, hairy vetch	Winter cover crop—no-till corn
	Bigflower vetch, crown vetch, alfalfa, lupine, arrowleaf clover, red clover	Winter cover crops preceding grain sorghum and cotton
Northeast	Alfalfa, birdsfoot trefoil, red clover	Legumes grown for hay or silage in crop rotations that include conventional or no-till corn as feed grain or silage; also used as living mulches
North Central	Soybean, pea	Grown in 1-year rotation with nonlegume, possibly using conservation tillage methods; peas may precede soybeans in a double-cropping system
	Alfalfa, red clover, white clover, alsike clover	Grown for 2 years or more in 3- to 5-year rotations with small grains or corn, possibly by use of conservation tillage methods
	Birdsfoot trefoil, crown vetch, sweet clover	Used for forage, silage, or pasture
Great Plains	Native legumes	Rangeland for grazing
Pacific Northwest	Dry pea, lentil, chickpea	Rotation or double cropped with grains
	Austrian winter pea	Green manure or alternated with winter wheat
	Alfalfa	Grown in rotation with winter wheat, spring barley, and winter peas
	Fava bean	Grown in rotation for silage
California	Dry bean, lima bean, blackeye pea, chickpea	Grown for grains in various rotations
	Alfalfa	Grown for seed on irrigated land and for erosion control and forage on steeply sloping soils
	Subterranean clover	Rangeland for grazing

SOURCE: Heichal, 1987, *Role of Legumes in Conservation Tillage Systems,* Soil Cons. Soc. Am.

quantities of N_2 during their short-lived activity. N availability to other organisms provided by blue-green algae is important to chemical weathering in the early stages of soil formation. N_2 fixation by blue-green algae is of economic significance in tropical rice soils.

There is a symbiotic relationship between *Anabaena azolla* (a blue-green alga) and *Azolla* (a water fern) in temperate and tropical waters. The blue-green algae located in leaf cavities of the water fern are protected from external adverse conditions and are capable of supplying all of the N needs of the host plant. An important feature of this association is the water fern's very large light-harvesting surface, a property that limits the N_2-fixing capacity of free-living blue-green algae. The organism *Beijerinckia,* found almost exclusively in the tropics, inhabits the leaf surfaces of many tropical plants and fixes N on these leaves rather than in the soil.

In southeast Asia, *Azolla* has been used for centuries as a green manure in wetland rice culture, as a fodder for livestock, as a compost for production of other crops, and as a weed suppressor. In California, the *Azolla-Anabaena* N-fixing association has supplied 105 kg N/ha per season, or about 75% of the N requirements of rice. When used as a green manure, it provided 50 to 60 kg N/ha and substantially increased yields over unfertilized rice.

Certain N_2-fixing bacteria can grow on root surfaces and to some extent within root tissues of corn, grasses, millet, rice, sorghum, wheat, and many other higher plants. *Azospirillum brasilense* is the dominant N-fixing bacterium that has been identified. Inoculation of cereal crops with Azospirillum can improve growth and N nutrition, although the response to inoculation is variable. In most of the studies in which inoculation was beneficial, the response was related to factors other than increased N_2 fixation. Some of the possibilities are increased root hair growth that enhances water and nutrient uptake and improved root permeability.

Azotobacter- and clostridium-inoculated seed may provide a maximum of 5 kg N/ha; therefore, these nonsymbiotic organisms are of little value to N availability in intensive agriculture.

Atmospheric N

N compounds in the atmosphere are deposited from rain and snow as NH_4^+, NO_3^-, NO_2^-, and organic N. Because of the small amount of NO_2^- present in the atmosphere, NO_3^- and NO_2^- are combined and reported as NO_3^-. About 10 to 20% of the NO_3^- is formed during atmospheric electrical discharges, with the remainder from industrial waste gases or denitrification from soil. NH_4^+ comes largely from industrial sites where NH_3 is used or manufactured. Ammonia also escapes (volatilization) from the soil surface. Organic N accumulates as finely divided organic residues swept into the atmosphere from the earth's surface.

Total N deposition in rainfall ranges between 1 and 50 lbs/a/yr, depending on the location (Fig. 4-11). Total N deposition is higher around areas of intense industrial activity and, as a rule, is greater in tropical than in polar or temperate zones. NH_4^+ deposition represents the majority of the total atmospheric N deposited and has increased with time, especially in highly populated and industrial regions. For example, in eastern North Carolina, NH_4^+ deposition has increased threefold over the last 24 years as a result of human and animal (hogs and poultry) population increases (Fig. 4-12). Figure 4-13 illustrates localized NH_4^+ deposition from a poultry operation that can depress soil pH and reduce crop yield potential if the field is not limed (Chapter 3). Soil has a pronounced capacity for adsorbing NH_3 gas from the atmosphere. In localized areas where atmospheric NH_3 concentrations are high, 50 to 70 lbs NH_3/a/yr may be adsorbed. Adsorption increases with increasing NH_3 concentration and temperature.

Industrial N_2 Fixation

To world food security and agricultural profitability, the industrial fixation of N_2 is by far the most important source of N to plants. Industrial N_2 fixation is based on the Haber-Bosch process:

$$3H_2 + N_2 \xrightarrow[1{,}200^\circ C,\ 500\ atm]{Catalyst} 2NH_3$$

The NH_3 produced can be used directly as a fertilizer (anhydrous NH_3), although numerous other fertilizer N products are manufactured from NH_3 (see pp. 150 to 153).

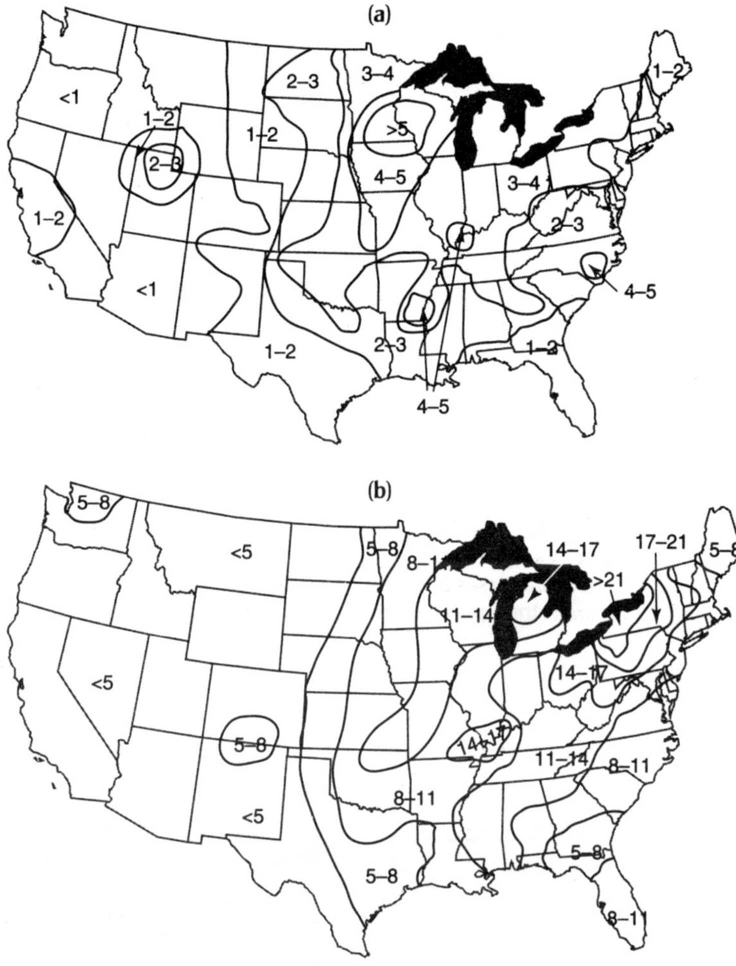

Figure 4-11 **Spatial distribution of NH_4^+ (a) and NO_3^- (b) in 2002. All units in kg/ha.** ***(National Atmospheric Deposition Program, 2002.)***

Forms of Soil N

Total soil N content ranges from $< 0.02\%$ in subsoils to $> 2.5\%$ in organic soils. The N concentration in the top 1 ft of most cultivated soils in the United States varies from 0.03 to 0.4%. Soil N occurs as inorganic or organic N, where about 95% of total N in surface soils is organic N.

Inorganic N Compounds

Inorganic soil N includes ammonium (NH_4^+), nitrite (NO_2^-), nitrate (NO_3^-), nitrous oxide (N_2O), nitric oxide (NO), and elemental N (N_2), which is inert except for its utilization by Rhizobia and other N-fixing microorganisms. For plants, NH_4^+, NO_2^-, and NO_3^- are the

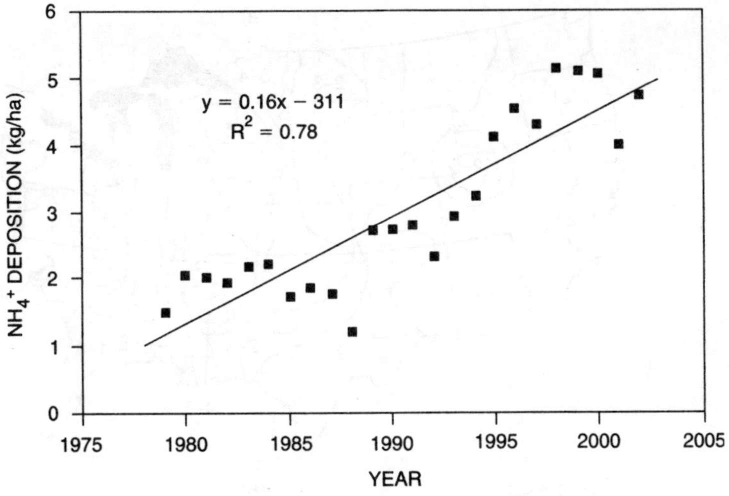

Figure 4-12 NH_4^+ deposition in Sampson County, North Carolina, has doubled over the last twenty years. This increase is likely caused by dramatic increases in urban population and confinement hog production. *(National Atmospheric Deposition Program, 2002.)*

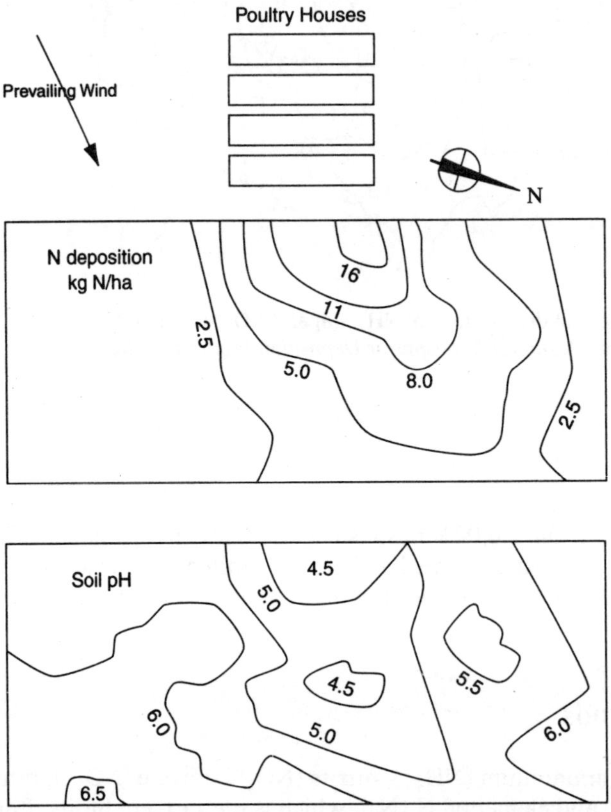

Figure 4-13 NH_3 produced from the poultry houses (20,000 animals) deposits NH_4^+ downwind and reduces soil pH. NH_4^+ deposition data were collected over 1 month. Field is approximately 20 acres and poultry houses had been operated for eighteen years before air and soil sampling in 1986. *(Speirs and Frost*, 1987, Research & Development in Agriculture.*)*

most important and are produced from aerobic decomposition of soil OM or from addition of N fertilizers. These forms represent 2 to 5% of total soil N. N_2O and NO are important N forms lost through denitrification.

Organic N Compounds

Organic soil N occurs as proteins, amino acids, amino sugars, and other complex N compounds. The proportion of total soil N in these various fractions is: bound amino acids, 20 to 40%; amino sugars such as the hexosamines, 5 to 10%; and purine and pyrimidine derivatives, < 1%. Very little is known about the chemical nature of the 50% or so of the organic N not found in these fractions. Proteins are commonly found in combination with clays, lignin, and other materials resistant to decomposition. The biological oxidation of free amino acids is an important source of NH_4^+. Relative to other forms, the quantities of free amino acids in soils are low.

N Transformations in Soils

Supplying sufficient NH_4^+ and NO_3^- to meet plant requirement depends on the quantity of N mineralized from soil organic N with the remainder provided through fertilizer or organic N applications. The amount of plant available N released from organic N depends on many factors affecting N mineralization, immobilization, and losses of NH_4^+ and NO_3^- from the soil.

N Mineralization

N *mineralization* is the conversion of organic N to NH_4^+ through two reactions, *aminization* and *ammonification* (Fig. 4-1). Mineralization occurs through the activity of heterotrophic microorganisms that require organic C for energy. Heterotrophic bacteria dominate the breakdown of proteins in neutral and alkaline environments, with some involvement of fungi, while fungi predominate in acid soils. The end products of the activities of one group furnish the substrate for the next and so on until the material is decomposed. Aminization converts proteins in residues to *amino acids, amines*, and *urea*. These are organic N compounds that are further converted to inorganic NH_4^+ by ammonification. A diverse population of aerobic and anaerobic bacteria, fungi, and actinomycetes is capable of converting the products of aminization to NH_4^+.

Step 1 Aminization

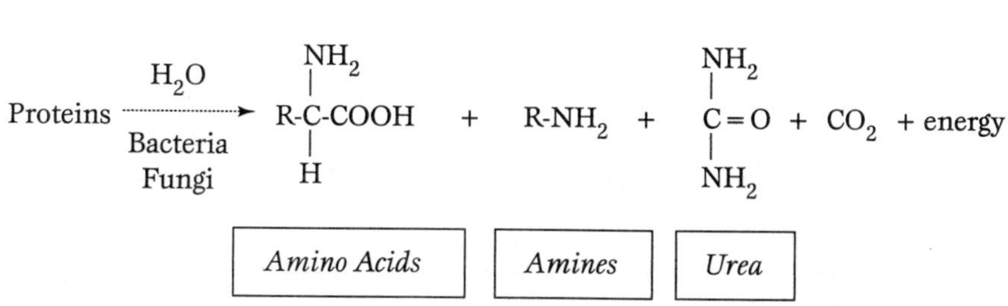

Step 2 Ammonification

$$R\text{-}NH_2 + H_2O \longrightarrow NH_3 + R\text{-}OH + \text{energy}$$

$$NH_3 \xrightarrow{+H_2O} NH_4^+ + OH^-$$

The NH_4^+ produced through ammonification is subject to several fates (Fig. 4-1). NH_4^+ can be:

- converted to NO_2^- and NO_3^- (*nitrification*),
- absorbed directly by higher plants (*N uptake*),
- utilized by heterotrophic bacteria to decompose residues (*immobilization*),
- fixed as biologically unavailable N in the lattice of certain clay minerals (*NH_4^+ fixation*), or
- converted to NH_3 and slowly released back to the atmosphere (*volatilization*).

Soil moisture content regulates the proportions of aerobic and anaerobic microbial activity (Fig. 4-14). Maximum aerobic activity and N mineralization occur between 50 and 70% water-filled pore space. Soil temperature also influences microbial activity and N mineralization (Fig. 4-14). Optimum soil temperature for microbial activity ranges between 25 and 35°C. Figure 4-10 illustrates the distribution in N mineralization throughout a growing season as influenced by soil temperature and moisture.

Soil OM contains about 5% N and during a growing season 1 to 4% of organic N is mineralized to inorganic N. As total soil N content increases, the quantity of N mineralized from soil organic N increases (Fig. 4-15). Therefore, soil and crop management strategies that conserve or increase soil OM will result in a greater contribution of mineralizable N to N availability to crops. The quantity of N mineralized during the growing season can be estimated. For example, if a soil contained 4% OM with 2% mineralization rate, then:

$$4\%\ \text{OM} \times (2 \times 10^6\ \text{lb soil/afs}) \times (5\%\ \text{N}) \times (2\%\ \text{N mineralized}) = 80\ \text{lbs N/a}$$

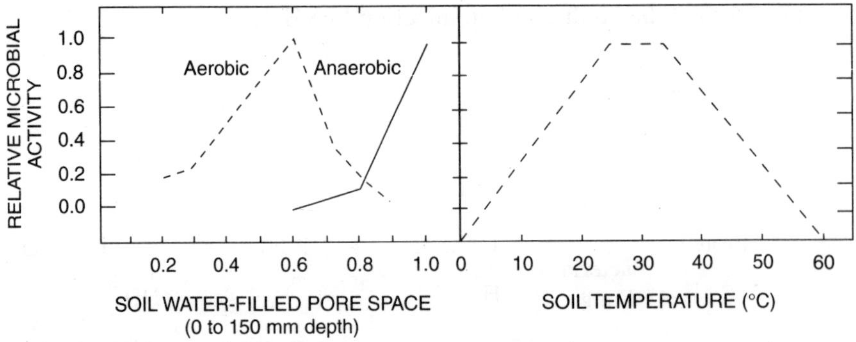

Figure 4-14 **Influence of soil moisture (water-filled pore space) and temperature on relative microbial activity in soil.** *(Doran and Smith*, 1987, SSSA Spec. Publ. 19.)

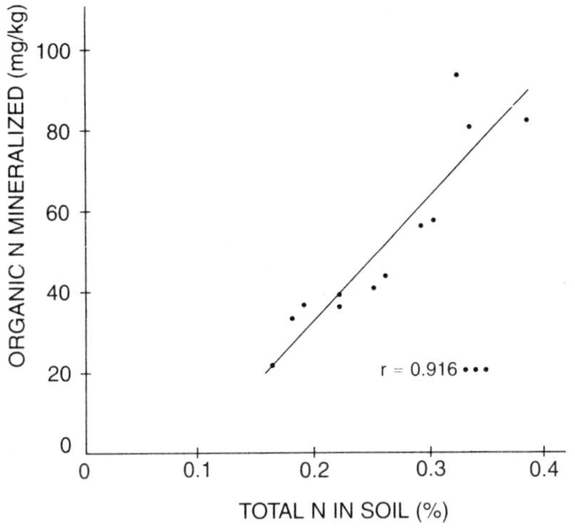

Figure 4-15 **Influence of total soil N on quantity of N mineralized.**

Thus, each year, 80 lbs N/a as NH_4^+ are mineralized, which can be utilized by plants or other soil N processes (Fig. 4-1).

N Immobilization

N immobilization is the conversion of inorganic N (NH_4^+ and NO_3^-) to organic N and is basically the reverse of N mineralization (Fig. 4-1). If decomposing OM contains low N, microorganisms will immobilize NH_4^+ and NO_3^- in the soil solution. The microbes need N in a C:N ratio of about 8:1; therefore, inorganic N in the soil is utilized by the rapidly growing population. N immobilization during crop residue decomposition can reduce NH_4^+ and NO_3^- to very low levels. Microorganisms compete effectively with plants for NH_4^+ and NO_3^- during immobilization, and plants can readily become N deficient. Fortunately, in most cropping systems, sufficient fertilizer N is applied to compensate for immobilization and crop requirements. If added organic material contains high N, immobilization will not proceed because the residue contains sufficient N to meet microbial demand, and inorganic N will increase from mineralization of organic N in the residue.

C:N Ratio Effects on Mineralization and Immobilization

The ratio of % C to % N (C:N ratio) defines the relative quantities of these two elements in crop residues and other fresh organic materials, soil OM, and soil microorganisms (Table 4-14). The N content of humus or stable soil OM ranges from 5.0 to 5.5%, whereas C ranges from 50 to 58%, giving a C:N ratio ranging between 9 and 12.

Whether N is mineralized or immobilized depends on the C:N ratio of the OM being decomposed by soil microorganisms. For example, a typical soil is mineralized at 0.294 mg N, as measured by plant uptake (Table 4-15). When residues of variable C:N ratio are added to the soil, N mineralization or immobilization would be indicated if plant uptake was greater or less than 0.294 mg N, respectively. In this study, a C:N ratio of approximately 20:1 was the dividing line between immobilization and mineralization.

Table 4-14 **C:N Ratios of Selected Organic Materials**

Organic Substances	*C:N Ratio*	*Organic Substances*	*C/N Ratio*
Soil microorganisms	8:1	Bitumens and asphalts	95:1
Soil OM	10:1	Coal liquids and shale oils	125:1
Sweet clover (young)	12:1	Oak	200:1
Barnyard manure (rotted)	20:1	Pine	300:1
Clover residues	23:1	Crude oil	400:1
Green rye	36:1	Sawdust (generally)	400:1
Corn/sorghum residues	60:1	Spruce	1,000:1
Grain straw	80:1	Fir	1,200:1
Timothy	80:1		

Table 4-15 **N Mineralized from Various Residues as Measured by Plant Uptake**

*Plant Residue**	*C:N Ratio*	*N Uptake (mg)*
Check soil	8:1	0.294
Tomato stems	45:1	0.051
Corn roots	48:1	0.007
Corn stalks	33:1	0.038
Corn leaves	32:1	0.020
Tomato roots	27:1	0.029
Collard roots	20:1	0.311
Bean stems	17:1	0.823
Tomato leaves	16:1	0.835
Bean stems	12:1	1.209
Collard stems	11:1	2.254
Collard leaves	10:1	1.781

*Residues above the dashed line have a C:N ratio > 20:1. Residues below the dashed line have a C:N ratio < 20:1.
SOURCE: Iritani and Arnold, 1960, *Soil Sci.*, 89:74.

The progress of N mineralization and immobilization following residue addition is illustrated in Figure 4-16. During the initial stages of the decomposition of fresh organic material there is a rapid increase in the number of heterotrophic organisms, indicated by the increased evolution of CO_2. If the C:N ratio of the fresh material is > 20:1, N immobilization occurs, as shown in the hatched area under the top curve of Figure 4-16. As residue decay proceeds, the residue C:N ratio decreases, due to decreasing C (respiration as CO_2) and increasing N (N immobilized from soil solution). Microbial activity eventually decreases as the residue C supply decreases (decreasing CO_2 evolution). Ultimately a new equilibrium is reached, accompanied by mineralization of N (indicated by the hatched area under the top curve in Figure 4-16). The result is that the final soil level of inorganic N may be higher than the original level, as a result of additional N content in the residue.

Generally, when organic residues with C:N > 20:1 are added to soil, soil N is immobilized during the initial decomposition process. For residues with C:N < 20:1 there is a release of mineral N early in the decomposition process. Soil OM may also increase, depending on the quantity and type of residue added and the quantity of OM loss through oxidation (mineralization) or physical soil loss (Chapter 13). The time required for residue decomposition depends on the quantity of OM added, inorganic soil N supply, resistance of the residue to microbial attack (a function of the amount of lignins, waxes, and fats present), and soil temperature and moisture.

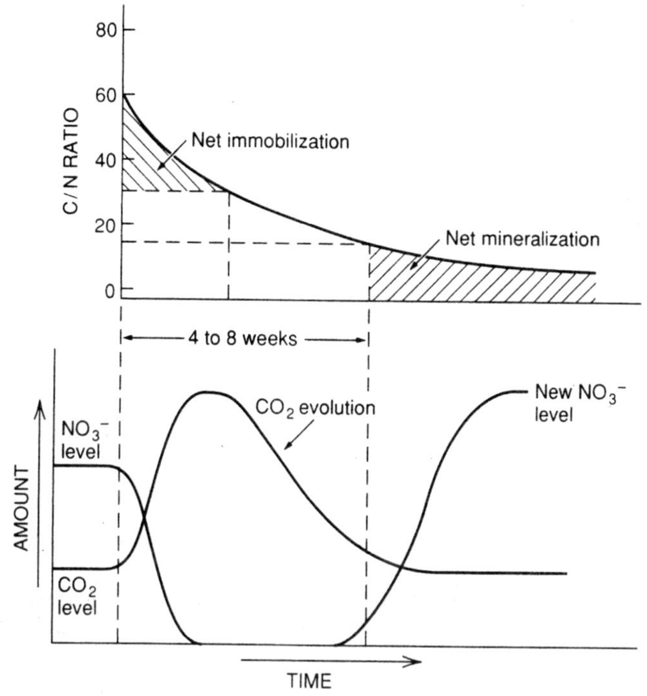

Figure 4-16 **General description of N mineralization and immobilization following addition of residue to soil.** *(Adapted from B. R. Sabey, Univ. of Illinois.)*

The N content of the residue being added to soil also can be used to predict whether N is immobilized or mineralized (Fig. 4-17). N mineralization occurs with residue N content > 2.0% under aerobic conditions.

When high C:N residues are added to soil, N in the residue and inorganic soil N are used by the microorganisms during residue decomposition. The quantity of inorganic soil N immobilized by the microbes can be estimated. For example, assume 3,000 lbs/a residue and C:N = 60 (40% C).

$$3{,}000 \text{ lbs residue} \times 40\% \ \ \text{C} = 1{,}200 \text{ lbs C in the residue}$$

Microbial activity will utilize 35% of the residue C (increasing microbial biomass), while the remaining 65% is respired as CO_2 (Fig. 4-16). Thus, the microbes will use 315 lbs C in the residue:

$$1{,}200 \text{ lbs C in the residue} \times 35\% \ = 420 \text{ lbs C used by microbes}$$

The increasing microbial population will require N governed by microbe C:N = 8:1 (Table 4-14):

$$\frac{420 \text{ lbs C}}{\text{X lbs N}} = \frac{8}{1}$$

$$\text{X} = 52.5 \text{ lb N/a}$$

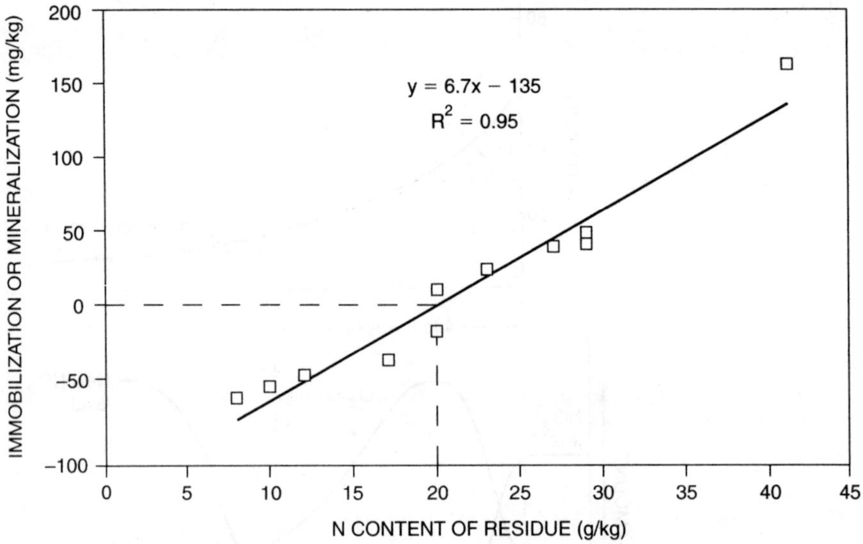

Figure 4-17 **Effect of N content of organic materials on apparent N immobilization or mineralization.** *(Goos, 1995,* J. Nat. Resources Life Sci. Educ. *24:68–70.)*

needed by microbes to degrade the 420 lbs C or 1,200 lbs residue. The microbes use the N in the residue during decomposition determined by:

$$\frac{1{,}200 \text{ lbs C}}{\text{X lbs N}} = \frac{60}{1}$$

$$\text{X} = 20 \text{ lbs N/a in residue}$$

If the residue N content were known (assume 0.67 % N), the lbs N/a would be determined by:

$$3{,}000 \text{ lbs residue} \times 0.67\,\%\,\text{N} = 20 \text{ lbs N}$$

Thus, the quantity of N immobilized is:

$$52.5 \text{ lbs N needed by microbes} - 20 \text{ lbs N in residue} = 32.5 \text{ lbs N/a immobilized}$$

Therefore, at least 32.5 lbs N/a will be needed to compensate for immobilization of inorganic N. Routine fertilizer N recommendations usually account for N immobilization requirements.

Large amounts of small grain straw, corn stalks, or other high C:N residues incorporated into soils with low inorganic N content will result in N immobilization by microorganisms as residues are decomposed. If crops are planted immediately after residue incorporation, they may become N deficient. Deficiencies can be prevented by adding sufficient N to supply the needs of the microorganisms and the growing crop.

N Mineralization and Immobilization Effects on Soil OM

The C:N ratio of undisturbed topsoil is about 10 or 12. Generally, C:N narrows in the subsoil because of lower C content. An uncultivated soil has a relatively stable soil microbial population, a relatively constant amount of plant residue returned to the soil, and usually a low rate of N mineralization. If the soil is disturbed with tillage, the increased O_2 supply increases N mineralization rate. Continued cultivation without the return of adequate crop residues ultimately leads to a decline in soil OM content. The influence of soil and crop management on soil OM and its relationship to soil and crop productivity is discussed in Chapter 13.

Any change in soil OM content dramatically reduces the quantity of N mineralized, and thus native soil N availability to crops. The differences in N mineralization can be readily calculated. For example, suppose that a virgin soil has a 5% OM content, and as the soil is cultivated (conventional tillage) the rate of OM loss is 4% per year. The quantity of N mineralized in the first year is:

$$(5\%\ \text{OM}) \times (2 \times 10^6\ \text{lbs/afs}) \times (4\%\ \text{OM loss/yr}) \times (5\%\ \text{N in OM})$$
$$= 200\ \text{lbs N/a/yr mineralized}$$

Notice that the 200 lbs N/a would meet or exceed the quantity of N required by most crops. Now assume that after 50 years of cultivation, the OM declined to 2.5% or one-half the original level, as depicted in Figure 4-18. Assume that 2% of the OM oxidizes per year; thus, the quantity of N mineralized is:

$$(2.5\%\ \text{OM}) \times (2 \times 10^6\ \text{lbs/afs}) \times (2\%\ \text{OM loss/yr}) \times (5\%\ \text{N in OM})$$
$$= 50\ \text{lbs N/a/yr mineralized}$$

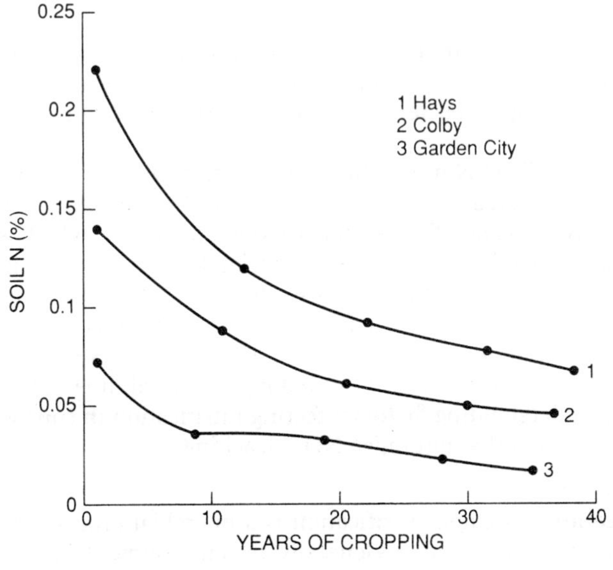

Figure 4-18 Decline in total soil N with years of cropping at three locations in Kansas. Each site was in wheat-fallow-wheat, with all residues incorporated with tillage. Total soil N represents soil OM, since 95% of total N is organic N. *(Haas and Evans, 1957,* USDA Tech. Bull. no. 1164.*)*

The estimated N mineralized illustrates that cultivation of virgin soils mineralized sufficient N to optimize yields of most crops, especially at lower yield levels experienced 50 years ago. The excess N not utilized by the crop was subject to several losses, which include leaching and denitrification. However, at present yield levels, mineralization of 50 lbs N/a is insufficient and fertilizer or manure N is needed to optimize yields.

Nitrification

A portion of the NH_4^+ in soil is converted to NO_3^- through microbial oxidation or *nitrification* (Fig. 4-1). Nitrification is a two-step process where NH_4^+ is converted to NO_2^- and then to NO_3^-. Oxidation of NH_4^+ to NO_2^- is represented by:

Step 1

$$2NH_4^+ + 3O_2 \xrightarrow{\textit{Nitrosomonas}} 2NOH_2^- + 2H_2O + 4H^+$$

(−3) .... (+3) increasing oxidation of N

Step 2

$$2NO_2^- + O_2 \xrightarrow{\textit{Nitrobacter}} 2NO_3^-$$

(+3) .... (+5) increasing oxidation of N

Net Reaction

$$NH_4^+ + 2O_2 \rightarrow NO_3^- + H_2O + 2H^+$$

Nitrosomonas and *nitrobacter* are autotrophic bacteria that obtain their energy from the oxidation of N and C from CO_2. Other autotrophic bacteria (*nitrosolobus, nitrospira,* and *nitrosovibrio*), and some heterotrophic bacteria, can oxidize NH_4^+ and other reduced N compounds (i.e., amines).

The source of NH_4^+ can be from N mineralization or N fertilizers or manures containing or forming NH_4^+. Nitrification reaction rates in well-drained soils are $NO_2^- \rightarrow NO_3^- >> NH_4^+ \rightarrow NO_2^-$. As a result, NO_2^- generally does not accumulate in soils, which is fortunate since NO_2^- is toxic to plant roots. Both reactions require molecular O_2; thus, nitrification occurs rapidly in well-aerated soils. The reactions also show that nitrification of 1 mole of NH_4^+ produces 2 moles of H^+. Increasing soil acidity with nitrification is a natural process, although soil acidification is accelerated with continued application of NH_4^+-containing or NH_4^+-forming fertilizers (Fig. 4-19). Since NO_3^- is readily produced, it is very mobile and subject to leaching losses. Understanding factors affecting nitrification in soils will provide insight into management practices that minimize NO_3^- leaching.

Factors Affecting Nitrification Because nitrification is a microbial process, soil environmental conditions influence nitrification rate. Generally, the environmental factors favoring

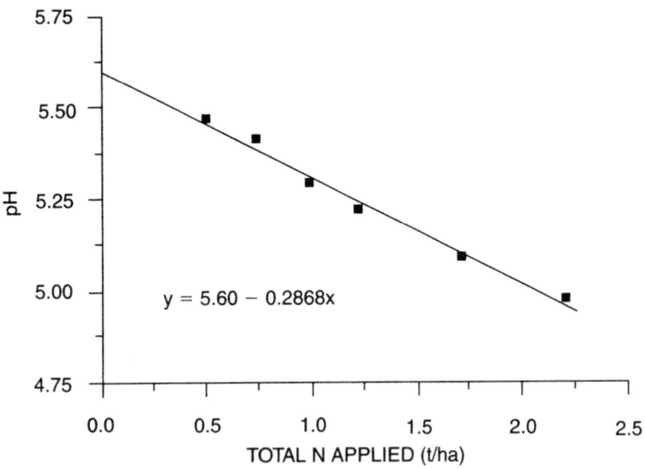

Figure 4-19 **The effect of NH_4^+ fertilizer on soil pH (0 to 8 in. depth).** ***(Rasmussen and Rohde, 1989,*** **Soil Sci. Soc. Am. J.,** ***53:119.)***

the growth of most agricultural plants are those that also favor the activity of nitrifying bacteria. Several factors influence nitrification in soils.

Supply of NH_4^+. A supply of NH_4^+ is the first requirement for nitrification. If conditions do not favor mineralization of NH_4^+, or if NH_4^+-containing or NH_4^+-forming fertilizers are not added to the soils, nitrification is mimimal. Temperature and moisture levels that enhance nitrification are also favorable to mineralization (Fig. 4-14).

Population of Nitrifying Organisms. Soils differ in their ability to nitrify NH_4^+ even under similar temperature, moisture, and NH_4^+ content. Variation in nitrifier population results in differences in the lag time between addition of NH_4^+ and buildup of NO_3^-. Because of the tendency of microbial populations to multiply rapidly with an adequate C supply, total nitrification is not affected by the number of organisms initially present, provided that temperature and moisture conditions are favorable for sustained nitrification.

Soil pH. Nitrification takes place over a wide range in pH (4.5 to 10), although the optimum pH is 8.5. Nitrifying bacteria need an adequate supply of Ca^{+2}, $H_2PO_4^-$, and micronutrients. The influence of soil pH and Ca^{+2} on activity of nitrifiers supports the importance of liming.

Soil Aeration. Aerobic nitrifying bacteria will not produce NO_3^- in the absence of O_2 (Fig. 4-20). Maximum nitrification occurs at the same O_2 concentration in the aboveground atmosphere. Soil conditions that permit rapid gas diffusion are important for maintaining optimum soil aeration. Soils that are coarse textured or possess good structure facilitate rapid gas exchange and ensure an adequate supply of O_2 for nitrifying bacteria. Incorporation of crop residues and other organic amendments will help maintain or improve soil aeration.

Soil Moisture. Bacteria are sensitive to soil moisture. Nitrification rates are generally highest at field capacity or 1/3 bar matric suction (70 to 80% of total pore space). N mineralization and nitrification are reduced when soil moisture exceeds field capacity and between

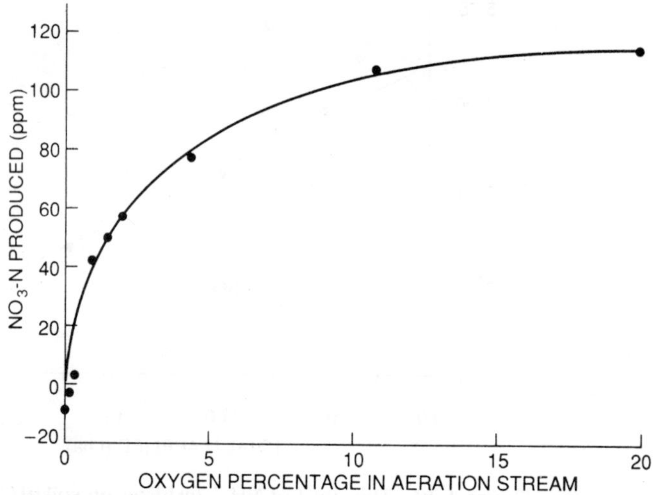

Figure 4-20 **Production of NO_3^- incubated with added $(NH_4)_2SO_4$ and aerated with varying O_2 levels.** ***(Black, 1957,*** **Soil-Plant Relationships.** ***Reprinted with permission of John Wiley & Sons, Inc., New York.)***

15 bars and air dryness. For example, in a soil incubated at the wilting point (15 bars), more than half of the NH_4^+ is nitrified in 28 days (Fig. 4-21). At 7 bars, 100% of NH_4^+ is converted to NO_3^- at the end of 21 days. Soil moisture and soil aeration are closely related in their effects on nitrification.

Soil Temperature. Most biological reactions are influenced by temperature. The temperature coefficient, Q_{10}, is 2 over the range of 5 to 35°C. Thus, a twofold change in mineralization or nitrification rate is associated with a shift of 10°C (Fig. 4-22).

Optimum soil temperature for nitrification of NH_4^+ to NO_3^- is 25 to 35°C, although some nitrification occurs over a wide temperature range (Fig. 4-23). For off-season application of NH_3 or NH_4^+-containing or NH_4^+-forming fertilizers, winter soil temperatures should be low enough to retard NO_3^- formation, thereby reducing the risk of leaching and denitrification losses. Fall NH_4^+ applications are most efficient when minimum air temperatures are below 40°F (4.4°C) or when soil temperatures are below 50°F (10°C).

Even if temperatures are occasionally high enough to permit nitrification of fall-applied NH_4^+, this is not detrimental if leaching does not occur. In many areas, moisture movement through the soil profile during the winter months is insufficient to leach NO_3^-. For example, NH_4^+ sources may be applied in late summer or early fall in the Great Plains before winter wheat planting. The same is true for spring cereal crops in the northern Plains. Improved positioning and distribution of N will often result from its overwinter movement in dry regions. In humid areas water movement through the soil profile is excessive, and NO_3^- losses occur. Whether NH_4^+ can be applied in the fall without significant NO_3^- loss depends on local soil and weather conditions.

It is possible to apply NH_4^+ sources in the fall in cool and/or dry climates to soils of fine texture without appreciable loss by leaching, provided that temperatures remain below 40°F. The presence of NH_4^+ does not ensure its loss against leaching. It is necessary that the soil has a sufficiently high CEC to retain the added NH_4^+ and prevent loss in percolating water. Sandy soils with low CEC permit appreciable movement of NH_4^+ into the subsoil.

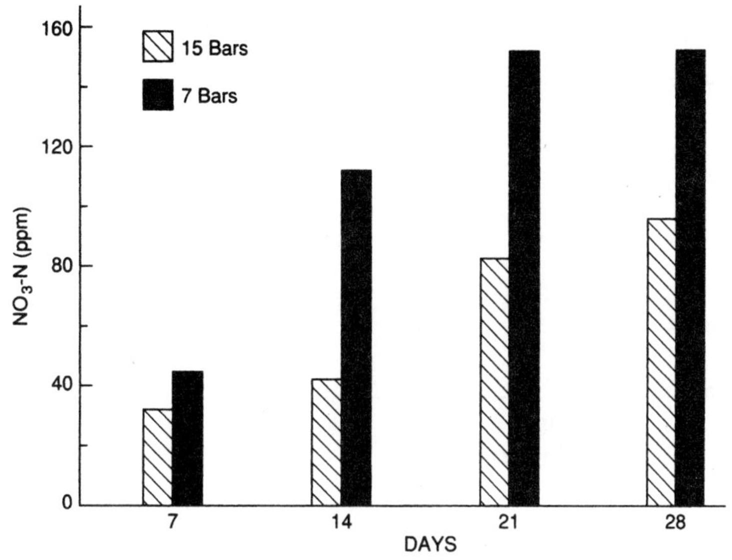

Figure 4-21 **Effect of moisture levels near the wilting point on the nitrification of 150 ppm of N applied as $(NH_4)_2SO_4$.** *(Justice et al., 1962* SSSA Proc, *26:246.)*

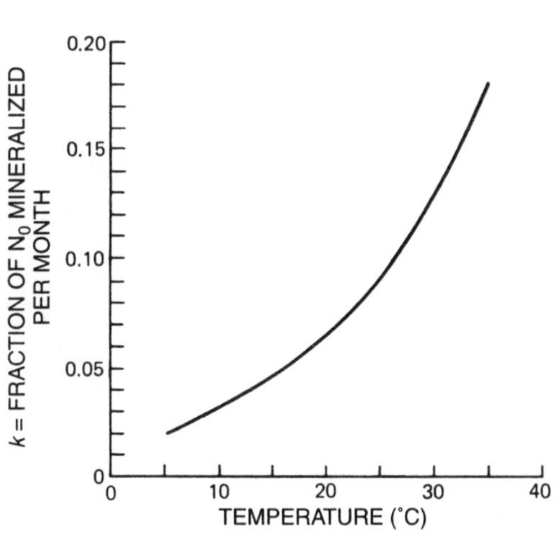

Figure 4-22 Fraction of N mineralized per month, ***k*** in relation to temperature (*k* was estimated graphically for observed average monthly air temperatures). *(Stanford et al., 1977,* Agron. J. *69:303.)*

Nitrate Leaching

NO_3^- is very soluble in water and is not strongly adsorbed to the AEC. Consequently, it is highly mobile and subject to leaching losses when both soil NO_3^- content and water movement are high (Fig. 4-24). N leaching is considered a major pathway of N loss in humid climates and under irrigated cropping systems. NO_3^- leaching must be carefully controlled because of the serious impact on the environment. High NO_3^- levels in surface runoff and water percolating through the soil can pollute drinking water sources and stimulate unwanted plant and algae growth in lakes and reservoirs. Some of the factors that influence the magnitude of NO_3^- leaching losses are (1) rate, time, source, and method of N fertilization; (2) intensity of cropping and crop N uptake; (3) soil profile characteristics that affect percolation; and

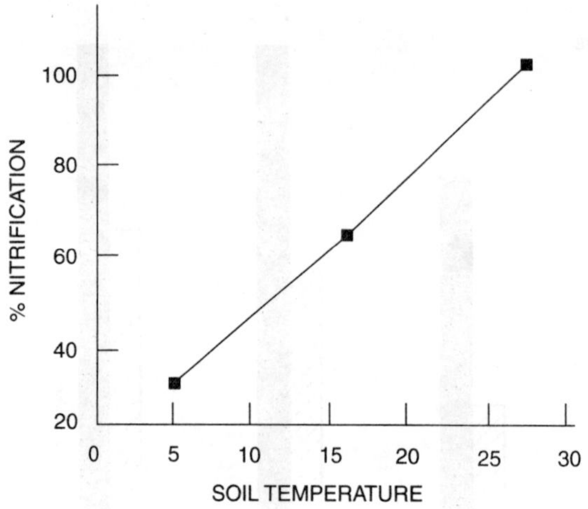

Figure 4-23 Nitrification as affected by temperature. *(Chandra, 1962,* Can. J. Soil *Sci., 42: 314.)*

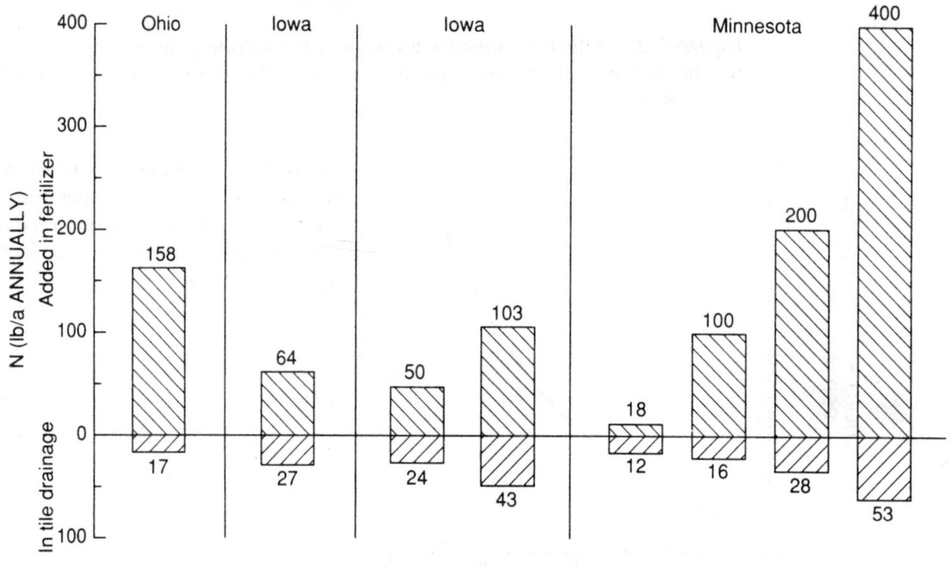

Figure 4-24 N added in fertilizer and lost as NO_3^- in tile drainage water in experiments in Ohio, Iowa, and Minnesota. *(CAST, 1985,* Agric. and Groundwater Qual., Report no. 103, *Ames, IA.)*

(4) quantity, pattern, and time of precipitation and/or supplemental irrigation. It is important to match crop N needs with soil and applied N so that leachable NO_3^- is minimized.

Figure 4-24 illustrates NO_3^- leaching into water draining from tile lines located several feet below the soil surface. Generally, NO_3 leaching losses in tile-drained systems can approach 60% of applied fertilizer or manure N, while under natural-drainage systems values between 10 and 30% are common. In general, increased leaching potential is related to N rates exceeding crop yield potential (Fig. 4-25). Long-term studies with irrigated corn illustrated increased profile N content above the optimum N rate, especially when corn yield was reduced by P deficiency (Fig. 4-26). Correcting the P deficiency increased yield and N uptake, decreasing profile N by 66%.

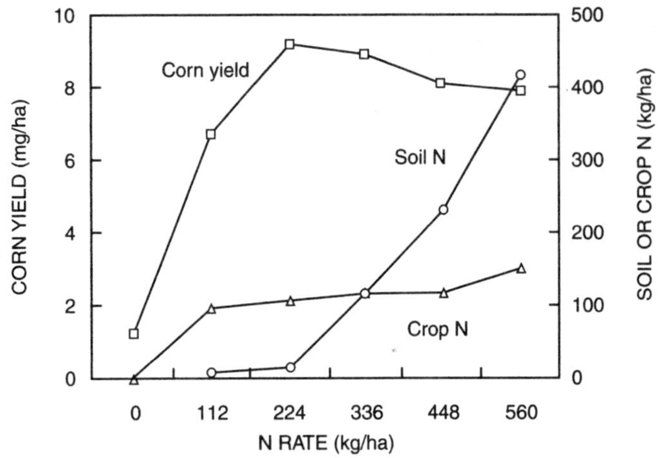

Figure 4-25 **Typical relationship between N rate, crop yield, and N accumulation in the soil profile.**

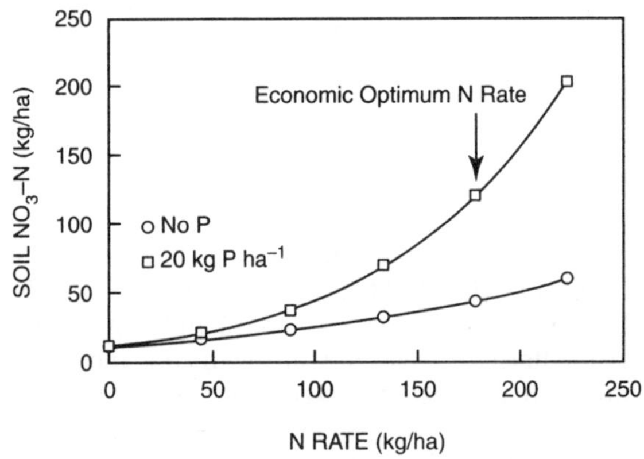

Figure 4-26 **Influence of N rate on soil NO_3^- content (0 to 3 m depth) after 30 years of irrigated corn production. Economic optimum N rate occured at 180 kg N·ha^{-1}. Addition of P reduced soil NO_3^-.** *(Schlegel et al., 1996,* J. Prod. Agric. *9:114.)*

One of the most important factors related to NO_3^- leaching is applying N synchronous with high crop N demand. The same principle holds for matching peak N uptake periods with peak N mineralization (Fig. 4-10). Figure 4-27 illustrates the basic components of the hydrologic cycle for a humid region. Increasing N leaching potential occurs when inorganic profile N is present during periods of low evapotranspiration (low crop water and N demand) that coincides with periods of high precipitation, soil water content, and drainage water. Timing N applications to avoid periods of high water transport through the profile reduces leaching potential.

The quantity of residual fertilizer N (N not recovered by the crop) can be substantially reduced with legumes in the crop rotations (10 to 30% reduction) and/or cover crops (20 to 80% reduction).

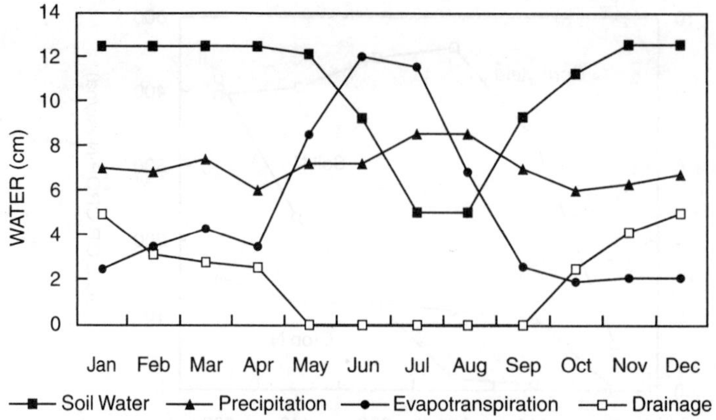

Figure 4-27 Typical soil-plant-water cycle for a humid region, sandy loam soil in the southeast U.S. Soil water content in surface 1 m and water drainage below 1m.

NO_3^- leaching is a natural process, and even under natural or uncultivated systems some N transport below the root zone occurs. In agricultural systems, proper soil, crop, and nutrient management present little or no risk of NO_3^- contamination of surface and groundwater. However, poor management practices may result in substantial leaching losses of applied N. Chapters 10 and 13 discuss N-management strategies for maximizing crop productivity and minimizing the contribution of N leaching on water quality.

Ammonium Fixation

Certain clay minerals, particularly vermiculite and mica, are capable of fixing NH_4^+ by replacement with cations in the expanded lattices of clay minerals (Fig. 4-28). Fixed NH_4^+ can be replaced by cations that expand the lattice (Ca^{+2}, Mg^{+2}, Na^+, H^+) but not by those that contract it (K^+). Coarse clay (0.2 to 2 mm) and fine silt (2 to 5 mm) are important fractions in fixing added NH_4^+. The moisture content and temperature of the soil affect NH_4^+ fixation (Table 4-16). Alternate cycles of wetting-drying and freezing-thawing are believed to contribute to the stability of recently fixed NH_4^+.

The presence of K^+ often restricts NH_4^+ fixation since K^+ can also fill fixation sites (Chapter 6). Consequently, K fertilization before NH_4^+ application can reduce NH_4^+ fixation.

The availability of fixed NH_4^+ ranges from negligible to relatively high. Clay fixation of NH_4^+ provides some degree of protection against rapid nitrification and subsequent leaching. Although the agricultural significance of NH_4^+ fixation is not great, it is important in certain soils. For example, selected soils from Oregon and Washington fixed 1 to 30% of the applied anhydrous NH_3. In certain soils of eastern Canada, relatively large portions of

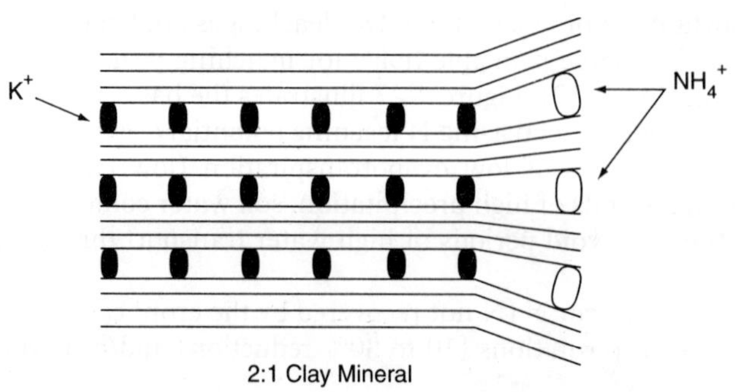

Figure 4-28 Diagram of an expanding clay mineral capable of fixing native or applied NH_4^+.

Table 4-16 Average Native and Added Fixed NH_4^+ Under Moist, Frozen, and Dry Conditions

		Applied NH_4^+ Fixed		
Soil Horizons	*Native NH_4^+ Fixed*	*Moist*	*Frozen*	*Dried*
		meq/100 g		
Gray-brown podzolic soils				
$A_p + A_1$	0.54	0.08	0.14	0.68
$A_2 + A_3$	0.41	0.06	0.06	0.35
$B_1 + B_2$	0.60	0.15	0.25	0.82
Brunizem soils				
$A_p + A_1$	0.64	0.07	0.10	0.56
A_3	0.65	0.07	0.11	0.72
$B_1 + B_2$	0.60	0.15	0.16	0.67

SOURCE: Walsh et al., 1960, *Soil Sci.*, 89:183.

fertilizer NH_4^+ can be fixed, often ranging from 14 to 60% in surface soil and as high as 70% in subsurface soil. Native fixed NH_4^+ is significant in many of these soils and can amount to 10 to 30% of the total fixation capacity.

Gaseous Losses of N

The major losses of N from the soil are due to crop removal and leaching; however, under certain conditions, inorganic N can be converted to gases and lost to the atmosphere (Fig. 4-1). The primary pathways of gaseous N losses are by denitrification and NH_3 volatilization.

Denitrification

When soils become waterlogged, O_2 is excluded and anaerobic conditions occur (Fig. 4-14). Some anaerobic organisms obtain their O_2 from NO_2^- and NO_3^-, with the accompanying release of N_2 and N_2O. Although several possible mechanisms exist (Table 4-16), the most probable biochemical pathway for denitirifcation is:

$$NO_3^- \rightarrow NO_2^- \rightarrow NO \rightarrow N_2O\uparrow \rightarrow N_2\uparrow$$

Figure 4-29 shows examples of NO_2^- and NO_3^- loss and formation of N_2 and N_2O by denitrification.

Large populations of denitrifying microorganisms exist, the most common being the bacteria *Pseudomonas, Bacillus*, and *Paracoccus*, and several autotrophs (*Thiobacillus denitrificans* and *Thiobacillus thioparus*). Denitrification potential is high in most field soils, but conditions must arise that cause a shift from aerobic respiration to a denitrifying metabolism involving NO_3^- as an electron acceptor in the absence of O_2. N_2O and N_2 loss is highly variable because of fluctuations in environmental conditions between seasons and years. N_2 loss predominates, sometimes accounting for about 90% of the total, while N_2O loss is greater under less reduced conditions.

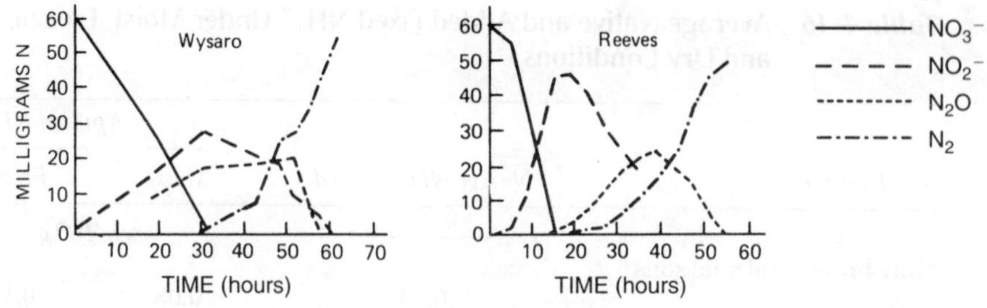

Figure 4-29 **Sequence and magnitude of N products formed and utilized during anaerobic denitrification of Wysaro clay (pH 6.1) and Reeves loam (pH 7.8) at 30°C.** *(Cooper and Smith, 1963,* Soil Sci. Soc. Am. J., *27:659.)*

Factors Affecting Denitrification

Decomposable OM. Decomposable soil OM or C enhances denitrification potential in soil (Fig. 4-30). The reactions with available C required for microbial reduction of NO_3^- to N_2O or N_2 are:

$$4(CH_2O) + 4NO_3^- + 4H^+ \rightarrow 4CO_2 + 2N_2O + 6H_2O$$
$$5(CH_2O) + 4NO_3^- + 4H^+ \rightarrow 5CO_2 + 2N_2 + 7H_2O$$

Under field conditions, freshly added crop residues can stimulate denitrification. Carbonaceous exudates from active roots support denitrifying bacteria growth in the rhizosphere.

Soil Water Content. Waterlogging causes denitrification by impeding the diffusion of O_2 through soil. Higher soil water content increases N loss through denitrification (Fig. 4-31). Rapid conversion of NO_3^- to N_2O or N_2 occurs when rain saturates a warm soil. Denitrification losses of 10 to 30 lbs N/a following saturation have been measured. Saturation during snowmelt in the spring is also suspected of causing major denitrification losses of N. Duration of snow cover during warming conditions encourages denitrification associated with spring thawing.

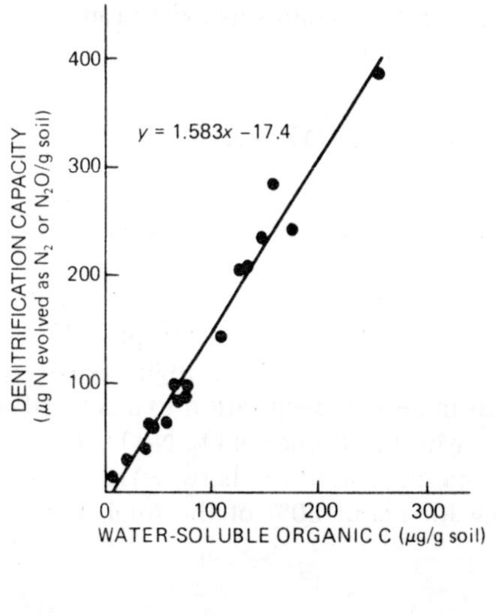

Figure 4-30 **Relationship between denitrification capacity and water-soluble organic C.** *(Burford and Bremner, 1975,* **Soil Biol. Biochem.,** *7:389.)*

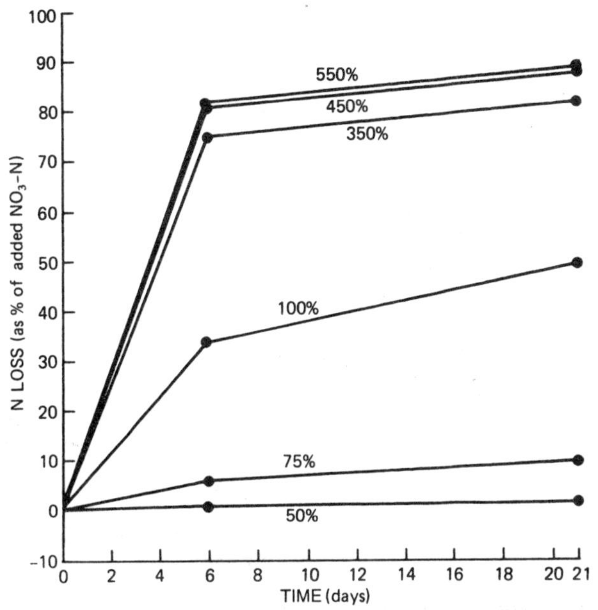

Figure 4-31 **Effect of soil water content (% water-holding capacity) on denitrification in soil.** *(Bremner and Shaw, 1958,* J. Agr. Sci.[Camb.] *51:40.)*

In flooded rice soils, NO_3^- fertilizers are generally ineffective because of denitrification. Some NO_3^- is always present in paddy soils, since NH_4^+ in the aerobic zone of the plant-soil-water system is converted to NO_3^-. When NO_3^- diffuses into anaerobic parts of the soil, it is rapidly denitrified.

Aeration. Formation of NO_3^- and NO_2^- depends on an ample supply of O_2. Denitrification proceeds only when the O_2 supply is too low to meet microbiological requirements. Denitrification can occur in well-aerated soils, presumably in anaerobic microsites where the biological O_2 demand exceeds supply (Fig. 4-32). Denitrification occurs with a low

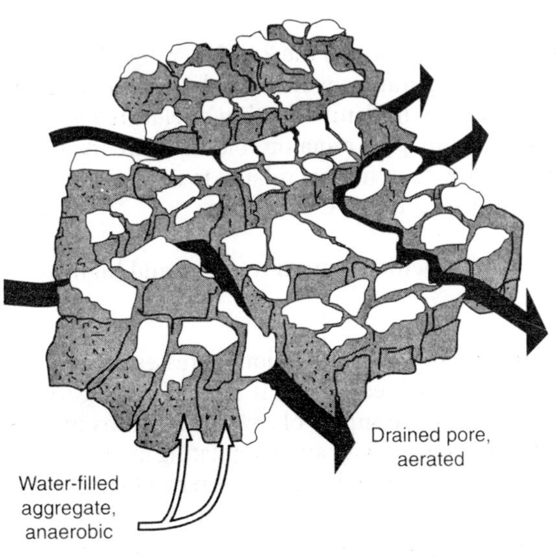

Figure 4-32 **Diagram of microsites within an aerated soil that represent anaerobic, water-saturated aggregates in which native or applied N can be denitrified.**

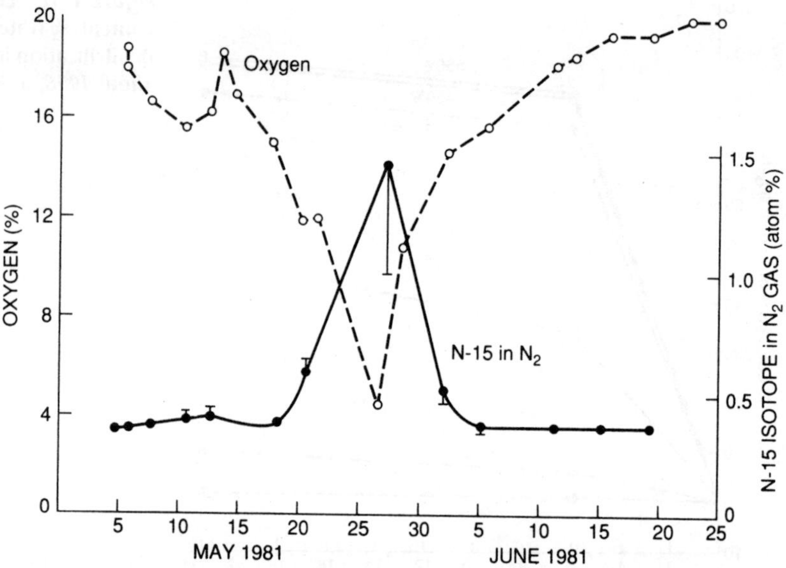

Figure 4-33 **Relationship between production of N_2 with decreasing O_2 concentration (15-cm soil depth). 100 kg N/ha were applied on May 5. Release of N_2 peaked when soil O_2 dropped to 5% after 60 mm of rain. Total N loss averaged about 20% of the N applied.** *(Colburn et al., 1984,* J. Soil Sci., *35:542.)*

rate of O_2 diffusion into the soil and a high microbial respiratory demand. Denitrification losses are generally observed when O_2 content is < 10 to 15% soil air (Fig. 4-33).

Soil pH. Denitrifying bacteria are sensitive to low pH, thus, microbial denitrification is negligible at $<$ pH 5.0 but increases with pH (Fig. 4-34). At pH $<$ 6.0 to 6.5, N_2O represents more than half of the N loss. Formation of NO occurs at pH $<$ 5.5. NO_2 may be the first gas detectable in neutral or slightly acidic soil, but it is reduced by microbes to N_2 at pH $>$ 6.

Temperature. Denitrification increases rapidly in the 2 to 5°C range. Denitrification will proceed at slightly higher rates when temperature is increased to 25 to 60°C, but is inhibited by temperatures $>$ 60°C. The increase in denitrification at elevated soil temperatures suggests that thermophilic microorganisms play a major role in denitrification. Thus, denitrification losses coinciding with spring thawing are related to accelerated denitrification rates when soils are quickly warmed from 2 to 12°C or higher.

NO_3^- Level. NO_3^- must be present for denitrification to occur and high NO_3^- increases denitrification potential.

Presence of Plants. Under field conditions, denitrification increases because of the release of readily available C in root exudates and sloughed-off root tissues. Denitrification in most fertilized soil-cropping systems is controlled by the supply of organic C. Plants may also increase denitrification by consuming O_2 through root activity and stimulating microbial activity in the rhizosphere. On the other hand, plants can restrict denitrification by (1) uptake of NH_4^+ and NO_3^-; (2) reducing soil water content with resultant increase in O_2 supply; and (3) directly increasing O_2 in the rhizosphere of certain plants that transport O_2 (e.g., paddy rice).

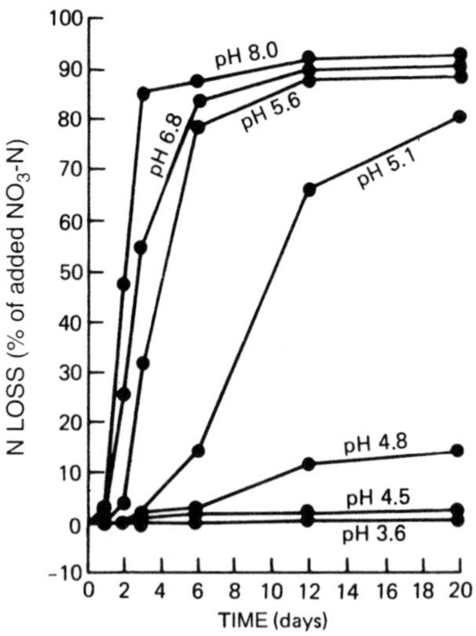

Figure 4-34 Effect of soil pH on denitrification. *(Bremner and Shaw, 1958,* J. Agr. Sci. [Camb.], *51:40.)*

Nitrite (NO_2^-) in Soil In addition to microbial denitrification, denitrification of soil and fertilizer N also occurs through chemical reactions involving NO_2^- (Table 4-17). Although NO_2^- does not usually accumulate in soil, detectable amounts occur in calcareous soils and in localized soil zones containing NH_4^+ or NH_4^+-forming fertilizers.

NO_2^- is toxic to plants and microorganisms. For example, *nitrobacter* activity is reduced due to NO_2^- formation under high soil pH and NH_4^+ levels. At pH $\geq$ 7.5 to 8.0, conversion of NH_4^+ to NO_2^- exceeds conversion of NO_2^- to NO_3^-, but at neutral pH the reverse is true. Although NO_2^- buildup in soil is favored by high pH, its breakdown to N_2O and N_2 is

Table 4-17 **Gaseous Losses of N from Soils**

Form of N Lost	*Source of N*	*General Reaction*
N and NO_2 gases	Denitrification of NO_3^-	$NO_3^- \rightarrow NO_2^- \rightarrow NO \rightarrow N_2O\uparrow \rightarrow N_2\uparrow$
	Nitrification of NH_4^+	$NH_4^+ \rightarrow NH_2OH \rightarrow H_2N_2O_2 \rightarrow NO_2^- \rightarrow NO_3^-$; $H_2N_2O_2 \downarrow N_2O$
	Reactions of NO_2^- with	
	NH_4^+	$NH_4^+ + NO_2^- \rightarrow N_2\uparrow + 2H_2O$
	Amino acids	$NO_2^- + NH_2R \rightarrow N_2\uparrow + R{-}OH + OH^-$
	Lignin	$NO_2^- + \text{lignin} \rightarrow N_2\uparrow + N_2O\uparrow + CH_3ONO$
	Decomposition of NO_2^-	
	H^+	$3NO_2^- + 2H^+ \rightarrow NO + NO_3^- + H_2O$
	Fe^{+2}	$Fe^{+2} + NO_2^- + 2H^+ \rightarrow 2H^+ + Fe^{+3} + NO + H_2O$
	Mn^{+2}	$Mn^{+2} + NO_2^- + 2H^+ \rightarrow 2H^+ + Mn^{+3} + NO + H_2O$
NH_3	Fertilizers	
	anhydrous NH_3	NH_3 (liquid) $\rightarrow NH_3$ (gas)
	urea	$(NH_2)_2CO + H_2O \rightarrow 2NH_3\uparrow + CO_2$
	NH_4^+ salts	$NH_4^+ + OH^- \rightarrow NH_3\uparrow + H_2O$ (pH > 7)
	Decomposition of residues	Organic N $\rightarrow NH_4^+ \rightarrow NH_3\uparrow$

SOURCE: Modified from Kurtz, 1980, ASA Spec. Publ. 38, p. 5.

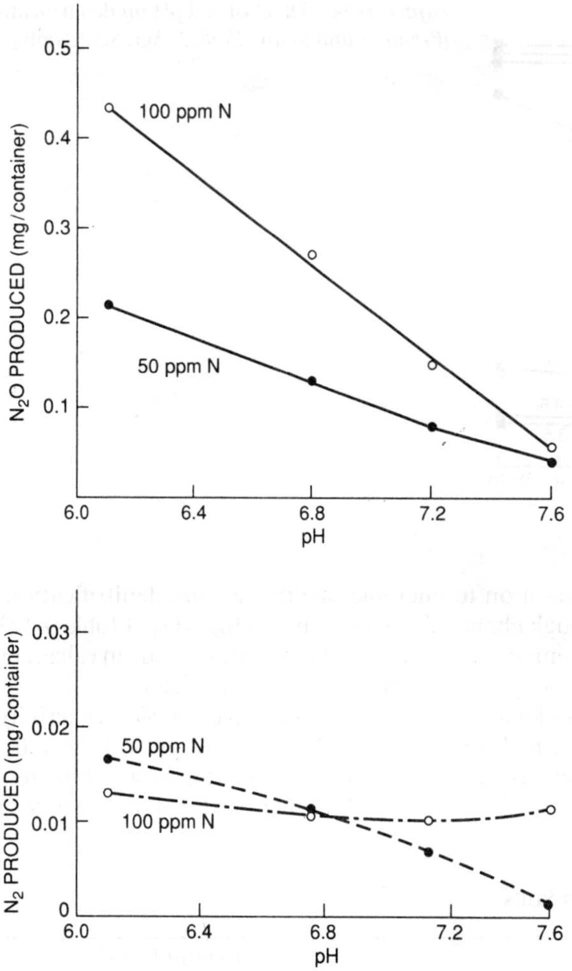

Figure 4-35 **Effect of pH on increasing N_2O (top) and N_2 (bottom) production with increasing application of NO_2^- as $NaNO_2$.** *(Christianson et al., 1979,* Can. J. Soil Sci., *59:147.)*

restricted by high soil pH (Fig. 4-35). NO_2^- formed in the fall may undergo chemical denitrification, even if soils freeze.

High rates of band-applied urea, anhydrous NH_3, or $(NH_4)_2HPO_4$ fertilizers cause temporary increases in NH_4^+ and pH, which encourages NO_2^- accumulation in the band, regardless of initial soil pH. Diffusion and/or dilution of NH_4^+ in the fertilizer bands will restore conditions suitable for conversion of NO_2^- to NO_3^-. NO_2^- can diffuse beyond the fertilizer band to a soil environment, where *nitrobacter* will readily convert it to NO_3^-.

Agricultural and Environmental Significance of Denitrification Under reducing conditions, NO_3^- is subject to denitrification losses to the atmosphere. Since the earth's atmosphere is largely N_2 and the oceans are virtually NO_3^- free, denitrification is responsible for returning N_2 to the atmosphere. Two categories of N loss by denitrification exist: (1) rapid and extensive flushes associated with heavy rains, irrigation, and snowmelt; and (2) continuous small losses over extended periods in anaerobic microsites. Generally, as soil water-filled pore space increases > 60%, loss of NO, N_2O, and N_2 increase. N loss estimates vary widely but are usually < 15% of N applied to crops. Under conditions of high soil NO_3^-, temperature, and water content, denitrification losses can reach 1 lb N/ac/day. Generally, denitrification losses range from 2 to 25% of fertilizer N applied in well-drained soils, compared to 6 to 55% in poorly drained soils. With fall-applied N, when heavy winter snows persist into late spring, N deficiencies can occur. N fertilizer use efficiency can be reduced 25 to 50% under these conditions.

In systems where fertilizer N enters drainage water, controlled drainage and riparian buffer systems can denitrify relatively large quantities of NO_3 (Chapter 13). Thus, field measures of denitrification of fertilizer N applied to the soil surface would be relatively low compared to total eventual denitrification in the system.

Worldwide increase in N fertilizer use has increased emissions of N_2O from soils and contributed to deterioration of the ozone layer. Although there is evidence that denitrification of fertilizer-derived NO_3^- is responsible for N_2O emission, contributions from natural transformations of soil OM and fresh crop residues also contribute to N_2O emission.

Volatilization of NH_3

NH_3 is a natural product of N mineralization of which only small amounts are volatilized compared to NH_3 volatilization from surface-applied N fertilizers and manure (Fig. 4-1). The reaction is:

$$NH_4^+ \leftrightarrows NH_3 + H^+ \ (pK_a\ 9.3) \tag{1}$$

Understanding the soil, environmental, and N fertilizer-management factors influencing volatilization reactions is essential to minimize NH_3 loss.

Factors Affecting Volatilization

Soil pH. Volatilization of NH_3 depends on the quantity of NH_3 and NH_4^+ in the soil solution, which is dependent on pH (Fig. 4-36). At pH 9.3 (pK_a 9.3), NH_3 and NH_4^+ concentrations are equal with NH_3, increasing with increasing pH. Appreciable quantities of NH_3 loss

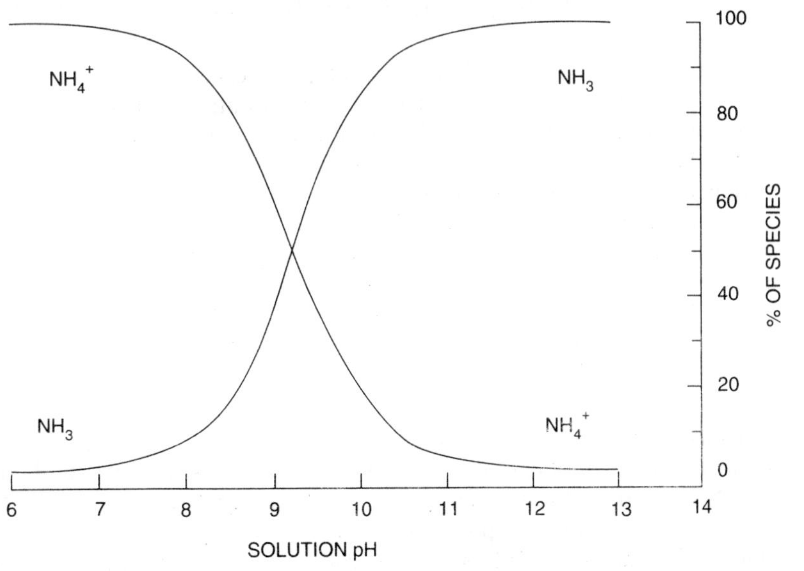

Figure 4-36 Influence of pH on the proportion of NH_3 and NH_4^+ in solution.

occur when soil solution pH > 7.5. When NH_4^+ fertilizers are added to acidic or neutral soils, little or no NH_3 volatilization occurs because soil solution pH is not increased. Recall that soil pH decreases slightly when the NH_4^+ is nitrified to NO_3^-. When NH_4^+-forming fertilizers (e.g., urea) are added to acidic or neutral soils, solution pH around the urea granule increases during hydrolysis:

$$CO(NH_2)_2 + H^+ + 2H_2O \rightarrow 2NH_4^+ + HCO_3^- \qquad (2)$$

Solution pH increases above 7 because H^+ is consumed in the reaction; thus, the $NH_4^+ \leftrightarrows NH_3$ equilibrium shifts to the right (Eq. 1) to favor NH_3 volatilization loss. Therefore, in neutral and acidic soils, NH_4^+-containing fertilizers are less subject to NH_3 loss than urea and urea-containing fertilizers.

N Source. In calcareous soils, the $CaCO_3$ buffers solution pH around 7.5; thus, NH_4^+-containing fertilizers may be subject to NH_3 volatilization losses. For example, when $(NH_4)_2SO_4$ is applied to a calcareous soil, the reaction is:

$$(NH_4)_2SO_4 + CaCO_3 + 2H_2O \rightarrow 2NH_4^+ + Ca^{+2} + 2HCO_3^- + 2OH^- \qquad (3)$$

$$\downarrow$$

$$NH_4^+ + HCO_3^- \rightarrow NH_3 + CO_2 + H_2O \qquad (4)$$

Solution pH increases because of the OH^- produced. The Ca^{+2} and OH^- further react with $(NH_4)_2SO_4$:

$$(NH_4)_2SO_4 + Ca^{+2} + 2OH^- \rightarrow 2NH_3 + H_2O + CaSO_4 \qquad (5)$$

When all three equations (Eqs. 3, 4, and 5) are combined, the overall reaction is:

$$(NH_4)_2SO_4 + CaCO_3 \rightarrow 2NH_3 + CO_2 + H_2O + CaSO_4 \qquad (6)$$

Since $CaSO_4$ is slightly soluble, the reaction proceeds to the right and NH_3 volatilization is favored due to increasing pH driven by precipitation of insoluble Ca precipitates. Similar reactions occur with other NH_4^+ fertilizers that produce insoluble Ca precipitates (e.g., $[NH_4]_2HPO_4$). In comparison, volatilization losses are reduced with NH_4^+ fertilizers that produce soluble Ca reaction products (e.g., NH_4NO_3, NH_4Cl) (Fig. 4-37).

Generally, NH_3 volatilization losses in calcareous soils are greatest with urea fertilizers and the NH_4^+ salts that form insoluble Ca precipitates. NH_3 losses also increase with increasing fertilizer rate and with liquid compared with dry N sources.

NH_3 volatilization of N in animal waste can be as high as 40% depending on waste source and N content (see Chapter 10). Immediate incorporation of broadcast manure will reduce volatilization losses.

N Placement. NH_3 volatilization is much greater with broadcast compared to subsurface or surface band applications (Table 4-18). The data show increased crop response to fertilizer N when urea-ammonium nitrate (UAN) is band applied compared with surface broadcasting. Immediate incorporation of broadcast N greatly reduces the NH_3 volatilization potential. Some of the N losses from broadcast UAN with high surface residue cover is due to immobilization.

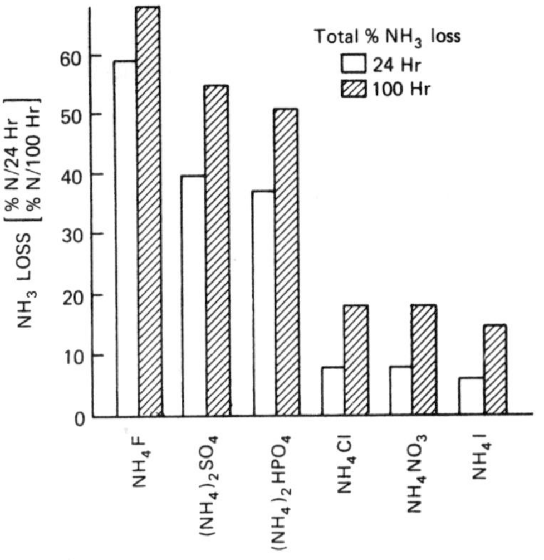

Figure 4-37 **Total NH_3 loss as influenced by anions of several NH_4^+ fertilizers. NH_4-N was surface applied at 550 kg N/ha.** *(Fenn and Kissel, 1973, SSSAJ, 37:855.)*

Table 4-18 **No-Till Corn Grain Yield as Affected by UAN Rate and Method of Application**

		Surface Band	
N Rate	*Broadcast*	*Unincorporated*	*Incorporated*
kg/ha		*t/ha*	
90	5.61	7.40	7.87
180	6.77	8.34	8.84
270	7.18	8.69	9.66
Mean	6.52	8.14	8.46

SOURCE: Touchton and Hargrove, 1982, *Agron.* J., 74:825.

Buffer Capacity (BC). Soil BC greatly influences NH_3 volatilization loss (Fig. 4-38). Soil pH and subsequent NH_3 loss will be less in a soil with high BC compared with low BC because of increased pH buffering capacity adsorption of NH_4^+ on the CEC. Soil BC will increase with increasing CEC and OM content.

Environment. NH_3 losses are influenced by environmental conditions during the reaction of urea and NH_4^+ salts with soil. Volatilization increases with increasing temperature up to about 45°C, which is related to higher reaction rates and urease activity. With a dry soil surface, microbial activity and volatilization reaction rates are reduced. Maximum potential NH_3 loss occurs when the soil surface is at or near field-capacity moisture content and when slow drying conditions exist for several days. Water evaporation from the soil surface encourages NH_3 volatilization.

Crop Residues. Surface crop residues increase potential NH_3 volatilization by maintaining wet, humid conditions at the soil surface and by reducing the quantity of urea diffusing into the soil. Crop residues also have a high urease activity (Fig. 4-39). Partial residue incorporation can significantly reduce NH_3 losses from surface-applied urea fertilizer.

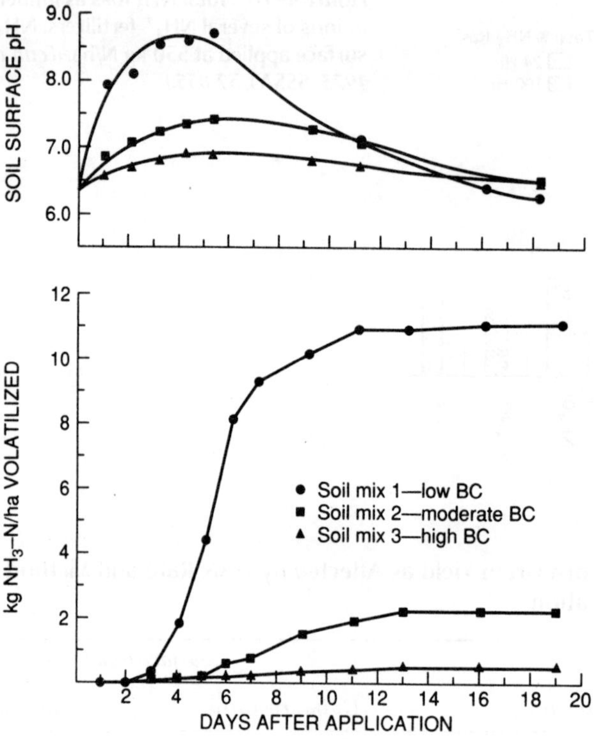

Figure 4-38 **Soil BC effects on soil pH and NH_3 volatilization after N fertilizer application.** ***(Ferguson et al., 1984,*** **SSSAJ,** ***48:578.)***

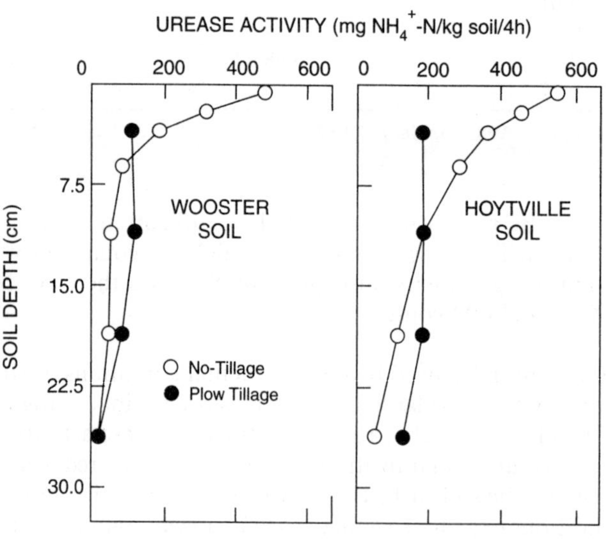

Figure 4-39 **Distribution of urease activity in soil profiles as affected by tillage.** ***(Dick, 1984,*** **SSSAJ,** ***48:569.)***

Agricultural and Environmental Significance of Volatilization Although substantial losses of NH_3 have been measured in laboratory studies, their validity should be closely examined. It should be recognized that experimental systems will impose artificial conditions of air movement, temperature, and relative humidities quite different from those occurring naturally. For example, NH_3 volatilization losses as high as 70% of fertilizer N have been reported from laboratory studies. Field studies conducted under a wide range of conditions show that volatilization losses with $(NH_4)_2SO_4$ broadcast on a calcareous soil can be about 50% of the fertilizer N applied, while NH_3 volatilization losses can be as high as 25% with urea. In an acidic soil, NH_3 losses are greater for urea than for $(NH_4)_2SO_4$. Typical NH_3 losses in arable systems are usually < 25% in low-pH soil and about double this amount in high-pH soils. Soil and environmental conditions conducive to maximizing NH_3 losses are high soil pH, low buffer capacity, broadcast/unincorporated urea containing fertilizer or manures, and warm/moist surface soil conditions. In flooded rice systems, NH_3 loss has been reported as high as 75% of applied N.

NH_3 Exchange by Plants

NH_3 absorption and loss occurs in plant leaves. The quantity depends on soil-surface wetness and extent of evaporation, which influence the amount of NH_3 released into the air coming into contact with plant canopies. Field crops exposed to air containing normal levels of atmospheric NH_3 may obtain as much as 10% of their N requirement by direct absorption of NH_3. Plant seedlings are a natural sink for atmospheric NH_3, absorbing about 40% of the NH_3 from air containing 1 ppm NH_3. NH_3 produced near the ground surface of grass-clover pasture can be completely absorbed by the plant cover. NH_3 volatilization from plant foliage also occurs during ripening and senescence, with values ranging between 10 and 50 lbs N/ac/yr.

N Sources for Crop Production

Both organic and inorganic N sources supply the N required for optimum crop growth. Efficient management of N inputs requires understanding N cycling and transformations in soils (Fig. 4-1). Management practices that minimize N losses and maximize the quantity of applied N recovered by the crop will increase production efficiency and reduce potential impacts of N use on the environment. Nutrient management technologies are discussed in greater detail in Chapter 10, but the commonly available N sources used in agricultural production systems and their reactions with soil are presented here.

Organic N Forms

Before 1850, virtually all of the fertilizer N consumed in the United States was primarily animal manure and legume N. Presently these materials account for 35% of the total N use in the United States (Table 4-6). However, depending on the rate of manure applied, considerable quantities of N and other nutrients are added with manure. A complete discussion of fertilization with manure is found in Chapter 10. The average N concentration in organic materials is typically between 1 to 13%.

Manure The total quantity of manure produced annually in the United States is nearly 200 million tons (dry weight), with about 60% produced and deposited by grazing animals. The remaining 40% is produced in confinement animal feeding operations (CAFO). Approximately 16 million acres (8%) of cropland were fertilized with manure. Average annual manure production ranges between 4 and 16 tons of manure per animal (Table 4-19). The quantity of N in manure and the availability to plants varies greatly and depends on (1) nutrient content of the animal feed, (2) method of manure handling

Table 4-19 Annual Manure Production by Selected Animals and N Content

		Waste Component		*N Form*				
Animal Species	*Manure* Production*	*Feces*	*Urine*	*Amino Acid*	*Urea*	*NH_4^+*	*Uric Acid*	*Other*
	t/yr	*% of Total*						
Poultry	4.5	25	75	27	04	8	61	01
Sheep	6.0	50	50	21	34	<1.5	—	43
Horse	8.0	60	40	24	25	<1.0	—	49
Beef	8.5	50	50	20	35	<0.5	—	44
Dairy	12	60	40	23	28	<0.5	—	49
Swine	16	33	67	27	51	<0.5	—	22

*Based on 1,000-lb animal weight.

and storage, (3) quantity of added materials (i.e., bedding, water, and so on), (4) method and time of application, (5) soil properties, and (6) intended crop. Most wastes exiting the animal contain 75 to 90% water. Storage and handling usually reduce water content in solid-storage systems and increase water content in liquid systems, such as the lagoon storage common with swine production.

With total N contents ranging between < 1 and 6%, 50 to 75% of the total N is organic N, while the remaining 25 to 50% is NH_4^+ (Table 4-19). Thus, manure N availability to plants depends on mineralization of the organic N in the manure. The mineralization process is the same as described previously for soil OM.

Organic N in manure is composed of stable and unstable forms (Fig. 4-40). Urea and uric acid (Table 4-19) are the main components of unstable organic N and are readily mineralized to plant available NH_4^+. Since NH_4^+ can be converted to NH_3 under optimum soil and environmental conditions, significant volatilization losses of manure N are possible, ranging from 15 to 40% of total N. In lagoon systems, 60 to 90% of total manure N can be lost through denitrification and volatilization during storage and land application. The remaining stable organic N will mineralize in the first and subsequent years after application. The less resistant stable organic N will generally mineralize in the year of application. This fraction represents 30 to 60% of total manure N, depending on manure type and placement. Subsurface injection results in greater N mineralization (and N availability) than surface-applied manure (Table 4-20). The more resistant stable organic N mineralizes slowly over the next several years, where about 50, 25, and 12.5% of the N mineralized in the first year is mineralized in the second, third, and fourth years, respectively.

N mineralization rates vary between manures sources (Fig. 4-41). The kinetics of N mineralization from manure, legume, or native soil OM can often be described by a first-order rate equation:

$$N_{min} = N_0 (1 - e^{-kt})$$

where N_{min} = amount of N mineralized at time, t

N_0 = the total mineralizable N

k = rate constant

t = time

This equation indicates larger quantities of N mineralized initially, with decreasing N mineralized with time (Fig. 4-42).

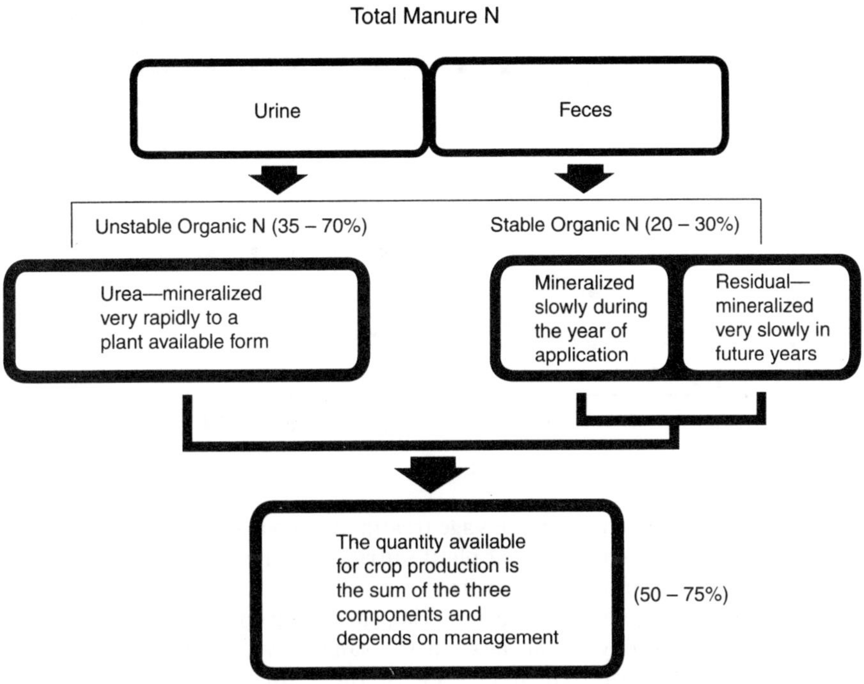

Figure 4-40 **Form and relative availability of N in manure.** *(***Bulletin 308,** ***1986, Univ. Maryland.****)*

Table 4-20 Mineralization Factors for Selected Animal Wastes and Storage/Handling Methods*

	Mineralization Factor[†]	
Animal	*Solid Storage*[††]	*Liquid Storage*[††]
Swine	0.50–0.60	0.30–0.35
Beef cattle	0.25–0.35	0.25–0.30
Dairy cattle	0.25–0.35	0.25–0.30
Sheep	0.25–0.35	—
Poultry	0.50–0.60	0.50–0.70
Horses	0.20–0.35	—

*Factors represent the proportion of organic N mineralized in the first year of application.
[†]Mineralization factors are reduced for surface application compared with subsurface injection.
[††]Higher factors in a storage column represent anaerobic liquid storage and solid manure without bedding or litter added. Lower factors in a storage column represent aerobic liquid storage and solid manure with bedding or litter added.

Legume Legumes can provide substantial proportions of plant available N to crop production (Table 4-7). Please refer to the material on N_2 fixation in this chapter.

Sewage Sludge About 75% of the sewage handled by municipal treatment plants is of human origin, and the remaining 25% is from industrial sources. The end products of all sewage treatment processes are sewage sludge and sewage effluent. Sewage sludge refers to

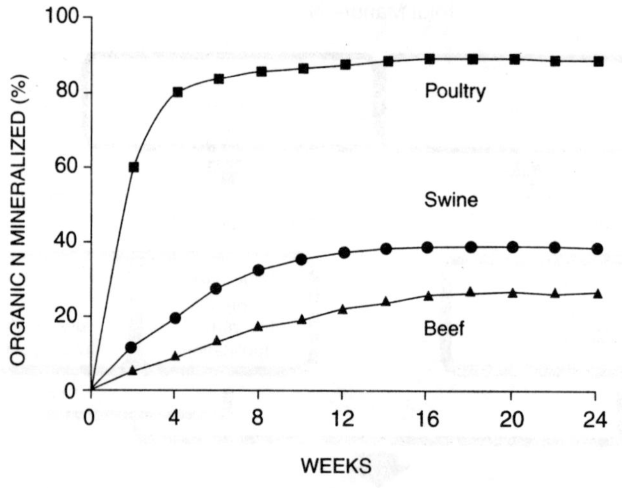

Figure 4-41 **N mineralization of organic N in selected liquid animal manures applied to a sandy soil.** ***(Van Faassen, 1987, Netherlands. In v.d. Meer [ed.],*** **Animal Manure on Grassland and Fodder Crops,** ***Martinus Nijhoff Publ. Dordrecht, Netherlands.)***

the solids produced during sewage treatment. Sewage effluent is essentially clear water containing low concentrations of plant nutrients and traces of OM, which may be chlorinated and discharged into surface waters.

Sludge is a heterogeneous material, varying in composition from one city to another and even from one day to the next in the same city. Sewage sludge contains < 1 to 3% N (Chapter 10). Approximately 25% of the municipal sludge produced is land applied, although very little is applied to land used for food production.

Before developing plans for land application of sludge, it is essential to obtain representative samples of the sludge over a period of time and determine its typical chemical analysis (Table 10-20). Sewage sludge is disposed of by (1) application on cropland by approved methods; (2) incineration, with loss of OM and N; and (3) burial in landfill sites, where it will produce methane for many years (Chapter 10).

Inorganic N Sources

Manufactured fertilizers are the most important sources of N to plants. Over the last 30 years, world N consumption has increased from 22 to 85 million metric tons. In the United States,

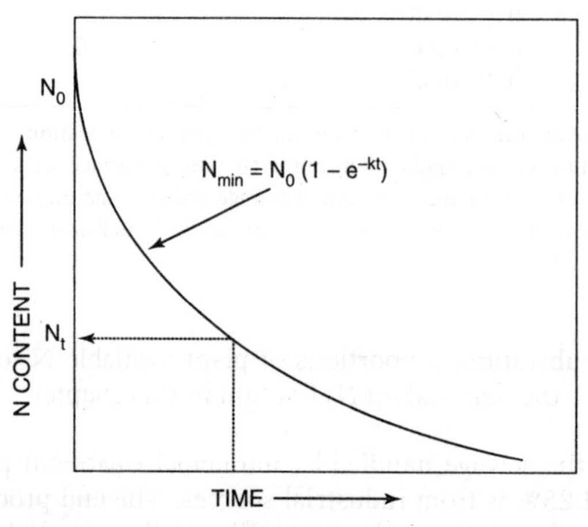

Figure 4-42 **General first-order kinetics of N mineralization. The quantity of N mineralized (N_{min}) at any time (t) decreases with time as the quantity of initial mineralizable N (N_0) decreases.**

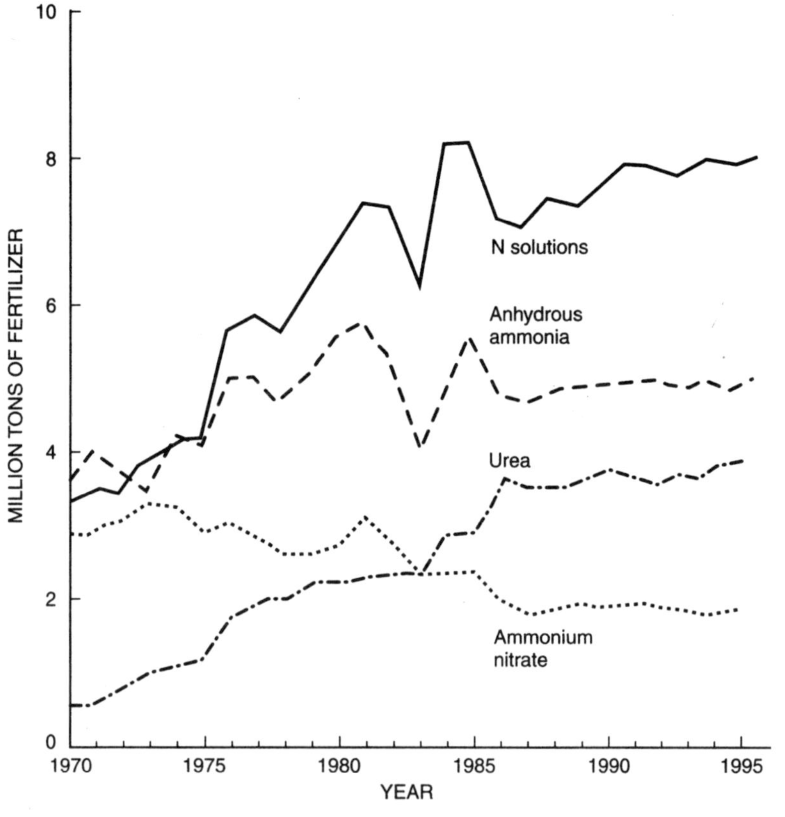

Figure 4-43 **Common N sources used in the U.S.** *(USDA, 1994.)*

anhydrous NH_3, urea, and N solutions currently account for about 70% of total N (Fig. 4-43). Anhydrous NH_3 is the basic building block for almost all chemically derived N fertilizer materials. Most of the NH_3 is produced by reacting N_2 and H_2 gases (Haber-Bosch process; see p. 114. From NH_3 many different fertilizer N compounds are manufactured. A few materials do not originate from NH_3 but they constitute only a small percentage of N fertilizers. For convenience, the various N compounds are grouped into three categories: ammoniacal, nitrate, and slowly available (Table 4-21).

NH_4^+ or NH_4^+ Forming Sources

Anhydrous NH_3. Anhydrous NH_3 contains 82% N, the highest N content of fertilizer (Table 4-21). In some respects NH_3 behaves like water, since they both have solid, liquid, and gaseous states. The affinity of anhydrous NH_3 for water is apparent from its solubility (Table 4-22). As a result, NH_3 is rapidly absorbed by water in human tissue. Because NH_3 is very irritating to the eyes, lungs, and skin, safety precautions must be taken with anhydrous NH_3. Safety goggles, rubber gloves, and an NH_3 gas mask are required safety equipment. A large container of water attached to NH_3 application equipment is required for washing skin and eyes exposed to NH_3. Current regulations require certification for anyone applying NH_3.

Under normal atmospheric conditions, anhydrous NH_3 boils and escapes to the atmosphere. To prevent escape, it is stored under pressure and/or refrigeration (−28°F). When liquid NH_3 is released from a pressurized tank, it expands rapidly, vaporizes, and produces

Table 4-21 Composition of Some Common Soluble Fertilizer N Sources

N Source	Nutrient Content (%)							Physical State
	N	P_2O_5	K_2O	CaO	MgO	S	Cl	
NH_4^+ or NH_4^+ forming								
Anhydrous ammonia	82	—	—	—	—	—	—	Gas
Aqua ammonia	20–25	—	—	—	—	—	—	Liquid
Ammonium chloride	25–26	—	—	—	—	—	66	Solid
Ammonium nitrate	33–34	—	—	—	—	—	—	Solid
Ammonium sulfate	21	—	—	—	—	24	—	Solid
Monoammonium phosphate	11	48–55	—	2	0.5	1–3	—	Solid
Diammonium phosphate	18–21	46–54	—	—	—	—	—	Solid
Ammonium phosphate-sulfate	13–16	20–39	—	—	—	3–14	—	Solid
Ammonium polyphosphate	10–11	34–37	—	—	—	—	—	Liquid
Ammonium thiosulfate	12	—	—	—	—	26	—	Liquid
Urea	45–46	—	—	—	—	—	—	Solid
Urea-sulfate	30–40	—	—	—	—	6–11	—	Solid
Urea-ammonium nitrate	28–32	—	—	—	—	—	—	Liquid
Urea-ammonium phosphate	21–38	13–42	—	—	—	—	—	Solid
Urea phosphate	17	43–44	—	—	—	—	—	Solid
NO_3^-								
Calcium nitrate	15	—	—	34	—	—	—	Solid
Potassium nitrate	13	—	44	0.5	0.5	0.2	1.2	Solid
Sodium nitrate	16	—	—	—	—	—	0.6	Solid

Table 4-22 Properties of Anhydrous NH_3

Properties	
Color	Colorless
Odor	Pungent, sharp
Molecular weight	17.03
Weight per gallon of liquid at 60°F	5.15 lbs
Boiling point	228°F
One gallon of liquid at 60°F expands to	113 standard ft^3 of vapor
Solubility in water at 60°F	0.578 lb/lb of water
Toxicology	*ppm N*
Slight detectable odor	1
Detectable odor but no adverse effects on unprotected workers for ≤ 8 hr exposure	25
Noticeable irritation of eyes and nasal passages	100
Irritation to eyes and throat; no direct adverse effects, but exposure should be avoided	400–700
May be fatal after short exposure	2,000
Convulsive coughing, respiratory spasms, strangulation, and asphyxiation	5,000+

a white cloud of water vapor formed by water condensation in the air surrounding NH_3 as it vaporizes (Chapter 10). Because anhydrous NH_3 is a gas at atmospheric pressure, some may be lost to the atmosphere during and after application. If the soil is hard or full of clods during application, the slit behind the applicator blade will not close or fill, and some NH_3 will escape to the atmosphere.

Anhydrous NH_3 convertors are often used to reduce the need for deep injection and preapplication tillage. The convertors serve as depressurization chambers for compressed anhydrous NH_3 stored in the applicator tank. Anhydrous NH_3 freezes as it expands in the convertors, separating liquid NH_3 from the vapor and greatly reducing the pressure. The temperature of liquid NH_3 is about $-32°C$ ($-26°F$). Approximately 85% of the anhydrous NH_3 turns to liquid; the remainder stays in vapor form. The liquid flows by gravity through regular application equipment into the soil. Vapor collected at the top of the convertor is injected into the soil in the usual manner.

NH_3 Retention Zones. As a gas, NH_3 escapes to the atmosphere if it does not react rapidly with water and various organic and inorganic soil components through several possible reactions:

- $NH_3 + H^+ \rightarrow NH_4^+$
- $NH_3 + H_2O \rightarrow NH_4^+ + OH^-$
- Reaction with OH^- groups and tightly bound water of clay minerals
- Reaction with water of hydration around exchangeable cations on CEC
- Reaction with OM
- NH_4^+ fixation by expanding clay minerals
- Adsorption by clay minerals and organic components through H bonding

Immediately after NH_3 injection, a localized zone high in both NH_3 and NH_4^+ is created (Fig. 4-44). The horizontal, roughly circular- to oval-shaped zone is about 2 to 5 in. in diameter, depending on several factors influencing NH_3 retention:

Soil moisture content → NH_3 retention increases with soil moisture content, with maximum NH_3 retention occurring at or near field capacity. As soils become drier or wetter than field capacity, they lose their ability to hold NH_3 (Fig. 4-45). The size of the initial retention zone decreases with increasing soil moisture. Diffusion of NH_3 from the injection zone is impeded by high soil moisture, because of the strong affinity of NH_3 for water.

Clay content → NH_3 retention increases with the clay content. NH_3 diffusion is greater in sandy soils than in clay soils due to larger pores in coarse-textured soils and lower retention capacity of soil colloids.

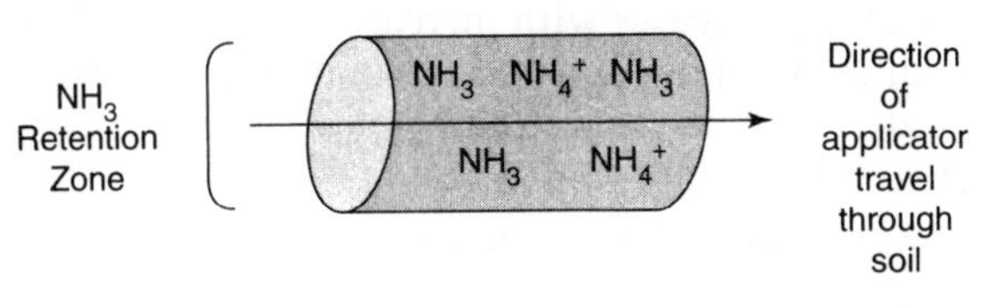

Figure 4-44 **Diagram of an NH_3 retention zone.**

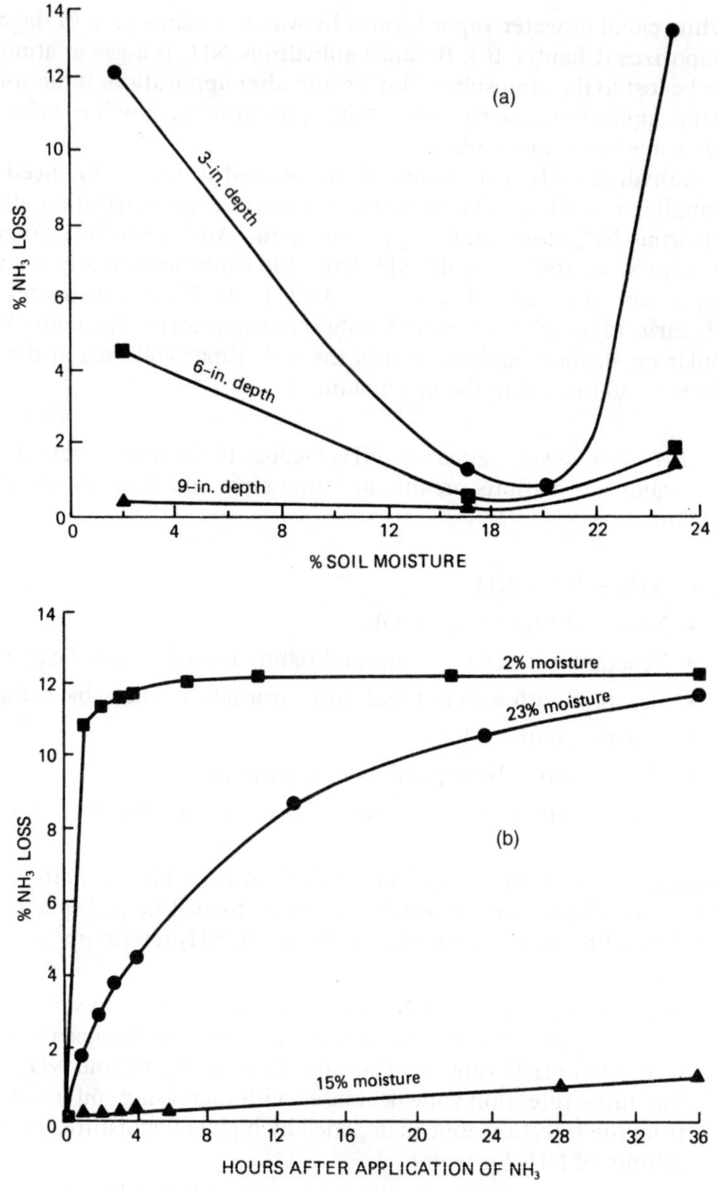

Figure 4-45 **NH_3 loss from a silt loam soil as influenced by soil moisture content and depth of application (a) and time (b). Anhydrous NH_3 applied at 100 lbs N/a on 40-in. row spacing.** *(Stanley and Smith, 1956,* SSSAJ, *20:557.)*

Injection depth → NH_3 retention increases with increasing depth of injection and varies considerably, depending on soil properties and conditions. Deeper injection depths are required for sandy soils compared to clay soils. In dry soil, NH_3 loss declines with increasing placement depth (Fig. 4-45).

Injection spacing → At a given N rate, NH_3 applied per unit volume of soil decreases with decreasing injection spacing. With the greater retention achieved with narrow

Table 4-23 Effect of NH_3 on Fungi, Bacteria, and Actinomycetes in the NH_3 Injection Zone

	Bacteria		*Actinomycetes*		*Fungi*	
Days after Treatment	*Check*	*NH_3*	*Check*	*NH_3*	*Check*	*NH_3*
	---x 10^6/g soil---					
0	2.3	0.3	1.5	0.4	20.1	5.1
3	1.3	6.3	0.9	1.0	20.2	10.4
10	3.1	9.2	0.9	2.0	15.0	9.3
24	1.3	4.2	0.5	1.3	22.7	9.2
31	4.5	3.4	0.4	1.0	20.0	13.3
38	0.9	0.9	0.3	0.7	24.0	4.0

SOURCE: Eno and Blue, 1954, *Soil Sci. Soc. Am. J.*, 18:178.

spacings, there is less chance of NH_3 loss, especially in sandy soils with limited NH_3-retention capacity.

Soil OM → NH_3 retention increases with increasing soil OM. At least 50% of the NH_3-retention capacity is due to OM.

Temporary changes in soil chemical, biological, and physical conditions occur in the NH_3 retention zone. High NH_3 and NH_4^+ levels (≈ 1,000 to 3,000 ppm) produce high soil pH (≥ 9) and osmotic potential (≥ 10 bar), resulting in partial and temporary sterilization of soil within the retention zone (Table 4-23). NH_3 is toxic to microorganisms, higher plants, and animals. It can readily penetrate cell membranes, which are relatively impermeable to NH_4^+. Bacterial activity is probably affected most by free NH_3, while fungi are depressed by high pH. Partial sterilization in the retention zone can persist for several weeks. As a consequence of reduced microbial activity, nitrification of NH_4^+ to NO_2^- and NO_3^- will be reduced until conditions return to normal.

High NH_3, NH_4^+, and NO_2^- concentrations can severely damage germinating seedlings (Fig. 4-46). Concentrations > 1,000 ppm NH_3 near the seed substantially reduce corn population. Deeper injection offsets the harmful effects of high rates of NH_3 more than extending the time for the NH_3 effects to dissipate. Closer injection spacing would also reduce the injurious effect of high NH_3 rates.

The OH^- produced by the reaction of NH_3 with H_2O will dissolve or solubilize soil OM. Most of these effects on OM are only temporary. Solubilization of OM may temporarily increase the availability of nutrients associated with OM.

Contrasting beneficial and harmful effects on soil structure have been reported following the use of anhydrous NH_3. Several long-term studies have shown no difference among N sources on soil physical properties. Impairment of soil structure is not expected to be serious or lasting except in situations involving low-OM soils, in which any loss of OM would likely be harmful.

Aqua NH_3. The simplest N solution is aqua NH_3, which is made by forcing compressed NH_3 gas into water. It has a pressure of less than 10 lb/in.^{2} and is composed of 25 to 29% NH_3 by weight. Transportation and delivery costs limit aqua NH_3 production to small, local fluid-fertilizer plants. Aqua NH_3 is used for direct soil applications or to produce other liquid fertilizers. The NH_3 will volatilize quickly at temperatures above 50°F; thus, aqua NH_3

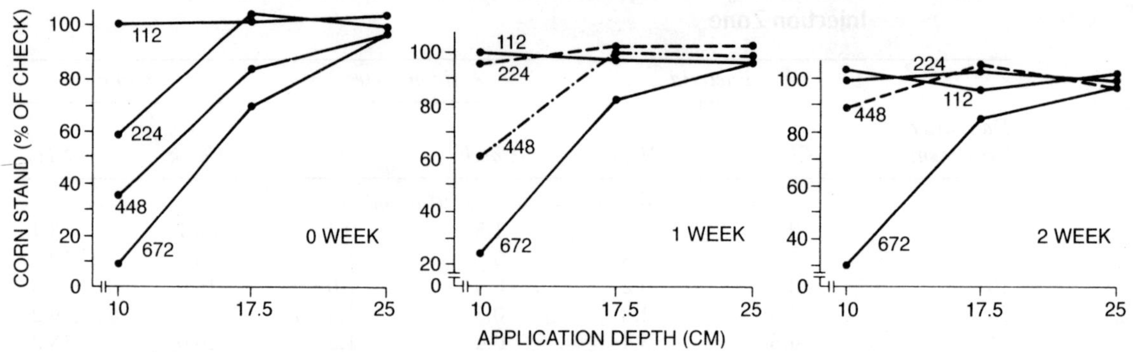

Figure 4-46 **Effect of time, depth, and rate of NH_3 application on a stand 27 days after planting (numbers by lines are kg/ha of N).** *(Colliver and Welch, 1970,* Agron. J., *62:341.)*

is usually injected into soil to depths of 2 to 4 in. At temperatures over 50°F, surface applications of aqua NH_3 should be immediately incorporated into the soil.

Nonpressure N Solutions. Of the liquid N fertilizers used for direct application, nonpressure N solutions are most common, representing ~24% of total N consumption in the United States (Fig. 4-43). Some advantages of N solutions include:

- It is easier and safer to handle and apply than other N fertilizers (especially NH_3).
- It is applied more uniformly and accurately than solid N sources.
- Many pesticides are compatible with N solutions, allowing simultaneous application.
- It is applied through various types of irrigation systems.
- Excellent sources of N for use in formulation of fluid N, P, K, and S fertilizers.
- Lower cost of production than most solid N sources.

N solutions are usually produced from urea, NH_4NO_3, and water and are referred to as UAN (urea-ammonium nitrate) solutions (Table 4-24). Each UAN solution has a specific salting-out temperature, below which dissolved fertilizer salts precipitate. The salting-out temperature determines feasibility of outside winter storage and the time of year for application. Salting-out temperatures vary with N concentration in solution (Table 4-24).

Ammonium Nitrate (NH_4NO_3). NH_4NO_3 contains 33 to 34% N. Global use of NH_4NO_3 has declined since 1985 and for internal security reasons it is now banned in some countries. NH_4NO_3 dissolves to NO_3^- and NH_4^+ and is readily available to crops. Several disadvantages of NH_4NO_3 include:

- Hygroscopic compound (absorbs water) that results in caking during storage.
- High risk of explosion when combined with oxidizable C (oil, diesel fuel, gasoline, etc.).
- Less effective for flooded rice than urea or NH_4^+ fertilizers.
- More prone to leaching and denitrification than NH_4^+ products.

Table 4-24 **Physical and Chemical Characteristics of UAN**

Composition by weight (%)	*Grade (% N)* 28	30	32
Ammonium nitrate	40.1	42.2	43.3
Urea	30.0	32.7	35.4
Water	29.9	25.1	20.3
Density (g/cm^3) at 60°F	1.28	1.30	1.32
Salting-out temperature	−18 (+1)	−10 (+14)	−2 (+28)

Ammonium Sulfate [$(NH_4)_2SO_4$]. Ammonium sulfate represents only about 2% of total N fertilizer use in the United States. The advantages of $(NH_4)_2SO_4$ include low hygroscopicity and source of both N and S. The strongly acid-forming reaction of $(NH_4)_2SO_4$ in soil can be advantageous in high-pH soils and for acid-requiring crops, although is undesirable in acid soil in need of liming. The main disadvantage of $(NH_4)_2SO_4$ is its relatively low N content (21% N) compared to other sources. $(NH_4)_2SO_4$ can be an economical N source particularly when S is also required.

Ammonium Phosphates. Monoammonium ($NH_4H_2PO_4$) and diammonium [$(NH_4)_2HPO_4$] phosphates are more important P sources than N sources (see Chapter 5).

Ammonium Chloride (NH_4Cl). NH_4Cl contains 25% N. The majority of NH_4Cl is used in Japan, China, India, and Southeast Asia. Some of its advantages include a higher N concentration than $(NH_4)_2SO_4$ and superiority over $(NH_4)_2SO_4$ for rice. NH_4Cl is an excellent N source for Cl^- responsive crops (i.e., coconut, oil palm, kiwifruit, etc.). NH_4Cl is as acid-forming as $(NH_4)_2SO_4$ per unit of N and, thus, is undesirable in acid soils requiring lime. Other shortcomings are its low N content compared to urea or NH_4NO_3, and its high Cl^- content, which limits its use to Cl^--tolerant crops.

Ammonium Bicarbonate (NH_4HCO_3). This low analysis N source (19% N) has been used almost exclusively in China. In 1998, about 42 million metric tons or about 50% of total N use were applied.

Urea [$CO(NH_2)_2$]. Favorable manufacturing, handling, storage, and transportation economics make urea a competitive N source. It is the most widely used N source and its worldwide urea use is almost five times that of NH_4NO_3. Urea represents about 20% of total N use in the United States (Fig. 4-43). Granular urea has noteworthy characteristics, including (1) less tendency to stick and cake than NH_4NO_3, (2) lack of sensitivity to explosion, and (3) less corrosive to handling and application equipment. Substantial savings in handling, storage, transportation, and application costs are possible because of urea's high N content.

During manufacturing, biuret (NH_2-CO-NH-CO-NH_2) concentration in urea is kept low due to its phytotoxicity. Biuret levels of 2% can be tolerated in most fertilizers, unless applied to sensitive crops (i.e. citrus, pineapple, and other crops) where $< 0.25\%$ is recommended. Solutions made from urea containing 1.5% biuret are acceptable for foliar application on corn and soybeans. Urea high in biuret should not be placed near or in the seed row.

Behavior of Urea in Soils. When applied to soil, urea is hydrolyzed by the enzyme urease to NH_4^+. Depending on soil pH, NH_4^+ may form NH_3, which can be volatilized at the soil surface by:

$$CO(NH_2)_2 + H^+ + 2H_2O \xrightarrow{\text{Urease}} 2NH_4^+ + HCO_3^-$$

$$NH_4^+ \longrightarrow NH_3 + H^+$$

Urea hydrolysis proceeds rapidly in warm, moist soils, with most of the urea transformed to NH_4^+ in several days.

Urease, an enzyme that catalyzes urea hydrolysis, is abundant in soils. Large numbers of bacteria, fungi, and actinomycetes in soils possess urease. Urease activity increases with the size of the soil microbial population and with OM content. The presence of fresh plant residues often results in abundant supplies of urease (Fig. 4-39).

Urease activity is greatest in the rhizosphere where microbial activity is high. Rhizosphere urease activity varies depending on the plant species and the season of the year. Although temperatures up to 37°C favor urease activity, urea hydrolysis occurs at temperatures down to 2°C or less. As a result, a portion of fall-applied or early winter-applied urea may be converted to NH_3 or NH_4^+ before the spring.

The effects of soil moisture on urease activity are generally small in comparison to the influence of temperature and pH. Hydrolysis rates are highest at soil moisture contents optimum for plants.

Free NH_3 inhibits the enzymatic action of urease. Since significant concentrations of free NH_3 can occur at > pH 7, temporary inhibition of urease by NH_3 occurs after the addition of urea because soil pH in the immediate vicinity of the dissolving urea granule may reach pH 9.0. High rates of band-applied urea could create conditions restrictive to urea hydrolysis.

Management of Urea Fertilizers. Careful management of urea and urea-based fertilizers will reduce the potential for NH_3 volatilization losses and increase the effectiveness of urea fertilizers. Surface applications of urea are most efficient when they are washed into the soil or applied to soils with low potential for volatilization. Conditions for best performance of surface-applied urea are cold, dry soils at the time of application and/or the occurrence of significant precipitation, probably more than 0.25 cm (0.1 in.), within the first 3 to 6 days following application. Movement of soil moisture containing dissolved NH_3 and diffusion of moisture vapor to the soil surface during the drying process probably contribute to NH_3 volatilization at or near the soil surface.

Incorporation of broadcast urea minimizes NH_3 losses by increasing the volume of soil to retain NH_3. Also, NH_3 not converted in the soil must diffuse over much greater distances before reaching the atmosphere. If soil and other environmental conditions appear favorable for NH_3 volatilization, deep incorporation is preferred over shallow surface tillage.

Band placement of urea results in soil changes comparable to those produced by applications of anhydrous NH_3. Diffusion of urea from banded applications can be 2.5 cm (1 in.) within two days, while appreciable NH_4^+ can be observed at distances of 3.8 cm (1.5 in.) from the band. After dilution or dispersion of the band by moisture, hydrolysis begins within three to four days or less under favorable temperature conditions.

Placement of urea with the seed at planting should be carefully controlled because of the toxic effects of free NH_3 on germinating seedlings (see reactions above). The harmful effects of urea placed in the seed row can be eliminated or greatly reduced by banding at least 2.5 cm (1 in.) directly below and/or to the side of the seed row of most crops. Seed-placed urea should not exceed 5 to 10 lbs N/a.

The effect on germination of urea placed near seeds is influenced by available soil moisture. With adequate soil moisture in medium-textured loam soils at seeding time, urea at 30 lbs N/a can be used without reducing germination and crop emergence. However, in low-moisture, coarse-textured (sandy loam) soils, urea at 10 to 20 lbs N/a often reduces both germination and crop yields. Seedbed moisture is less critical in fine-textured (clay and clay loam) soils, and urea can usually be drilled in at rates of up to 30 lbs N/a.

To summarize, the effectiveness of urea depends on the interaction of many factors, which cause some variability in the crop response to urea. However, if managed properly, urea will be about as effective as the other N sources.

Urea-Based Fertilizers. Urea phosphate [$CO(NH_2)_2H_3PO_4$] is a crystalline product formed by the reaction of urea with phosphoric acid. The common grade is 17-44-0, which is primarily used to produce other grades of lower analysis. Urea phosphates with lower purity standards may be adequate for production of suspension fertilizers and for fertigation. Urea has also been combined with $(NH_4)_2HPO_4$ into a solid 28-28-0.

Granular urea sulfate with grades ranging from 40-0-0-4 to 30-0-0-13 have been produced. The N:S ratio may vary from 3:1 to 7:1, providing enough flexibility to correct N and S deficiencies in crops. Although numerous urea-based fertilizers have been produced in pilot plants, they are not commonly used in North America.

NO_3^- Sources. In addition to NH_4NO_3, sodium nitrate ($NaNO_3$), potassium nitrate (KNO_3), and calcium nitrate $Ca(NO_3)_2$, should be mentioned because of their importance in certain regions. NO_3^- sources are soluble and thus mobile in the soil (Table 4-21). They are quickly available to crops and are susceptible to leaching. Unlike NH_4^+ fertilizers, NO_3^- salts of Na^+, K^+, and Ca^{+2} are not acid forming. Because NO_3^- is often absorbed by crops more rapidly than the accompanying cation, HCO_3^- and organic anions are exuded from roots, resulting in a slightly higher soil solution pH. Prolonged use of $NaNO_3$, for example, will maintain or even raise the original soil pH.

At one time $NaNO_3$ (16% N) was a major source of N in many countries. Most of it originated in large natural deposits in Chile, where $NaNO_3$ production continues to be a major industry.

Potassium nitrate (KNO_3, 13% N) contains two plant nutrients and is a common source in horticultural crops such as tomatoes, potatoes, tobacco, leafy vegetables, citrus fruits, peaches, and other crops. KNO_3 properties that make it attractive include moderate salt index, rapid NO_3^- uptake, favorable N/K_2O ratio, negligible Cl^- content, and alkaline reaction in soil.

Calcium nitrate [$Ca(NO_3)_2 + NH_4NO_3$, 15% N, 19% Ca] is a significant source of Ca and readily available NO_3^-, and is a common fertilizer for winter-season vegetable production and in foliar sprays for celery, tomatoes, and apples. On sodic soils, Ca^{+2} can displace Na^+ on the CEC.

$CaCO_3$-NH_4NO_3 (26% N and 10% Ca) is often referred to as calcium ammonium nitrate (CAN). CAN eliminates potential combustion hazards of NH_4NO_3 and is popular in Europe and South Africa.

Slowly Available N Compounds. Because the crop recovery of soluble fertilizer N is $\approx$ 40 to 60%, development of N fertilizer products that potentially minimize fertilizer N losses through volatilization and leaching have been developed (Table 4-25). N products that reduce the nitrification and volatilization potential release soluble N (NH_4^+ and NO_3^-) over several weeks or months, which increases % fertilizer N recovered by the

Table 4-25 **Slow-Release N Products Used to Reduce Potential N Losses by Volatilization, Leaching, and Denitrification**

N Source	*Base Compound*	*Common Name(s)*	*N Content*	*N Process*	*Inhibition Duration*
			-- % --		*--weeks--*
Nitrapyrin	2-chloro-6(trichloromethyl) pyridine	N- Serve	–	nitrification, denitrification	2–6
DCD	dicyandiamide	Didin, SuperN, UMAXX, UFLEXX	–	nitrification, denitrification	12–14
NBPT	n-butyl-thiophosphoric triamide	Agrotain	–	volatilization	2
S-coated urea	urea	SCU	32–38	volatilization	4–12
Polymer/S coated urea	urea	PolyPlus, Poly-S, Tricote,	32–38	volatilization	6–16
Polymer-or resin-coated urea	urea	Polyon, Osmocote, RLCU, Meister, Agriform, Multicote	38–44	volatilization	
Urea-formaldehyde	ureaforms	Nitroform, UF, Blue Chip, Powder Blue, Methex, FLUF	≥ 35	volatilization, leaching	10–30+
	methylene urea	Nutralene	39–40		7–12
	methylol urea	RESI-GROW, GP-4340	30		6–10
	polymethylene urea	CORON	12 or 28		7–9
Isobutylidene diurea	isobutylidine urea	IBDU	31	volatilization, leaching	10–16
Triazone	triazone/urea	N-Sure	28	volatilization, leaching	6–9
Crotonylidene Diurea	urea/crotonaldehyde	Crotodur, CDU	34	volatilization, leaching	6–12
Melamine	2,4,6 triamino-1,3,5-triazine	Nitrazine	50–60	volatilization, leaching	

plant and reduces N transport to surface and groundwaters, as well as gaseous N loss to the atmosphere. Slow-release N products reduce the need for repeated applications of conventional water-soluble products, and reduce hazards of injury to germinating crops when used at high rates with or near the seed.

The ideal product would be one that releases N in synchrony with crop N (Fig. 4-10) need throughout the growing season. Most materials developed for controlled N-release involve:

- nitrification and urease inhibitors, and
- low water solubility compounds that undergo chemical and/or microbial decomposition to release plant available N.

Most slow-release products are more expensive than water-soluble N fertilizers (Table 4-21); therefore, they are commonly used in horticulture and turfgrass applications.

Nitrification and Urease Inhibitors. Certain compounds are toxic to nitrifying bacteria and will, when added to the soil, temporarily inhibit nitrification. A nitrification inhibitor should (1) be nontoxic to plants, other soil organisms, fish, and mammals; (2) block conversion of NH_4^+ to NO_3^- by inhibiting *Nitrosomonas* activity; (3) not interfere with transformation of NO_2^- to NO_3^- by *Nitrobacter*; (4) be compatable with liquid and dry N sources; (5) maintain inhibition for several weeks to months; and (6) be relatively inexpensive. Nitrification inhibitors can also lower denitrification N losses by reducing the amount of NO_3^- available for denitrification.

N-Serve (nitrapyrin) and DCD (dicyandiamide) are the most common nitrification inhibitors that reduce N losses when conditions are suitable for rapid nitrification to NO_3^- (Table 4-25). If soil and environmental conditions are favorable for NO_3^- losses, treatment with an inhibitor often increases fertilizer N efficiency. Generally, coarse-textured, low-OM soils are responsive to nitrification inhibitors added to N fertilizers (Fig. 4-47); however, crop responses are also possible on poorly drained soils with a high denitrification potential. Although circumstances favoring loss of NO_3^- are generally known, it is difficult to predict when and how much N will be lost. Also, protective action is unlikely when conditions conducive for NO_3^--leaching develop after the inhibitor has degraded. When conditions are optimum, yield responses on corn can be 2 to 20 bu/a.

DCD has been tested as both a nitrification inhibitor and a slow-release N source. DCD is readily soluble and stable in anhydrous NH_3, and nitrification is effectively inhibited for up to 3 months by the addition of 15 kg/ha of DCD. Urea containing 1.4% DCD (by weight) and UAN solution with 0.8% DCD are currently available in North America for increasing the effectiveness of fertilizer N.

Compounds that are effective urease inhibitors should be (1) effective at low concentrations, (2) relatively nontoxic to higher forms of life, (3) inexpensive, (4) compatible with urea, and (5) as mobile in soil as urea. Prospects for improving the effectiveness of urea through urease inhibition do not appear as promising as subsurface band placement; however, broadcast application may be the only option in certain systems (i.e., turf) where urease inhibitors reduce N loss.

The most common urease inhibitor is Agrotain (NBPT). NBPT is used with surface-broadcast applications of urea granules or UAN solution. Yield responses up to 5 to 20 bu/a of corn have been observed (Table 4-26). The higher yield responses occur under conditions of high N volatilization potential (see pp. 137 to 141) and where urea is broadcast in heavy

Table 4-26 **Effect of NBPT on Corn Yield**

N Treatment	*N Rate* 100	150	200
		bu/a	
No N	76	76	76
Urea Broadcast	114	127	143
Urea Broadcast + NBPT	131	142	158
UAN Broadcast	129	151	150
UAN Broadcast + NBPT	144	158	160
UAN Subsurface Band	145	156	157

SOURCE: Mengel, 1989, Purdue Univ. (personal communication)

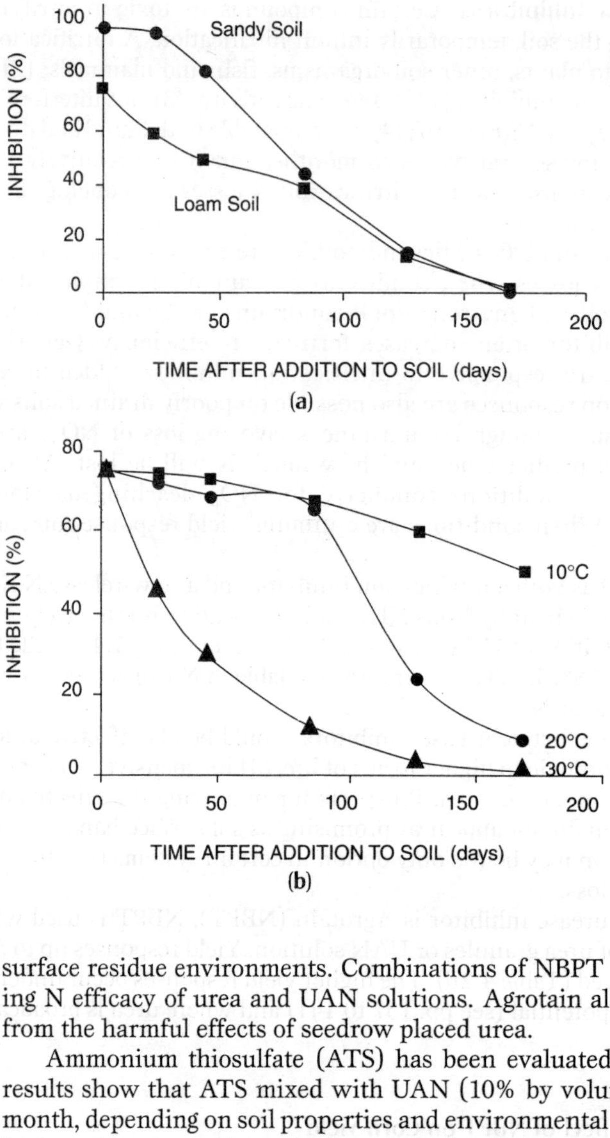

Figure 4-47 **Persistence of nitrapyrin in soil as affected by soil texture (a) and soil temperature (b).** *(McCarty and Bremner, 1990,* **Comm. Soil Sci. Plant Anal.** *21:639–48.)*

surface residue environments. Combinations of NBPT and DCD are available for improving N efficacy of urea and UAN solutions. Agrotain also provides protection to seedlings from the harmful effects of seedrow placed urea.

Ammonium thiosulfate (ATS) has been evaluated as a urease inhibitor. Laboratory results show that ATS mixed with UAN (10% by volume) will inhibit urease for about a month, depending on soil properties and environmental conditions. Results from field studies have been inconsistent in demonstrating increased N fertilizer efficiency with ATS.

Low Water Solubility Compounds Requiring Decomposition. These urea-based fertilizers are only slightly soluble in soil solution, where the rate of N release is related to their water solubility and to the rate of microbial activity and hydrolysis. While representing a small proportion of total fertilizer N use (< 4%), adoption of slow-release N products is increasing due to their potential benefit in reducing N loss to the environment and improving N nutrition in some cropping systems.

Sulfur-coated urea (SCU) is a controlled-release N fertilizer consisting of an S shell around each urea granule with N content of 22 to 38%. Dissolution rate depends on thickness of the S coating. S must be oxidized by soil microorganisms before the urea is exposed and subsequently hydrolyzed. Where cracks and imperfections exist in the S coating, additional coating with wax or polymer sealant can improve control of N release rate (Table 4-26). Soil microbes degrade the sealant to expose the S coating that is degraded through microbial oxidation. Coating degradation rate will increase with soil temperature and moisture, increasing N release.

SCU has the greatest potential for use where multiple applications of soluble N sources are needed during the growing season, particularly on sandy soils under high rainfall or irrigation. It is advantageous for use on sugarcane, pineapple, grass forages, turf, ornamentals, fruits such as cranberries and strawberries, and rice under intermittent or delayed flooding. SCU might also find general use under conditions in which urea decomposition losses are significant. Another advantage of SCU is its plant available S content (12 to 22% S).

Several slow-release N sources are comprised of urea reacted with organic compounds capable of inhibiting microbial activity and hydrolysis of urea to reduce volatilizaiton and nitrification. These products are characterized by their solubility in water given by:

$$\mathrm{AI} = \frac{\%\ \mathrm{CWIN} - \%\ \mathrm{HWIN}}{\%\ \mathrm{CWIN}} \times 100$$

where AI = activity index

% CWIN = % cold water insoluble

% HWIN = % hot water insoluble

Most products exhibit an AI of $\geq 50\%$, where the water insoluble (WIN) component is usually $> 60\%$..

The best-known products in this category are ureaforms made by reacting urea with formaldehyde (Table 4-25). Conversion of ureaformaldehyde and related products to plant available N is a multistep process, involving dissolution and microbial decompositon. Once in the soil solution, products are converted to plant available N through either microbial decomposition or hydrolysis. Microbial decomposition is the primary mechanism of N release with the carbon in the methylene urea polymers providing the site for microbial activity. Environmental factors such as soil temperature, moisture, pH, and aeration affect the rate of N release. Consumption of ureaform is primarily in turfgrass, landscaping, ornamental, horticulture, and greenhouse crops and as an aid in overcoming planting shock of transplanted coniferous seedlings.

Triazone is a controlled-release N compound containing between 28 to 30% N. Because of the closed-ring structure and strong C-N bonds, N is released slowly. Triazone is predominately used as a foliar-applied N source, exhibiting excellent absorption properties with no toxicity to plants.

Polymer-coated fertilizers (PCFs) represent the most technically advanced state of the art in terms of controlling product longevity and improving nutrient efficiency (Table 4-25). Because most polymer-coated products release by diffusion through a semipermeable membrane, the rate of release can be altered by composition of the coating and the coating thickness. In recent research, the fertilizer N source being coated has also been shown to influence the rate of N release. Polymer coatings can be categorized as either thermoset resins or thermoplastic resins. Because of the relatively high cost of the coatings on most polymer-coated products, their use has been restricted mostly to high-value applications.

Study Questions

1. Describe the major functions of N in plants and how they might relate to distinctive visual deficiency symptoms.
2. Do crops utilize both NH_4^+ and NO_3^-? Which is the preferred form of N? Does the stage of growth influence crop uptake of either NH_4^+ or NO_3^-?
3. Identify an important soil property that can be altered by uptake of NH_4^+ or NO_3^-.
4. How is atmospheric N made usable to higher plants (exclude synthetic N fixation)?
5. What are the various microorganisms responsible for N fixation?
6. What soil property can exercise considerable influence on the survival and growth of *Rhizobia* in soil? Describe at least two practical ways of improving the effectiveness of growth and performance of *Rhizobia*.
7. Describe how to distinguish between effective and noneffective nodules on legume roots. Describe the location and appearance of effective nodules.
8. Define ammonification and nitrification. What factors affect these reactions in soils?
9. Why does intensive cultivation of land lead to a rapid decomposition of OM? How does this influence N availability in both the short- and long-term?
10. What is the difference between N fixation and nitrification?
11. Nitrification is a two-step reaction. What are the two steps and what organisms are responsible for each? Why is nitrification important and this phenomenon a mixed blessing?
12. If leaching losses of N are to be minimized after fall application of NH_4-N, soil temperatures during winter months should not rise above what point? As a general rule, is fall application of NO_3^- fertilizers to a spring planted crop a sound practice? Why or why not?
13. What is NH_4^+ fixation? What are the soil conditions under which it occurs? How important is NH_4^+ fixation to N availability?
14. Barley straw was incorporated a week before planting fall wheat. At planting, you applied 20 lbs N/a, 10 lbs P/a, and 30 lbs K/a fertilizer. The wheat germinates and turns yellow. Tests show low NO_3^- in the tissue. What is wrong with the wheat? What would you advise?
15. In what forms may N gas be lost from soil? Discuss the conditions under which each form is lost, and write the reactions involved. Can there be large losses of N gases from soil? How would you prevent or minimize the various gaseous losses of N?
16. Classify the various forms of N fertilizers. What are the most important sources of N?
17. What developments have resulted in the great increase in urea use?
18. List changes in soil properties influenced in the injection zone of anhydrous NH_3.
19. What conditions favor NO_2^- accumulation? Describe the harmful effects of NO_2^- on crops.
20. Ammonium volatilization of urea in soils can be an important N loss mechanism. The reaction is: $NH_2\text{-}C\text{-}NH_2 + 2H_2O \rightarrow (NH_4)_2CO_3 \rightarrow 2NH_3 + H_2O + CO_2$
    a. Volatilization losses of urea fertilizer applied to the soil can occur if not properly managed. List the factors/conditions that would maximize the potential for NH_3 volatilization.
    b. What urea management recommendations would you make to minimize NH_3 volatilization.
    c. What other source of urea (besides urea fertilizer) is subject to volatilization?

21. What is urease and why is it important? How do urease inhibitors reduce N loss?

22. What are the important factors governing the selection of fertilizer N source?

23. Why does NH_4-N have an acidifying effect on the soil?

24. Describe the conditions in which nitrification inhibitors have the greatest potential for increasing the efficiency of N fertilizer management.

25. A crop consultant recommends 80 lbs N/a to a sorghum crop in a soybean-sorghum rotation. The following data are available:

Previous Soybean Crop	Sorghum Crop	Soil Data
30 bu/a grain yield	100 bu/a yield goal	2% OM
40 lbs residue/bu	56 lbs/bu test weight	1% OM degradation rate
40% residue C	75 lbs residue/bu	20 lbs/a profile N content
30:1 C:N ratio	1.8% grain N	30 lbs N/a soybean credit
	0.6% residue N	

Is the recommendation accurate? Show all work.

26. A turf specialist annually applies 100 lbs N/a as $(NH_4)_2SO_4$ to turfgrass. Initial soil pH was 6.8 and the CEC = 14 meq/100 g. After 20 years would the soil pH drop below 6.8 if 2 ton/a $CaCO_3$ were applied every 4 years? If so, by how much?

27. A soil contains 1.5% OM with an annual decomposition rate of 1%. The farmer wanted to increase OM to 2%. How many years will it take if he produces 8,000 lbs/yr crop residue (80:1 C:N; 40% C; 80% of residue N used to make OM)?

Selected References

Barber, S. A. 1984. *Soil nutrient bioavailability: A mechanistic approach*. New York: John Wiley & Sons.

Boswell, F. C., J. J. Meisinger, and N. L. Case. 1985. Production, marketing, and use of nitrogen fertilizers (pp. 229–292). In O. P. Engelstad (Ed.), *Fertilizer technology and use*. Madison, Wis.: Soil Science Society of America.

Follett, R. F. (Ed.). 1989. Nitrogen management and groundwater protection. In *Developments in agricultural managed-forest ecology #21*. New York: Elsevier.

Follett, R. H., L. S. Murphy, and R. L. Donahue. 1981. *Fertilizers and soil amendments*. Englewood Cliffs, N.J.: Prentice-Hall.

Hauck, R. D. 1984. *Nitrogen in crop production*. American Society of Agronomy, Madison, Wis.

Hauck, R. D. 1985. Slow-release and bioinhibitor-amended nitrogen fertilizers (pp. 293–322). In O. P. Engelstad (Ed.), *Fertilizer technology and use*. Madison, Wis.: Soil Science Society of America.

Power, J. F., and R. I. Papendick. 1985. Organic sources of nitrogen (pp. 503–520). In O. P. Engelstad (Ed.), *Fertilizer technology and use*. Madison, Wis.: Soil Science Society of America.

Stevenson, F. J. (Ed.). 1982. *Nitrogen in agricultural soils*. Madison, Wis.: American Society of Agronomy.

Stevenson, F. J. 1986. *Cycles of soil*. New York: John Wiley & Sons.

CHAPTER 5

Phosphorus

Phosphorus (P) is less abundant in soils than N and K. Total P in surface soils varies from 0.005 to 0.15%. The average total P content of soils is lower in the humid Southeast than in the Prairie Provinces and Western states. Unfortunately, the quantity of total P in soils has little or no relationship to the availability of P to plants. Although prairie soils are often high in total P, many of them are characteristically low in plant available P. Therefore, understanding the relationships and interactions of the various forms of P in soils and the numerous factors that influence P availability is essential to efficient P management.

The P Cycle

Figure 5-1 illustrates the relationships between the various P forms in soils. The decrease in soil solution P with absorption by plant roots is buffered by both inorganic and organic P fractions in soils. Primary and secondary P minerals dissolve to resupply $H_2PO_4^-$ and HPO_4^{-2} in solution. Inorganic P adsorbed on mineral and clay surfaces as $H_2PO_4^-$ and HPO_4^{-2} (labile inorganic P) can also desorb to buffer solution P. Soil microorganisms digest plant residues containing P and produce organic P compounds that are mineralized through microbial activity to supply solution P.

Water-soluble fertilizer P applied to soil readily dissolves and increases P in soil solution. In addition to P uptake by roots, inorganic and organic P fractions buffer the increase in solution P through P adsorption on mineral surfaces, precipitation as secondary P minerals, and immobilization as microbial or organic P. Maintaining solution P concentration (*intensity*) for adequate P nutrition depends on the ability of labile P (*quantity*) to replace soil solution P taken up by the plant. The ratio of *quantity* to *intensity* factors defines buffer capacity (BC) or the relative ability of the soil to buffer changes in soil solution P (Chapter 2). The larger the BC, the greater the ability to buffer solution P. The P cycle can be simplified to the following relationship:

$$\text{Soil solution P} \leftrightarrows \text{labile P} \leftrightarrows \text{nonlabile P}$$

where labile and nonlabile P represent both inorganic and organic fractions (Fig. 5-1). Labile P is the readily available portion of the quantity factor that exhibits a high dissoci-

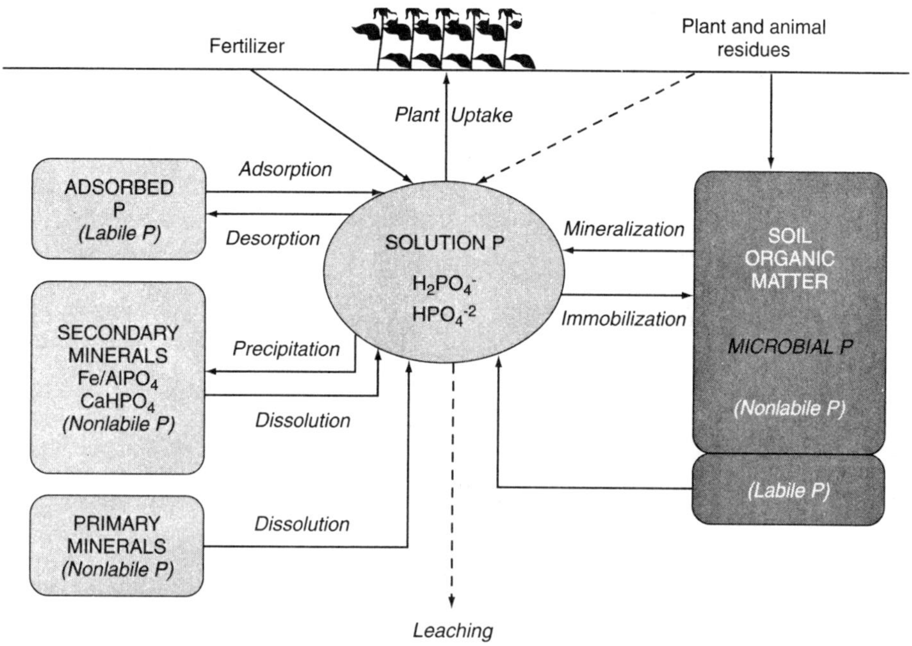

Figure 5-1 P cycle in soil.

ation rate and rapidly replenishes solution P. Depletion of labile P causes some nonlabile P to become labile, but at a slow rate. Thus, the quantity factor comprises both labile and nonlabile P fractions. Understanding the dynamics of P transformations in soils will provide the basis for sound management of soil and fertilizer P to ensure adequate P availability to plants.

Forms and Functions of P in Plants

Forms

P concentration in plants ranges between 0.1 and 0.5%, considerably lower than N and K. Plants absorb either H_2PO_4 or HPO_4^{-2} (orthophosphate) depending on soil pH (see p. 166). Plants also absorb soluble, low-molecular weight organic P compounds (i.e., nucleic acid and phytin) that are products of soil OM decomposition. Because of the instability of many organic P compounds in the presence of active microbes, their importance as sources of P for higher plants is limited.

Functions

Like N, P is involved in many vital plant growth processes.The most essential function is in energy storage and transfer. Adenosine di- and triphosphates (ADP and ATP) act as "energy

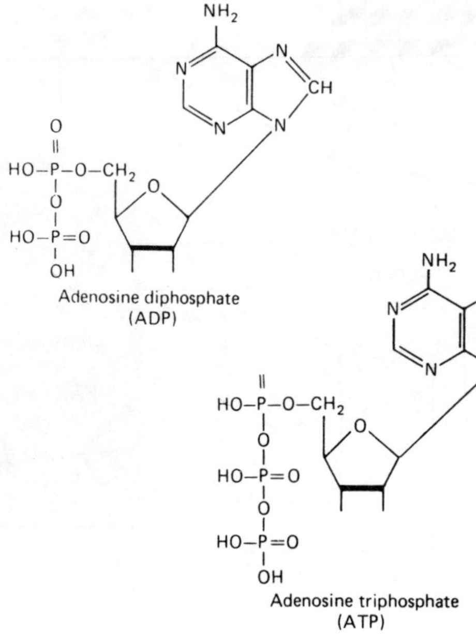

Figure 5-2 Structure of ADP and ATP.

currency" within plants (Fig. 5-2). When the terminal $H_2PO_4^-$ phosphate molecule from either ADP or ATP is split off, a large amount of chemical energy (12,000 cal/mol) is liberated. Energy obtained from photosynthesis and metabolism of carbohydrates is stored in phosphate compounds for subsequent use in growth and reproductive processes. Transfer of the energy-rich $H_2PO_4^-$ molecules from ATP to energy-requiring substances in the plant is known as phosphorylation. In this reaction ATP is converted to ADP. ADP and ATP are formed and regenerated in the presence of sufficient P. Almost every metabolic reaction of any significance involves $H_2PO_4^-$ derivatives (Table 5-1). As a result, P deficiency is associated with restricted growth and development.

P is an essential element in deoxyribonucleic acid (DNA) and ribonucleic acid (RNA) that contain the genetic code of the plant to produce proteins and other compounds essential for plant structure, seed yield, and genetic transfer. Phospholipids, phosphoproteins, coenzymes, and nucleotides are important structural components of membrane chemistry and related functions. Thus, P is essential for vigorous growth and development of reproductive parts (fruits, seeds, etc.).

Adequate P is associated with increased root growth. When soluble $H_2PO_4^-$ is applied in a band, plant roots proliferate extensively in P-treated soil. Similar observations are made

Table 5-1 **Processes and Functions of ADP and ATP in Plants**

Membrane transport	Generation of membrane electrical potentials
Cytoplasmic streaming	Respiration
Photosynthesis	Biosynthesis of cellulose, pectins, hemicellulose, and lignin
Protein biosynthesis	Lipid biosynthesis
Phospholipid biosynthesis	Isoprenoid biosynthesis → steroids and gibberellins
Nucleic acid synthesis	

with both NO_3^- and NH_4^+ applied in a band near roots (Fig. 5-3). The increased root proliferation should encourage extensive exploitation of the treated soil areas for nutrients and water. P also enhances crop maturity, particularly in grain crops, and reduces the time required for grain ripening (Fig. 5-4).

Adequate P increases straw strength in cereals and increases N_2-fixation capacity of legumes. The quality of certain fruit, forage, vegetable, and grain crops is improved and disease resistance enhanced under adequate P availability. The effect of P on raising the tolerance of small grains to root-rot diseases is particularly noteworthy. Also, the risk of winter damage to small grains can be decreased with sufficient P, particularly on low-P soils and with unfavorable growing conditions.

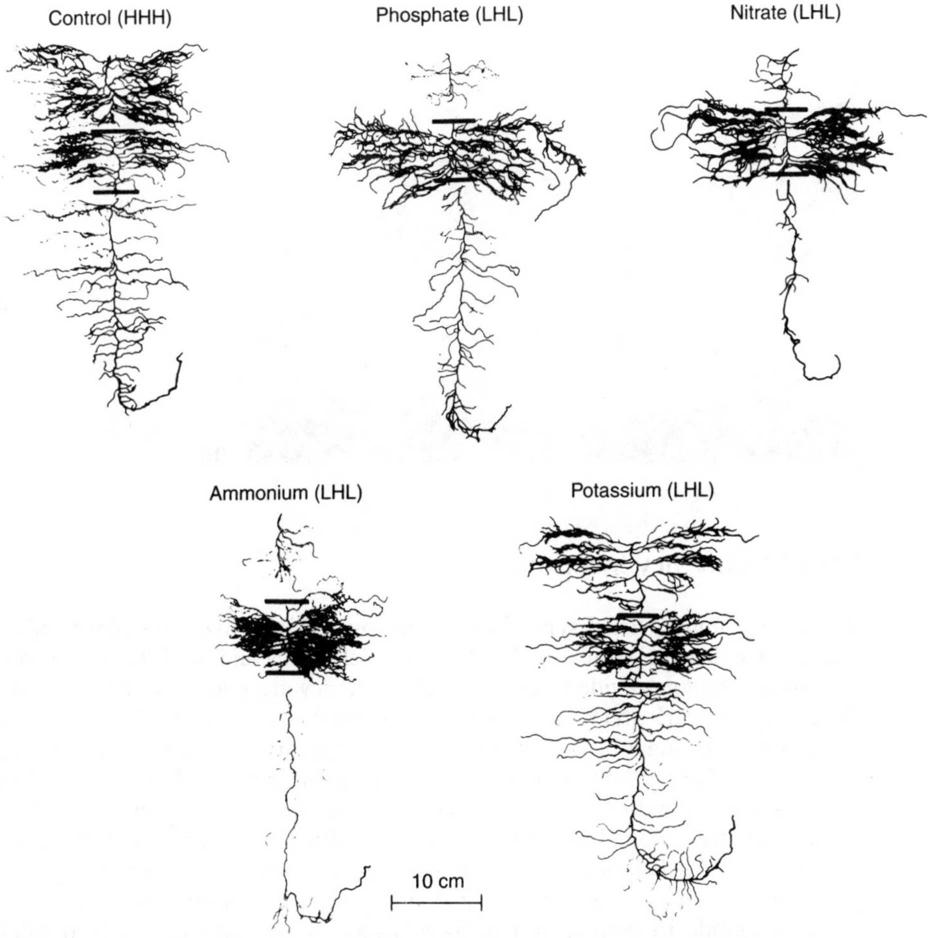

Figure 5-3 **Effect of a localized supply of phosphate, nitrate, ammonium, and potassium on root form. Control plants (HHH) received the complete nutrient solution to all parts of the root system. The other roots (LHL) received the complete nutrient solution only in the middle zone, the top and bottom being supplied with a solution deficient in the specified nutrient.** ***(Drew, 1975,*** **New Phytol.,** ***75:486.)***

(a)

(b)

Figure 5-4 Effect of P fertilization on grain sorghum (a) and winter wheat (b) maturity. Notice the advanced maturity of both crops receiving the P (left) in contrast to those that received no P (right).

Visual Deficiency Symptoms

The most common visual symptoms include overall stunting of the plant and a darker green coloration of leaves. Because of the effect of P deficiency on retarding overall growth, the obvious foliar symptoms evident with N or K deficiency are seldom observed. With increasing P deficiency, the dark green color changes to a grayish-green to bluish-green metallic lustre. In some crops (i.e., sugar beets), dark green leaves appear in the early seedling stage, developing to brown, netted veining in older leaves as the plant matures. Purple leaf coloration is commonly associated with P deficiency in corn and other grasses. Symptoms appear on lower leaf tips and progress along leaf margins until the entire leaf is purple. Lower leaves are necrotic under severe P deficiency. The purple color is due to accumulation of sugars that enhances synthesis of anthocyanin (a purple pigment) in the leaf (see color plates).

P is mobile in plants, and is translocated from older to newly developing tissues. Consequently, early growth stage responses to P are common. In the reproductive stage, P is translocated to fruit and seeds. Thus, P deficiencies late in the growing season affect both seed development and crop maturity.

P-deficiency symptoms can appear in P-sensitive crops emerging under cool, wet conditions, even in soils with sufficient plant available P. Reduced P diffusion in cool soils combined with small root systems in young plants causes the P-deficiency systems. Increasing soil temperature and expanding root growth usually corrects the P deficiency. When this condition is anticipated, starter P applications can prevent early season P deficiency (Chapter 10).

Forms of Soil P

Solution P

The amount of $H_2PO_4^-$ and HPO_4^{-2} present in solution depends on soil pH (Fig. 5-5). At pH 7.2, $H_2PO_4^- \approx HPO_4^{-2}$. Below this pH, $H_2PO_4^- > HPO_4^{-2}$, whereas $HPO_4^{-2} > H_2PO_4^-$ above pH 7.2. Plant uptake of HPO_4^{-2} is much slower than with $H_2PO_4^-$. Average soil solution P concentration is ~0.05 ppm and varies widely among soils. Soil solution P concentration required by most plants varies from 0.003 to 0.3 ppm and depends on the crop species and level of production (Table 5-2). Maximum corn grain yields may be obtained with 0.01 ppm P if yield potential is low, but 0.05 ppm P is needed with high-yield potential (Figure 5-6).

The actively absorbing surface of plant roots is the young tissue near the root tips. Relatively high concentrations of P accumulate in root tips, followed by a zone of lesser accumulation, where cells are elongating, and then by a second region of higher concentration, where the root hairs are developed. Rapid replenishment of solution P is important where roots are actively absorbing P.

As roots absorb P from soil solution, diffusion and mass flow transport additional P to the root surface (Chapter 2). Mass flow in low-P soils provides only a small portion of the requirement. For example, assume a transpiration ratio[1] of 400 and 0.2% P in the crop. If the average solution concentration is 0.05 ppm P, then the quantity of P moving to the plant by mass flow is:

$$\frac{400 \text{ g } H_2O}{\text{g plant}} \times \frac{100 \text{ g plant}}{0.2 \text{ g P}} \times \frac{0.05 \text{ g P}}{10^{-6} \text{ g } H_2O} \times 100 = 1\%$$

In fertilized soil with a solution concentration of 1 ppm P, mass flow contributes 20% of the total requirement. The very high P concentrations that exist temporarily in and near fertilizer bands are expected to encourage further P uptake by mass flow, as well as P diffusion. For example, P concentrations between 2 and 14 ppm occur in soil-fertilizer reaction zones. Since mass flow contributes $<$ 20% of P delivered to the root surface, P diffusion is the primary mechanism of P transport especially in low-P soils (Chapter 2).

Inorganic Soil P

As organic P is mineralized to inorganic P or as P is added to soil, inorganic P in solution not absorbed by roots or immobilized by microorganisms can be *adsorbed* to mineral surfaces (labile P) or *precipitated* as secondary P compounds (Fig. 5-1). Surface adsorption and precipitation reactions are collectively called P *fixation* or retention. The extent of

[1]Transpiration ratio = weight of H_2O transpired per unit plant weight.

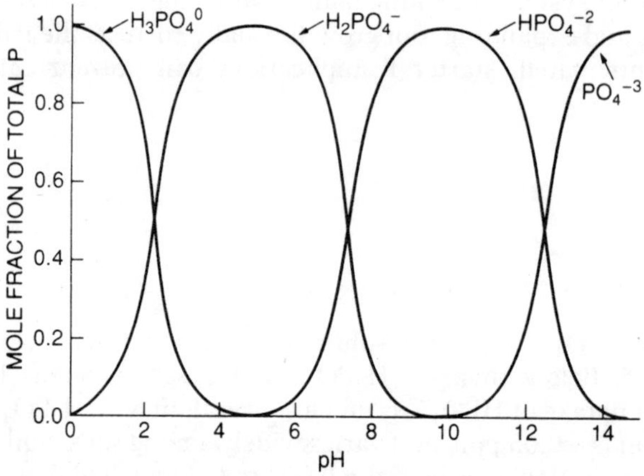

Figure 5-5 **Influence of pH on the distribution of orthophosphate species in solution.**

Table 5-2 **Estimated Soil Solution P Concentration Associated with 75 and 95% of Maximum Yield of Selected Crops**

	Approximate Soil Solution P (ppm) for Two Yield Levels	
Crop	*75 % Maximum Yield*	*95 % Maximum Yield*
Cassava	0.003	0.005
Peanuts	0.003	0.01
Corn	0.008	0.025
Wheat	0.009	0.028
Cabbage	0.012	0.04
Potatoes	0.02	0.18
Soybeans	0.025	0.20
Tomatoes	0.05	0.20
Head lettuce	0.10	0.30

SOURCE: Fox, 1982, *Better Crops Plant Food*, 66:24.

inorganic P fixation depends on many factors, most importantly soil pH (Fig. 5-7). In acid soils, inorganic P precipitates as Fe/Al-P secondary minerals and/or is adsorbed to surfaces of Fe/Al oxide and clay minerals. In neutral and calcareous soils, inorganic P precipitates as secondary minerals of Ca-P and Mg-P in high-Mg soils and/or is adsorbed to surfaces of clay minerals and $CaCO_3$.

P retention is a continuous sequence of precipitation and adsorption. With low-solution P concentrations, adsorption dominates, while precipitation reactions proceed when solution P exceeds the solubility product (K_{sp}) of the specific P-containing mineral (Chapter 2). Where water-soluble fertilizers are applied, soil solution P concentration increases greatly depending on P rate and method of application (band vs. broadcast). Both adsorption and precipitation reactions proceed, to some extent, immediately following fertilizer P addition. P precipitation reactions occur as solution P exceeds a specific mineral solubility, while adsorption occurs when adsorption capacity is not saturated with P. Regardless of the contributions of adsorption and precipitation, understanding P-fixation processes is important for optimum P nutrition and efficient fertilizer P management.

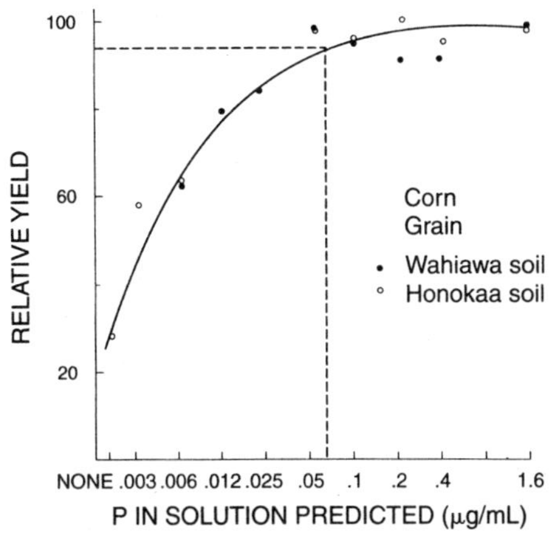

Figure 5-6 **Influence of inorganic P in soil solution on corn grain yield.** ***(Fox, 1981,*** **Chemistry in the Soil Environment,** ***p. 232, ASA, 1981.)***

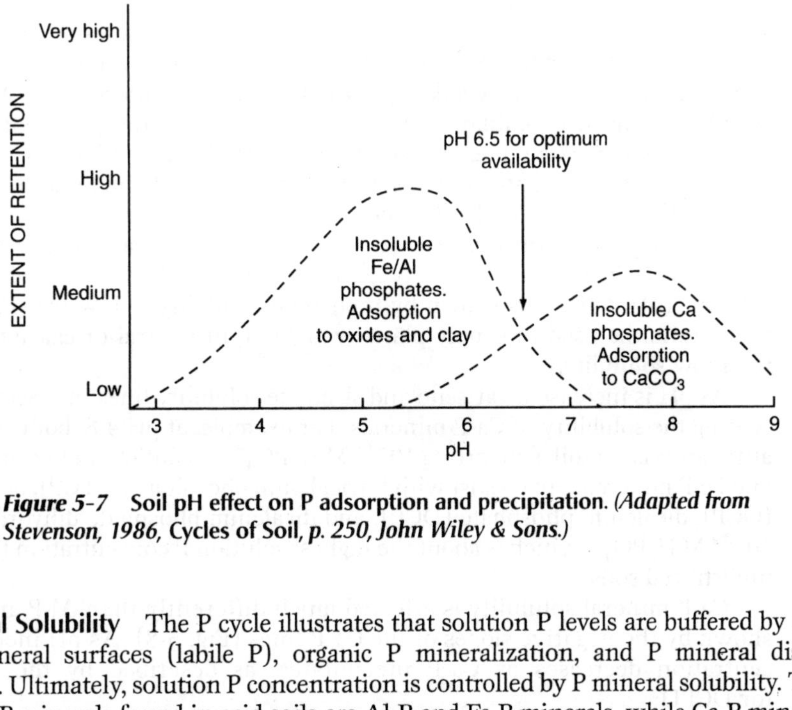

Figure 5-7 **Soil pH effect on P adsorption and precipitation.** ***(Adapted from Stevenson, 1986,*** **Cycles of Soil,** ***p. 250, John Wiley & Sons.)***

P Mineral Solubility The P cycle illustrates that solution P levels are buffered by adsorbed P on mineral surfaces (labile P), organic P mineralization, and P mineral dissolution (Fig. 5-1). Ultimately, solution P concentration is controlled by P mineral solubility. The most common P minerals found in acid soils are Al-P and Fe-P minerals, while Ca-P minerals predominate in neutral and calcareous soils (Table 5-3). Mineral solubility represents the ion concentration maintained in the soil solution by a specific mineral. Each P mineral will support specific ion concentrations that depend on the solubility product (K_{sp}) of the mineral. For example, $FePO_4 \cdot 2H_2O$ will dissolve according to:

$$FePO_4 \cdot 2H_2O + H_2O \leftrightarrows H_2PO_4^- + H^+ + Fe(OH)_3 \qquad (1)$$

As $H_2PO_4^-$ decreases with P uptake, strengite dissolves to resupply or maintain solution $H_2PO_4^-$ concentration. This reaction also shows that as H^+ increases (decreasing pH),

Table 5-3 **Common P Minerals Found in Acid, Neutral, and Calcareous Soils**

*Acid soils**	
Variscite	$AlPO_4 \cdot 2H_2O$
Strengite	$FePO_4 \cdot 2H_2O$
Neutral and calcareous soils	
Dicalcium phosphate dihydrate (DCPD)	$CaHPO_4 \cdot 2H_2O$
Dicalcium phosphate (DCP)	$CaHPO_4$
Octacalcium phosphate (OCP)	$Ca_4H(PO_4)_3 \cdot 2.5H_2O$
b-tricalcium phosphate (b-TCP)	$Ca_3(PO_4)_2$
Hydroxyapatite (HA)	$Ca_5(PO_4)_3OH$
Fluorapatite (FA)	$Ca_5(PO_4)_3F$

*Minerals are listed in order of decreasing solubility.

$H_2PO_4^-$ decreases. Therefore, specific P minerals present in soil and the concentration of solution P supported by these minerals are dependent on solution pH.

The relationship between the solubility of the common P minerals and solution pH is shown in Figure 5-8. The y-axis represents the concentration of $H_2PO_4^-$ or HPO_4^{-2} in soil. $H_2PO_4^-$ is the predominant ion < pH 7.2, while HPO_4^{-2} predominates > pH 7.2 (Fig. 5-5). The x-axis represents solution pH. At pH 4.5, $AlPO_4 \cdot 2H_2O$ and $FePO_4 \cdot 2H_2O$ control $H_2PO_4^-$ concentration in solution. Increasing pH increases $H_2PO_4^-$ concentration because the Al-P and/or Fe-P minerals dissolve according to equation 1, which is also depicted in the diagram as a positive slope. Increasing P availability is often observed when acid soils are limed. Also, hydroxyapatite or fluorapatite can be used as a fertilizer in low pH soils (pH < 4.5), as shown by their high solubility at low pH (Fig. 5-8). In contrast, they cannot be used to supply plant available P in neutral or calcareous soils because of their low solubility.

As pH is increased, variscite and strengite solubility lines intersect several lines, representing the solubility of Ca-P minerals. For example, at pH 4.8, both strengite and fluorapatite can exist in soil, supporting $10^{-4.5}$ M $H_2PO_4^-$ in solution. Between pH 6.0 and 6.5, Al-P and Fe-P minerals can coexist with b-tricalcium phosphate (b-TCP), octacalcium phosphate (OCP), dicalcium phosphate (DCP), and dicalcium phosphate dihydrate (DCPD) at about $10^{-3.2}$ M $H_2PO_4^-$, which is about the highest solution P concentration that can exist in most unfertilized soils.

Ca-P mineral solubility is affected much differently than Al-P and Fe-P minerals, as shown by the negative slopes of the Ca-P lines (Fig. 5-8). As pH increases, $H_2PO_4^-$ concentration decreases as Ca-P precipitates, as described by the following equation for DCPD:

$$CaHPO_4 \cdot 2H_2O + H^+ \leftrightarrows Ca^{+2} + H_2PO_4^- + 2H_2O \tag{2}$$

For example, assume that a soil contains b-TCP at pH 7.0. If pH decreases, $H_2PO_4^-$ increases until ≈ pH 6.0 as b-TCP dissolves. If pH < 6.0, strengite and/or variscite will precipitate and decrease $H_2PO_4^-$. The Ca-P lines (Fig. 5-8) change slopes at > pH 7.2 because $H_2PO_4^-$ predominates in solution compared with HPO_4^{-2}. The solubility lines represent only HPO_4^{-2} at > pH 7.2. Above pH 7.8, Ca-P solubility lines exhibit a positive slope, which means that

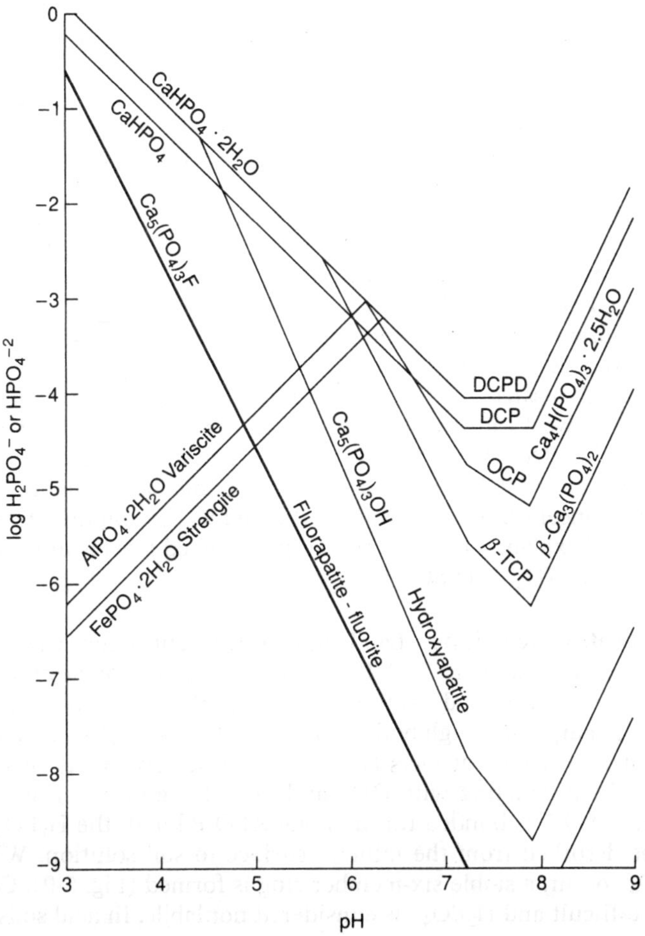

Figure 5-8 **Solubility of Ca, Al, and Fe phosphate minerals in soils. *(Lindsay, 1979,* Chemical Equilibria in Soils, *Wiley Interscience, p.181.)***

as pH increases above 7.8, HPO_4^{-2} concentration increases. The change in solubility is due to the competing reaction of $CaCO_3$ solubility given by

$$CaHPO_4 \cdot 2H_2O + H^+ \leftrightarrows Ca^{+2} + H_2PO_4^- + 2H_2O \quad (3)$$

$$Ca^{+2} + CO_2 + H_2O \leftrightarrows CaCO_3 + 2H^+$$

$$CaHPO_4 \cdot 2H_2O + CO_2 \leftrightarrows Ca^{+2} + H_2PO_4^- + H^+ + H_2O + CaCO_3 \quad (4)$$

$CaCO_3$ precipitation occurs at pH 7.8 and above. As solution Ca^{+2} decreases with $CaCO_3$ precipitation in soils (Eq. 3), DCPD will dissolve (Eq. 2) to resupply solution Ca^{+2}. When DCPD dissolves, $H_2PO_4^-$ increases (Eq. 4), which is the sum of Equations 2 and 3. All Ca-P minerals (Table 5-3) behave similarly in calcareous soils. Even though these P-solubility relationships show solution P concentration increasing above pH 7.8, P availability to plants actually decreases. $H_2PO_4^-$ released to solution by dissolution of Ca-P minerals will adsorb to the precipitating $CaCO_3$.

P minerals that support the lowest P concentration (lowest P solubility) are the most stable in soils. For example, apatite minerals (TCP and OCP) are more stable than DCPD in slightly acid and neutral soils. Therefore, the P mineral-solubility relationships (Fig. 5-8) can be used to understand the fate of inorganic P applied to soils (see pp. 189–194).

An important fertilizer P source is monocalcium phosphate [MCP, $Ca(H_2PO_4)_2$], which is very soluble in soil. When MCP dissolves, $H_2PO_4^-$ concentration is much higher than P concentrations supported by native P minerals (Fig. 5-8). Because soil P minerals have lower solubility, $H_2PO_4^-$ from fertilizer will likely precipitate as these minerals. For example, in an acid soil, fertilizer $H_2PO_4^-$ reacts with solution Al^{+3} and Fe^{+3} to form $AlPO_4$ and $FePO_4$ compounds, respectively. As a result, solution $H_2PO_4^-$ decreases once the precipitation reactions begin. In neutral and calcareous soils, fertilizer $H_2PO_4^-$ initially precipitates as DCDP and DCP within the first few weeks after application. After 3 to 5 months, OCP begins to precipitate, with b-TCP forming after 8 to 10 months. After long periods of time, apatite minerals eventually form.

Thus, after MCP is applied to soil, reactions occur that decrease the elevated solution $H_2PO_4^-$ concentration as insoluble P minerals precipitate. These reactions cannot be controlled and explain why plant recovery of applied P is lower than recovery of soluble nutrients such as NO_3^- and SO_4^{-2}.

P Adsorption Reactions Labile inorganic P represents $H_2PO_4^-$ and/or HPO_4^{-2} adsorbed to mineral surfaces (Fig. 5-1). In acid soils, Al and Fe oxide and hydroxide minerals are primarily involved in P adsorption. Because of the acidic solution, the mineral surface has a net (+) charge, although both (+) and (−) sites exist (Chapter 3). The predominance of (+) charges readily attracts $H_2PO_4^-$ and other anions. P ions adsorb to the Fe/Al oxide surface by interacting with OH^- and/or OH_2^+ groups on the mineral surface (Fig. 5-9). When $H_2PO_4^-$ is bonded through one Al-O-P bond, the $H_2PO_4^-$ is considered labile and can be desorbed from the mineral surface to soil solution. When two Al-O bonds with $H_2PO_4^-$ occur, a stable six-member ring is formed (Fig. 5-9). Consequently, desorption is more difficult and $H_2PO_4^-$ is considered nonlabile. In acid soils, P adsorption also readily

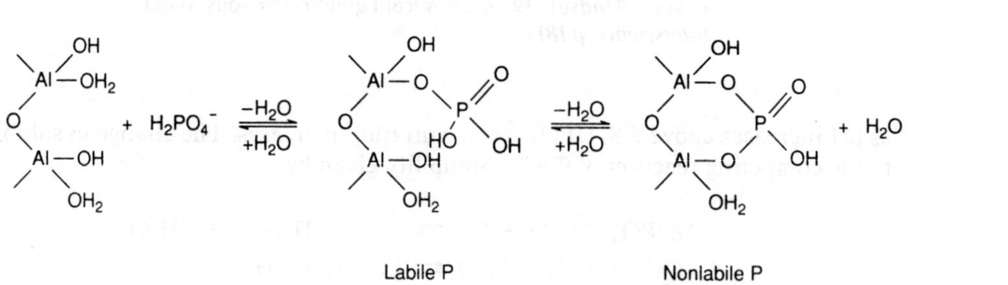

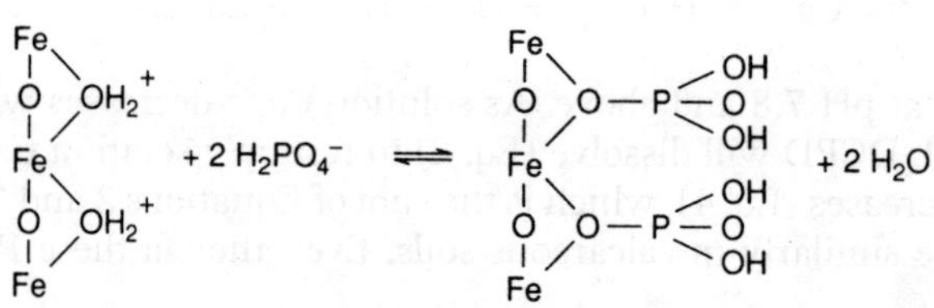

Figure 5-9 **Mechanism of P adsorption to Al/Fe oxide surface. Phosphate bonding through one Al-O bond results in labile P; however, bonding through two Fe-O or Al-O bonds produces a stable structure that results in very little desorption of P.**

occurs on the broken edges of kaolinite clay minerals (Fig. 2-7). Again, exposed OH^- groups can exchange for $H_2PO_4^-$ similarly to surface exchange with Fe/Al oxides. Cations held to the surface of silicate clay minerals also influence P adsorption by developing a small (+) charge near the mineral surface saturated with cations. This small (+) charge attracts small quantities of anions such as $H_2PO_4^-$. As discussed earlier, precipitation of Al-P minerals in acid soils and Ca-P minerals in neutral and calcareous soils occurs at high P concentrations.

In calcareous soils, small quantities of P can be adsorbed through replacement of CO_3^{-2} on the $CaCO_3$ surfaces. At low P concentrations, surface adsorption predominates; however, at high P concentrations, Ca-P minerals precipitate on the $CaCO_3$ surface. Other minerals, mostly $Al(OH)_3$ and $Fe(OH)_3$, contribute to adsorption of solution P in calcareous soils.

Adsorption Equations. The Freundlich and Langmuir equations have been used to describe P adsorption in soils. These equations are helpful for understanding the relationship between the quantity of P adsorbed per unit soil weight and the concentration of P in solution. Adsorption equations have the general form:

$$q = f(c)$$

where q is the quantity of P adsorbed and is a function (f) of the solution P concentration (c).

The Freundlich equation is represented by:

$$q = ac^b$$

where a and b are coefficients that vary among soils, and q and c are the same as previously defined. This equation does not predict or include a maximum adsorption capacity and therefore is most reliable with low solution P concentrations (Fig. 5-10). According to the Freundlich equation, P adsorption decreases with increasing P concentration. Since P adsorption data exhibit a maximum P adsorption capacity at some solution P concentration, another equation is needed to describe situations in which the adsorption sites

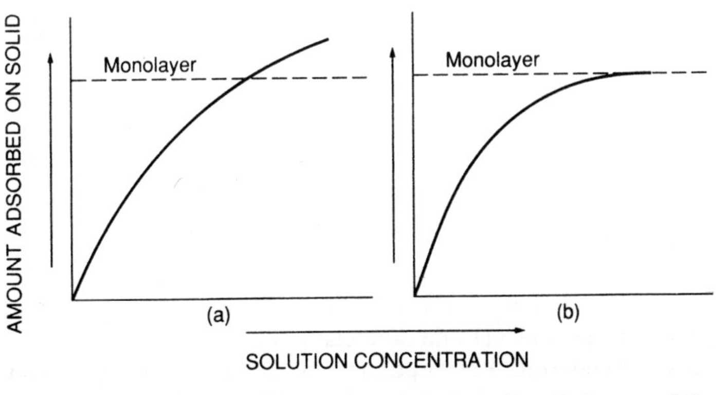

Figure 5-10 **Graphical representation of adsorption isotherms of the Freundlich (a) and Langmuir (b) equations used to describe P adsorption in soils.**

are saturated with P. The Langmuir equation includes a term for the maximum P adsorption described by:

$$q = \frac{abc}{1 + ac}$$

where q, c, and a are defined as before and b is the P adsorption maximum (Fig. 5-10). The P adsorption maximum in the Langmuir equation implies that a monolayer of P ions is adsorbed on the surface of the mineral, which occurs at relatively higher solution P concentrations than described by the Freundlich equation. The equation also shows that further increases in solution P concentration do not increase P adsorption. Although this does not occur with all soils, the Langmuir equation frequently has been used to quantify P adsorption.

Adsorption equations provide no information about adsorption mechanisms. They are incapable of showing whether Fe/Al oxides, silicate clays, or $CaCO_3$ dominate adsorption reactions. P adsorption is extremely slow, decreasing with time. In general, desorption appears to become very slow after about 2 days. The extent of desorption depends on the nature of the adsorption complex at the surface of the Fe/Al oxides. Formation of ring structures limits P adsorption (Figure 5-9).

Factors Influencing P Fixation in Soils Many physical and chemical properties of soil influence P solubility and adsorption reactions in soils. Consequently, these soil properties also affect solution P concentration, P availability to plants, and fertilizer P recovery by crops.

Soil Minerals. Adsorption and desorption reactions are affected by the type of mineral surfaces in contact with solution. Fe/Al oxides are abundant in acid soils and have the capacity to adsorb large amounts of solution P. Fe/Al oxides occur as discrete particles in soils or as coatings or films on other soil particles. They also exist as amorphous Al hydroxy compounds between the layers of expandable Al silicates. In soils with significant Fe/Al oxide contents, the less crystalline or the more amorphous the oxides, the larger their P-fixation capacity because of greater surface area.

P is adsorbed to a greater extent by 1:1 clays (e.g., kaolinite) than by 2:1 clays (e.g., montmorillonite) because of the higher amounts of Fe/Al oxides associated with kaolinitic clays that predominate in highly weathered soils. Kaolinite has a larger number of exposed OH groups in the Al layer that can exchange with P. In addition, kaolinite develops pH-dependent charges on its edges that can adsorb P (Fig. 2-7).

Figure 5-11 shows the influence of clay mineralogy on P adsorption. First, compare the three soils with > 70% clay content. Compared with the Oxisol and Andept soils, very little P adsorption occurred in the Mollisol, composed mainly of montmorillonite, with only small amounts of kaolinite and Fe/Al oxides. The Oxisol soils contained Fe/Al oxides and exhibited considerably more P adsorption capacity compared with the Mollisol soils. Greatest P adsorption occurred with the Andept soils, composed principally of Fe/Al oxides and other minerals.

Soils containing large quantities of clay will fix more P than soils with low clay content (Fig. 5-11). In other words, the more surface area exposed with a given type of clay, the greater the tendency to adsorb P. For example, compare the three Ultisol soils with 6, 10, and 38% clay. A similar relationship is evident in the Oxisol soils (36, 45, and 70% clay) and the Andept soils (11 and 70% clay).

In calcareous soils, P adsorption to $CaCO_3$ surfaces occurs; however, much of the adsorption is attributed to Fe oxide impurities. The amount and reactivity of $CaCO_3$ will influence P fixation. Impure $CaCO_3$ with large surface area exhibits greater P adsorption and more rapid precipitation of Ca-P minerals. Calcareous soils with highly reactive $CaCO_3$ and a high Ca-saturated clay content will exhibit low solution P levels, since P can readily precipitate or adsorb.

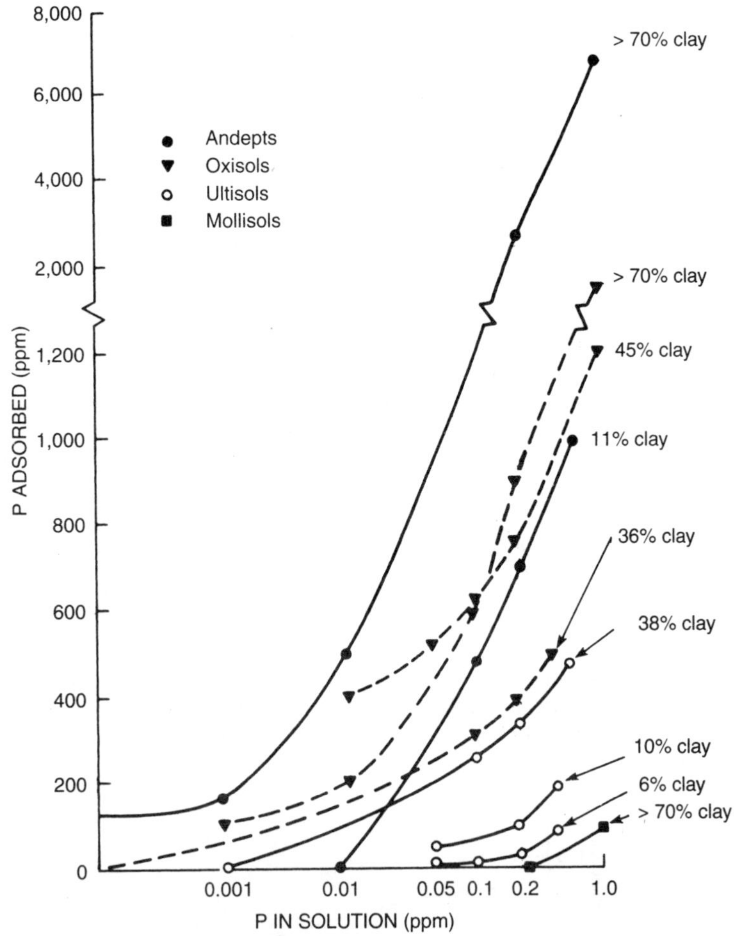

Figure 5-11 **P adsorption influenced by clay content.** *(Sanchez and Uehara, 1980,* **The Role of Phosphorus in Agriculture,** *p. 480, ASA, Madison, Wis.)*

In relative terms, acid soils fix two times more P per unit surface area of soil than neutral or calcareous soils. The P adsorbed is held with five times more bonding energy in acid soils than in calcareous soils.

To maintain a given level of solution P in soils with a high fixation capacity, it is necessary to add larger quantities of P fertilizers (Fig. 5-12). In any one soil, solution P concentration increases with increasing P additions. Larger additions of P are required to reach a given solution P concentration in fine-textured compared with coarse-textured soils. Consequently, high-clay soils often require more fertilizer P than loam soils to optimize yields.

Soil pH. P adsorption by Fe/Al oxides declines with increasing pH. Gibbsite [$Al(OH)_3$] adsorbs the greatest amount of P at pH 4 to 5. P adsorption by goethite (FeOOH) decreases steadily between pH 3 and 12 (Fig. 5-13).

P availability in most soils is at a maximum near pH 6.5 (Figure 5-7). At low pH values, P fixation is largely from reaction with Fe/Al oxides and precipitation as $AlPO_4$ and $FePO_4$. As pH increases, activity of Fe and Al decreases, which reduces P adsorption/ precipitation

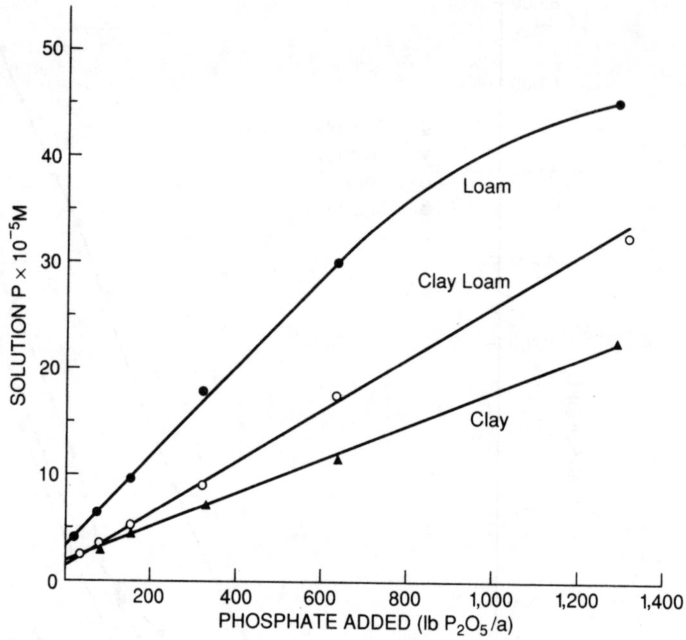

Figure 5-12 **P solubility (the mean activity of DCP in solution) as a function of the amounts of P added to three calcareous soils of different texture.** *(Cole et al., 1959,* SSSA Proc., *23:119.)*

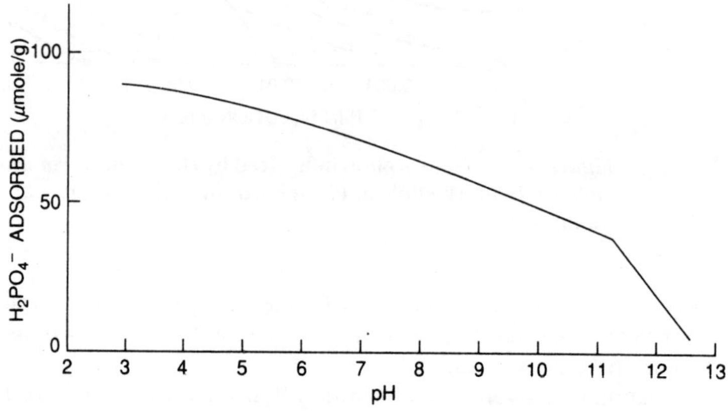

Figure 5-13 **The adsorption of P by Fe oxide (goethite) as influenced by soil pH.** ***(Adapted from Hingston et al., 1968,*** **Trans. 9th Int. Cong. Soil Sci.,** ***1:1459–61.)***

and increases solution P concentration. Above pH 7.0, Ca^{+2} precipitates with P as Ca-P minerals (Fig. 5-8) and P availability decreases. Minimum P adsorption at pH 6.0 to 6.5 (Fig. 5-7) corresponds with the pH range of maximum P solubility (Fig. 5-8). Liming acidic soils generally increases P solubility. Overliming can depress P solubility due to the formation of insoluble Ca-P minerals.

Cation Effects. Divalent cations on the CEC enhance P adsorption relative to monovalent cations. For example, clays saturated with Ca^{+2} retain greater amounts of P than those saturated with Na^{+} or other monovalent ions. Divalent cations increase the accessibility of (+)-charged edges of clay minerals to P. This occurs at pH < 6.5, because at greater soil pH Ca-P minerals would precipitate.

Concentration of exchangeable Al^{+3} is also an important factor in P adsorption in soils since 1 meq of exchangeable Al^{+3}/100 g of soil may precipitate up to 100 ppm P in solution. Strong correlations between P adsorption and exchangeable Al^{+3} have been observed (Fig. 5-14). The following illustrates how hydrolyzed Al^{+3} can adsorb soluble P.

Step 1 Cation Exchange

$$\text{Clay}\left.\begin{matrix} Al^{+3} \\ Al^{+3} \end{matrix}\right. + 3Ca^{+2} \leftrightharpoons \text{Clay}\left.\begin{matrix} Ca^{+2} \\ Ca^{+2} \\ Ca^{+2} \end{matrix}\right. + 2Al^{+3}$$

Step 2 Hydrolysis

$$Al^{+3} + 2H_2O \leftrightharpoons Al(OH)_2{}^{+} + 2H^{+}$$

Step 3 Precipitation and/or Adsorption

$$Al(OH)_2{}^{+} + H_2PO_4{}^{-} \leftrightharpoons Al(OH)_2H_2PO_4$$

Anion Effects. Both inorganic and organic anions can compete with P for adsorption sites, resulting in decreased P adsorption. Weakly held inorganic anions such as $NO_3{}^{-}$ and Cl^{-} are of little consequence, whereas adsorbed OH^{-}, $H_3SiO_4{}^{-}$, $SO_4{}^{-2}$, and $MoO_4{}^{-2}$ can be competitive. The anion adsorption strength determines the competitive ability. For example, $SO_4{}^{-2}$ is unable to desorb much $H_2PO_4{}^{-}$, since $H_2PO_4{}^{-}$ is capable of forming a stronger bond than is $SO_4{}^{-2}$.

Organic anions from sources such as organic waste materials and wastewater treatment can affect P adsorption-desorption reactions in soils. The impact of organic anions on reduction of adsorbed P is related to their molecular structure and pH. Organic anions form

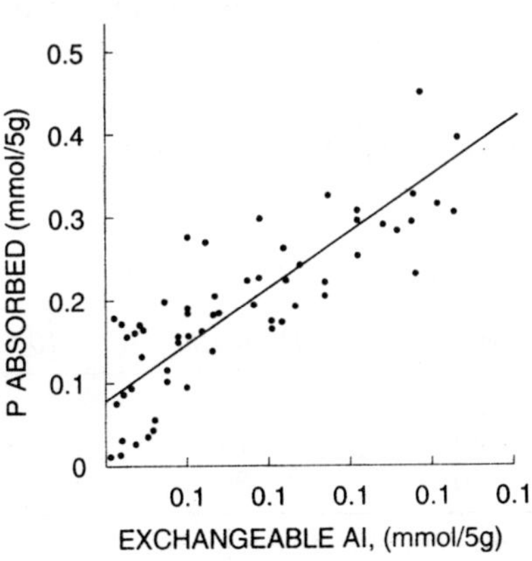

Figure 5-14 **Effect of exchangeable Al on the amount of P adsorbed by suspended clay.** ***(Coleman et al., 1960,*** **Soil Sci.,** ***90:1. Reprinted with permission of The Williams & Wilkins Company, Baltimore.)***

stable complexes with Fe and Al, which reduces adsorbed P. Oxalate and citrate can be adsorbed on soil surfaces similarly to $H_2PO_4^-$. Some of the effects of organic anions on P adsorption are partially responsible for the beneficial action of OM on P availability.

Extent of P Saturation. In general, P adsorption is greater in soils with little P adsorbed to mineral surfaces. As fertilizer P is added and the quantity of P adsorption increases, the potential for additional P adsorption decreases. When all adsorption sites are saturated with $H_2PO_4^-$, further adsorption will not occur and recovery of applied fertilizer P should increase.

Soil OM. Organic compounds in soils increase P availability by (1) formation of organophosphate complexes that are more easily assimilated by plants, (2) anion replacement of $H_2PO_4^-$ on adsorption sites, (3) coating of Fe/Al oxides by humus to form a protective cover and reduce P adsorption, and (4) increasing the quantity of organic P mineralized to inorganic P.

Organic anions produced from OM decomposition form stable complexes with Fe and Al, preventing their reaction with $H_2PO_4^-$. These complex ions exchange for P adsorbed on Fe/Al oxides. Anions that are most effective in replacing $H_2PO_4^-$ are citrate, oxalate, tartrate, and malate.

Organic P compounds can move to a greater depth than can inorganic P in soil solution. Continued application of manure results in elevated P levels at 2- to 4-ft depths. In contrast, application of the same quantity of P as inorganic fertilizer P results in less downward movement.

Time and Temperature. P adsorption in soils follows two distinct patterns: an initial rapid reaction followed by a much slower reaction. Adsorption reactions involving exchange of P for anions on Fe/Al oxide surface are rapid. The slower reactions involve (1) formation of covalent Fe-P or Al-P bonds on Fe/Al oxide surfaces (Fig. 5-10) and (2) precipitation of a P compound for which the solubility product has been exceeded. These slow reactions involve a transition from more loosely bound to more tightly bound adsorbed P, which is less accessible to plants.

The initial compounds precipitated during the reaction of fertilizer P in soils are relatively unstable and will usually change with time into more stable and less soluble compounds (see p. 189). Table 5-4 shows the percentage of DCPD converted to OCP as a function of time and temperature. Conversion of 70% or more of the DCPD occurred after 10 months at 10°C and after only 4 months at 20 and 30°C.

Generally, P adsorption increases with higher temperatures. P adsorption in soils of warm regions is generally greater than in soils of temperate regions. These warmer

Table 5-4 **Percentage of DCPD Hydrolyzed to OCP as a Function of Time and Temperature**

Temperature (°C)	*Percentage OCP Present at* *1 Month*	*2 Months*	*4 Months*	*10 Months*
10	<5	20	20	70
20	<5	40	75	100
30	<5	30	80	100

SOURCE: Sheppard and Racz, 1980, *Western Canada Phosphate Symp.*, p. 170.

climates also give rise to soils with higher Fe/Al oxides contents. Mineralization of P from soil OM or crop residues depends on soil biological activity, which increases with increasing temperature. Usually, mineralization rates double with each 10°C increase in temperature.

Flooding. In most soils there is an increase in available P after flooding, largely due to a conversion of Fe^{+3}-P minerals to more soluble Fe^{+2}-P minerals. Other mechanisms include dissolution of occluded P, increased mineralization of organic P in acid soils, increased solubility of Ca-P in calcareous soils, and greater P diffusion. These changes in P availability explain why response to applied P by irrigated rice is usually less than an upland crop grown on the same soil.

Fertilizer P Management Considerations An important practical consequence of P adsorption and precipitation reactions is the time after application during which the plant is best able to utilize the added P. On soils with high P-fixation capacity, this period may be short, whereas with other soils it may last for months or even years. The reaction time will determine whether fertilizer P should be applied at one time in the rotation or in smaller, more frequent applications. Adsorption of fertilizer P is greater in fine-textured soils because the reactive mineral surface area is greater than in coarse-textured soils.

Also important is P placement in the soil. If fertilizer P is broadcast and incorporated, P is exposed to a greater amount of soil; hence, more P fixation occurs than if the same amount of P is band applied. Band placement reduces contact between soil and fertilizer, with a subsequent reduction in P adsorption (see Chapter 10). Although this is only one factor to consider in P fertilizer placement, it is very important for crops grown on low-P soils with a high-P adsorption capacity, where band placement generally increases plant utilization of fertilizer P.

Organic Soil P

Organic P represents about 50% of total soil P in soils and typically varies between 15 to 80% (Table 5-5). Like OM, soil organic P decreases with depth, and the distribution with depth also varies among soils (Fig. 5-15). P content in soil OM ranges from 1 to 3%.

Table 5-5 **Range in Organic P Levels in Various Soils**

	Organic P	
Location	*mg/g*	*% Total P*
Australia	040–900	—
Canada	080–710	09–54
Denmark	354	61
England	200–9200	22–74
New Zealand	120–1360	30–77
Nigeria	160–1160	—
Scotland	200–9200	22–74
Tanzania	005–1200	27–90
United States	4–85	03–52

SOURCE: Stevenson, 1986, *Cycles of Soil*, p. 260, John Wiley & Sons.

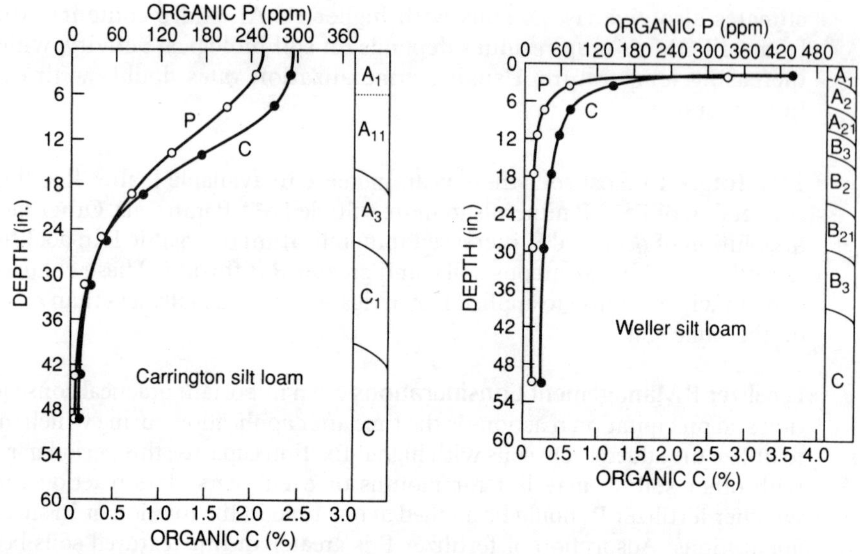

Figure 5-15 **Distribution of organic P and C with depth in two Mollisol soils in Iowa.** *(Stevenson, 1986,* Cycles of Soil, *p.261, John Wiley & Sons.)*

Therefore, if a soil contains 4% OM in the surface 6 in. (assume 1% OM degradation rate), the organic P content is:

$$2 \times 10^6 \text{ lbs soil/afs} \times 0.01 \times 0.04 = 800 \text{ lbs organic P/afs}$$

Soil organic P generally increases with increasing organic C and/or N; however, the C:P and N:P ratios are more variable among soils than C:N ratio. Soils are characterized by C:N:P:S ratio, which also varies among soils (Table 5-6). Average C:N:P:S ratio in soil is 140:10:1.3:1.3.

Most soil organic P compounds are esters of orthophosphate ($H_2PO_4^-$) including inositol phosphates (10 to 50%), phospholipids (1 to 5%), and nucleic acids (0.2 to 2.5%). Inositol phosphates represent a series of phosphate esters ranging from monophosphate up to hexaphosphate.

Table 5-6 **Organic C:N:P:S Ratio in Selected Soils**

Location	*Number of Soils*	*C:N:P:S*
Iowa	6	110:10:1.4:1.3
Brazil	6	194:10:1.2:1.6
Scotland*		
Calcareous	10	113:10:1.3:1.3
Noncalcareous	40	147:10:2.5:1.4
New Zealand†	22	140:10:2.1:2.1
India	9	144:10:1.9:1.8

*Values for S given as total S.

†Values for subsurface layers (35–53 cm) were 105:10:3.5:1.1.

SOURCE: Stevenson, 1986, *Cycles of soil*, p. 262, John Wiley & Sons.

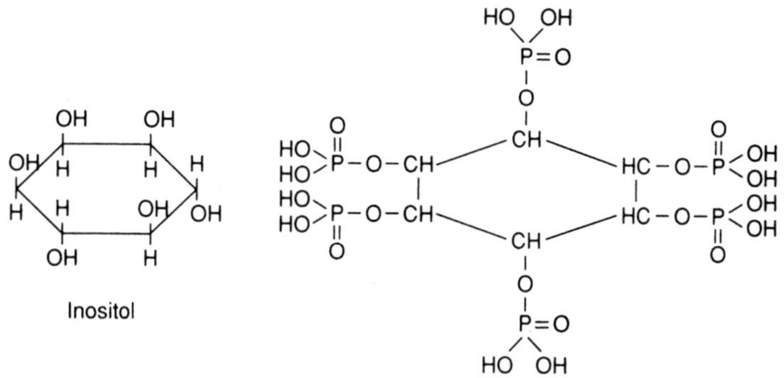

Figure 5-16 **Chemical structure of inositol and inositol phosphate (phytic acid).**

Phytic acid (myoinositol hexaphosphate) has six $H_2PO_4^-$ groups attached to each C atom in the benzene ring (Fig. 5-16). Successive replacement of $H_2PO_4^-$ with OH^- represents the other five phosphate esters. For example, the pentaphosphate ester has five $H_2PO_4^-$ groups and one OH^-. Inositol hexaphosphate is the most common phosphate ester and comprises ≈ 50% of total soil organic P. Most inositol phosphates and nucleic acids in soils are products of microbial degradation of plant residues. Two distinct nucleic acids, RNA and DNA, are released into soil in greater quantities than inositol phosphates. Since nucleic acids are rapidly degraded by soil microbes, they represent a small portion of total soil organic P. The common phospholipids are derivatives of glycerol and are insoluble in water, but also readily degraded by soil microbes. Thus, phospholipids also represent a small proportion of total organic P. The remaining soil organic P compounds originate from microbial activity, where, for example, bacterial cell walls contain large amounts of stable P esters.

P Mineralization and Immobilization in Soils In general, P mineralization and immobilization are similar to N in that both processes occur simultaneously in soils and can be depicted as follows:

$$\text{Organic P} \underset{\textit{Immobilization}}{\overset{\textit{Mineralization}}{\rightleftarrows}} \text{Inorganic P } (H_2PO_4^-/HPO_4^{-2})$$

Soil organic P originates from plant and animal residues, which are degraded by microorganisms to produce other organic compounds and release inorganic P (Fig. 5-1). Phosphatase enzymes catalyze the mineralization reaction of organic P by:

$$\text{R}-\text{O}-\underset{\underset{\text{O}}{|}}{\overset{\overset{\text{O}}{\|}}{\text{P}}}-\text{O}^- + H_2O \xrightarrow{\textit{Phosphatase}} \text{H}-\text{O}-\underset{\underset{\text{O}}{|}}{\overset{\overset{\text{O}}{\|}}{\text{P}}}-\text{O}^- + \text{R-OH}$$

The quantity of P mineralized in soils increases with increasing organic P content (Fig. 5-17). In contrast, the quantity of inorganic P immobilized is inversely related to soil organic P, such that as the ratio of soil organic C:P increases (i.e., decreasing organic P), P immobilization increases (Fig. 5-18). Evidence of organic P mineralization can be provided by measuring changes in soil organic P during the growing season (Fig. 5-19). Organic P content decreases with crop growth and increases again after harvest.

Residue C:P ratio determines the predominance of P mineralization over immobilization, just as C:N influenced N mineralization and immobilization. The following guidelines have been suggested:

C:P Ratio	*Mineralization/Immobilization*
< 200	Net mineralization of organic P
200–300	No gain or loss of inorganic P
> 300	Net immobilization of inorganic P

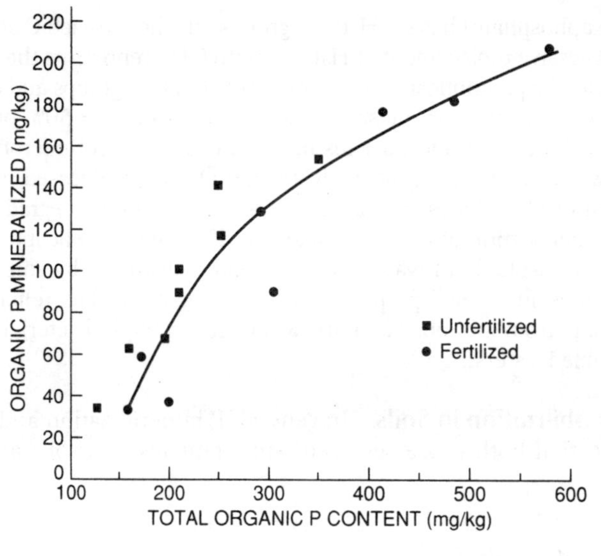

Figure 5-17 **Mineralization of organic P in soil as influenced by total organic P.** *(Sharpley, 1985,* SSSAJ, *49:907.)*

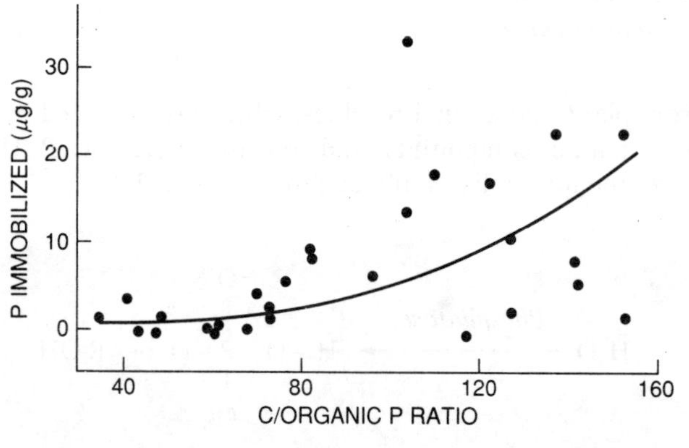

Figure 5-18 **Relationship between organic P immobilization and C:P ratio in the soil.** *(Enwezor, 1967,* Soil Sci., *103:62.)*

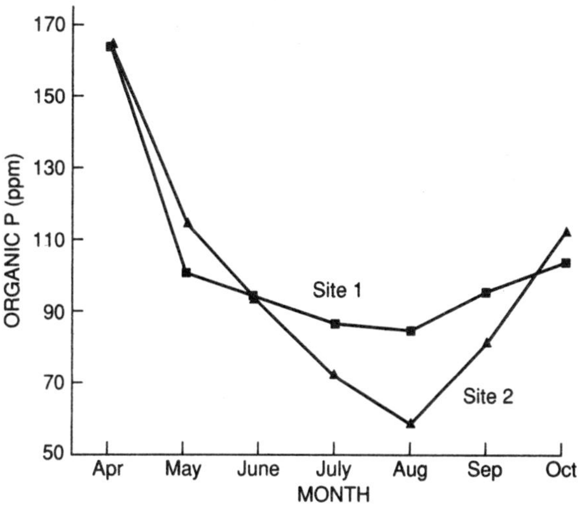

Figure 5-19 Changes in soil organic P over a cropping season for two locations. *(Dormaar, 1972,* Can. J. Soil. Sci., *52:107.)*

Expressed as % residue P, net P immobilization occurs when residue P $< 0.2\%$ and net mineralization occurs with $> 0.3\%$ residue P. When residues are added to soil, net P immobilization occurs during the early stages of decomposition, followed by net P mineralization as the C:P ratio of the residue decreases. P mineralization/immobilization processes are similar to N (Fig. 4-1).

Other factors affecting the quantity of P mineralization/immobilization are temperature, moisture, aeration, pH, cultivation intensity, and P fertilization. The environmental effects are similar to those described for N mineralization/immobilization, since both are microbial processes (see Chapter 4).

Inorganic fertilizer P can be immobilized to organic P by microorganisms. The quantity of P immobilized varies widely, with values of 25 to 100% of applied P reported. Continued fertilizer P applications can increase organic P content and subsequently increase P mineralization. Increases of 3 to 10 lbs/a/yr in organic P with continued P fertilization are possible. In general, organic P will accumulate with P fertilization when C and N are available in quantities relative to the C:N:P ratio of soil OM. Inorganic P will likely accumulate if C and N are limiting.

Further evidence of organic P mineralization is provided by the decrease in organic P with continued cultivation. When virgin soils are brought under cultivation, the soil OM decreases (see Chapter 13). As soil OM is oxidized, organic P is mineralized to inorganic P. For example, in the northern Plains, organic C and P decreased an average of 38 and 21% after 60 and 70 years of cultivation, respectively (Table 5-7). Studies in the Midwest showed that after 25 years of cultivation, mineralization reduced organic P 24% in the surface soil, which was less than the loss in organic C and N. In the southern Plains, organic P losses are greater because of increased soil temperature. In temperate regions, the decline in organic P with cultivation is generally less than that of organic C and N because of fewer loss mechanisms for P, resulting in comparatively greater conservation of organic P. Under higher temperature and moisture regimes, equal losses of organic C, N, and P have been observed.

Measuring organic P cycling in soils is more difficult than for N because inorganic P produced through mineralization can be removed from solution by (1) P adsorption to clay and other mineral surfaces and (2) P precipitation as secondary Al-, Fe-, or Ca-P minerals. However, the quantity of P mineralized during a growing season varies widely among

Table 5-7 Organic P Loss with Cultivation in Canadian Prairie Soils

Soil Association	*Native Prairie*	*60–70 Years of Cultivation*	*C or P Loss*
	mg/g		%
Blaine Lake			
Organic C	48	33	32
Total P	0.82	0.72	12
Organic P	0.65	0.53	18
Inorganic P	0.18	0.20	
Sutherland			
Organic C	38	24	37
Total P	0.766	0.66	12
Organic P	0.50	0.41	17
Inorganic P	0.26	0.25	
Bradwell			
Organic C	32	17	46
Total P	0.75	0.53	29
Organic P	0.45	0.32	29
Inorganic P	0.30	0.21	29

SOURCE: Tiessen et al., 1982, *Agron. J.*, 74:831.

Table 5-8 Organic P Mineralized in a Growing Season for Several Soils

Location	*Land Use*	*Soil*	*Period*	*Organic P*	*Mineralized*
			yr	*kg/ha/yr*	% /*yr*
	Slightly weathered, temperate soils				
Australia	Grass	—	4	6	4
	Wheat	—	55	0.3	0.3
Canada	Wheat	Silt loam	90	7	0.4
		Sandy loam	65	5	0.3
England	Grassland	Silt and sandy loam	1	7–40	1.3–4.4
	Arable	Silt and sandy loam	1	2–11	0.5–1.7
	Woodland	Silt loam	1	22	2.8
	Cereal crop	—	—	0.5–8.5	—
	Deciduous forest	Brown earth	1	9	1.2
	Grass	Brown earth	1	14	1.0
Iowa	Row crops	Clay loam	80	9	0.7
Maine	Potatoes	Silt loam	50	6	0.9
Minnesota	Alfalfa	Silty clay loam	60	12	1.2
Mississippi	Cotton	Silt loam	60	5	1.0
	Soybean	Silty clay loam	40	8	1.0
New Mexico	Row crops	Loam	30	2	0.4
Texas	Sorghum	Clay	60	7	1.0
	Weathered, tropical soils				
Honduras	Corn	Clay	2	6–27	6–12
Nigeria	Bush	Sandy loam	1	123	24
	Cocoa	Sandy loam	1	91	28
Ghana	Cleared shaded	Ochrosol fine	3	141	6
	Tropical half shaded	Sandy loam	3	336	17
	Rainforest exposed		3	396	17

SOURCE: Stewart and Sharpley, 1987, SSSA Spec. Publ. No. 19, p. 111.

soils (Table 5-8). Large quantities of organic P are mineralized in tropical, high-temperature environments. In the Midwest, organic P mineralization probably contributes about 4 to 10 lbs/a/yr of plant available P.

Immobilization and mineralization processes for P, C, N, and S cycling are similar and related. For example, if adequate amounts of N, P, and S are added to soils to which crop residues are returned, some of the added nutrients may be immobilized. Continued cropping of soils without the addition of N, P, and S results in their depletion in soils through mineralization. If N, P, or S is present in insufficient amounts, the synthesis of soil OM may be reduced.

P Sources

Organic P

Animal and municipal wastes are excellent sources of plant available P, with manure accounting for 98% of organic P applied to cropland. The form and content of P in fresh animal waste varies greatly depending on P content of the feed and animal type. Typically, inorganic P ranges from 0.3 to 2.4% of the dry weight, while organic P ranges from 0.1 to 1% (Table 5-9). In fresh manure, organic P represents 30 to 70% of total P. As discussed in relation to N, manure storage and handling change the nutrient content of manure. Mineralization of organic P during storage usually increases inorganic P content and decreases organic P. For example after 3 to 4 months of liquid swine waste storage, inorganic P increased from 60 to 70% to 85% of fresh manure dry weight (Table 5-10). Additional information on P content in manures and manure management can be found in Chapter 10.

Table 5-9 **P Content of Selected Animal Wastes**

Animal	*Total P*	*Inorganic P*
	---------- *% of Dry Matter* ----------	
Swine	1.5–2.5	0.8–2.0
Beef cattle	0.7–1.2	0.5–0.8
Dairy cattle	0.5–1.2	0.3–1.0
Poultry	0.9–2.2	0.3–1.2
Horses	0.4–1.4	0.2–0.8

Table 5-10 **Distribution of P Fractions in Liquid Swine Manure After Three to Four Months of Storage**

Animal	*Total P (% dry matter)*	*% of Total P*
Total inorganic P	1.5–2.0	85
Total organic P	0.2–0.3	15
Inorganic P in solution	0.01–0.20	5
Organic P in solution	0.01–0.03	<4
Microbial P	0.02–0.04	<2

SOURCE: Van Faassen, 1987, in V. D. Meer (Ed.), *Animal Manure on Grassland Crops*, pp. 27–45.

P content in sewage sludge ranges from 2 to 4%, with most present as inorganic P (Table 10-21). Thus, 40 to 80 lbs P/a would be applied per ton of material. If 80% is inorganic P and plant available during the first year, then 32 to 64 lbs P/a would be applied per ton. Because of relatively high transportation and processing expenses, application rates generally exceed 1 t/a, and therefore the total amount of P applied can greatly exceed typical crop requirements.

Microbial P Fertilization Phosphate-solubilizing bacilli and other rhizobacteria are abundant in soil and may be readily isolated from plant rhizospheres. The rhizobacteria colonizing plant roots and stimulating plant growth are known as *plant growth promoting bacteria* (PGPR). *Bacillus* spp. are among the most abundant P-solubilizers and have the advantage of forming stress-resistant spores, a necessary requirement for developing seed inoculants.

Research initiated in the 1980s showed that *Penicillium bilaii* can solubilize native mineral soil mineral P, as well as added rock phosphate (RP) and various specific P-containing minerals. The mode of action is apparently due to release of organic acids or other chelating agents and phytohormonal effects on root development. A commercial inoculant (JumpStart) is currently used to treat seed for significant acreages of canola/mustard, peas, lentils and other crops in western Canada. An Australian company has registered a similar P-solubilizing fungi, *Penicillium radicum,* and it is being evaluated in the Northern Great Plains. One important property of Penicillium is their activity at low temperatures, 3 to 4°C, where root development and P availability are usually limited.

Inorganic P

P Fertilizer Terminology Terms used to describe P content in fertilizers are *water soluble, citrate soluble, citrate insoluble, available*, and *total* P (as P_2O_5). A small sample is first extracted with water, and the P contained in the filtrate represents the fraction that is water soluble. The remaining water-insoluble material is extracted with 1 N ammonium citrate to determine citrate-soluble P. The sum of water-soluble and citrate-soluble P represents plant available P. The P remaining after the water and citrate extractions is citrate-insoluble P. The sum of available and citrate-insoluble P represents total P.

P Content of Fertilizers Fertilizer P content is expressed as P_2O_5 instead of elemental P. Although attempts have been made to change from % P_2O_5 to % P, most still express P concentration in fertilizers as % P_2O_5. Similarly, the concentration of K in fertilizers is usually expressed as % K_2O instead of % K. As a matter of interest, N was formerly guaranteed as % NH_3 rather than as % N, as is now done.

The conversion between % P and % P_2O_5 is:

$$\% P = \% P_2O_5 \times 0.43$$
$$\% P_2O_5 = \% P \times 2.29$$

The conversion factors are derived from the ratio of molecular weights of P and P_2O_5:

$$\frac{2 \times P(\text{g/mole})}{P_2O_5(\text{g/mole})} = \frac{2 \times 31}{142} = 0.43$$

P Fertilizer Sources Rock phosphate (RP) is the primary raw material for P fertilizers. The major RP deposits are found in the United States, Morocco, China, and Russia, representing nearly 70% of total world production. The United States produces nearly 30% of the world's RP. RP minerals are apatites [$Ca_{10}(PO_4)_6(X)_2$], where X is either F^-, OH^- or Cl^-. Fluorapatite [$Ca_{10}(PO_4)_6(F)_2$] is the most common RP. RP contains numerous impurities of CO_3, Na, and Mg. Common P fertilizers are produced from either acid- or heat-treated RP to increase water-soluble P (Table 5-11).

Rock Phosphate. The most reactive RPs are those containing francolite, a CO_3-F apatite. After several processing and purification steps, RP contains numerous minor constituents such as CO_3, Na, and Mg and variable amounts of heavy metal impurities including Cd which might be harmful to human health. Sedimentary RPs are highest in Cd with levels up to 300 mg/kg of P_2O_5, of which ~ 60 to 80% can be retained in P fertilizers. The European Union is considering drastic three-step measures over a 15-year period to restrict Cd to 60, 40, and finally 20 mg/kg of P_2O_5.

None of the P is water soluble, although the citrate solubility varies from 5 to 17% of total P. Finely ground RP can supply sufficient plant available P in low pH soils (Fig. 5-8) when applied at 2 to 3 times the rates of superphosphate. At these rates several years of residual availability has been observed. RP is used extensively for plantation crops such as rubber, oil palm, and cacao grown on very acid soils.

Warm climates, moist soils, and long growing seasons increase the effectiveness of RP. Ground RP is sometimes used for restoration of low-P soils on abandoned farms and on newly broken lands. For these purposes, a heavy initial application is recommended (1 to 3 t/a), which may be repeated at 5- to 10-year intervals.

In situations where RP reactivity is inadequate for immediate crop response and the P-fixation capacity of the soil quickly renders soluble P fertilizer unavailable to plants, partially acidulated RP can increase the water-soluble P content and improve the short-term crop response to RP. Partially acidulated RP is produced by treating RP with 10 to 20% of the quantity of H_3PO_4 used for the manufacture of triple superphosphate or by reacting it with 40 to 50% of the amount of H_2SO_4 normally used in the production of single superphosphate.

Phosphoric Acid. Phosphoric acid (H_3PO_4), or green or wet-process acid, contains 17 to 24% P (39 to 55% P_2O_5) and is produced by reacting RP with H_2SO_4. The reaction also produces gypsum ($CaSO_4 \cdot 2H_2O$) that can be used as a S and Ca fertilizer, an amendment for sodic soils, and for other industrial purposes. H_3PO_4 can also be made by heating RP in an electric furnace to produce elemental P that is reacted with O_2 and H_2O to form H_3PO_4. H_3PO_4 produced by burning is termed white or furnace acid and is produced mostly for nonagricultural uses. White acid has a much higher degree of purity than green acid; however, the high energy cost involved in manufacturing makes it expensive and limits its use in agriculture.

Agricultural-grade green acid is used to acidulate RP to make Ca and NH_4 phosphates (see following discussion). It can also be injected in soil or irrigation water, particularly in alkaline and calcareous areas. Almost all wet acid is used to manufacture P fertilizers.

Calcium Phosphates. Ca phosphate fertilizers—single superphosphate, triple superphosphate, and enriched superphosphates—were once the most important P sources. Unlike H_3PO_4 and NH_4^+ phosphates, superphosphates have no appreciable effect on soil pH.

Single superphosphate (SSP) is manufactured by reacting H_2SO_4 with RP:

$$\underset{\text{Rock phosphate}}{[Ca_3(PO_4)_2]_3 \cdot CaF_2} + \underset{\text{Sulfuric acid}}{7H_2SO_4} \rightarrow \underset{\text{Monocalcium phosphate}}{3Ca(H_2PO_4)_2} + \underset{\text{Gypsum}}{7CaSO_4} + \underset{\text{Hydrofluoric acid}}{2HF}$$

Table 5-11 **Common Ortho- and Polyphosphate Fertilizers**

Fertilizer	Frequently Used Abbreviations	Analysis (%)				% Total Available P	P Compound
		N	P_2O_5	K_2O	S		
Rock phosphate	RP	—	25–40	—	—	14–65	$[Ca_3(PO_4)_2]_3 \cdot CaF_x \cdot (CaCO_3)_x \cdot (Ca(OH)_2)_x$
Single superphosphate	SSP	—	16–22	—	11–12	97–100	$Ca(H_2PO_4)_2$
Phosphoric (green) acid	—	—	48–53	—	—	100	H_3PO_4
Triple superphosphate	TSP or CSP	—	44–53	—	1–1.5	97–100	$Ca(H_2PO_4)_2$
Ammonium phosphates							
Monoammonium phosphate	MAP	11–13	48–62	—	0–2	100	$NH_4H_2PO_4$
Diammonium phosphate	DAP	18–21	46–53	—	0–2	100	$(NH_4)_2HPO_4$
Ammonium polyphosphate*	APP	10–15	35–62	—	—	100	$(NH_4)_3HP_2O_7 \cdot NH_4H_2PO_4$
Urea-ammonium phosphate*	UAP	21–34	16–42	—	—	100	$(NH_4)_3HP_2O_7 \cdot NH_4H_2PO_4$
Potassium phosphates							
Monopotassium phosphate	—	—	51	35	—		KH_2PO_4
Dipotassium phosphate	—	—	41	54	—		K_2HPO_4

*Contain a mixture of ortho- and polyphosphates.

SOURCE: Mortvedt et al., 1999, Fertilizer Technology and Application, Meister Publishing Co. *Fertilizers and Soil Amendments*, p. 131, Prentice-Hall.

SSP contains 7 to 9.5% P (16 to 22% P_2O_5) although unpopular in the United States and is 90% water soluble. SSP is an excellent source of P and S (12% S); because of its low P content (Fig. 5-20), it is an important P source worldwide.

Triple superphosphate (TSP) contains 17 to 23% P (44 to 52% P_2O_5) and is produced by treating RP with H_3PO_4:

$$\underset{\text{Rock phosphate}}{[Ca_3(PO_4)_2]_3 \cdot CaF_2} + \underset{\text{Phosphoric acid}}{12H_3PO_4} + 9H_2O \rightarrow \underset{\text{Monocalcium phosphate}}{9Ca(H_2PO_4)_2} + \underset{\text{Calcium fluoride}}{CaF_2}$$

TSP was manufactured to increase the P content of SSP, although TSP contains $< 1\%$ S. TSP is an excellent source of P and was the most common P source used in the United States until the 1960s, when NH_4^+ phosphates became popular (Fig. 5-20). Its high P content is an advantage because transportation, storage, and handling costs make up a large fraction of total fertilizer cost. TSP is manufactured in both granular and nongranular form with the granular product used in blending with other materials and in direct soil application.

Ammonium Phosphates. Ammonium phosphates are produced by reacting wet-process H_3PO_4 with NH_3 (Fig. 5-21). Monoammonium phosphate (MAP) contains 11 to 13% N and 21 to 24% P (48 to 55% P_2O_5); however, the common grade is 11-22-0 (11-52-0).

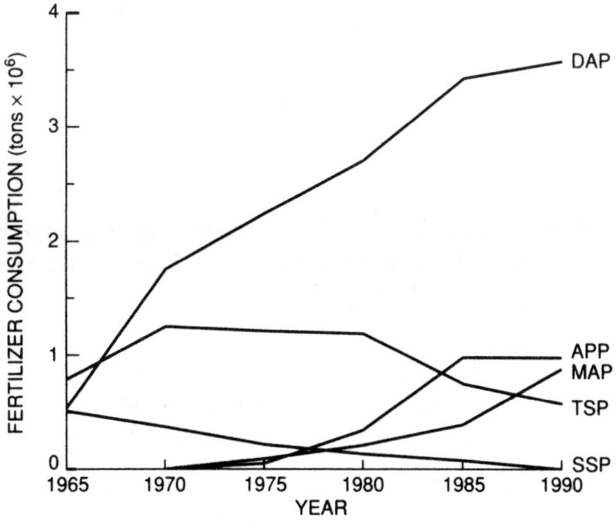

Figure 5-20 Use of common P fertilizers in the United States. DAP, diammonium phosphate; APP, ammonium polyphosphate; MAP, monoammonium phosphate; TSP, triple superphosphate; SSP, single superphosphate. *(USDA ERS, 1990.)*

$$\underset{\text{Ammonia}}{NH_3} + \underset{\text{Orthophosphoric acid}}{H_3PO_4} \longrightarrow \underset{\text{Monoammonium phosphate}}{NH_4H_2PO_4}$$

$$\underset{\text{Ammonia}}{2\,NH_3} + \underset{\text{Orthophosphoric acid}}{H_3PO_4} \longrightarrow \underset{\text{Diammonium phosphate}}{(NH_4)_2HPO_4}$$

$$\underset{\text{Ammonia}}{3\,NH_3} + \underset{\text{Pyrophosphoric acid}}{H_4P_2O_7} \longrightarrow \underset{\text{Triammonium pyrophosphate}}{(NH_4)_3HP_2O_7}$$

Figure 5-21 Reactions of ammonia with ortho- and pyrophosphate to produce monoammonium phosphate (MAP), diammonium phosphate (DAP), and ammonium polyphosphate (APP). *(Mortvedt et al., 1999,* Fertilizer Technology and Application, *p. 45, Meister.)*

Diammonium phosphate (DAP) contains 18 to 21% N and 20 to 23% P (46 to 53% P_2O_5); the most common grade is 18-20-0 (18-46-0). Although MAP use has increased significantly in the last decade, DAP is more widely used than any other P fertilizer in the United States (Fig. 5-19). Increased interest in and use of NH_4^+ phosphates result from increased P uptake when NH_4^+ is placed with P fertilizer (see Chapter 10).

Both MAP and DAP are granular, water-soluble fertilizers with the advantage of high nutrient content, which minimizes shipping, handling, and storage costs. They can be used for formulating solid fertilizers by bulk blending or in manufacturing suspension fertilizers. MAP and DAP are also used for direct application as starter fertilizers. Row or seed placement of DAP can cause seedling injury and inhibit root growth through NH_3 produced according to:

$$(NH_4)_2HPO_4 \rightarrow 2\ NH_4^+ + HPO_4^{-2}\quad (pH\ 8.5)$$
$$\downarrow$$
$$NH_4^+ + OH^- \rightarrow NH_3 + H_2O$$

These problems are especially common in calcareous or high-pH soils. Adequate separation of seed and DAP is usually all that is required to eliminate seedling damage. In most cases, the N rate should not exceed 15 to 20 lbs N/a as DAP applied with the seed. Seedling injury with MAP is seldom observed except in sensitive crops such as canola/rapeseed and flax.

Initial soil reaction pH with DAP is about 8.5, which favors NH_3 production (Fig. 4-36), whereas the reaction pH with MAP is 3.5. Except for the differences in reaction pH and seedling injury when applied with the seed, few agronomic differences exist between MAP and DAP. Reports of improved crop response to MAP compared with DAP on high-pH or calcareous soils are generally not substantiated. Low-reaction pH with MAP has been claimed to increase micronutrient availability in calcareous soils, but this has not been consistently demonstrated.

Ammonium Polyphosphate. Ammonium polyphosphate (APP) is manufactured by reacting pyrophosphoric acid, $H_4P_2O_7$, with NH_3 (Fig. 5-22). Pyrophosphoric acid is pro-

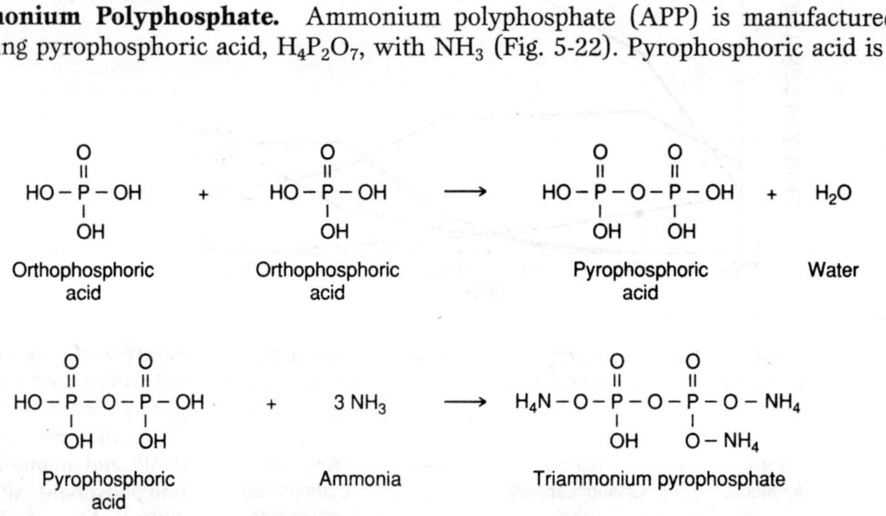

Figure 5-22 **Reaction of two orthophosphate molecules to produce pyrophosphate. The reaction can continue to form longer chain products called polyphosphates. Ammonium of pyro- and polyphosphates produces ammonium polyphosphate (APP).** *(Mortvedt et al., 1999,* **Fertilizer Technology and Application,** *p. 46.)*

duced from dehydration of wet-process acid. Polyphosphate is a term used to describe two or more orthophosphate ions ($H_2PO_4^-$) combined together, with the loss of one H_2O molecule per two $H_2PO_4^-$ (Fig. 5-22). APP is a liquid containing 10 to 15% N and 15 to 16% P (34 to 37% P_2O_5), with about 75 and 25% of the P present as polyphosphate and orthophosphate, respectively. The most common APP grade is 10-15-0 (10-34-0).

Liquid APP is a competitive P source and can be directly applied or mixed with other liquid fertilizers. Commonly, UAN and APP are combined and subsurface band applied. One unique property of APP is the chelation or sequestering reaction with metal cations, which maintains higher concentrations of micronutrients in APP than are possible with $H_2PO_4^-$ solutions (Fig. 5-23). APP can maintain 2% Zn in solution compared with only 0.05% Zn with $H_2PO_4^-$.

A granular fertilizer, urea-ammonium phosphate (UAP), is produced by reacting urea with APP. The fertilizer grade is 28-12-0 (28-28-0), containing 20 to 40% polyphosphate. UAP can be easily blended with other granular fertilizers. Like DAP, seedling damage occurs when UAP is applied with the seed.

Potassium Phosphate. Potassium phosphate products include KH_2PO_4 and K_2HPO_4 (Table 5-11). They are water soluble and commonly used in the horticulture industry. Their high P and K content makes them attractive materials for requiring both P and K. In addition, they are ideally suited for solanaceous crops such as potatoes, tomatoes, and many leafy vegetables that are sensitive to high levels of Cl^- associated with KCl (see Chapter 6). Their low salt index reduces injury to germinating seeds and to young seedlings when they are placed in or close to the seed row.

Behavior of P Fertilizers in Soils

Fertilizer P Reactions Numerous characteristics of soil and P-fertilizer source determine the soil-fertilizer reactions that influence fertilizer P availability to plants. Many of the factors that affect native P availability, discussed earlier, also influence fertilizer P reactions in soil and P availability. P fertilizer added to soil initially increases solution P but subsequently solution P decreases through influences of mineral, adsorbed (labile), and organic P fractions (Fig. 5-1).

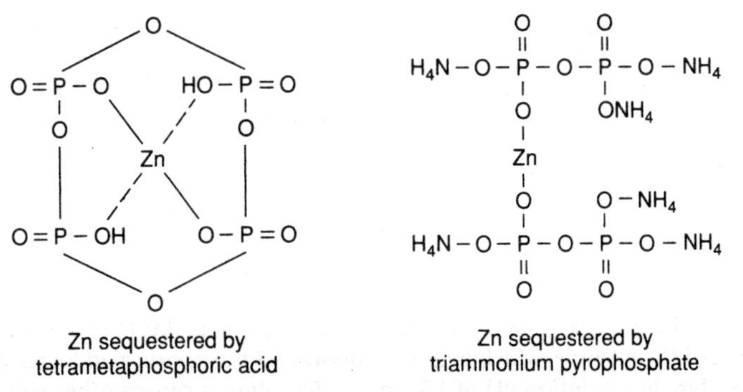

Figure 5-23 Sequestering of Zn by polyphosphate molecules can maintain a greater Zn concentration in solution than orthophosphate. *(Mortvedt et al., 1999,* Fertilizer Technology and Application, *p. 47, Meister.)*

The Ca- and NH_4- P fertilizers are 90 to 100% water soluble and dissolve rapidly when placed in moist soil. Water sufficient to initiate dissolution moves to the granule or droplet by either capillary or vapor transport. A nearly saturated solution of the P-fertilizer material forms in and around fertilizer granules or droplets (Figs. 5-24, 5-25, and 5-26). While water is drawn into the fertilizer, the fertilizer solution moves into the surrounding soil. Movement of water inward and fertilizer solution outward continues to maintain a nearly saturated solution as long as the original salt remains. Initial P diffusion from the fertilizer seldom exceeds 3 to 5 cm (Fig. 5-24). Diffusion of fertilizer P reaction products away from the dissolving granule increases with increasing soil moisture content. Extensive reaction zones combined with thorough distribution of the reaction products are factors that should enhance absorption of P by plant roots encountering reaction zones.

As the saturated P solution moves into the first increments of soil, the chemical environment is dominated by the solution properties rather than by soil properties. Solutions

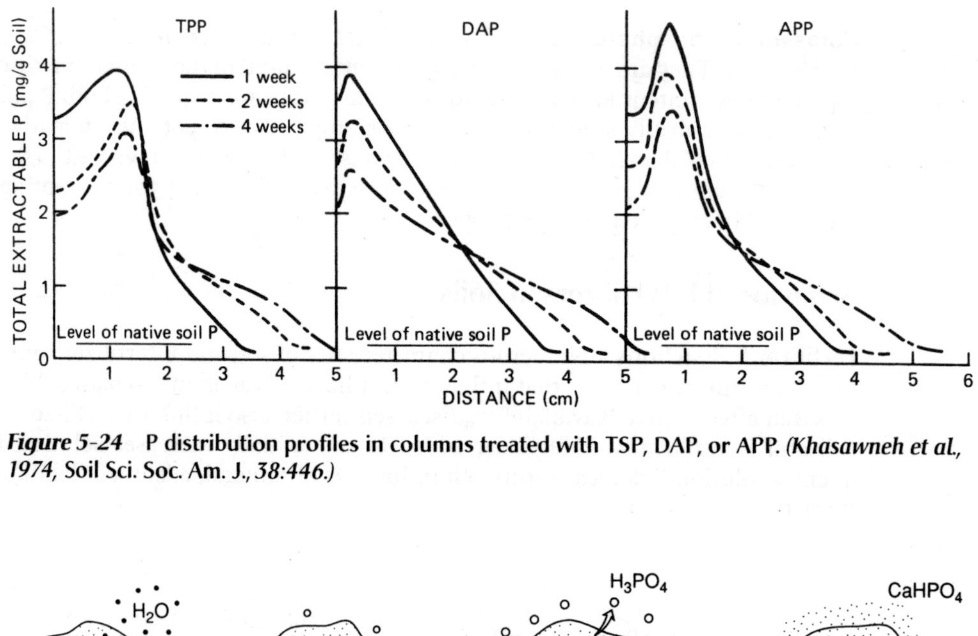

Figure 5-24 **P distribution profiles in columns treated with TSP, DAP, or APP. *(Khasawneh et al., 1974,* Soil Sci. Soc. Am. J., *38:446.)***

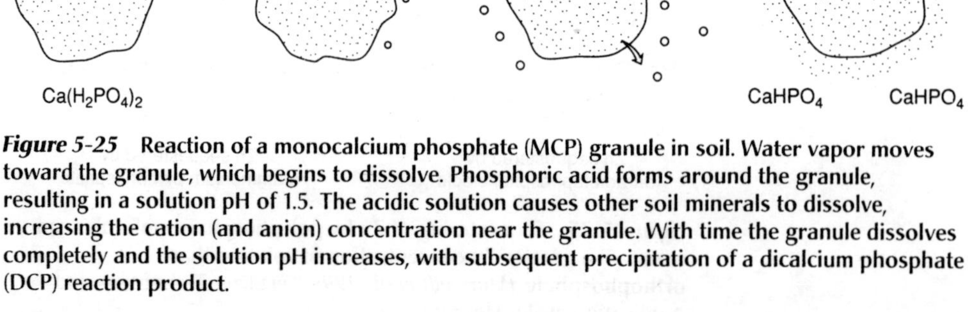

Figure 5-25 **Reaction of a monocalcium phosphate (MCP) granule in soil. Water vapor moves toward the granule, which begins to dissolve. Phosphoric acid forms around the granule, resulting in a solution pH of 1.5. The acidic solution causes other soil minerals to dissolve, increasing the cation (and anion) concentration near the granule. With time the granule dissolves completely and the solution pH increases, with subsequent precipitation of a dicalcium phosphate (DCP) reaction product.**

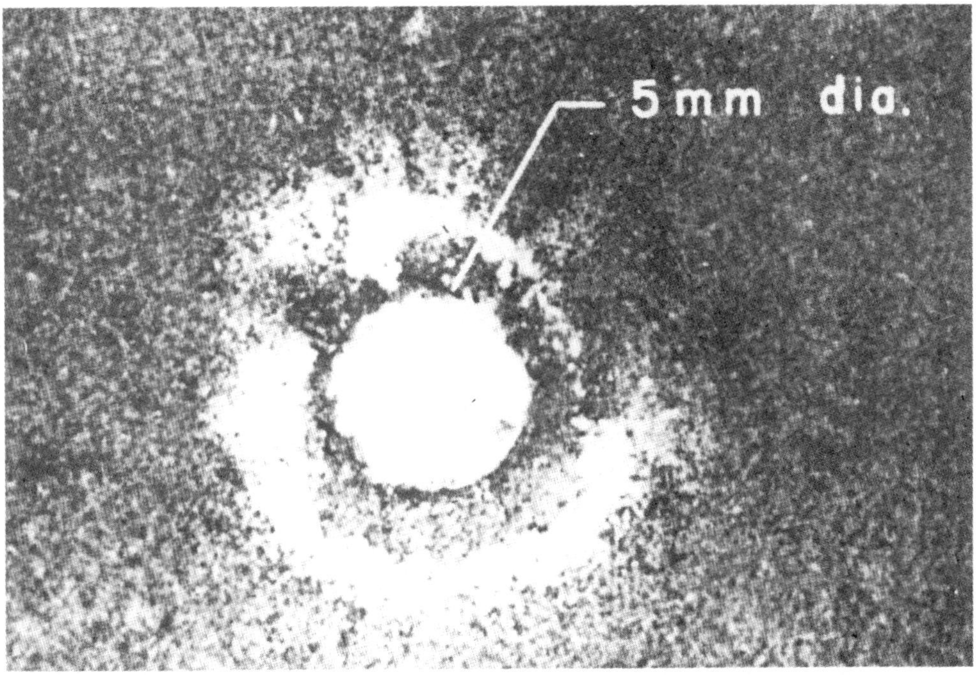

Figure 5-26 Distribution of monocalcium phosphate (MCP) reaction products after 14 days' reaction at 5°C in the Bradwell very-fine sandy loam. *(Hinman et al., 1962,* Can. J. Soil Sci., *42:229.)*

Table 5-12 Fertilizer P Sources and Their Reaction Chemistry in Soils

			Composition of Saturated Solution			
					Predominant	
Compound	*Formula*	*Symbol*	*pH*	*P (m/l)*	*Cation*	*m/l*
Highly water soluble						
Monocalcium phosphate	$Ca(H_2PO_4)_2$	TSP	1.5	4.5	Ca	1.3
Monoammonium phosphate	$NH_4H_2PO_4$	MAP	3.5	2.9	NH_4	2.9
Ammonium polyphosphate	$(NH_4)_3HP_2O_7$	APP	6.0	6.8	NH_4	10.2
Diammonium phosphate	$(NH_4)_2HPO_4$	DAP	8.5	3.8	NH_4	7.6
*Sparingly soluble**						
Dicalcium phosphate	$CaHPO_4$	DCP	6.5	≈0.002	Ca	0.001
Dicalcium phosphate dihydrate	$CaHPO_4 \cdot 2H_2O$	DCPD	6.5	≈0.002	Ca	0.001
Hydroxyapatite	$Ca_{10}(PO_4)_6(OH)_2$	HA	6.5	$\approx 10^{-5}$	Ca	0.001

*Compounds not used as fertilizers.

SOURCE: Sample et al., 1980, in F. E. Khasawneh et al. (Eds.), *Phosphorus in Agriculture*, p.275, ASA, Madison, Wis.

formed from water-soluble P fertilizers have pH values from 1.5 to 8.5 and contain from 2.9 to 6.8 ml/l of P (Table 5-12). When the concentrated P solution diffuses from the granule and moves into the surrounding soil, the soil components are altered by the solution; at the same time, the solution's composition is changed by its contact with soil. Some soil minerals may be dissolved by the concentrated P solution, resulting in the release of cations such as Fe^{+3}, Al^{+3}, Mn^{+2}, K^{+}, Ca^{+2}, and Mg^{+2}. Cations from exchange sites can be displaced by these cations in the concentrated solutions. P reacts with these cations to form specific compounds, referred to as soil-fertilizer reaction products.

For example, after monocalcium phosphate [MCP, $Ca(H_2PO_4)_2$] is added to soil, water diffuses toward the granule (Fig. 5-25). As MCP dissolves, H_3PO_4 forms near the granule and lowers pH to 1.5 (Table 5-12). Other soil minerals in contact with H_3PO_4 may dissolve, increasing solution cation concentration near the granule. Subsequently, the solution pH will increase as H_3PO_4 is neutralized. Within a few days or weeks, DCP and/or DCPD will precipitate as the initial fertilizer reaction product (Fig.5-8). Depending on the native P minerals initially present in the soil, OCP, TCP, HA, or Fe/AlPO4 may eventually precipitate.

Precipitation reactions are favored by high P concentrations that exist near the dissolving P fertilizer. Adsorption reactions are expected to be most important at the periphery of the soil-fertilizer reaction zone, where P concentrations are lower (Fig. 5-24). Although both precipitation and adsorption occur, precipitation accounts for most of the P being retained near the dissolving granule. Precipitation of DCP occurs near the MCP granule, where 20 to 34% of the applied P will remain as DCP for several weeks (Fig. 5-26).

Although initial reaction products are unstable and are usually transformed with time into more stable but less water-soluble P compounds, they will have a favorable influence on P availability. Some of the initial reaction products will provide solution P concentrations 1,000 times those in untreated soil. The rate of change of the initial reaction products is influenced by soil properties and environmental factors. For example, after initial DCP formation (a few weeks), formation of OCP may take several months. Further transformation to TCP or HA may take longer. The residual value of fertilizer P depends on the nature and reactivity of long-term reaction products.

In acid soils, reaction products formed from MCP include DCP and eventually $AlPO_4$ and/or $FePO_4$ precipitates (Fig. 5-8). In calcareous soil, DCP and OCP are the dominant initial reaction products. Because MAP has a reaction pH of 3.5 compared with pH 8.5 for DAP, P should be more soluble near the dissolving granule (Table 5-12). The acid pH with MAP may temporarily reduce the rate of P reaction product precipitation in calcareous soils. Although differences in pH among the various P fertilizers cause differences in reaction product chemistry, the overall effect is temporary because the volume of soil influenced by the P granule or droplet is small. Differences in availability of P sources to crops are small compared with differences in other P management factors such as P rate and placement.

APP applied to soil reacts similarly to granular P fertilizers. Reaction pH is 6.2 and both precipitation and adsorption of the polyphosphate and $H_2PO_4^-$ present initially, plus that formed by hydrolysis of the polyphosphate, occur as described earlier for native $H_2PO_4^-$.

Chemical and biological reaction of polyphosphate with H_2O (hydrolysis) produces $H_2PO_4^-$ and various shortened polyphosphate fragments that undergo further hydrolysis to $H_2PO_4^-$. Polyphosphate hydrolysis proceeds slowly in sterile solutions at room temperature; however, in soils where both mechanisms function, hydrolysis is rapid.

Several factors control hydrolysis rates in soils, with enzymatic activity provided by plant roots and microorganisms being the most important. Phosphatase associated with plant roots and rhizosphere organisms is responsible for biological hydrolysis of polyphosphates.

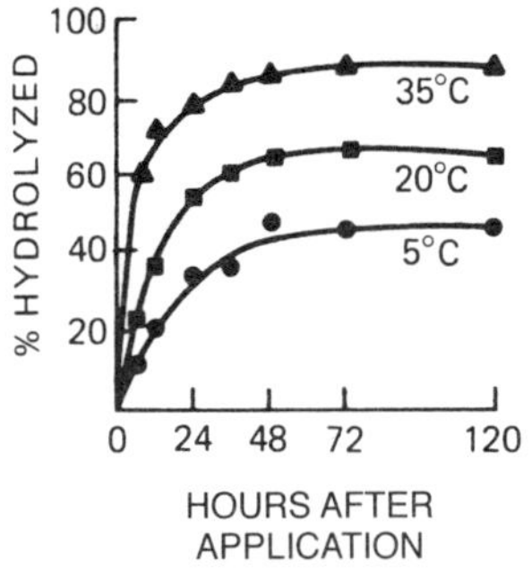

Figure 5-27 Effects of temperature on hydrolysis of water-soluble pyrophosphate (200 ppm).
(Chang and Racz, 1977, Can. J. Soil Sci., *57:271.)*

Temperature, moisture, soil C, pH, and various conditions that encourage microbial and root growth favor phosphatase activity and polyphosphate hydrolysis. Temperature is the most important environmental factor, where hydrolysis of pyro- and polyphosphate increases substantially as soil temperature increases from 5 to 35°C (Fig. 5-27).

Polyphosphates are as effective as $H_2PO_4^-$ sources for crops. Plants can absorb polyphosphates directly. Because polyphosphates have the ability to form metal complexes, they are effective in mobilizing Zn in soils (Fig. 5-23). Complexing Zn with polyphosphate is temporary because hydrolysis is usually very rapid.

Interaction of N with P N promotes P uptake by plants by (1) increasing top and root growth, (2) altering plant metabolism, and (3) increasing P solubility and availability. Increased root mass is largely responsible for increased crop uptake of P. NH_4^+ fertilizers have a greater stimulating effect on P absorption than NO_3^-. Greater effectiveness of fertilizer P can occur when fertilizer application places P close to NH_4^+ sources. For example, agronomic advantages, often resulting in 5 to 6 bu/a yield increases of winter wheat, can be gained by simultaneously injecting anhydrous NH_3 and APP solution into the soil (see Chapter 10).

Effect of Granule or Droplet Size Fertilizer P availability to plants is influenced by the granule or droplet size and the water solubility of the P fertilizer. Since water-soluble P is rapidly converted to less-soluble P reaction products, decreasing contact between soil and fertilizer generally improves the plant response to P fertilizer. Increasing granule or droplet size and/or band application of the fertilizer decreases soil-fertilizer contact and maintains a higher solution P concentration for a longer time compared with broadcast P and/or fine particle size.

Soil Moisture Soil moisture content influences the effectiveness and availability of applied P. At field capacity, 50 to 80% of the water-soluble P can diffuse from the fertilizer granule within 24 hours. Even at 2 to 4% moisture, 20 to 50% of the water-soluble P moves out of the granule within the same time.

Rate of Application Even though fertilizer P eventually forms less-soluble P compounds, the P concentration in solution increases with P application rate. With time the P concentration decreases as less soluble P compounds precipitate. The duration of elevated solution P levels depends on the rate of P fertilizer applied, the method of P placement, the quantity of P removed by the crop, and the soil properties that influence P availability.

Modification of Chemistry in Soil Fertilizer Reaction Zones Modification of the environment around fertilizer P particles or bands of fluid P by coatings or additions of a specific family of polymers with CECs of over 1.6 eq/100 g has been investigated since 1999 on a wide range of crops and soil conditions. Higher yields and improved crop uptake of P have been obtained and attributed to decreased interference of cations such as Al, Fe, Ca, and Mg known to adversely affect P availability, as discussed previously.

Residual P Residual fertilizer P availability can persist for years depending on P rate applied, crop P removal, and soil properties that influence P reaction product chemistry. P-fixation reactions influence residual P availability in acid soils more than in basic soils (Table 5-13). These data, show that $< 50\%$ of fertilizer P was plant available after 6 months over a wide range in soil properties; however, residual P availability was lower in weathered, acid soils compared to slightly weathered and calcareous soils.

With increasing P rate the initial and residual fertilizer P availability increases (Fig. 5-28). After more than 10 to 12 years, soil test P had decreased to its initial level except with the highest P rate. P fertilizer is usually recommended when $NaHCO_3$ soil test levels are < 15 ppm. These data demonstrate that relatively high P rates are needed to substantially increase and maintain residual available P over a long time period.

Figure 5-29 illustrates the change in plant available P with P rates based on crop need. First, plant removal of P in the unfertilized soil caused initial soil test P to decrease substantially over six years. Annual application of 50 kg/ha P maintained the soil test P at 2 to 3 ppm above the initial soil test level, whereas the intermediate P rate (25 kg/ha P) resulted in soil test levels between 0 and 50 kg/ha P annual rates. Triennial application of 75 kg/ha P increased available P in the first year; however, soil test P subsequently decreased below the initial soil test level until the next triennial application. Similarly, 75 kg/ha P applied only in the first year maintained soil test P at or above the initial level during the first 3 years, followed by decreasing soil test P in subsequent years. These data illustrate the importance of soil testing for accurately determining when additional fertilizer P is needed for optimum production.

Table 5-13 **Influence of Soil Properties on Residual Fertilizer P Availability***

		% Available after Six Months	
Soil Type and Related Properties†	*Number of Soils*	*Mean*	*Range*
Calcareous			
$CaCO_3$	56	45	11–72
Slightly Weathered			
Base Saturation	80	47	7–74
Soil Test P			
pH			
Moderately Weathered	27	32	6–51
Clay Content			
Soil Test P			
Soil OM			
Highly Weathered	40	27	14–54
Clay Content			
Extractable Al and Fe			

*Resin extractable P measured six months after P application.
†Primary soil properties influencing residual P availability.
SOURCE: Sharpley, 1991, *Soil Sci. Soc. Am. J.* 55:1038.

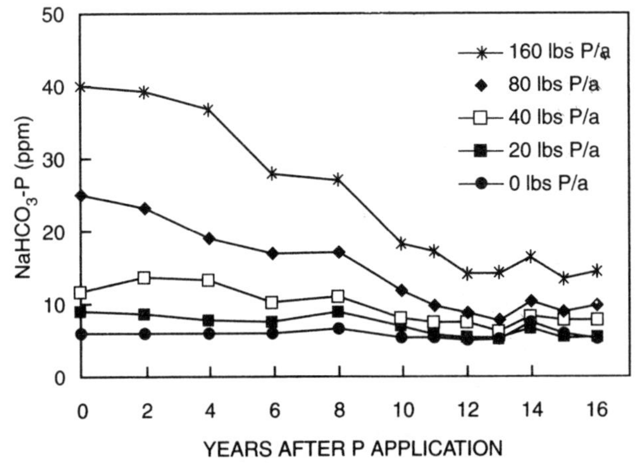

Figure 5-28 **Residual effect of single applications of P on the $NaHCO_3$ extractable P over 16 years of production.** *(Havlorson, 1989,* Soil Sci Soc. Am. J., *53:839.)*

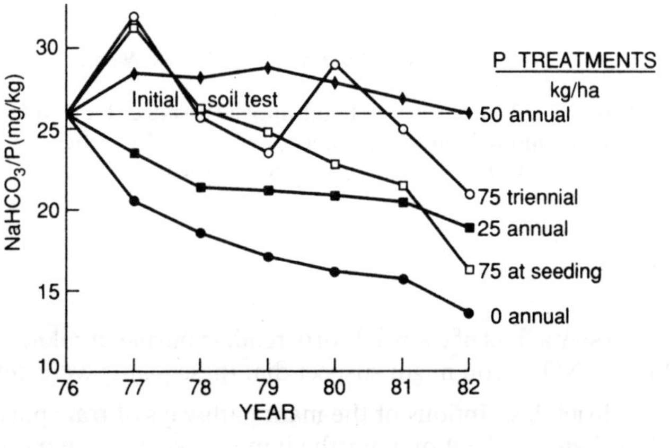

Figure 5-29 **Influence of broadcast fertilizer P on buildup or decline in soil test P over six years.** ***(Havlin et al., 1984,*** **SSSAJ,** ***48:332.)***

P placement also influences the quantity of residual fertilizer P (Fig. 5-30). On this low-P soil, soil test P for broadcast (BC) P applied at 15 and 45 lbs P_2O_5/a was no different from that of the unfertilized soil, indicating that the applied fertilizer P not taken up by the crop had been converted to P compounds with a solubility similar to that of the native P minerals. However, increasing band-applied (KN) P from 15 to 75 lbs/a P_2O_5 dramatically increased soil test P in the band, indicating that the solubility of the P reaction products is greater than that of the native P minerals and that they persist for several years after application.

There is some question about the need for additional P even when residual P levels are high. Low rates of P in starter fertilizers placed with or near the seed row are potentially beneficial on high-P soils when the crop is stressed by cold, wet conditions and diseases such as root rots. Although residual P contributes significantly to crop yields, additional banding of P may be required to maximize crop production (Chapter 10).

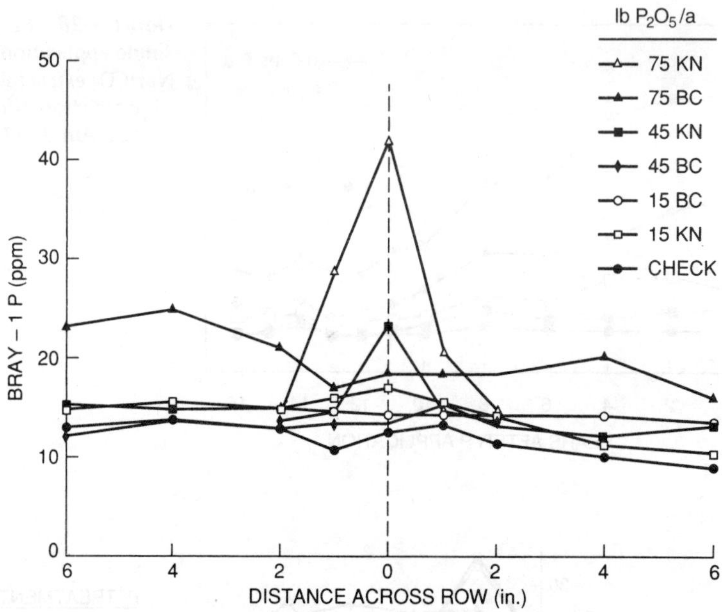

Figure 5-30 **Influence of band-applied fertilizer P on soil test P in the band 23 months after application. KN-knifed P 1 in. below the seed; BC-broadcast P.** ***(Havlin et al., 1990,*** **Proc. FFF Symposium,** ***p. 213.)***

Study Questions

1. If you saw a field of dwarfed corn, reddish purple in color, and the corn plant tissue tested high in NO_3^-, you might suspect that these plants were deficient in what nutrient?
2. Give brief descriptions of the main pathways of transporting soil P to plant roots. Can phosphate fertilization alter the importance of these pathways?
3. Compare typical soil solution concentrations of P in unfertilized soil with the required soil solution levels for high yields.
4. Define P intensity and quantity factors. What is labile soil P?
5. Is soil organic P available to plants?
6. How is P availability influenced by soil pH?
7. What are two important factors that influence the P uptake by plants? What is P retention or fixation? Why is it important agriculturally? Is fixed P totally lost to plants?
8. What are the various mechanisms of P retention in acid mineral soils?
9. What soil properties influence fixation of fertilizer P and what can be done to reduce the amount of P fixation?
10. Refer to Figure 5-8 (P solubility diagram) and answer the following:
    a. A soil contains TCP and Strengite minerals. The soil pH would be _____ and the soil solution P concentration would be _____ M.
    b. After 20 years of fertilizer N use the soil pH dropped 2 units. The P mineral present at this pH would be _____ and the solution P concentration would be _____ M.

c. Assuming the critical P level is 10^{-4} M, the minimum pH for adequate P supply to plants would be ______.

d. The initial soil pH is 8. Circle one answer in each group. If the pH is slowly decreased, the concentration of P in solution will (increase, decrease, not change) until about pH (7.2, 6.2, 7.8), at which point the solution P level generally (increases, decreases, or stays the same) until pH (7.0, 6.0, 5.0) at which point solution P (increases, decreases, stays the same).

e. A soil contains octacalcium phosphate and variscite. What is the soil pH range where solution P would be enough for adequate P availability (assume the critical P level is 10^{-4} M). Soil pH = ___–___.

f. Why does the the P solubility increase above pH 7.8 for the Ca-phosphate minerals?

g. Fertilizer P is added to a soil at pH 7.2. The P compound in this soil is hydroxyapatite. What is the initial P compound the precipitates in the soil and what is the final P compound to precipitate?

11. What is the original source of most fertilizer P?

12. What acids are commonly used to acidify RP? Why does acid treatment of RP render the P more plant-available?

13. Describe the soil and management conditions that you might expect an appreciable downward movement of P through the soil profile.

14. Under what soil conditions would the band placement of P result in its greatest utilization by the plant? If there were no such thing as P fixation, what method of fertilizer placement would probably result in the greatest utilization by plants? Why?

15. Under what types of soil and cropping conditions might the use of RP give satisfactory results? Explain.

16. What advantages or disadvantages exist with high-analysis sources as DAP, MAP, and TSP?

17. What is residual P? Why is it important agriculturally?

18. What are polyphosphates? Describe the hydrolysis reaction of polyphosphates.

19. Briefly describe the sequence of events that takes place during the dissolution of P fertilizers.

20. Describe how the presence of N improves plant utilization of P fertilizers. Which of the two forms, NH_4^+ or NO_3^-, is more beneficial?

21. What are typical distances for the initial movement of P from fertilizer application sites? Will P in the reaction zones eventually become more uniformly distributed in the soil?

Selected References

Barber, S. A. 1984. *Soil nutrient bioavailability: A mechanistic approach*. New York: John Wiley & Sons.

Khasawneh, F. E. (Ed.). 1980. *The role of phosphorus in agriculture*. Madison, Wis.: American Society of Agronomy, Crop Science Society of America, Soil Science Society of America.

Lindsay, W. L. 1979. *Chemical equilibria in soils*. New York: John Wiley & Sons.

Mortvedt, J.J., L.S. Murphy, and R.H. Follett. 1999. *Fertilizer technology and application.* Willoughby, Ohio: Meister Publishing Co.

Stevenson, F. J. 1986. *Cycles of soil: Carbon, nitrogen, phosphorus, sulfur, micronutrients.* New York: John Wiley & Sons.

Young, R. D., D. G. Westfall, and G. W. Colliver. 1985. Production, marketing, and use of phosphorus fertilizers (pp. 324–76). In O. P. Englestad (Ed.), *Fertilizer technology and use.* Madison, Wis.: Soil Science Society of America.

CHAPTER 6

Potassium

Potassium (K) is absorbed by plants in larger amounts than any other nutrient except N. Although total soil K content exceeds crop uptake during a growing season, in most cases only a small fraction of it is available to plants. Total soil K content ranges between 0.5 to 2.5% and is lower in coarse-textured soils formed from sandstone or quartzite and higher in fine-textured soils formed from rocks high in K-bearing minerals.

Soils of the Southeast and Northwest are highly leached and have a low K content. In contrast, soils of the Midwest and Western states generally have a high K content because these soils are formed from geologically young parent materials and conditions of lower rainfall. In tropical soils, total K content is generally low because of greater weathering by high rainfall and temperatures, thus K deficiency frequently occurs after a few years of cropping a virgin soil.

The K Cycle

Listed in increasing order of plant availability, soil K exists in four forms:

mineral	5,000–25,000 ppm (0.5 to 2.5%)
nonexchangeable	50–750 ppm
exchangeable	40–600 ppm
solution	1–10 ppm

Mineral K accounts for 90 to 98% of the total soil K, whereas slowly available (nonexchangeable) and readily available (exchangeable and solution) represents 1 to 10% and 0.1 to 2%, respectively. K cycling or transformations among K forms in soils are dynamic (Fig. 6-1). Because of K removal by crop uptake and leaching, there is a continuous but slow transfer of K from primary minerals to exchangeable and slowly available forms. With applications of large amounts of fertilizer K, some reversion to slowly available forms will occur.

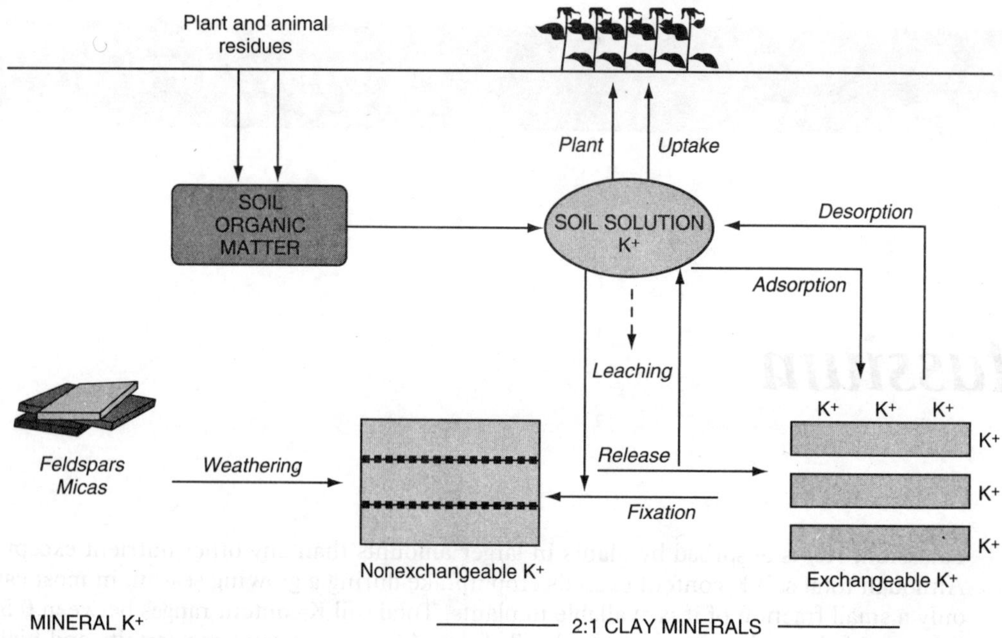

Figure 6-1 **K cycling in soils.**

Exchangeable and solution K equilibrate rapidly, whereas nonexchangeable K equilibrates very slowly with exchangeable and solution forms. Transfer of K from the mineral fraction to more available forms is extremely slow in most soils, and this K is considered essentially unavailable to crops during a single growing season.

Functions and Forms of K in Plants

Forms

K is absorbed by plant roots as K^+ and its tissue concentration ranges from 0.5 to 6% in dry matter.

Functions

Unlike N, P, and most other nutrients, K is not a component of biochemical compounds in the plant. K exists solely in solution or bound to (−) charges on tissue surfaces. As a result, K^+ has functions particularly related to solution ionic strength in plant cells. K is involved in water relations, charge balance, and osmotic pressure in cells and across membranes, which explains its high mobility in the plant.

K is important for many crop quality characteristics due to its involvement in synthesis and transport of photosynthates to plant reproductive and storage organs (grain, fruit, tubers, etc.), and subsequent conversion into carbohydrates, proteins, oils, and other products.

In fruit and vegetable crops (citrus, bananas, tomatoes, potatoes, onions, etc.), adequate K enhances fruit size, color, taste, and peel thickness, which is important for storage and shipping quality.

K deficiency influences metabolic processes primarily related to photosynthesis, and synthesis and translocation of enzymes. The increase in dark respiration under K deficiency reduces plant growth and crop quality.

Photosynthesis and Energy Relations K is essential to photosynthesis through several functions, including:

- ATP synthesis
- production and activity of specific photosynthetic enzymes (i.e. RuBP carboxylase)
- CO_2 absorption through leaf stomates
- maintenance of electroneutrality during photophosphorylation in chloroplasts

Plants require K for the photosynthetic transfer of radiant energy into chemical energy through production of ATP (photophosphorylation). Energy from ATP is required for metabolic processes in plants that produce carbohydrates, proteins, lipids, oils, vitamins, and other compounds essential for crop productivity and quality. K nutrition for optimum photosynthesis, measured by CO_2 absorption, varies with the crop, where 1.7 to 2.0% leaf K is needed in corn (Fig. 6-2) and 3.0 to 3.2% K is needed in alfalfa (Fig. 6-3). Increased

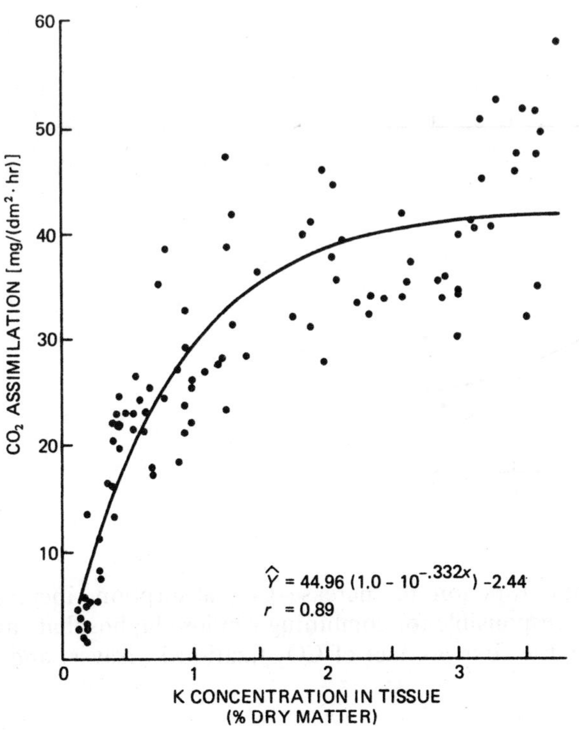

Figure 6-2 **Adequate K in corn leaves increases photosynthesis as measured by CO_2 fixation.** ***(Smid and Peaslee, 1976, Agron. J., 68:907.)***

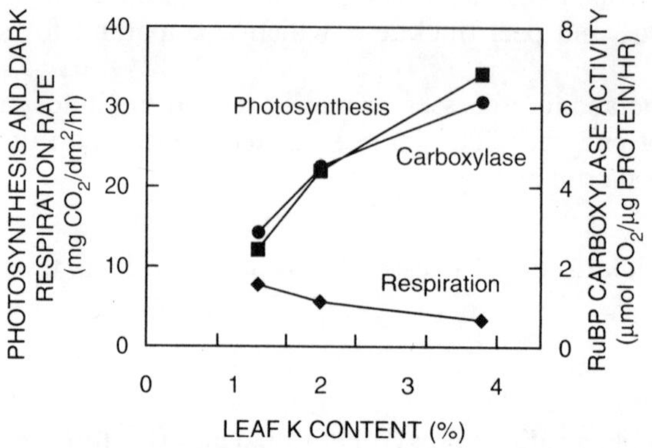

Figure 6-3 **Relationship between K nutrition and rate of photosynthesis and dark respiration as measured by CO_2 exchange in alfalfa.** *(Marschner, 1995,* **Mineral Nutrition of Higher Plants.** *[2nd ed.], Academic Press, London.)*

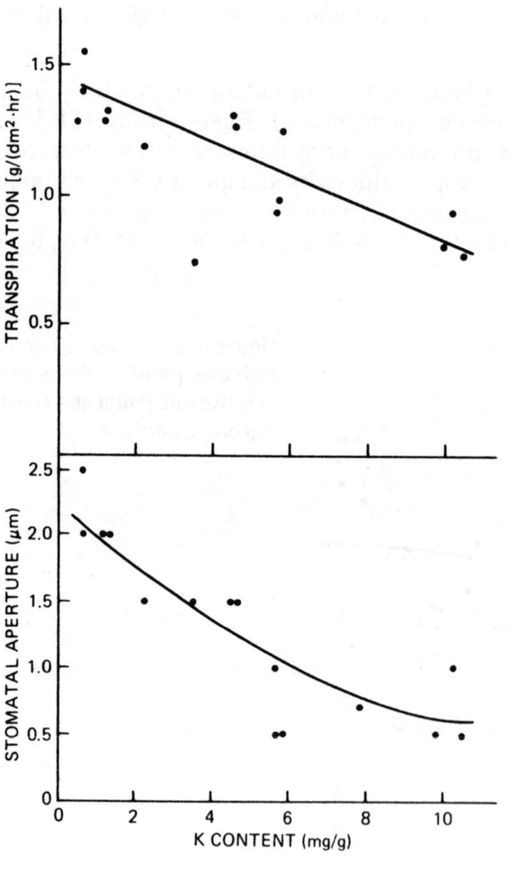

Figure 6-4 **Improved K nutrition reduced transpiration rate of peas due to smaller stomatal apertures.** *(Brag, 1972,* **Physiol. Plant.,** *26:254.)*

K supply influences stomatal function to increase CO_2 absorption, increases RuBP carboxylase enzyme activity responsible for combining ribulose biphosphate and CO_2 to produce 3-phosphoglycerate, the first product of CO_2 fixation in leaves, and decreases dark respiration (Fig. 6-4).

Enzyme Activation K is involved in activation of enzymes important to energy utilization, starch synthesis, N metabolism, and respiration. These enzymes are abundant in meristematic tissue at the growing points, both above and below ground level, where cell division occurs rapidly and where primary tissues are formed. For example, the starch synthetase enzyme converts sugars into starch, which is critical to starch accumulation in grains, fruits, and vegetables. Decreased starch conversion causes soluble sugar accumulation that affects fruit quality. Also, K influences the nitrogenase enzyme required for reduction of atmospheric N_2 to NH_3 in *Rhizobium* (Chapter 4). N_2 reduction depends on carbohydrate supply, where K enhances carbohydrate transport to nodules for amino acids synthesis.

Translocation of Assimilates Once CO_2 is assimilated into sugars during photosynthesis, they are transported from leaves to fruits, roots, tubers, seeds, and grains where they are stored or used for growth. Translocation of sugars uses energy from ATP that requires K for its synthesis. Sugar translocation is greatly reduced in K-deficient plants where, for example, normal translocation rate in sugarcane leaves is $\approx$ 2.5 cm/min that is reduced to half in K-deficient plants. Under adequate K nutrition, osmotic potential of the phloem sap, water flow rate, and sucrose concentration are higher than in K-deficient plants. K is also important as a counterion (maintaining electrical balance) for NO_3^- transport in the xylem.

Water Relations K provides much of the osmotic "pull" that draws water into plant roots. K-deficient plants are less able to withstand water stress, mostly because of their inability to fully utilize available water. Maintenance of plant turgor is essential for optimum photosynthetic and metabolic processes. Stomatal opening occurs when there is an increase of turgor pressure in the guard cells surrounding each stoma, which is brought about by an influx of K. Malfunctioning of stomata due to K deficiency is related to lower rates of photosynthesis and less efficient water use. Transpiration, or water loss through stomata, accounts for most plant water use. K can affect the rate of transpiration and water uptake through regulation of stomatal openings (Fig. 6-2).

Visual Deficiency Symptoms

Typical K-deficiency symptoms in alfalfa consist of white spots on the leaf edges, whereas chlorosis and necrosis of the leaf edges are observed with corn and other grasses (see color plates inside book cover). Since K is mobile in the plant, visual deficiency symptoms usually appear first in the lower leaves, progressing toward the top leaves as deficiency severity increases. K deficiency can also occur in young leaves of high-yielding, fast-maturing crops such as cotton and wheat. Dry weather-induced K-deficiency symptoms appear on leaves in the middle of the plant where leaf tips and eventually the whole leaf exhibit chlorosis.

Another K-deficiency symptom is weakening of straw, which causes lodging in small grains and stalk breakage in corn (Fig. 6-5) and sorghum. Table 6-1 shows how seriously stalk breakage can affect production through impaired yields and harvesting losses. K stress can increase the degree of crop damage by bacterial and fungal diseases, insect and mite infestation, and nematode and virus infection (Fig. 6-6). K-deficient soybeans are highly

Figure 6-5 Response of corn to K on a low-K soil. Note the poor growth and lodged condition of the crop on the right. *(Courtesy of the Potash & Phosphate Institute.)*

Table 6-1 Effect of N and K on Corn Yield and Lodging

K_2O Applied	N Applied 0	80	160
----------lb/a----------			
		Grain Yield (bu/a)	
0	48	33	38
80	73	116	119
160	59	122	129
		Lodging (%)	
0	9	57	59
80	4	3	8
160	4	4	4

SOURCE: Schulte, 1975, Proc. Wisconsin Fert. and Aglime Conf., p. 58.

susceptible to pod and stem blight caused by the fungus *Diaporthe sojae L.* (Table 6-2). Higher rates of K as either KCl or K_2SO_4 markedly decreased the incidence of disease in each variety. Lack of K in wetland rice greatly increases the severity of foliar diseases such as stem rot, sheath blight, and brown leaf spot.

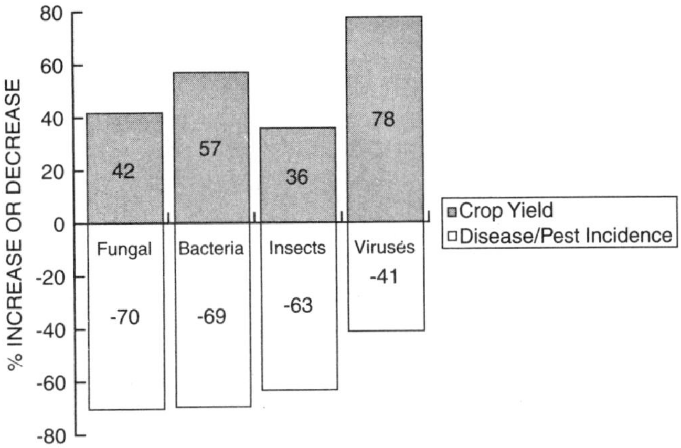

Figure 6-6 **Summary of over 2,400 research projects demonstrating the positive effect of adequate K nutrition on crop yield and resistance to diseases and insect infestation. *(Perrenoud, 1990,* Potassium and Plant Health, *IPI Research Topics No. 3., Switzerland.)***

Table 6-2 **Effect of K on Soybean Yield and Disease**

KCl or K_2SO_4 g/pot	*Seeds per Plant*		*Diseased Seed (%)**	
	Var. A	*Var. B*	*Var. A*	*Var. B*
0	254	200	87	62
2	262	207	65	58
10	275	209	21	33
40	264	200	13	14

*Percentage of gray, moldy seed (*D. sojae* infected).
SOURCE: Crittenden and Svec, 1974, *Agron. J.*, 66: 697.

In citrus fruits and vegetables, K deficiency appears through decreased size, reduced peel or skin thickness, increased skin cracking, and discolorations on skins. K deficiency also contributes to poor storage and shelf-life characteristics.

Forms of Soil K

Soil Solution K

Plant roots absorb K^+ from the soil solution (Fig. 6-1). Solution K^+ concentration for optimum plant growth varies, depending on the crop and yield level, ranging between 1 and 10 ppm K^+. The higher values are commonly found in arid or saline soils. Under field conditions, K^+ varies considerably due to concentration and dilution through evaporation and precipitation. K^+ uptake is influenced by the presence of other cations, particularly Ca^{+2} and Mg^{+2}. In acid and sodic soils, Al^{+3} and Na^+ reduce K^+ uptake, respectively. The activity ratio (AR_e^k)

$$\frac{K^+ \text{ activity}}{\sqrt{Ca^{+2} + Mg^{+2} \text{activity}}}$$

represents the ratio of cations in solution in equilibrium with exchangeable cations and provides an estimate of readily available K. Soils with similar values may have different capacities for maintaining AR_e^k while K^+ is being depleted by plant uptake or leaching. Thus, to describe K availability both solution (intensity) and exchangeable K (capacity) must be evaluated, as discussed in Chapter 2.

The quantity of K transported to the root surface by diffusion and mass flow is related to K intensity. The relative contribution of mass flow to K absorption can be estimated. For example, if the K concentration in the crop is 2.5% and the transpiration ratio is 400 g H_2O/g plant, transpirational water should contain > 60 ppm K for mass flow to provide sufficient K. Since most soils contain 1 to 10 ppm solution K, mass flow contributes ≈ 10% of crop K requirement. Mass flow could supply more K to crops grown in soils naturally high in water-soluble K or where fertilizer K has increased solution K. K diffusion is a slow process compared with mass flow and is limited to distances of only 1 to 4 mm (Table 6-3). Diffusion accounts for ≈ 90% of K absorption by roots. K diffusion to roots can be seen from autoradiographs made by using ^{86}Rb, which closely resembles K (Fig. 6-7). Since K absorption occurs within only a few millimeters of the root, K that is farther away, although possibly plant available, is not positionally available.

Exchangeable K

Like other exchangeable cations, K^+ is held around negatively-charged soil colloids by electrostatic attraction to three types of exchange sites or binding positions (Fig. 6-8). The planar position (*p*) on the outside surfaces is rather unspecific for K, whereas the edge (*e*) and inner (*i*) positions have a high K^+ specificity. Under field conditions, soil solution K concentrations are buffered more readily by K^+ held to *p* positions; however, K^+ held on all 3 positions contributes to solution K.

Because of the major role of exchangeable K in buffering changes in solution K, the relationship between exchangeable K (quantity) and solution K (intensity), or Q:I ratio defined in Chapter 2, is used to quantify K buffering in soils. Labile soil K (held in *p* positions) may be more reliably estimated by Q:I than by 1 N NH_4OAc exchangeable K.

Table 6-3 **Mechanisms and Rate of K Transport in Soils**

Situation	*Mechanism*	*Rate (cm/day)*
In profile	Mainly mass flow	Up to 10
Around fertilizer source	Mass flow and diffusion	< 0.1
Around root	Mainly diffusion	0.01–0.1
Out of clay interlayers	Diffusion	10^{-7}

SOURCE: Tinker, 1978, *Potassium in Soils and Crops*, Potash Research Institute of India, New Delhi.

Figure 6-7 Left, corn roots growing through soil. Right, autoradiograph showing the effect of corn roots on ^{86}Rb distribution in the soil. Lighter areas are where ^{86}Rb concentration is reduced by root uptake of ^{86}Rb. *(Barber, 1985, in R. D. Munson (Ed.),* Potassium in Agriculture, *ASA, CSSA, SSSA, Madison, Wis.)*

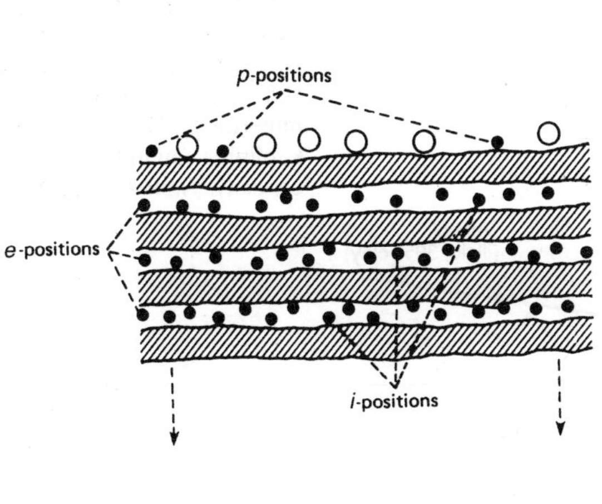

Figure 6-8 Binding sites for K on 2:1 clay minerals such as mica, vermiculite, and chlorite. *(Mengel and Haeder, 1973,* Potash Rev., *11:1.)*

Q:I measures the ability of soil to maintain the K^+ intensity and is proportional to CEC. A high Q:I signifies good K buffering capacity, whereas a low Q:I suggests a need for K fertilization. Liming can increase Q:I, presumably as a result of the increase in pH-dependent CEC. When Q:I values are low, small changes in exchangeable K produce large differences in solution K^+. In sandy soils, where BC is small, intense leaching or rapid plant growth can deplete available K (Fig. 6-9). In addition, the BC of kaolinitic soils is lower than in mica clays (Fig. 6-10).

In general, the relation between exchangeable and solution K^+ is a good measure of availability of labile K to plants. Soil-testing laboratories use extractants (e.g., NH_4OAc) to quantify both solution and exchangeable K. The ability of a soil to maintain the activity ratio against depletion by plant roots and leaching is governed partly by labile K pool, rate of release of fixed or nonexchangeable K, and diffusion and transport of K^+ in solution.

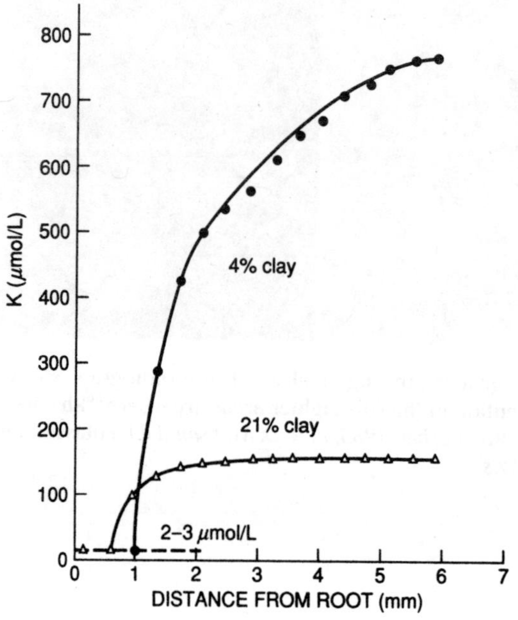

Figure 6-9 **K concentration in the soil solution around a maize root in two soils after 3 days. The initial exchangeable K content was 0.17 meq/100 g in the loamy soil (21% clay) and 0.37 meq/100 g in the sandy soil (4% clay). Because of the lower BC of the sandy soil, the difference in solution K concentrations was greater than for exchangeable K.** ***(Claassen and Jungk, 1982,*** **Soil Sci. Soc. Am. J.** ***41:1322.)***

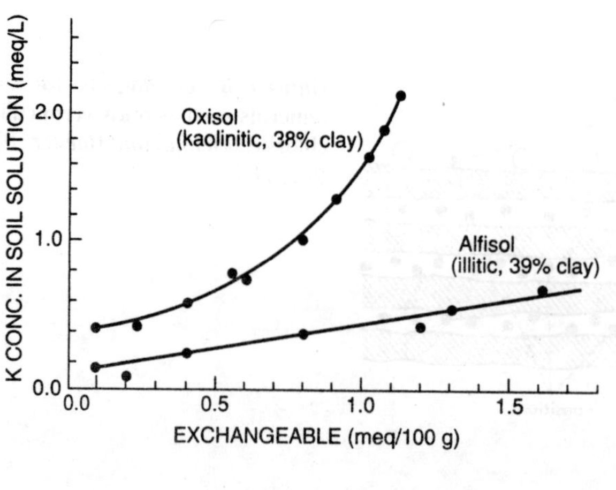

Figure 6-10 **Relationship between exchangeable-K and solution-K concentration of two soils with the same clay content but different clay mineralogy. The steeper slope of the kaolinitic soil indicates less buffer capacity.** ***(Nemeth, unpublished.)***

Nonexchangeable and Mineral K

The remaining soil K is comprised of *nonexchangeable* and *mineral* K. Although nonexchangeable K reserves are not always immediately available, they can contribute significantly to maintenance of exchangeable or labile K. A portion of nonexchangeable K becomes available as the exchangeable and solution K^+ are removed by cropping or lost by leaching during the growing season. However, nonexchangeable K release is generally too slow to meet crop demand during the growing season.

K Release The rate of nonexchangeable K release to solution and exchangeable K is largely governed by weathering of K-bearing micas and feldspars. K feldspars are orthoclase and microcline ($KAlSi_3O_8$) and the micas are muscovite [$KAl_3Si_3O_{10}(OH)_2$], biotite [$K(Mg,Fe)_3AlSi_3O_{10}(OH)_2$], and phlogopite [$KMg_2Al_2Si_3O_{10}(OH)_2$]. The ease of weathering depends on mineral properties and the environment. The relative K availability from these minerals is biotite, which is greater than muscovite, which is greater than potassium feldspars. Feldspars have a three-dimensional crystal structure, with K located throughout the mineral lattice. K can be released from feldspars only by destruction of the mineral.

K feldspars are the largest natural K reserve in many soils. In moderately weathered soils, there are usually considerable quantities of K feldspars. They often occur in much smaller amounts or may even be absent in strongly weathered soils such as those in humid tropical areas.

The micas are 2:1 layer silicates (Chapter 2). K^+ resides mainly between the silicate layers (Figure 6-11). Bonding of interlayer K is stronger in dioctahedral than in trioctahedral micas; therefore, K release generally occurs more readily with biotite than with muscovite. Gradual release of K from positions in the mica lattice results in the formation of hydrous mica and eventually vermiculite (Figure 6-11). There is also an increase in CEC following transformation of mica.

K release from mica is both a cation exchange and a diffusion process, requiring time for the exchanging cation to reach the site and for the exchanged K^+ to diffuse. Low K^+ concentration in solution favors interlayer K release. Thus, depletion of K^+ by root adsorption

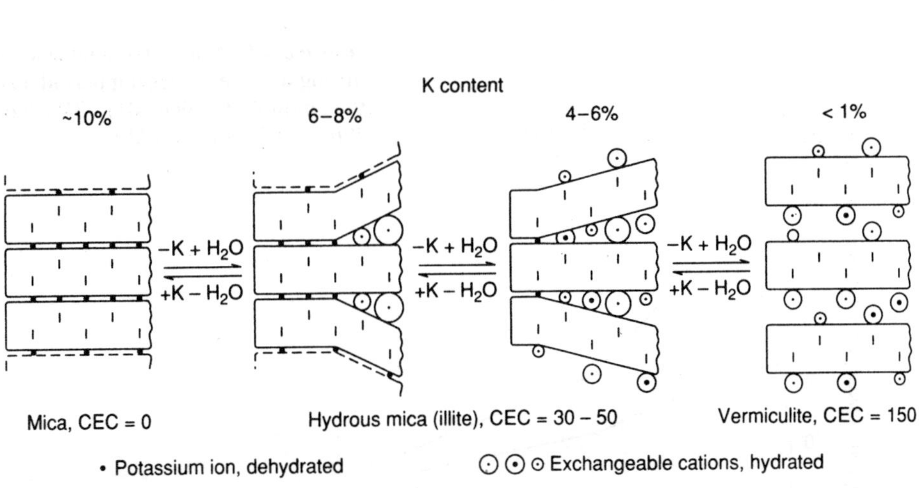

Figure 6-11 **Schematic weathering of micas and their transformation into clay minerals: A matter of K release and fixation.** *(McLean, 1979,* **Potassium in Soil and Crops,** *Potash Research Institute of India, New Delhi, pp. 1–13.)*

or leaching may induce nonexchangeable K release. K release can occur from all interlayer locations, or it may come only from alternate interlayers, leading to formation of interstratified mica-vermiculite.

K Fixation K fixation represents the reentrapment of K^+ between the layers of 2:1 clays, predominately hydrous mica (Figure 6-11). The 1:1 minerals such as kaolinite do not fix K. K^+ is sufficiently small to enter the interlayer regions, where it is firmly held by electrostatic forces. NH_4^+ has nearly the same ionic radius as K^+ and can also be fixed (Chapter 4). Cations such as Ca^{+2} and Na^+ have larger ionic radii than K^+ and do not move into the interlayer positions. Because NH_4^+ can be fixed by clays in a manner similar to K^+, its presence will alter both fixation of added K and release of fixed K. Just as the presence of K^+can block the release of fixed NH_4^+, the presence of NH_4^+ can block the release of fixed K^+ (Figure 6-12). NH_4^+ held in the interlayer positions further traps K^+ already present.

K fixation is generally more important in fine-textured soils. Although fixation reactions are not considered a serious factor in limiting crop response to either applied NH_4^+ or NH_4^+, increasing K^+ concentration in soils with a high fixation capacity will obviously encourage greater fixation.

Air drying some soils high in exchangeable K can result in fixation and a decline in exchangeable K. In contrast, drying of field-moist soils low in exchangeable K, particularly subsoils, will frequently increase exchangeable K. The release of K upon drying is thought to be caused by cracking of the clay edges and exposure of interlayer K, which can then be released to exchange sites. The effects of wetting and drying on the availability of K under field conditions is difficult to quantify. They are important, however, in soil testing. Soil test procedures call for the air drying of samples before analysis. Drying can substantially modify soil test K values and subsequent recommendations for K fertilization.

Freezing and thawing of moist soils may also be important in K release and fixation. With alternate freezing and thawing, mica clays release K, whereas in soils low in these clays, particularly those high in exchangeable K, no K release is observed. Freezing and thawing may play a significant role in the K supply of certain soils, depending on their clay mineralogy and degree of weathering.

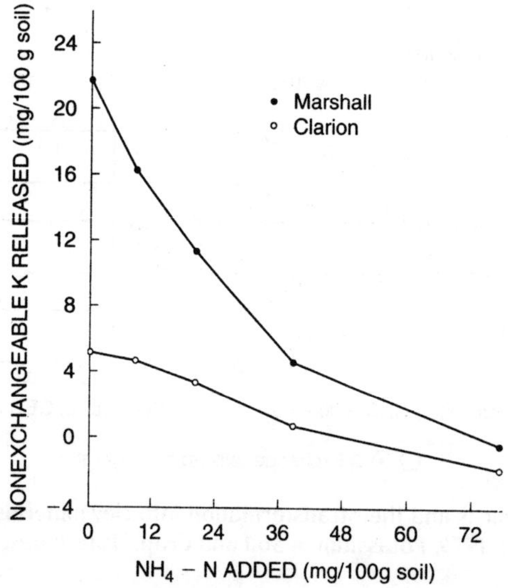

Figure 6-12 **Nonexchangeable K released during a 10-day cropping period as influenced by the amount of added NH_4^+. *(Welch and Scott, 1961,* SSSA Proc., *25:102.)***

Retention of K in less available or fixed forms is of considerable practical significance. As with P, the conversion of K to slowly available or fixed forms reduces its immediate value as a plant nutrient. However, it must not be assumed that K fixation is completely unfavorable. K fixation results in conservation of K, which can become available over a long period of time and thus is not entirely lost to plants, although plants vary in their ability to utilize slowly available K.

Factors Affecting K Availability

Clay Minerals and CEC

The greater the proportion of high K clay minerals, the greater the potential K availability in a soil. Soils containing vermiculite, montmorillonite, or mica have more K than soils containing mainly kaolinitic clays, which are more highly weathered and low in K. Intensively cropped montmorillonitic soils may be low in K and require K fertilization for optimum crop production.

Finer-textured soils usually have a higher CEC and can hold more exchangeable K; however, a higher exchangeable K does not always result in higher solution K. Solution K^+ in the finer-textured soils (loams and silt loams) may be considerably lower than that in coarse-textured soils at any given level of exchangeable K (Fig. 6-10).

Exchangeable K

Determination of exchangeable K is a measure of K availability. Many studies show the relationship between soil test K and response to applied K. Fertilizer applications of K can be adjusted downward with increasing levels of available soil K (Fig. 6-13). In general, the amount of K needed to increase exchangeable K 1 ppm may vary (1 to 50 lbs K/a), depending on the soil. The wide difference is related in part to the variation in K-fixation potential among soils. Fortunately, some of the K that is fixed may be subsequently released to crops, but the release may be too slow for high levels of crop production.

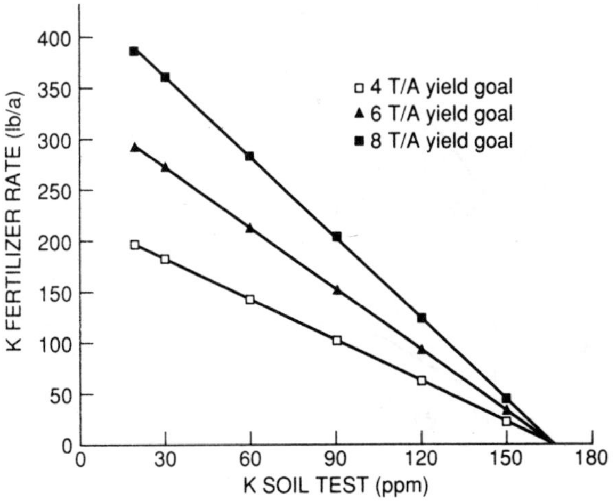

Figure 6-13 **K fertilizer recommendations for alfalfa in the northern Plains. Fertilizer K rate decreases with increasing soil test K and decreasing alfalfa yield goal.**

Environment

Soil Moisture With low soil moisture, water films around soil particles are thinner and discontinuous, resulting in a more tortuous path for K^+ diffusion to roots. Increasing K levels or moisture content in the soil will increase K diffusion. Soil moisture can have substantial effects on K transport in soil (Fig. 6-14). Increasing soil moisture from 10 to 28% increases total transport by up to 175%.

Soil Temperature The effect of temperature on K uptake is due to changes in both K availability and root activity. Low temperatures restrict plant growth and rate of K uptake. For example, K influx into corn roots at 15°C (59°F) was only about one-half that at 29°C (84°F) (Fig. 6-15). In the same study, root growth was eight times greater at 29°C than at 15°C. K concentration in the shoot was 8.1% at 29°C and 3.7% at 15°C.

Providing high K levels to increase K uptake at low temperatures overcomes some of the adverse effect of low temperature on diffusion. Temperature effects are probably a major reason for crop responses to band-applied fertilizer for early season crops. The beneficial effect of K fertilization of barley grown on soils high in available K is attributed mainly to improvement in K supply under cool soil conditions (Table 6-4).

Soil Aeration Normal root function is strongly dependent on an adequate O_2 supply. Under high soil moisture or in compact soils, root growth is restricted, O_2 supply is reduced,

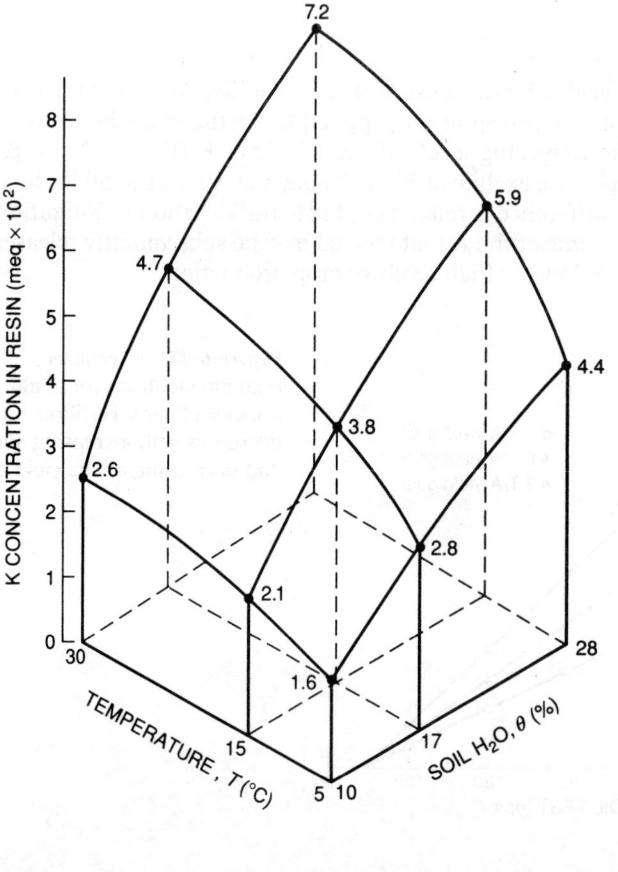

Figure 6-14 **Diffusion of K in silt loam as influenced by temperature and soil moisture.** ***(Skogley, 1981, Proc. 32nd Annu. Northwest Fert. Conf., Billings, Montana.)***

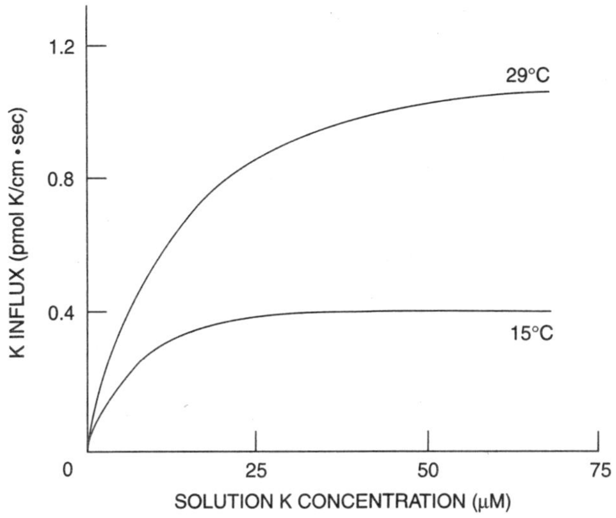

Figure 6-15 **Rate of K influx into young corn roots is increased by higher temperature and K concentration in solution.** *(Ching and Barber, 1979,* Agron. J., *71:1040.)*

Table 6-4 **Effect of K Fertilization on Barley Seedlings Grown on High-K Montana Soils**

Seeding Date	*K_2O* (lb/a)*	*Yield (bu/a)*
April 6	00	48
	20	55
May 6	00	36
	20	42
June 3	00	30
	20	33

*N at 60 lbs/a/yr and P_2O_5 at 25 lbs/a/yr.
SOURCE: Dubbs, 1981, *Better Crops Plant Food*, 65: 27.

and K absorption is slowed. The inhibitory action of poor aeration on nutrient uptake is most pronounced with K.

Soil pH In low pH soils, toxic amounts of exchangeable Al^{+3} and Mn^{+2} create an unfavorable root environment for nutrient uptake. When acid soils are limed, exchangeable Al^{+3} is converted to insoluble $Al(OH)_3$. The reduction in exchangeable Al^{+3} reduces competition with K^+, enabling K^+ to compete with Ca^{+2} for vacant exchange sites. As a consequence, greater amounts of K^+ can be adsorbed to CEC. Leaching losses of K will also likely be reduced.

Both Ca^{+2} and Mg^{+2} compete with K^+ for uptake; thus, soils high in one or both may require K fertilization for optimum K nutrition. The AR_e^k illustrates that K^+ uptake would be reduced as Ca^{+2} and Mg^{+2} are increased; conversely, Ca^{+2} and Mg^{+2} would be reduced as K^+ is increased. Thus, the K^+ availability is somewhat more dependent on its concentration relative to Ca^{+2} and Mg^{+2} than on the total quantity of K present.

K Leaching

In most soils, K leaching losses are small, except in coarse-textured or organic soils in humid regions or under irrigation. In the humid tropics, K leaching is recognized as a major factor in limiting productivity. Under natural vegetation, leaching is low (0 to 5 lbs/a/yr). On cleared land after fertilizer application, 35% of applied K may be leached with cropping, and much higher losses occur on bare land. In these soils emphasis should be placed on annual or split applications rather than on buildup of soil K.

K source can influence the amount of K leached (Table 6-5). Compared with KCl, the SO_4^{-2} and PO_4^{-2} sources exhibit greater anion adsorption to (+) exchange sites. Thus, with fewer anions in solution available for leaching, fewer K^+ would be leached. Remember that solutions must be electrically neutral, (−) charges = (+) charges; therefore, for every one (−) charge leached, one (+) charge must also be leached.

The specific cations adsorbed to the CEC also influence K leaching. Consider the following:

$$\text{Clay}\left]\begin{array}{l}K^{+}\\K^{+}\\Al^{+3}\\K^{+}\\K^{+}\end{array}\right. + \; CaSO_4 \;\leftrightarrows\; \text{Clay}\left]\begin{array}{l}Al^{+3}\\Ca^{+2}\\K^{+}\\K^{+}\end{array}\right. + \; K_2SO_4$$

If the CEC is nearly saturated with K^+ (usually not the case), and a neutral salt (e.g., $CaSO_4$) is added, some of the adsorbed K^+ will be replaced by Ca^+. The amount of replacement will depend on the type and amount of salt added and the quantity of adsorbed K^+. On some soils used for perennial crop production, $CaSO_4$ is applied to encourage K^+ desorption and transport into the subsoil to increase K availability deeper in the profile.

In this example, KCl is added to a soil saturated with Ca^{+2} and Al^{+3} (common in acid soils):

$$\text{Clay}\left]\begin{array}{l}Ca^{+}\\Al^{+3}\\Al^{+3}\end{array}\right. + \; KCl \;\leftrightarrows\; \text{Clay}\left]\begin{array}{l}K^{+}\\1/2Ca^{+2}\\Al^{+3}\\Al^{+3}\end{array}\right. + \; 1/2CaCl_2$$

Because Ca^{+2} is easier displaced than Al^{+3}, the added K^+ replaces some of the Ca^{+2}. This reaction illustrates an important point: the greater the degree of Ca^{+2} saturation, the

Table 6-5 **Influence of K Source on Leaching Loss in Turf**

	Water Applied (in.)				
K Source	*10*	*20*	*50*	*75*	*100*
	% of K applied leached below root zone				
Potassium chloride, KCl	17	75	91	91	94
Potassium sulphate, K_2SO_4	0	15	53	79	79
Potassium phosphate, K_3PO_4	0	0	0	18	33

SOURCE: Sartain, 1988, *Soil Sci. Fert. Sheet.*, SL52, Univ. of Florida, Gainesville, Fla.

greater the K^+ adsorption. This is consistent with the previous example, where Ca^{+2} from $CaSO_4$ replaces K^+, but less readily replaces Al^{+3} (*lyotropic series* in Chapter 2). In such cases, there will be a net transfer of K^+ to the soil solution. Sandy soils with a high % BS lose less exchangeable K^+ by leaching than soils with a low % BS, because the added K^+ will exchange with Ca^{+2} easier than in an acid soil with low % BS. Liming increases % BS, thus decreasing exchangeable K^+ loss.

Sources of K

Organic K

K in organic wastes (manures and sewage sludge) occurs predominately as soluble inorganic K^+. In animal waste, K content ranges between 0.2 and 2% (4 to 40 lbs K/t) of dry matter (Table 10-17). The average K content in sewage sludge is 10 lbs K/t. Therefore, waste materials can supply sufficient quantities of plant available K, depending on the rate applied. Most waste application rates are governed by the quantity of N or P applied to minimize impacts of land application of waste on surface and groundwater quality. If low waste rates are utilized on K-deficient soils, additional K may be needed.

Inorganic K Fertilizers

Deposits of soluble K salts are found well beneath the earth's surface, but also in the brines of dying lakes and seas (Fig. 6-16). Many of these deposits have high purity and lend themselves to mining of agricultural and industrial K salts or potash. The world's largest high-grade potash deposit is in Canada, extending 450 miles long by 150 miles wide, with a depth of 3,000 to 7,000 ft.

Like P, fertilizer K content is presently guaranteed as K oxide (K_2O) equivalent (Table 6-6). Converting between % K and % K_2O is accomplished by:

$$\%K = \%K_2O \times 0.83$$

$$\%K_2O = \%K \times 1.2$$

Potassium Chloride (KCl) Fertilizer-grade KCl contains 50 to 52% K (60 to 63% K_2O) and varies in color from pink or red to brown or white, depending on the mining and recovery process. KCl is the most common K fertilizer used for direct application and for manufacture of N-P-K fertilizers. When added to the soil, it readily dissolves in water.

Potassium Sulfate (K_2SO_4) K_2SO_4 is a white solid containing 42 to 44% K (50 to 53% K_2O) and 17% S. Its global consumption has been increasing and now represents about 7% of total potash use. K_2SO_4 is produced in several different ways, including reacting KCl with SO_4-containing salts or H_2SO_4 and recovery from natural brines. It is commonly used on Cl^- sensitive crops such as potatoes and tobacco and for tree fruits and vegetables. Its behavior is similar to KCl in soil but has the advantages of supplying S and having a lower salt index.

Potassium Magnesium Sulfate (K_2SO_4, $MgSO_4$) Potassium magnesium sulfate is a double salt containing 18% K (22% K_2O), 11% Mg, and 22% S. It has the advantage of supplying both Mg and S and is frequently included in mixed fertilizers for soils deficient in Mg and S. It reacts as would any other neutral salt when applied to the soil.

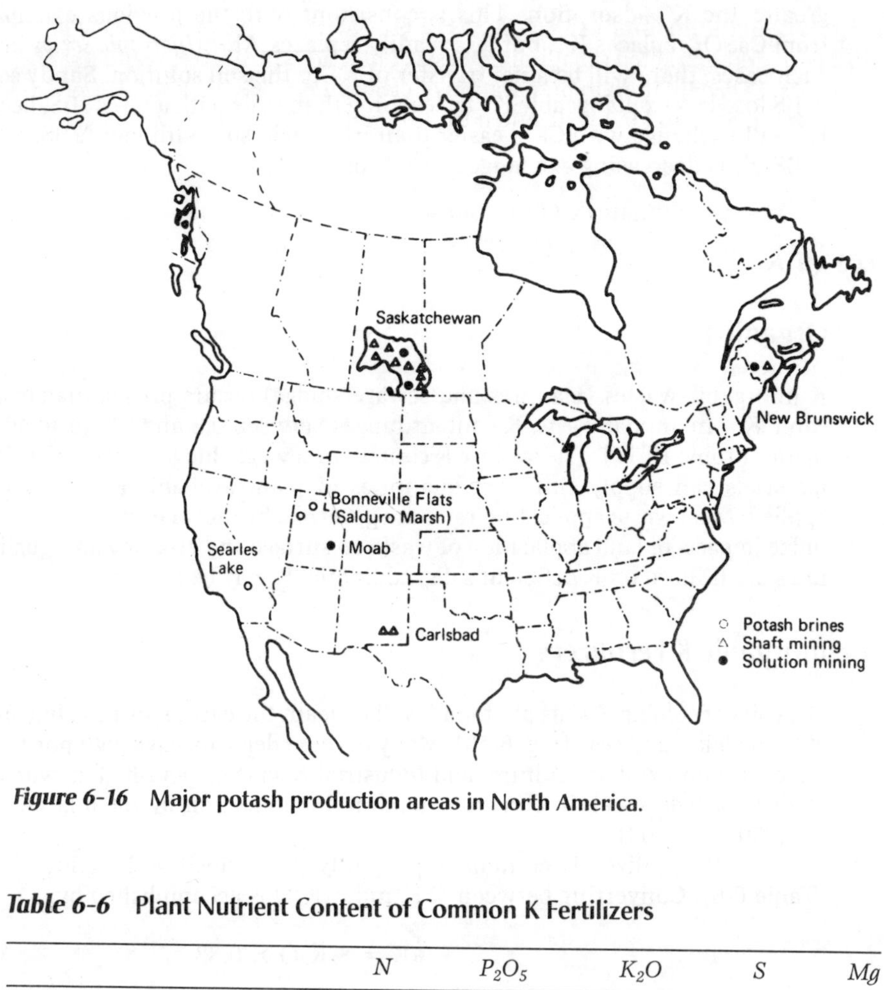

Figure 6-16 **Major potash production areas in North America.**

Table 6-6 Plant Nutrient Content of Common K Fertilizers

Material	*N*	*P_2O_5*	*K_2O*	*S*	*Mg*
			%		
Potassium chloride	—	—	60–62	—	—
Potassium sulfate	—	—	50–52	17	—
Potassium magnesium sulfate	—	—	22	22	11
Potassium nitrate	13	—	44	—	—
Potassium hydroxide	—	—	83	—	—
Potassium carbonate	—	—	,68	—	—
Potassium orthophosphates	—	30–60	30–50	—	—
Potassium polyphosphates	—	40–60	22–48	—	—
Potassium thiosulfate	—	—	25	17	—
Potassium polysulfide	—	—	22	23	—

Potassium Nitrate (KNO_3) KNO_3 contains 13% N and 37% K (44% K_2O). Agronomically, it is an excellent source of fertilizer N and K. KNO_3 is marketed largely for use on fruit trees and on crops such as cotton and vegetables. If production costs can be lowered, it might compete with other sources of N and K for use on crops of a lower value.

Potassium Phosphates ($K_4P_2O_7$, KH_2PO_4, K_2HPO_4) Several K phosphates have been produced and marketed on a limited basis. Their advantages are (1) high analysis, (2) low salt index, (3) adaptation to preparation of clear fluid fertilizers high in K_2O, (4) polyphosphate as a P source, and (5) well suited for use on potatoes and other crops sensitive to excessive amounts of Cl^-.

Potassium Carbonate (K_2CO_3), Potassium Bicarbonate ($KHCO_3$), and Potassium Hydroxide (KOH) These salts are used primarily for the production of high-purity fertilizers for foliar application or other specialty uses. The high cost of manufacture has precluded their widespread use as commercial fertilizers.

Potassium Thiosulfate ($K_2S_2O_3$) and Potassium Polysulfide (KS_x) Analysis of these liquid fertilizers, $K_2S_2O_3$ and KS_x, is 0-0-25-17 and 0-0-22-23, respectively. $K_2S_2O_3$ is compatible with most liquid fertilizers and is well suited for foliar application and drip irrigation.

Study Questions

1. What processes transport K to the plant root surface?
2. Why do K-deficiency symptoms commonly appear on old growth first?
3. What factors control the amount of K present in the soil solution? How does exchangeable K buffer K in solution? What is the activity ratio (AR^k), and what does it measure?
4. Under what soil conditions is there most likely to be reversion of available or added K to less-available forms?
5. What effect will liming an acid soil have on K leaching or retention?
6. Why does the addition of gypsum to an acid soil not result in an increased conservation of K?
7. Describe K fixation in soil. How does fixed K become available to plants?
8. Is K released more readily from feldspar than from the K-bearing micas? Do members of the mica group have similar abilities to supply K? In which soil particle-size fractions are feldspar and micas usually found?
9. Describe the changes that occur when mica minerals weather in soils. Why could exchangeable K increase with transformation of mica to montmorillonite or vermiculite?
10. Why might continuous cropping at high-yield levels deplete available K over time and increase the probability of a response to K?
11. Can plant uptake of available soil K be impaired by soil and environmental factors? If so, list the principal factors.
12. Name the common sources of fertilizer K. Under what soil conditions might you prefer to use K_2SO_4-$MgSO_4$ rather than KCl and dolomite or KCl alone?
13. Are there situations where KCl will be more effective than K_2SO_4 or KNO_3?
14. A sandy soil has a CEC = 5 meq/100 g and a 6% K saturation. An alfalfa crop yields 5 t/a/yr at 3% K content. Calculate initial exchangeable K and estimate final exchangeable K after one crop.

15. Two soils have CEC of 5 meq/100 g and 25 meg/100 g. Both have 5% exchangeable K content. Calculate the exchangeable K content for both soils in lbs/a. Using the crop data in Question 14, how many years can each soil be cropped before all the exchangeable K is removed? Assume that 1% of the CEC is resupplied by nonexchangeable K release each year after the first year.

Selected References

Barber, S. A. 1984. *Soil nutrient bioavailability: A mechanistic approach.* New York: John Wiley & Sons.

Barber, S. A., R. D. Munson, and W. B. Dancy. 1985. Production, marketing, and use of potassium fertilizers (pp. 377–410). In O. P. Englestad (Ed.), *Fertilizer technology and use.* Madison, Wis.: Soil Science Society of America.

Mortvedt, J. J., L. S. Murphy, and R.H. Follett. 1999. Willoughby, Ohio: *Fertilizer Technology and Application.* Meister Publ. Co.

Munson, R. D. (Ed.). 1985. *Potassium in agriculture.* Madison, Wis.: Soil Science Society of America.

CHAPTER 7

Sulfur, Calcium, and Magnesium

Sulfur (S), calcium (C), and magnesium (Mg) are secondary macronutrients required in relatively large amounts for good crop growth. S and Mg are needed by plants in about the same quantities as P, whereas for many plant species, the Ca requirement is greater than that for P. S reactions in soil are very similar to N reactions, which are dominated by organic or microbial fractions in the soil (Chapter 4). In contrast, Ca^{+2} and Mg^{+2} are associated with the soil clay fraction and behave similarly to K^{+} (Chapter 6).

Sulfur (S)

The S Cycle

S is the most abundant element in the earth's crust, averaging 0.06 to 0.10%. The original source of soil S is metal sulfide minerals that, when exposed to weathering, S^{-2} oxidizes to SO_4^{-2}. The SO_4^{-2} is precipitated as soluble and insoluble SO_4^{-2} salts in arid or semiarid climates, utilized by living organisms, reduced by microorganisms to S^{-2} or S^0 under anaerobic conditions, and/or transported through runoff to the sea. Oceans contain approximately 2,700 ppm SO_4^{-2}, whereas natural waters range from 0.5 to 50 ppm SO_4^{-2} but may reach 60,000 ppm (6%) in saline lakes and sediments.

Soil S is present in organic and inorganic forms, although ≈ 90% of total S in noncalcareous surface soils exists as organic S. Solution and adsorbed SO_4^{-2} represents readily plant available S. S cycling in the soil-plant-atmosphere system is similar to N in that both have gaseous components and their occurrence in soils is mainly associated with OM (Fig. 7-1).

Forms and Functions of S in Plants

Forms S is absorbed by plant roots almost exclusively as sulfate (SO_4^{-2}). Small quantities of SO_2 can be absorbed through plant leaves and utilized within plants, but high concentrations are toxic. Thiosulfate ($S_2O_3^{-2}$) can also be absorbed by roots. Typical S

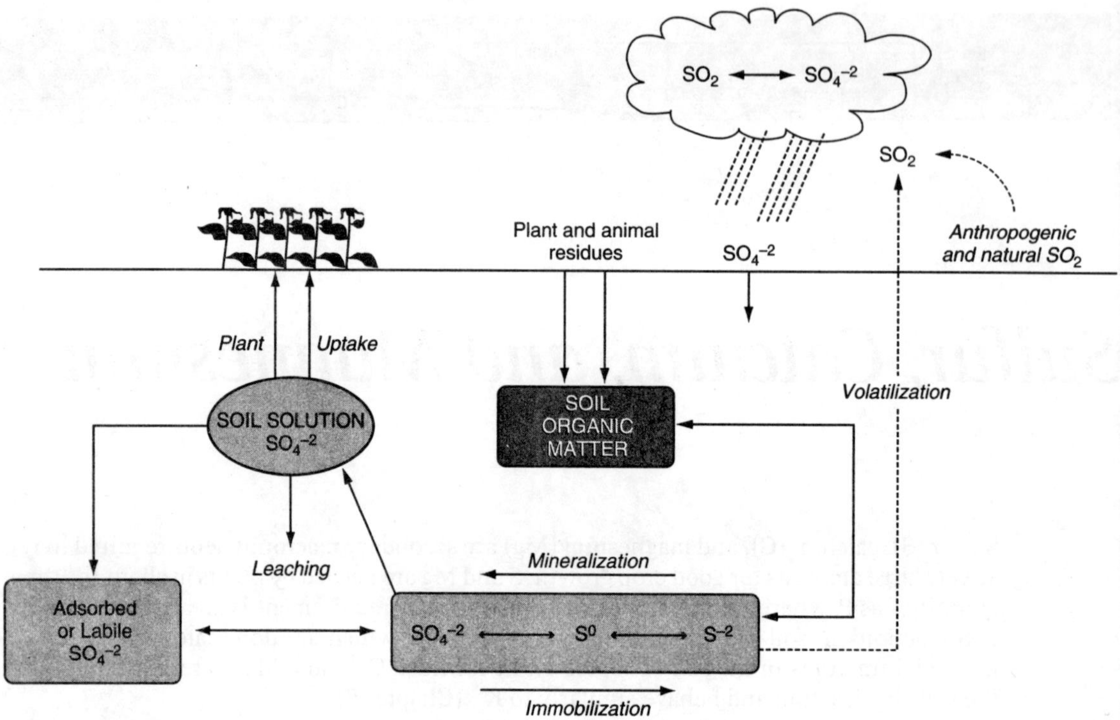

Figure 7-1 **Simplified version of the overall S cycle.**

concentrations in plants range from 0.1 to 0.5%. S content increases in the order *Gramineae* is less than *Leguminosae*, which is less than *Cruciferae* and is reflected in the differences in S content of their seeds: 0.18 to 0.19%, 0.25 to 0.3%, and 1.1 to 1.7%, respectively. Much of the SO_4^{-2} is reduced in the plant to —S—S and —SH forms, although SO_4^{-2} occurs in plant tissues and cell sap.

Functions S is required for synthesis of S-containing amino acids cystine, cysteine, and methionine, which are essential components of protein that comprise about 90% of the S in plants. Cysteine and methionine content increases with increasing S content in leaves (Fig. 7-2). S-deficient plants accumulate nonprotein N as NH_2 and NO_3^- (Table 7-1). An N:S ratio of 9:1 to 12:1 is needed for effective N use by rumen microorganisms. Increasing S nutrition narrows the N:S ratio and improves animal nutrition (Table 7-1). With S deficiency in vegetables, NO_3^- accumulates in leaves, reducing food quality (Fig. 7-3). In this example, NO_3^- accumulated in lettuce only when plants exhibited visual S-deficiency symptoms ($<$ 2.5 mg S/g).

One of the main functions of S in proteins is the formation of disulfide (—S—S—) bonds between polypeptide chains within a protein causing the protein to fold. Disulfide linkages are important in determining the configuration and catalytic or structural properties of proteins.

S is needed for synthesis of coenzyme A, which is involved in oxidation and synthesis of fatty acids, synthesis of amino acids, and oxidation of intermediates of the citric acid cycle.

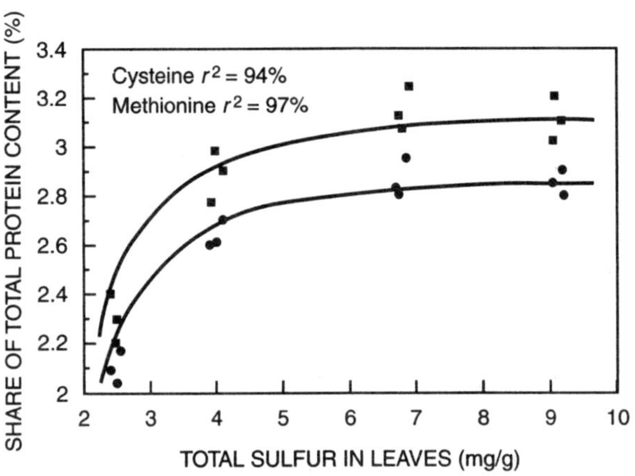

Figure 7-2 **Relations between the S nutritional status of borecole and the concentration of cysteine and methionine in leaf protein.** *(Schung, 1990,* Sulphur in Agric., *Washington, D.C.: The Sulphur Institute, 14:2–7.)*

Table 7-1 **Effects of Elemental S on Yield and Quality of Orchard Grass**

*Sulfur**	*Yield (t/ac) of Cutting*		*Nonprotein N (%) in Cutting*		*Nitrate N (%) in Cutting*		*N/S Ratio in Cutting*	
(lbs/a)	*1*	*3*	*1*	*3*	*1*	*3*	*1*	*3*
0	1.67	0.79	1.05	1.22	0.064	0.211	21.3	21.4
20	1.66	1.13	0.64	0.85	0.037	0.184	15.3	18.7
40	1.62	1.17	0.59	0.49	0.051	0.144	14.3	14.8
80	1.51	1.29	0.51	0.44	0.037	0.137	12.2	13.4
100	1.51	1.23	0.49	0.37	0.033	0.106	10.8	10.0

*S applied in 1965 and 1967, harvested in 1968. 100 lbs N/a applied after each cutting.
SOURCE: Baker et al., 1973, *Sulphur Inst. J.*, 9:15.

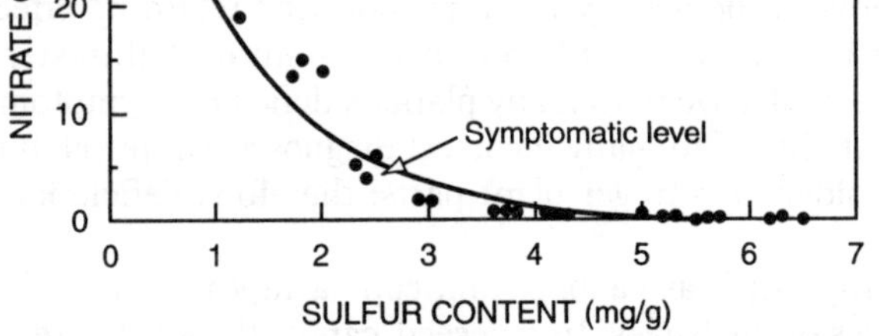

Figure 7-3 **Influence of S nutrition on the NO_3^- concentrations in lettuce dry matter.** *(Schung, 1990,* Sulphur in Agric., *Washington, D.C.: The Sulphur Institute, 14:2–7.)*

Although not a constituent, S is required for the synthesis of chlorophyll (Table 7-2). S is a vital part of the ferredoxins, an Fe-S protein in the chloroplasts. Ferredoxin has a significant role in NO_2^- and SO_4^{-2} reduction, the assimilation of N_2 by root nodule bacteria, and free-living N-fixing soil bacteria. S occurs in volatile compounds responsible for the characteristic taste and smell of plants in the mustard and onion families.

Table 7-2 **Effect of S Nutrition on Chlorophyll Content of Kenland Red Clover**

Applied Sulfate	*Chlorophyll Content*
(ppm S)	(% dry weight)
0	0.49
5	0.54
10	0.50
20	1.02
40	1.18

SOURCE: Rendig et al., 1968, *Agron. Abstr. Annu. Meet.*, Am. Soc. Agron., p. 109.

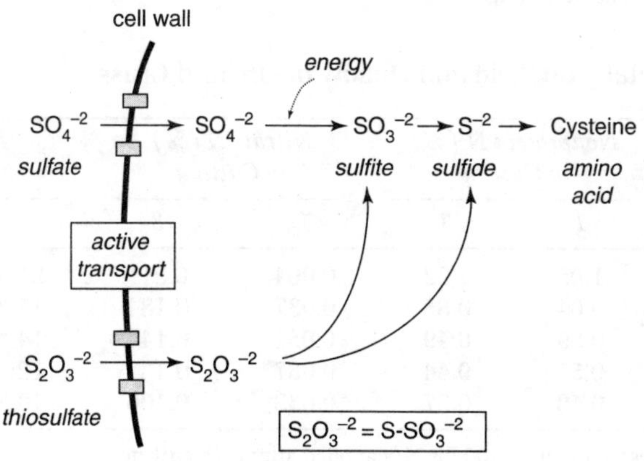

Figure 7-4 **Proposed model of absorption of thiosulfate that may require less energy to convert to amino acids than absorption of sulfate. *(Hooper, 2000,* Best Sulfur Products, *Fresno, CA: Pima Research Co.)***

SO_4^{-2} uptake is not inhibited by other anions (NO_3^- or $H_2PO_4^{-2}$), but is inhibited by chromate and selenate (Chapter 8). When plants absorb thiosulfate ($S_2O_3^{-2}$), less energy may be required by the plant in conversion to S^{-2} and cysteine (Fig. 7-4). Therefore, $S_2O_3^{-2}$ as a fertilizer source may exhibit a yield advantage over SO_4^{-2} sources, especially at low S rates.

Visual S-Deficiency Symptoms S deficiency has a pronounced retarding effect on plant growth and is characterized by uniformly chlorotic plants—stunted, thin-stemmed, and spindly (see color plates inside book cover). In many plants S-deficiency symptoms resemble N deficiency and have undoubtedly led to many incorrect diagnoses. Unlike N, however, S is not easily translocated from older to younger plant parts; therefore, deficiency symptoms occur first in younger leaves.

S-deficient cruciferous crops such as cabbage and canola/rapeseed initially develop a reddish color on the undersides of the leaves. In rapeseed/canola the leaves are also cupped inward. As the deficiency progresses in cabbage, reddening and purpling of both upper and lower leaf surfaces occurs; the cupped leaves turn back on themselves, presenting flattened-to-concave surfaces on the upper side. Paler-than-normal blossoms and severely impaired seed set also characterize S-deficiency symptoms in rapeseed.

Forms of S in Soil

Solution SO_4^{-2} SO_4^{-2} reaches roots by diffusion and mass flow. In soils containing ≥ 5 ppm SO_4^{-2}, total S requirement of most crops can be supplied by mass flow. Concentrations of 3 to 5 ppm SO_4^{-2} in solution is sufficient for most crops, although some (rapeseed/canola, alfalfa, broccoli, etc.) require higher solution S. SO_4^{-2} concentrations of 5 to 20 ppm are common in many North American soils. Sandy, low-OM soils often contain < 5 ppm SO_4^{-2}. Except for soils in dry areas that may have accumulations of SO_4^{-2} salts, most soils contain less than 10% of total S as SO_4^{-2}. Large seasonal and year-to-year fluctuations in SO_4^{-2} can occur due to the influence of environmental conditions on organic S mineralization, downward or upward movement of SO_4^{-2} in soil water, and SO_4^{-2} uptake by plants. SO_4^{-2} content of soils is also affected by the application of S-containing fertilizers and by SO_4^{-2} deposition in precipitation and irrigation.

Like NO_3^-, SO_4^{-2} can be readily leached through the soil profile. Increasing the quantity of percolation water increases potential SO_4^{-2} leaching. Another factor influencing SO_4^{-2} loss is the nature of the cation in solution. SO_4^{-2} leaching losses will be greater with monvalent compared to divalent cations in solution. Leaching losses are least in acid soils with appreciable exchangeable Al^{+3} and AEC to adsorb SO_4^{-2}.

Adsorbed SO_4^{-2} Adsorbed SO_4^{-2} is an important fraction in highly weathered, humid-region soils containing large amounts of Al/Fe oxides. Many Ultisol (red-yellow Podzol) and Oxisol (Latosol) soils contain up to 100 ppm adsorbed SO_4^{-2} and can significantly contribute to S nutrition of plants. Possible mechanisms of SO_4^{-2} adsorption include:

- (+) charges on Fe/Al oxides or on clay edges, especially kaolinite, at low pH (Chapter 2);
- adsorption to Al(OH)x complexes (Chapter 3); and
- (+) charges on soil OM at low pH.

Reserves of adsorbed SO_4^{-2} in subsoils result from SO_4^{-2} leaching from surface soil, accounting for ≈30% total subsoil S compared to ≈10% in surface soil. Although crops utilize subsoil-adsorbed SO_4^{-2}, S deficiency can occur during early growth stages until root development is sufficient to explore the subsoil. Deep-rooted crops (e.g., alfalfa, clover, lespedeza, etc.) are unlikely to have temporary shortages of available S.

Factors Affecting SO_4^{-2} Adsorption/Desorption

- *Clay Minerals.* SO_4^{-2} adsorption increases with clay content. In general, SO_4^{-2} adsorption in kaolinite is greater than mica, which is greater than montmorillonite. Under low pH and high Al^{+3} saturation, SO_4^{-2} adsorption with kaolinite is approximately equal to mica, which is much greater than montmorillonite.
- *Hydrous Oxide.* Fe/Al oxides are responsible for most SO_4^{-2} adsorption in soils.
- *Soil OM.* Increasing soil OM content increases SO_4^{-2} adsorption potential.
- *Soil Depth.* SO_4^{-2} adsorption capacity is often greater in subsoils due to higher clay and Fe/Al oxide content.
- *Soil pH.* SO_4^{-2} adsorption potential decreases with increasing pH (< AEC), and is negligible at pH > 6.0.

- *Solution SO_4^{-2}.* Adsorbed SO_4^{-2} is in equilibrium with solution SO_4^{-2}, thus increasing solution SO_4^{-2} will increase adsorbed SO_4^{-2}.
- *Competing Anions.* SO_4^{-2} is considered to be weakly held, with adsorption strength decreasing in the order $OH^- > H_2PO_4^- > SO_4^{-2} > NO_3^- > SO_4^{-2}$. For example, $H_2PO_4^-$ will displace SO_4^{-2}, but SO_4^{-2} has little effect on $H_2PO_4^-$. Cl^- has little effect on SO_4^{-2} adsorption.

Of these factors, the amount and type of clay, pH, soil OM, and presence of other anions exert the greatest influence on SO_4^{-2} adsorption.

SO_4^{-2} Reaction with $CaCO_3$ S occurs as a coprecipitate ($CaCO_3$-$CaSO_4$) impurity in calcareous soils. Availability of SO_4^{-2} coprecipitated with $CaCO_3$ increases with decreasing pH ($CaCO_3$ more soluble), decreasing $CaCO_3$ particle size, and increasing soil moisture content. Grinding calcareous soil samples will render SO_4^{-2} accessible to chemical extraction. Consequently, more S will be extracted by a particular soil test procedure than is available under field conditions.

Reduced Inorganic S (S^{-2} and S^0) Sulfides do not exist in well-drained soils. Under waterlogged, anaerobic conditions, H_2S accumulates as OM decays or from added SO_4^{-2}. In contrast, S^{-2} does not accumulate in normal soil. S^{-2} accumulation is limited primarily to coastal regions influenced by seawater. In normal submerged soils well-supplied with Fe, the H_2S liberated from OM is almost completely removed from solution by reaction with Fe^{+2} to form FeS, which undergoes conversion to pyrite (FeS_2). The dark color observed on the shores of the Black Sea is caused by the accumulation of FeS_2. If H_2S is not subsequently precipitated by Fe and other metals, it escapes to the atmosphere. The effect of waterlogging on the production of H_2S in a rice paddy soil increases with both time and added OM (Fig. 7-5).

In some tidal marshlands, large quantities of reduced S compounds accumulate. When these areas are drained, oxidization of S compounds to SO_4^{-2} will reduce pH to < 3.5 by the reaction:

$$FeS_2 + H_2O + 3^1/_2O_2 \rightarrow Fe^{+2} + 2SO_4^{-2} + 2H^+$$

Elemental S^0 is not a direct product of SO_4^{-2} reduction but is an intermediate formed during chemical oxidation of S^{-2}, and may accumulate in soils when oxidation of reduced S is interrupted by periodic flooding.

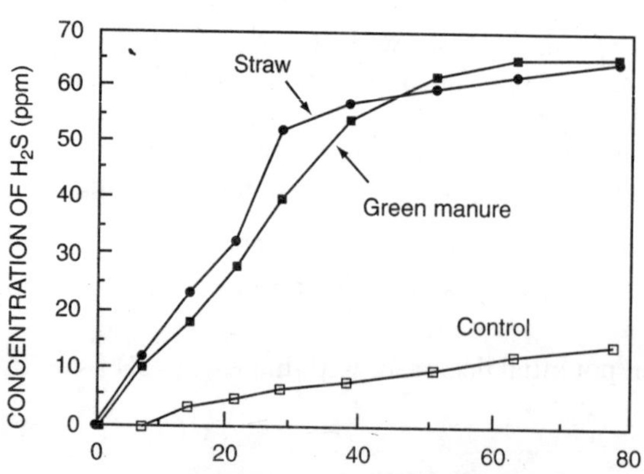

Figure 7-5 **Effect of OM on H_2S emission in a saturated soil.** *(Mandal, 1961,* Soil Sci., *91:121.)*

As noted, S^0, S^{-2}, and other inorganic S compounds can be chemically oxidized in the soil, but these are generally slow reactions. Biological oxidation of S^0 is enhanced in well-aerated soils previously treated with reduced S sources. The rate of biological S^0 oxidation depends on soil microbial activity, characteristics of the S source, and soil environmental conditions.

Factors Affecting S^0 Oxidation

1. *Soil Microbes.* Heterotrophic fungi and bacteria capable of oxidizing S^0 represent 3 to 37% of the total heterotrophic population in soils. S^0 oxidation is greater in the rhizosphere, where there are larger and more diverse populations of S^0-oxidizing heterotrophs, many of which are also plant-growth promoting rhizobacteria (PGPR), than beyond the rhizosphere. The most important group of S-oxidizing bacteria, particularly *Thiobacillus sp.*, are the most activé S-oxidizers while other microorganisms including fungi (e.g., *Fusaarium sp.*) and actinomycetes (e.g., *Streptomyces sp.*) are also important. *Thiobacillus* are autotrophic bacteria that obtain their energy from S^0 oxidation and C from CO_2. Photolithotrophic S bacteria oxidize S^{-2} but use light for energy. Addition of S^0 to soil encourages the growth of S^0-oxidizing microorganisms. The reaction mediated by *Thiobacilli* is:

$$CO_2 + S^0 + 2^1/_2O_2 + 2H_2O \rightarrow CH_2O + 2SO_4^{-2} + 2H^+$$

2. *Soil Temperature.* Increasing soil temperature increases S^0 oxidation rate (Fig. 7-6). Optimum temperature is between 25 and 40°C. At temperatures above 55 to 60°C, microbial activity decreases.
3. *Soil Moisture and Aeration.* S^0-oxidizing bacteria are mostly aerobic, and their activity will decline if O_2 is lacking due to waterlogging. S^0 oxidation is favored by soil moisture

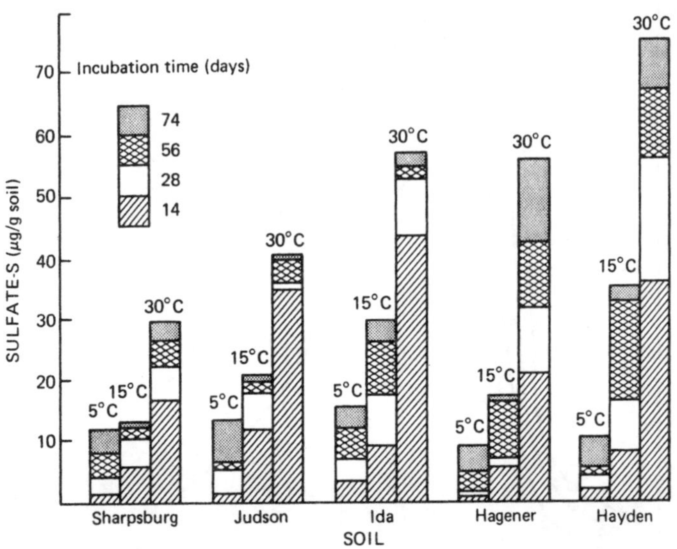

Figure 7–6 **Effects of temperature and incubation time on oxidation of S^0 in soils.** *(Nor and Tabatabai, 1979,* Soil Sci. Soc. Am. J., *41:739.)*

levels near field capacity (Fig. 7-7). Also evident is the decline in oxidizing activity when soils are either excessively wet or dry. Dry soils retain their ability to oxidize S^0, but a lag period can follow rewetting before they regain full capacity.

4. *Soil pH.* Generally, microbial S^0 oxidation occurs over a wide range in soil pH. The optimum for some *Thiobacillus* is often near pH 2.0 to 3.5, while others prefer near neutral or even slightly alkaline conditions.

Organic S As described in Chapter 4, there is a close relationship between organic C, total N, and total S in soils. The C:N:S ratio in most well-drained, noncalcareous soils is approximately 120:10:1.4. Differences in C:N:S among and within soils are related to variations in parent material and other soil-forming factors, such as climate, vegetation, leaching intensity, and drainage. The N:S ratio in most soils falls within the narrow range of 6 to 8:1. The organic S fraction governs the production of plant available SO_4^{-2} (Fig. 7-1). Three groups of S compounds in soil include *HI-reducible S, C-bonded S*, and *residual S* (Table 7-3).

- *HI-reducible S* is soil organic S that is reduced to H_2S by hydriodic acid (HI). The S occurs in ester and ether compounds that have C—O—S linkages (e.g., arylsulfates, alkylsulfates, phenolic sulfates, sulfated polysaccharides, and sulfated lipids). HI-reducible S ranges between 27 and 59% of organic S.
- *Carbon-bonded S* occurs as S-containing amino acids (cystine and methionine), which accounts for 10 to 20% of total organic S. More oxidized S forms, including

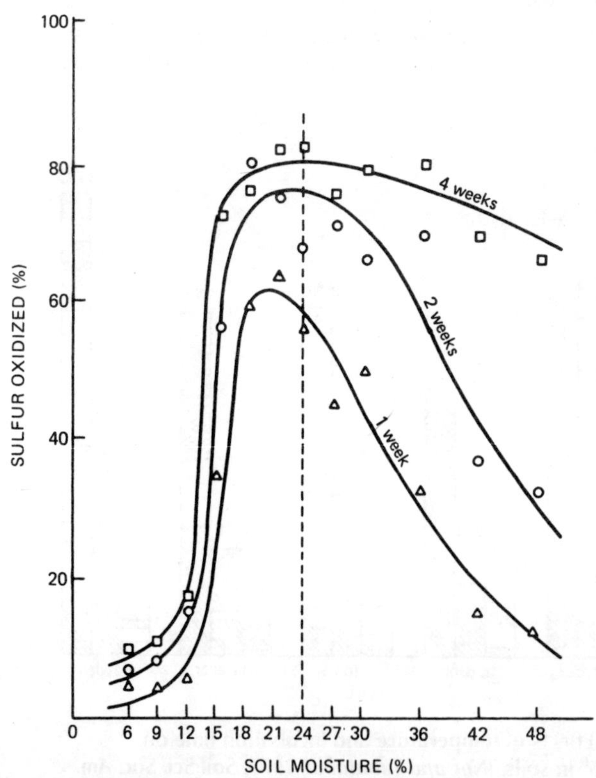

Figure 7–7 **Percentage of added S^0 oxidized at various moisture contents with time. Dashed line is field moisture capacity.** ***(Kittams and Attoe, 1965,*** **Agron. J.,** ***57:331.)***

Table 7-3 Fractionation of Organic S in Surface Soils

	HI-Reducible S		*C-Bonded S*		*Residual S*	
Location[*]	*Range*	*Mean*	*Range*	*Mean*	*Range*	*Mean*
	------- % *of Total* -------					
Quebec, Canada (3)	44–78	65	12–32	24	0–44	11
Alberta, Canada (15)	25–71	49	12–32	21	7–45	30
Australia (15)	32–63	47	22–54	30	3–31	23
Iowa, U.S. (24)	36–66	52	5–20	11	21–53	37
Brazil (6)	36–70	51	5–12	07	24–59	42

[*]Figures in parentheses refer to number of samples.
SOURCE: Biederbeck, in *Soil Organic Matter,* M. Schnitzer and S. U. Khan (Eds.), 1978, New York: Elsevier.

sulfoxide, sulfones, and sulfenic, sulfinic, and sulfonic acids, are also included in this fraction.

- *Residual S* represents the remaining organic S fraction and generally represents 30 to 40% of total organic S.

S Mineralization and Immobilization. S mineralization is the conversion of organic S to inorganic SO_4^{-2} and immobilization is the reverse reaction, similar to N mineralization (Chapter 4).

$$\text{amino acid} + 2H_2O \xrightarrow[\text{heterotrophs}]{O_2} S^{-2} + CO_2 + NH_4^+$$

$$S^{-2} \rightarrow S^{O} + 1\tfrac{1}{2}O_2 + H_2O \leftrightarrows SO_4^{-2} + 2H^+$$

Any factor that affects microbial activity influences mineralization and immobilization of S. When plant and animal residues are returned to soil, they are digested by microorganisms, converting some organic S to SO_4^{-2}; however, most of the S remains as organic S and eventually becomes part of soil humus (Fig. 7-1). The S supply to plants depends largely on SO_4^{-2} released from OM and from plant and animal residues. Approximately 2 to 15 lbs/a of S as SO_4^{-2} is mineralized each year from the organic fraction.

Factors Affecting S Mineralization and Immobilization

1. *S content of OM.* Like N, S mineralization or immobilization depends on S content of the decomposing material:

C:S ratio in crop residue	
< 200:1	mineralization
200 – 400	no change
> 400:1	immobilization

Smaller amounts of SO_4^{-2} are liberated from low-S-containing residue. Fresh organic residues commonly have C:S ratios of about 50:1. Where large amounts of straw, stover, or other OM are returned to the soil, adequate N and S availability is necessary to promote rapid decomposition of the straw. Otherwise, a temporary N or S deficiency may be induced in the following crop. Increasing total soil S content or OM also increases S mineralization (Fig. 7-8).

2. *Soil temperature.* S mineralization is impeded below 10°C, increases with higher temperatures from 20 to 40°C, and decreases at > 40°C. In samples representing 12 major soil series, more S was released during incubation at 35°C than at 20°C (Figs. 7-8 and 7-9). An average Q_{10} of 1.9 occurred in these soils. The temperature effect on S mineralization is consistent with the relatively greater S content of soils in northern climates.
3. *Soil moisture.* S mineralization in soils incubated at low (< 15%) and high (> 40%) moisture content is reduced compared with the optimum moisture content of 60% of field capacity. Gradual moisture changes between field capacity and wilting point have little influence on S mineralization. However, drastic differences in soil moisture conditions can produce a flush of S mineralization in some soils. Increased availability of S due to soil wetting and drying may explain observations of increased plant growth after dry periods in S-deficient soils.

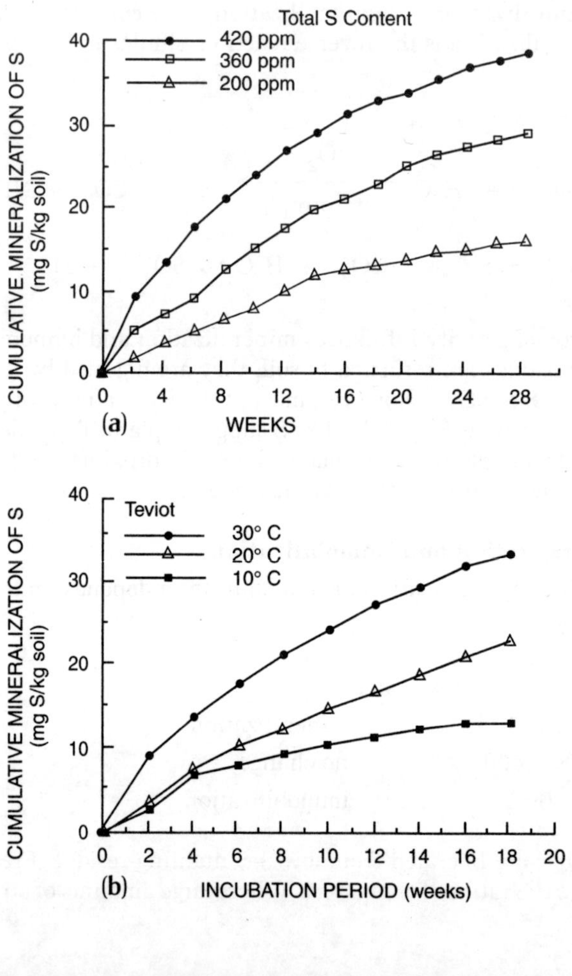

Figure 7-8 **Increasing total S content (a) or increasing soil temperature (b) increases S mineralization.** ***(Ghani, 1994,*** **Sulphur in Agric.,** ***Washington, D.C.: The Sulphur Institute, 18:13–18.)***

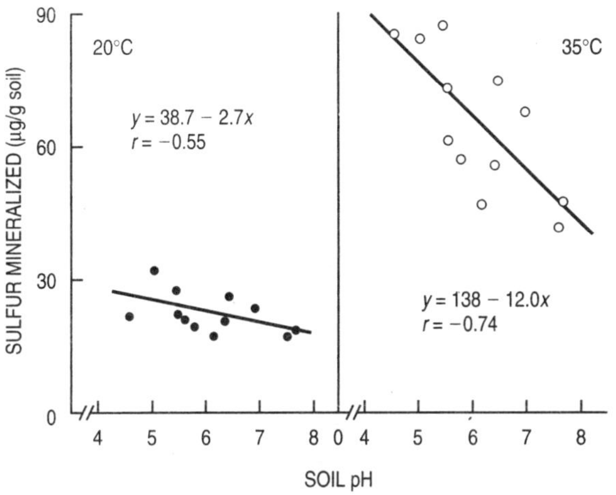

Figure 7–9 Relationship between total S mineralized and pH of soils incubated at 20 or 35°C. *(Tabatabai and Al-Khafaji, 1980,* Soil Sci. Soc. Am. J. *44:1,000.)*

4. *Soil pH.* Although in some soils mineralization decreases with increasing soil pH (Fig. 7-9), generally S mineralization is directly proportional to pH up to 7.5. Near-neutral soil pH is normally expected to encourage microbial activity and S mineralization.
5. *Presence or absence of plants.* Soils generally mineralize more S with the presence of growing plants than without, due to stimulated microbial activity in the rhizosphere through excretion of amino acids and sugars from plant roots. Immobilization of added SO_4^{-2} has been observed in uncropped soils.
6. *Time and cultivation.* As with N, when soil is first cultivated, its S content declines rapidly. With time, an equilibrium is reached that is characteristic of the climate, cultural practices, and soil type. Before reaching this point, S mineralization gradually diminishes and becomes inadequate to meet plant needs. The C:N:S ratio of virgin soils is larger than those of corresponding cultivated surface soils. Reduction of this ratio with cultivation suggests that S is relatively more resistant to mineralization than C and N or that losses of organic C and N are proportionately greater than S.
7. *Sulfatase activity.* As much as 50% of total S in surface soils may be present as organic S esters. Sulfatase enzymes that hydrolyze esters and release SO_4^{-2} are important in the mineralization process by:

$$R\text{-}O\text{-}SO_3^- + H_2O \xrightarrow{\text{sulfatase}} R\text{-}OH + HSO_4^-$$

HI-reducible ester sulfates are natural substrates for sulfatase enzymes in soil.

Sulfur Volatilization. Volatile S compounds are produced through microbial transformations under both aerobic and anaerobic conditions. Where volatilization occurs, the volatile S compounds are dimethyl sulfide (CH_3SCH_3), carbon disulfide (CS_2), methyl mercaptan (CH_3SH), and/or dimethyl disulfide (CH_3SSCH_3). CH_3SSCH_3 accounts for 55 to 100% of S volatilized. In low OM soils, S volatilization is negligible and generally increases with increasing OM content. The amount of S volatilized represents $< 0.05\%$ of the total S present in soil and is relatively insignificant under field conditions.

Like NH_3, volatile S evolves from growing plants. Losses range from 0.3 to 6.0% of total plant S. Volatile S released by plants may affect the palatability of forage plants to grazing animals. S losses from forages when they are dried in haymaking or pelleting might also influence quality and palatability.

Practical Aspects of S Transformations. Crops grown on coarse-textured soils are generally more susceptible to S deficiency because these soils often have low OM contents (< 1.2 to 1.5% OM) and are subject to SO_4^{-2} leaching. Leaching losses of SO_4^{-2} can be especially high on coarse-textured soils under conditions of high rainfall or irrigation. Under such conditions, SO_4^{-2}-containing fertilizers may have to be applied more frequently than on fine-textured soils or under lower rainfall conditions. In more humid regions, a fertilizer containing both SO_4^{-2} and S^0 may be required to extend the period of S availability to crops.

Added S can be immobilized in some soils, particularly those that have a high C:S or N:S ratio. In contrast, S mineralization is favored in soils with a low C:S or N:S ratio. S availability generally increases with increasing OM content.

S Sources

Atmospheric S SO_2 is released into the air, oxidizes to SO_4^{-2}, and is deposited in soil through precipitation. Nearly 70% of the S compounds in the atmosphere are due to natural processes. In localized areas, SO_4^{-2} content of soils can be increased by direct adsorption of SO_2 and the fallout of dry particulates. In addition, plants absorb SO_2 by diffusion into the leaves. However, exposure to as little as 0.5 ppm SO_2 can cause visible injury to the foliage of sensitive vegetation. Volatile S compounds are also released through volcanic activity, tidal marshes, and decaying OM.

Atmospheric SO_2 also results from combustion of fossil fuels and other industrial processes such as ore smelting, petroleum refining, and others. The amount of SO_4^{-2} deposited in rainfall in the United States ranges from 1 lb/a per year in rural areas to ≈50 lbs/a near industrial areas. SO_2 emissions are partly responsible for the acid rainfall and snowfall in industrialized regions (Chapter 3). Because of the concern over air pollution, the Clean Air Act was created to substantially reduce SO_2 emissions. As a result, atmospheric deposition of SO_4^{-2} has decreased ≈50% since 1980 (Fig. 7-10). As SO_4^{-2} deposition continues to decline, increasing frequency of S deficiency may be expected.

S in Irrigation Water Most irrigation water contains SO_4^{-2}. If S deficiency is expected, a water sample should be analyzed for SO_4^{-2} prior to use of S fertilizers. Generally, a response to additional S is expected if the irrigation water contains < 5 lbs S/acre-ft of water or 5 ppm SO_4^{-2}.

Organic S Because of the lower S requirement of most crops compared with N, most animal and municipal wastes contain sufficient quantities of plant available S. Typical S content in organic wastes ranges from 0.2 to 1.5%, or 5 to 25 lbs/t dry weight of S. With typical application rates ranging between 2 and 20 t/a, S applications would range between 10 and 250 lbs/a of S.

Inorganic S SO_4^{-2} materials applied to the soil surface and moved into the profile with rainfall or irrigation are immediately plant available unless immobilized by microbes degrading high C:S or N:S residues. Studies comparing the effectiveness of SO_4^{-2} sources (Table 7-4) suggest that one SO_4^{-2} source is generally equal to any other (provided that the accompanying cation is not Zn, Cu, or Mn, which must be applied sparingly) and the factor determining election should be cost per unit of S applied.

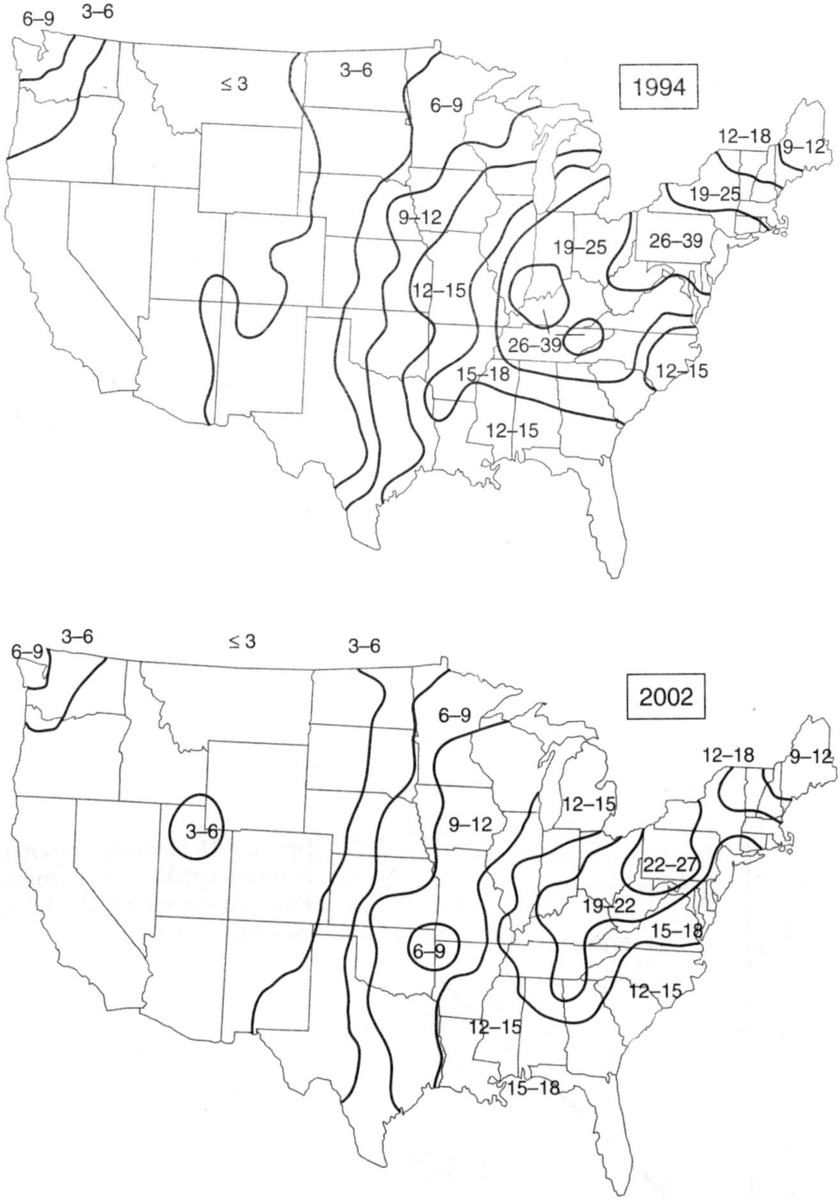

Figure 7–10 **Distribution and decrease in SO_4^{22} deposition (kg SO_4^{22}/ha) in the United States between 1994 and 2002.** ***(National Atmospheric Deposition Program, 2002, Washington, D.C.)***

Elemental S^0. S^0 is a yellow, water-insoluble solid. When finely ground S^0 is mixed with soil it is oxidized to SO_4^{-2} by soil microorganisms (see the discussion on p. 225). The effectiveness of S^0 in supplying S to plants compared with SO_4^{-2} depends on S^0 particle size; rate, method, and time of application; S^0 oxidizing potential; and environmental conditions. S^0 oxidation rates increase as particle size is reduced. As a general rule, 100% of S^0 must pass through a 16-mesh screen, and 50% of that should, in turn, pass through a 100-mesh screen.

Table 7-4 **S-Containing Fertilizer Materials**

Material	*Formula*	*Plant Nutrient Content (%)*				
		N	P_2O_5	K_2O	*S*	*Other*
Ammonium polysulfide	NH_4S_x	20	-	-	45	
Ammonium sulfate	$(NH_4)_2SO_4$	21	-	-	24	
Ammonium thiosulfate	$(NH_4)_2S_2O_3$	12	-	-	26	
Calcium polysulfide	CaS_x	-	-	-	22	6 (Ca)
Calcium thiosulfate	CaS_2O_3	-	-	-	10	6 (Ca)
Ferrous sulfate	$FeSO_4 \cdot H_2O$	-	-	-	19	33 (Fe)
Gypsum	$CaSO_4 \cdot 2H_2O$	-	-	-	19	24 (Ca)
Magnesium sulfate	$MgSO_4 \cdot 7H_2O$	-	-	-	13	10 (Mg)
Potassium-magnesium sulfate	$K_2SO_4 \cdot MgSO_4$	-	-	22	22	11 (Mg)
Potassium polysulfide	KS_x	-	-	22	23	
Potassium sulfate	K_2SO_4	-	-	50	18	
Potassium thiosulfate	$K_2S_2O_3$	-	-	25	17	
Sulfur	S^0	-	-	-	100	
Sulfur (granular w/additives)	S^0	0–7	-	-	68–95	
Sulfuric acid (100%)	H_2SO_4	-	-	-	33	
Superphosphate, single	$Ca(H_2PO_4)_2 \cdot CaSO_4 \cdot 2H_2O$	-	20	-	14	
Superphosphate, triple	$Ca(H_2PO_4)_2 \cdot CaSO_4 \cdot 2H_2O$	-	46	-	1.5	
Urea-sulfur	$CO(NH_2)_2 + S$	38	-	-	10–20	
Urea-sulfuric acid	$CO(NH_2)^2 + H_2SO_4$	10–28	-	-	9–18	
Zinc sulfate	$ZnSO_4 \cdot H_2O$	-	-	-	18	36 (Zn)

SOURCE: Bixby and Beaton, 1970, *Tech. Bull. 17,* Washington, D.C.: The Sulphur Institute.

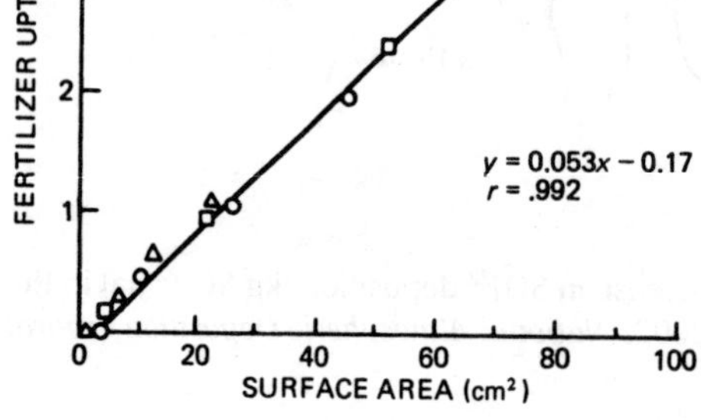

Figure 7-11 **Influence of surface area of applied S^0 on the uptake of S by canola.** *(Janzen et al., 1982, Proc. Alberta Soil Sci. Workshop, p. 229, Edmonton, Alberta.)*

The finer the S^0 particle size, the greater the surface area and the faster the SO_4^{-2} formation. Thus, increasing S^0 surface area results in increased SO_4^{-2} availability to crops (Fig. 7-11).

When finely ground S^0 is mixed with soil possessing a high oxidizing potential, it is usually just as effective as other S sources. However, to assure adequate S availability, S^0 should be incorporated into the soil as far ahead of planting as possible. Application of heavier

S^0 rates will increase surface area exposed to S^0oxidizing organisms, which should increase plant available S. Placement of S^0 can often affect oxidation rate, with broadcast incorporation being superior to banding. Uniform distribution of S^0 particles throughout the soil will provide greater exposure to oxidizing microorganisms and minimize any potential problems caused by excessive acidity.

Dispersible, Granular S^0 Fertilizers. Water dispersible, granular S^0 fertilizers, such as S-bentonite (approximately 90% S) and micronized granular S (95% S) have several important advantages, including high S analysis resulting in savings in costs of transportation and handling; wide distribution of S^0 particle sizes with varying degrees of controlled availability to plants; low susceptibility to leaching losses in areas of high and intense rainfall; and excellent durable physical forms that are well-suited for direct application or blending with most common granular fertilizers except those containing NO_3-N. S-bentonite is manufactured by adding bentonite to molten S^0, whereas micronized granular S^0 consists of 100% < 74-mm-(200-mesh-) sized particles bound together with a water soluble binder.

Dispersion of S^0-bentonite into readily oxidized finely divided S^0occurs gradually in soil following wetting and swelling of the bentonite component. Micronized, granular S^0 disperses rapidly and completely upon wetting in soil. Dispersion of both S sources is enhanced by exposure to precipitation and freezing/thawing before soil incorporation. Thus, fertilization practices involving broadcast applications are usually more dependable than banding.

Because of the uncertainty of adequate formation of SO_4^{-2} from S^0-bentonite in the first growing season after application, it should be applied well in advance of planting, with a period of exposure at the soil surface before incorporation. When applied just before seeding of high-S-requiring crops and on S-deficient soils, some SO_4^{-2} should also be provided.

S^0 Suspensions. The addition of finely ground S^0 to water containing 2 to 3% attapulgite clay results in a suspension containing 40 to 60% S. These suspensions can be applied directly to the soil or combined with suspension fertilizers.

Ammonium Sulfate [$(NH_4)_2SO_4$ or AS]. This solid fertilizer containing 24% S and 21% N was previously described on page 146 (Table 7-4). AS is used predominately when both N and S are required (see Chapter 4).

Potassium Sulfate (K_2SO_4) and Potassium Magnesium Sulfate (K_2SO_4, $MgSO_4$). Both materials were discussed in Chapter 6 and are commonly used when both S and K are required.

Ammonium Thiosulfate [$(NH_4)_2S_2O_3$, or ATS]. ATS is a clear liquid containing 12% N and 26% S and is a popular S-containing product (Table 7-4). ATS is compatible with N solutions and complete (N-P-K) liquid mixes, which are neutral to slightly acidic in pH.

ATS can be applied directly to soil, in mixtures, or through either sprinkler or open-ditch irrigation systems. When applied to the soil, ATS forms colloidal S and $(NH_4)_2SO_4$. The SO_4^{-2} is immediately available, whereas the S^0 must be oxidized to SO_4^{-2}, thus extending the availability to the crop. Potassium thiosulfate (KTS) behaves similarly to ATS.

Ammonium Polysulfide (NH_4S_x). Ammonium polysulfide is a red to brown to black solution having a H_2S odor. It contains approximately 20% N and 45% S (Table 7-4). In addition to use as a fertilizer, it is used for reclaiming high-pH soils and for treatment of irrigation water to improve water penetration into the soil. Ammonium polysulfide is recommended for mixing with anhydrous NH_3, aqua NH_3, and UAN solutions. The simultaneous application of ammonium polysulfide and anhydrous NH_3 is popular in some areas for providing both N and S. Normally, it is considered incompatible with phosphate-containing liquids. This material has a low vapor pressure, and it should be stored at a pressure of 0.5 psi to prevent loss of NH_3 and subsequent precipitation of S^0. Potassium polysulfide (0–0–22–23) has been used on a limited basis in sprinkler and flood irrigation systems for salt removal and to supply K.

Calcium Polysulfide (CaS_x) and Calcium Thiosulfate (CaS_2O_3). Calcium polysulfide (22% S, 6% Ca) and calcium thiosulfate (10% S, 6% Ca) are clear, odorless solutions. They are commonly used in soils to reduce exchangeable Na content and improve water infiltration, while supplying S.

Urea-Sulfuric Acid. Two typical grades used as acidifying amendments, as well as sources of N, contain 10% N and 18% S and 28% N and 9% S, respectively (Table 7-4). They can be applied directly to the soil or added through sprinkler systems. Because urea-sulfuric acid formulations have pH values between 0.5 and 1.0, the equipment used must be made from stainless steel and other noncorrosive materials. Workers must wear protective clothing.

Fertilizer Use Guidelines For purposes of convenience, recommendations for the use and proper application of common S-containing fertilizers are summarized in Table 7-5.

Calcium (Ca)

In acid, humid-region soils, Ca^{+2} and Al^{+3} dominate the CEC, while in neutral and calcareous soils Ca^{+2} occupies the majority of the exchange sites. As with any other cation, exchangeable and solution Ca^{+2} are in dynamic equilibrium and provide the majority of plant available Ca^{+2} (Fig. 7-12). If solution Ca^{+2} is decreased by leaching or plant uptake, Ca^{+2} will desorb from the CEC to resupply solution Ca^{+2}. Other soluble cations replace the desorbed Ca^{+2}, or Ca minerals dissolve to provide additional exchangeable and solution Ca^{+2}. Conversely, if solution Ca^{+2} is increased, the equilibrium shifts in the opposite direction, with adsorption of Ca^{+2} on the CEC. The fate of solution Ca^{+2} is less complex than that of K^+. Ca^{+2} may be (1) leached by drainage water, (2) absorbed by organisms, (3) adsorbed to CEC, or (4) reprecipitated as a secondary Ca compound, particularly in arid climates.

Forms and Functions of Ca in Plants

Plants absorb Ca^{+2} from the soil solution, where mass flow and root interception are the primary mechanisms of Ca transport to the root surface. Ca deficiency is uncommon but can occur in highly leached and unlimed acid soils. In soils abundant in Ca^{+2}, excessive accumulation in the vicinity of roots can occur. Ca^{+2} in plants ranges between 0.2 and 1.0%.

Ca^{+2} is essential to cell wall membrane structure and permeability. Low Ca^{+2} weakens cell membranes (i.e., plasmalemma), resulting in increased permeability, loss of cell contents, and failure of the nutrient-uptake mechanisms. Ca^{+2} and other cations neutralize organic acids formed during during normal cell metabolism. Ca^{+2} is important to N metabolism and protein formation by enhancing NO_3^- uptake. Ca^{+2} also provides some regulation of cation uptake. For example, K^+ and Na^+ uptake are equivalent in absence of Ca^{+2}, but in its presence K^+ uptake greatly exceeds Na^+ uptake.

Table 7-5 Guidelines for Use of S Fertilizers

Materials	*Guideline*	*Remarks*
Ammonium phosphate–S^0 Urea–S^0 Dispersible, granular S^0; flake S and porous granular S	Direct application and bulk blends, apply materials several months before growing season; fall applications are encouraged, allowances made for dispersion before incorporation of broadcast applications	As starter or preplant, SO_4^{-2} should be included; dispersion of water-degradable granular S at the soil surface before incorporation improves effectiveness; incorporate 4 to 5 months preplant; apply preplant or on severely S-deficient soils, SO_4^{-2} should be included.
Ammonium sulfate	Direct application and to some extent for bulk blending; effective anytime	Segregates in bulk blends unless physical properties are improved by granulation; where leaching losses expected, apply shortly before planting
Ammonium nitrate-sulfate; ammonium phosphate-sulfate; potassium sulfate; potassium magnesium-sulfate	Direct application and bulk blends; effective anytime	Where significant SO_4^{-2} leaching is expected, apply shortly before planting or growing season
Calcium sulfate (gypsum)	Direct application; effective anytime	Difficulties encountered in application (dustiness, clogging)
Ammonium thiosulfate Potassium thiosulfate	Direct application and blending with fluid fertilizers; broadcast preplant or applied in starters; topdress on certain growing crops; add through open-ditch and irrigation systems	Blended with neutral fluid P products, all N solutions, and most micronutrient solutions
Ammonium polysulfide Potassium polysulfide	Direct application and blending with N solutions; injected into soil; broadcast applications with H_2O dilution; single preplant applications; repeated applications at low rates through open-ditch irrigation systems	Ammonium polysulfide not suitable for mixing with P-containing fluids
Sulfuric acid	Mixing with ammonium polyphosphate and anhydrous ammonia for clear liquid blends	Applied directly to crops for weed control purposes
Suspensions containing S^0	Direct application and simultaneous application with other fertilizers, suspensions applied 2 to 3 months before growing season	As starter or preplant; include SO_4^{-2} (15 to 20% of total S applied)
Suspensions containing SO_4^{-2}	Effective anytime	Where leaching losses expected, apply preplant or before beginning of growing season

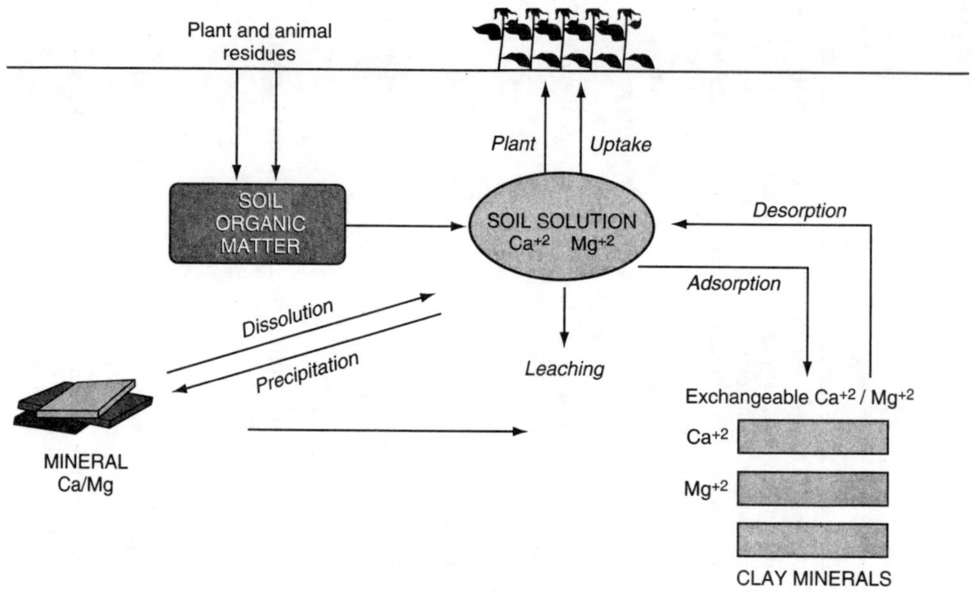

Figure 7-12 Ca and Mg cycling in soil.

Ca^{+2} is essential for cell elongation and division. Ca^{+2} deficiency reduces development of terminal buds of shoots and apical tips of roots, which causes plant growth to cease. For example, in corn, Ca^{+2} deficiency prevents emergence and unfolding of new leaves, while leaf tips are almost colorless and covered with a sticky gelatinous material that causes them to adhere to one another.

Ca^{+2} is essential for translocation of carbohydrates and nutrients. Accumulation of carbohydrates in leaves under Ca^{+2} stress decreases carbohydrate content of stems and roots, which impairs normal root function (i.e., nutrient absorption) because of low energy supply. As a result, Ca^{+2} deficiency results in malformation of storage tissues in many fruits and vegetable crops.

While Ca^{+2} is important for translocation, Ca^{+2} is generally immobile in the plant. Following absorption, Ca^{+2} moves with transpirational water in the xylem. Once in the leaves, very little Ca^{+2} translocation in the phloem occurs, resulting in poor Ca^{+2} supply to roots and storage organs. Since Ca^{+2} cannot be redistributed within the plant, it is critical that a continuous supply of Ca^{+2} is available for root absorption to support normal growth and fruit development. Soil conditions that reduce root growth (e.g., Al^{+3} toxicity, P deficiency, diseases, etc.) will limit root access to Ca^{+2} and induce deficiency. Problems related to inadequate Ca^{+2} uptake more commonly occur in plants that have small root systems than with plants having more highly developed root systems.

Deficiency symptoms are primarily exhibited in meristematic regions (i.e., areas of rapid cell division) of leaves, stems, and roots. Ca^{+2} deficiency causes deformed tissues and death of the growing points including buds, blossoms, and root tips. Leaf tips and margins are chlorotic and/or necrotic, a condition commonly refered to as *die back* or *tip burn*. The gelatinous material secreted causes leaf tips to stick together in some crops. Ca^{+2} deficiency will cause poor nodulation by N-fixing bacteria on legume roots, where nodule tissues are white to grayish green compared to the pink/red color found in normal legume nodules. Under severe Ca^{+2} deficiency, root development is slow and root tips develop a dark color and die.

Low Ca^{+2} uptake combined with limited translocation of carbohydrates causes distinct symptoms in fruits and vegetable crops. Examples are blossom end rot in peppers and tomatoes, deformed watermelons, bitter pit in apples, internal brown spot in potatoes, black heart in peanuts, black heart in celery, and cavity spot in carrots. Ca^{+2} deficiency results in discolored and softer fruit with inferior shelf life and marketability. Crop quality in leafy vegetable crops is reduced through burning of leaf tips and margins (e.g., lettuce, cabbage, spinach).

Ca in Soil

The Ca concentration of the earth's crust is about 3.5%. Ca in soils originated from the minerals from which the soil was formed. Anorthite ($CaAl_2Si_2O_3$) is the most important primary source of Ca, although pyroxenes and amphiboles are also common. Small amounts of Ca may also originate from biotite, apatite, and certain borosilicates.

Total Ca^{+2} content in soils varies widely depending on region. Ca^{+2} normally ranges from 0.7 to 1.5% in noncalcareous soils of humid temperate regions; however, highly weathered, tropical soils contain much lower amounts of Ca, from 0.1 to 0.3%. Calcareous soils in semiarid and arid regions contain 1 to 30% Ca, predominately as $CaCO_3$ (Chapter 3). Dolomite [$CaMg(CO_3)_2$] and gypsum ($CaSO_4 \cdot 2H_2O$) also may be present.

Generally, coarse-textured, humid-region soils formed from low-Ca minerals are low in plant available Ca. Fine-textured soils formed from high-Ca minerals are much higher in both exchangeable and total Ca. However, in humid regions, even soils formed from limestones are frequently acidic in the surface layers because of removal of Ca and other cations by excessive leaching. As water containing dissolved CO_2 percolates through the soil, the H^+ formed ($CO_2 + H_2O \leftrightarrows H^+ + HCO_3^-$) displaces $Ca^{+2}$and other basic cations on the CEC. If considerable volumes of water percolate through the soil profile, as in humid regions, soils gradually become acidic (Chapter 3). Where leaching occurs, Na^+ is lost more readily than Ca^{+2} (Chapter 2); however, since exchangeable and solution Ca^{+2} are greater than Na^+ in most soils, the quantity of Ca^{+2} lost is also much more. Ca is often the dominant cation in drainage waters and various surface waters. Ca^{+2} leaching ranges from 75 to 200 lbs/a per year. Since Ca^{+2} is adsorbed on the CEC, losses by erosion may be considerable in some soils.

Ca^{+2} in the soil solution of temperate-region soils ranges from 30 to 300 ppm. In higher-rainfall areas, solution Ca^{+2} varies from 5 to 50 ppm. About 15 ppm solution Ca^{+2} is adequate for most crops. Solution Ca^{+2} higher than necessary for optimum plant growth has little effect on Ca^{+2} uptake, because uptake is genetically controlled. Although solution Ca^{+2} is about 10 times greater than K^+, its uptake is usually lower than K^+. The limited capacity for Ca^{+2} uptake is due to its absorption being confined to root tips where cell walls of the endodermis are still unsuberized.

The most important factors in determining Ca^{+2} availability to plants are:

- Total Ca supply
- Soil pH
- CEC
- % Ca^{+2} saturation on CEC
- Type of soil clay
- Ratio of solution Ca^{+2} to other cations

Total Ca in low CEC, acid soils can be too low to provide sufficient plant available Ca^{+2}, requiring Ca fertilization or liming. In addition, low soil pH (high Al^{+3} and H^+) impedes

Ca^{+2} uptake (Fig. 7-13). For example, as pH decreases, higher Ca^{+2} concentrations are required to maintain root growth (Table 7-6).

In soils not containing $CaCO_3$, $CaMg(CO_3)_2$, or $CaSO_4 \cdot 2H_2O$, solution Ca^{+2} concentration depends on the amount of exchangeable Ca^{+2}. In acid soils, Ca^{+2} is not readily available to plants at low % Ca saturation. For example, a low-CEC soil with 1,000 ppm exchangeable

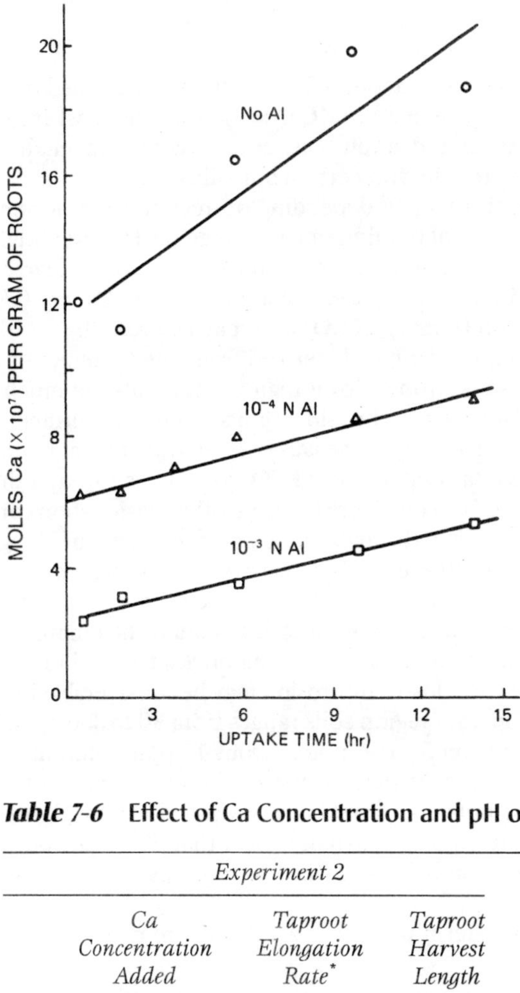

Figure 7-13 **Influence of Al^{13} on the rate of Ca uptake in wheat roots.** *(Johnson and Jackson, 1964,* Soil Sci. Soc. Am. J., *28:381.)*

Table 7-6 **Effect of Ca Concentration and pH on Root Elongation in Nutrient Solution**

	Experiment 2					*Experiment 3*	
	Ca Concentration Added	*Taproot Elongation Rate**	*Taproot Harvest Length*	*Oven Dry Wt.*		*Ca Concentration Added*	*Taproot Elongation Rate*
pH	**ppm**	**mm/hr**	**mm**	**mg**	**pH**	**ppm**	**mm/hr**
5.6	0.05	2.66	461	0.20	4.75	0.05	0.11
	0.50	2.87	453	0.23		0.50	0.91
	2.50	2.70	455	0.32			
4.5	0.05	0.04	024	0.54	4.00	2.50	0.44
	0.50	1.36	270	0.26		5.00	1.26
	2.50	2.38	422	0.31			

*Elongation rate during first 4 hr in solution. Harvested 7½ days after entering the solution.
SOURCE: Lund, 1970, *Soil Sci. Soc. Am. J.*, 34:457.

Ca^{+2} but representing a high %Ca saturation can supply plants with more Ca^{+2} compared to a high-CEC soil with 2,000 ppm exchangeable Ca^{+2} and a low %Ca saturation. Thus, as %Ca saturation decreases in proportion to total CEC, the amount of Ca^{+2} absorbed by plants also decreases. High Ca^{+2} saturation indicates a favorable pH for plant growth and microbial activity and will usually reflect low exchangeable Al^{+3} in acid soils and Na^{+} in sodic soils. Many crops respond to Ca applications when Ca saturation is $< 25\%$ of CEC.

The type of clay influences Ca^{+2} availability; 2:1 clays require higher %Ca saturation than 1:1 clays. Specifically, montmorillonitic clays require $> 70\%$ Ca saturation for adequate Ca availability, whereas kaolinitic clays are able to supply sufficient Ca^{+2} at 40 to 50% Ca saturation.

Ca Sources

The primary Ca sources are liming materials such as $CaCO_3$, $CaMg(CO_3)_2$, and others that are applied to neutralize soil acidity (Chapter 3). In situations where Ca is required without the need for correcting soil acidity, gypsum is used. Gypsum ($CaSO_4 \cdot 2H_2O$) deposits are found at several locations in North America, and large amounts of by-product gypsum are produced in the manufacture of phosphoric acid (Chapter 5). Gypsum has little effect on soil pH; hence, it may have value with crops that prefer acid soil yet need considerable Ca. It is widely used on sodic soils in arid climates (Chapter 3).

Ca is present in several fertilizer materials including triple superphosphate (12 to 14% Ca), ordinary superphosphate (18 to 20% Ca), calcium nitrate (19% Ca), and lime-ammonium nitrate (10% Ca). Synthetic chelates such as CaEDTA contain approximately 3 to 5% Ca, while some of the natural complexing substances used as micronutrient carriers contain 4 to 12% Ca. Chelated Ca can also be foliarly applied to crops. Rock phosphate contains about 35% Ca, and when applied at high rates to acid tropical soils, substantial amounts of Ca are supplied. Animal and municipal wastes contain approximately 2 to 5% Ca by dry weight and are excellent Ca sources.

Magnesium (Mg)

Like Ca, Mg occurs predominantly as exchangeable and solution Mg^{+2} (Fig. 7-12). Mg^{+2} absorption by plants depends on the amount of solution Mg^{+2}, soil pH, %Mg saturation on the CEC, quantity of other exchangeable ions, and the type of clay. Mg in soil solution may be (1) lost in percolating waters, (2) absorbed by living organisms, (3) adsorbed on the CEC, or (4) reprecipitated as a secondary mineral, predominantly in arid climates.

Forms and Functions of Mg in Plants

Mg is absorbed by plants as Mg^{+2} from the soil solution and, like Ca^{+2}, is supplied to plant roots by mass flow and diffusion. Root interception contributes much less Mg^{+2} to uptake than Ca^{+2}. The quantity of Mg^{+2} taken up by plants is usually less than that of Ca^{+2} or K^{+}.

Mg^{+2} concentration in crops varies between 0.1 and 0.4%. Mg^{+2} is a primary constituent of chlorophyll, and without chlorophyll photosynthesis would not occur (Fig. 4-2). Chlorophyll usually accounts for 15 to 20% of the total Mg^{+2} content of plants. Mg also serves as a structural component in ribosomes, stabilizing them in the configuration necessary for protein synthesis. Under Mg^{+2} deficiency, protein N decreases while nonprotein N generally increases in plants.

Mg is associated with transfer reactions involving phosphate-reactive groups. Mg is required for maximal activity of almost every phosphorylating enzyme in carbohydrate metabolism. Most reactions involving phosphate transfer from adenosine triphosphate (ATP) require Mg^{+2}. Since the fundamental process of energy transfer occurs in photosynthesis, glycolysis, the citric acid or Krebs cycle, and respiration, Mg^{+2} is important throughout plant metabolism.

Because of the mobility of plant Mg^{+2} and its ready translocation from older to younger plant parts, deficiency symptoms often appear first on the lower leaves. In many plants, Mg^{+2} deficiency causes interveinal chlorosis in leaves, where only leaf veins remain green. Under severe Mg^{+2} deficiency, leaf tissue becomes uniformly chlorotic to necrotic. In other plants (e.g., cotton), lower leaves develop a reddish-purple cast, gradually turning brown and finally necrotic (see color plates).

Grass Tetany Low Mg content in forage crops, particularly grasses, used for animal feed may cause grass tetany (hypomagnesemia), which is an abnormally low level of blood Mg. Low soil Mg, or high rates of NH_4^+ or K^+ fertilizers, may depress Mg^{+2} uptake. For example, Mg content of young corn plants is markedly reduced when NH_4^+ rather than NO_3^- is applied. Because grass tetany often occurs in the spring, NH_4^+may be greater than NO_3^-, particularly under extended cool-weather conditions. In addition, the high protein content of ingested forages (and other feeds) can depress Mg absorption by the animal, especially cattle.

Soil Mg may be increased through application of dolomitic limestone, if liming is advisable, or through the use of Mg-containing fertilizers. Including legumes in the forage program is advisable because legumes exhibit higher Mg contents than grasses. The animal diet can also be supplemented with Mg salts to help prevent grass tetany.

Mg in Soil

Mg constitutes 1.93% of the earth's crust; however, total soil Mg content ranges from 0.1% in coarse, humid-region soils to 4% in fine-textured, arid, or semiarid soils formed from high-Mg minerals. Soil Mg originates from weathering of several Mg-bearing minerals including biotite, dolomite, hornblende, olivene, and serpentine. Mg also occurs in the clay minerals chlorite, illite, montmorillonite, and vermiculite. Substantial amounts of epsomite ($MgSO_4 \cdot 7H_2O$) and bloedite ($Na_2MgSO_3 \cdot 4H_2O$) may occur in arid or semiarid soils.

Soil solution Mg^{+2} concentration typically ranges from 5 to 50 ppm in temperate-region soils, although Mg^{+2} concentrations between 120 and 2,400 ppm have been observed. Mg^{+2}, like Ca^{+2}, can be leached with potential losses of 5 to 60 lbs/a/yr. Mg leaching losses depend on soil Mg content, rate of weathering, intensity of leaching, and plant uptake. Leaching of Mg^{+2} is often a severe problem in sandy soils, particularly following KCl or K_2SO_4 fertilization (Table 7-7). As with Ca^{+2}, Mg^{+2} erosion losses can be considerable in some soils.

Mg in clay minerals is slowly depleted by leaching and exhaustive cropping. Vermiculite has a high Mg content, and it can be a significant Mg source in soils. Conditions in which Mg is likely to be deficient include acid, sandy, highly leached soils with low CEC; calcareous soils with inherently low Mg levels; acid soils receiving high rates of liming materials low in Mg; high rates of NH_4^+ or K^+ fertilization; and crops with a high Mg demand. Coarse-textured, humid-region soils exhibit the greatest potential for Mg deficiency. These soils

Table 7-7 **Influence of K Fertilizer Salts on Desorption of Exchangeable Mg in Sandy Soils**

	Initial Exchangeable Mg (% of CEC)		
	0.56	*0.59*	*0.22*
		% desorbed	
KCl	12.1	6.8	31.4
K_2SO_4	4.3	6.1	30.4
K_2CO_3 or $KHCO_3$	< 0.1	< 0.1	1.6
KH_2PO_4	< 0.1	< 0.1	2.6

SOURCE: Hogg, 1962, *New Zealand J. Sci.*

normally contain low total and exchangeable Mg^{+2}, and are likely deficient when they contain < 25 to 50 ppm exchangeable Mg^{+2}. Exchangeable Mg^{+2} normally accounts for 4 to 20% of the CEC. Mg saturation for optimum plant growth coincides closely with this range, but in most instances, Mg saturation should be ≈7 to 10%. Excess Mg can occur in soils formed from serpentine minerals or influenced by groundwaters high in Mg. Normal Ca nutrition can be disrupted when exchangeable $Mg^{+2} > Ca^{+2}$.

Reduced Mg^{+2} uptake in many strongly acid soils is caused by high levels of exchangeable Al^{+3}. Al saturation of 65 to 70% is often associated with Mg deficiency. Mg deficiencies can also occur in soils with a high Ca:Mg ratio of 10:1 to 15:1. In many sandy, humid-region soils, continued use of high-Ca liming materials may increase the Ca:Mg ratio and induce Mg deficiency on certain crops.

High levels of exchangeable K^+ can interfere with Mg uptake by crops. Generally, the recommended K:Mg ratios are < 5:1 for field crops, 3:1 for vegetables and sugar beets, and 2:1 for fruit and greenhouse crops.

Competition between NH_4^+ and Mg^{+2} can also reduce Mg uptake. NH_4^+-induced Mg^{+2} stress is greatest when high rates of NH_4^+ fertilizers are applied to soils with low exchangeable Mg^{+2}. The mechanism of this interaction involves the H+ released when NH_4^+ is absorbed by roots, as well as the direct effect of NH_4^+.

Mg Sources

In contrast to Ca, few primary nutrient fertilizers contain Mg, with the exception of $K_2SO_4 \cdot MgSO_4$ (Chapter 6). Dolomite is commonly applied to low-Mg acid soils. $K_2SO_4 \cdot MgSO_4$ and $MgSO_4$ (Epsom salt) are the most widely used materials in dry fertilizer formulations (Table 7-4). Other materials containing Mg are magnesia (MgO, 55% Mg), magnesium nitrate [$Mg(NO_3)_2$, 16% Mg], magnesium silicate (basic slag, 3 to 4% Mg; serpentine, 26% Mg), magnesium chloride solution ($MgCl_2 \cdot 10H_2O$, 8 to 9% Mg), synthetic chelates (2 to 4% Mg), and natural organic complexing substances (4 to 9% Mg).

$MgSO_4$, $MgCl_2$, $Mg(NO_3)_2$, and synthetic and natural Mg chelates are well suited for application in clear liquids and foliar sprays. Mg deficiency of citrus trees in California is frequently corrected by foliar applications of $Mg(NO_3)_2$. In tree-fruit regions, $MgSO_4$ solutions are foliar applied to supply Mg. $K_2SO_4 \cdot MgSO_4$ is the most widely used Mg additive in suspensions. A special suspension grade (100% passing through a 20-mesh screen) is available commercially. Mg content in animal and municipal wastes is similar to S content and can therefore be used to supply sufficient Mg.

Study Questions

1. S is an integral part of which amino acids?
2. What mechanism(s) are involved in transport of solution S to plant roots?
3. What is the importance of the C:N:P:S ratio on S availability?
4. What are the soil conditions under which S leaching would be expected?
5. Describe soil and climatic conditions where S deficiencies are most likely to occur.
6. Discuss SO_4^{2-} adsorption by soils, with emphasis on the factors affecting this phenomenon.
7. What are the three broad groups of organic S compounds in soil? Which of these compounds contributes most to mineralizable S?
8. What are the factors affecting the oxidation of S^0 in soils? What soil microorganisms are responsible for S oxidation?
9. What factors influence the type and amount of S fertilizer needed by crops?
10. When using granular S^0 fertilizer, what conditions will increase rate of oxidation and ultimate plant availability?
11. A corn producer irrigates 4 times each season with 2 inches of water (12 ppm S). The total above-ground biomass (grain plus residue) weighs 4 t/a (2.5% N, 12:1 N:S). The soil contains 2% OM, which declines at a rate of 1% per year. Does the crop need additional S?
12. An irrigation water sample contains 12 ppm S. How many acre-feet of irrigation water would you need to apply 16 lbs S/a?
13. The soil contains 2% O.M with 2% loss each year (N:S = 8:1). A clover crop grown on this soil yields 5 ton/a (N:S = 12:1, 3% N content).
    a. How many pounds SO_4^{-2}/afs are mineralized each year?
    b. Does this crop need S fertilization (assume that all available S comes from the OM)?
    c. How many pounds of gypsum/afs would be required per year?
14. Why is a deficiency of Ca sometimes observed under very dry soil conditions?
15. In what ways do Mg- and K-deficiency symptoms resemble each other? In what ways are they dissimilar? What function of Mg in plants is unique?
16. What is the primary transport mechanism of Mg^{2+} and Ca^{2+} to the root surface?
17. Are deficiencies of Ca and Mg common? What conditions are conducive to deficiencies?
18. Why is it desirable to have a high degree of Ca saturation on the CEC?
19. Why is soil acidity usually associated with impaired uptake of Ca and Mg?
20. What are some incidental sources of plant-nutrient Ca?
21. An acid soil has a CEC of 10 meq/100 g. Ca and Mg saturation are 40 and 2%, respectively. Calculate the pounds of $CaCO_3$ and $MgSO_4$ needed to increase Ca and Mg saturation to 65 and 8%, respectively.

Selected References

Barber, S. A. 1984. *Soil nutrient bioavailability: A mechanistic approach.* New York: John Wiley & Sons.

Beaton, J. D., Fox, R. L., and Jones, M. B. 1985. Production, marketing, and use of sulfur products, In O. P. Englestad (Ed.), *Fertilizer technology and use* (pp. 411–454). Madison, Wis.: Soil Science Society of America.

Mortvedt, J. J., Murphy, L. S., and Follett, R. H. 1999. *Fertilizer technology and application.* Willoughby, Ohio: Meister Publishing.

Mortvedt, J. J., and Fox, F. R. 1985. Production, marketing, and use of calcium, magnesium, and micronutrient fertilizers. In O. P. Englestad (Ed.), *Fertilizer technology and use.* Madison, Wis.: Soil Science Society of America.

Tabatabai, M. A. (Ed.). 1986. *Sulfur in agriculture.* No. 27. Madison, Wis.: ASA, CSSA, Soil Science Society of America.

CHAPTER 8

Micronutrients

Micronutrients are equally important in plant nutrition as macronutrients; they simply occur in plants and soils in much lower concentrations. Plants grown in micronutrient-deficient soils exhibit similar reductions in productivity as those grown in macronutrient-deficient soils. Micronutrients in soil are (1) elements in primary and secondary minerals, (2) adsorbed to mineral and OM surfaces, (3) incorporated in OM and microorganisms, and (4) incorporated in solution (Fig. 8-1). Depending on the micronutrient, some forms are more important than others in buffering micronutrients in soil solution. Understanding the relationships and dynamics among these forms is essential for optimizing plant productivity in micronutrient-deficient soils.

Iron (Fe)

Fe Cycle

Plant available Fe is governed primarily through organic and mineral fractions in soils (Fig. 8-2). Fe minerals dissolve to buffer reductions in solution Fe caused by plant uptake. Solution Fe can be immobilized by microorganisms and complexed by organic compounds in the soil solution. Because solution Fe concentration is low compared to Ca^{+2}, Mg^{+2}, K^{+}, and Na^{+} (and Al^{+3} in acid soils), micronutrient cations like Fe are not adsorbed on the CEC. Thus, adsorbed Fe has little effect on plant available Fe.

Fe in Plants

Fe is absorbed by roots as Fe^{+2} and Fe^{+3}. Because Fe can exist in two oxidation states, it accepts or donates an electron ($Fe^{+3} + e^{-} \leftrightarrows Fe^{+2}$), depending on oxidation potential. Transfer of electrons between organic molecules and Fe provides the electrochemical potential for many enzymatic transformations in plants. Several of these enzymes are involved in chlorophyll synthesis, and when Fe is deficient, chlorophyll production is reduced, which results in the characteristic chlorosis symptoms of Fe stress (see color plates).

Fe is a structural component of porphyrin molecules: cytochromes, hemes, hematin, ferrichrome, and leghemoglobin. These substances are involved in oxidation-reduction

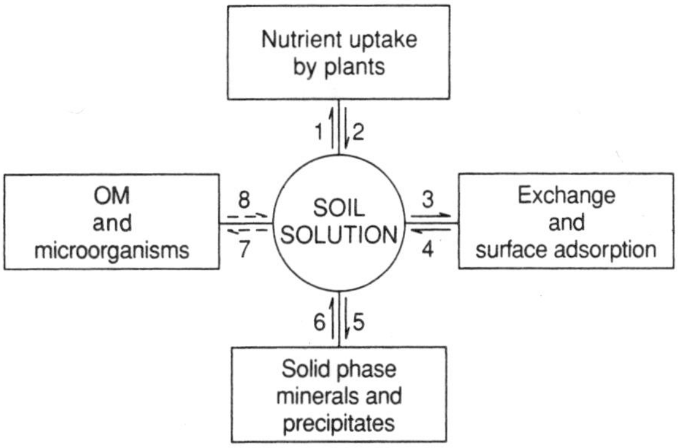

Figure 8-1 Relationships between various forms of micronutrients in soils. Reactions 1 and 2 represent plant absorption and exudation, respectively; reactions 3 and 4 represent adsorption and desorption, respectively; reactions 5 and 6 represent precipitation and dissolution, respectively; and reactions 7 and 8 represent immobilization and mineralization, respectively. All of these processes interact to control micronutrient concentration in soil solution. *(Lindsay, 1972,* Micronutrients in Agriculture*, p. 42, Madison, WI: ASA.)*

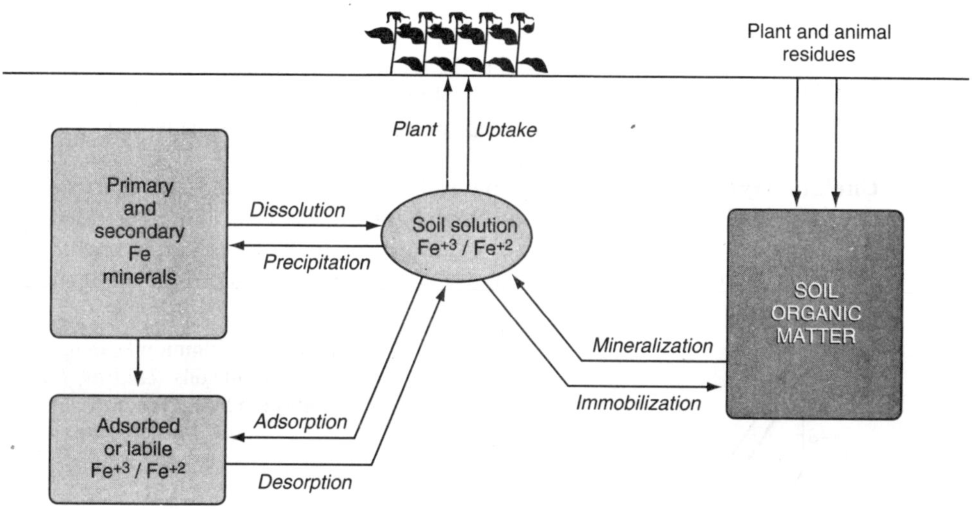

Figure 8-2 Fe cycling in soils.

reactions in respiration and photosynthesis. As much as 75% of cell Fe is associated with the chloroplasts, and up to 90% of Fe in leaves occurs with lipoprotein of the chloroplast and mitochondria membranes.

Fe-containing cytochromes in the chloroplasts function in photosynthetic reduction processes where ferrodoxin, an Fe-S protein, is an electron acceptor. Ferredoxins are the first stable compound of the photosynthetic electron transport chain. Reduction of O_2 to H_2O during respiration is also a common function of Fe compounds. Fe is a constituent of nitrogenase, the enzyme essential for N_2 fixation by N-fixing microorganisms. Fe may also be capable of partial substitution for Mo involved in NO_3^- reductase in soybeans.

The sufficiency range of Fe in plant tissue is between 50 and 250 ppm. Generally, when tissue Fe content < 50 ppm, deficiency is likely to occur. Fe deficiency symptoms appear first in the young leaves, because Fe is not mobile in the plant. Young leaves develop interveinal chlorosis, which progresses rapidly over the entire leaf. In severe cases, leaves turn entirely white and necrotic.

Fe toxicity can be observed under certain conditions. For example, in rice grown on poorly drained or submerged soils, leaf bronzing symptoms occur with > 300 ppm Fe in rice leaves.

Fe in Soil

Mineral Fe Fe is the fourth most abundant element, comprising about 5% of the earth's crust. Common primary and secondary Fe minerals are olivene [$(Mg, Fe)_2SiO_4$], siderite ($FeCO_3$), hematite (Fe_2O_3), goethite ($FeOOH$), and magnetite (Fe_3O_4)]. Total Fe in soil varies widely from 0.7 to 55%. The solubility of common Fe minerals in soil is very low, only 10^{-6} to 10^{-24} M Fe^{+3} in solution, depending on pH (Fig. 8-3). "Soil Fe" represents an amorphous $Fe(OH)_3$ precipitate that more closely reflects Fe solubility in most soils.

Soil Solution Fe Compared with other cations, solution Fe^{+3} concentration is very low. In well-drained, oxidized soils, solution $Fe^{+2} < Fe^{+3}$ (Fig. 8-4). Soluble Fe^{+2} increases significantly when soils become waterlogged. The pH-dependent relationship for Fe^{+3} in soil solution is:

$$Fe(OH)_3 + 3H^+ \leftrightarrows Fe^{+3} + 3H_2O$$

For each 1 pH unit increase, Fe^{+3} concentration decreases a thousandfold. In contrast, Fe^{+2} decreases a hundredfold for each unit increase in pH, which is similar to other divalent cations (Fig. 8-4). Over the normal soil pH range, total solution Fe is not sufficient to meet plant Fe requirements, even in acid soils, where Fe deficiencies occur less frequently than in high-pH and calcareous soils (Fig. 8-5). Obviously, another mechanism that increases Fe availability to plants exists; otherwise, crops grown on almost all soils would be Fe deficient.

Chelate Dynamics Numerous natural organic compounds in soil, or synthetic compounds added to soils, are able to complex, or *chelate*, Fe^{+3} and other micronutrients. The concentration of Fe in solution and Fe transported to the root by mass flow and diffusion can be greatly increased through Fe complexes with natural organic chelating compounds in the

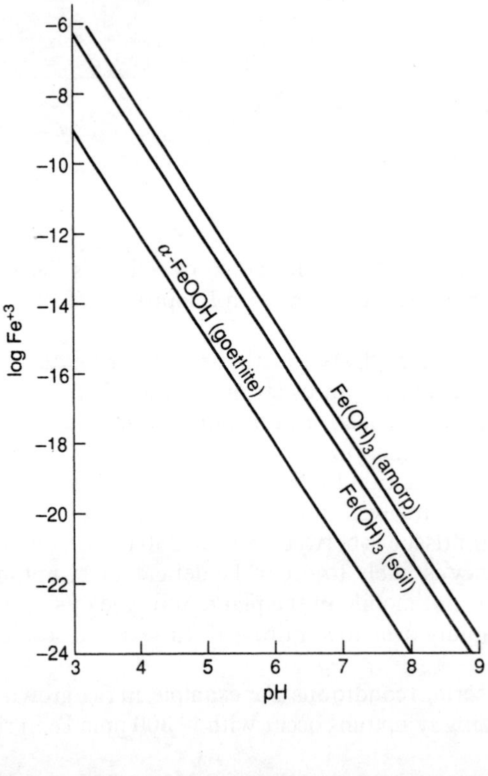

Figure 8-3 **Common Fe minerals that control solution Fe in soils. *(Lindsay, 1979,* Chemical Equilibria in Soils, *New York: John Wiley & Sons.)***

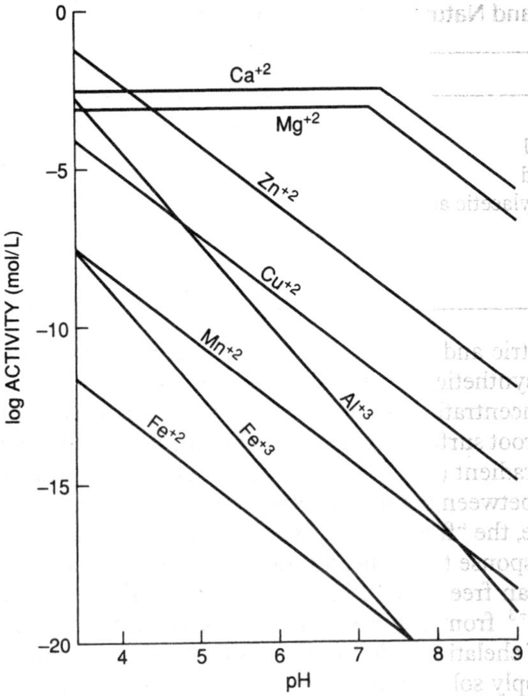

Figure 8-4 **Influence of pH on solution Fe^{13} concentration relative to other cations.** ***(Lindsay, 1981,*** **Chemistry in Soil Environment,** ***p. 189, Madison, WI: ASA.)***

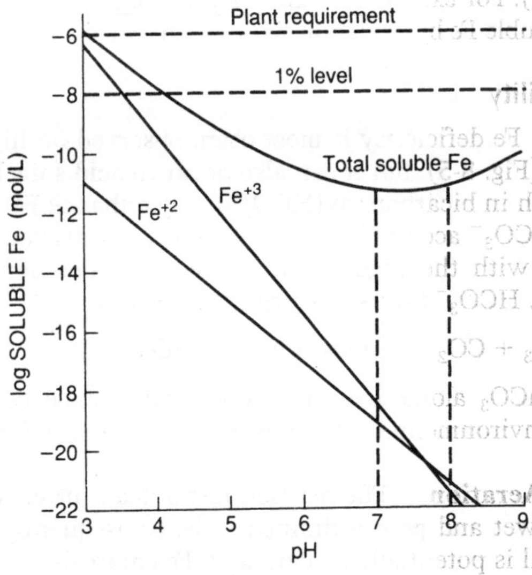

Figure 8-5 **Influence of pH on total solution Fe concentration and its relationship to Fe required by plants.** ***(Lindsay, 1974,*** **Plant Root and Its Environment,** ***p. 508, Univ. Press of Virginia.)***

soil. Chelate is a term derived from a Greek word meaning "claw." Chelates are soluble organic compounds that bond with metals such as Fe, Zn, Cu, and Mn, increasing their solubility and supply to plant roots. Natural organic chelates in soils are products of microbial activity and degradation of soil OM and plant residues. Root exudates are also capable of complexing micronutrients. Many natural organic chelates have not been identified;

Table 8-1 Common Synthetic and Natural Chelate Compounds

Name	*Formula*	*Abbreviation*
Ethylenediaminetetraacetic acid	$C_{10}H_{16}O_8N_2$	EDTA
Diethylenetriaminepentaacetic acid	$C_{14}H_{23}O_{10}N_3$	DTPA
Cyclohexanediaminetetraacetic acid	$C_{14}H_{22}O_8N_2$	CDTA
Ethylenediaminedi-o-hydroxyphenylacetic acid	$C_{18}H_{20}O_6N_2$	EDDHA
Citric acid	$C_6H_8O_7$	CIT
Oxalic acid	$C_2H_2O_4$	OX
Pyrophosphoric acid	$H_4P_2O_7$	PPA

however, compounds such as citric and oxalic acids have chelating properties (Table 8-1). Molecular structures of several synthetic chelates are shown in Figure 8-6.

During plant uptake, the concentration of chelated Fe or other micronutrients is greater in the bulk solution than at the root surface; thus, chelated Fe diffuses to the root surface in response to the concentration gradient (Fig. 8-7). At the root surface, Fe^{+3} dissociates from the chelate through interaction between organic cell wall compounds and the chelate. After Fe^{+3} dissociates from the chelate, the "free" chelate will diffuse away from the root back to the "bulk" solution, again in response to a concentration gradient (free chelate concentration near the root is greater than free chelate in bulk solution). The free chelate subsequently complexes another Fe^{+3} from solution. As the *unchelated* Fe^{+3} concentration decreases in solution because of chelation, additional Fe is desorbed from mineral surfaces or Fe minerals dissolve to resupply solution Fe. The chelate-micronutrient "cycling" is an extremely important mechanism in soils that greatly contributes to plant available Fe and other micronutrients (Fig. 8-7). For example, Fe diffusion to sorghum roots is encouraged by higher concentration of soluble Fe by chelation with EDDHA (Fig. 8-8).

Factors Affecting Fe Availability

Soil pH and Bicarbonate. Fe deficiency is most often observed on high-pH and calcareous soils in arid regions (Fig. 8-5), but it can also occur in acid soils low in total Fe. Irrigation water and soils high in bicarbonate (HCO_3^-) may enhance Fe deficiency, due to high pH associated with HCO_3^- accumulation. Calcareous soil pH ranges from 7.3 to 8.5 (Chapter 3), coinciding with the highest incidence of Fe deficiency and lowest solubility of soil Fe (Fig. 8-5). HCO_3^- forms in calcareous soils by:

$$CaCO_3 + CO_2 + H_2O \leftrightarrows Ca^{+2} + 2HCO_3^-$$

Although the presence of $CaCO_3$ alone does not necessarily induce Fe deficiency, its interaction with certain soil environmental conditions is related to Fe deficiency.

Excessive Water and Poor Aeration. The reaction just noted is promoted by accumulation of CO_2 in excessively wet and poorly drained soils. Consequently, any compact, heavy-textured, calcareous soil is potentially Fe deficient. Fe chlorosis is often associated with cool, rainy weather when soil moisture is high and soil aeration is poor. Also, root development and nutrient absorption are reduced under cool, wet conditions, which contributes to Fe stress. High pH or HCO_3^--induced chlorosis often disappears when these soils dry. Flooding and submergence of soils where HCO_3^- formation is of no concern can improve Fe availability by increasing Fe^{+2} concentration.

Organic Matter. Although lime-induced Fe deficiency occurs in wet soils, low-OM, calcareous soils are often low in plant available Fe. This deficiency occurs especially on

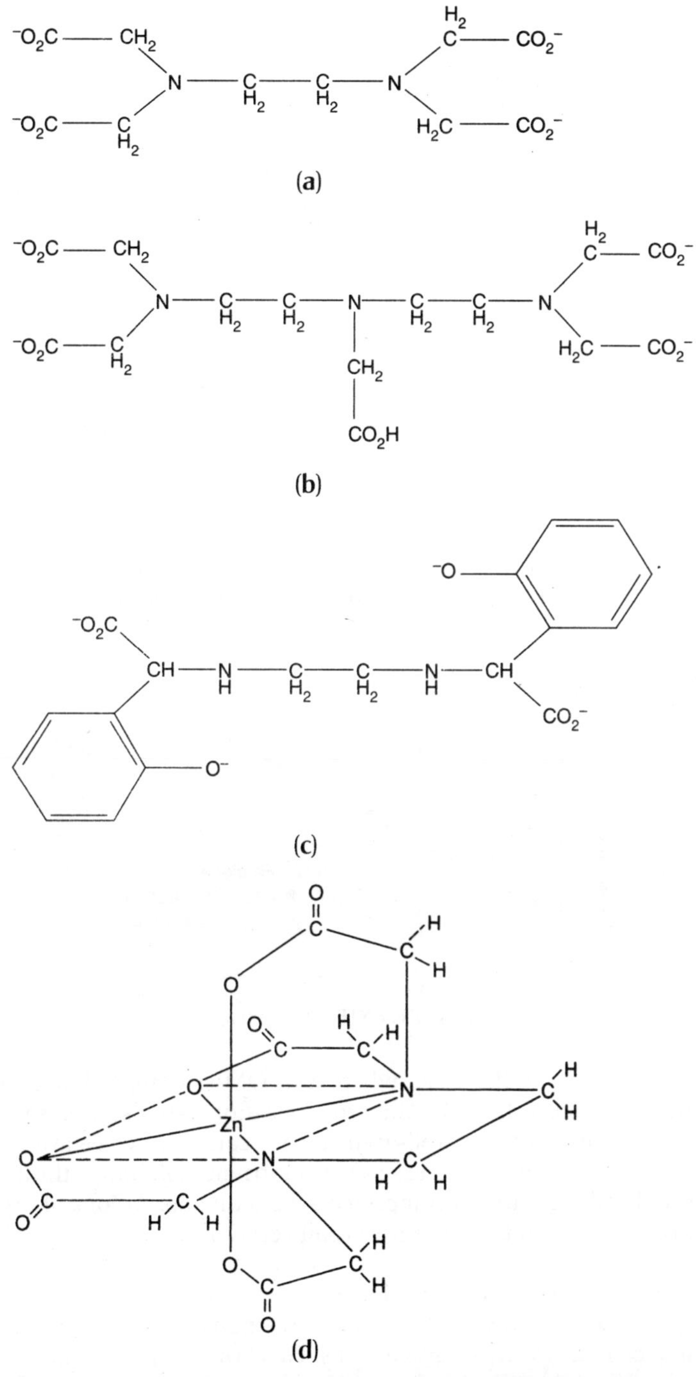

Figure 8-6 The structure of EDTA (a), DTPA (b), EDDHA (c), and Zn-EDTA (d). *(Follett et al., 1981,* Fertilizers and Soil Amendments *Englewood Cliffs, NJ: Prentice-Hall.)*

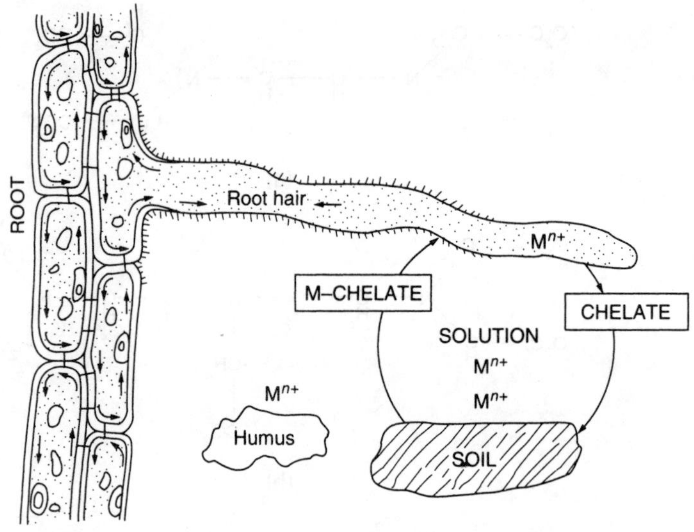

Figure 8-7 **Cycling of chelated micronutrients (M) in soils.** ***(Lindsay,1974,*** **Plant Root and Its Environment,** ***p. 517, Univ. Press of Virginia.)***

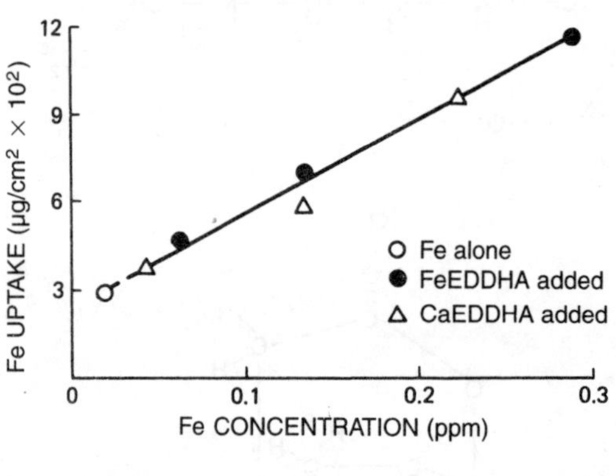

Figure 8-8 **Fe uptake by sorghum roots as influenced by solution Fe and chelate treatment.** ***(O'Connor et al., 1971,*** **Soil Sci. Soc. Am. J.,** ***35:407.)***

eroded portions of the field where the OM-rich topsoil has been removed, exposing calcareous subsoils. Land leveling for irrigation can also expose calcareous, low-OM subsoils. Additions of OM to well-drained soils can improve Fe availability. Organic materials such as manure may increase micronutrient solubility through chelation reactions. Improved soil structure in compacted soils with applications of organic wastes should also increase Fe availability by improved soil aeration.

Interactions with Other Nutrients. Metal cations can interact with Fe to induce Fe deficiency. For example, high soil Cu following extended use of $CuSO_4$ as a fertilizer or fungicide can induce Fe stress in sensitive crops. Fe-sensitive crops exhibit Fe chlorosis when grown on soils high in Mn. Fe deficiency in soybeans can occur due to low Fe:(Cu+Mn) ratio in plants. In addition to Fe deficiency caused by excess Cu, Mn, Zn, and Mo, Fe-P interactions have been observed in some plants, probably related to precipitation of Fe-P minerals.

Plants receiving NO_3^- are more likely to develop Fe stress than those receiving NH_4^+. When a strong acid anion (NO_3^-) is absorbed and replaced with a weak acid (HCO_3^-), the

Table 8-2 **Sensitivity of Crops to Fe Deficiency***

Sensitive	*Moderately Tolerant*	*Tolerant*
Azalea	Alfalfa	Alfalfa
Beans, snap	Asparagus	Barley
Berries	Barley	Corn
Blueberries	Cabbage	Cotton
Broccoli	Corn	Flax
Cauliflower	Cotton	Grasses
Citrus	Field beans	Millet
Field beans	Field peas	Oats
Flax	Flax	Potato
Forage sorghum	Forage legumes	Rice
Fruit trees	Fruit trees	Soybean
Grain sorghum	Grain sorghum	Sugar beet
Grapes	Grasses	Wheat
Maple trees	Oats	
Mint	Orchard grass	
Ornamentals	Ornamentals	
Peanuts	Rice	
Pin oak	Soybean	
Raspberries	Sweet corn	
Rhododendron	Tomato	
Soybean	Turfgrasses	
Spinach	Wheat	
Strawberries		
Sudan grass		
Vegetables		
Walnut		

*Some crops are listed under two or three categories because of variations in soil, growing conditions, and differential response varieties of a given crop.

pH of the root zone increases, particularly in low-buffered systems, which decreases Fe availability. Thus, Fe solubility and availability are favored by the acidity that develops when NH_4^+ is utilized by plants.

Plant Factors. Although diffusion of both Fe^{+3} and Fe^{+2} to the root occurs, Fe^{+3} is reduced to Fe^{+2} before absorption. Plant genotypes differ in their ability to take up Fe and are classified according to their sensitivity or tolerance to low levels of available Fe (Table 8-2). Fe-efficient varieties should be selected where Fe deficiencies are likely to occur.

The ability of plants to absorb and translocate Fe appears to be a genetically controlled adaptive process that responds to Fe deficiency or stress. Roots of Fe-efficient plants alter their environment to improve Fe availability and uptake by (1) excretion of H^+ and organic acids from roots, (2) excretion of chelating compounds from roots, and (3) enhanced rate of Fe^{+3} to Fe^{+2} reduction at root surface.

Some plants exhibit a unique mechanism to tolerate low Fe availability. For example, grass roots release amino acids called *phytosiderophores* with a high affinity for Fe^{+3}. Phytosiderophore-Fe complexes enhance Fe transport to root surfaces and absorption by root cells (Fig. 8-9).

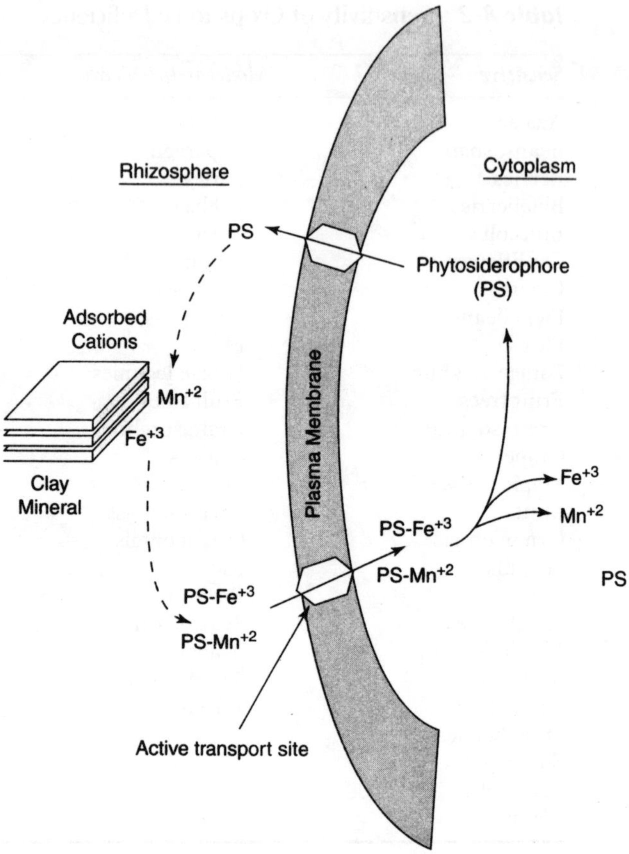

Figure 8-9 **Mechanism of enhancing Fe and Mn availability and transport through phytosiderophore complexes.**

Fe Sources

Organic Fe Most animal wastes contain small quantities of plant available Fe, typically ranging from 0.02 to 0.1%. Although sufficient plant available Fe can be provided through manure application at appropriate rates, the major benefit of organic waste application is increased OM and associated chelation effects. Enhanced Fe chelation may supply sufficient plant available Fe, even if the manure contains no Fe. In contrast, municipal waste can contain as much as 5% Fe (Table 8-3).

Inorganic Fe Fe chlorosis is one of the most difficult micronutrient deficiencies to correct in the field. In general, soil applications of inorganic Fe are not effective in correcting Fe deficiency in high pH soils because of rapid precipitation of insoluble $Fe(OH)_3$ (Fig. 8-3). For example, when $FeSO_4 \cdot 7H_2O$ and Fe-EDDHA were applied, only 20% was plant available (DTPA extractable) after 1 week, compared with 70% and 25% plant available Fe with FeEDDA after 7 and 14 weeks, respectively (Fig. 8-10). Inorganic Fe applications to Fe-deficient acid soils can provide sufficient Fe (Table 8-3).

Fe deficiencies are corrected mainly with foliar application of inorganic Fe (Table 8-4). One application of a 2% $FeSO_4$ solution at 15 to 30 gal/a is usually sufficient to alleviate mild chlorosis. However, several applications 7 to 14 days apart may be needed to remedy

Table 8-3 **Sources of Fe Fertilizer**

Source	*Formula*	*% Fe*
Ferrous sulfate	$FeSO_4 \cdot 7H_2O$	19
Ferric sulfate	$Fe_2(SO_4)_3 \cdot 4H_2O$	23
Ferrous oxide	FeO	77
Ferric oxide	Fe_2O_3	69
Ferrous ammonium phosphate	$Fe(NH_4)PO_4 \cdot H_2O$	29
Ferrous ammonium sulfate	$(NH_4)_2SO_4 \cdot FeSO_4 \cdot 6H_2O$	14
Iron ammonium polyphosphate	$Fe(NH_4)HP_2O_7$	22
Iron chelates	NaFeEDTA	5–14
	NaFeEDDHA	6
	NaFeDTPA	10
Natural organic materials		5–10

SOURCE: Mortvedt et al. (Eds.), 1972, *Micronutrients in Agriculture*, p. 357, Madison, WI: Soil Sci. Soc. Am.

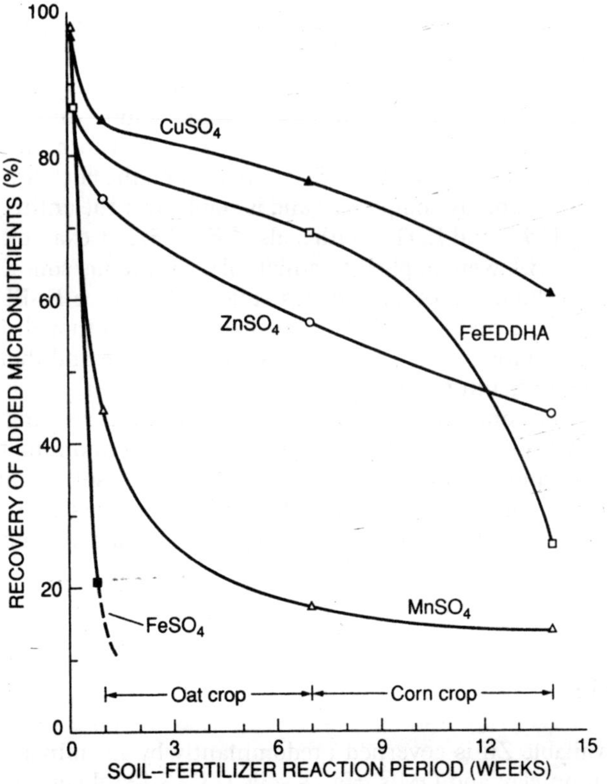

Figure 8-10 **Recovery of micronutrients in soils fertilized with various inorganic micronutrient fertilizers.** ***(Follett and Lindsay, 1971,*** **Soil Sci. Soc. Am. J.,** ***35:600–602.)***

Table 8-4 **Examples of Fe Management for Selected Crops**

Crop	*Fe Source*	*Fe Rate*	*Application Method*	*Remarks*
Vegetables	Fe chelates	0.5–1.0 lbs/a	Foliar	Wet foliage, repeat as needed
Citrus	Fe chelates	12–24 g/tree	Foliar	
Grain sorghum and corn	$FeSO_4 \cdot 7H_20$	0.70–1.2 lbs/100 L	Foliar	Three sprays of 125 L/a
Field (dry) beans	$FeSO_4 \cdot 7H_20$	595 g Fe/100 L H_2O 80–125 L/a	Foliar	Two-week intervals until symptoms disappear
Deciduous fruits	Fe polyflavonoid	60–100 g /100 L H_2O	Foliar	Wet foliage, repeat as needed
Soybeans	FeEDDHA	0.15 lbs/a	Foliar	Spray band over row at second trifoliate
Cotton	$FeSO_4 \cdot 7H_2O$	1.0 lb Fe/100 L H_2O	Foliar	Wet plants, repeat as needed
Turfgrass	$FeSO_4 \cdot 7H_2O$ Fe chelates	0.5–1.0 lbs/a or 0.025 lbs/1,000 ft^2	Foliar or soil	Foliar more effective, soil apply chelates

more severe Fe deficiencies. Fe salts injected directly into trunks and limbs of fruit trees are effective in controlling Fe chlorosis.

With the exception of $FeSO_4$, perhaps the most widely used Fe sources are the synthetic chelates (Table 8-3). These materials are water soluble and can be applied to soil or foliage. Chelated Fe is protected from the soil reactions that form insoluble $Fe(OH)_3$. The specific chelate applied depends on the micronutrient and the chelate stability in the soil (Fig. 8-11). EDDHA will strongly complex Fe and is stable over the entire pH range. DTPA can be used for soil < pH 7.5 and EDTA with soils < pH 6.5. For example, when Fe-EDTA, Fe-DTPA, and Fe-EDDHA were applied to a high pH, calcareous soil, EDDHA provided more plant available Fe than the other chelates (Fig. 8-12). Since Fe-EDDHA is the most stable Fe chelate, it is the preferred chelate fertilizer source, although Fe-DTPA has also been used (Fig. 8-10). Unfortunately, Fe chelates are expensive and their use is usually restricted to high-value horticultural crops.

Local root zone acidification can be effective in correcting Fe deficiencies in calcareous and high-pH soils. Several S products, such as S^0, ammonium thiosulfate, sulfuric acid, sulfur dioxide, and ammonium polysulfide, will lower soil pH and increase solution Fe concentration. Complexing with polyphosphate fertilizers also increases Fe availability, but Fe-EDDHA is more effective than polyphosphate at the same Fe rates.

Zinc (Zn)

Zn Cycle

Plant available Zn is governed predominantly by Zn mineral solubility, soil OM, and Zn adsorbed on clay and OM surfaces soils (Fig. 8-13). Primary and secondary minerals dissolve to initially provide solution Zn, which is then adsorbed onto the CEC, incorporated into microbial biomass, or complexed by organic compounds in solution. Like Fe, chelated Zn is important to the transport of Zn to root surfaces for uptake.

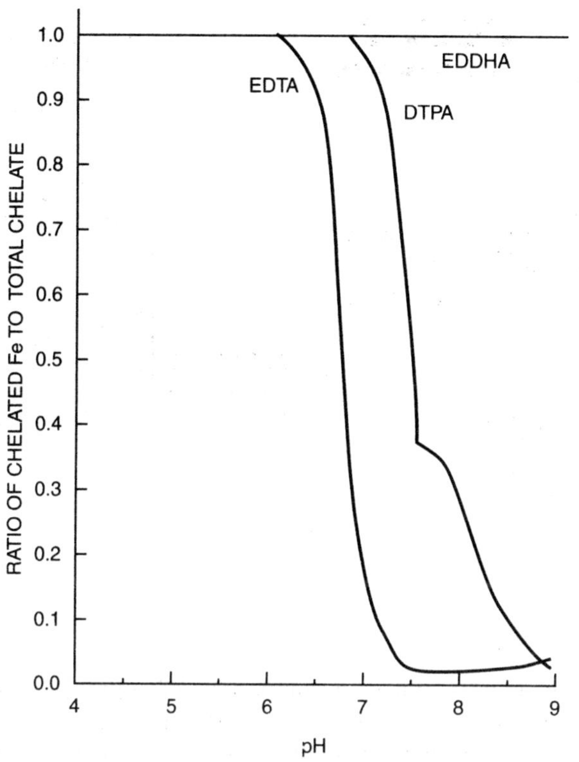

Figure 8-11 Stability of synthetic chelates with Fe in soils. *(Norvell, 1972,* Micronutrients in Agriculture, *Madison, WI: ASA.)*

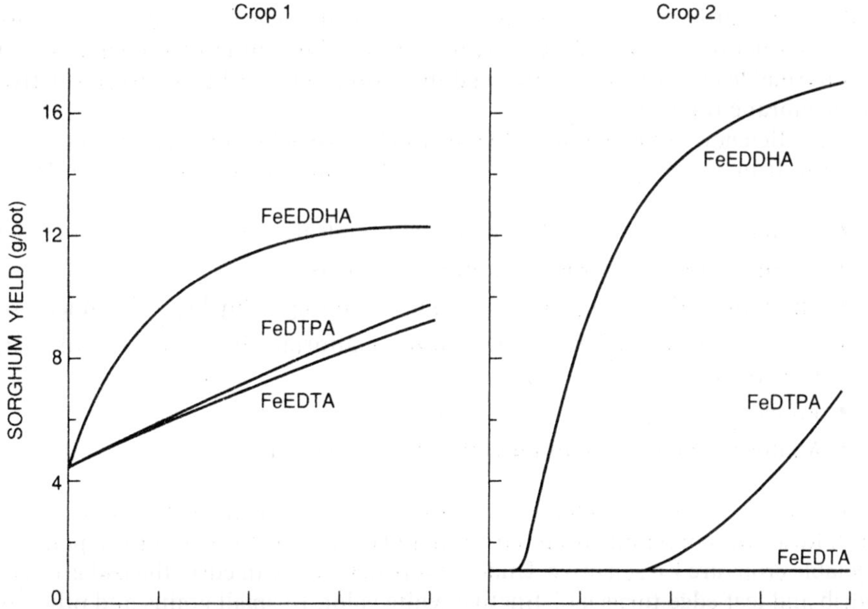

Figure 8-12 Effectiveness of synthetic Fe chelates in supplying Fe to Fe-deficient sorghum. *(Lindsay, 1974,* Plant Root and Its Environment, *p. 511, Univ. Press of Virginia.)*

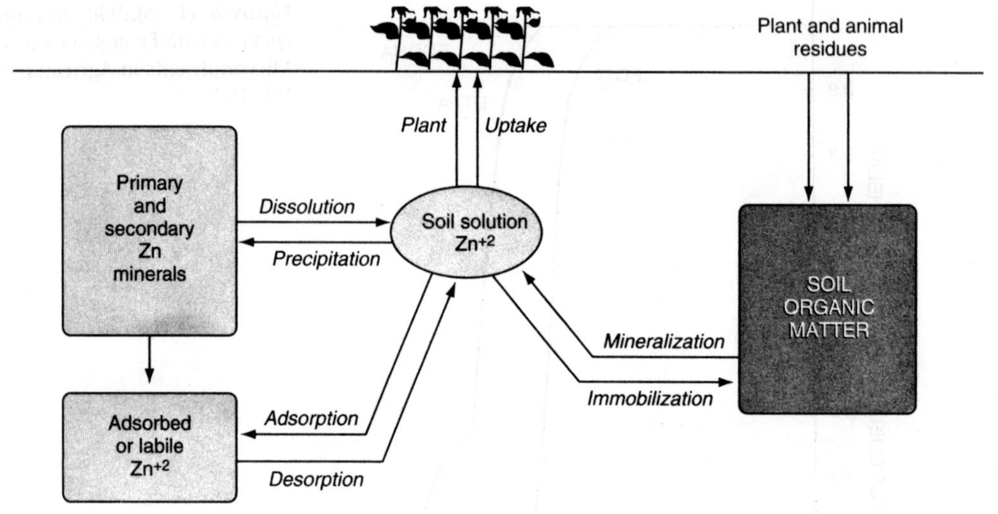

Figure 8-13 Zn cycle in soils.

Zn in Plants

Plant roots absorb as a cation (Zn^{+2}) and as a component of synthetic and natural organic complexes. Zn is involved in many enzymatic activities, but it is not known whether it acts as a functional, structural, or regulatory cofactor. Zn is important in the synthesis of tryptophane, a component of some proteins and a compound needed for the production of growth hormones (auxins) such as indoleacetic acid. Reduced growth hormone production in Zn-deficient plants causes shortening of internodes and smaller-than-normal leaves. Zn also is involved in chlorophyll synthesis, enzyme activation, and cell membrane integrity.

Zn deficiency can be identified by distinctive visual symptoms in leaves, but also can appear in fruit or storage organs, and in overall plant growth. Common symptoms include:

- Light green, yellow, or white areas between leaf veins, particularly in older leaves.
- Eventual tissue necrosis in chlorotic leaf areas.
- Shortening of stem or stalk internodes, resulting in bushy, rosetted leaves.
- Small, narrow, thickened leaves, often malformed by growth of only part of leaf tissue.
- Premature foliage loss.
- Malformation of fruit, often with little or no yield.

Zn deficiency causes characteristic *rosetting* or clustering of small leaves at the top of the plant. Rosetting commonly occurs in fruit and citrus trees. Corn, cotton, potato, and other vegetable crops are Zn sensitive. Under severe deficiency in corn, the leaf area between the midrib and leaf edge turns a distinctive white color. In small grains and other grasses, Zn deficiency depresses tillering, and the midrib at the base of young leaves becomes chlorotic. Eventually, older leaves exhibit brown spots or leaf tips turn yellow-orange, eventually progressing to the entire leaf. Under moderate Zn deficiency, symptoms may disappear after several weeks, although plant maturity is sufficiently delayed to limit yield.

Zn concentration in plants ranges between 25 and 150 ppm. Deficiencies of Zn are usually associated with concentrations of less than 10 to 20 ppm, depending on the crop, and toxicities will occur when the Zn leaf concentration exceeds 400 ppm. Zn toxicity reduces or ceases root growth, resulting in yellowing leaves and eventual plant death. Peanut and soybean are sensitive to high Zn, while most crops are tolerant.

Zn deficiencies are widespread throughout the world, especially in rice cropland of Asia. Soil conditions most associated with Zn deficiencies are acid, sandy soils low in Zn; neutral, basic, or calcareous soils; fine-textured soils; soils high in available P; some organic soils; and subsoils exposed by land leveling or by wind and water erosion.

Zn in Soil

Mineral Zn Zn content of the lithosphere is about 80 ppm, and Zn in soil ranges from 10 to 300 ppm (50 ppm average). Igneous rocks contain ≈ 70 ppm Zn, while sedimentary rocks (shale) contain more Zn (95 ppm) than limestone (20 ppm) or sandstone (16 ppm). Franklinite ($ZnFe_2O_4$), smithsonite ($ZnCO_3$), and willemite (Zn_2SiO_4) are common Zn-containing minerals (Fig. 8-14). Zn mineral solubility in soils often resembles the solubility represented by "soil Zn."

Soil Solution Zn Soil solution Zn^{+2} is low, ranging between 2 and 70 ppb, with more than half complexed by OM. Above pH 7.7, $ZnOH^+$ becomes the most abundant species (Fig. 8-15). Zinc solubility is pH dependent, decreasing with increasing pH, given by:

$$\text{Soil-Zn } 2H^+ \leftrightarrows Zn^{+2}$$

As a result of Zn^{+2} interactions with OM, thirtyfold reductions in solution Zn^{+2} for every unit pH increase between 5 to 7 typically have been observed.

Diffusion predominately transports Zn^{+2} to plant roots. Complexing agents or chelates from root exudates or from decomposing organic residues facilitate Zn^{+2} diffusion to roots (Fig. 8-7). Diffusion of chelated Zn^{+2} (and other micronutrients) can be significantly greater than that of unchelated Zn^{+2} (Fig. 8-16).

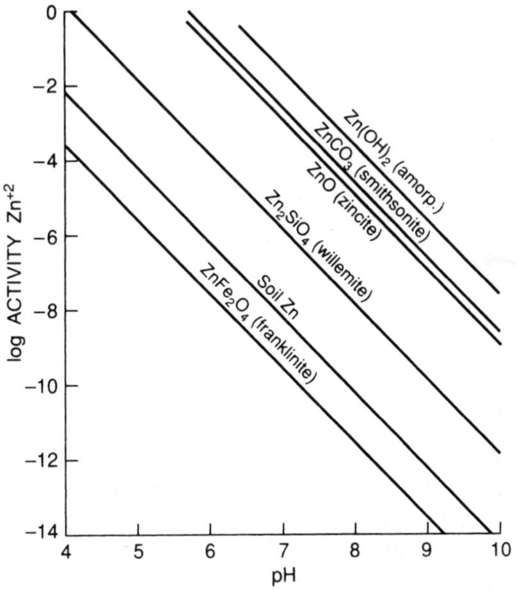

Figure 8-14 **Solubilities of common Zn minerals in soils.** *(Lindsay, 1979,* **Chemical Equilibria in Soils,** *New York: John Wiley & Sons.)*

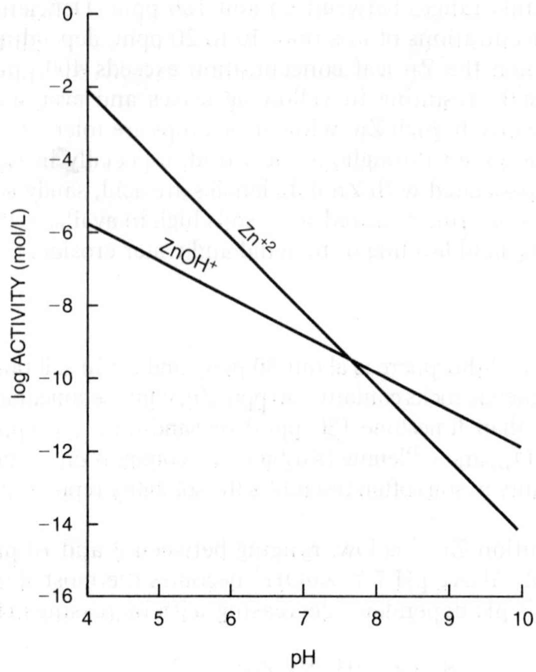

Figure 8-15 **Common Zn species in soil solution as influenced by pH.** ***(Lindsay, 1979,*** **Chemical Equilibria in Soils,** ***New York: John Wiley & Sons.)***

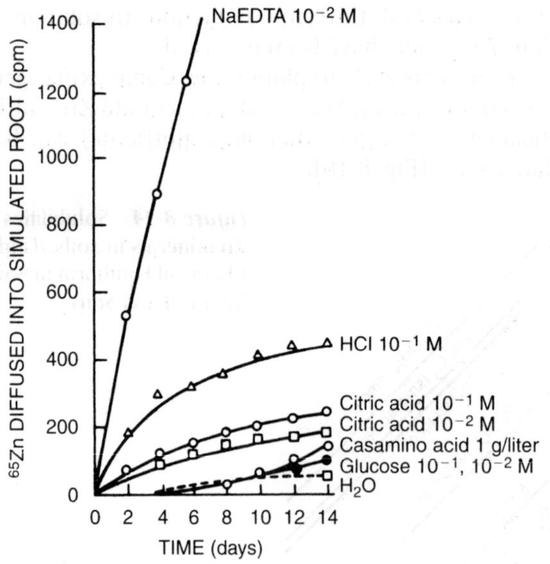

Figure 8-16 **Effect of various complexing agents and acids on accumulative Zn diffusion into a simulated root.** ***(Elgawhary et al., 1970, SSSAJ, 34:211.)***

Factors Affecting Zn Availability

Soil pH. Zn^{+2} availability decreases with increased soil pH (Fig. 8-15). Most pH-induced Zn deficiencies occur in neutral and calcareous soils, although not all of these soils exhibit Zn deficiency because of increased availability from Zn^{+2} chelation (Fig. 8-7). At high pH, Zn precipitates as insoluble amorphous soil Zn, $ZnFe_2O_4$, and/or $ZnSiO_4$, which reduces solution Zn^{+2} (Fig. 8-14). Liming acid soils, especially those low in Zn, will reduce Zn^{+2} uptake, which is related to pH effect on Zn^{+2} solubility. Zn^{+2} adsorption on $CaCO_3$, clay minerals, Al/Fe oxides, and OM surfaces also reduces solution Zn^{+2}, which increases with increasing pH (greater CEC).

Zn Adsorption The mechanism of Zn^{+2} adsorption on oxide surfaces is depicted as:

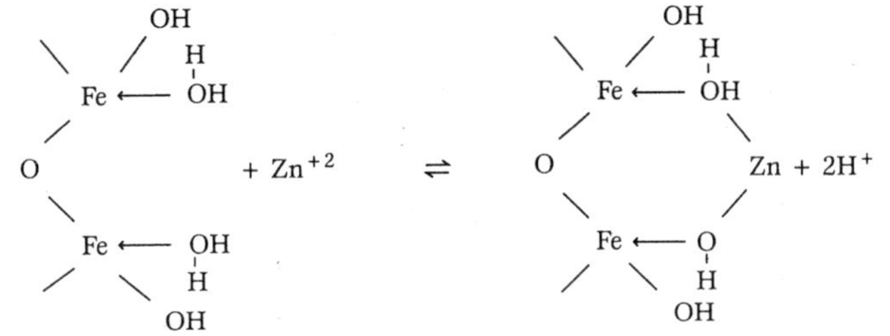

Zn^{+2} adsorption also occurs on the CEC of clay minerals, but does not occur to any great extent, at least compared to Ca^{+2} and Mg^{+2}. Zn is strongly adsorbed by magnesite ($MgCO_3$), and to a lesser extent dolomite [$CaMg(CO_3)_2$], where Zn is adsorbed into the crystal surface at sites normally occupied by Mg atoms. Zn adsorption by $CaCO_3$ is partly responsible for reduced Zn^{+2} availability in calcareous soils, where Zn availability decreases with increasing $CaCO_3$ content (Fig. 8-17).

Soil OM Zn^{+2} forms stable complexes with high-molecular-weight organic compounds (i.e., lignin, humic and fulvic acids) that exist as soluble or insoluble complexes. With insoluble complexes, Zn availability will be reduced as in Zn-deficient peats and humic soils. Formation of soluble chelated Zn complexes enhances availability by keeping Zn^{+2} in solution (Fig. 8-7). Substances present in or derived from freshly applied organic materials also have the capacity to chelate Zn^{+2}.

Interaction with Other Nutrients Other metal cations, including Cu^{+2}, Fe^{+2}, and Mn^{+2}, inhibit Zn^{+2} uptake, possibly because of competition for the same carrier site in the casparian

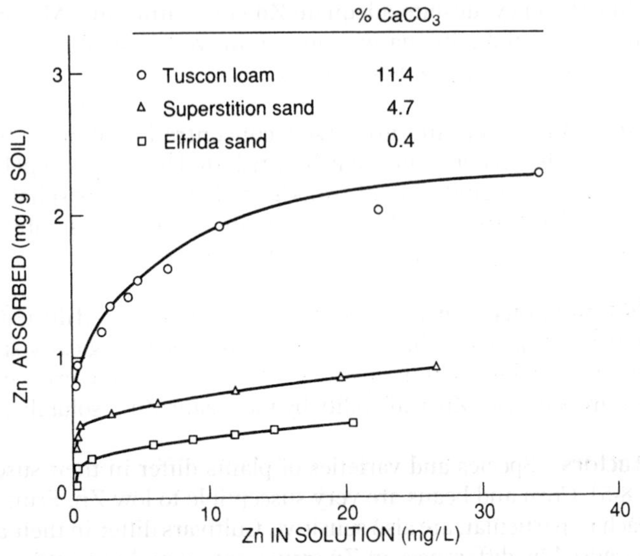

Figure 8-17 **Zn adsorption by calcareous soils.** *(Udo et al., 1970,* Soil Sci. Soc. Am. J., *34:405.)*

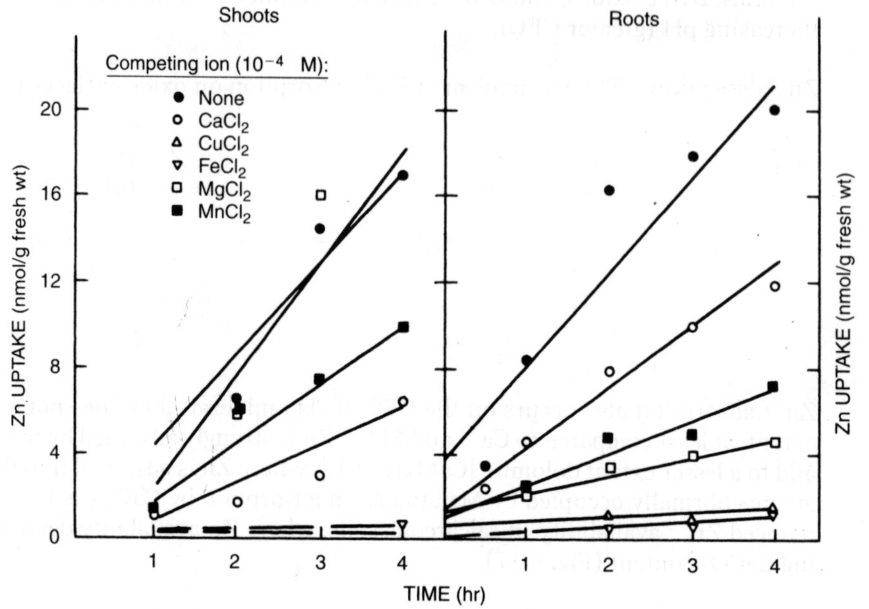

Figure 8-18 **Effect of competing ions on Zn uptake in shoots and roots of rice seedlings.** ***(Giordano et al., 1974,*** **Plant Soil,** ***41:637.)***

bands or plasmalemma (Chapter 2). The antagonistic effect is especially prevalent with Cu^{+2} and Fe^{+2} (Fig. 8-18).

High P-availability can induce Zn deficiency, commonly in soils that are marginally Zn deficient. With Zn-deficient plants, cellular regulation of P uptake is impaired, causing absorption of toxic levels of P and transportation to plant tops, creating symptoms resembling Zn deficiency, despite adequate Zn concentrations. Mycorrhizae can increase P and micronutrient uptake by many plants; however, P fertilization can suppress mycorrhizal uptake of Zn and induce Zn deficiency.

Flooding When soils are submerged, concentration of many nutrients increases, but not Zn. In acid soils, Zn deficiency may be attributed to increased pH under reducing conditions and subsequent precipitation of franklinite ($ZnFe_2O_4$) or sphalerite (ZnS). Decreasing pH in submerged, calcareous soils would usually increase Zn solubility. However, with high pH and poor aeration, potential Zn deficiency is aggravated.

Climatic Conditions Zn deficiencies are more pronounced during cool, wet seasons and often disappear in warmer weather. Climatic conditions during early spring that can contribute to Zn deficiency are low light intensity, low temperature, and excessive moisture. Increasing soil temperature increases Zn availability by increasing Zn^{+2} solubility and diffusion.

Plant Factors Species and varieties of plants differ in their susceptibility to Zn deficiency (Table 8-5). Corn and beans are very susceptible to low Zn. Fruit trees in general, and citrus and peach in particular, are also sensitive. Cultivars differ in their ability to take up Zn, which may be caused by differences in Zn translocation and utilization, different accumulations of nutrients that interact with Zn, and differences in roots and mycorrhizal infection.

Table 8-5 **Crop Sensitivity to Zn Deficiency**

High Sensitivity	*Mild Sensitivity*	*Low Sensitivity*
Apples	Alfalfa	Asparagus
Beans, lima beans	Barley	Carrots
Castor bean	Clover	Forage grasses
Citrus	Cotton	Mustard and other crucifers
Corn	Grapes	Oats
Flax	Lettuce	Peas
Fruit trees (deciduous)	Potato	Peppermint
Grapes	Sorghum	Rye
Hops	Sugar beet	Safflower
Onion	Tomato	
Pecan	Wheat	
Pine		
Rice		
Soybean		
Sudan grass		
Sweet corn		

Table 8-6 **Sources of Fertilizer Zn**

Source	*Formula*	*% Zn*
Zinc sulfate monohydrate	$ZnSO_4 \cdot H_2O$	35
Zinc oxide	ZnO	78
Zinc carbonate	$ZnCO_3$	52
Zinc phosphate	$Zn_3(PO_4)_2$	51
Zinc chelates	$Na_2ZnEDTA$	14
Natural organics	—	1–5

SOURCE: Mortvedt et al., (Eds.), 1972, *Micronutrients in Agric.*, p.371, Madison, WI: Soil Sci. Soc. Am.

Zn Sources

Organic Zn Most animal wastes contain small quantities of plant available Zn, typically ranging from 0.01 to 0.05%. With large manure-application rates, sufficient plant available Zn can be provided. As a result of Zn additions to animal diets, combined with continual manure applications to the same fields, plant available Zn can increase to very high levels. In some cases, extremely high Zn levels have prohibited production of sensitive crops (e.g., peanuts). The primary benefit of organic waste application is increased OM and associated natural chelation properties that increase solution Zn concentration and plant availability. Zn content in municipal waste varies greatly depending on the source, with an average Zn content of 0.5%.

Inorganic Zn Zinc sulfate ($ZnSO_4$) is the most common Zn fertilizer source, although use of Zn chelates has increased (Table 8-6). Inorganic Zn sources are satisfactory fertilizers because they are soluble in soils. Fertilizer Zn rates depend on the crop, Zn source, method of application, and severity of Zn deficiency. Rates usually range from 1 to 10 lbs/a with inorganic Zn and from 0.5 to 2.0 lbs/a with chelate or organic Zn sources (Table 8-7). For most field and vegetable crops, 10 lbs/a is recommended in clay and loam soils and 1 to 5 lbs/a in sandy soils. In most cropping situations, applications of 10 lbs/a of Zn can be effective for 3 to 5 years.

Table 8-7 Examples of Zn Management for Selected Crops

Crop	*Zn (lb/a)*	*Source*	*Application Method*	*Comments*
Corn	4–10 1–2	$ZnSO_4$, ZnO $ZnSO_4$, ZnO, Zn chelate	Broadcast Banded	Reduce rates for higher soil test Zn levels
Sorghum	3–9 1–2	$ZnSO_4$, ZnO $ZnSO_4$, ZnO, Zn chelate	Broadcast Banded	Reduce rates for higher soil test Zn levels
Soybean	2–3 1–2	$ZnSO_4$, ZnO $ZnSO_4$, ZnO, Zn chelate	Broadcast Banded	Reduce rates for higher soil test values
Rice	7–10 1	$ZnSO_4$, ZnO $ZnSO_4$, ZnO, Zn chelate	Broadcast preplant banded	Reduce rates for higher soil test values
Dry beans	3–4 0.5–3	$ZnSO_4$, ZnO $ZnSO_4$, ZnO, Zn chelate	Broadcast Banded	Reduce rates for higher soil test values
Citrus	0.5 lbs Zn/ 100 L H_2O	$ZnSO_4$	Foliar	Wet foliage, repeat until symptoms disappear
Pecans	30–60 g Zn/100 L H_2O; 400 L/a of trees	$Zn(NO_3)_2$	Foliar	5 applications starting at bud break, repeated weekly
Snap beans, onion, lima beans, potato	0.5–1.0 0.2–0.5 0.1	Zn chelate	Broadcast Banded Foliar	Repeat foliar until symptoms disappear or leaf analysis confirms adequate Zn
Turfgrass	0.44 lbs/a 0.01 lbs/1,000 ft^2	$ZnSO_4$ or chelate	Foliar or broadcast	Annual foliar or (3–4) 4 years soil appl.

Because of limited Zn mobility in soils, broadcast Zn should be thoroughly incorporated into the soil; however, band application may be more effective, especially in fine-textured and very low-Zn soils. The efficiency of band-applied Zn can be improved by combining with acid-forming N and S fertilizers.

With perennial crops, preplant soil applications of Zn are effective at rates between 20 and 100 lbs/a. Soil applications are of only limited value after these crops have been established. Foliar Zn application is recommended for turfgrass. Foliar applications are also used in tree crops. Sprays containing 10 to 15 lbs/a of Zn are usually applied to dormant orchards, whereas 2 to 3 lbs/a can be foliar applied to growing crops. Damage to foliage can be prevented by adding lime to the solution or by using less-soluble materials such as ZnO or $ZnCO_3$. Other methods include seed coatings, root dips, and tree injections. The former treatment may not supply enough Zn for small-seeded crops, but dipping potato seed pieces in a 2% ZnO suspension is satisfactory.

Foliar applications of chelates and natural organics are particularly suitable for rapid recovery of Zn-deficient seedlings. Chelated Zn can be used in high-analysis liquid fertilizers because of their high solubility and compatibility. ZnEDTA or ZnDTPA can be soil applied; however, high cost usually limits their use. In general, Zn chelates are more effective than inorganic Zn at similar rates of application (Table 8-8). Foliar-applied Zn is more effective than soil-applied Zn.

Copper (Cu)

Cu Cycle

The relationships involved in Cu cycling in soils are very similar to those described for Fe and Zn. Soil solution Cu and plant available Cu are governed predominantly by solution pH and Cu adsorbed on clay and OM surfaces (Fig. 8-19). Primary and secondary minerals dissolve to initially supply solution Cu, which is then adsorbed onto the CEC, incorporated into microorganisms, and complexed by organic compounds in solution. A significant "pool" of organically complexed Cu in equilibrium with solution Cu contributes to Cu^{+2} diffusion to plant roots.

Table 8-8 Comparison of Zn Sources and Application Methods on Leaf Zn Content of Selected Crops*

		Soil-Applied	Foliar Applied		
		$ZnSO_4$	$ZnSO_4$		ZnEDTA
Crop	*Control*	*(20 kg/ha)*	*(0.5 kg/ha)*	*(1.0 kg/ha)*	*(0.42 kg/ha)*
	mg Zn/kg				
Alfalfa	22	37	39	50	43
Ryegrass	18	28	46	61	63
Wheat	17	21	31	41	51
Barley	21	30	43	43	54

*Zn application rates shown in parentheses.
SOURCE: Gupta, 1989, *Can. J. Soil Sci.*, 69: 473.

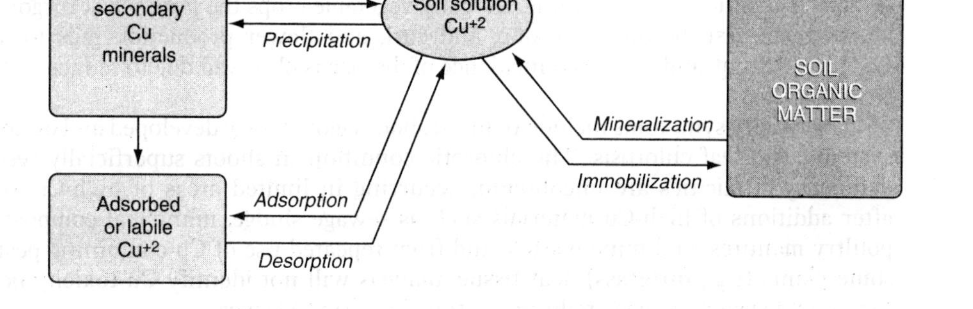

Figure 8-19 Cu cycle in soils.

Cu in Plants

Plants absorb Cu^{+2} and as a component of either natural or synthetic organic complexes. Normal Cu concentration in plant tissue ranges from 5 to 20 ppm. Deficiencies are probable at < 4 ppm Cu. Once absorbed, Cu^{+2} is readily reduced to Cu^{+} and donates an electron to reduce O_2. The ease with which Cu accepts and donates electrons enables it to function in many oxidation-reduction reactions in the plant.

Photosynthesis and Respiration Both photosynthesis (reduction of CO_2 to carbohydrates) and respiration (oxidation of carbohydrates to CO_2) involve the transfer of electrons that requires Cu. Fe and Mn are also involved in electron transport, but they cannot replace Cu. Electron transport reactions involved in photosynthesis and respiration produce adenosine triphosphate (ATP), which is the primary energy source for synthesis of proteins, lipids, cell wall membranes, and for active nutrient uptake (Chapter 2). Approximately 50% of Cu in the chloroplast is found in *plastocyanin,* a protein involved in energy transfer in photosynthesis reactions. Cu is part of the enzyme *cytochrome oxidase* that catalyzes electron transfer in the transfer of electrons in respiration.

Lignin Formation in Cell Walls Lignin is a constituent in cell walls that imparts strength and rigidity, essential for erect stature of plants. Several enzymes (polyphenol oxidase and diamine oxidase) important to synthesis of lignin contain Cu. Cu deficiency results in deformed leaves and stems, which increases potential for lodging. Lignin also aids natural plant resistance to diseases. Cu-deficient plants are more susceptible to disease.

Carbohydrate and Lipid Metabolism If photosynthesis is impeded by Cu deficiency during the vegetative growth stage, then carbohydrate production and plant growth are reduced. During the reproductive growth stage, carbohydrates accumulate because Cu deficiency impedes pollination and seed set. Reduced seed development, even under reduced photosynthesis, causes carbohydrates to accumulate since carbohydrate storage organs (seeds, fruits, etc.) are not present. Cu deficiency also alters lipid structure in cell membranes that is essential for low temperature tolerance and resistence to other environmental stresses.

Cu Deficiency and Toxicity Although Cu deficiencies are not as common as other micronutrient deficiencies, they do occur in sensitive crops grown on low-Cu soils. Symptoms of Cu deficiency vary with the crop, but chlorosis in young leaves is a common symptom, because of the Cu-containing enzyme function in the chloroplasts. In corn and small grains, young leaves become yellow and stunted, and as the deficiency progresses, young leaves turn pale and older leaves die back. In advanced stages, necrosis along leaf tips and edges appears, similar to the result of K deficiency. Stem melanosis, take-all root rot, and ergot infection can occur in Cu-deficient small grains. In many vegetable crops the leaves lack turgor, develop a bluish-green cast, become chlorotic, and curl, and flower production fails to take place. Lodging, wilting, and increased incidence of disease is observed due to reduced lignification with low Cu.

Cu toxicity symptoms include reduced shoot vigor, poorly developed and discolored root systems, and leaf chlorosis. The chlorotic condition in shoots superficially resembles Fe deficiency. Toxicities are uncommon, occurring in limited areas of high-Cu availability; after additions of high-Cu materials such as sewage sludge, municipal composts, pig and poultry manures, and mine wastes; and from repeated use of Cu-containing pesticides. In some plants (e.g., turfgrass), leaf tissue analysis will not identify Cu toxicity because the severe root system damage reduces Cu translocation to leaves.

Cu in Soil

Mineral Cu Cu concentration in the earth's crust averages about 50 to 70 ppm. Igneous rocks contain 10 to 100 ppm Cu, while sedimentary rocks contain 4 to 45 ppm Cu. Cu concentration in soils ranges from 1 to 40 ppm and averages about 9 ppm Cu. Total soil Cu may be 1 or 2 ppm in deficient soils. Malachite [$Cu_2(OH)_2CO_3$] and cupric ferrite ($CuFe_2O_4$) are important Cu-containing primary minerals (Fig. 8-20). Secondary Cu minerals include oxides, carbonates, silicates, sulfates, and chlorides, but most are too soluble to persist. The "soil Cu" line represents Cu solubility in most soils and is close to $CuFe_2O_4$ (Fig. 8-20).

Soil Solution Cu Solution Cu concentration is usually low, ranging between 10^{-8} and 10^{-6} M (Fig. 8-21). The dominant solution species are Cu^{+2} at pH < 7 and $Cu(OH)_2^0$ at pH > 7 (Fig. 8-21). Cu^{+2} solubility is pH dependent, increasing with decreasing pH, as shown by:

$$Cu^{+2} + 2H_2O \leftrightarrows Cu(OH)_2^0 + 2H^+$$

Cu is supplied to plant roots by diffusion of organically bound, chelated Cu, similar to chelated Fe diffusion (Fig. 8-7). Organic compounds in the soil solution are capable of chelating solution Cu^{+2}, which increases the solution Cu^{+2} concentration above that predicted by Cu mineral solubility.

Adsorbed Cu Cu^{+2} is chemically adsorbed to surfaces of clays; OM; and Fe, Al, or Mn oxides. With the exception of Pb^{+2} and Hg^{+2}, Cu^{+2} is the most strongly adsorbed divalent metal to Fe/Al oxides. The adsorption mechanism with oxides is unlike electrostatic attraction of Cu^{+2} on the CEC of clay particles, and involves formation of Cu-O-Al or Cu-O-Fe surface bonds (Fig. 8-22). This *chemisorption* process is controlled by the quantity of surface OH^- groups.

Cu adsorption increases with increasing pH due to (1) increased pH-dependent sites on clay and OM, (2) reduced competition with H^+, and (3) a change in the hydrolysis state of

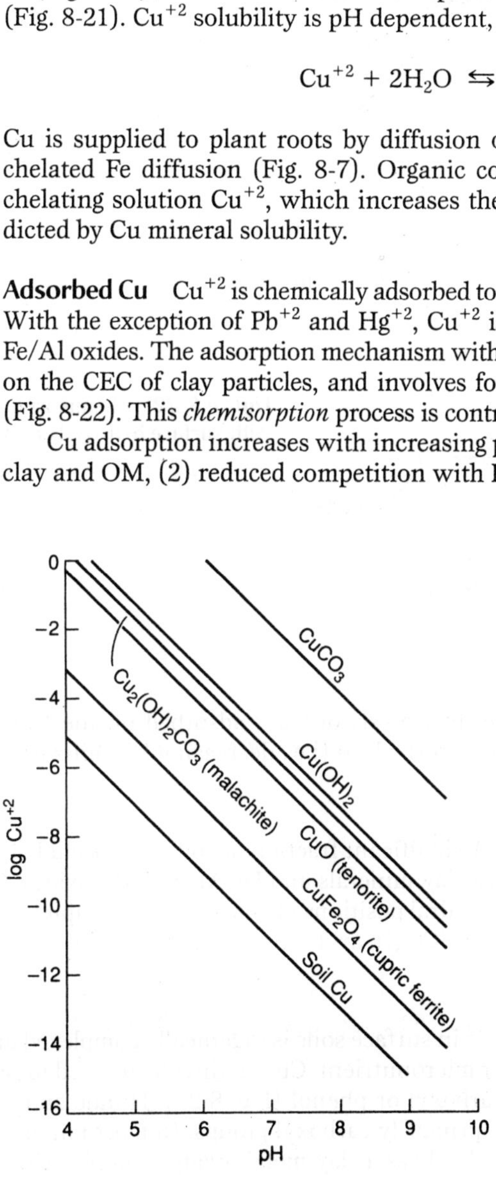

Figure 8-20 **Common Cu mineral solubility in soils. *(Lindsay, 1979,* Chemical Equilibria in Soils, *New York: John Wiley & Sons.)***

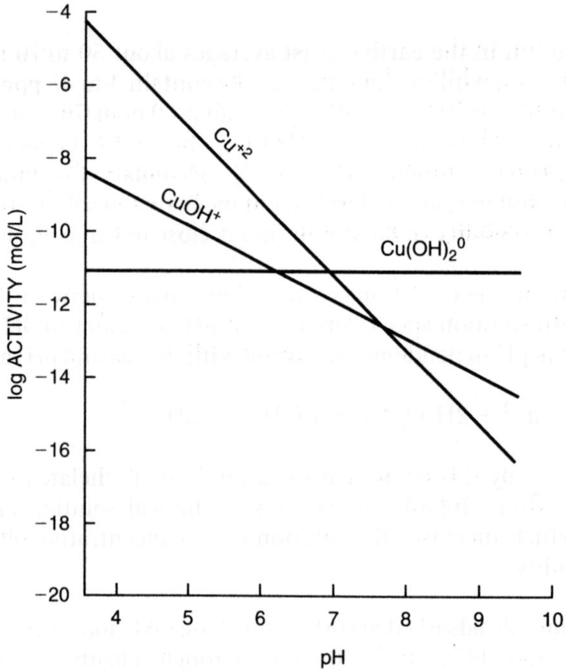

Figure 8-21 **Common Cu species in soil solution as influenced by pH. (*Lindsay, 1979,* Chemical Equilibria in Soils, *New York: John Wiley & Sons.*)**

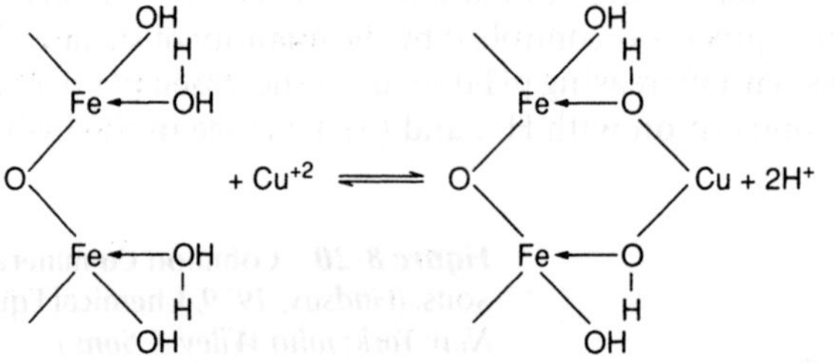

Figure 8-22 **Chemisorption of Cu^{+2} with surface hydroxyls on $Fe(OH)_3$.**

Cu in solution. As the pH is raised, hydrolysis of Cu^{+2} adsorbed on the CEC decreases exchangeable Cu^{+2} and increases chemisorbed Cu (i.e., decreasing H^+ shifts equilibrium to the right in Fig. 8-22).

Occluded and Coprecipitated Cu A significant fraction of soil Cu is occluded, or buried, in various mineral structures, such as clay minerals and Fe, Al, and Mn oxides. Cu is capable of isomorphic substitution in octahedral positions of silicate clays (Chapter 2). It is present as an impurity within $CaCO_3$ and $MgCO_3$ in arid soils and within $Al(OH)_3$ and $Fe(OH)_3$ in acid soils.

Organic Cu Most of the soluble Cu^{+2} in surface soils is organically complexed and is more strongly bound to OM than any other micronutrient. Cu^{+2} is directly bonded to two or more organic functional groups, chiefly carboxyl or phenol (Fig. 8-23). Humic and fulvic acids contain multiple Cu^{+2} binding sites, primarily carboxyl groups. In most mineral soils, OM is intimately associated with clay, probably as a clay-metal-organic complex (Fig. 8-24).

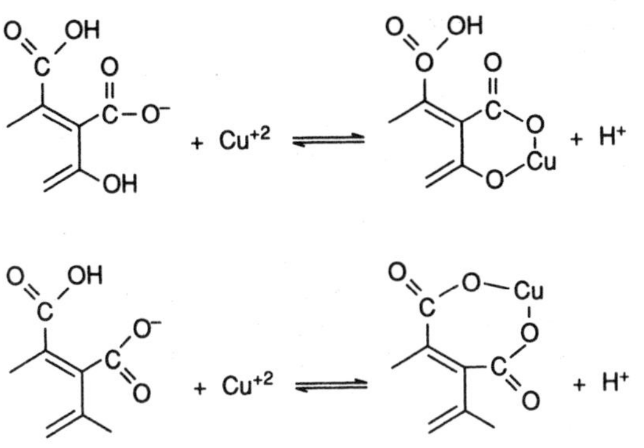

Figure 8-23 Mechanism of Cu complexed by organic matter. *(Stevenson and Ardakani, 1972,* Micronutrients in Agriculture, *p. 90, Madison, WI: Amer. Soc. Agron.)*

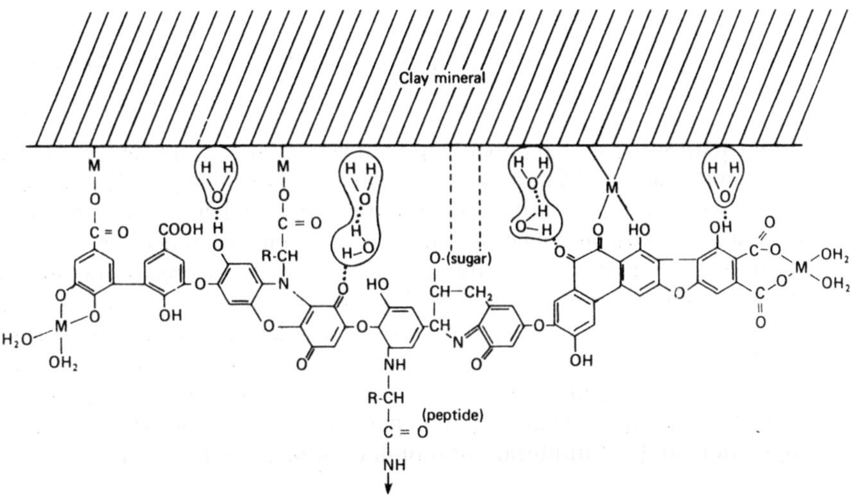

Figure 8-24 Schematic diagram of the clay-OM-metal (M) complex. *(Stevenson and Fitch, 1981, in J. F. Loneragan (Ed.),* Copper in Soils and Plants, *p. 70, New York: Academic Press.)*

At $\leq$ 8% soil OM, both organic and mineral surfaces are involved in Cu adsorption, while at $>$ 8% OM, binding of Cu takes place mostly on organic surfaces. Thus, Cu deficiency frequently occurs in peat and muck soils. For soils with similar clay and OM contents, the contribution of OM to complexing of Cu is highest with 1:1 versus 2:1 clays.

Factors Affecting Cu Availability

Texture The potential for Cu deficiency is the highest in excessively leached, coarse-textured soils.

Soil pH Solution Cu decreases with increasing pH due to decreased mineral solubility and increased adsorption.

Interactions with Other Nutrients High Zn, Fe, and P concentrations in soil solution can depress Cu absorption by roots and intensify Cu deficiency. Increased growth response to N or other nutrients may be proportionally greater than Cu uptake, which dilutes

Table 8-9 **Crop Sensitivity to Cu Deficiency**

High Sensitivity		*Mild Sensitivity*		*Low Sensitivity*	
Alfalfa	Lettuce	Apples	Cucumber	Apples	Potato
Beets	Onion	Barley	Oats	Beans	Rapeseed
Canary Seed	Rice	Blueberries	Parsnips	Beans, snap	Rye
Carrots	Spinach	Broccoli	Radishes	Canola	Soybean
Citrus	Sudan grass	Cabbage	Strawberries	Forage grasses	Turfgrasses
Flax	Wheat	Cauliflower	Sweet corn	Grapes	
		Celery	Timothy	Lupine	
		Clover	Tomato	Peas	
		Corn	Turnip		

Cu concentration in plants. Also, increasing N in plants impedes Cu translocation from older to newer leaves.

Plant Factors Crops vary greatly in their sensitivity to Cu (Table 8-9). Among small grains, rye tolerates low soil-Cu, whereas wheat is highly sensitive. Rye absorbs nearly twice as much Cu as wheat under the same conditions. Varietal differences in tolerance to low Cu can be as large as those among crop species. Genotypic differences are related to (1) differences in Cu absorption rates, (2) greater soil exploration due to greater root mass and/or root hairs, (3) increased Cu solubility due to root exudate influence on soil pH or redox potential, (4) more efficient Cu transport from roots to shoots, and/or (5) lower Cu requirement.

Severe Cu deficiency may also occur in crops planted into soils with actively degrading, high C:N residues and is related to (1) Cu complexing with organic compounds originating from decomposing residue, (2) competition for available Cu by a stimulated microbial population, and (3) inhibition of root development and the ability to absorb Cu.

Cu Sources

Organic Cu Although most animal wastes contain small quantities of plant available Cu (0.002 to 0.03%), elevated Cu levels occur in swine manure because of Cu added to the feed. Consequently, continued application might create toxic levels of soil Cu, especially with sensitive crops like peanut. With most manures, average application rates provide sufficient plant available Cu. As with Fe and Zn, the primary benefit of organic waste application is increased OM and associated natural chelation properties that increase Cu availability. Cu content in municipal waste is ≈ 0.1%, but varies greatly depending on source.

Inorganic Cu The most common Cu source is $CuSO_4 \cdot 5H_2O$, although CuO, mixtures of $CuSO_4$ and $Cu(OH)_2$, and Cu chelates are also used (Table 8-10). $CuSO_4$ is soluble in water and is compatible with most fertilizers. $CuNH_4PO_4{\cdot}H_2O$ is slightly water soluble, but can be suspended and soil or foliar applied.

Soil and foliar applications are both effective, but soil applications are more common, with Cu rates of 1 to 20 lbs/a needed to correct deficiencies (Table 8-11). Effectiveness is increased by thoroughly mixing Cu fertilizers into the root zone or by banding near the seed row. Potential root injury exists with high band-applied Cu rates. Additions of Cu can be ineffective when root activity is restricted by excessively wet or dry soil, root pathogens, toxicities, and deficiencies of other nutrients. Residual Cu fertilizer availability can persist for 2 or more years, depending on the soil, crop, and Cu rate.

Table 8-10 **Common Cu Fertilizers**

Source	*Formula*	*% Cu*
Copper sulfate	$CuSO_4 \cdot 5H_2O$	25
Copper sulfate monohydrate	$CuSO_4 \cdot H_2O$	35
Copper acetate	$Cu(C_2H_3O_2)_2 \cdot H_2O$	32
Copper ammonium phosphate	$Cu(NH_4)PO_4 \cdot H_2O$	32
Copper chelates	Na_2Cu EDTA	13
Organics	-	< 0.5

Table 8-11 **Effect of Cu Fertilizers on Barley Yield**

Source	*Application*		*Cu Rate*	*Yield*
			---------- *kg/ha*	----------
$CuSO_4$	Fall	Broadcast/	10	3,070
	Spring	Incorporate	10	2,370
	Spring		5	1,890
CuEDTA	Spring	Broadcast/	2	2,960
	Spring	Incorporate	1	2,700
	Foliar		1	2,100

SOURCE: Manitoba Agric. Agdex No. 541 MG#1853, 1990.

Table 8-12 **Examples of Cu Management for Selected Crops**

Crop	*Cu Source*	*Cu Rate* (lb/a)*	*Application Method*	*Comments*
Small grains	$CuSO_4 \cdot 5H_2O$	1–5	Banded	Several years residual
	or CuO	3–12	Broadcast	availability, increase rate
	Cu chelates	0.5–2.0	Banded	on high-OM soil
	Cu chelates	0.1% solution	Foliar	Annual application
Corn	$CuSO_4 \cdot 5H_2O$	3–12	Broadcast	Several years residual
	or CuO	1–2	Banded	availability, increase rate
	Cu chelates	0.2–0.4		on high-OM soil
Soybeans	$CuSO_4 \cdot 5H_2O$	2–4	Broadcast	Several years residual availability, increase rate
		1–2	Banded	on high-OM soil
Citrus	$CuSO_4 \cdot 5H_2O$	5–20	Broadcast	Repeat in 5 years
		0.1% solution	Foliar	Annual application
Turfgrass	$CuSO_4 \cdot 5H_2O$	0.13	Foliar	Annual as needed
	Cu chelates			

*Overapplication of Cu can result in Cu toxicity.

Cu application in foliar sprays is confined mainly to emergency treatment of deficiencies identified after planting. In some areas, however, Cu is included in regular foliar spraying programs. Cu chelates (CuEDTA) can be used as a foliar Cu fertilizer; however, soil application is more effective (Table 8-12). The data in Table 8-12 also show that fall-applied $CuSO_4$ is more effective than spring applications to barley, likely because the material has more time to dissolve and move into the root zone.

Manganese (Mn)

Mn Cycle

The equilibrium among solution, exchangeable, organic, and mineral forms determines Mn availability to plants (Fig. 8-25). The major processes are Mn oxidation-reduction and complexing solution Mn with natural organic chelates. Like Fe, the continuous cycling of OM significantly contributes to soluble Mn. Factors influencing the solubility of soil Mn include pH, redox, and organic complexation. Soil moisture, aeration, and microbial activity influence redox, while complexation is affected by OM and microbial activity.

Mn in Plants

Plants absorb Mn^{+2} and low-molecular-weight organically complexed Mn. Mn concentration in plants typically ranges from 20 to 500 ppm, while Mn deficient plants contain < 15 to 20 ppm Mn. Mn must be reduced to Mn^{+2} for absorption by roots by:

$$MnO_2 + 4H^+ + 2e^- \xrightarrow{\text{microbes}} Mn^{+2} + 2H_2O$$

Low-molecular-weight organic compounds are exuded by roots into the rhizosphere. Microbial degradation of these exudates establishes reducing conditions and provides electrons to reduce Mn to Mn^{+2} for absorption.

Mn^{+2} enters root cells through the plasmalemma by a specific transporter protein that establishes an electrical gradient where the cell wall is more (+) than the cell interior. Few other cations compete with Mn^{+2} for transport across membranes, which is unique since other cations do compete with each other (e.g., Cu^{+2} and Zn^{+2}). However, high concentrations of Ca^{+2} and Mg^{+2} adsorbed to apoplasmic (root) cell walls, especially in high-pH soils, can reduce Mn^{+2} adsorption to cell walls and eventual transport into the cell.

Mn is essential to photosynthesis reactions, enzyme activation, and root growth.

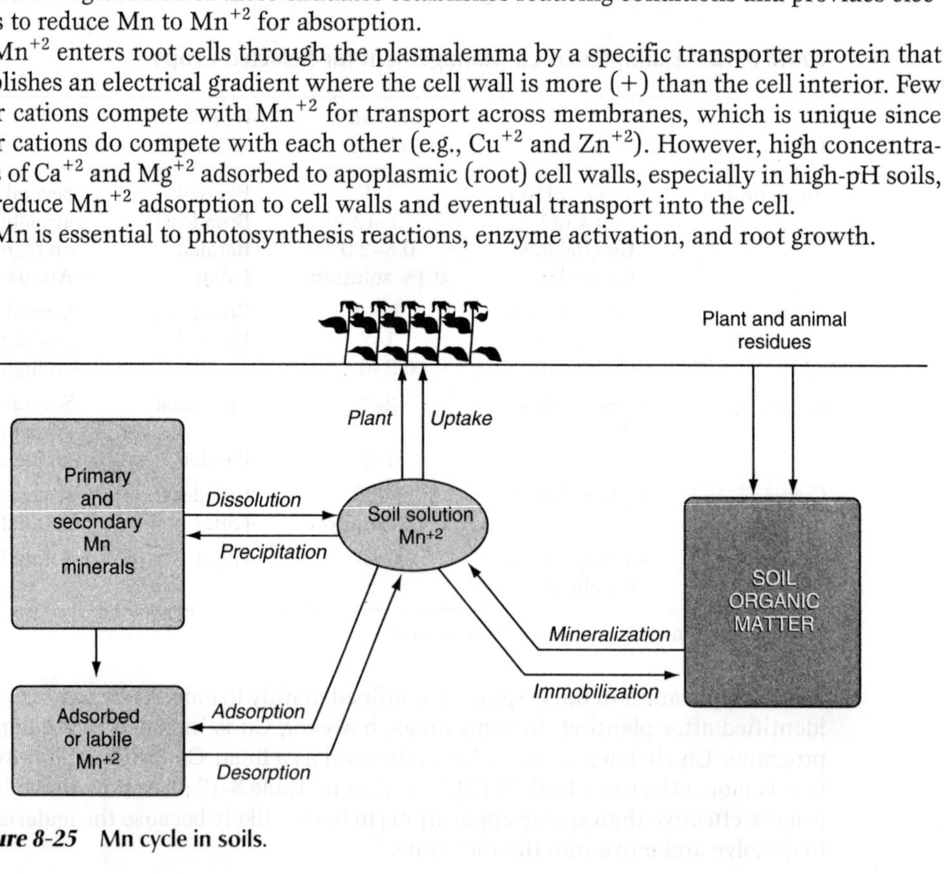

Figure 8-25 Mn cycle in soils.

O_2 and Photosynthesis Most O_2 in the atmosphere originates from Mn-facilitated electron transport in photosynthesis. Photosynthetic reduction of CO_2 to carbohydrates [$(CH_2O)_n$], given by:

$$CO_2 + 2H_2O \xrightarrow{\text{light}} (CH_2O)_n + O_2 + H_2O$$

involves several electron transfer steps. When chlorophyll absorbs light energy it is oxidized (loses an electron) and provides the energy to reduce CO_2. The oxidized chlorophyll accepts electrons from a Mn-containing protein. When Mn donates electrons to chlorophyll, the oxidized Mn protein will oxidize H_2O to produce O_2:

$$2H_2O + 4Mn^{+3} \longrightarrow 4Mn^{+2} + O_2 + 4H^+$$

The reduced Mn protein again donates electrons to another photo-oxidized chlorophyll. Therefore, Mn is essential to electron transfer through chlorophyll to reduce CO_2 to carbohydrate and produce O_2 from H_2O.

Reducing agents formed in cellular reactions can donate an electron to O_2, forming the superoxide free radical O_2^-. Free radicals are highly reactive and toxic to cellular metabolic reactions (e.g., chlorophyll degradation). Superoxide dimutase (SOD) enzymes are produced to readily convert O_2^- to O_2. Fe-SOD and CuZn-SOD occur in chloroplasts, while Mn-SOD occurs in mitochondria. This protection mechanism is especially important in plants grown under high light intensity where potential free radical production and photo-oxidative damage is the greatest.

Mn and Lignin Synthesis Like Cu, Mn activates several enzymes that synthesize several amino acids and phenols important to lignin production. In addition to lignin, these compounds are used to synthesize phenolic acids and alcohols that provide resistance to infection by pathogens.

Mn Deficiency and Toxicity Because of its essential role in photosynthesis, root and shoot growth rates are substantially reduced in Mn-deficient plants. As a result, N and P accumulate, which increases potential for root and leaf diseases. Mn deficiency also restricts formation of lignin and phenolic acids that also help reduce incidence of diseases. Soil fungi that generally do not infect plant roots can cause disease in Mn-deficient plants. Grasses low in Mn are often more susceptible to root-rot diseases.

Mn is immobile in the plant, so younger leaves initially exhibit defiency symptoms. Mn deficiency produces interveinal chlorosis in most crops. In some crops, low-Mn-related chlorosis of younger leaves can be mistaken for Fe deficiency. Mn deficiency of several crops has been described by such terms as gray speck of oat, marsh spot of pea, and speckled yellows of sugar beet.

Mn toxicity occurs in sensitive crops grown on acid soils. Crinkle leaf in cotton is commonly observed. Liming will readily correct this problem.

Mn in Soil

Mineral Mn Mn concentration in the earth's crust averages 1,000 ppm, and Mn is found in most Fe-Mg rocks. Mn, when released through weathering of primary rocks, will combine with O_2 to form secondary minerals, including pyrolusite (MnO_2), hausmannite (Mn_3O_4), and manganite ($MnOOH$). Pyrolusite and manganite are the most abundant (Fig. 8-26).

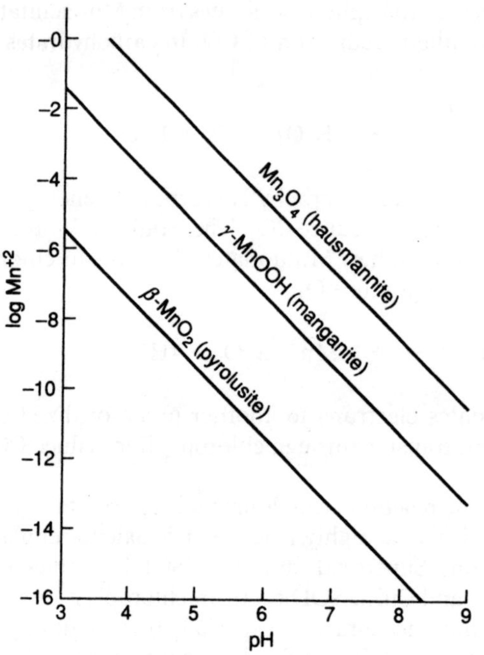

Figure 8-26 **Common Mn mineral solubilities in well-aerated soils. Reducing conditions will increase Mn solubility.** ***(Lindsay, 1979,*** **Chemical Equilibria in Soils,** ***New York: John Wiley & Sons.)***

Total Mn in soils generally ranges between 20 and 3,000 ppm and averages about 600 ppm. Mn in soils occurs as various oxides and hydroxides coated on soil particles, deposited in cracks and veins, and mixed with Fe oxides and other soil constituents.

Soil Solution Mn Mn^{+2} is the common form in solution; its concentration decreases hundredfold for each unit increase in pH, similar to the behavior of other divalent metal cations (Fig. 8-27). Mn^{+2} concentration is predominantly controlled by MnO_2, and ranges from 0.0 to 1 ppm, with organically complexed Mn^{+2} comprising about 90% of solution Mn^{+2} (Fig. 8-26). Mn^{+2} moves to the root surface by diffusion of chelated Mn^{+2}, similar to Fe (Fig. 8-7).

Solution Mn^{+2} is increased under acid, reducing (low O_2) conditions. In extremely acid soils ($pH < 5$), increased Mn^{+2} solubility causes Mn toxicity in sensitive crops (Fig. 8-27).

Mn^{+2} can leach from coarse-textured, acid soils. Mn deficiency in poorly drained mineral and organic soils is often attributed to low Mn levels resulting from Mn^{+2} leaching. Sand-based materials used in golf green construction are also commonly low in Mn.

Factors Affecting Mn Availability

Soil pH Management practices that influence soil pH affect Mn^{+2} availability and uptake. Liming acid soils decreases solution and exchangeable Mn^{+2} by precipitation as MnO_2 (Fig. 8-26). On the other hand, low Mn availability in high-pH and calcareous soils and in overlimed, poorly buffered, coarse-textured soils can be overcome by acidification through the use of acid-forming N or S materials. High pH also favors the formation of less available organic complexes of Mn.

Excessive Water and Poor Aeration Waterlogged soils exhibit reduced O_2 and lower redox potential, which increases soluble Mn^{+2}, especially in acid soils. Mn availability can

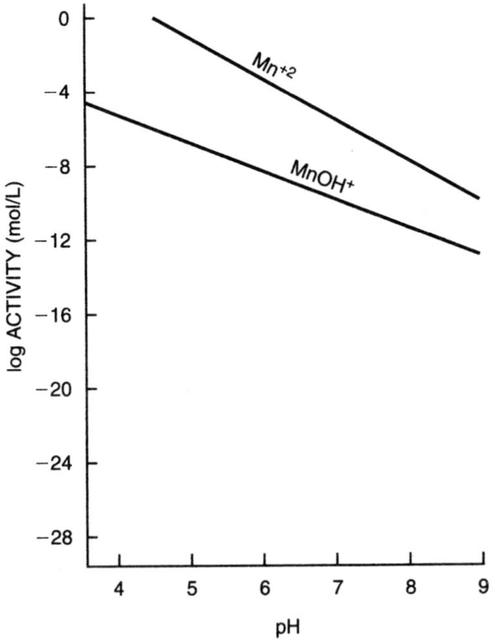

Figure 8-27 **Common Mn species in solution as influenced by pH.** *(Lindsay, 1979,* **Chemical Equilibria in Soils,** *New York: John Wiley & Sons.)*

be increased by poor aeration in compact soils and by local accumulations of CO_2 around roots and other soil microsites. The resulting low-redox conditions will render Mn more available without appreciably affecting the redox potential or pH of the bulk soil.

Soil OM Low Mn^{+2} availability in high-OM peats and muck soils is attributed to the formation of unavailable chelated Mn^{+2} compounds. In contrast, addition of natural organic materials such as peat moss, compost, and wheat and clover straw will increase solution and exchangeable Mn^{+2} in mineral soils. The important role of chelation was discussed earlier.

Interaction with Other Nutrients High levels of Cu, Fe, or Zn can reduce Mn^{+2} uptake by plants. Addition of acid-forming NH_4^+ fertilizers will enhance Mn uptake by decreasing soil pH. Neutral salts applied to acid soils also can increase Mn availability. The relative order of increasing available Mn is $KCl > KNO_3 > K_2SO_4$. KCl can increase Mn uptake to produce toxicity in sensitive crops.

Climatic Effects Wet weather increases Mn^{+2}, whereas dry conditions encourage oxidation to less available forms. Dry weather either induces or aggravates Mn deficiency, particularly in fruit trees. In contrast, wet weather is one of the conditions usually associated with Mn deficiency in oats. Increasing soil temperature during the growing season improves Mn uptake, presumably because of greater plant growth and root activity.

Plant Factors For satisfactory Mn nutrition, solution and exchangeable Mn should be 2 to 3 ppm and 0.2 to 5 ppm, respectively. Several plant species exhibit differences in sensitivity to Mn deficiency, caused by differences in plant metabolism (Table 8-13). Reductive capacity at the root may be the factor restricting Mn uptake and translocation. There may also be significant differences in the amounts and properties of root exudates generated by plants, which can influence Mn^{+2} availability. Plant characteristics pertinent to Fe-efficient plants may similarly influence plant tolerance to low Mn.

Table 8-13 **Crop Sensitivity to Mn Deficiency***

High Sensitivity		*Moderate Sensitivity*		*Low Sensitivity*	
Alfalfa	Peas	Barley	Oats	Barley	Rice
Apples	Potato	Broccoli	Parsnip	Blueberries	Rye
Beans, snap	Radish	Cabbage	Potato	Corn	Soybean
Citrus	Raspberries	Carrot	Rice	Cotton	Turfgrass
Cucumber	Soybean	Cauliflower	Rye	Field beans	Wheat
Fruit trees	Spinach	Celery	Soybean	Fruit trees	
Grapes	Strawberries	Corn	Sweet corn		
Lettuce	Sugar beet	Cotton	Tomato		
Oats	Tomato	Field beans	Turnip		
Onion	Wheat	Fruit trees	Wheat		

*Some crops are listed under two or three categories because of variation in soil, growing conditions, and differential response of varieties of a given crop.

Table 8-14 **Common Mn Fertilizers**

Source	*Formula*	*% Mn*
Manganese sulfate	$MnSO_4 \cdot 4H_2O$	26–28
Manganous oxide	MnO	41–68
Manganese chloride	$MnCl_2$	17
Natural organic	—	< 0.2
Manganese chelates	MnEDTA	5–12

Mn Sources

Organic Mn Mn concentration in most animal wastes is similar to Zn, ranging from 0.01 to 0.05% Mn. Average application rates of most manures will provide sufficient plant available Mn. As with Fe, Zn, and Cu, the primary benefit of organic waste application is increased OM and associated natural chelation properties increasing Mn availability. As with the other micronutrients, Mn content in municipal waste varies greatly depending on the source. On the average, Mn content is about half the Cu content (0.05%).

Inorganic Mn Manganese sulfate ($MnSO_4 \cdot 4H_2O$) is the most common Mn source and is soil or foliar applied (Table 8-14). In addition to inorganic Mn fertilizers, natural organic complexes and chelated Mn are available and are usually foliar applied. Manganese oxide is only slightly water soluble and must be finely ground to be effective. Rates of Mn application range from 1 to 40 lbs/a; higher rates are recommended for broadcast application, while lower rates are band and foliar applied (Table 8-15). Band-applied Mn is generally more effective than broadcast Mn, and band treatments are usually one-half broadcast rates. Oxidation to less available forms of Mn is delayed with band-applied Mn. Applications at higher rates are needed on organic soils. Band application of Mn in combination with N-P-K fertilizers is commonly practiced.

Broadcast application of Mn chelates and natural organic complexes is not normally advised because soil Ca or Fe can replace Mn in these chelates, and the freed Mn is usually converted to unavailable forms. Also, the more available chelated Ca or Fe may enhance Mn deficiency. Lime or high-pH-induced Mn deficiencies can be rectified by acidification by use of S or other acid-forming materials.

Table 8-15 Examples of Mn Management for Selected Crops

Crop	*Mn Source*	*Rate (lb/a)*	*Application Method*	*Comments*
Soybean	$MnSO_4 \cdot 4H_2O$	15–40 2–10	Broadcast Banded	Annual application
	$MnSO_4 \cdot 4H_2O$ MnEDTA	0.1–0.3 0.2–0.5	Foliar	Repeat as needed during season
Sugar beet	$MnSO_4 \cdot 4H_2O$	20–80	Broadcast	Annual application
Onion	$MnSO_4 \cdot 4H_2O$ or MnO	25–40 10–20	Broadcast Banded	Annual application
Citrus, nuts	$MnSO_4 \cdot 4H_2O$ or MnO	0.2–0.4 lbs Mn/ 100 L H_2O	Foliar	Repeat as needed
Vegetables Snap beans Spinach Cauliflower Celery Lettuce	$MnSO_4 \cdot 4H_2O$ or MnO	2–10	Banded	Annual application
Corn, oats	$MnSO_4 \cdot 4H_2O$ or MnO	15–40 2–10	Broadcast Banded	Annual application
Potato	$MnSO_4 \cdot 4H_2O$	2–10	Banded	Annual application
Turfgrass	$MnSO_4 \cdot 4H_2O$ MnEDTA	0.5–1.0 0.0125–0.025 lbs/1,000 ft^2	Foliar	Repeat as needed

Boron (B)

B Cycle

Soil B exists in rocks and minerals, adsorbed on clay surfaces and Fe/Al oxides, combined with OM, and in soil solution (Fig. 8-28). Understanding B cycling between solid and solution phases is important because of the narrow range in solution B separating deficiency and toxicity in crops.

B in Plants

B absorbed by plants is predominately undissociated boric acid (H_3BO_3). The anion forms ($H_2BO_3^-$, HBO_3^{-2}, BO_3^{-3}, and $B_4O_7^{-2}$) exist when soil pH > 7, although plants absorb these less readily than H_3BO_3. Active B uptake (against a concentration gradient) across the plasma membrane requires co-absorption of H^+. As inside cell pH is greater than outside cell pH, H^+ readily moves across the membrane, sometimes accompanied by H_3BO_3. This relationship helps explain why B uptake is reduced in alkaline soils where the H^+ gradient is smaller.

Once inside root cells, H_3BO_3 is readily transported in the xylem to leaves, where much of it occurs in cell walls. B translocation in the phloem from leaves to other plant parts is restricted, thus B accumulates, especially in older leaves. This explains why B toxicity symptoms first appear in older leaf tips. This is consistent with B-deficiency symptoms first appearing in apical meristems and other plant parts receiving water and nutrients through the phloem.

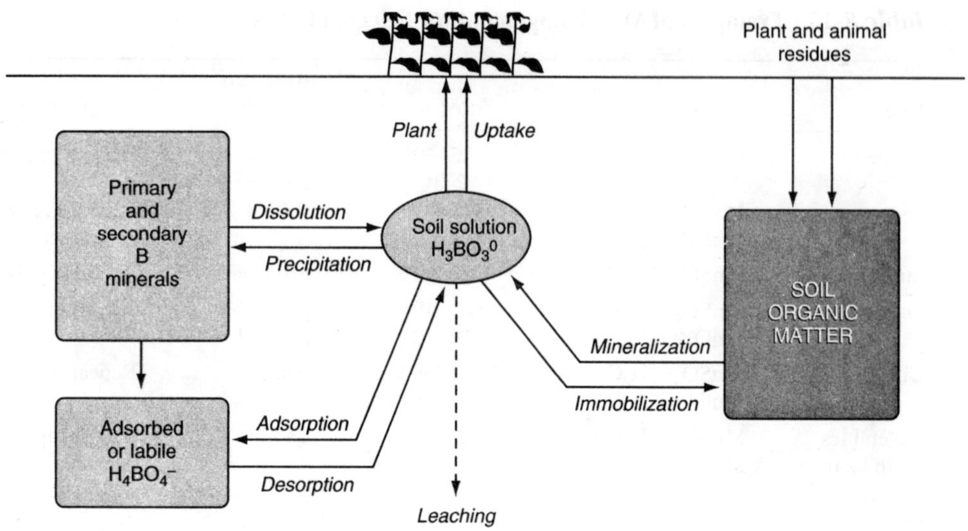

Figure 8-28 **Boron cycle in soils.**

B Functions and Deficiency Symptoms Although required for higher plants and some algae, B is not needed by animals, fungi, or microorganisms. The primary function of B is in plant cell wall structural integrity. B provides cross links between cell wall polysaccharides that gives structure to the cell wall—important for cell expansion, regulation of H^+ transport, retention of cellular Ca^{+2}, and control of lignin production following cell expansion. B linkages are flexible to enable cell wall expansion. Under B deficiency, normal cell wall expansion is disrupted. These functions are different in dicots and monocots, where grasses are less dependent on B for cell wall structure, although it is still important. Cell wall stability is especially important during pollen tube growth that is essential for seed development. Grass seed yield is reduced under B deficiency, even though other deficiency symptoms are absent. B is essential to transport of photosynthetic sugars to rapidly developing meristematic (growing) tissues, such as root tips, leaves, buds, storage, and conductive tissues.

Also, cell wall structure is essential for normal transport of water, nutrients, and organic compounds to new growth. Thus, B deficiency commonly appears as a structural deformity in actively growing regions. For example, in legumes, rosetting of new leaves is a common B-deficiency symptom caused by decreased cell division in apical regions. B is also needed for normal development of legume root nodules. B deficiency affects reproductive growth more than vegetative growth. Adequate B increases flower production and retention, and seed and fruit development.

Since B is not readily translocated from older to actively growing tissues, the first visual deficiency symptom is cessation of terminal bud growth, followed by death of the young leaves. In B-deficient plants the youngest leaves become pale green, losing more color at the base than at the tip. The basal tissues break down and, if growth continues, leaves have a twisted appearance.

B-deficiency symptoms often appear in the form of thickened, wilted, or curled leaves; a thickened, cracked, or water-soaked condition of petioles and stems; and a discoloration, cracking, or rotting of fruit, tubers, or roots. Internal cork of apple is caused by B deficiency. Low B in citrus fruits results in uneven thickness of the peel, lumpy fruit, and gummy deposits in the fruit. The breakdown of internal tissues in root crops gives rise to darkened areas referred to as brown heart or black heart. For example, *hollow-heart* in peanut occurs when low B limits Ca translocation that inhibits cell wall development and cell division. Some conifers exhibit striking B-deficiency symptoms including distorted branches and main stems, resin bleeding, and death of major branches.

Serious yield reductions in small grains occurs in Asia and elsewhere due to B deficiency causing male sterility, as exhibited by poorly developed anthers and nonviable pollen grains. Also, low B in shoots of pulse crops results in reduced seed germination and seedling vigor.

B concentration in monocots and dicots varies between 6 to 18 ppm and 20 to 60 ppm, respectively. B deficiency often occurs with < 20 ppm in mature leaf tissue of most crops. B toxicity to plants is uncommon in most arable soils unless it has been added in excessive amounts in fertilizers. In arid regions, however, B toxicity may occur naturally or may develop because of a high B content in irrigation waters.

B in Soil

Mineral B B is one of two nonmetal micronutrients. It occurs in low concentrations in the earth's crust and in most igneous rocks (< 10 ppm). Among sedimentary rocks, shales have the highest B content (≤ 100 ppm), present in clay minerals. Total B concentration in soils varies between 2 and 200 ppm and frequently ranges from 7 to 80 ppm. Less than 5% of total soil B is plant available.

The main B mineral in soils is *tourmaline*, a borosilicate, and relatively insoluble. Thus, buffering of solution B is slow and explains the increasing frequency of B deficiencies, especially under intensive cropping systems. In arid climates, B is usually sufficient because of greater mineral stability in a low-weathering environment.

Soil Solution B H_3BO_3 is the predominant solution species over the pH range from 5 to 9. At pH > 9, $H_2BO_3^-$ hydrolyzes to $H_4BO_4^-$. B can be transported from the soil solution to absorbing plant roots by both mass flow and diffusion. About 0.1 ppm B in solution is considered adequate for most monocots.

Adsorbed B B adsorption and desorption can buffer solution B, which reduces B leaching potential. It is a major form of B in alkaline, high-B soils. Primary B adsorption sites are Si—O and Al—O bonds at clay mineral edges and surfaces of Fe/Al oxy and hydroxy compounds. Increasing pH, clay content, OM, and Fe/Al compounds favors $H_2BO_3^-$adsorption. B-adsorption capacities generally follow the order mica is greater than montmorillonite which is greater than kaolinite.

Organically Complexed B OM represents a large potential source of plant available B in soils, which increases with increasing OM. The B-OM complexes are probably

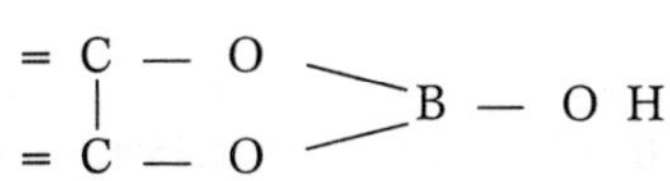

or

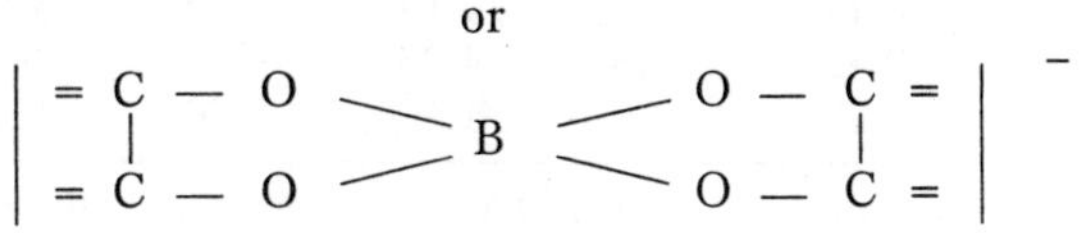

Factors Affecting B Availability

Soil pH B availability decreases with increasing soil pH, especially at pH > 6.3 to 6.5 (Table 8-16). Liming acid soils can cause a temporary B deficiency in susceptible plants with the severity depending on crop, soil moisture status, and time elapsed after liming. Lime effect on B availability is caused by B adsorption on freshly precipitated $Al(OH)_3$, with maximum adsorption at pH 7. Moderate liming can be used to depress B availability and plant uptake on high B soils. Heavy liming of soils high in OM may encourage OM decomposition and release of B, increasing B uptake.

Soil OM Higher B availability in surface soils compared with subsurface soils is related to increased soil OM. Applications of OM to soils can increase B in plants and even cause phytotoxicity.

Soil Texture Coarse-textured, well-drained soils are low in B, and crops with a high requirement respond to B applications of ≥ 3 lbs/a. Sandy soils with fine-textured subsoils generally do not respond to B in the same manner as those with coarse-textured subsoils. B added to soils remains soluble, and up to 85% can be leached in low-OM, sandy soils. Fine-textured soils retain B longer than coarse-textured soils because of greater B adsorption. The fact that clay retains more B than sand does not imply that B uptake in clays is greater than sands. At equal solution B concentration, plants absorb more B from sandy soils than from fine-textured soils, where B uptake can be impeded by higher levels of available Ca.

Interactions with Other Elements When Ca availability is high, plants can tolerate higher B availability. Under low Ca supply, many crops exhibit lower B tolerance. Greater Ca^{+2} supply in alkaline and recently overlimed soils restricts B availability; thus, high solution Ca^{+2} protects crops from excess B. The Ca:B ratio in leaf tissues has been used to assess B status of crops, where B deficiency for most crops is likely when Ca:B ratio is greater than 1,200:1.

B deficiency in sensitive crops (e.g., alfalfa) can be aggravated by K fertilization to the extent that B is needed to prevent yield loss, since Ca^{+2} displaced from the CEC by K^+ can interfere with B absorption.

Soil Moisture B deficiency is often associated with dry weather, where low soil moisture reduces B release from OM and B uptake through reduced B transport (diffusion and mass flow) to absorbing root surfaces.

Table 8-16 **B Uptake and %B Recovery in Tall Fescue at Five Soil pH Levels**

	Amount of Added B (mg/pot)						
	0	*4.5*	*8.9*	*17.8*	*4.5*	*8.9*	*17.8*
Soil pH	*B Uptake (mg/pot)*				*% Recovery*		
4.7	0.47	1.85	4.15	9.40	30.7	41.3	50.2
5.3	0.45	1.92	4.45	9.51	32.7	44.9	50.9
5.8	0.44	1.98	4.14	9.10	34.2	41.6	48.7
6.3	0.45	1.98	4.03	9.37	34.0	40.2	50.1
7.4	0.22	0.80	1.40	3.76	12.9	13.3	19.9

SOURCE: Peterson and Newman, 1976, *Soil Sci. Soc. Am. J.*, 40:280.

Table 8-17 **Crop Sensitivity to B Deficiency**

High Sensitivity		*Moderate Sensitivity*		*Low Sensitivity*	
Alfalfa	Peanut	Apple	Cotton	Asparagus	Pea
Cauliflower	Sugar beet	Broccoli	Lettuce	Barley	Peppermint
Celery	Table beet	Cabbage	Parsnip	Bean	Potato
Rapeseed	Turnip	Carrot	Radish	Blueberry	Rye
Conifers	Apple	Clover	Spinach	Cucumber	Sorghum
Canola	Broccoli	Grapes	Tomato	Corn	Spearmint
Turnip		Raspberries	Strawberries	Grasses	Soybean
		Turnip		Oat	Sudan grass
				Onion	Sweet corn
					Wheat

SOURCE: Robertson et al., 1976, Mich. Coop. Ext. Bull. E-1037.

Table 8-18 **Common B Fertilizers**

Source	*Formula*	*% B*
Borax	$Na_2B_4O_7 \cdot 10H_2O$	11
Boric acid	H_3BO_3	17
Colemanite	$Ca_2B_6O_{11} \cdot 5H_2O$	10–16
Sodium pentaborate	$Na_2B_{10}O_{16} \cdot 10H_2O$	18
Sodium tetraborate	$Na_2B_4O_7 \cdot 5H_2O$	14–15
Solubor	$Na_2B_4O_7 \cdot 5H_2O + Na_2B_{10}O_{16} \cdot 10H_2O$	20–21

Plant Factors Because of the narrow range between sufficient and toxic levels of available soil B, the sensitivity of crops to excess B is important (Table 8-17). Genetic variability contributes to differences in B uptake. Investigations with tomatoes revealed that susceptibility to B deficiency is controlled by a single recessive gene. Tomato variety T3238 is B inefficient, while the variety Rutgers is B efficient. Corn hybrids exhibit similar genetic variability related to B uptake.

B Sources

Organic B B content in animal waste ranges between 0.001 and 0.005%. Thus, with most manures, average application rates will provide sufficient plant available B. Similar to other micronutrients, increasing OM and associated chelation properties with waste application will increase B availability. B content in municipal waste is also low ($\approx$ 0.01% B).

Inorganic B B is one of the most widely applied micronutrients. Sodium tetraborate ($Na_2B_4O_7 \cdot 5H_2O$) is the most common B source, containing $\approx$ 15% B (Table 8-18). Solubor is a highly concentrated, soluble B source that can be foliar applied as a liquid or dust. It is also used in liquid and suspension fertilizers. Solubor is preferred to borax because it dissolves more readily. The Ca borate mineral colemanite is often used on sandy soils because it is less soluble and less subject to leaching than the sodium borates.

The common B application methods are broadcast, banded, or applied as a foliar spray or dust. In the first two methods, B fertilizer is usually mixed with N-P-K-S products and soil applied. B salts can also be coated on dry fertilizer materials.

B fertilizers should be uniformly soil applied because of the narrow range between deficiency and toxicity. Segregation of granular B sources in dry fertilizer blends must be avoided. B application with fluid fertilizers eliminates segregation.

Foliar B application is practiced for perennial tree-fruit crops, often in combination with pesticides other than those formulated in oils and emulsions. B may also be included in sprays of chelate, Mg, Mn, and urea. Foliar applications of B with pesticides are also used in cotton and peanuts.

B fertilization rates depend on plant species, soil cultural practices, rainfall, liming, soil OM, and other factors. Application rates of 0.5 to 3 lbs/a are generally recommended. The B rate also depends on application method. For example, B for vegetable crops is 0.4 to 2.7 lbs/a broadcast, 0.4 to 0.9 lbs/a banded, and 0.09 to 0.4 lbs/a foliar applied.

Chloride (Cl)

Cl Cycle

Nearly all chloride (Cl^-) in soils exists in soil solution (Fig. 8-29). The mineral, adsorbed, and organic fractions contain negligible quantities of Cl^-. Because of its high solubility and mobility in soils, appreciable Cl^- leaching can occur when rainfall or irrigation exceeds evapotranspiration. Plant-growth limiting Cl deficiencies are generally rare in areas of significant atmospheric Cl^- deposition (Fig. 8-30). Interaction of wind and sea water (≈ 4% NaCl) introduces Cl^- into the atmosphere. Compared to annual crop Cl^- requirement (≈ 4 to 8 lbs/a), atmospheric deposition supplies adequate Cl^-, although in coastal areas deposition is much greater.

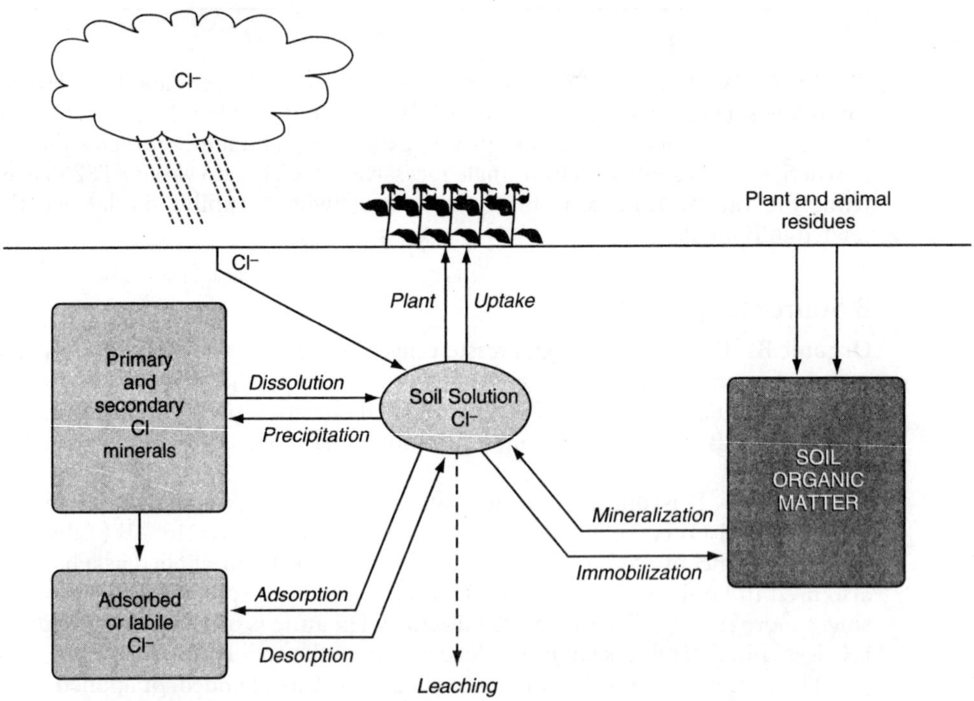

Figure 8-29 Cl cycle in soils.

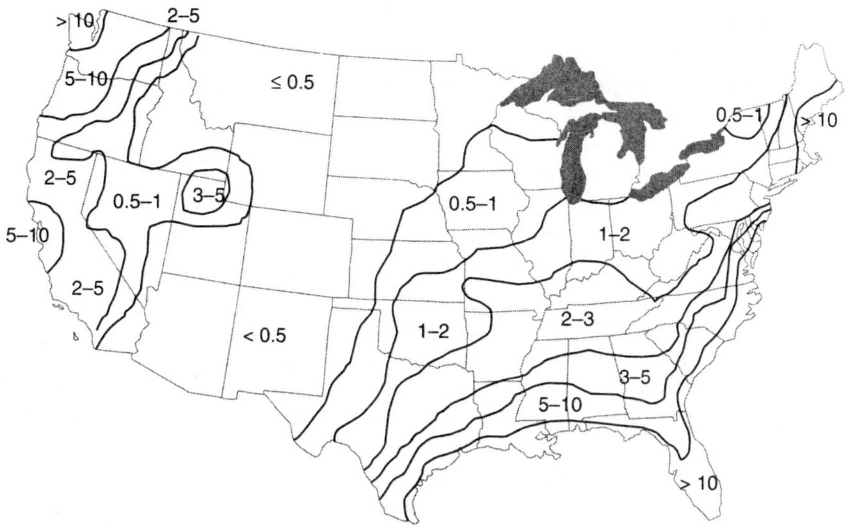

Figure 8-30 Distribution in Cl² depositon (kg Cl²/ha) in the U.S. National Atmospheric Deposition Program. *(2002, Washington, D.C.)*

Table 8-19 **Crop Sensitivity to Cl Deficiency**

High Sensitivity	*Mild Sensitivity*	*Low Sensitivity*
Avocado	Cotton	Barley
Legumes	Oats	Corn
Lettuce	Potato	Spinach
Peach	Soybean	Sugar beet
Tobacco	Wheat	Tomato

Cl in Plants

Cl^- is absorbed by plants through roots and leaves. Active transport of Cl^- across plasma membranes occurs through other anion transporters (i.e., NO_3^-, SO_4^{-2}, $H_2PO_4^-$). Cl^- is readily transported in plant tissues. Cl^- concentration in plants is about 0.2 to 2.0%, although levels as high as 10% are possible. All of these values usually exceed the strictly nutritional need of most plants. Tissue concentrations of 0.5 to 2.0% of sensitive crops can be toxic. Similar reductions in yield and quality can occur when $Cl^- \geq 4\%$ in tolerant crops (Table 8-19).

Cl Functions Cl^- primarily is involved in osmotic and cation neutralization, which are important to the biochemical process. Over 100 Cl^--containing organic compounds are known in plants; however, their functions are not well understood.

O_2 and Photosynthesis. Cl^- is important to the function of Mn in photosynthetic production of carbohydrates from CO_2 and evolution of O_2 (see *O_2 and Photosynthesis* under *Mn*). Cl^- will maintain electroneutrality when Mn^{+3} donates its electrons during photosynthetis (see page 271). This function of Cl^- is essential for photosynthesis as evidenced by the ≈ 10% Cl^- in the chloroplasts.

Cell Turgor. For rapid gas exchange (CO_2 in and O_2 / H_2O out) by leaves during active photosynthesis (daylight), the epidermal guard cells of stomates are turgid, caused by K^+ pumped from neighboring cells into the guard cells. K^+ transport into the guard cells must be balanced by organic anions or Cl^-, depending on plant species. Observations that loss of leaf turgor is a Cl^--deficiency symptom support the concept that Cl^- is an active osmotic agent. Some of the favorable actions of Cl^- fertilization are attributed to increased water potential and moisture relations. In other cells, inadequate osmotic adjustment reduces cell turgor pressure that inhibits cell enlargement and cell division. Reduction in cell expansion reduces leaf size, a common Cl^--deficiency symptom.

Solute Concentration in Vacuoles. For plants to absorb and use nutrients efficiently, the nutrients accumulate in vacuoles until transported to growing plant organs. Cl^- is essential for maintaining electrical balance in tonoplasts. Under saline conditions, Cl^- is especially critical in balancing high Na^+, and maintaining proper water status.

Cl^- Deficiency and Toxicity Symptoms Chlorosis in younger leaves and an overall wilting of the plants are the two most common Cl^--deficiency symptoms. Necrosis in some plant parts, leaf bronzing, and reduction in root and leaf growth may also be observed. Tissue concentrations below 70 to 700 ppm are usually indicative of Cl^- deficiency. However, higher concentrations may be beneficial for disease suppression and moisture relationships. Cl^- response in small grains in the Great Plains occurs about 50% of the time when plant Cl^- is between 0.12 and 0.4%.

Excess Cl^- can be harmful, and crops vary widely in their tolerance to Cl^- toxicity (Table 8-19). Leaves become thickened and tend to roll with excessive Cl^-. Storage quality of tuber crops is reduced by excessive Cl^-. The principal effect of excess Cl^- is an increase in osmotic pressure of soil water that reduces water uptake.

Cl in Soil

Mineral Cl Cl concentration is 0.02 to 0.05% in the earth's crust, and it occurs primarily in igneous and metamorphic rocks. Soil Cl^- commonly exists as soluble salts such as NaCl, $CaCl_2$, and $MgCl_2$. Cl^- is often the principal anion in saline soil solutions. Solution Cl^- ranges from 0.5 ppm in acid soils to $>$ 6,000 ppm in saline/sodic soils. The majority of Cl^- in soils originates from salts trapped in parent material, from marine aerosols, and from volcanic emissions. Nearly all of soil Cl^- has been in the oceans at least once, being returned to the land by uplift and subsequent leaching of marine sediments or by oceanic salt spray carried in rain or snow. Annual Cl^- depositions of 12 to 35 lbs/a are common and may increase to more than 100 lbs/a in coastal areas (Fig. 8-30). The quantity of Cl^- deposition depends on the amount of sea spray, which is related to temperature; wind strength, frequency, and duration sweeping inland from the sea; topography of the coastal region; and the amount, frequency, and intensity of precipitation. Salty droplets or dry salt dust may be whirled to great heights by strong air currents and carried over long distances. Cl^- concentration in precipitation is decreased in inland areas.

Solution Cl^- Cl^- is very soluble in soils. Because of Cl^- mobility it will accumulate where the internal drainage of soils is restricted and in shallow groundwater where Cl^- can be moved by capillarity into the root zone and deposited at or near the soil surface. Problems of excess Cl^- occur in some irrigated areas and are usually the result of interactions of:

- high Cl^- in the irrigation water,
- insufficient water to leach accumulated Cl^-,

- poor physical properties and drainage conditions for effective leaching, and
- high water table and capillary Cl^- movement into the root zone.

Environmental damage in localized areas from high Cl^- concentrations has resulted from road deicing, water softening, saltwater spills associated with the extraction of oil and natural gas deposits, and disposal of feedlot wastes and various industrial brines.

Plant Responses

Depression of Cl^- uptake by high concentrations of NO_3^- and SO_4^{-2} has been observed in a number of plants (Fig. 8-31). Here potato yields increase as Cl^- in petioles increases from 1.1 to 6.9% and NO_3^- decreases. Although beneficial effects of Cl^- on plant growth are not fully understood, improved plant-water relationships and inhibition of plant diseases are two important factors. The negative interaction between Cl^- and NO_3^- has been attributed to competition for carrier sites at root surfaces.

The effect of Cl^- fertilization on root and leaf disease suppression has been observed on a number of crops (Table 8-20). Several mechanisms have been suggested and include (1) increased NH_4^+ uptake through inhibition of nitrification by Cl^-, which reduces take-all root disease by decreased rhizosphere pH, or (2) competition between Cl^- and NO_3^- for uptake. Plants low in NO_3^- are less susceptible to root rot diseases. In some regions, Cl^- response in some crops has not been related to disease suppression. For example, in semiarid regions, Cl^- deficiency is caused by low soil Cl^-, with the probability of a Cl^- response increasing with decreasing water-extractable soil Cl^- (Table 8-21).

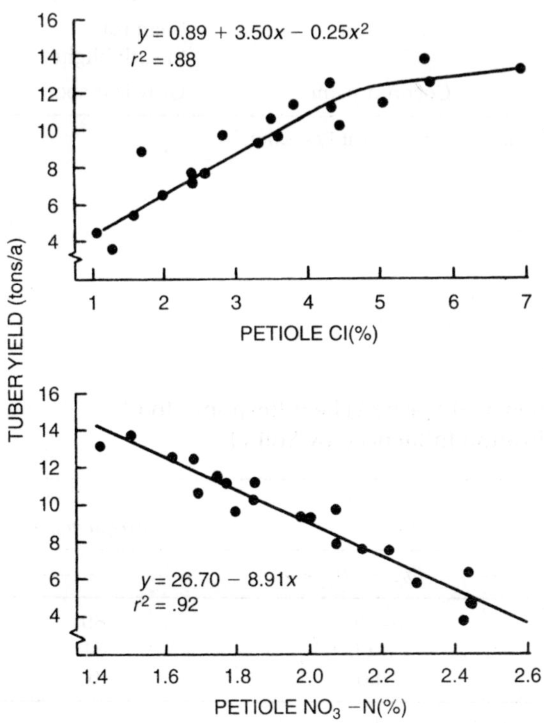

Figure 8-31 **Relationship between potato yield and Cl^2 and NO_3^2 concentration in petioles.** ***(Jackson et al., 1981, unpublished data, Oregon State Univ.)***

Table 8-20 Diseases Suppressed by Cl Fertilization

Location	*Crop*	*Suppressed Disease*
Oregon	Winter wheat	Take-all
		Septoria
	Potato	Hollow heart
		Brown center
North Dakota	Winter wheat	Tanspot
	Spring wheat	Common root rot
	Barley	Common root rot
		Spot blotch
	Durum wheat	Common root rot
South Dakota	Spring wheat	Leaf rust
		Tanspot
		Septoria
New York	Corn	Stalk rot
California	Celery	Fusarium yellows
Saskatchewan	Spring wheat	Common root rot
	Barley	Common root rot
Manitoba Take	Spring wheat	Take-all
Alberta	Barley	Common root rot
		Net blotch
Germany	Winter wheat	Take-all
Great Britain	Winter wheat	Stripe rust
India	Pearl millet	Downy mildew
Indonesia	Rice	Stem rot
		Sheath blight
Philippines	Coconut palm	Gray leaf spot

SOURCE: Fixen, 1987, 2nd National Wheat Res. Conf.

Table 8-21 Frequency of Spring Wheat Response to Cl Fertilization Influenced by Soil Cl

	Soil Cl Content	*Yield Response Frequency*
Category	---------- *lb/a−2 ft* ----------	---------- % ----------
Low	0–30	69
Medium	31–60	31
High	>60	0

SOURCE: Fixen, 1979, *J. Fert. Issues*, 4:95.

Cl Sources

Organic Cl Because of the solubility and mobility of Cl^-, most animal and municipal wastes are low in Cl^-.

Inorganic Cl When additional Cl^- is desirable, it can be supplied by the following sources:

- Ammonium chloride (NH_4Cl) 66% Cl
- Calcium chloride ($CaCl_2$) 65% Cl
- Magnesium chloride ($MgCl_2$) 74% Cl
- Potassium chloride (KCl) 47% Cl
- Sodium chloride (NaCl) 60% Cl

Rates of Cl^- vary, depending on the crop, method of application, and purpose of addition (i.e., for correction of nutrient deficiency, disease suppression, or improved plant water status). Where take-all root rot of winter wheat is suspected, banding 35 to 40 lbs/a of Cl^- with or near the seed at planting is recommended. Broadcasting 75 to 125 lbs/a of Cl^- has effectively reduced crop stress from take-all and by leaf and head diseases (e.g., stripe rust and septoria). Plant nutrient Cl^- requirements for high yields of most temperate-region crops are usually satisfied by only 4 to 10 lbs/a.

Molybdenum (Mo)

Mo Cycle

The main forms of Mo in soil include primary and secondary minerals, exchangeable Mo held by Fe/Al oxides, Mo in soil solution, and organically bound Mo. Although Mo is an anion in solution, the relationships between these forms are similar to those of other metal cations (Fig. 8-32).

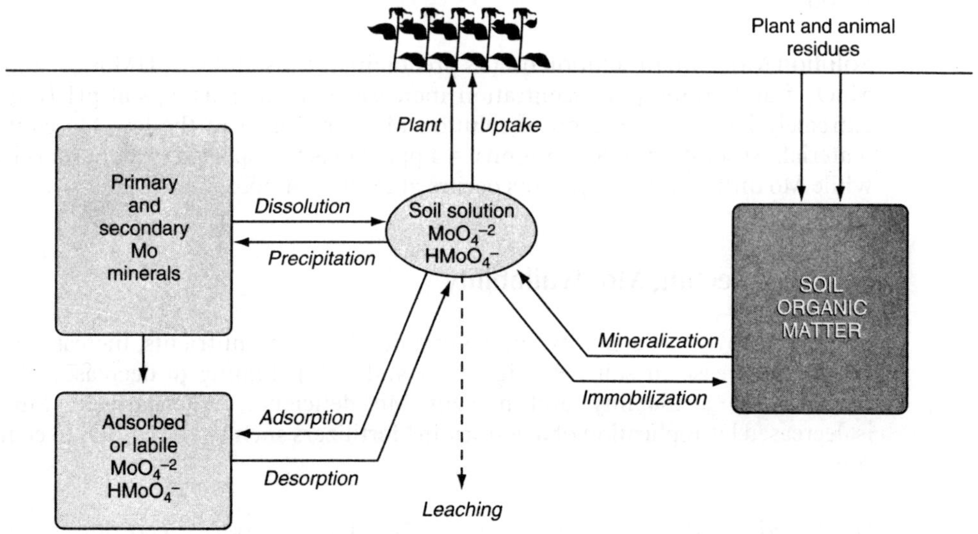

Figure 8-32 Mo cycle in soils.

Mo in Plants

Mo is absorbed as the weak acid molybdate (MoO_4^{-2}) that can form complexes with other anions such as phosphomolybdate. Mo complexation may explain why Mo can be absorbed in relatively large amounts without any apparent toxicity.

Mo content of plants is normally low (< 1 ppm), because of the extremely low MoO_4^{-2} in solution. In some cases, Mo levels in crops may exceed 1,000 ppm. Mo-deficient plants contain < 0.2 ppm.

Mo is an essential component of NO_3^- reductase, an enzyme concentrated in chloroplasts, which catalyzes the conversion of NO_3^- to NO_2^-. Mo also is a structural component of nitrogenase, the enzyme essential to N_2 fixation by root-nodule bacteria of leguminous crops, by some algae and actinomycetes, and by free-living, N_2-fixing organisms. Mo concentrations in legume nodules can be ten times higher than in leaves. Mo requirement of plants decreases with increasing inorganic N availability. Mo is also reported to have an essential role in Fe absorption and translocation in plants, which explains why a common Mo-deficiency symptom is similar to interveinal chlorosis in Fe deficiency.

Excessive amounts of Mo are toxic, especially to grazing cattle or sheep. High-Mo forage may occur on wet, high-pH, and high-OM soils. Molybdenosis, a disease in cattle, is caused by an imbalance of Mo and Cu in the diet when the Mo content of the forage is > 5 ppm. Mo toxicity causes stunted growth and bone deformation in the animal and can be corrected by oral feeding of Cu, injections of Cu, or the application of $CuSO_4$ to the soil. Other practices used to decrease Mo toxicity are application of S or Mn and improvement of soil drainage.

Mo in Soil

Mineral Mo The average Mo concentration in the earth's crust is ≈ 2 ppm, and typically ranges from 0.2 to 5 ppm in soils. Soil minerals controlling solution MoO422 concentration are PbMoO4 and CaMoO4 (Fig. 8-33). CaMoO4 predominates in both acidic and calcareous soils. Mo solubility in soils generally follows soil Mo, which is close to the solubility of PbMoO4.

Solution Mo Mo in solution occurs predominantly as MoO_4^{-2}, $HMoO_4^-$, and $H_2MoO_4^{-2}$. MoO_4^{-2} and $HMoO_4^-$ concentration increases with increasing soil pH (Fig. 8-34). The extremely low concentration of solution Mo is reflected in the low Mo content of plant material. At solution concentrations > 4 ppb, Mo is transported to plant roots by mass flow, while Mo diffusion to plant roots occurs at levels < 4 ppb.

Factors Affecting Mo Availability

Soil pH MoO_4^{-2} availability, unlike that of other micronutrients, increases about tenfold per unit increase in soil pH (Figs. 8-34 and 8-35). Liming to decrease soil acidity will increase Mo availability and prevent Mo deficiency. Alternatively, Mo availability is decreased by application of acid-forming fertilizers such as $(NH_4)_2SO_4$ to coarse-textured soils.

Fe/Al Oxides Mo is strongly adsorbed to Fe/Al oxide surfaces, a portion of which becomes unavailable to the plant. Soils high in Fe/Al oxides tend to be low in available Mo.

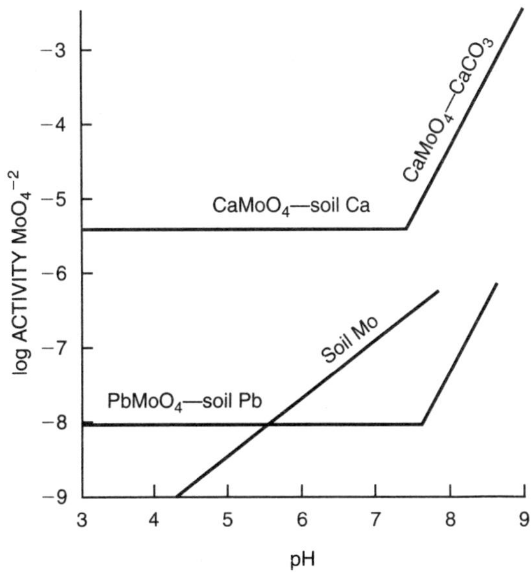

Figure 8-33 Mo mineral solubilities, which increase with increasing pH. *(Lindsay, 1979,* Chemical Equilibria in Soils, *New York: John Wiley & Sons.)*

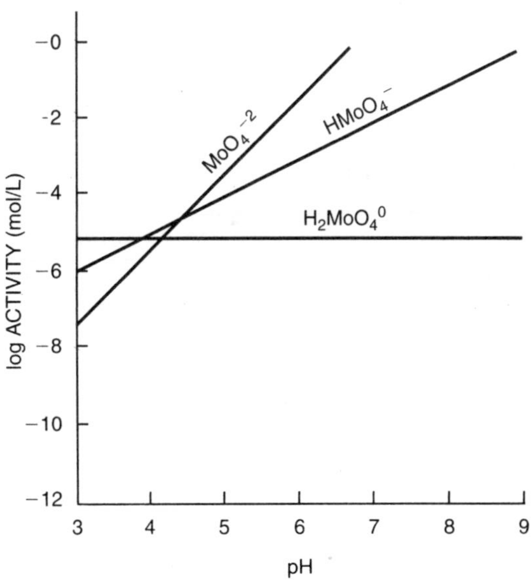

Figure 8-34 Common Mo species in soil solution as influenced by pH. *(Lindsay, 1979,* Chemical Equilibria in Soils, *New York: John Wiley & Sons.)*

Interactions with Other Nutrients P enhances Mo absorption by plants, probably due to exchange of adsorbed MoO_4^{-2}. In contrast, high levels of solution SO_4^{-2} depress Mo uptake by plants (Table 8-22). On soils with marginal Mo deficiencies, application of SO_4^{-2} fertilizers may induce Mo deficiency.

Both Cu and Mn can also reduce Mo uptake; however, Mg has the opposite effect and will encourage Mo absorption. NO_3^- encourages Mo uptake, while NH_4^+ sources reduce Mo uptake. The effect of NO_3^- nutrition may be related to release of OH^- by roots that would increase Mo solubility.

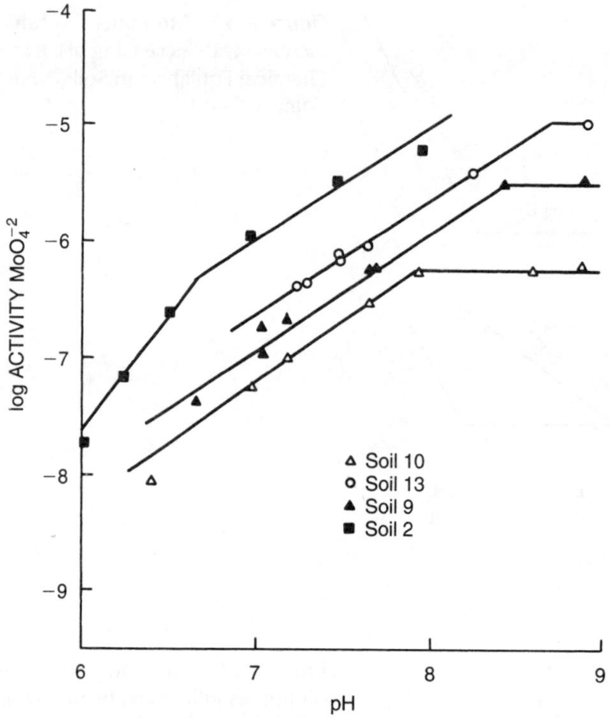

Figure 8-35 pH dependence of Mo solubility in Colorado soils. (*Vlek and Lindsay, 1977,* Soil Sci. Soc. Am. J., *41:42.*)

Table 8-22 **Effect of S and Mo on the Yield and S and Mo Content of Brussels Sprouts**

Treatment	*Yield (g/pot)*	*Tissue Content* Mo (ppm)	*Tissue Content* S (%)
*Sulfur**			
0 ppm S	12.6	5.09	0.25
50 ppm S	13.8	0.88	0.60
100 ppm S	13.8	0.50	0.70
Molybdenum			
0 ppm Mo	12.7	0.08	0.53
Seed treated w/Mo	13.6	0.16	0.49
2.5 ppm Mo	13.9	6.23	0.51

*S treatments did not alter soil pH or the exchangeable Mo content.
SOURCE: Gupta, 1969, *Sulphur Inst. J.*, 5:4.

Climate Mo deficiency is accentuated under dry conditions, probably due to reduced mass flow or diffusion under low-soil-moisture content.

Plant Factors Crops vary in their sensitivity to low solution Mo (Table 8-23). Mo-efficient and Mo-inefficient varieties of alfalfa, cauliflower, corn, and kale have been identified. The differing levels of susceptibility of cauliflower varieties to Mo deficiency is related to their abilities to extract soil Mo.

Table 8-23 **Crop Sensitivity to Mo Deficiency**

High Sensitivity	*Mild Sensitivity*	*Low Sensitivity*	
Alfalfa	Beet	Apple	Oats
Broccoli	Broccoli	Asparagus	Potato
Brussels sprouts	Cabbage	Barley	Raspberries
Cauliflower	Cotton	Beans	Ryegrass
Clover	Peas	Blueberries	Soybean
Legumes	Potato	Carrot	Sugar beet
Lettuce	Radish	Celery	Sweet Corn
Onion	Tomato	Corn	Tomato
Rapeseed	Turnip	Flax	Turfgrass
Spinach		Grapes	Wheat

Table 8-24 **Sources of Mo Fertilizer**

Sources	*Formula*	*% Mo*
Ammonium molybdate	$(NH_4)_6Mo_7O_{24} \cdot 2H_2O$	54
Sodium molybdate	$Na_2MoO_4 \cdot 2H_2O$	39
Molybdenum trioxide	MoO_3	66
Molybdenum frits	Fritted glass	1–30

SOURCE: Mortvedt, 1980, *Farm Chem.*, 143:42.

Mo Sources

Organic Mo Only small quantities of Mo occur in animal wastes (0.0001 to 0.0005% Mo), although with most manures, average application rates will provide sufficient plant available Mo. Mo content in municipal waste is usually low, averaging 0.0001% Mo.

Inorganic Mo Mo fertilizers, shown in Table 8-24, are applied at low rates (0.5 to 5 oz/a). Mo solutions are soil or foliar applied, or applied as a seed coating. The optimum Mo rate depends on the application method, with lower rates used in the latter two methods. Seeds treated with a solution of sodium molybdate before seeding are widely used because of the low application rates needed. Seed treatments with a slurry or dust are also effective. To obtain satisfactory distribution of the small quantities of Mo applied to soil, Mo sources are sometimes combined with N-P-K fertilizers. Foliar spray applications with NH_4 or Na molybdate are also effective in correcting deficiencies. Mo application to clovers will in some cases increase the yield equivalent to that achieved with the addition of limestone. Since liming can be more expensive, Mo fertilization is often preferred.

Nickel (Ni)

Ni is the latest nutrient to be established (in 1987) as an essential nutrient to higher plants since the recognition of Cl^- in 1954. Ni content of plants normally ranges from 0.1 to 1.0 ppm. It is readily taken up by most species as Ni^{+2}. Ni is the metal component of urease that catalyzes the reaction $CO(NH_2)_2 + H_2O \leftrightarrows 2\ NH_3 + CO_2$. Apparently, Ni is essential for plants supplied with urea and for those in which ureides are important in N metabolism.

Table 8-25 **Effect of Ni Supply on Germination and Yield of Barley**

Ni in Solution	*Germination*	*Ni Concentration*	*Total Grain Wt*
(mM)	*(%)*	*(μg/g dry wt)*	*(g dry wt)*
0.0	11.6	7.0	7.3
0.6	56.6	63.8	7.5
1.0	94.0	129.2	8.4

SOURCE: Brown et al., 1987, *Plant Physiol.* 85:801.

Ni is beneficial to N metabolism in legumes. Nodule weight and seed yield of soybeans have been stimulated by Ni.

Ni-deficient plants accumulate toxic levels of urea in leaf tips because of reduced urease activity. Ni-deficient plants may develop chlorosis in the youngest leaves that progresses to necrosis of the meristem. Ni may also be involved in plant diseases caused by faulty N metabolism.

Ni has been demonstrated as essential to small-grain crops (Table 8-25). The data show increasing barley germination and grain yield with increasing Ni in solution.

High levels of Ni may induce Zn or Fe deficiency because of cation competition. Application of some sewage sludge may result in elevated levels of Ni in crop plants.

Plant genes have recently been identified from wild mustard, *Thlaspi goesingense,* that enable plants to accumulate high levels of Ni. Currently over 350 plants are known to hyper-accumulate metals from soil contaminated with Ni, Cu, Zn, Cd, Se, and/or Mn. Tissue concentrations of 1% Ni are 1,000 times greater than normal levels.

Beneficial Elements

In addition to the 17 essential nutrients, several elements are benefical to some plants but are not considered necessary for completion of the plant life cycle.

Cobalt (Co)

Co in Plants Co is essential for the growth of symbiotic microorganisms such as *Rhizobia,* free-living N_2-fixing bacteria, and blue-green algae. Co concentration in plants ranges from 0.02 to 0.5 ppm. N_2 fixation in alfalfa can be enhanced by only 10 ppb Co. Co forms a complex with N, important for synthesis of vitamin B_{12} coenzyme. Co is also important in the synthesis of vitamin B_{12} in ruminant animals; thus, soil is an important source of plant Co for animals. Because Co behaves similarly to Fe or Zn, excess Co produces visual symptoms similar to Fe and Mn deficiencies.

Co in Soils Average total Co concentration in the earth's crust is $\approx$ 40 ppm. Soils formed on granitic glacial materials are low in total Co, ranging 1 to 10 ppm. Much higher levels (100 to 300 ppm Co) are present in Mg-rich ferromagnesian minerals. Sandstones and shales are normally low in Co, with concentrations $<$ 5 ppm. Total Co in soils typically ranges from 1 to 70 ppm and averages about 8 ppm. Co deficiencies in ruminants are often associated with forages produced on soils containing $<$ 5 ppm total Co.

Co can be beneficial to some plants grown on (1) acid, highly leached, sandy soils with low total Co; (2) some highly calcareous soils; and (3) some peaty soils. Co^{+2} is adsorbed on exchange sites and occurs as clay-OM complexes similar to those of the other metal cations (Fig. 8-24). Solution Co is often < 0.5 ppm.

Co availability decreases with greater adsorption capacity of Fe/Al/Mn oxides. Co can replace Mn in the surface of these minerals. Co availability is favored by increasing acidity and waterlogging conditions, which decompose Mn oxide; therefore, liming and drainage reduce Co availability.

Co Fertilizer Co deficiency of ruminants can be corrected by (1) adding it to feed, salt licks, or drinking water; (2) drenching; (3) using Co bullets; and (4) fertilizing forage crops with small amounts of Co. Co fertilization with 1.5 to 3 oz/a as $CoSO_4$ is recommended. Soils low in available Co for satisfactory nodulation and N_2 fixation by clover and alfalfa require applications of 0.5 to 2 oz/a of Co. Superphosphate, with small amounts of $CoSO_4$, has also been used to increase Co concentration in subterranean clover.

Sodium (Na)

Na in Plants Na is essential for halophytic plants that accumulate salts in vacuoles to maintain turgor and growth. The beneficial effects of Na on plant growth are often observed in low-K soils, because Na^+ can partially replace K^+. Crops have been categorized according to their potential for Na uptake (Table 8-26). Growth of crops with high and medium ratings will be favorably influenced by Na^+.

Plants absorb Na^+, where concentration in leaf tissue varies from 0.01 to 10%. Many C_4 plants require Na, which is specifically involved in water relations. Many C_4 plants occur naturally in arid, semiarid, and tropical conditions, where stomatal closure to prevent water loss is essential for growth and survival. As a result, CO_2 entry is also restricted when stomata are closed. Efficiency of photosynthetic CO_2 conversion is greater in C_4 compared to C_3 plants, where the ratio of CO_2 assimilated to H_2O transpired by C_4 plants is often double that of C_3 plants. It is also noteworthy that C_4 plants are often found in saline habitats.

Sugar beets are particularly responsive to Na, with concentrations in leaf tips up to ≥ 10%. Na influences water relations and increases drought resistance in sugar beets. In low Na soils, beet leaves are dark green, thin, and dull in hue. Plants wilt more rapidly and may grow horizontally from the crown. There may also be an interveinal necrosis similar to K deficiency. Some of the Na effects may also be due to Cl^-, as NaCl is the common Na source.

Na in Soils Na content in the earth's crust is about 2.8%, while soils contain 0.1 to 1%. Low Na in soils indicates weathering of Na from Na-containing minerals. Very little exchangeable

Table 8-26 **Na Uptake Potential of Various Crops**

High	*Medium*	*Low*	*Very Low*
Fodder beet	Cabbage	Barley	Buckwheat
Mangold	Coconut	Flax	Maize
Spinach	Cotton	Millet	Rye
Sugar beet	Lupins	Rape	Soybean
Swiss chard	Oats	Rubber	Swede
Table beet	Potato	Wheat	Turnip

and mineral Na occurs in humid-region soils. Na is common in most arid and semiarid region soils, where it exists as NaCl, Na_2SO_4, Na_2CO_3, and Na salts that especially accumulate in poorly drained soils, contributing to soil salinity and sodicity (Chapter 3).

Soil solutions contain between 0.5 and 5 ppm Na^+ in temperate regions. Solution and exchangeable Na^+ varies greatly among soils. In humid-region soils the proportion of exchangeable Na^+ to other cations is low. Exchangeable Na^+ can be utilized by crops. Sugar beets respond to fertilization when exchangeable $Na^+ < 0.05$ meq/100 g. In arid regions and if soils are irrigated with sodic waters, exchangeable Na^+ is greater than K^+.

Na Sources Responses to Na have been observed in crops with a high uptake potential (Table 8-26). The Na demand of these crops appears to be independent of, and perhaps even greater than, their K demand. The important Na-containing fertilizers are:

- K fertilizers with NaCl impurities,
- $NaNO_3$ (about 25% Na), and
- multiple-nutrient fertilizers with Na.

Silicon (Si)

Si in Plants Plants absorb Si as silicic acid ($H_4SiO_4^0$). Cereals and grasses contain 0.2 to 2.0% Si, while broadleaves contain 0.02 to 0.2% Si. Si concentrations of 2 to 20% occur in Si-rich plants like sedges, nettles, horsetails, and some grasses. Si impregnates the walls of epidermal and vascular cells, where it strengthens tissues, reduces water loss, and retards fungal infection. With large accumulations of Si, intracellular deposits called *plant opals* can occur.

The role of Si in root functions is likely related to drought tolerance. Although no biochemical role for Si in plant development has been positively identified, it has been proposed that enzyme-Si complexes that act as protectors or regulators of photosynthesis and enzyme activity form in sugarcane. Si can suppress the activity of invertase in sugarcane, resulting in greater sucrose production. A reduction in phosphatase activity is believed to provide a greater supply of essential high-energy precursors needed for optimum cane growth and sugar production.

The beneficial effects of Si have been attributed to partial remediation of toxic effects of high soil Mn^{+2}, Fe^{+2}, or Al^{+3}; plant disease resistance; greater stalk strength and resistance to lodging; increased availability of P; and reduced transpiration.

Freckling, a necrotic leaf spot condition, is a symptom of low Si in sugarcane receiving direct sunlight. Ultraviolet radiation seems to be the causative agent in sunlight since plants kept under plexiglass or glass do not freckle. There are suggestions that Si in the sugarcane plant filters out harmful ultraviolet radiation.

In rice, Si also helps maintain leaf erectness, increases photosynthesis through improved light interception, and results in greater resistance to diseases and insect pests. The oxidizing capacity of rice roots and accompanying tolerance to high Fe and Mn depends on Si. Si additions are beneficial at Si contents of rice straw at < 11%. Heavy N rates render rice plants more susceptible to fungal attack due to decreased Si in the straw. Often, Si materials are applied under high fertilizer N use.

Si in Soils Si is the second most abundant element in the earth's crust, averaging 28%, while Si in soils ranges between 23 and 35%. Unweathered sandy soils can contain as much as 40% Si, compared with as little as 9% Si in highly weathered tropical soils. Major sources of Si include primary and secondary Si minerals, where quartz (SiO_2) is the most common, comprising 90 to 95% of all sand and silt fractions.

Low-Si soils exist in intensively weathered, high-rainfall regions that exhibit low total Si, high Al, low %BS, and low pH. In addition, they all have extremely high P-fixing capacity due to high AEC and Fe/Al oxide content. Plant available Fe^{+2} and Mn^{+2} may also be high in these soils.

$H_4SiO_4{}^0$ is the principal Si species in solution. Solution Si concentrations of < 0.9 to 2 ppm are insufficient for proper nutrition of sugarcane. By comparison, 3 to 37 ppm solution Si occurs in most soils. Si levels adequate for rice production are ≈ 100 ppm. Solution Si concentration is largely controlled by pH-dependent adsorption reactions. Si is adsorbed on the surfaces of Fe/Al oxides. Si leaching in highly weathered soils will reduce solution Si and Si uptake.

Si Sources Primary Si fertilizers include:

- Calcium silicate slag ($CaAl_2Si_2O_8$) — 18 to 21% Si
- Calcium metasilicate ($CaSiO_3$) — 31% Si
- Sodium metasilicate ($NaSiO_3$) — 23% Si

Minimum rates of at least 5,000 lbs/a of $CaSiO_3$ are broadcast applied and incorporated before planting sugarcane (Fig. 8-36). Annual $CaSiO_3$ applications of between 500 and 1,000 lbs/a applied in the row have also improved sugarcane yields. Liming to increase Ca and decrease acidity does not improve sugarcane production to the same extent as Si fertilization. Rates of 1.5 to 2.0 t/ha of silicate slag usually provide sufficient Si for rice produced on low-Si soils.

Selenium (Se)

Se in Plants Se is not essential for plants, but it is required by animals. A greater frequency of livestock nutritional disorders caused by low Se occurs after cold, rainy summers than after hot, dry ones. High summer temperatures are amenable to increased Se concentration in forages.

Plant species differ in Se uptake. Certain species of *Astragalus* absorb many times more Se than do other plants growing in the same soil, because they utilize Se in an amino acid

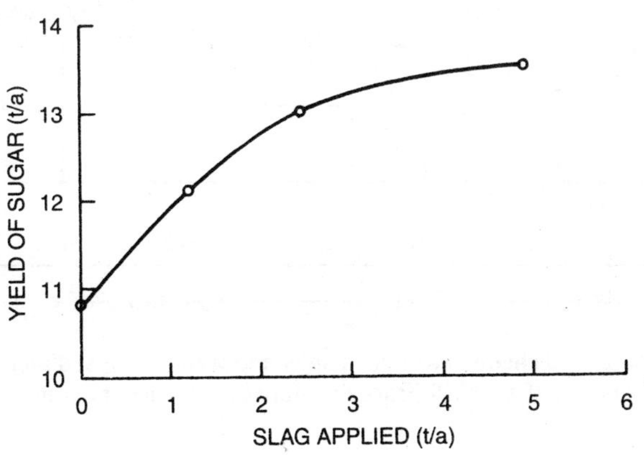

Figure 8-36 **Effect of Se slag on sugar yield from sugarcane grown on an acid, volcanic soil. Mean results for plant and ratoon crops combined.** *(Ayres, 1966,* Soil Sci., *101:216.)*

specific to this species. Plants such as the cruciferae (e.g., cabbage, mustard) and onions, which require large amounts of S, absorb intermediate amounts of Se, while grasses and grain crops absorb low to moderate amounts of Se.

Se in Soil Se occurs in very small amounts in nearly all materials of the earth's crust. It averages only 0.09 ppm in rocks and is found mainly in sedimentary minerals. Se is similar in behavior to S; however, it has 5 oxidation states (see the following list). Total Se in most soils is between 0.1 and 2 ppm. High-pH, calcareous soils formed from sedimentary shale in semiarid regions exhibit high-Se soils and produce high-Se vegetation that is toxic to livestock.

Forms of Se present in soil are selenides (Se^{-2}), elemental Se^0, selenites (Se^{+4}), selenates (Se^{+6}), and organic Se compounds (Fig. 8-37). Se species in soils and sediments are closely related to redox potential, pH, and solubility.

Selenides (Se^{-2}). Selenides are largely insoluble and are associated with S^{-2} in soils of semiarid regions where weathering is limited. They contribute little to Se uptake.

Elemental Se (Se^0). Se^0 is present in small amounts in some soils. Significant amounts may be oxidized to selenites and selenates by microorganisms in neutral and basic soils.

Selenites (SeO_3^{-2}). A large fraction of Se in acid soils may occur as stable complexes of selenites with Fe oxides. The low solubility of Fe-selenite complexes is apparently responsible for the nontoxic levels of Se in plants growing on acid, high-Se soils. Plants absorb selenite but generally to a lesser extent than selenate.

Selenates (SeO_4^{-2}). Selenates are frequently associated with SO_4^{-2} in arid-region soils. Other Se forms will be oxidized to SeO_4^{-2} under these conditions. Only limited quantities of SeO_4^{-2} occur in acid and neutral soils. Selenates are highly

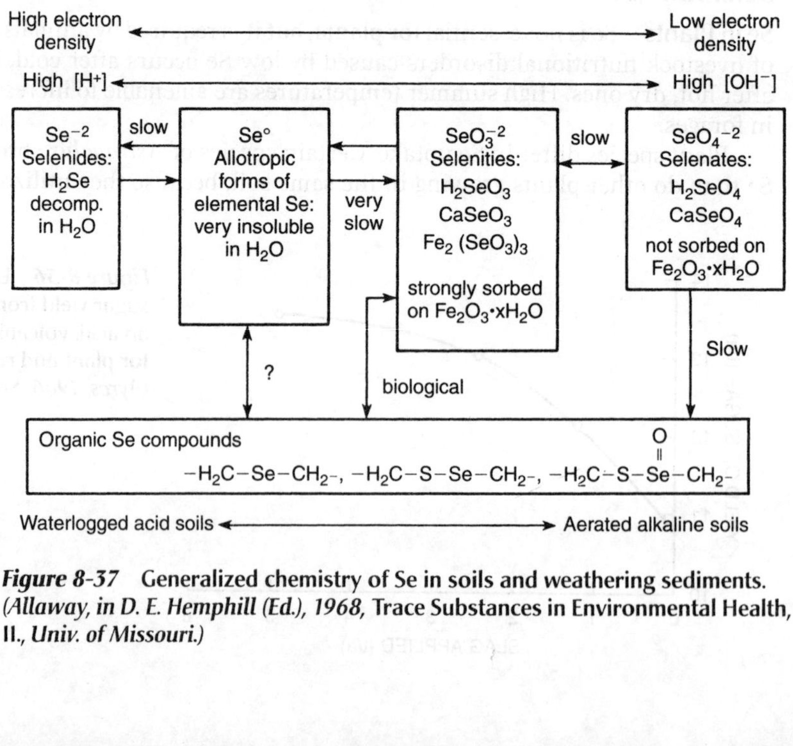

Figure 8-37 **Generalized chemistry of Se in soils and weathering sediments.** ***(Allaway, in D. E. Hemphill (Ed.), 1968,*** **Trace Substances in Environmental Health, II.,** ***Univ. of Missouri.)***

soluble and readily available to plants and are largely responsible for Se toxicity in plants grown on high-pH soils. Most of the water-soluble Se in soils probably occurs as selenates.

Organic Se. As much as 40% of total Se in some soils occurs as organically complexed Se. Soluble organic Se compounds are liberated through the decay of residues from Se accumulator plants. Se in plant residue is stable in dry regions, and much of it remains plant available. Organic Se is more soluble in basic than acid soils, which would enhance availability in semiarid-region soils.

Low-Se uptake is usually caused by low total Se in the soil parent material or low-Se availability in acid and poorly drained soils. Solution Se is lowest at slightly acid to neutral pH and increases under both more acid and basic soil pH. High soil pH facilitates the oxidation of SeO_3^{-2} to the more soluble SeO_4^{-2}. Increased yields with N and S fertilization may lower Se concentration in crops through dilution. There has been some concern about increased incidence and severity of Se deficiencies in cattle due to the negative interaction of SO_4^{-2} on SeO_4^{-2} uptake by crops. Fertilization with S^0 products depresses Se uptake less than fast acting SO_4 sources.

Se Sources Although Se deficiency disorders such as muscular dystrophy or white muscle disease in cattle and sheep can be corrected by therapeutic measures, there is interest in Se fertilization to produce forages adequate in Se for grazing animals, rather than to satisfy any particular plant requirements. Se fertilization is acceptable if precautions are taken:

- To avoid Se toxicity to grazing animals, Se topdressing is not recommended.
- High Se levels in edible animal tissue should be prevented.
- Protection against Se deficiency should be provided for at least one grazing season following application during the dormant season.

Fertilization with SeO_3^{-2} is preferred because it is slower acting and less likely to result in excessive Se levels in plants. SeO_4^{-2} can be used if rapid Se uptake is desired. Addition of Na selenite at 1 oz Se/a is satisfactory for forages. Foliar application of Na selenite at 6 g Se/a is an efficient way to increase Se in plants used for animal feed.

Se is also present in P fertilizers produced from rock phosphate. Superphosphate containing 20 or more ppm Se may provide sufficient Se to plants in Se-deficient areas to protect livestock from Se-deficiency.

Vanadium (V)

Low concentrations of V are beneficial for growth of microorganisms, animals, and higher plants. Although it is considered to be essential for green algae, there is still no decisive evidence that V is necessary for higher plants. V may partially substitute for Mo in N_2 fixation by *Rhizobia.* It may also function in biological oxidation-reduction reactions. Increases in growth attributable to V have been reported for asparagus, rice, lettuce, barley, and corn. V requirement of plants is < 2 ppb, whereas normal V concentration in plant material averages about 1 ppm.

Study Questions

1. Identify the essential micronutrients in plants. What other elements are beneficial to some plants but are not essential? Which micronutrients are metals and nonmetal ions?
2. Give the principal anion and cation forms absorbed by plant roots for each micronutrient.
3. For each micronutrient, describe the influence of soil solution pH on nutrient availability.
4. For which micronutrients does adsorption to clay and Fe/Al oxide surfaces affect buffering changes in nutrient concentration in solution and plant availability? What adsorption mechanisms are important in calcareous soils?
5. Flooding and submergence influence the solubility and availability of which micronutrients?
6. Explain how microbial activity influences the solubility and availability of micronutrients.
7. Give examples of nutrient interactions important in micronutrient uptake (a) among heavy metal cations, (b) between N and at least 3 other elements, (c) between P and at least 3 other elements, and (d) between K and at least 2 other nutrients.
8. How do climatic factors influence plant availability of B, Mn, Mo, and Zn?
9. Describe the mechanism that enables Fe-efficient plants to tolerate low-Fe soils.
10. Explain why soluble Fe^{+3} decreases a thousandfold and soluble Zn^{+2} a hundredfold for every 1 unit increase in soil pH.
11. Over the normal range in soil pH, solution Fe is 1,000 or more times lower than that required by plants for normal growth. Explain why most soils, regardless of pH, are not deficient in Fe. Explain why soil-applied inorganic Fe fertilizers are ineffective in correcting Fe deficiencies, whereas inorganic Zn fertilizers are commonly applied. Describe alternative methods which can be used to correct Fe deficiency.
12. Your county extension agent told you that $FeCl_3$ could be soil applied to a calcareous soil because HCl (hydrochloric acid) produced by the following reaction would keep the soil acid and Fe^{+3} in solution: $FeCl_3 + 3H_2O \rightarrow Fe^{+3} + 3OH^- + 3HCl$. Is this good or bad advice? Explain your answer.
13. What deficiencies are best controlled by foliar treatments of micronutrient fertilizers?
14. What micronutrient deficiencies are best corrected soil applications of micronutrients?
15. Acidification of high-pH and calcareous soils in localized zones such as fertilizer bands can be helpful in the treatment of what micronutrient deficiencies?
16. How is the availability of micronutrients affected by soil OM?
17. What essential function does Mn play in photosynthesis?
18. What soil and environmental condition would increase the potential for micronutrient toxicities?
19. Why is the behavior of Mo in soils different from the behavior of the other microelements?
20. Why is Cl^- not commonly deficient in soils?
21. How is a Co deficiency in animals commonly remedied?
22. In what ways is Se important in soils?
23. Which of the microelements are frequently applied as chelates?
24. What precaution must be observed in applying Cu, Zn, B, Co, Mo, and Se to crops?

25. Turf managers frequently use Fe to "green up" fairways. Calculate the quantity of FeEDTA needed to apply 0.3 lbs Fe/1,000 ft^2. If a 0.1% solution were prepared, how many gallons/1,000 ft^2 are needed to apply the same rate of Fe?

26. A grower wants to apply 5 lbs Zn/a. Calulate the amount of $ZnSO_4$ and ZnEDTA needed.

Selected References

Barber, S. A. 1984. *Soil nutrient bioavailability: A mechanistic approach.* New York: John Wiley & Sons.

Epstein, E. 1972. *Mineral nutrition of plants: Principles and perspectives.* New York: John Wiley & Sons.

Mengel, K., and Kirkby, E. A. 1987. *Principles of plant nutrition.* Bern, Switzerland: International Potash Institute.

Mortvedt, J. J., and Cox, F. R. 1985. Production, marketing, and use of calcium, magnesium, and micronutrient fertilizers. In O. P. Engelstad (Ed.), *Fertilizer technology and use* (pp. 455–482). Madison, WI: Soil Science Society of America.

Mortvedt, J. J., et al. (Eds.). 1991. *Micronutrients in agriculture.* No. 4. Madison, WI: Soil Science Society of America.

Mortvedt, J. J., Murphy, L. S., and Follett, R. H. 1999. *Fertilizer technology and application.* Meister Publishing. Willoughby, OH.

Ršmheld, V., and Marscher, H. 1991. Function of micronutrients in plants. In J. J. Mortvedt et al. (Eds.), *Micronutrients in Agriculture.* No. 4. Madison, WI: Soil Science Society of America.

CHAPTER 9

Soil Fertility Evaluation

Optimum productivity of a cropping system depends on an adequate supply of plant nutrients. The quantity of nutrients required by plants varies depending on many interacting factors, including (1) plant species and variety, (2) yield level, (3) soil properties, (4) environment, and (5) management. Thus, the quantity of additional nutrient needed to optimize yield will vary. Continued nutrient removal, with little or no replacement, ensures future nutrient-related yield loss.

When soil does not supply sufficient nutrients for optimum productivity, nutrients must be applied. The proper nutrient rate is determined by knowing the nutrient requirement of the crop (Table 9-1) and the potential nutrient supply of the soil. Diagnostic techniques, including identification of deficiency symptoms and soil and plant tests, are used to determine potential nutrient deficiency and the quantity of nutrients needed to optimize yield. By the time a plant exhibits deficiency symptoms, a reduction in yield potential has occurred; thus, quantifying soil capacity to supply nutrients before planting is essential for optimum plant growth and yield.

Quantifying nutrient requirements by soil and plant analysis depends on careful sampling and analytical methods calibrated for the representative crops and soils in a specific region. Knowing the relationship between test results and crop nutrient response is essential for providing an accurate nutrient recommendation. Several techniques are commonly employed to assess the nutrient status of a soil:

- nutrient-deficiency symptoms of plants,
- tissue analysis from plants growing on the soil,
- biological tests where plants growth is used as a measure of soil fertility, and
- soil analysis.

Nutrient-Deficiency Symptoms of Plants

Plants are integrators of all growth factors (Fig. 9-1). Therefore, careful observation of the growing plant can help identify a specific nutrient stress (see color plates inside book cover). A nutrient-deficient plant will exhibit characteristic symptoms because normal plant

Table 9-1 Typical Nutrient Uptake Levels for Selected Agricultural and Horticultural Crops

Crop	*Yield*	*N*	*P*	*K*	*Ca*	*Mg*	*S*	*Cu*	*Mn*	*Zn*
	unit/a	*lbs/a*								
Grains										
Barley (grain)	60 bu	65	14	24	2	6	8	0.04	0.03	0.08
Barley (straw)	2 ton	30	10	80	8	2	4	0.01	0.32	0.05
Canola	45 bu	145	32	100	—	—	28	—	—	—
Corn (grain)	200 bu	150	40	40	6	18	15	0.08	0.10	0.18
Corn (stover)	6 tons	110	12	160	16	36	16	0.05	1.50	0.30
Flax	25 bu	65	8	29	—	—	12	—	—	—
Oats (grain)	80 bu	60	10	15	2	4	6	0.03	0.12	0.05
Oats (straw)	2 tons	35	8	90	8	12	9	0.03	—	0.29
Peanuts (nuts)	2 tons	140	22	35	6	5	10	0.04	0.30	0.25
Peanuts (vines)	2.5 tons	100	17	150	88	20	11	0.12	0.15	—
Rye (grain)	30 bu	35	10	10	2	3	7	0.02	0.22	0.03
Rye (straw)	1.5 tons	15	8	25	8	2	3	0.01	0.14	0.07
Sorghum (grain)	80 bu	65	30	22	4	7	10	0.02	0.06	0.05
Sorghum (stover)	4 tons	80	25	115	32	22	—	—	—	—
Soybean (grain)	50 bu	188	41	74	19	10	23	0.05	0.06	0.05
Soybean (stover)	3 tons	89	16	74	30	9	12	—	—	—
Sunflower	50 bu	70	13	30	—	—	12	—	—	—
Wheat (grain)	60 bu	70	20	25	2	10	4	0.04	0.10	0.16
Wheat (straw)	2.5 tons	45	5	65	8	12	15	0.01	0.16	0.05
Forages and Turf										
Alfalfa	6 tons	350	40	300	160	40	44	0.10	0.64	0.62
Bent grass	2 tons	230	22	100	—	—	—	—	—	—
Bluegrass	2 tons	60	12	55	16	7	5	0.02	0.30	0.08
Bromegrass	4 tons	140	22	180	—	15	15	—	—	—
Clover	6 tons	320	40	260	—	—	—	—	—	—
Coastal Bermuda	8 tons	400	45	310	48	32	32	0.02	0.64	0.48
Cowpea	2 tons	120	25	80	55	15	13	—	0.65	—
Fescue	3.5 tons	135	18	160	—	13	20	—	—	—
Orchard grass	6 tons	300	50	320	—	25	35	—	—	—
Red Clover	2.5 tons	100	13	90	69	17	7	0.04	0.54	0.36
Ryegrass	5 tons	215	44	200	—	40	—	—	—	—
Sorghum—Sudan	8 tons	320	55	400	—	47	—	—	—	—
Soybean	2 tons	90	12	40	40	18	10	0.04	0.46	0.15
Timothy	4 tons	150	24	190	18	6	5	0.03	0.31	0.20
Vetch	6 tons	360	38	250	—	—	—	—	—	—
Fruits and Vegetables										
Apples	500 bu	30	10	45	8	5	10	0.03	0.03	0.03
Bean, Dry	30 bu	75	25	25	2	2	5	0.02	0.03	0.06
Bell Peppers	180 cwt	137	52	217	—	43	—	—	—	—
Cabbage	20 tons	130	35	130	20	8	44	0.04	0.10	0.08
Onion	7.5 tons	45	20	40	11	2	18	0.03	0.08	0.31
Peach	600 bu	35	20	65	4	8	2	—	—	0.01
Peas	25 cwt	164	35	105	—	18	10	—	—	—
Potato (sweet)	300 bu	40	18	96	4	4	6	0.02	0.06	0.03
Potato (white)	15 tons	90	48	158	5	7	7	0.06	0.14	0.08

(continued)

Table 9-1 (Continued)

Crop	*Yield*	*N*	*P*	*K*	*Ca*	*Mg*	*S*	*Cu*	*Mn*	*Zn*
	unit/a					*lbs/a*				
Snap Bean	4 tons	138	33	163	—	17	—	—	—	—
Spinach	5 tons	50	15	30	12	5	4	0.02	0.10	0.10
Sweet Corn	90 cwt	140	47	136	—	20	11	—	—	—
Tomato	20 tons	120	40	160	7	11	14	0.07	0.13	0.16
Turnip	10 tons	45	20	90	12	6	—	—	—	—
Other Crops										
Cotton (seed+lint)	1.3 tons	63	25	31	4	7	5	0.18	0.33	0.96
Cotton (stalk +leaf)	1.5 tons	57	16	72	56	16	15	0.05	0.06	0.75
Sugar beet	20 tons	200	20	320	—	50	25	—	—	—
Sugarcane	40 tons	180	40	250	—	25	22	—	—	—
Tobacco (burley)	2 tons	145	14	150	—	18	24	—	—	—
Tobacco (flue cure)	1.5 tons	85	15	155	75	15	12	0.03	0.55	0.07

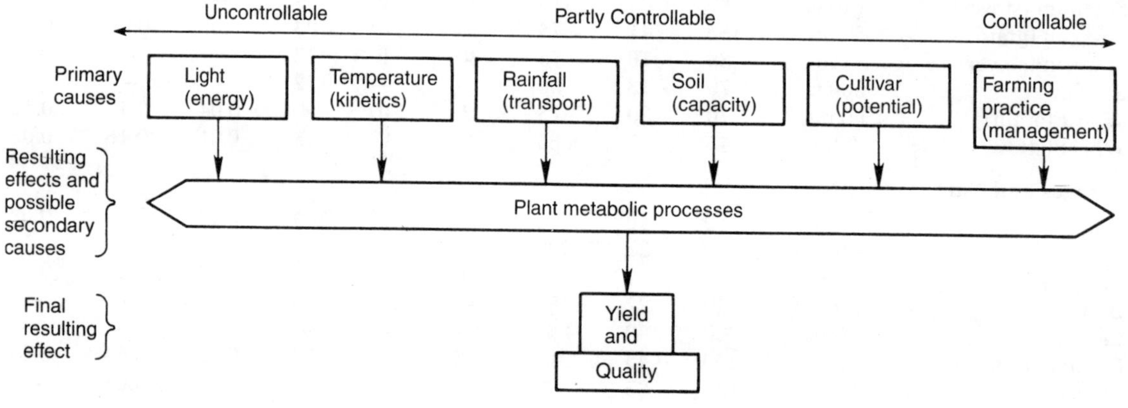

Figure 9-1 **Schematic representation of the interrelationships between crop yield and quality, metabolic process, and external and genetic factors.** ***(Beaufils, 1973,*** **Soil Sci. Bull. 1,** ***Pietermaritzburg, South Africa Univ. of Natal.)***

processes are inhibited. Visual evaluation of nutrient stress should be used only to support or direct other diagnostic techniques (i.e., soil and plant analysis).

In addition to leaf symptoms, nutrient deficiencies have a marked effect on root growth (Fig. 9-2). Plant roots receive less attention because of the difficulty of observing them; however, considering that roots absorb nutrients, inspection of root growth is an important diagnostic tool. Effects of nutrients on root growth are described in Chapters 2 to 5.

Each symptom must be related to some nutrient function in the plant (Chapters 4 to 8). A nutrient may have several functions, making it difficult to identify the reason for a particular deficiency symptom. For example, with N deficiency, plant leaves become pale green or light yellow. When N is limiting, chlorophyll production and leaf greenness is reduced, allowing yellow pigments (carotene and xanthophylls) to prevail. Several nutrient deficiencies produce pale-green or yellow leaves, thus the symptom must be further related to a particular leaf pattern or location.

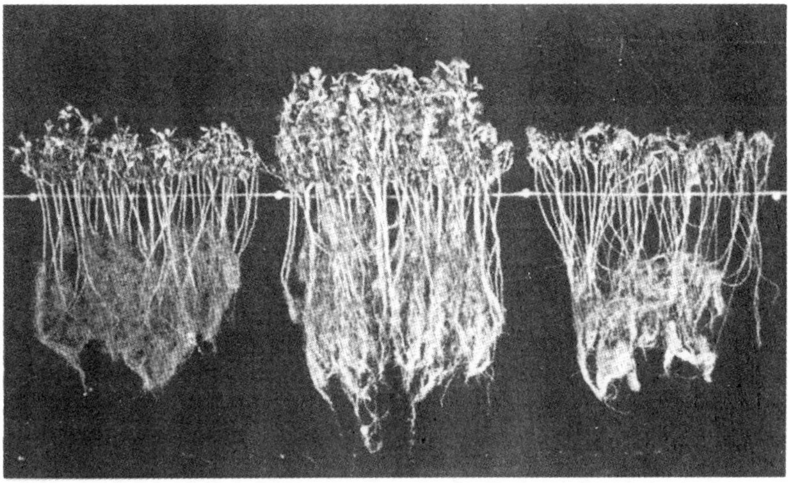

Figure 9-2 **Omitting P (left) or K (right) reduced the growth of alfalfa roots as well as tops the spring after seeding in soil deficient in P and K.** ***(Courtesy Potash & Phosphate Inst., Atlanta, Ga.)***

Visual deficiency symptoms can be related to factors other than nutrient stress. Precautions in interpreting nutrient deficiency symptoms include:

1. The visual symptom may be caused by more than one nutrient. For example, N-deficiency symptoms may be identified, although S deficiency may also be apparent.
2. Deficiency of one nutrient may be related to toxicity or imbalance of another. For example, Mn deficiency may be induced by excessive Fe in soils that are marginally deficient in Mn. Also, plants poorly supplied with P may have lower N needs compared to those with adequate P. In other words, once one limiting factor is eliminated, a second factor may appear (Liebig's Law of the Minimum).
3. It is difficult to distinguish among the deficiency symptoms in the field, because disease, insect, or herbicide damage can resemble certain micronutrient deficiencies. For example, leaf hopper damage can be confused with B deficiency in alfalfa.
4. A visual symptom may be caused by more than one factor. For example, sugars in corn combine with flavones to form anthocyanins (purple, red, and yellow pigments), and their accumulation may be caused by an insufficient supply of P, low soil temperature, insect damage to the roots, or N deficiency.

Nutrient deficiency symptoms appear when nutrient supply is so low that the plant cannot function properly. In such cases, supplemental nutrients were needed long before the symptoms appeared. If the symptom is observed early, it might be corrected during the growing season with foliar or sidedress applications. However, yield is often reduced below optimum if adequate nutrients are not available at planting. Diagnosis of nutrient deficiency late in the growing season can still be useful in correcting the deficiency the following year.

A simple, easy-to-use leaf color chart has been developed for effective N management of irrigated rice in Asia. Crop N status is periodically assessed by comparing rice leaf color with four panels of critical colors in the chart. Farmers are alerted to the best time for top-dressing N as plants begin to show N-deficiency symptoms. Rating of turf quality is often done by means of a color chart.

With most nutrients, significant responses can be obtained even though no recognizable symptoms have appeared. The question, then, is how to identify *hidden hunger*, the nutrient status when deficiency symptoms are not visible but nutrient levels are considerably under those needed for optimum yield. Soil and plant analysis is essential to nutrient-management programs to avoid yield loss from nutrient stress.

Nutrients may be present in sufficient quantities under ideal conditions, but in drought, excessive moisture, or unusual temperature conditions, plants may be unable to absorb adequate nutrients. For example, with cooler temperatures, nutrient uptake is generally reduced because

- mass flow of nutrients is reduced by decreased growth rate and transpiration,
- diffusion rate decreases with declining temperature and a lower concentration gradient, and
- mineralization of organic, complexed nutrients is reduced.

Nutrient-deficiency symptoms appearing during early growth may disappear as the growing season progresses, or there may be no measurable yield benefit from nutrient additions. For example, P may improve early crop growth, but at harvest there may be no measurable yield response. Such occurrences are probably related to seasonal effects or to root penetration into soil areas having higher fertility levels.

To assure that nutrients do not limit plant growth, nutrient availability should be high enough to take advantage of optimum growing conditions and to prevent climate-related nutrient stress. Plant nutrient analysis can be an invaluable tool in identifying hidden hunger or verifying the nutrient stress suspected from the visual deficiency symptom.

Plant Analysis

Plant analysis methods include tests on fresh tissue in the field and tissue analysis performed in the laboratory. Plant analyses are based on the relationship between nutrients in a plant and nutrient availability in the soil. Since a nutrient shortage will limit growth, other nutrients may accumulate, regardless of their supply. For example, if NO_3^- in the plant is low, P content may be high. This is no indication, however, that under adequate N supply, P would be adequate. Plant analyses are performed for the following reasons:

- to identify deficiency symptoms and to determine nutrient shortages before they appear as symptoms,
- to aid in determining the nutrient supplying capacity of the soil (employed in conjunction with soil tests and management history),
- to aid in determining the effect of nutrient addition on the nutrient supply in the plant, and
- to study the relationship between nutrient status of the plant and crop performance.

Tissue Tests

Rapid nutrient analysis on fresh tissue is important in diagnosing the nutrient needs of growing plants. The nutrient concentration in the cell sap can be a good indication of nutrient supply at the time of testing. Through the proper application of tissue testing, it is possible to anticipate or forecast certain nutrient-related production problems while the crop is still in the field.

Tissue tests are easy to conduct and interpret, and many tests can be made in a few minutes. Because laboratory tests take longer, there is a tendency to guess rather than send samples to the laboratory. It is important to recognize that application of nutrients to correct a nutrient stress identified with a tissue test may not be feasible because (1) the deficiency may have already caused yield loss, (2) the crop may not respond to the applied nutrient at the specific growth stage tested, (3) the crop may be too large to apply nutrients, and (4) climatic conditions may be unfavorable for fertilization and/or for the crop to benefit from nutrient additions.

Cell Sap Tests Semiquantitative estimates of plant N, P, and K can be rapidly obtained with simple plant-tissue tests conducted in the field. Plant leaves or stems are chopped up and extracted with reagents specific for each nutrient. Plant tissue can also be squeezed with pliers to transfer plant sap to filter paper and color-developing reagents are then added. The color intensity of the cell sap/reagent mix is compared with a standard chart that indicates very low, low, medium, or high nutrient content. Plant tissue test kits are readily available and inexpensive. It is essential to test the plant part that gives the best indication of nutrient status (Fig. 9-3). In general, the conductive tissue of the latest mature leaf is used for testing, while immature leaves at the top of the plant are avoided. Time of day can affect tissue N concentrations. To reduce variability, samples should be collected in the morning. Plant nutrient content varies; thus, test 10 to 15 plants and average the results. Also, test plants from deficient areas and compare them with plants from normal areas.

If a plant is discolored or stunted and tissue tests show high N, P, and K content, then some other factor is limiting growth. Further diagnostic tests are essential to identify limiting growth factor(s). Thus, accurate tissue-test interpretation can only occur if other growth factors are nonlimiting (e.g., moisture, disease, etc.). Generally, low to medium N, P, or K levels early in the growing season means yield will likely be less than optimum. At bloom stage, medium to high levels are adequate in most crops. Recommended sampling times are similar to those for total tissue analysis.

Total Analysis Total analysis is performed on the whole plant or specific plant parts (e.g., petioles, stems, leaves) in the laboratory. After sampling, the plant material is dried, ground, and the nutrient content determined following wet digestion with concentrated acid or dry ashing in a high-temperature oven. With total analysis, content of all elements, essential and nonessential, can be determined. As in tissue tests, the plant part selected is important, with the most recently matured leaf preferred (Table 9-2).

Care must be taken in treatment of the samples before analysis. Samples should be kept cold or refrigerated and protected from contamination by soil, dust, fertilizer materials, and so on.

Sampling Time. Growth stage is important in plant analysis because nutrient status and demand varies during the season. Nutrient concentration in vegetative parts usually decreases with maturity (Fig. 9-4). Misinterpretation of plant analysis results are common if sampling time is not identified correctly. For example, corn leaves sampled at silking would be considered N deficient if compared with normal 4 to 6 leaf-stage

Sampling Chart

Plant	Test	Part to sample	(To avoid hidden hunger) Minimum level
Corn			
Under 15 in.	NO_3	Midrib, basal leaf	High
	PO_4	Midrib, basal leaf	Medium
	K	Midrib, basal leaf	High
15 in. to ear showing	NO_3	Base of stalk	High
	PO_4	Midrib, first mature leaf*	Medium
	K	Midrib, first mature leaf*	High
Ear to very early dent	NO_3	Base of stalk	High
	PO_4	Midrib, first below ear	Medium
	K	Midrib, first below ear	Medium
Soybeans			
Early growth to midseason	NO_3	Not tested	
	PO_4	Pulvinus (swollen base of petiole), first mature leaf*	High High
	K	Petiole, first mature leaf	High
Midseason to good pod development	PO_4	Pulvinus, first mature leaf	Medium
	K	Petiole, first mature leaf	Medium
Cotton			
To early bloom	NO_3	Petiole, basal leaf*	High
	PO_4	Petiole, basal leaf*	High
	K	Petiole, basal leaf*	High
Boll setting to 2/3 maturity	NO_3	Petiole, first mature leaf*	High
	PO_4	Petiole, first mature leaf*	High
	K	Petiole, first mature leaf*	High
2/3 maturity to maturity	NO_3	Petiole, first mature leaf*	Medium
	PO_4	Petiole, first mature leaf*	Medium
	K	Petiole, first mature leaf*	Medium
Alfalfa			
Before first cutting	PO_4	Middle 1/3 of stem	High
	K	Middle 1/3 of stem	High
Before other cuttings	PO_4	Middle 1/3 of stem	Medium
	K	Middle 1/3 of stem	Medium
Small Grains			
Shoot stage to milk stage	NO_3	Lower stem	High
	PO_4	Lower stem	Medium
	K	Lower stem	Medium

*First Mature Leaf—Avoid the immature leaves at the top of the plant. Take the most recently fully matured leaf near the top of the plant.

Figure 9-3 **Part of the plant used for tissue tests.** *(Wickstrom et al, 1964,* **Better Crops Plant Food,** *47(3):18.)*

N concentration (Table 9-3). In most agricultural crops the two best sampling times coincide with peak periods of dry matter and plant nutrient accumulation. The first peak occurs during the maximum vegetative growth period (Fig. 10-1), with the second peak during the reproductive stage. Plants from both deficient and normal areas should be sampled to compare results.

Table 9-2 **Plant Sampling Guidelines for Selected Agricultural and Horticultural Crops**

Crop	*Sampling Time*	*Plant Part Sampled*	*Sample #*
Field Crops			
Alfalfa	Early bloom	Top 6 in. or upper 1/3 of plant	20–30
Canola	Before seed set	Newest mature leaf	50–60
Clover	Before bloom	Upper 1/3 of plant	30–40
Corn/sweet corn	Seedling stage	All above-ground material	25–30
	Before tasseling	Fully mature leaf from top of plant	15–20
	Tasseling to silking	Leaf blow and opposite ear	15–20
Cotton	Full bloom	Newest mature leaf from main stem	30–40
Grasses/forage mixes	Stage of best quality	Upper leaves	40–50
Peanuts	Before or at bloom	Newest mature leaf	40–50
Small grains	Seedling stage	All above-ground material	25–40
	Before heading	Uppermost leaf blades	25–40
Sorghum	Before or at heading	Leaf from top of plant	20–30
Soybean	Before or at bloom	Newest mature leaf from top of plant	20–30
Sugar beet	Midseason	Newest mature leaf, center of whorl	30–40
Sunflower	Before heading	Newest mature leaf	20–30
Tobacco	Before bloom	Top fully developed leaf	8–10
Vegetable Crops			
Asparagus	Maturity	18–30 inches above ground line	10–20
Beans	Seedling stage	All above-ground portions	20–30
	Before or at bloom	Newest mature leaf	20–30
Beets, table	Mature	Young mature leaf	20–30
Broccoli	Before heading	Newest mature leaf	12–20
Brussels sprouts	Midseason	Newest mature leaf	12–20
Cabbage, cauliflower	Before heading	Newest mature leaf, center of whorl	10–20
Celery	Midseason	Outer petiole of newest mature leaf	12–20
Cucumber	Before fruit set	Newest mature leaf	12–20
Eggplant	Early fruiting	Young mature leaf	15–25
Garlic	Bulbing	Young mature leaf	25–35
Lettuce, spinach	Midseason	Newest mature leaf	15–25
Melons	Before fruit set	Newest mature leaf	15–25
Peas	Before or at bloom	Leaves from node from top	40–60
Peppers	Midseason	Recently mature leaf	25–50
Potato	Before or at bloom	Leaf from growing tip	25–30
Pumpkin/Squash	Early fruiting	Young mature leaf	15–25
Radishes	Midgrowth to harvest	Young mature leaf	40–50
Root crops (carrot, beet, onion)	Before root or bulb enlargement	Newest mature leaf	25–35
Sweet potato	Midseason	Leaf from tip center	20–30
	Before root enlargement	Mature leaves	25–35
Tomato (field)	Early-midbloom	Leaf from growing tip	15–25
Tomato (trellis or indeterminate)	Midbloom from 1st–6th cluster stage	Petiole of leaf below or opposite top cluster	15–25

(*continued*)

Table 9-2 **(Continued)**

Crop	*Sampling Time*	*Plant Part Sampled*	*Sample #*
Ornamentals and Flowers			
Carnation	Newly planted	4th–5th leaf pair from base of plant	20–30
	Established	5th–6th leaf pair from base of plant	20–30
Chrysanthemum	Before or at bloom	Top leaves on flowering stem	20–30
Poinsettia	Before or at bloom	Newest mature leaf	15–25
Rose	At bloom	Newest mature compound leaf on flowering stem	25–30
Trees and shrubs	Current year growth	Newest mature leaf	30–70
Turf	Active growth	Leaf blades—avoid soil contamination	2 cups
Fruit and Nut Crops			
Apple, pear, almond, apricot, cherry, prune, plum	Midseason	Leaves from current year growth—nonfruiting, nonexpanding spurs	50–100
Blueberries	First week of harvest	Young mature leaf	50–70
Cantaloupe	Early fruiting	Fifth leaf from tip	25–35
Grapes	At bloom	Petioles or leaves adjacent to basal clusters at bloom	50–100
Lemon, lime	Midseason	Mature leaf from last growth flush, nonfruiting terminals	30–40
Orange	Midseason	Spring cycle leaf, 4–7 months old, nonfruiting terminals	25–35
Peach, nectarine	Midseason	Midshoot leaflets/leaves	25–100
Pecan	Midseason	Midshoot leaflets/leaves	25–60
Pistachios	Mid- to late season	Terminal leaflets, nonfruiting shoots	25–60
Raspberries	Midseason	Newest mature leaf, laterals of primocanes	30–50
Strawberries	Midseason	Newest mature leaves	25–40
Walnut	6–8 weeks after bloom	Terminal leaflets/leaves from nonfruiting shoots	25–40
Watermelon	Midgrowth	Newest mature leaf	15–25

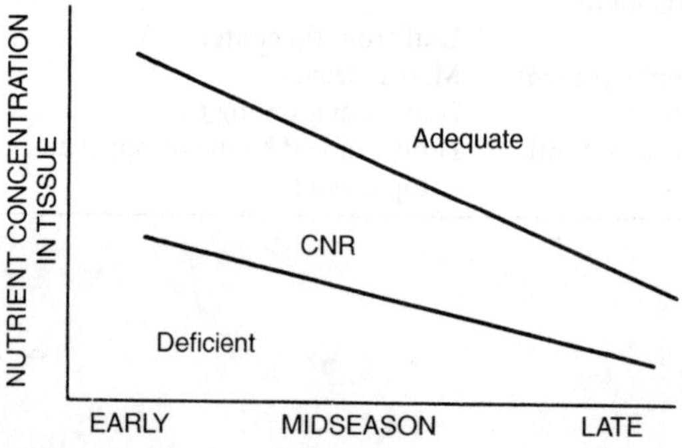

Figure 9-4 **General relationship between nutrient concentration in leaves over the growing season.** ***(Dow and Roberts, 1982, Agron. J., 74:401.)***

Table 9-3 Critical Nutrient Ranges for Selected Crops

Corn				
Nutrient	*Whole Plant 24–45 Days**	*Third Leaf, 45–80 Days†*	*Earleaf Green Silks‡*	*Earleaf Brown Silks§*
N, %	4.0–5.0	3.5–4.5	3.0–4.0	2.8–3.5
P, %	0.40–0.60	0.35–0.50	0.30–0.45	0.25–0.40
K, %	3.0–5.0	2.0–3.5	2.0–3.0	1.8–2.5
Ca, %	0.51–1.60	0.20–0.80	0.20–1.0	0.20–1.2
Mg, %	0.30–0.60	0.20–0.60	0.20–0.80	0.20–0.80
S, %	0.18–0.40	0.18–0.40	0.18–0.40	0.18–0.35
B, ppm	6–25	6–25	5–25	5–25
Cu, ppm	6–20	6–20	5–20	5–20
Fe, ppm	40–500	25–250	30–250	30–250
Mn, ppm	40–160	20–150	20–150	20–150
Zn, ppm	25–60	20–60	20–70	20–70

*Seedlings 6 to 16 in. tall; 24 to 45 days after planting.
† Third leaf from top; plants over 12 in. tall; before silking.
‡Seventy to ninety days after planting.
§Grain in developing stage up to "roasting ear."
SOURCE: Schulte and Kelling, 1985, *National Corn Handbook,* NCH-46, Purdue Univ. Coop. Ext. Service.

Soybean		Small Grain	
Nutrient	*Sufficiency Range**		*Sufficiency Range*
N, %	4.3–5.5	winter / spring grains	1.75–3.0 / 2.0–3.0
P, %	0.3–0.5		0.20–0.50
K, %	1.7–2.5		1.5–3.0
Ca, %	0.4–2.0	barley / all other	0.30–1.2 / 0.20–0.50
Mg, %	0.3–1.0		0.15–0.50
S, %	0.4–0.8		0.15–0.40
Mn, ppm	21–100		25–100
Fe, ppm	51–350		40–250
Zn, ppm	21–50		15–70
Cu, ppm	10–30		5–25
B, ppm	21–55		
Mo, ppm	1.0–5.0		

*Upper fully developed trifoliate leaves sampled before pod set.

(continued)

Table 9-3 (Continued)

Alfalfa

Plant Part	*N*	*P*	*K*	*S*	*Ca*	*Mg*
	%					
Top 6 in.	4.0–5.0	0.20–0.30	1.8–2.4	0.18–0.30	0.8–1.5	0.2–0.3
Upper 1/3	—	0.18–0.22	1.7–2.0	0.20–0.30	—	—
Whole tops	—	0.20–0.25	1.5–2.2	0.20–0.24	1.4–2.0	0.28–0.32
N:S tops	—	—	—	12–17	—	—

Turfgrass

Nutrient	*Bermuda-grass*	*Coastal Bermuda*	*Creeping Bentgrass*	*Fescue*	*Kentucky Bluegrass*	*Perennial Ryegrass*	*St. Augustine-grass*
N, %	4.0–6.0	1.8–2.2	4.5–6.0	2.8–3.4	2.4–2.8	3.34–5.1	1.9–3.0
P, %	0.25–0.6	0.2–0.3	0.3–0.6	0.26–0.32	0.24–0.3	0.35–0.55	0.2–0.5
K, %	1.5–4.0	1.8–2.1	2.2–2.6	2.5–2.8	1.6–2.0	2.0–3.42	2.5–4.0
Ca, %	0.5–1.0	0.4–0.7	0.5–0.75	0.4–0.6	0.25–0.55	0.25–0.51	0.3–0.5
Mg, %	0.13–0.4	0.2–0.3	0.25–0.3	0.12–0.28	0.28–0.33	0.16–0.32	0.15–0.25
S, %	0.2–0.5	0.28–0.4	—	0.24–0.5	0.26–0.45	0.27–0.56	—
Fe, ppm	50–500	—	100–300	—	—	97–934	50–300
Mn, ppm	25–300	—	50–100	—	—	30–73	40–250
Cu, ppm	5–50	—	8–30	—	—	6–38	10–20
Zn, ppm	20–250	—	25–75	—	—	14–64	20–100
B, ppm	6–30	—	8–20	—	—	5–17	5–10
Mo, ppm	0.1–1.2	—	—	—	—	0.5–1.0	—

Fruits and Vegetables

Crop	*N*	*P*	*K*	*Ca*	*Mg*	*S*	*Fe*	*B*	*Cu*	*Zn*	*Mn*	*Mo*
	%							*ppm*				
Apples	1.9–2.3	0.1–0.4	1.2–1.8	0.8–1.6	0.25–0.45	0.2–0.4	50–200	30–50	6–12	20–50	25–135	> 0.1
Asparagus	2.4–3.8	0.25–0.5	1.5–2.4	0.4–1.0	0.25–0.3	—	40–250	40–100	5–25	20–60	25–160	—
Bean, snap	5.0–6.0	0.25–0.75	2.2–4.0	1.5–3.0	0.25–0.7	—	50–300	20–60	7–30	20–60	50–300	> 0.4
Beets, table	3.5–5.0	0.25–0.5	3.0–4.5	2.5–3.5	0.30–1.0	—	50–200	30–80	5–15	15–30	70–200	—
Blueberries	1.7–2.1	0.10–0.4	0.4–0.7	0.35–0.8	0.12–0.25	0.12–0.3	70–200	25–70	5–20	9–30	50–600	—
Broccoli	3.2–5.5	0.3–0.7	2.0–4.0	1.2–2.5	0.23–0.4	0.3–0.75	50–150	30–100	4–10	20–80	25–150	0.3–0.5
Brussels sprouts	3.1–5.5	0.3–0.75	2.0–4.0	1.0–2.5	0.25–0.75	0.3–0.75	60–300	30–100	5–15	25–200	25–200	0.25–1.0
Cabbage	3.6–5.0	0.33–0.75	3.0–5.0	1.1–3.0	0.4–0.75	0.3–0.75	30–200	25–75	5–15	20–200	25–200	0.4–0.7
Cantaloupe	4.5–5.5	0.3–0.8	4.0–5.0	2.3–3.0	0.35–0.8	0.25–1.0	40	50–300	25–60	7–30	20–200	50–250
Carrot	2.5–3.5	0.2–0.3	2.8–4.3	1.4–3.0	0.3–0.5	—	50–300	30–100	5–15	25–250	60–200	0.5–1.5
Cauliflower	3.3–4.5	0.33–0.80	2.6–4.2	2.0–3.5	0.27–0.50	—	30–200	30–100	4–15	20–250	25–250	0.5–0.8
Celery	2.5–3.5	0.3–0.5	4.0–7.0	0.6–3.0	0.20–0.50	—	30–70	30–60	5–8	20–70	100–300	—
Cucumber	4.5–6.0	0.3–1.3	3.5–5.0	1.0–3.5	0.3–1.0	0.3–0.7	50–300	25–60	5–20	25–100	50–300	—
Eggplant	4.2–5.0	0.45–0.6	5.7–6.5	1.7–2.2	0.25–0.35	—	—	20–30	4–6	30–50	15–100	—
Garlic	3.4–4.5	0.28–0.5	3.0–4.5	1.0–1.8	0.23–0.35	—	—	—	—	—	—	
Grapes	1.6–2.8	0.2–0.46	1.5–2.0	1.2–2.5	0.3–0.4	—	40–180	25–50	5–10	25–100	25–100	0.2–0.4
Lettuce	2.5–4.0	0.4–0.6	6.0–8.0	1.4–2.0	0.5–0.7	—	50–500	30–100	7–10	26–100	30–90	> 0.1
Onion	5.0–6.0	0.35–0.5	4.0–5.5	1.5–3.5	0.3–0.5	0.50–1.0	60–300	30–45	5–10	20–55	50–65	—
Peas	4.0–6.0	0.3–0.8	2.0–3.5	1.2–2.0	0.3–0.7	0.2–0.4	50–300	25–60	5–10	25–100	30–400	> 0.6
Peppers	3.5–4.5	0.3–0.7	4.0–5.4	0.4–0.6	0.30–1.50	—	60–300	30–100	10–20	30–100	26–300	—
Potato (leaf)	3.5–4.5	0.25–0.5	4.0–6.0	0.5–0.9	0.25–0.5	0.2–0.35	30–150	20–40	5–20	20–40	20–450	—
Potato (petiole)	—	0.22–0.4	8.0–10.0	0.6–1.0	0.3–0.55	0.2–0.35	50–200	20–40	4–20	20–40	30–300	—
Pumpkin/ Squash	4.0–6.0	0.35–1.0	4.0–6.0	1.0–2.5	0.3–1.0	—	60–300	25–75	6–25	20–200	50–250	—
Radish	3.0–6.0	0.30–0.70	4.0–7.5	3.0–4.5	0.50–1.20	0.20–0.40	50–200	30–50	6–12	20–50	25–130	—
Raspberries	2.2–3.5	0.20–0.50	1.1–3.0	0.6–2.5	0.25–0.80	0.20–0.30	50–200	25–300	4–20	15–60	25–300	—
Spinach	4.2–5.2	0.30–0.60	5.0–8.0	0.6–1.2	0.60–1.00	—	60–200	25–60	5–25	25–100	30–250	> 0.5
Strawberry	2.1–2.9	0.2–0.35	1.1–2.5	0.6–1.8	0.25–0.7	0.2–0.3	90–150	25–60	6–20	20–50	30–100	—
Sweet corn	2.8–3.5	0.25–0.4	1.8–3.0	0.6–1.1	0.2–0.5	0.2–0.75	50–300	8–25	5–25	20–100	30–300	0.9–1.0
Tomato	4.0–6.0	0.25–0.8	2.9–5.0	1.0–3.0	0.4–0.60	0.4–1.2	40–200	25–60	5–20	20–50	40–250	—
Watermelon	2.0–3.0	0.2–0.3	2.5–3.5	2.5–3.5	0.6–0.8	—	100–300	30–80	4–8	20–60	60–240	—

SOURCE: C. J. Rosen and R. Eliason, 1996, *Nutrient Management for Commercial Fruit & Vegetable Crops in Minnesota,* Univ. of Minnesota, DG-05886-GO.

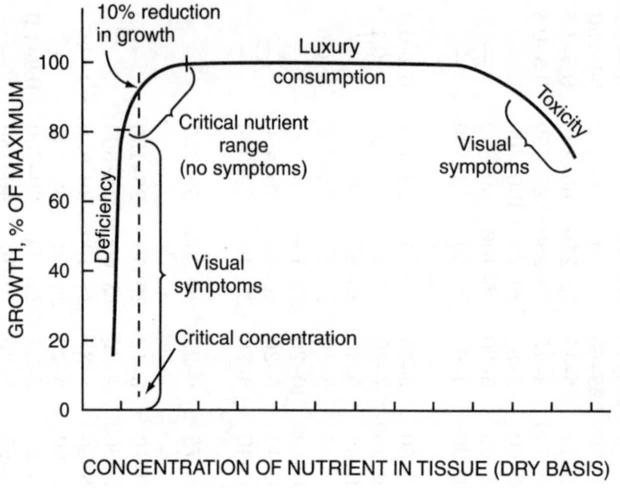

Figure 9-5 **Relationship between plant nutrient concentration and crop yield. Critical nutrient range (CNR) represents an economic yield loss without visual deficiency symptoms.**

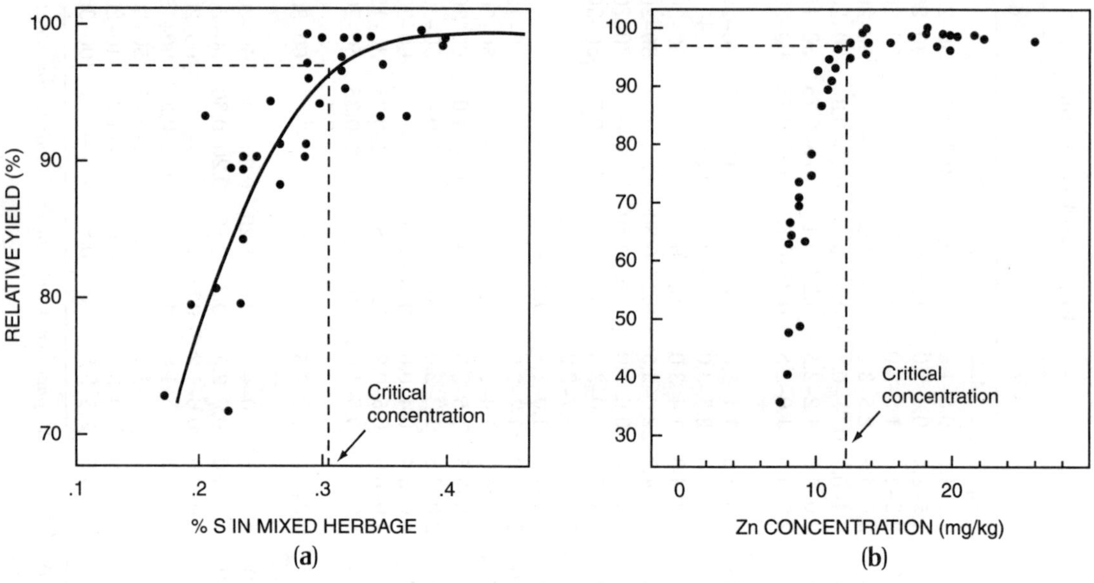

Figure 9-6 **Influence of increasing S concentration in forage on clover yield (a) and increasing Zn concentration in leaves on wheat growth (b).**

Interpretation. Plants that are *severely* deficient in an essential nutrient exhibit a visual deficiency symptom (Fig. 9-5). Plants that are *moderately* deficient usually exhibit no visual symptoms, although yield potential is reduced. Added nutrients will maximize yield potential and increase plant nutrient concentration. *Luxury consumption* represents nutrient absorption in excess of that required for optimum growth. Thus, as nutrient supply increases, plant nutrient concentration increases without an increase in yield. Nutrient toxicity occurs when plant growth and yield decrease with increasing plant nutrient concentration.

The critical nutrient concentration (CNC) is commonly used in interpreting plant analysis results (Fig. 9-6). The CNC is located in that portion of the curve where the plant nutrient concentration changes from deficient to adequate; therefore, CNC is the nutrient level below which crop yield, quality, or performance is unsatisfactory. For example, CNCs in corn are about 3% N, 0.3% P, and 2% K in the leaf opposite and below the uppermost ear at silking time (Table 9-3). For crops such as sugar beets or malting barley, in which excessive concentrations of N seriously affect quality, the CNC for N is a maximum rather than a minimum.

It is difficult to establish an exact CNC since considerable variation exists in the transition zone between deficient and adequate nutrient concentrations. Consequently, critical nutrient range (CNR) is used, which is the range in nutrient concentration at a specific growth stage above which nutrient supply is adequate and below which nutrient deficiency occurs (Fig. 9-5). CNRs have been developed for most of the essential nutrients in many crops (Table 9-3).

Relationship Between Yield and Plant Nutrient Content. When a nutrient is deficient, increasing nutrient availability will increase plant nutrient content and crop yield until CNR is exceeded (Fig. 9-5). For example, applied N increased % N (or grain protein) in wheat (Fig. 9-7) and in corn (Fig. 9-8). Above the CNR, % N increases with no yield advantage.

Plant analysis interpretations based on the CNR and sufficiency-range concepts have limitations. Unless the crop sample is taken at the proper growth stage, the analytical results will have little value (Fig. 9-4). Also, considerable skill in the diagnostician is needed to interpret crop analysis results relative to overall production conditions.

Nutrient Ratios. Plant nutrient ratios can be used to assess crop nutrient balance. For example, N:P, N:S, K:Mg, K:Ca, Ca+Mg:K, and other ratios are commonly used. When a nutrient ratio is optimal, optimum yield occurs unless some other limiting factor reduces yield. When a ratio is low, a response to the nutrient in the numerator may be obtained. If the nutrient in the denominator is excessive, yield response to application of the nutrient in the numerator may or may not occur. When the ratio is too high, the reverse is true. Optimum

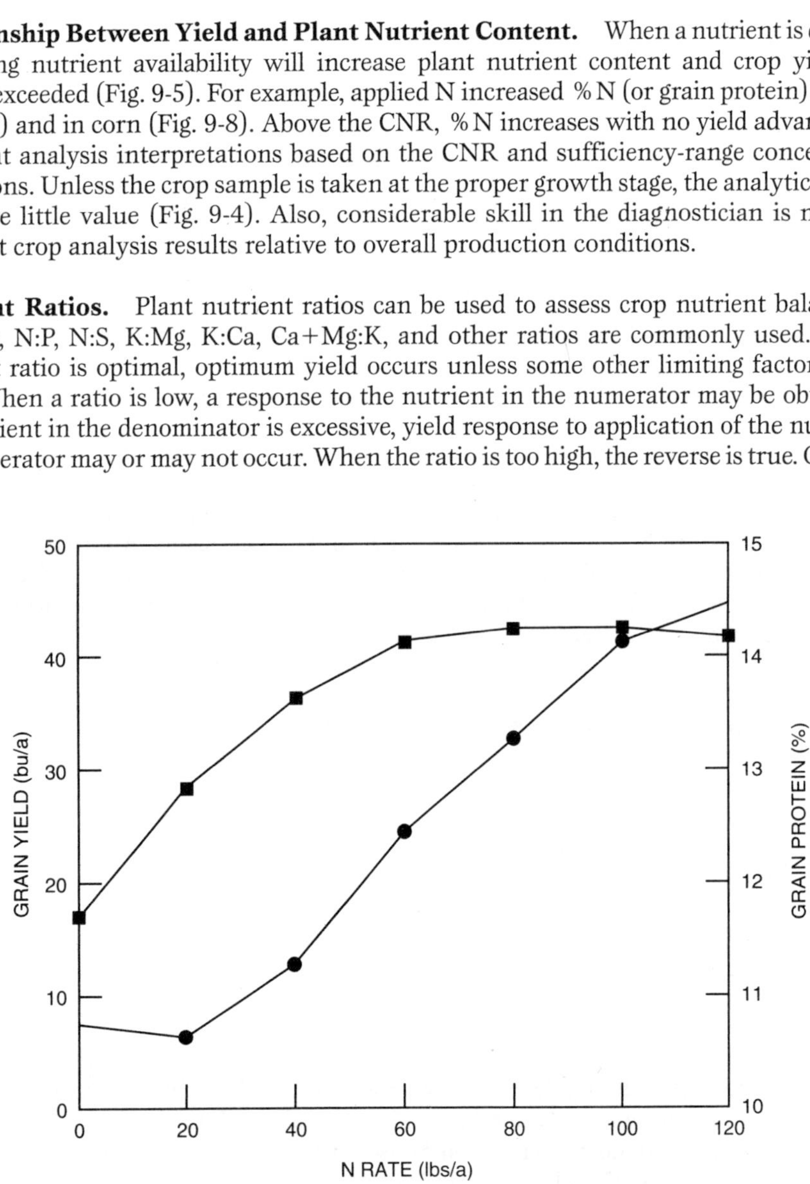

Figure 9-7 Influence of N rate on dryland wheat yield (■) and grain protein content (●). *(Halvorson et al., 1976, N.D.* Farm Res, *33:3–9.)*

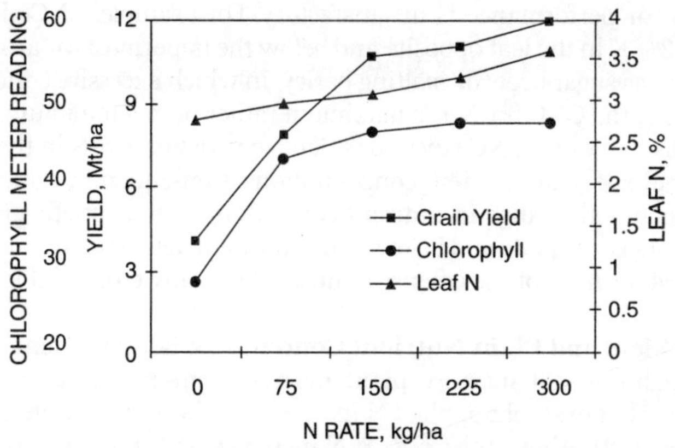

Figure 9-8 **Relationship between irrigated corn grain yield, tissue N, and chlorophyll readings at V8 growth stage. Chlorophyll readings were obtained with a handheld chlorophyll meter.** *(Schepers et al., 1992,* **Great Plains Soil Fert. Conf.,** *p.42.)*

nutrient ratios are established similar to sufficiency levels for individual nutrients (Fig. 9-9). These data illustrate that when S concentration $< 0.12\%$ or N:S < 17, wheat grain yield will likely respond to S fertilization.

Caution should be exercised in interpreting nutrient ratios. For example, when N:S = 17 (Fig. 9-9), three possibilities exist:

- both N and S are optimal,
- both N and S are excessive, or
- both N and S are deficient.

It is not possible to determine from the ratio alone which of the three situations exists in the plant. All that can be said is that the two nutrients are in relative balance. When N:S >17, either N could be excessive or S could be deficient. Alternatively, when N:S < 17, either N could be deficient or S could be excessive. Where N:S > 17, a response to applied S will be obtained only if S is deficient. If N is excessive and S is normal, additional S may not improve the yield. The same is true with N when N:S < 17. This analysis demonstrates why a yield response is not always obtained when a ratio is outside the optimum range.

Tissue Tests for In-Season N Adjustments. Plant analysis is used in many crop systems to determine appropriate nutrient application rates during the growing season. Petiole NO_3 analysis is advised in cotton production to enhance yield and N-use efficiency (Fig. 9-10). Petiole samples of the newest mature cotton leaf are collected at or near first bloom stage and are either sent to a laboratory for NO_3^- analysis or quick-tested using in-field colorimetric analysis of the petiole tissue sap. For example, if first bloom petiole samples tested 0.2% $NO_3^-{-}N$ (Fig. 9-10), then a foliar application of 5 lbs/a of N would be recommended. Usually three foliar applications are required to optimize cotton yield. As the cotton plant matures, petiole NO_3^- declines. Thus, it is essential to identify the growth stage accurately.

In potato, petiole NO_3^- determined 50 to 55 days after emergence is used as a guide for sidedress or topdress N to maximize yield and recovery of applied N (Fig. 9-11). When petiole NO_3^- concentrations are < 1.5 to 2.0%, additional N is recommended. Petiole NO_3^- sufficiency levels will vary depending on crop (Table 9-4) and in some cases the variety (Table 9-5).

In winter wheat, N uptake at mid- (GS25) and late-tillering (GS30) are critical growth stages for maximizing yield and N-use efficiency (Fig. 10-2). When tiller density is < 100 tillers/ft^2 at GS25 and/or % N in leaves at GS30 is $< 4.5\%$, additional N is required to optimize yield (Fig. 9-12).

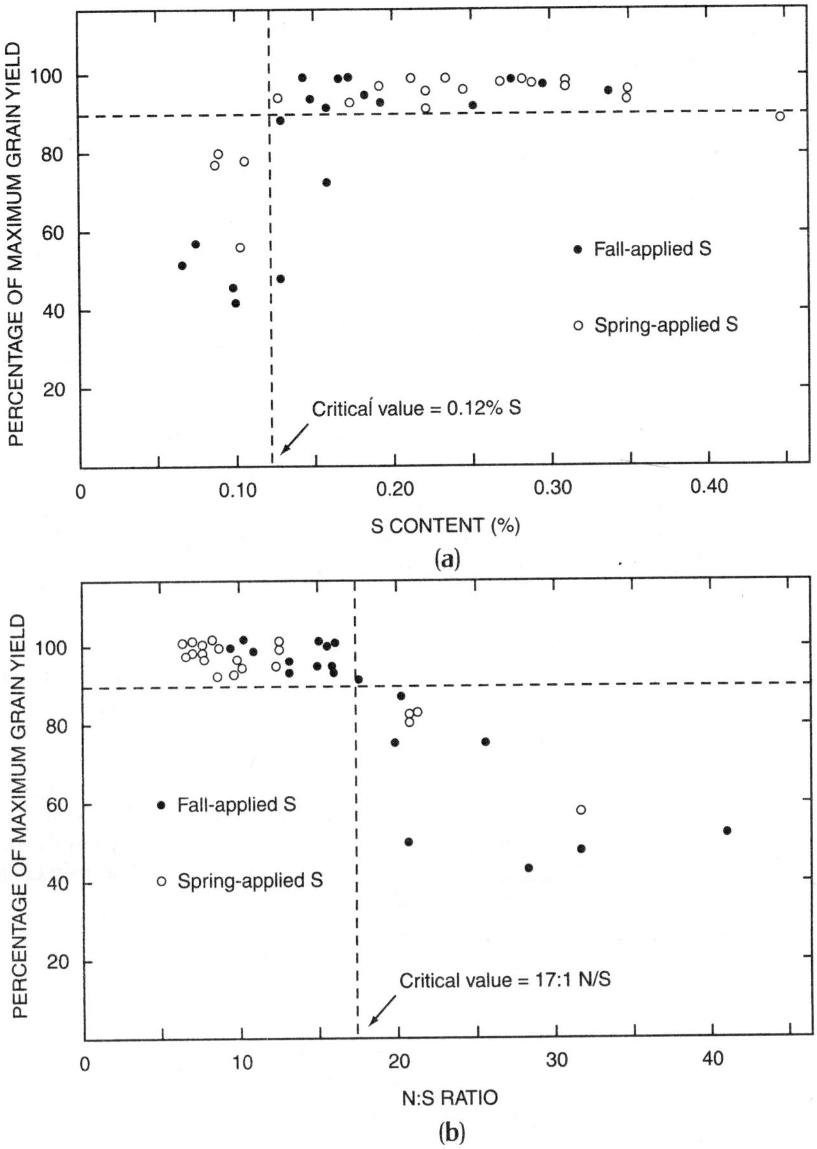

Figure 9-9 **Relationship between winter wheat grain yield and S concentration (a) and N:S ratio (b). N and S were determined in whole plant samples collected at boot stage.**

Sensor-Based Tissue Analysis

Chlorophyll Meters for Plant Nutrient Status. Use of a handheld chlorophyll meter provides a nondestructive method to assess the nutrient status of the crop. Measurements involve placing the handheld chlorophyll meter on a leaf surface, the quantity of light (650 nm) transmitted through the leaf is measured. Increasing chlorophyll content results in decreasing light transmittance. In practice, chlorophyll readings from nutrient-deficient

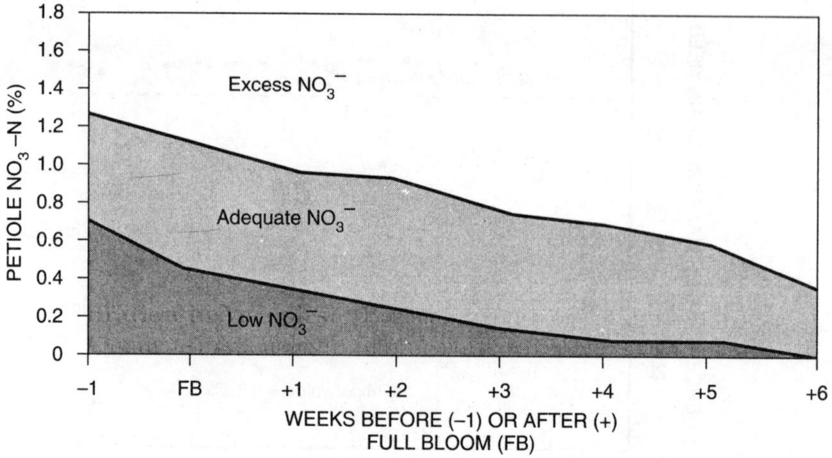

Figure 9-10 Cotton petiole NO_3^- concentration as influenced by sampling time. Foliar N applications would be recommended when petiole NO_3- is low. *(Courtesy Dr. Steve Hodges, 1997, Dept. Soil Science, NCSU.)*

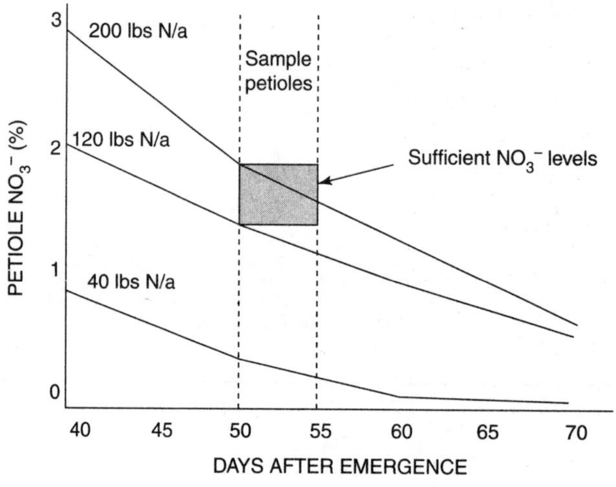

Figure 9-11 Influence of N rate on petiole NO_3 concentration. Optimum petiole NO_3^- concentration is 1.5–2.0% at 50–55 days after emergence. *(Wolkowski et al., 1995,* Nitrogen management on sandy soils, *Madison, WI: Univ. Wisconsin Coop. Ext.* Publ. A3634.*)*

leaves are compared to readings from reference plants where nutrients are nonlimiting. The primary advantage of using a chlorophyll meter is its ability to detect nutrient stress before deficiency symptoms are visible.

Leaf chlorophyll content is highly correlated with % N in the leaf, particularly over the range of yield response to fertilizer N (Fig. 9-8). Increasing N rate increases grain yield and leaf N, but chlorophyll readings do not increase with increasing N applied above that required for optimum yield (Fig. 9-8). Also, chlorophyll readings decrease with plant maturity (Fig. 9-13). For N-management purposes, chlorophyll readings have greater value at an early growth stage because the potential crop response to in-season N applications is greater.

Table 9-4 **Petiole and Midrib NO_3-N Sufficiency Ranges for Selected Vegetable Crops on a Dry Weight and Sap Basis**

			NO_3-N	
Crop	*Tissue*	*Growth Stage*	*% in dry weight*	*ppm in sap*
Broccoli	Midrib	Buttoning	0.9–1.2	800–1100
Cabbage	Midrib	Heading	0.7–0.9	NA
Carrots	Petiole	Midgrowth	0.75–1.0	550–750
Cauliflower	Midrib	Buttoning	0.7–0.9	NA
Celery	Petiole	Midgrowth	0.7–0.9	500–700
Cucumber	Petiole	First blossom	0.75–0.9	800–1000
		Early fruit set	0.5–0.75	600–800
		First harvest	0.4–0.5	400–600
Eggplant	Petiole	Initial fruit	NA	1200–1600
		First harvest	NA	1000–1200
Lettuce	Midrib	Heading	0.6–0.8	NA
Muskmelon	Petiole	First blossom	1.2–1.4	1000–1200
		Initial fruit	0.8–1.0	800–1000
		First mature fruit	0.3–0.5	700–800
Peppers	Petiole	First flower	1.0–1.2	1400–1600
		Early fruit set	0.5–0.7	1200–1400
		Fruit 3/4 size	0.3–0.5	800–1000
Potato	Petiole	Vegetative	1.7–2.2	1200–1600
		Tuber bulking	1.1–1.5	800–1100
		Maturation	0.6–0.9	400–700
Tomato	Petiole	Early bloom	1.4–1.6	1000–1200
		Fruit 1 in. diameter	1.2–1.4	400–600
		Full ripe fruit	0.6–0.8	300–400
Watermelon	Petiole	Early fruit set	0.75–0.9	1000–1200
		Fruit 1/2 size	NA	800–1000
		First harvest	NA	600–800

NA = not applicable.
SOURCE: C.J. Rosen and R. Eliason, 1996, *Nutrient Management for Commercial Fruit & Vegetable Crops in Minnesota,* Univ. of Minnesota, DG–05886-GO.

To help reduce inherent variability in chlorophyll readings in the field, an N-sufficiency index (NSI) is calculated:

$$\text{NSI} = \frac{\text{(average meter reading from unknown area)}}{\text{(average meter reading from area with adequate N)}} \times 100\%$$

When NSI $< 95\%$, additional N is required for optimum corn yield. Chlorophyll readings also can be interpreted directly. For example, in-season N applications would be recommended when chlorophyll meter readings are below 43, 44, and 37 for corn, wheat, and rice, respectively. Chlorophyll meter readings can also be used as a postmortem diagnostic, where low readings would indicate that additional N would have increased yield.

The chlorophyll meter can also be used to identify S deficiency (Fig. 9-14). Chlorophyll meter values of < 45 in the flag leaf indicate S-deficient wheat; these readings are comparable to those for N in corn and wheat (Fig. 9-8).

Table 9-5 **Petiole NO_3-N Sufficiency Ranges at Different Growth Stages for Two Russet Potato Varieties***

Growth Stage	*Description*	*N Sufficiency Range (%)*
	Ranger Russett	
I	Emergence until tuberization	2.0–2.2
II	Tuberization	1.8–2.0
III	Tuber bulking	1.8–2.0
IV	Maturation	1.3–1.5
	Gem Russett	
I	Emergence thru tuberization	2.1–2.3
II	Tuberization	2.1–2.3
III	Early tuber bulking	1.6–1.9
IV	Late tuber bulking	1.0–1 .3
V	Maturation	0.6–1.1

*To convert NO_3^- to NO_3-N, multiply by 0.226.
SOURCE: S. L. Love, 1998, *Cultural Management of Ranger (CIS919) and Gem (CIS1093) Russet Potatoes,* Coop. Ext. System, Univ. of Idaho.

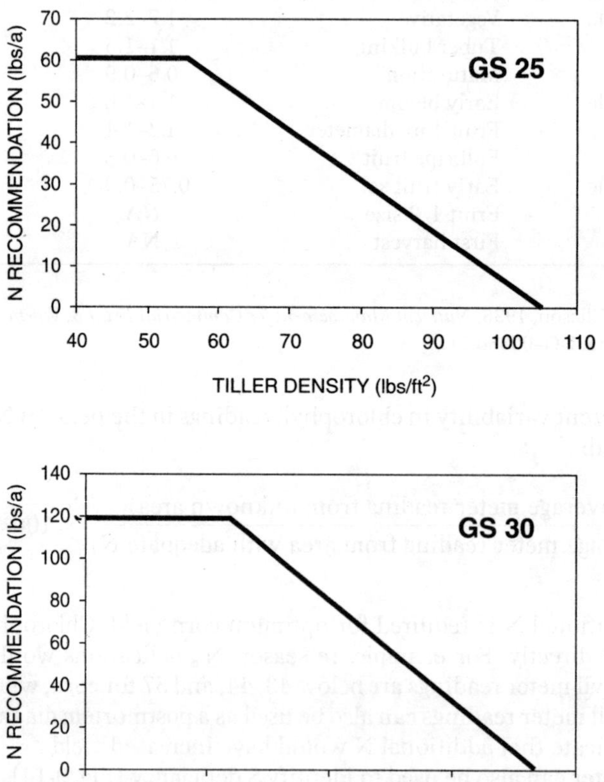

Figure 9-12 **Use of tiller density at GS 25 and tissue N concentration at GS 30 to quantify split N application rates to optimize winter wheat yield and N-use efficiency. *(Alley et al., 1996, Virginia Coop. Ext.,* Publ. No. 424-026.*)***

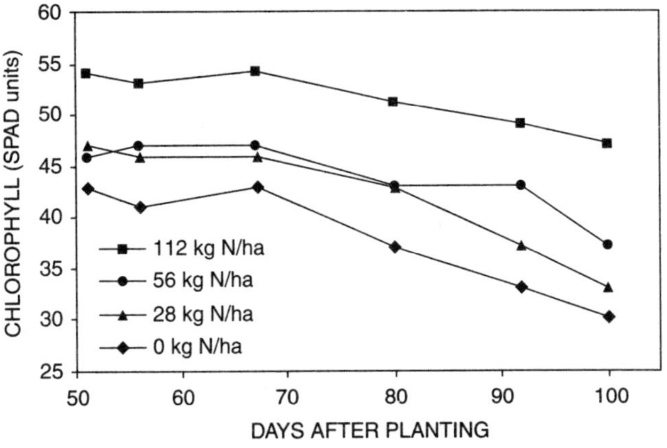

Figure 9-13 **Effect of N rate and crop maturity on chlorophyll meter readings in corn. May 12, 1998 planting data.** ***(Havlin, 1994, unpublished data).***

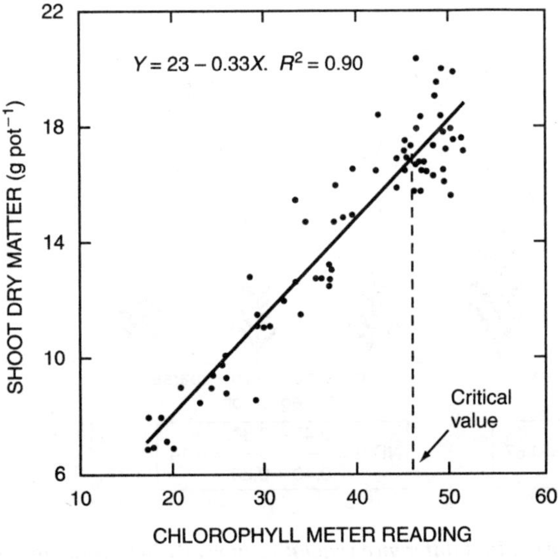

Figure 9-14 **Relationship between chlorophyll content in flag leaves and shoot dry-matter influence by S supply.**

Chlorophyll meter readings identified K deficiency in cotton, where values < 42 represented $\leq 1\%$ K (Fig. 9-15). However, at this leaf K content, it is usually too late to correct K deficiency and realize optimum yield.

Remote Sensing for Crop N Status. Remote sensing applications in production agriculture have advanced rapidly over the last several decades. Visible and near-infrared sensors are commonly used to detect plant stress related to nutrients, water, and pests. When light energy (green, blue, red, and near-infrared wavelengths) strikes a leaf surface, blue and red wavelengths are absorbed by chlorophyll, while green and near-infrared wavelengths are reflected. The reflected light is monitored by an optical sensor. The contrast of light reflectance and absorption by leaves enables assessment of the quantity and quality of vegetation (Fig 9-16). Chlorotic, nutrient-stressed leaves absorb less light energy. A common index used to evaluate vegetation cover is the normalized difference vegetation index, or NDVI, calculated by:

$$\text{NDVI} = \frac{\text{NIR} - \text{PAR}}{\text{NIR} + \text{PAR}}$$

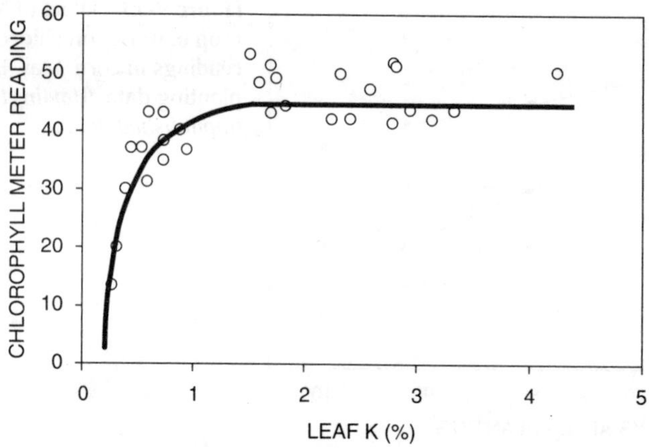

Figure 9-15 **Relationship between leaf K content and chlorophyll meter readings with cotton grown over a range of soil K availability. *(Reddy et al., 2000,* Potassium Nutrition of Cotton, *Mississippi State Univ.,* Bull. 1094.)**

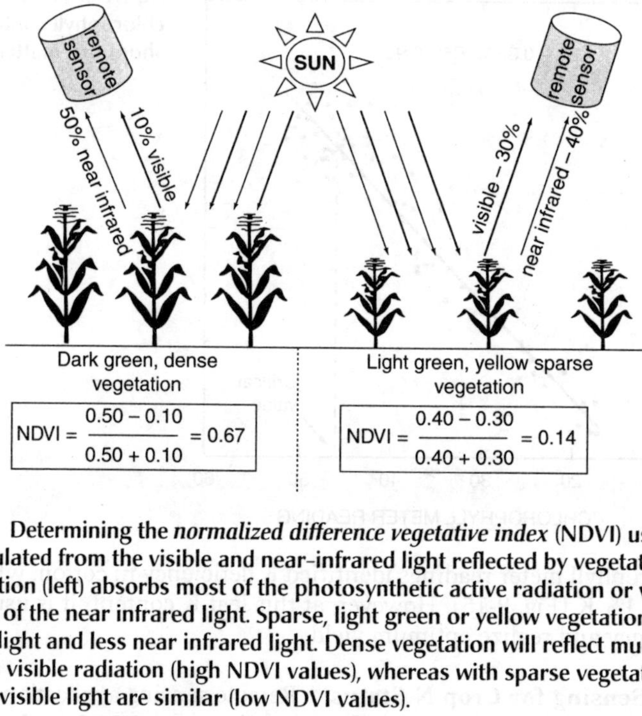

Figure 9-16 **Determining the *normalized difference vegetative index* (NDVI) using an optical sensor. NDVI is calculated from the visible and near-infrared light reflected by vegetation. Dense, dark green vegetation (left) absorbs most of the photosynthetic active radiation or visible light and reflects most of the near infrared light. Sparse, light green or yellow vegetation (right) reflects more visible light and less near infrared light. Dense vegetation will reflect much greater near infrared than visible radiation (high NDVI values), whereas with sparse vegetation reflected near infrared and visible light are similar (low NDVI values).**

NDVI is based on the principle that growing plants strongly absorb photosynthetically active radiation (PAR) or visible light, while strongly reflecting near infrared (NIR) radiation. NDVI increases with increasing leaf greenness and with green leaf biomass (Fig. 9-16).

NDVI is highly correlated with plant N status; thus, remote sensing of growing crops can be used to identify in-season N requirements. For example, in wheat, NDVI measured at tillering is highly correlated to N uptake (Fig. 9-17). This information is used to predict grain yield potential for purposes of estimating topdress N rates (Fig. 9-18). This method is readily incorporated into real-time, leaf-reflectance-guided variable topdress N applications to increase yield and N-use efficiency. Field evaluation of these remote sensing methods showed that prediction of wheat response to topdress N was positively correlated to measured N response. In addition, sensor-based N application increased N-use efficiency and net return (Table 9-6).

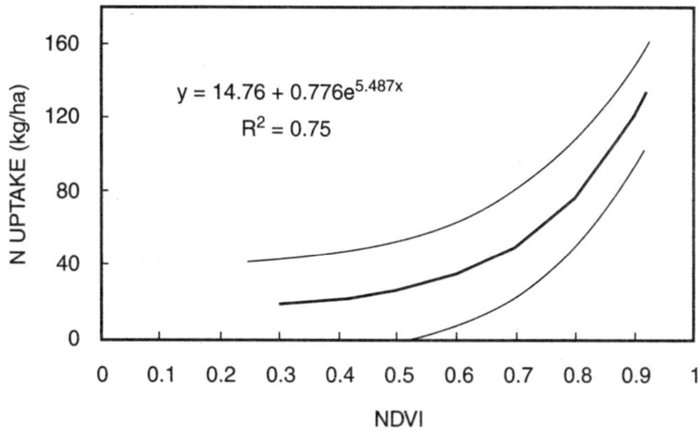

Figure 9-17 **Relationship between the normalized difference vegetation index (NDVI) at late tillering in winter wheat and plant N uptake. Dashed lines represent variation in the data collected from three sites over three years.** *(Raun et al., 2002,* Agron. J. *94:815.)*

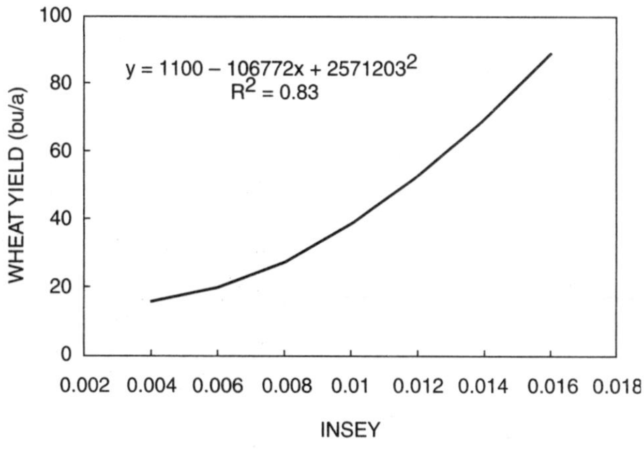

Figure 9-18 **Relationship between measured wheat yield and in-season estimated yield (INSEY) determined from NDVI measured at late tillering divided by accumulated growing degree days from planting to late tillering. INSEY is then used to determine N rate required to achieve the estimated yield.** *(Raun et al., 1999,* Agron J. *93:131.)*

Table 9-6 **Wheat Grain Yield Response to N Applied at Uniform Preplant and Late Tillering Compared to Midseason N Rates Determined by Remote Sensing**

N Rate	*Method*	*Grain Yield*	*NUE*	*Net Revenue*
kg ha^{-1}		kg/ha	%	\$/ha
0		1182		118
45	Midseason	1562	25	131
90	Midseason	1810	17	132
90	$^1/_2$ Preplant + $^1/_2$ Midseason	2105	22	161
90	Preplant	2063	22	157
43	Sensor NDVI / Midseason	1835	40	160
23	Sensor NDVI / $^1/_2$ Midseason	1619	50	149

SOURCE: Raun et al., 2002, *Agron. J.* 94:815–820.

Another method for estimating in-season N requirements involves the use of remote sensing to determine plant biomass. If tiller density is low (< 100 tillers/ft^2), N application at GS25 improves grain yield (Fig. 9-12). Tiller number can be determined by remote sensing using aerial infrared photographs at GS25 (Fig. 9-19). These data are then used in conjunction with tissue N estimated by NDVI to determine optimum N rates applied at GS30. Remote sensing techniques have also been established to estimate sidedress N rate required at pre-tassel stage in corn (Fig. 9-20). Field evaluation of this technique demonstrated a 35% reduction in N rate and a 50% increase in N-use efficiency.

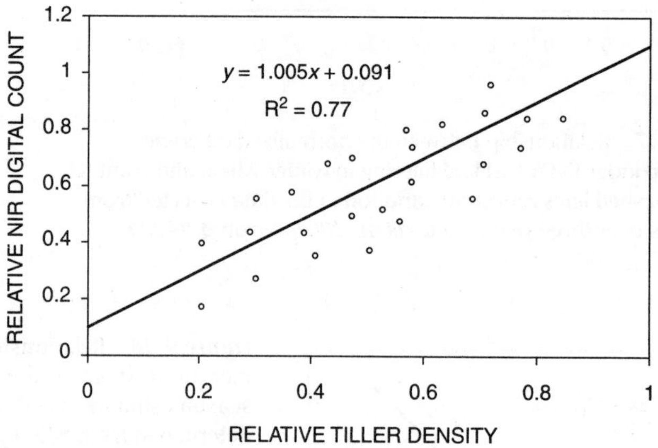

Figure 9-19 **Use of aerial infrared photography to determine tiller number in wheat at GS 25. Tiller number is used to estimate in-season N requirements.** *(Flowers et al., 2001,* Agron. J. *93:783.)*

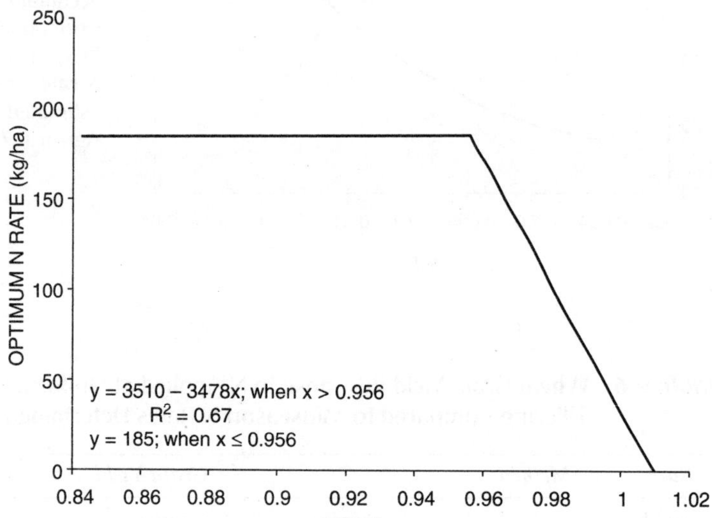

Figure 9-20 **Prediction of in-season sidedress N rates for corn using aerial color infrared photography at the pre-tassel growth stage. RGDVI represents the relative green difference vegetation index, which represents the NIR-green values divided by the value for a high N-rate reference plot.** *(Sripada, et al., 2003, "Remote Sensing Based In-Season Nitrogen Management Decisions in Corn: Model Development and Validation,"* Agron. Abstracts, *ASA, Madison, WI.)*

Post Mortem Tissue Tests

Stalk NO_3^- Test. The stalk NO_3^- test was developed to assess N sufficiency using a corn stalk sample collected at physiological maturity. The postmortem test enables a producer to assess excessive N use more effectively than additional N requirement. Stalk NO_3^- has been positively correlated with soil NO_3^- concentration.

At 1 to 3 weeks after black layer formation, 6 to 8-inch stalk sections are taken 8 to 14 inches above the soil surface from 10 to 12 plants. Samples are dried, ground, and analyzed for NO_3^-. Areas dissimilar in soil types and management should be sampled separately. General guidelines for interpreting stalk NO_3^- tests are:

Stalk NO_3–N (ppm N)	*Plant N Status*	*N Management Recommendations*
0–700	Low	Increase N rate
700–2,000	Optimal	N rate adequate for optimum productivity
> 2,000	Excess	N rate or availability exceeds crop requirement

Grain Analysis. Grain or other harvested plant parts are often collected to provide nutritional information to the grower. For example, wheat grain protein can be used to indicate if additional N was required for optimum yield (Fig. 9-21). When winter and spring wheat grain protein is < 11.5% and < 13.2%, respectively, additional N is needed to optimize yield.

Grain samples can be sent to a laboratory for analysis, although grain protein sensors have been developed using NIR transmittance that provide inexpensive and rapid results. Sensors can be installed in combines to monitor grain protein as the field is harvested. Grain protein measured in this way illustrates the high spatial correlation between grain

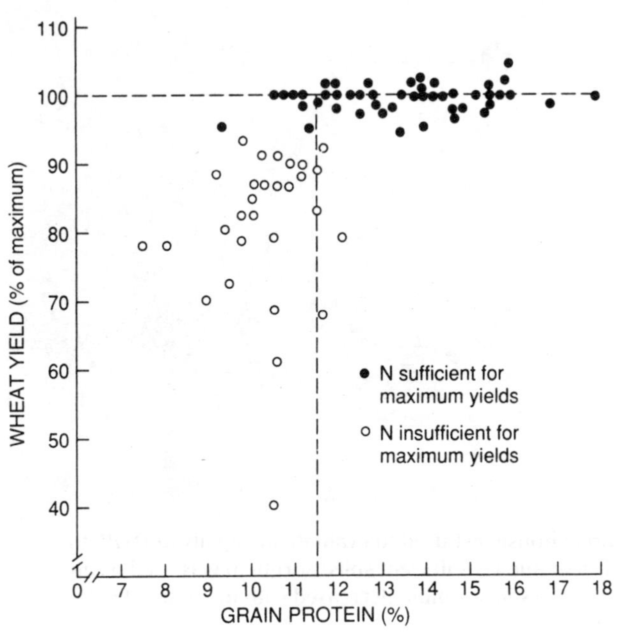

Figure 9-21 **Relationship between grain protein and N sufficiency in winter wheat.** *(Goos et al., 1982, Agron J., 74:130–133.)*

protein and soil-profile NO_3 content. Because temporal stability of this relationship is greater in regions where annual precipitation is < 750 mm, N application rates could be reduced in areas within fields that consistently exhibit high residual soil profile NO_3. While areas of high-profile NO_3 content are likely due to either high N mineralization or low yields (low N uptake), grain protein distribution can be used to help delineate variation in N requirements within fields. Although grain analysis can be very helpful in N management, it is a postmortem analysis. However, monitoring grain protein for several consecutive years provides information that improves the accuracy in estimating N requirements.

Greenhouse and Field Tests

Greenhouse Tests

Simple greenhouse tests involve growing plants in small amounts of soil to quantify nutrient availability. Generally, soils are collected from a field suspected of being deficient in a specific nutrient. For purposes of calibrating soil and plant tissue tests, a wide range of soils that differ in nutrient availability are selected. Selected nutrient rates are applied, and a crop is planted that is sensitive to the specific nutrient being evaluated. Crop response to increasing nutrient rate can be determined by measuring total plant yield and nutrient content. Figure 9-22 illustrates the use of a greenhouse test to separate Fe-deficient and Fe-sufficient soils. Soils were selected to represent a range in DTPA-extractable Fe. Sorghum plants show decreasing Fe deficiency as DTPA-extractable Fe increases.

Figure 9-22 **Greenhouse test used to evaluate the ability of DTPA to separate Fe-deficient and Fe-sufficient soils. Sorghum was used as an indicator crop. Fe stress in sorghum decreased with increasing DTPA-extractable Fe (ppm).**

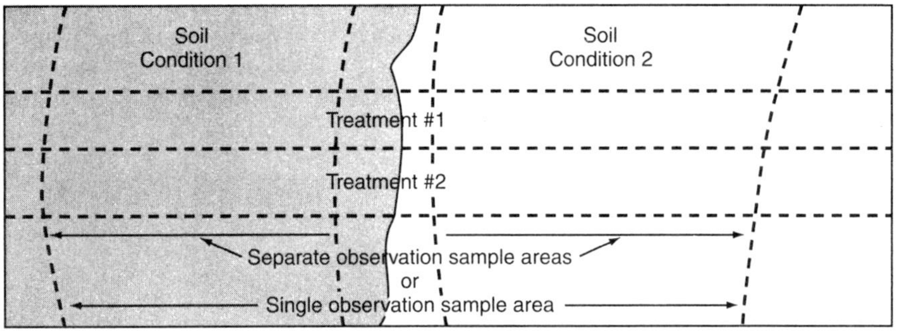

(a)

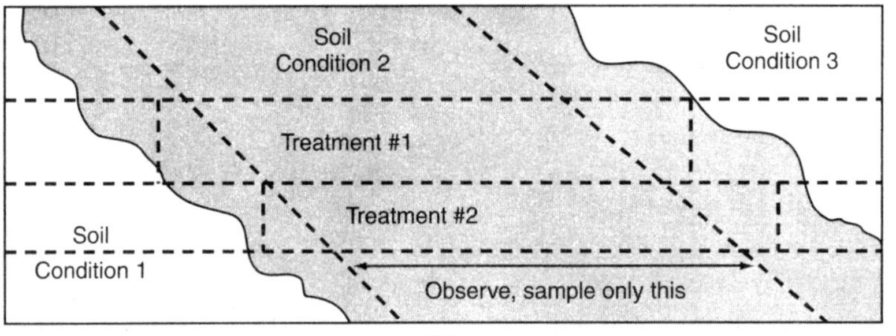

(b)

Figure 9-23 Example of strip tests located in a field with two (a) or three (b) soil types or conditions in the field.

Strip Tests

Narrow field strips where selected nutrient treatments have been applied can help verify the accuracy of management recommendations. The test results must be interpreted with caution if they are unreplicated. Replication of strip tests on several farms is also helpful. Figure 9-23 illustrates how a strip test of several nutrient rates might be located in the field. It is important to place treatments in as similarly uniform areas as possible. If several soil types or conditions occur in the same field, locate treatments so that each soil type occurs equally in each treatment. The use of a yield-monitoring combine to measure and record treatment yields makes strip tests a valuable tool in assessing the accuracy of management recommendations.

Field Tests

Measuring crop response to applied nutrients is commonly done by agricultural scientists developing nutrient recommendations. After the specific treatments are selected, they are randomly assigned to an area of land. The treatments are replicated several times to obtain more reliable results and to account for soil variations at the experimental site (Fig. 9-24). For example, when a range of increasing N rates are applied and a crop planted and harvested, the yield results are used in establishing N recommendations (see *Calibrating Soil Tests*). When many similar tests are conducted on well-characterized soils, recommendations can be extrapolated to other soils with similar characteristics.

Field tests are used in conjunction with greenhouse tests in the calibration of soil and plant tests. Field experiments are essential in establishing equations used to provide fertilizer

N RATE TREATMENTS (lbs/a)

0	40	80	120	160	Replicate 1
80	120	160	40	0	Replicate 2
120	80	0	160	40	Replicate 3
40	160	120	0	80	Replicate 4

Figure 9-24 **Example field plot design for evaluating crop response to applied N. Five N rates are replicated 4 times, with N rates randomly placed within each replicate.**

recommendations that will optimize crop yield. Plant analysis of samples collected from the various treatments can also help establish CNR. There can be difficulties with this technique when results from small plots exhibiting little spatial variability in soil properties are applied to large fields with greater variability.

Soil Testing

A soil test is a chemical extraction of a soil sample to estimate nutrient availability. Soil tests extract part of the total nutrient content that is related to (but not equal to) the quantity of plant available nutrient. Thus, a soil test level represents only an *index* of nutrient availability. Compared with plant analysis, soil tests determine relative nutrient status before planting.

As an index of nutrient availability, the quantity of nutrient extracted by the soil test is not equal to the quantity of nutrient absorbed by the crop, but they are closely related. For example, Figure 9-25 shows that soil test P varied from 20 to 80 ppm in a 6-a field. If soil test P is related to P availability, then the variability in %P in the crop should reflect the variability in extractable soil P. The spatial distribution of %P concentration in wheat grain reflects the distribution of plant available P as measured by soil test P (Fig. 9-25). Specifically, high and low soil test P results in high and low grain P, respectively. These data demonstrate the ability of a soil test to provide a reliable index of plant available nutrients.

Objectives of Soil Tests

Soil test information can be used in many ways:

1. *To provide an index of nutrient availability in soil.* The soil test or extractant is designed to extract a portion of the nutrient from the same "pool" (i.e., solution, exchange, organic, or mineral) used by the plant.

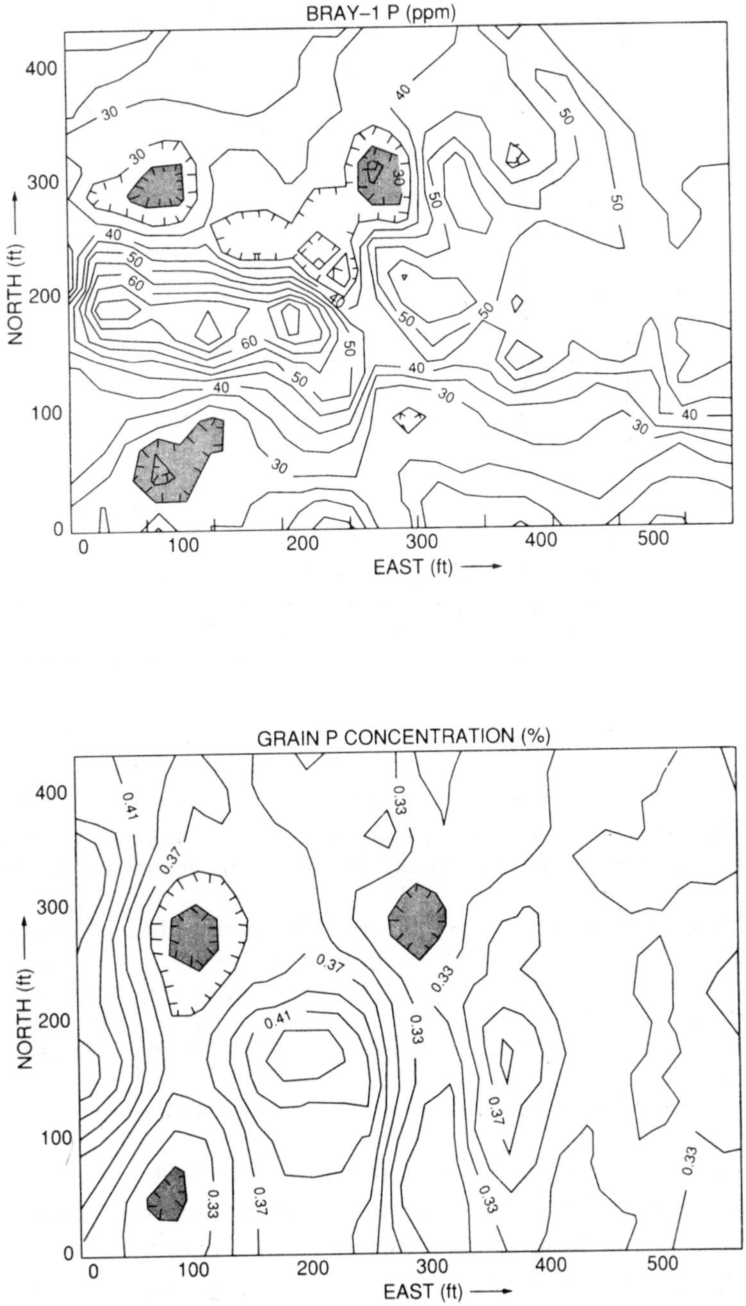

Figure 9-25 Spatial distribution of Bray-1 P and wheat grain P concentration over a 6-a field. Areas of high soil test P correspond to areas of high %P in the grain (left center region of both figures). Low Bray-1 P levels result in low %P in the grain (see two shaded areas above and one below high soil test P area). *(Havlin and Sisson, 1990,* Proc. Dryland Farming Conf, *pp. 406.)*

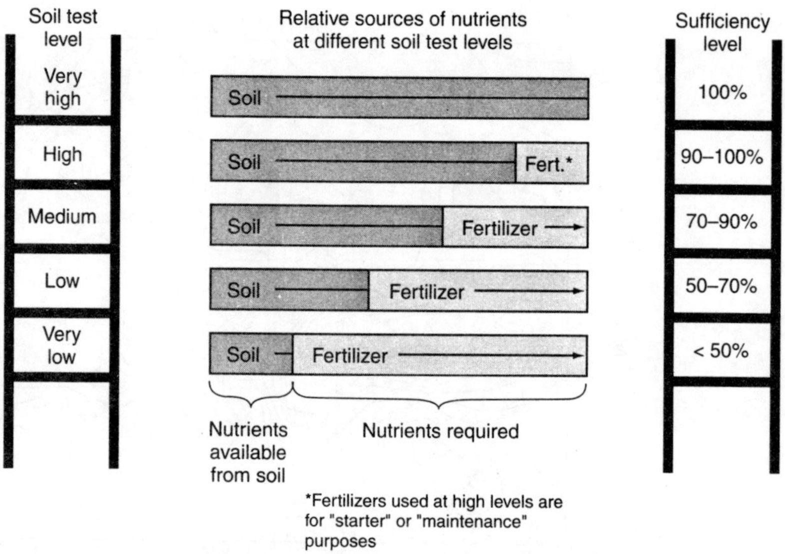

Figure 9-26 **As soil test levels decrease, nutrient rates applied for maximizing yield potentials increase. High soil test levels represent a 90 to 100% sufficiency in supplying adequate nutrients. A low soil test level represents a 50 to 70% sufficiency in supplying adequate nutrients.**

2. *To predict the probability of obtaining a profitable response to fertilizer or lime.* Although a response to applied nutrients will not always be obtained on low-testing soils because of other limiting factors, the probability of a response is greater than on high-testing soils.
3. *To provide a basis for development of fertilizer and lime recommendations.* These basic relations are obtained by careful laboratory, greenhouse, and field studies.

The objective of soil testing is to simply help predict the amount of nutrients needed to supplement native soil supply. For example, a soil testing high will require little or no additional nutrients in contrast to soil with a low test value (Fig. 9-26). Sufficiency levels are commonly used in soil testing, where a high soil test represents 90 to 100% sufficiency in supplying adequate plant nutrients from the soil. Sufficiency levels decrease with decreasing soil test levels.

The *soil testing–nutrient recommendation system* is comprised of four consecutive steps:

1. Collect a representative soil sample from the field.
2. Determine the quantity of plant available nutrient in the soil sample (soil test).
3. Interpret the soil test results (soil test calibration).
4. Estimate the quantity of nutrient required by the crop (nutrient recommendation).

Soil Sampling

The most critical aspect of soil testing is obtaining a soil sample that is representative of the field. Usually, a composite sample of only 1 pint of soil (about 1 lb) is taken from a field or sampling area that may represent, for example, a 10-a field or about 20×10^6 lbs of surface soil. Therefore, considerable opportunity exists for sampling errors. If the sample does

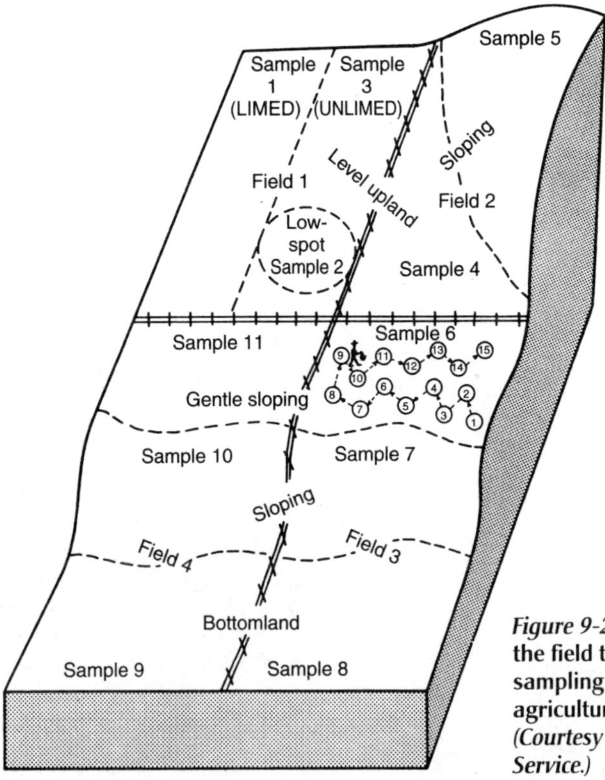

Figure 9-27 **Samples that are representative of the field to be fertilized are important. The sampling pattern recommended by the various agricultural agencies should be followed.** *(Courtesy of the Nebraska Agricultural Extension Service.)*

not represent the field, it is impossible to provide a reliable nutrient recommendation. Field-sampling errors are much greater than laboratory analysis errors.

Two common methods of soil sample collection are (1) sampling whole or parts of fields to provide "average" soil test value(s) or (2) sampling to describing spatial variability in soil test values. Currently, soil sampling to obtain the field-average soil test is commonly used, but site-specific nutrient management requires the spatial distribution of soil test values.

Field Average Sampling Each field should be subdivided into *sampling units* representing a relatively uniform area. Criteria used to delineate a sampling unit include soil types, slope, drainage, or past management (Fig. 9-27). Sampling units vary in size, but usually are < 40 a. Small areas within a sampling unit that are not representative of the unit should be omitted from the sample. Even in a relatively uniform area, variability in soil test levels exists. For example, recent lime or nutrient applications, or previous crop residues, may have been unevenly distributed. A sample taken entirely from areas high in these materials would not represent field average. To minimize sampling errors, 15 to 40 sample cores should be collected in the sampling unit (Fig. 9-27). Soil samples within each sampling unit are composited by mixing in a nongalvanized container, and a subsample is sent to the laboratory for analysis.

With the use of a geographic information system (GIS), sampling units and sampling sites within a unit can be identified. Pertinent digital data layers readily available from local, state, or federal agencies would include soil survey data (soil types), digital elevation, and an aerial photograph of the field. Other known spatial data (soil test data, yield maps, etc.) specific for the field may also be available and could be included. The GIS enables the user to overlay spatial data and delineate sampling units based on uniformity of field and soil characterists (Fig. 9-28). Sampling points within a sampling unit can also be identified in the GIS. With this information and a global positioning system (GPS) on the soil sampling vehicle, personnel can collect samples from the exact positions identified with the GIS.

On apparently uniform fields, nutrient levels still can be highly variable. More often, soil test values are not normally distributed (Fig. 9-29). When normally distributed, the average or *mean* soil test value is the same as the *mode,* the value that occurs most frequently. If soil test results do not follow a normal distribution, the data are skewed and the mean does not represent the most frequently occurring value or mode. Table 9-7 shows how the mean soil test level was consistently greater than the mode, which represents the largest per-

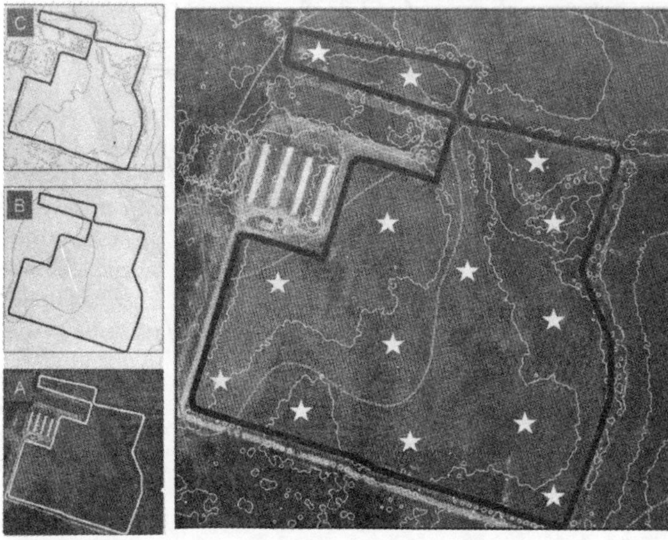

Figure 9-28 **Using geospatial data to guide field soil sampling. A represents the digital orthoimagery or aerial black/white photograph of a field, B is the digitized map of soil types obtained from NRCS Soil Survey data, and C is the elevation in the field obtained from remote sensing, where each contour represents a 2m change in elevation. These three data layers are then combined (large photo on the right) to identify locations in the field where soil samples will be collected (areas represented by the "stars").** ***(Courtesy D. Crouse, NC State University.)***

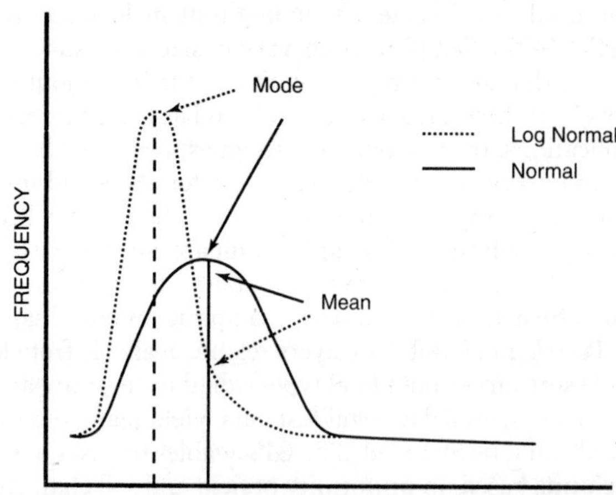

Figure 9-29 **Normal and log-normal distributions showing the mean and mode.**

Table 9-7 **Statistical Characteristics of Soil Tests from a 220-ft × 220-ft Sampling Grid (Samples)**

Nutrient	*Range*	*Mean*	*Mode*
	ppm		
NO_3-N	2–24	11	8
P	0–104	15	9
K	127–598	276	155
SO4-S	7–944	480	10

SOURCE: Penney et al., 1996, *Proc. Great Plains Soil Fert. Conf.* 6:126.

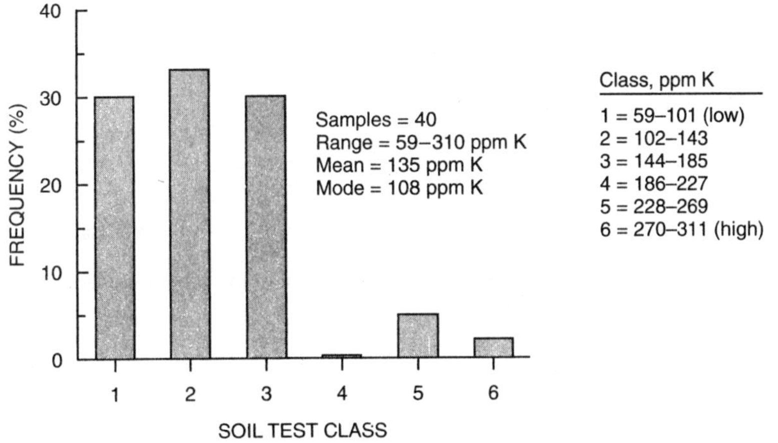

Figure 9-30 **Frequency distribution of soil test K from a 220-ft × 220-ft sampling grid. 30% of the field tested low enough to require K (Class 1) and another 33% was marginal in K status (Class 2). If K recommendations were based on the field mean, at least 30% of the field would have experienced K deficiency. *(Penney et al., 1996,* Proc. Great Plains Soil Fert. Conf, *6:126.)***

centage of the field. Nutrient rates based on mean soil test levels would then be lower than those based on the mode. Most soil test data are log normally distributed, where > 50% of the soil test values are less than the mean (Fig. 9-29). When this occurs, nutrient needs are underestimated. For example, the skewed distribution of soil test K results in no K recommended when 30% of the field tested low (Fig. 9-30).

Site-Specific Sampling Use of equipment capable of variably applying nutrients according to variability in soil test levels for a specific nutrient requires intensive, georeferenced field sampling. Georeferenced soil sampling refers to the use of the GPS to record the latitude and longitude of each sampling point.

Grid Sampling. Grid sampling consists of collecting equally spaced soil samples throughout the field and analyzing each sample separately (Fig. 9-31). Typically 2- to 3-a grids are used, representing 300-360-ft-square grids, respectively. Decreasing the grid size increases the number of samples collected and associated sampling and analysis costs, but improves the probability of accurately describing the true distribution. For example, in a comparison of grid sizes varying from 0.75 a (180-ft grid) to 7.5 a (570-ft grid), the ≤ 3.0 a grid adequately describes the spatial variability in soil test P (Fig. 9-32).

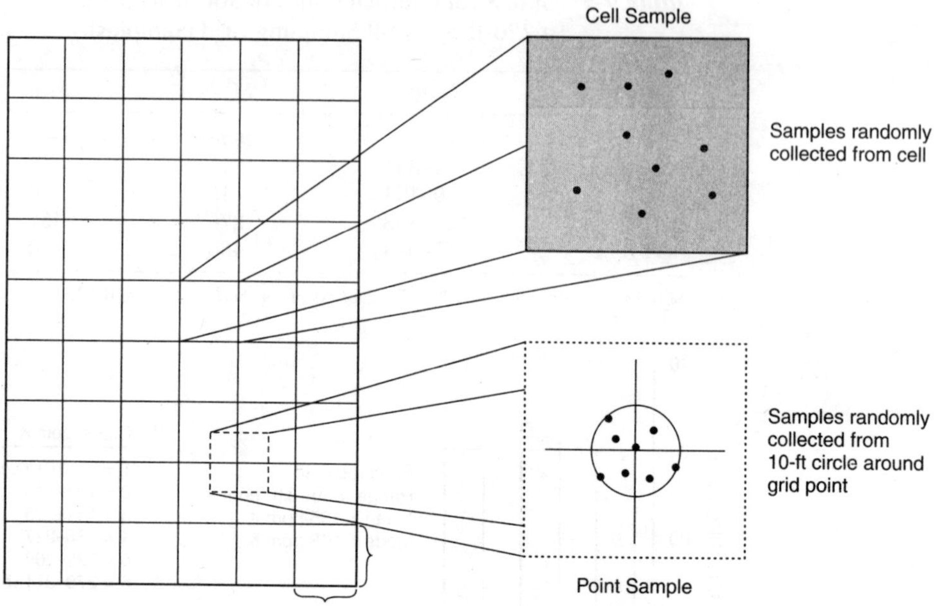

Figure 9-31 **Illustration of point and cell sampling schemes used for describing the spatial distribution of soil properties.**

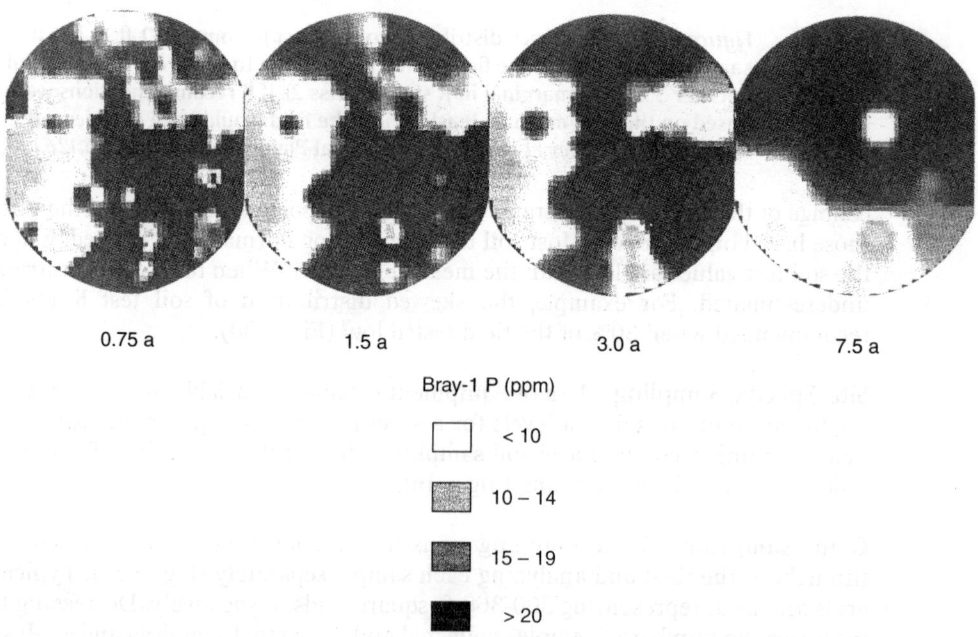

Figure 9-32 **Influence of grid size on the spatial distribution of soil test P (Bray-1) levels; ≤ 3 acre adequately described the variability.** ***(Havlin et al., 1996,*** **Agron. Abstracts,** ***p. 184.)***

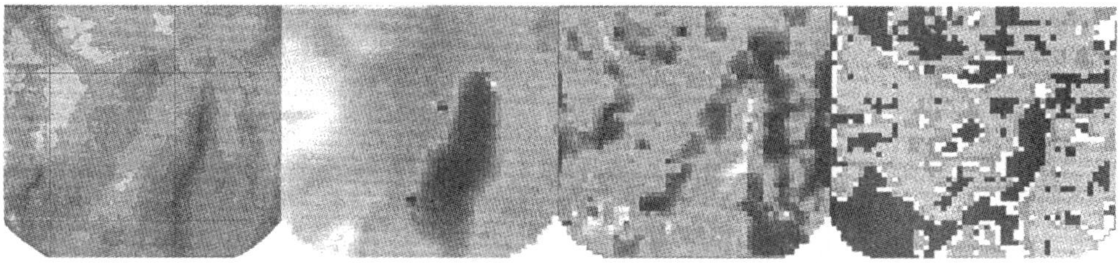

Figure 9-33 **The spatial distribution of soil color, using aerial black-and-white photography, is related to soil OM and soil test P. Dark soil color regions correspond to regions of high soil OM and Bray-1 P. Georeferenced soil sampling could be guided by the soil color map to reduce the samples required to grid-sample the field.** *(Courtesy of R. Ferguson and J. Schepers, 1995, Univ. of Nebraska.)*

Grid samples can be collected as *cell* or *point* samples (Fig. 9-31). With cell sampling, random samples are collected within each grid and composited. With large grids (e.g., 2-a), compositing samples within a cell will mask variability within the grid. To avoid the averaging that occurs with cell sampling, point samples can be collected (Fig. 9-31). With point sampling, 5 to 10 individual soil samples are composited from a 10- to 15-ft diameter circle centered over each intersection of the vertical and horizontal grid lines. Thus, with point sampling more within-field variability is quantified.

Directed Sampling. To reduce the cost of grid sampling, sampling locations can be identified by using other spatially variable parameters in the field. Figure 9-33 illustrates that soil color, OM, and elevation could be used to identify the spatial distribution of soil test P. Yield-monitored data and other remote sensing information could also help direct specific sampling locations.

Other Soil Sampling Considerations

Banded Nutrients. Band application of immobile nutrients (e.g., P and K) often results in higher concentration of residual nutrient in previous fertilizer bands for several years after application. Residual availability depends on application rate, soil chemical and physical properties, quantity of nutrient removed by the crop, crop rotation and intensity, and time after application. For example, increasing broadcast or band P-rate increased soil test P (Fig. 9-34). Band-applied P increased soil test P more than the same rate of broadcast P. Thus, if only the bands are sampled, the soil test P is much higher than if none of the bands are sampled (i.e., if only the between-band areas are sampled). Few guidelines have been established for soil sampling fields in which immobile nutrients have been band applied. In no-till systems where the band is undisturbed and its position is known, the following can be used:

$$S = \frac{8 \times \text{row spacing (in.)}}{12}$$

where S = ratio of off-band to on-band samples. Thus, for 12-in. band spacing, eight samples between the bands are required for every sample taken on the band. If the band position is

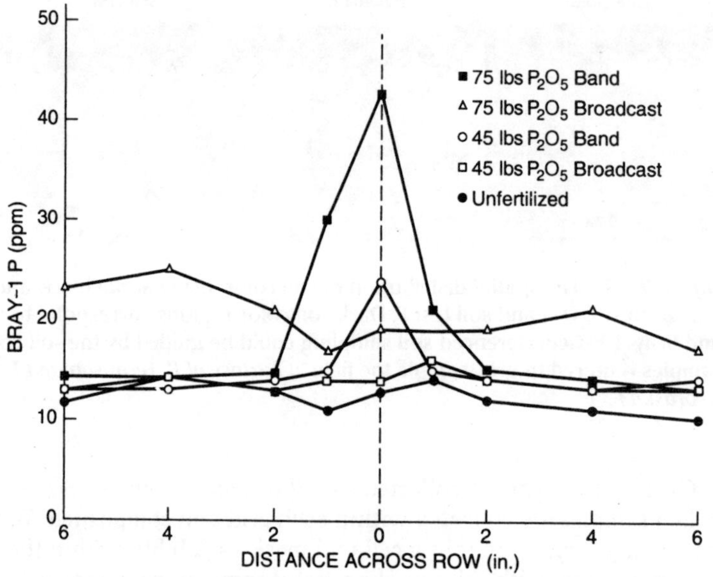

Figure 9-34 **Effect of P rate and placement on soil test P (Bray-1) levels measured in 1 in. increments perpendicular to the row. P fertilizer was broadcast and band applied (2 in. below the seed) at 15, 45, and 75 lbs P_2O_5/a at wheat planting in September 1986. Soils were sampled in August 1988. Soil test levels for the 15 lbs/a rate are not shown because they were similar to the unfertilized treatment.** ***(Havlin et al., 1989,*** **Proc. Fluid Fert. Foundation,** ***p. 193.)***

not known, then the sampling intensity should be increased to provide an adequate estimate of the average field soil test level.

Sampling Depth. For cultivated crops, samples are ordinarily taken to tillage depth that can vary from 6 to 12 in. (Fig. 9-35). Tillage generally mixes previous lime and nutrient applications in the tillage layer (Table 9-8). When lime and nutrients are broadcast on the surface in lawns, pastures, and no-till systems, considerable nutrient stratification occurs (Table 9-8, Table 9-9) Soil samples collected from the upper 2- or 4-in. depth is recommended. In low rainfall regions, preplant subsoil samples (2- to 4-ft depth) are routinely collected to determine NO_3^- content to adjust N recommendations (see *N Soil Tests*).

Sampling Time. Ideally, samples should be taken just before planting or early in the crop growth cycle. However, these times are often impractical due to the time involved in collecting samples, obtaining test results, and applying needed amendments. Consequently, samples are customarily taken any time soil conditions permit in the noncrop period. Samples from spring-planted crops are often taken after harvest. In drier regions where NO_3^- levels are used to assess soil N status, fall sampling is common.

Most recommendations call for testing each field about every 3 years, with more frequent testing on sandy soils. In most instances, this frequency is sufficient to assess soil pH and to determine whether the nutrient management program is adequate for optimum productivity. For instance, if soil test P is decreasing, P application rate can be increased. If it has risen to a satisfactory level, application may be reduced to maintenance rates (see *Immobile Nutrient Recommendations*).

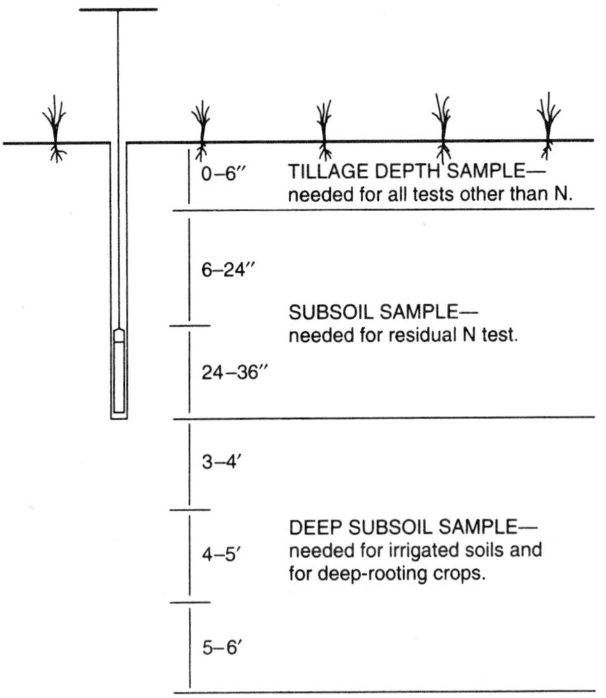

Figure 9-35 **Diagram of various soil sampling depths used for nutrient analyses.**

Table 9-8 Influence of Tillage on Stratification of Soil Test P and K

Soil Depth	*Plow*	*Chisel*	*No-Till*	*Plow*	*Chisel*	*No-Till*
	Bray-1 P			*KCl Extractable K*		
in.	*ppm*					
0–3	37	85	90	150	230	285
3–6	47	35	27	165	105	100
6–9	30	15	18	140	100	100
9–12	8	8	8	100	100	100

SOURCE: Mengel, 1990, *Agron. Guide AY-268*, Purdue Univ.

Table 9-9 Influence of Tillage and N Rate on Soil pH

Yearly N Rate lb/a	*No-Till*		*Plow*	
	0–2 in.	*2–6 in.*	*0–2 in.*	*2–6 in.*
0	5.75	6.05	6.45	6.45
75	5.20	5.90	6.40	6.35
150	4.82	5.63	5.85	5.83
300	4.45	4.88	5.58	5.43

SOURCE: Blevins et al., 1983, *Soil Tillage Res.* 3:36–46.

Table 9-10 **Common Soil Test Extractants and the Source of Nutrient Extracted from the Soil**

Plant Nutrient	*Common Extractants*	*Nutrient Source*
NO_3^-	KCl, $CaCl_2$	Solution
NH_4^+	KCl	Solution/CEC
$H_2PO_4^-$/ $H_2PO_4^-$	NH_4F/HCl (Bray-P)	Fe/Al-P mineral solubility
	$NH_4F/CH_3COOH/HNO_3$ (Mehlich-P)	Fe/Al-P mineral solubility
	$NaHCO_3$ (Olsen-P)	Ca-P mineral solubility
K^+	NH_4OAc	CEC
SO_4^{-2}	$Ca(H_2PO_4)_2$, $CaCl_2$	Solution/AEC
Zn^{+2}, Fe^{+3}, Mn^{+2}, Cu^{+2}	DTPA, EDTA	Zn, Fe, Mn, Cu mineral solubilty
$H_3BO_3^0$	Hot water	Solution
Cl^-	Water	Solution

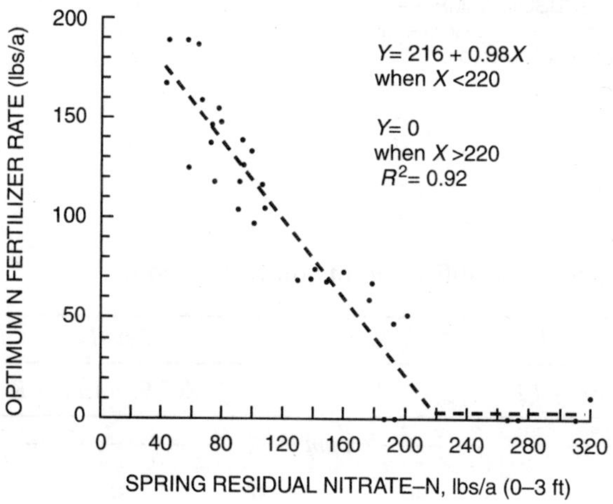

Figure 9-36 **Optimum N rates for corn based on preplant soil NO_3^- content. *(Bundy et al., 1995,* Wisconsin's Preplant Soil Nitrate Test, *Univ. of Wisconsin, A3512.)***

Soil Tests

The specific chemical extractants used in soil testing varies with the nutrient (Table 9-10). A soil test extractant removes a nutrient from similar reservoirs (i.e., CEC, OM, mineral solubility, etc.) that provide nutrients to growing plants (Fig. 2-1).

N Soil Tests NO_3^- occurs predominantly in the soil solution and NH_4^+ exists both in solution and on the CEC. A simple water extract of the soil sample would recover solution NO_3^- + NH_4^+. KCl (1 or 2 M) is commonly used, where Cl^- replaces small amounts of exchangeable NO_3^- absorbed to AEC and K^+ would remove exchangeable NH_4^+. Increasing KCl extractable NO_3^- decreases N required for optimum yield in some regions (Fig. 9-36).

Preplant Sampling. In many humid regions where annual precipitation exceeds evapotranspiration, leaching and denitrification reduce preplant profile NO_3^- to levels often unreliable for use in N recommendations of subsequent crops (Fig. 9-37). However, in the

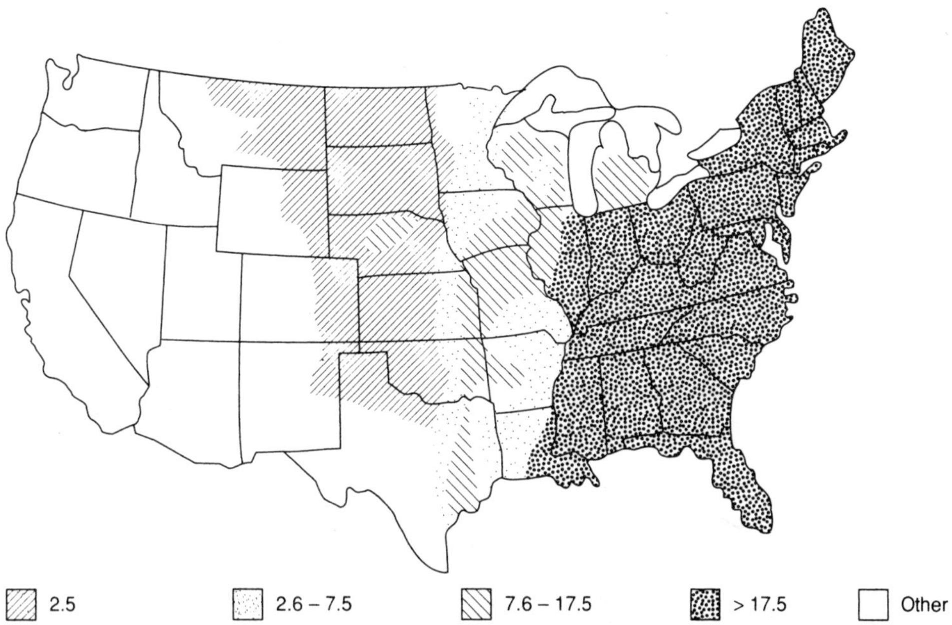

Figure 9-37 Use of residual profile NO_3^- analysis in determining N recommendations is more common in regions where average annual potential percolation (shading indicates values in cm) below the root zone < 17.5 cm. *(Hergert, 1987,* SSSA Spec. Publ. No. 21.*)*

North Central region of the United States preplant soil NO_3^- concentration is related to relative corn yield (Fig. 9-38). As soil NO_3^- increases, the additional N required for optimum yield decreases (Fig. 9-39).

In regions where evapotranspiration exceeds precipitation (Fig. 9-37), measuring preplant profile NO_3^- content is valuable in determining N requirements. Usually a 2- to 3-ft profile sample is collected before planting to provide plant available NO_3^- (Table 9-11). Determining soil profile NO_3^- is essential to accurately estimate supplemental N requirements in all cropping systems (Fig. 9-40)

In-season Sampling.

Pre-sidedress Soil NO_3^- Test (PSNT). As mineralization and nitrification rates increase in the spring, soil NO_3^- increases, which occurs just prior to the maximum N uptake period in corn (Fig. 9-41). Soil NO_3^-N determined in surface soil samples (0- to 12-in. depth) collected between corn rows when corn is about 12 in. tall is related to relative yield (Fig. 9-42). The critical soil NO_3^-N concentration below which sidedress N applications are recommended varies between regions, but is approximately 20 to 25 ppm NO_3^-N (Fig. 9-43). Previous legume crops or manure application greatly influences the quantity of extractable soil NO_3^-N (Fig. 9-44). Lower PSNT critical levels (13 to 15 mg · kg^{-1}) are appropriate in semiarid regions due to greater subsoil NO_3^-N. In soils amended with organic wastes (manure, sewage sludge, etc.), NH_4 + NO_3 analysis improves prediction of sidedress N response compared to soil NO_3^-N alone.

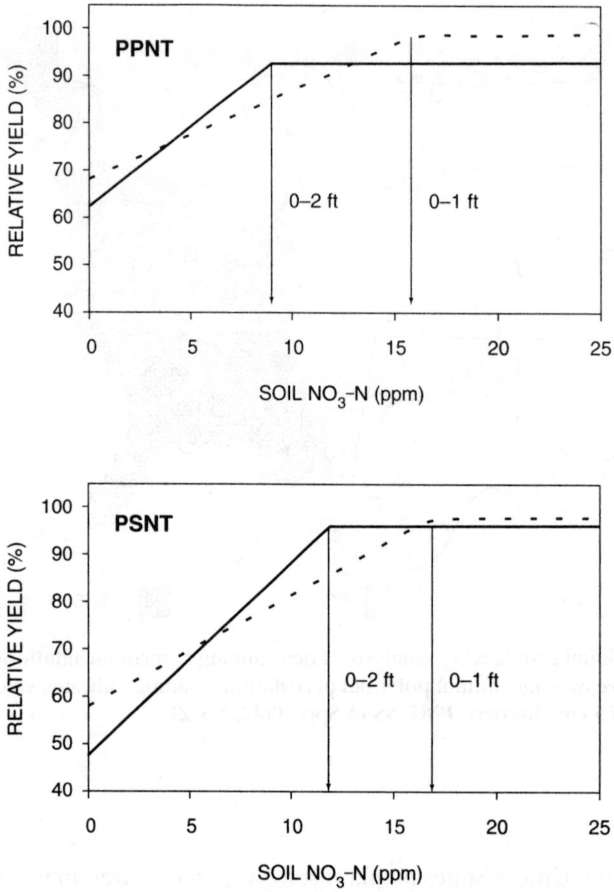

Figure 9-38 Relationship between soil NO_3-N concentration and relative corn yield. The preplant soil NO_3-N test (PPNT) and the presidedress soil NO_3-N test (PSNT) are based on 0- to 1-ft soil samples collected before planting and when corn is about 1-ft tall, respectively. Use of a 0- to 2-ft sample varies with states. The arrows represent the critical soil NO_3-N concentration above which no additional N is required. *(Adapted from Bundy et al., 1999, North Central Regional Res.* Publ. No. 342.*)*

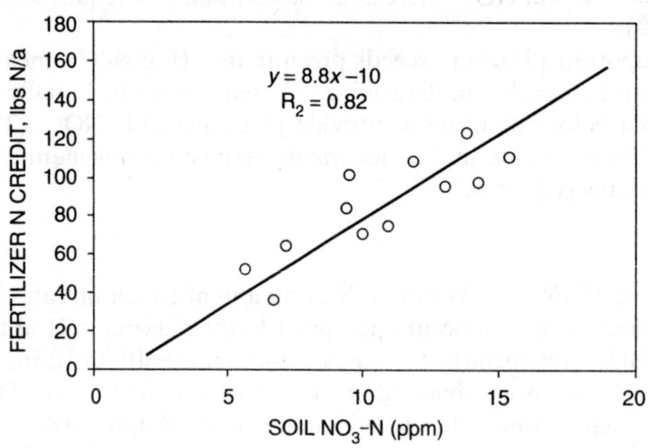

Figure 9-39 Quantity of fertilizer N credit for corn-based on preplant soil NO_3-N in a 0- to 2-ft sample. Generally the higher soil NO_3^- levels occur in cropping systems where manure is utilized or when overwinter or spring precipitation is low. *(Schmitt et al., 1998, Univ. Minnesota, FO-06514-GO.)*

The PSNT has also been adapted for vegetables where the critical level is similar to that used for corn (Fig. 9-45). Guidelines for in-season soil sampling with vegetables is also similar to corn (Table 9-12).

Other In-Season N Tests. As with the PSNT, sampling to determine soil NO_3-N is also useful in adjusting in-season N application rates in wheat (Fig. 9-46).

Table 9-11 N Recommendations for Dryland Winter Wheat Based on Soil Profile NO_3-N and OM Content for a 50 bu/a Yield Goal*

Soil NO_3-N, ppm†		*Soil OM, %*		
0–1 ft	*0–2 ft*	*0–1.0*	*1.1–2.0*	*>2.0*
		N rate, lbs/a		
0–3	0–5	75	75	75
4–6	6–9	75	70	50
7–9	10–12	75	45	25
10–12	13–15	50	20	0
13–15	15–18	25	0	0
>15	>18	0	0	0

*To adjust N rate for yield goals different from 50 bu/a, add or subtract 25 lbs N/a for each 10 bu/a difference, where maximum rate is 75 lbs N/a.

†NO_3-N concentration in the 0–1- or 0–2-ft sample depth.

SOURCE: Davis et al., 2002, *Fertilizing Winter Wheat,* Colorado State Univ. Coop. Ext. No. 0.544.

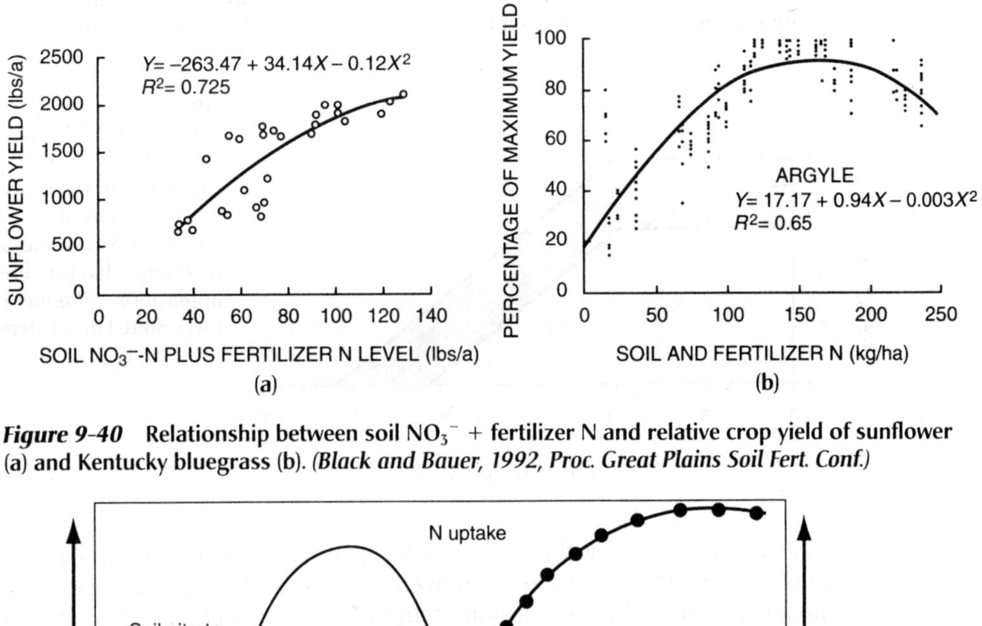

Figure 9-40 Relationship between soil NO_3^- + fertilizer N and relative crop yield of sunflower (a) and Kentucky bluegrass (b). *(Black and Bauer, 1992, Proc. Great Plains Soil Fert. Conf.)*

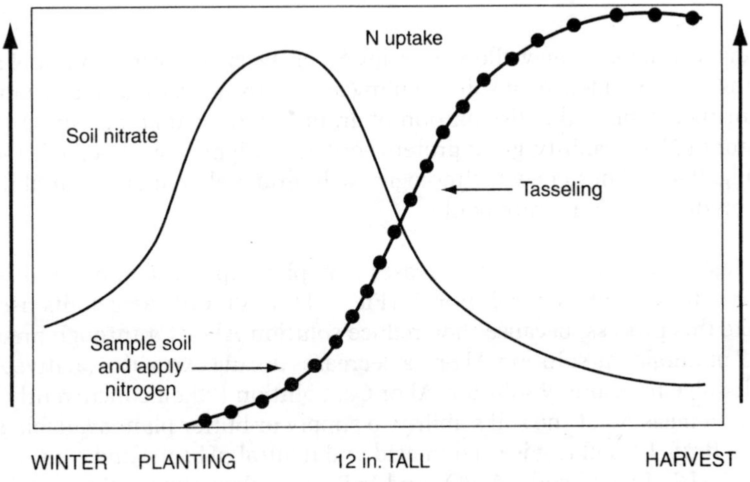

Figure 9-41 General distribution of soil NO_3^- and N uptake in corn.

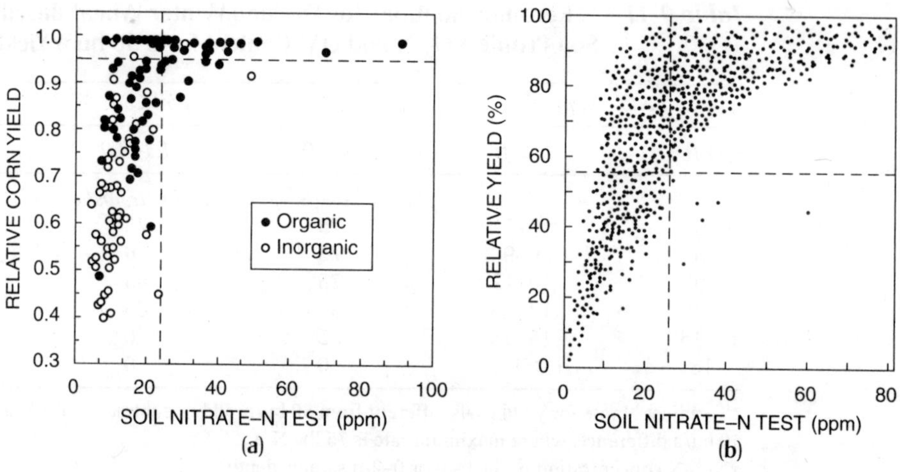

Figure 9-42 **Relationship between soil NO_3^- and relative corn yield in Pennsylvania (a) and Iowa (b). Organic indicates soils with a history of manure or legumes, whereas inorganic indicates soils without this history.** ***(Beegle, 1982, Proc. Indiana Ag. Chem. Conf.)***

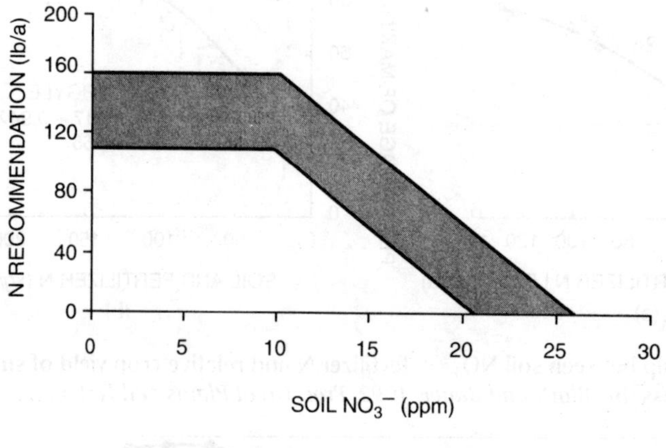

Figure 9-43 **Sidedress N recommendations for corn based on PSNT. At 10 ppm NO_3^- the range in N rates is 110–160 lbs/a, whereas at 20 ppm NO_3^-, 10–60 lbs N/a would be recommended for sidedress application.** ***(Blakmer et al., 1991, Iowa State Univ. Extension, p. 1381.)***

New technologies may allow description of the spatial variation in N availability while reducing the dependence on soil sampling and analysis. With a sensor mounted on a yield-monitoring combine, the distribution of grain protein can be measured (Fig. 9-47). As an indicator of N availability, grain protein content is highly correlated with soil-profile N content (Fig. 9-47). These new technologies will ultimately enhance our ability to more accurately predict crop N requirements.

P Soil Tests When solution P decreases with plant uptake, P minerals dissolve or adsorbed P desorbs to resupply soil solution P (Fig. 5-1). Chemical extractants used for P soil tests simulate this process, because they reduce solution Al or Ca through precipitation as Al-P or Ca-P minerals. As solution Al or Ca decreases during extraction, native Al-P or Ca-P minerals dissolve to resupply solution Al or Ca. Solution P then concurrently increases, which provides a measure of the soil's ability to supply or buffer plant available P.

The *Bray-1 P* soil test is used in acid and neutral pH soils and contains 0.025 M HCl + 0.03 M NH_4F. In acid soils, $AlPO_4$ and $FePO_4$ are the primary P minerals controlling P in

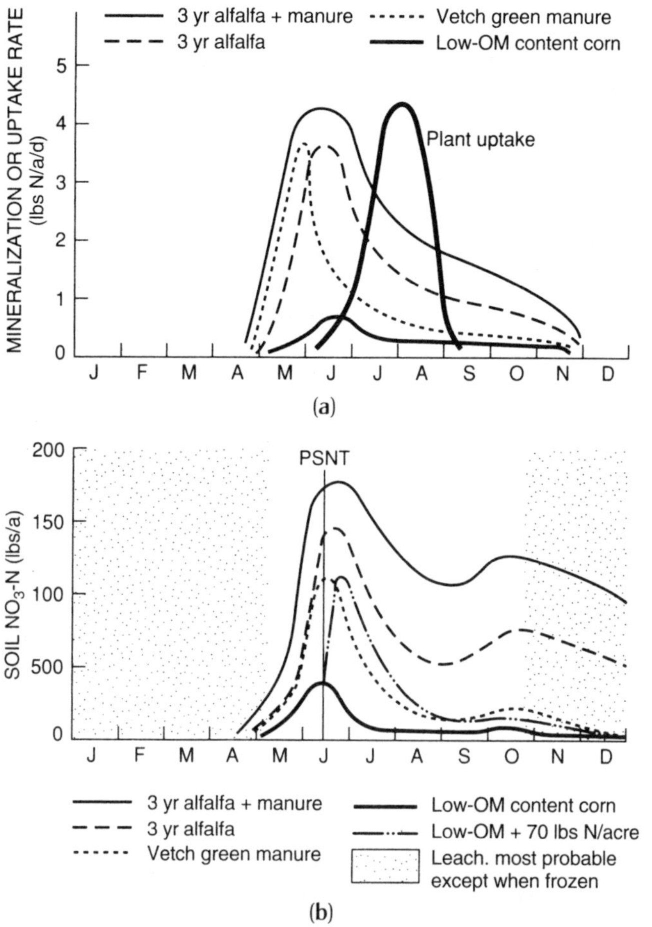

Figure 9-44 **Synchronization of N mineralization and crop N uptake (a) and subsequent accumulation of NO_3 (b) as influenced by previous crop and manure.** *(Magdoff, 1991,* Prod. Ag. *4:297–305.)*

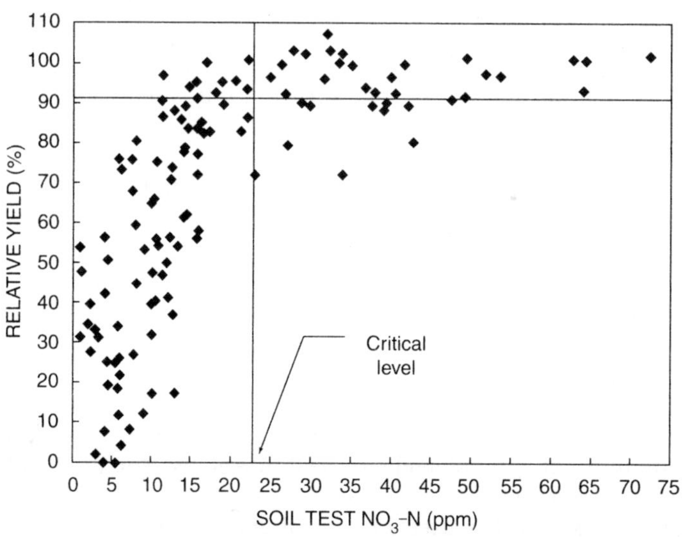

Figure 9-45 Relationship between PSNT and relative yield of cabbage. *(Heckman, 2003,* Rutgers Coop. Ext. Bull. E285.*)*

Table 9-12 **Guidelines for In-Season Soil Sampling Used for PSNT in Vegetables**

Crop	*Soil Sampling Time*
Sweet Corn, Field Corn	plants 6–10 in. tall
Cabbage, Cauliflower, Broccoli, Brussels sprouts	2 wks. post-transplant
Celery	2 wks. post-transplant, repeat in 3–4 wks.
Lettuce, Endive, Escarole	2 wks. post-transplant or after thinning at 2–4 leaf stage if direct seeded
Beet, Turnip, Rutabaga	after thinning at 2–4 leaf stage
Pumpkin, Winter squash, Cucumber, Muskmelon	when vines are 6 in. long
Spinach	at 2–4 leaf stage, repeat after cutting
Irish potato	when plants are 6 in. tall
Peppers, Tomato, Eggplant	at 1st fruit set, repeat after 3–4 wks

SOURCE: Heckman, 2003, Rutgers Coop. Ext. Bull. E285.

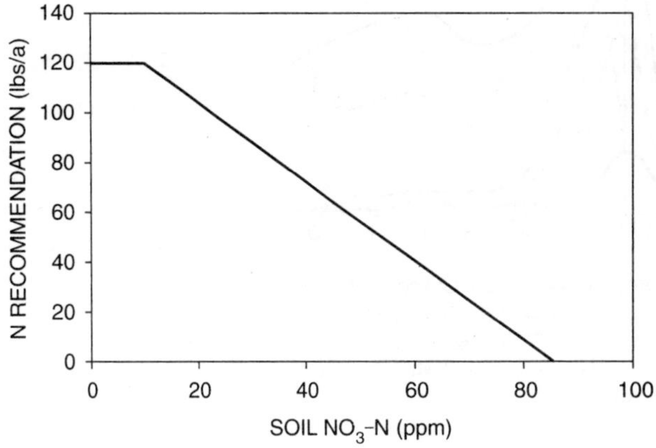

Figure 9-46 **Relationship between soil NO_3-N (0–3-ft depth) at mid-tillering (GS 25) and N required for optimum wheat yield.** *(Alley et al., 1996, Virginia Coop. Ext.,* **Publ. No. 424-026.***)*

solution (Fig. 5-8). During extraction, F^- and Al^{+3} precipitate as AlF_3. As Al^{+3} decreases, $AlPO_4 \cdot 2H_2O$ dissolves to buffer the loss of solution Al^{+3}, releasing $H_2PO_4^-$ into solution according to:

Step 1 $3F^- + Al^{+3} \rightarrow AlF_3 \downarrow$ [Al^{+3} decreases as AlF_3 precipitates]

Step 2 $AlPO_4 \cdot 2H_2O + 2H^+ \rightarrow Al^{+3} + H_2PO_4^- + 2H_2O$

The subsequent increase in solution $H_2PO_4^-$ during the extraction is measured, which represents an estimate of the soil's capacity to supply plant available P. The HCl in the extractant also dissolves Ca-P minerals present in slightly acid and neutral soils.

The *Mehlich–3P* soil test is also used in acid and neutral soil test and contains NH_4F, extracting P in the same manner as the Bray–1 P test. A *Mehlich–1* soil test (0.05M HCl + 0.0125M H_2SO_4) is used in some regions with more highly weathered, low-CEC soils. The quantity of P dissolved by these dilute acids from Fe-P and Al-P minerals is calibrated with P crop response.

The *Olsen* or *Bicarb-P* soil test is used in neutral and calcareous soils and contains 0.5 M $NaHCO_3$ buffered at pH 8.5. In these soils, Ca-P minerals control solution P concentration (Fig. 5-8). The HCO_3^- causes $CaCO_3$ to precipitate during extraction, which

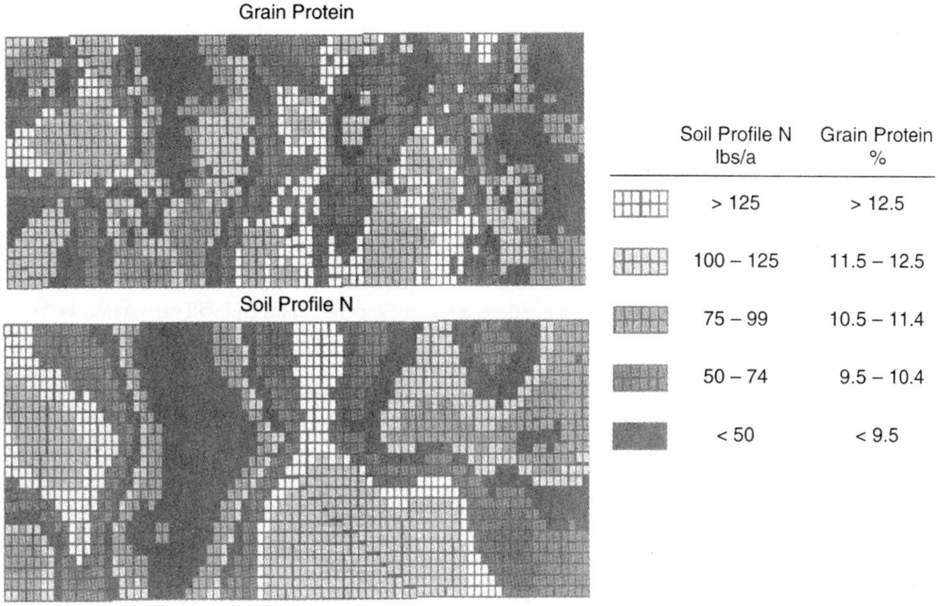

Figure 9-47 **Spatial distribution of soil profile N content is similar to that of wheat grain protein content determined with a grain protein sensor mounted on a yield-monitoring combine. Grain protein content is high where soil NO_3^- is high.**

reduces Ca^{+2} in solution. Consequently, Ca-P minerals dissolve to buffer solution Ca^{+2} and release $H_2PO_4^-$ into solution by:

Step 1 $HCO_3^- + Ca^{+2} \rightarrow CaCO_3 \downarrow + H^+$ [Ca^{+2} decreases as $CaCO_3$ precipitates]

Step 2 $CaHPO_4 \cdot 2H_2O + H^+ \rightarrow Ca^{+2} + H_2PO_4^- + 2H_2O$

As with the Bray–1 and Mehlich–3 tests, the increase in $H_2PO_4^-$ provides a measure of the soil's ability to supply plant available P.

The *Kelowna* (0.015N NH_4F + 0.25N HOAc) and *modified Kelowna* (0.015N NH_4F + 0.5N HOAc + 1N NH_4Oac) soil tests are recommended for plant available P on high-pH, calcareous soils in western Canada.

Although soil test calibrations differ among regions and crops, general sufficiency levels for the common P soil tests are shown in Table 9-13. These categories show that the Bray-1 and Mehlich P tests extract similar quantities of P, while the Olsen P test extracts about half as much P. The soil test level indicates the relative potential crop response to nutrient application. As soil test P increases, response to P fertilization decreases. Thus, 100% yield or no response to P fertilization occurs at high soil test P (Fig. 9-48). At lower soil test P levels, soybean would attain 100% at 10 ppm, while alfalfa would only reach 60% yield at 10 ppm soil test P.

K Soil Tests Exchangeable plus solution K^+ is usually extracted with 1 M NH_4OAc (Table 9-10)

$$\text{Clay-}K^+ + NH_4^+ \rightarrow \text{Clay-}NH_4^+ + K^+$$

Table 9-13 **Calibrations for the Bray-1, Mehlich III, and Olsen Soil Tests***

Sufficiency Level	*Bray-1*	*Mehlich-3*	*Olsen*	*P Recommendation*
	----	*ppm*	----	*lbs* P_2O_5/a
Very low	< 5	< 7	< 3	50–90
Low	6-12	8–14	4–7	30–50
Medium	13–25	15–28	8–11	10–30
High	26–40	29–50	12–20	0 (starter P if needed)
Very High	> 40	> 50	> 20	0

*P sufficiency levels and recommendations represent general values and will vary greatly between region and crop.

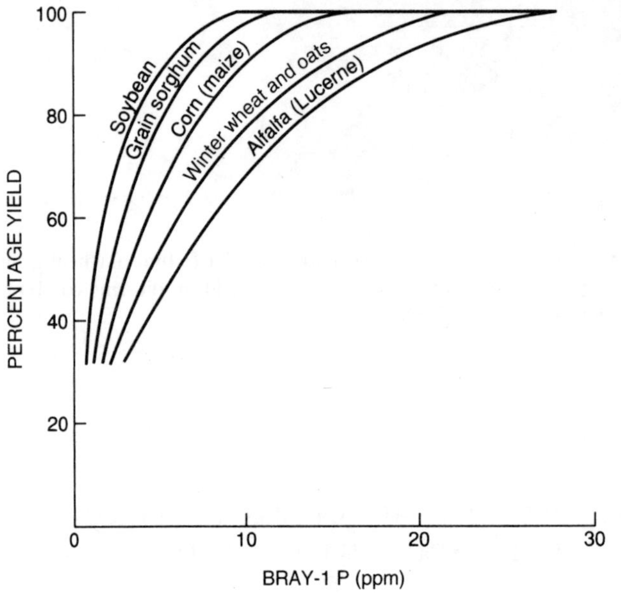

Figure 9-48 **Response of various crops to Bray-1 P.** ***(Olsen et al., 1984,*** **Nat. Corn Handbook.)**

This method will, however, extract some K^+ from soils with high K release and retention properties that is unavailable to crops. The NH_4OAc soil test extracts K^+ in concentrations related to K availability to plants; however, as with P, crops vary in their responsiveness to K (Fig. 9-49). A general calibration for the NH_4OAc soil test is shown in Table 9-14.

S Soil Tests Like NO_3^-, SO_4^{-2} is mobile in the soil; thus, in humid regions, extractable SO_4^{-2} has not been a reliable measure of S availability. In low rainfall regions; H_2O, $Ca(H_2PO_4)_2$, or $CaCl_2$ extractable SO_4^{-2} have been used with some success. Plant available SO_4^{-2} is supplied by OM mineralization during the growing season. Since organic S represents about 90% of total S in most soils, S soil tests that estimate mineralizable S might be more accurate in identifying S-deficient soils. $Ca(H_2PO_4)_2$ or KH_2PO_4 extractable S represents some mineralizable organic S + SO_4^{-2} and should be a better indicator of S availability (Fig. 9-50). In pastoral soils, extraction with 0.2 M KH_2PO_4 satisfactorily measures both currently available SO_4^{-2} and the very important contribution of labile organic S. A typical calibration of the S soil test for mixed grass pasture is shown in Table 9-15.

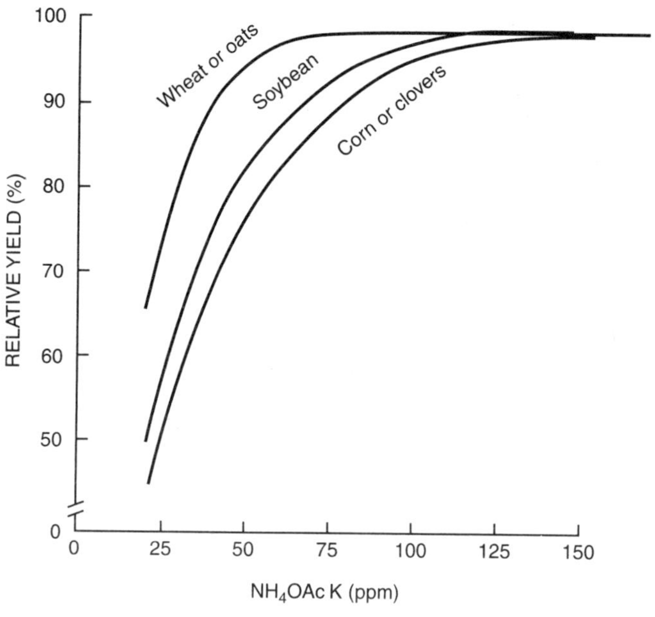

Figure 9-49 Relationship between NH_4OAc extractable K and relative yield of several crops.

Table 9-14 General Calibration of the NH_4OAc-K Soil Test*

Sufficiency Level	*NH_4OAc-K*	*K Recommendation*
	ppm	*lbs K_2O/a*
Very low	<40	120–160
Low	41–80	80–120
Medium	81–120	40–80
High	121–160	0–40
Very High	>160	0

*K sufficiency levels and recommendations represent general values and will vary greatly between region and crop.

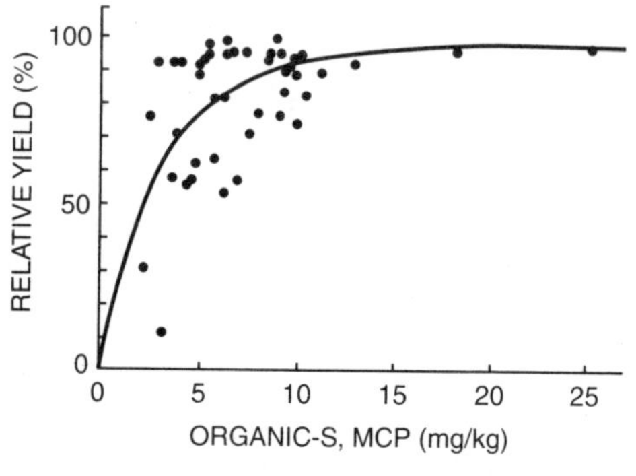

Figure 9-50 Relationship between relative annual yield of pasture and $Ca(H_2PO_4)_2$ -extractable organic S.

Where S soil tests are unreliable, recognizing that crop response to S is more likely on coarse-textured, low-OM soils is helpful in identifying potential S deficiency. Other factors to consider are (1) crop requirement for S, (2) crop history, (3) use of manures, (4) proximity to industrial S emissions, and (5) S content of irrigation water (Chapter 7).

Table 9-15 **Interpretation of SO_4 and Organic S Soil Test Values**

Soil S Status	*SO_4^{-2} (ppm)*	*Organic S (ppm)*	*S Recommendation*
Deficient	0–6	0–10	10–20 lbs/a of S
Adequate	7–12	10–20	0
Above optimum	> 12	> 20	0

SOURCE: Sulphur Institute, 1994.

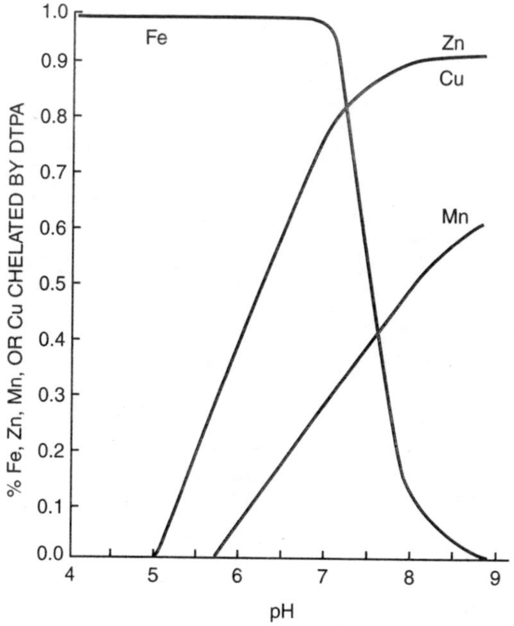

Figure 9-51 **Influence of soil pH on the amount of Fe, Zn, Mn, or Cu chelated with DTPA. Over the pH range of most soils (pH 5 to 8), DTPA complexes micronutrients in quantities related to crop response.**

Fe, Zn, Mn, Cu Soil Tests Chelate-micronutrient relationships and stability in soils are utilized in soil testing for micronutrients (Chapter 8). When EDDHA is added to soil, 100% is complexed with Fe over the soil pH range (Fig. 8-10). Therefore, EDDHA might make a good extractant for Fe; however, Fe-EDDHA is so stable that very few other micronutrient cations would be complexed with EDDHA. Although Fe-DTPA is not as stable at high pH as Fe-EDDHA (Fig. 8-11), the other micronutrients (i.e., Zn and Cu) exhibit stability with DTPA, especially at pH < 7 (Fig. 9-51).

Knowledge of chelate stability in soil provides the basis for developing the DTPA soil test for Fe, Zn, Cu, and Mn, which is used in most soil testing laboratories. EDTA is less effective in extracting micronutrients because it has a high affinity for Ca. In soils with pH > 6.5, EDTA would be ~100% complexed with Ca, with little remaining capacity to complex Fe, Zn, Cu, and Mn. Before chelate relationships were developed, the most common micronutrient soil test was based on an acid extraction, usually HCl. Although some laboratories still use acid-extractable micronutrient soil tests, the DTPA test is preferred. Excellent correlations exist between DTPA-extractable micronutrients and relative crop yield (Fig. 9-52). For example, DTPA effectively separates Zn-deficient from nondeficient soils (Fig. 9-53). About 90% of the soils testing < 0.65 ppm Zn responded to Zn, whereas 100% above this level did not respond. The DTPA soil test has been calibrated for most crops, and the general interpretation for DTPA-extractable micronutrients is shown in Table 9-16.

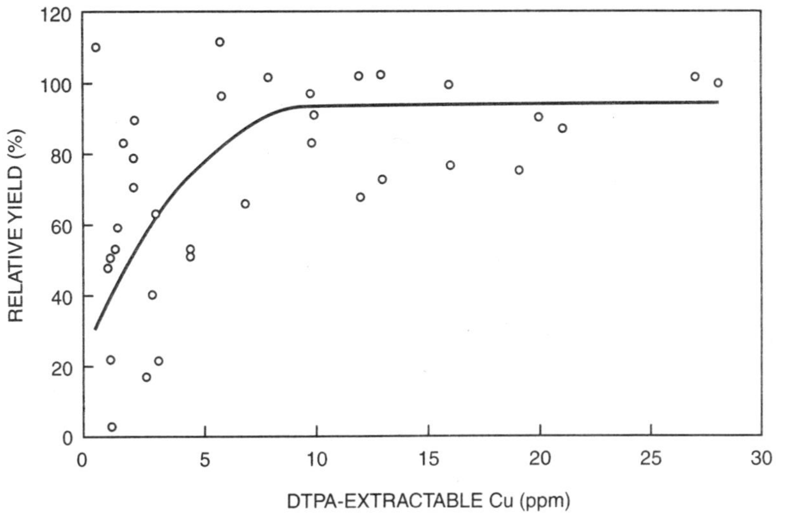

Figure 9-52 Relationship between DTPA-extractable Cu and relative barley yield.

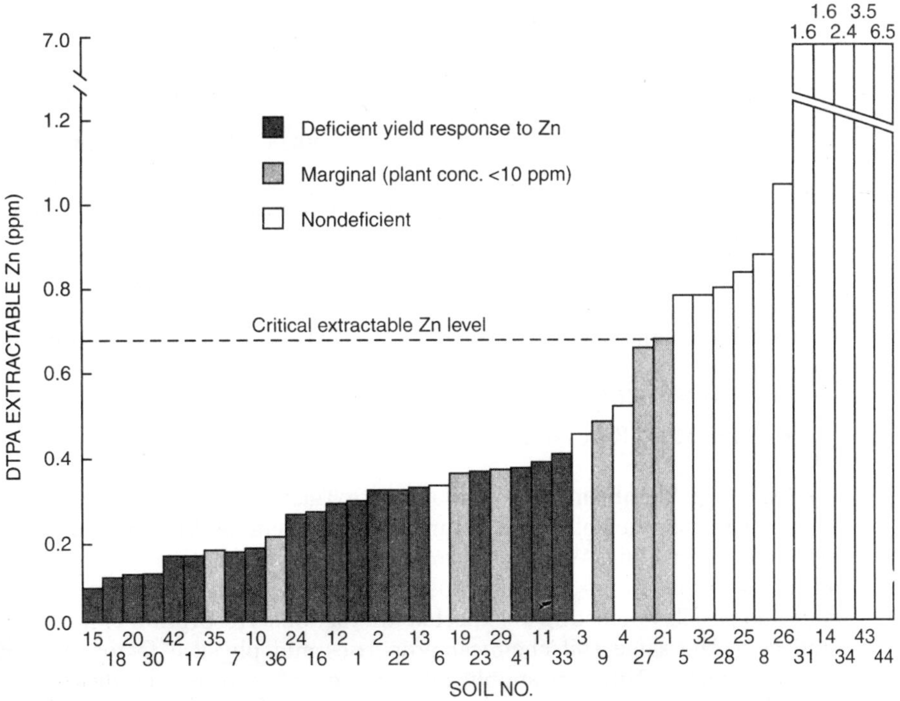

Figure 9-53 Corn response of forty soils to Zn as a function of DTPA soil test levels. *(Havlin and Soltanpour, 1981, SSSAJ, 45:70–75.)*

Table 9-16 DTPA-Extractable Fe, Zn, Cu, and Mn for Deficient, Marginal, and Sufficient Soils

Sufficiency	*Fe*	*Zn*	*Mn*	*Cu*
		ppm		
Low (deficient)	0–2.5	0–0.5	< 1.0	0–0.4
Marginal	2.6–4.5	0.6–1.0	—	0.4–0.6
High (sufficient)	> 4.5	> 1.0	> 1.0	> 0.6

B, Cl, and Mo Soil Tests Extraction with hot water is the most common soil test for B. Critical levels for most crops are ≤ 0.5 ppm B. When hot water-extractable B is > 4 to 5 ppm, B toxicity can occur.

Like NO_3^-, Cl^- is soluble, so extraction with water is used. Soil samples should be taken to at least a 2-ft depth. The critical water-extractable Cl^- level is 7 to 8 ppm for most crops.

No reliable Mo soil test has been developed, although both water and NH_4 oxalate extracts have been used. Mo deficiency is uncommon in the United States.

Multinutrient Soil Tests With the advance of analytical instruments capable of measuring elements simultaneously, soil tests have been developed that simultaneously extract macro- and micronutrients. Components of the Mehlich–3 soil test and their functions in extracting nutrients include:

- 0.2N CH_3COOH (acetic acid)—buffers solution at pH 2 to 3 to limit CaF_2 precipitation.
- 0.25N NH_4NO_3 (ammonium nitrate)—NH_4^+ exchanges for Ca^{+2}, Mg^{+2}, K^+, and Na^+ on CEC.
- 0.013N HNO_3 (nitric acid)—dissolves some Ca-P and micronutrient-containing minerals.
- 0.015N NH_4F (ammonium fluoride)—extracts P (as described in the section *P Soil Tests*); NH_4^+ exchanges for cations on CEC.
- 0.001 M EDTA (Table 8-1)—complexes Fe, Zn, Cu, and Mn.

For calcareous soils, the multielement NH_4HCO_3-DTPA soil test is based on:

- 1.0 M NH_4HCO_3 (ammonium bicarbonate)—NH_4^+ exchanges for K^+.
- 0.005 M DTPA (Table 8-1)—complexes Fe, Zn, Cu, and Mn.

Ion Exchange Membranes Simultaneous extraction of plant nutrients with ion exchange resins or membranes placed in intimate contact with soil provides an alternative to conventional soil testing. When used together, anion and cation exchange resins can absorb all important nutrients simultaneously while measuring the availability of nutrients over time and possibly detecting unexpected interactions. Absorption of nutrients to the resin is subject to the same soil chemical properties and physical factors that influence plant nutrient uptake. Nutrient supply rate or ion flux can also be measured by these resin procedures. Thus, these plant nutrient availability determinations are likely more biologically meaningful than those obtained by chemical extraction. They also have the advantage of elimination of collection, preparation, and treatment of soil samples. The simplicity of simultaneous elution of all ions from the resins and their subsequent instrumental analysis is both cost effective and time saving.

Calibrating Soil Tests

To identify the most efficient nutrient application rate from soil test results, soil tests must be calibrated against crop responses to applied nutrients in field experiments conducted over a wide range of soils. Yield responses from various rates of applied nutrients can then be related to the quantity of available nutrients indicated by the soil test. An accurately calibrated soil test (1) correctly identifies the degree of nutrient deficiency or sufficiency and (2) estimates of the nutrient rate required to optimize crop productivity.

Controlled experiments are initially conducted in the greenhouse to provide information about (1) the ability of a soil test to extract a nutrient in quantities related to the crop uptake (i.e., to identify the best extractants), and (2) the relationship between soil test level and relative yield. Figure 9-22 illustrates relative crop responsiveness to a range of DTPA-extractable Fe levels. When DTPA Fe is > 4.5 ppm normal growth is observed.

After greenhouse studies have been completed, field calibration experiments are conducted on the major soil series and crops in the region. For example, if a P soil test is being calibrated, 4 to 6 P rates will be applied and the crop response quantified by measuring yield (e.g., forage, grain, and fruit) and P content in the whole plant or plant part (Fig. 9-24). Yield response data can be expressed as *% yield* or *yield increase* (Fig. 9-54). Percent yield represents the ratio of yield in unfertilized soil to yield obtained where P is nonlimiting (fertilized soil). For example, 70% yield means that the unfertilized crop yield is 70% of that obtained at optimum P. Yield increase represents the yield increase obtained with optimum fertilization. Thus, as soil test P increases, % yield increases to 100%, or the soil test level where no difference in yield is observed between fertilized and unfertilized soil. Alternatively, as soil test P level increases, yield increase to P fertilization eventually declines to zero.

Generally, when % yield reaches 95 to 100% or when yield increase reaches 0 to 5%, the critical soil test level (CL) is obtained (Fig. 9-54). The CL represents the soil test level above which no yield response to fertilization will be obtained. Soil test CLs vary among

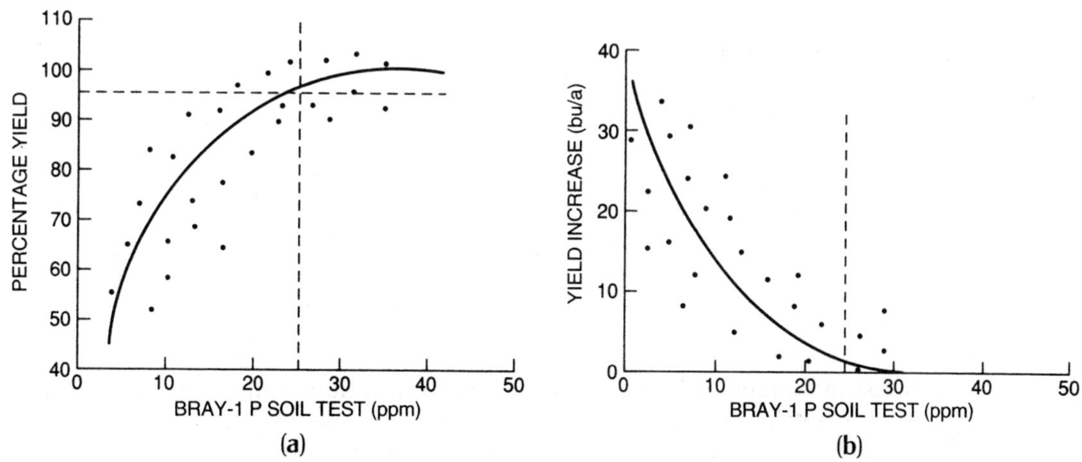

Figure 9-54 **Relationship between % yield (a) or yield increase (b) and Bray-1 P soil test level. The vertical dashed line represents the critical soil test level, or the soil test level below which crop response to added nutrient is expected.**

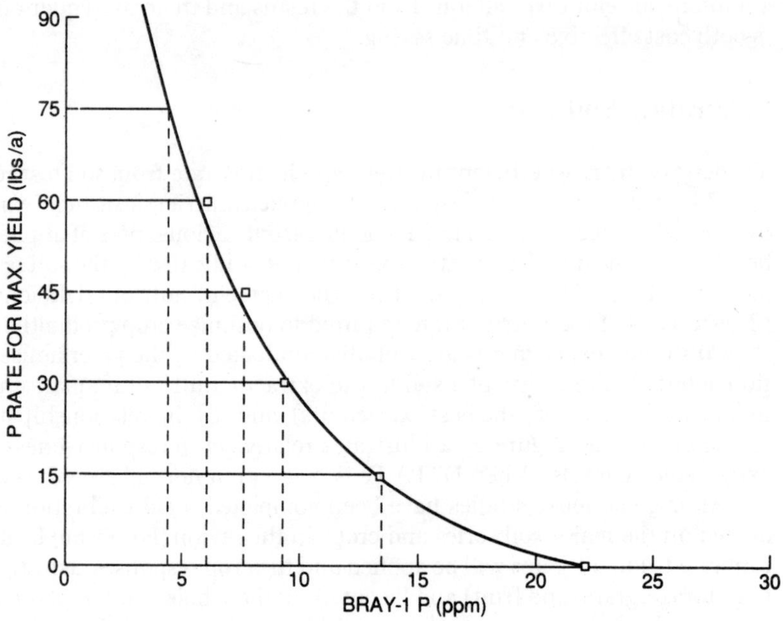

Figure 9-55 **Influence of soil test P level on P rate required for maximum yield.**

crops, climatic regions, and extractants. For example, CLs for the Bray–1 P, Olsen-P, and Mehlich-P tests are approximately 25, 13, and 28 ppm, respectively (Table 9-13).

Soil test calibration studies also provide data to establish fertilizer recommendations. For example, at each field location, P rate required for optimum yield can be determined and displayed (Fig. 9-55). Increasing soil test level corresponds to decreasing P rate required for optimum yield. These diagrams are used to establish nutrient rates associated with very low, low, medium, and high-soil test levels; however, an equation is commonly used to describe the relationship (Fig. 9-55).

Interpretation of Soil Tests

Many soil test reports, in addition to reporting exact measurements, classify the degree of nutrient sufficiency as very low, low, medium, high, or very high, based on the quantity of nutrient extracted, although the exact quantity is also reported. The probability of a response to fertilization increases with decreasing soil test level (Fig. 9-56). While nutrient availability is only one factor influencing plant growth, the probability of a response to applied nutrients increases with decreasing soil test level. For example, $>$ 85% of the fields testing very low may give a profitable increase; in the low category, increases may occur 60 to 85% of the time, whereas $<$ 15% will respond with very high ratings. These values are arbitrary, but they illustrate the concept of the probability of a response.

Soil test interpretation involves an economic evaluation of the relation between soil test level and nutrient response. However, the response may vary due to several factors, including soil, crop, expected yield, management level, and weather (Fig. 9-57). Factors A–D represent increasing yield potential or yield goal, where A and D are low- and high-yield levels, respectively. However, A–D also represent other factors, including climate and crop/variety. For example, increasing rainfall from drought (A) to optimum rainfall

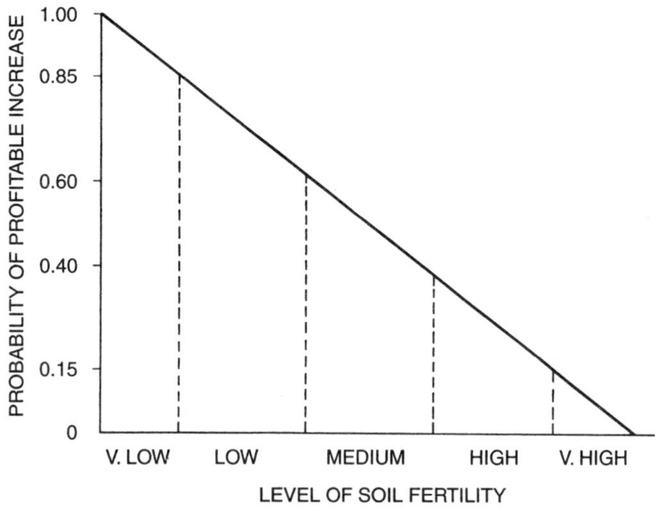

Figure 9-56 **The probability of obtaining a profitable response from nutrient addition increases with decreasing soil test level.**

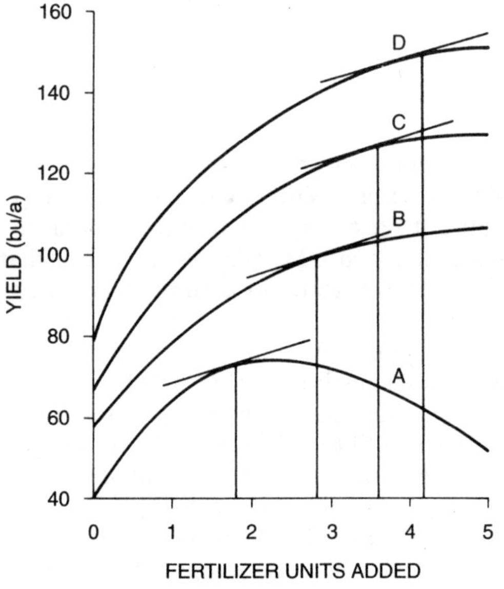

Figure 9-57 **Yield response to fertilization depends on yield potential, with "A" being the poorest and "D" the highest potential.**

(D) increases the yield potential and therefore the nutrient requirement. Different crops often respond differently to applied nutrients, where *A* might be a relatively unresponsive crop (e.g., soybeans) while *D* is extremely responsive (e.g., alfalfa or wheat) (Fig. 9-57).

Many soil test laboratories provide one recommendation, assuming best production practices for the region, and producers make adjustments as necessary. As technology and management practices improve, yield potential and recommendations increase. For the grower, the goal is to maintain plant nutrients at a level for sustained productivity and profitability, which means that nutrients should not be a limiting factor at any stage, from plant emergence to maturity.

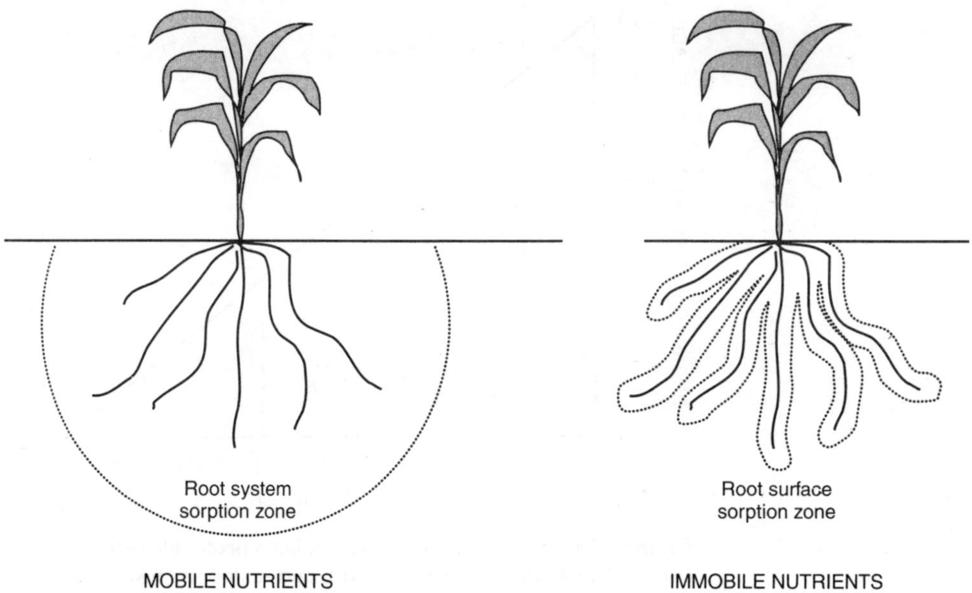

Figure 9-58 **Difference in nutrient extraction zones between mobile and immobile nutrients in the soil. For mobile nutrients, the soil test must estimate the total nutrient available in the root zone. For immobile nutrients, the soil test is an index of the quantity available to the plant.** ***(Courtesy B. Raun and G. Johnson, Oklahoma State Univ.)***

Nutrient Mobility Soil test interpretation for purposes of making nutrient recommendations is influenced by the mobility of the nutrient. With mobile nutrients, crop yield is proportional to the total quantity of nutrient present in the root zone, because of minimal interaction with soil constituents (e.g., CEC and OM) (Fig. 9-58). Recall that for NO_3^-, SO_4^{-2}, and Cl^-, a 2- to 3-ft profile sample is important for accurately assessing plant availability. In contrast, yield response to immobile nutrients (e.g., $H_2PO_4^-$, K^+, Zn^{+2}) is proportional to the concentration of nutrients near the root surface because these nutrients strongly interact with or are buffered by soil constituents (Fig. 9-58).

The mobility concept refers to the situation in which crop response to an increasing concentration of mobile nutrients is linear until the yield potential for the given environment is achieved or is limited by the depletion of the mobile nutrient or other yield limiting factors (Fig. 9-59). For example, if the profile N soil test indicated sufficient N available for only 100 bu/a, additional N would be recommended if the yield goal was 150 bu/a. N recommendations are usually based on yield goal, where the amount of N required to produce each unit of yield is known (i.e., 2.0 lbs N/bu of N for winter wheat, see p. 299). This concept is also evident when in-season N is recommended because better-than-average growing conditions increased yield potential above initial estimates provided before planting.

Nutrient-Response Functions The most common models used in fitting nutrient-response data are shown in Figure 9-59 and are given by the following:

Linear-plateau model:

$$Y = mx + b \quad \text{linear portion with slope} = m$$
$$Y = b \quad \text{plateau portion with slope} = 0$$

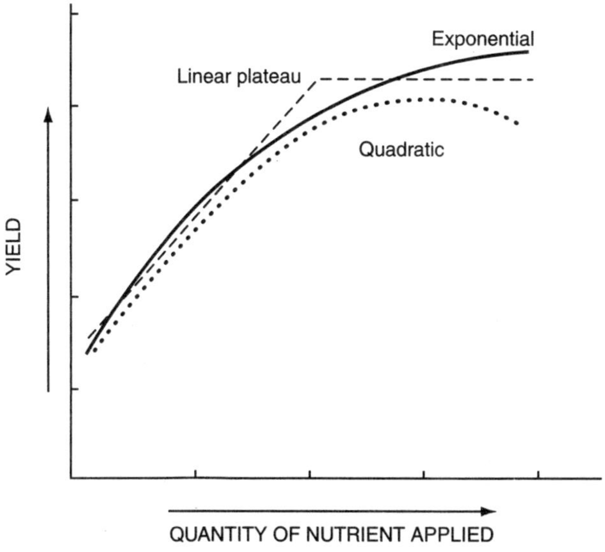

Figure 9-59 **Common equations used to describe crop response to applied nutrients.**

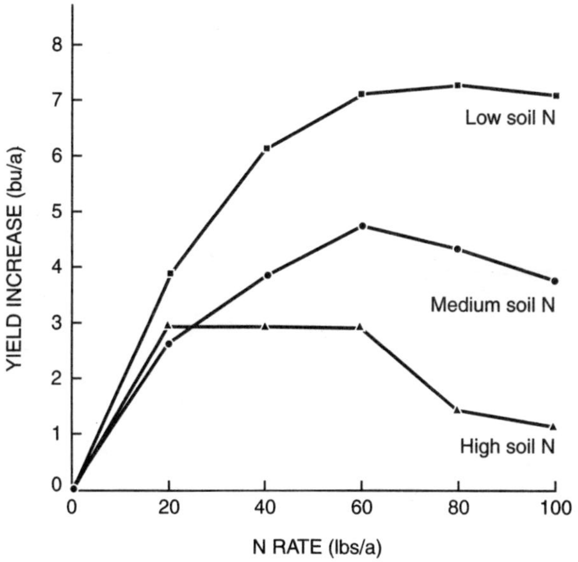

Figure 9-60 **Interaction between wheat grain yield response to fertilizer N and soil profile NO_3. *(Thompson, 1976,* Kansas Agric. Exp. Sta. Bull. 590.*)***

Exponential model:

$$Y = e^{x}$$

Quadratic model:

$$Y = a + bx - cx^2$$

where Y = yield, x = nutrient rate, and a, b, c, and m represent constants or coefficients.

All of these equations have been used to describe yield response to both immobile and mobile nutrients. Regardless of the equation used, the response function will vary with the crop (Fig. 9-48), yield potential (Fig. 9-57), soil test level (Figs. 9-60 and 9-61), previous crop (Fig. 9-62), year (Fig. 9-63), and other factors discussed in Chapter 10.

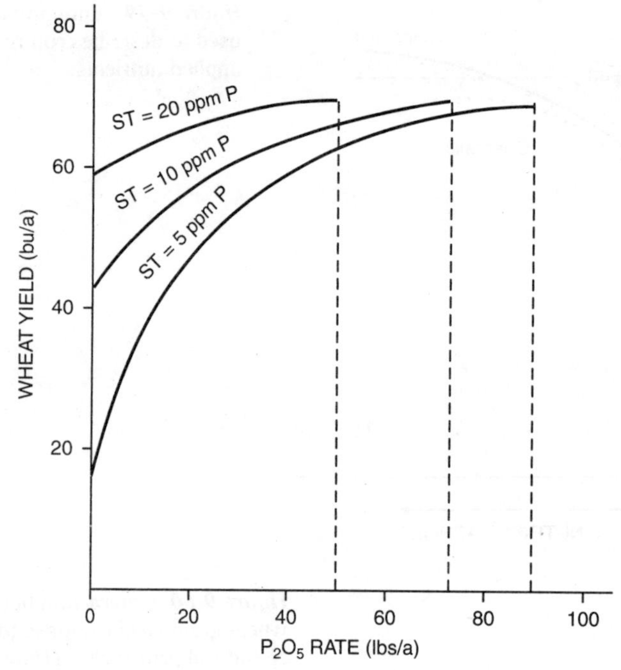

Figure 9-61 **Relationship between expected wheat yield and P_2O_5 rate at three soil test levels.**

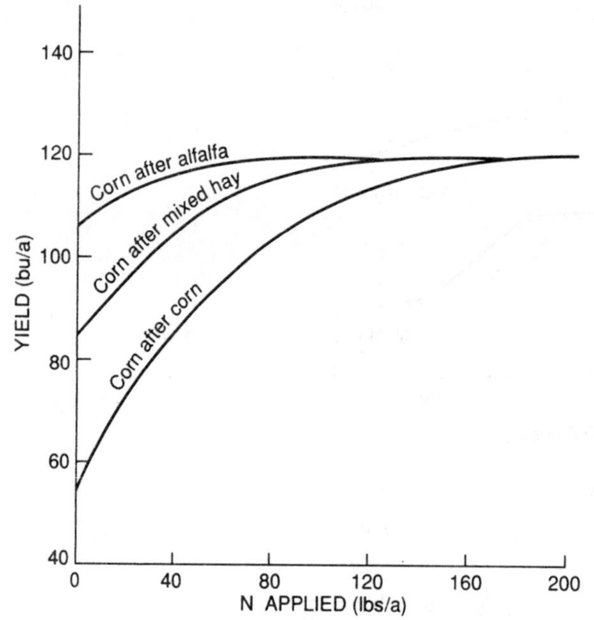

Figure 9-62 **Influence of previous crop on corn grain yield response to N fertilization.** ***(Barber, 1967,*** **SSSA Spec. Publ. No. 2.)**

N Recommendation Model With mobile nutrients, buildup and/or maintenance programs are not practical, because these nutrients can readily leach below the root zone in many soils. Preventing potential NO_3^- contamination of groundwater by leaching while providing sufficient N for profitable crop production requires accurate N recommendations. N recommendations require knowledge of the quantity of N needed by the crop and supplied by the soil. N recommendations are based on:

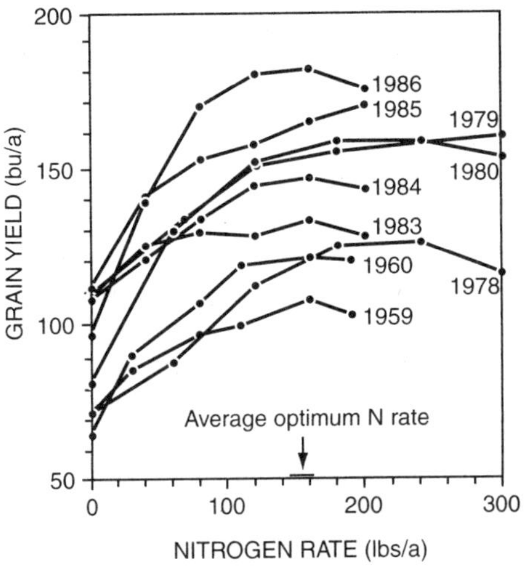

Figure 9-63 Typical corn yield response to applied N on Plano silt loam soils. Bar represents ± standard error of the mean of economically optimum N rates, *(Vanotti and Bundy, 1994,* J. Prod. Agric., *7:243.)*

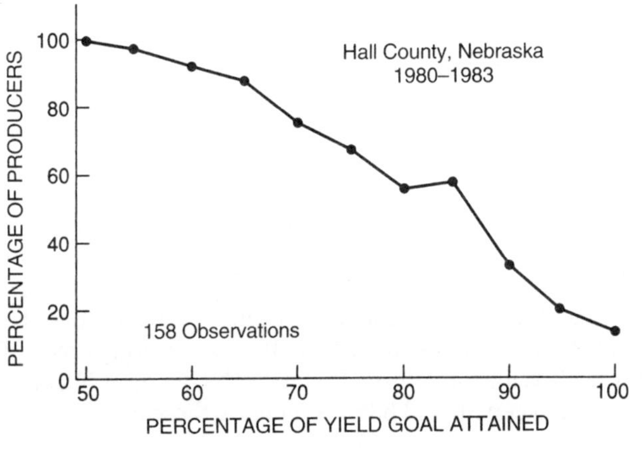

Figure 9-64 Producer success in attaining the yield goal for irrigated corn. *(Schepers and Martin, 1986,* Proc. Agric. Impacts on Groundwater, *Dublin, OH: Well Water Journal Publ. Co.)*

$$N_{REC} = N_{CROP} - N_{SOIL} - (N_{OM} + N_{PC} + N_{MN})$$

where N_{REC} = N recommendation
N_{CROP} = crop yield goal × N coefficient
N_{SOIL} = preplant soil NO_3^- content
N_{OM} = organic N mineralization
N_{PC} = previous legume crop N availability
N_{MN} = manure N availability

N_{CROP} represents the N required by the crop and involves estimating yield and N required to produce that yield (N coefficient). Underestimating the yield goal can cause considerable yield loss due to underfertilization. Alternatively, overestimating the yield goal results in overfertilization, which can greatly increase profile N content after harvest and increase N leaching potential. Surveys suggest that 80% of growers overestimate yield goal and thus apply excess N (Fig. 9-64). The N coefficient also varies among crops, regions, and climates (Table 9-1). For example, 1 bu of corn contains 0.7 lbs N. Applied N recovered by the grain varies between 40 and 70%; thus, usually 0.9 to 1.7 or an average value of 1.2 lbs N/bu grain is used for the N coefficient to determine N_{CROP}. With winter wheat, for example, a 1.8 to 2.4 lbs N/bu yield goal is used to estimate N_{CROP}. Thus, with a 60 bu/a yield goal, total N required by the crop would be 120 lbs/a (using 2.0 lbs N/bu).

The N_{CROP} estimate is reduced by potential N available in the soil. After adjustments for soil profile NO_3^- content, if necessary, N_{CROP} is adjusted for potential N availability from N_{OM}, N_{PC}, and N_{MN}. N_{MN} varies with rate applied and is approximately 5 lbs N/ton in the first year following manure application. Generally, 50% of the manure N is available in the first year, 25% in the second year, and none in the third year (Chapter 10). N_{PC} depends on the legume, legume yield, and length of time after the legume crop was rotated to the nonlegume crop (Chapter 4 and Chapter 13). N_{PC} from forage legumes is generally greater than grain legumes, although low-yielding forage legumes can fix less N_2 than high-yielding grain legumes (Table 4-6). The influence of N_{PC} on N_{CROP} for corn is shown in Figure 9-63. When nonlegume crops are grown on soils previously cropped to a forage legume, N_{PC} decreases with time (Fig. 4-9). Thus, N_{REC} is lower in the first year following the legume compared with subsequent years.

Few N_{REC} models include N_{OM} because of the difficulty in accurately estimating the N content of manure and the quantity of N mineralization under variable climate conditions from year to year. Although many tests have been evaluated, they have not always been highly correlated with N_{OM}. Some models reduce the N coefficient to account for N_{OM}. Alternatively, some N_{REC} models use % soil OM as an indicator of N_{OM} (Table 9-11). Credits for N_{OM} generally range from 20 to 80 lbs N/a.

N_{REC} Based on Average N-Response Data. Most N_{REC} systems are based on field trials that quantify crop response to a wide range of N rates (Fig. 9-24). The N-response data over many soils, soil and crop management inputs, and years are combined to develop an average N-response equation that uses average yield goals and average N coefficients (lb N/bu grain) In most situations, the actual N rate needed for optimum yield varies greatly between years. For example, Figure 9-65 shows typical variation in crop N response over years. Under dryland conditions, variation in yield response would likely be more extreme. Based on optimum N rate determined in each year, a two fold range in N coefficients was observed (Table 9-17). At the optimum N rate for each year, the N-use efficiency (NUE) or % N applied that was recovered in the grain ranged between 36 and 63%. Averaging these data results in 185 bu/a grain yield at 145 lbs/a average optimum N rate. To ensure that N is not limiting in high-yield years, average yield potential should be increased. Increasing optimum yield 10% or 204 bu/a raised the N requirement to 160 lbs/a, which decreased the N coefficient and NUE in 3 of

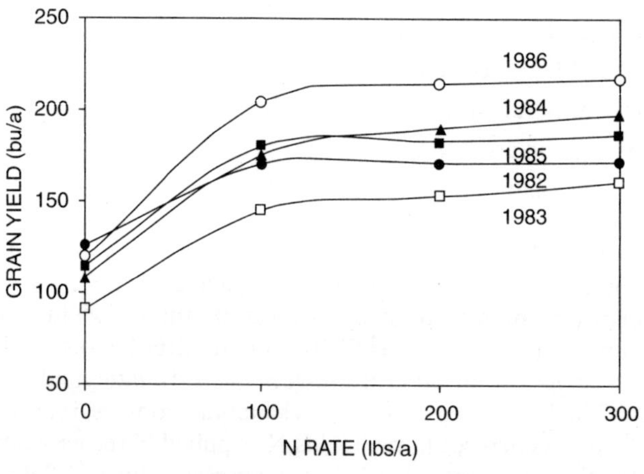

Figure 9-65 Variation in irrigated corn yield response to N. *(Bock and Hergert, 1991, in R. F. Follett et al. [eds],* Managing Nitrogen for Groundwater Quality and Farm Profitability, *pp. 140–164 Madison, WI: Soil Sci. Soc. Am.)*

Table 9-17 Variation in Irrigated Corn Yield Response to N and N-Use Efficiency Between Years

Year	*Optimum Yield*	*Yield No N*	*Optimum N rate*	*N Coefficient**	*NUE (optimum)†*	*NUE (Ave + 10%)‡*
	a	*b*	*c*	*a/c*	$(a_{1.4}-b_{1.2})/c$	$(a_{1.4}-b_{1.2})/c_{(ave+10\%)}$
	------- *bu/a* ---------		*lbs/a*	*lbs N/lbs grain*	--------------- % ---------------	
1982	170	126	95	100	51	30
1983	160	91	180	50	36	40
1984	195	109	180	61	44	50
1985	185	115	130	80	52	42
1986	215	120	140	86	63	55
Average	*185*	*112*	*145*	*71*	*49*	*44*

*(bu/a) × (56 lbs/bu) = lbs grain/a.

†In the NUE calculation, 1.2 and 1.4% grain N content was assumed for the unfertilized and fertilized treatments. NUE → % fertilizer N recovered in the grain at the optimum N rate → $(a_{1.4}-b_{1.2})/c$ represents [(fertilized yield*1.4% N – unfertilized yield*1.2% N)/optimum N rate]*100

‡NUE → % fertilizer N recovered in the grain at the average optimum N rate + 10% (160 lb N/a) → $(a_{1.4}-b_{1.2})/c_{(ave+10\%)}$ represents [(fertilized yield*1.4% N – unfertilized yield*1.2% N)/average optimum N rate + 10%]*100

SOURCE: Adapted from Bock and Hergert, 1991. In Follet et. al. (eds), *Managing Nitrogen for Groundwater Quality and Farm Profitability,* Madison, Wis.: Soil Sci. Soc. Am.

the 5 years. This estimate is quite conservative, as the N recommendation model currently used for irrigated corn in this region would have resulted in a 205 lbs N/a recommendation that would have further reduced NUE from 49 to 44%.

These data illustrate the difficulty in accurately estimating yield goal for a given year, so use of average yield estimates results in misapplication of N that significantly contributes to low NUE. While year-to-year variation in growing season environment greatly contributes to the error in predicting yield potential, these conditions also greatly influence the ability of the soil to provide mineralizable N. Therefore, methods used to improve the accuracy of estimated annual yield goal by inclusion of appropriate soil or crop measurements indicating between year variability in N_{OM} could provide significant increases in NUE. Many of these methods involve in-season soil and plant analysis discussed earlier (see *Tissue Tests* and *Soil Tests*).

Economic and Environmental Impacts. In general, when N rate exceeds N_{REC} for optimum crop yield, considerable quantities of residual N exist after harvest, which represents potentially leachable NO_3^- (Fig. 9-66). These data illustrate that when applied N exceeds N_{REC} (160 lbs N/a), residual profile NO_3^- increased. Since rooting depth is about 5 to 6 ft., a portion of profile NO_3^- moves below the root zone and is unavailable to the next crop. Groundwater contamination could occur as residual N leaches through the profile. Also, when $N_{REC} > 160$ lbs N/a, no additional income is generated. These data demonstrate the importance of accurately quantifying N_{REC} for optimum production, profitability (Chapter 12), and minimum environmental risk (Chapter 13).

Immobile Nutrient Recommendations With immobile nutrients, crop yield potential is limited by the quantity of nutrient available at the soil-root interface (Fig. 9-58). Generally, solution concentrations of immobile nutrients are low, and although some replenishment occurs through exchange, mineralization, and mineral solubility reactions, the solution concentration in the soil-root zone can be depleted to levels that limit yield. Plant growth and yield will be limited to the extent that the immobile nutrient is deficient. Immobile nutrient recommendations are based on sufficiency levels determined through soil testing. For example, with a medium

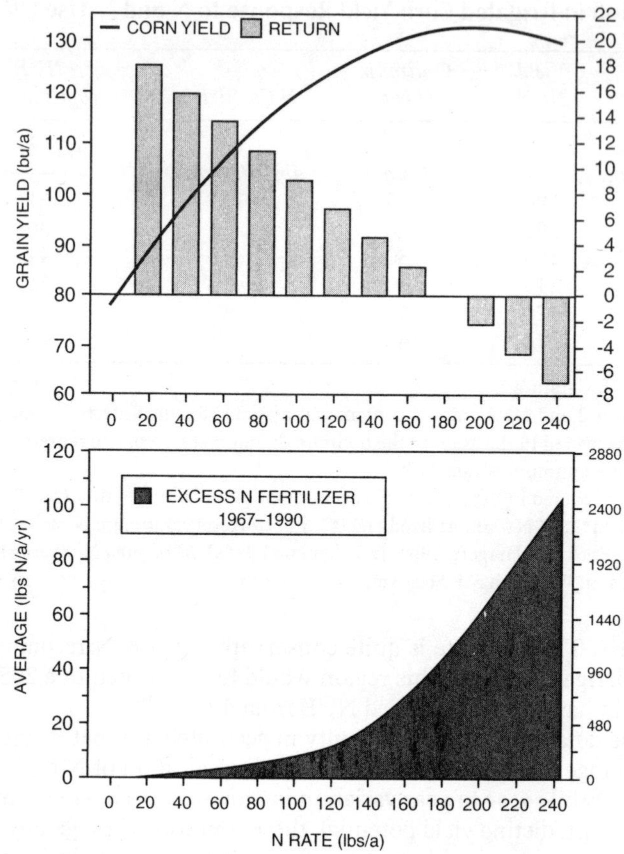

Figure 9-66 **Effect of N rate on corn yield, economic return, and amounts of excess N applied.** *(Vanotti and Bandy, 1994,* J. Prod. Agric. *7:243.)*

soil test level, 80% sufficiency in crop yield potential is expected (Fig. 9-26). Soil tests for immobile nutrients provide an index of nutrient availability that is generally independent of environment. In a good year, more roots will explore soil with similar soil test levels, and if these levels are < 100% sufficient, yield potential will not be attained. Examples of % sufficiency in relation to soil test levels are provided in Tables 9-13 and 9-14.

In contrast, some immobile nutrient recommendation models account for yield potential similarly to N recommendations. Incorporation of yield potential into the P or K recommendation, for example, is based on "replacement" of nutrients removed as a function of yield level. For instance, 70 bu/a wheat production would deplete soil test P if nutrients were applied for 40 bu/a yield potential. Alternatively, P rates applied for 70 bu/a production are inappropriate for 40 bu/a yields. Significant soil test P buildup would occur with overfertilization. As a result, some laboratories provide recommendations for immobile nutrients based on soil test level and yield potential (Table 9-18).

Table 9-18 N, P, and K Recommendations Based on Corn Yield Potential

	Yield Potential (bu/a)		
	100	140	180
	N Rate (lbs/a)		
	110	160	220
Bray-1 P (lbs P/a)	P_2O_5 Rate (lbs/a)*		
10	85	100	115
20	60	75	90
30–60	35	50	65
70	20	25	35
80	0	0	0
NH_4OAC-K (lbs K/a)	K_2O Rate (lbs/a)†		
100	195	210	220
150	145	160	170
200	95	110	120
250–310	45	60	70
330	25	30	35
350	0	0	0

*Values represent P soil test maintenance recommendations, where P rate will increase or decrease if buildup or drawdown of soil test P is advised, respectively.

†Values represent K rates for a CEC=20 meq/100 g, where K rate increases with increasing CEC or decreases with decreasing CEC.

SOURCE: Vitosh et al., 2002, Coop. Ext. Service Bulletin E–2567, Ohio State Univ., Columbus, OH.

Whether immobile nutrient recommendations include yield goal is not as important as a regular soil testing program that accurately monitors change in soil test level with time as nutrients are added and removed. Soil test history will guide adjustments in rates depending on whether soil test levels are increasing or decreasing. Soil test P or K buildup substantially above the the critical level is unnecessary, and with P, poses a potential risk to water quality (Chapter 13). Alternatively, decreasing soil test levels below the critical level that reduces yield is economically unsustainable and should be avoided. Figure 9-67 presents several management options for immobile nutrients.

Buildup. When the soil test is below the critical level (CL), it may be desirable to apply P or K at rates that increase soil test above the CL. Generally, applications of 10 to 30 lbs P_2O_5/a are required to increase soil test P level 1 ppm, depending on soil properties influencing P-fixation capacity (Chapter 5). Similarly, 5 to 15 lbs K_2O/a are needed to increase soil test K level 1 ppm, depending on CEC. When soil test is greater than CL, continued applications to further increase soil test are likely not needed, where it may be possible, depending on the crop, to draw down the soil test level. Although this can be a viable option, soil test levels can decline rapidly; thus, annual soil testing is recommended.

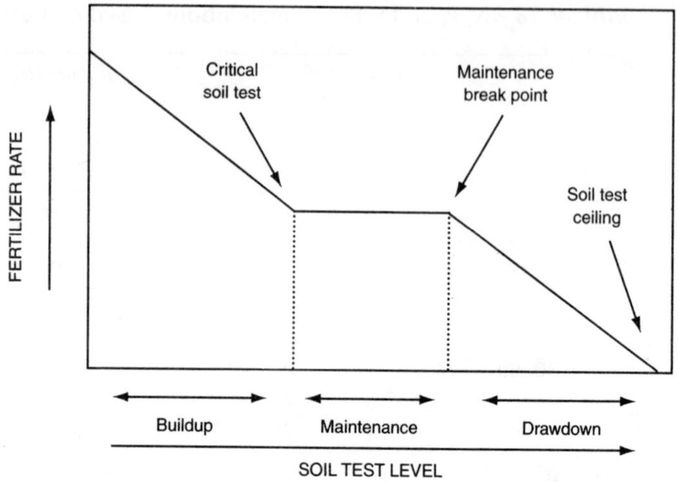

Figure 9-67 **Diagram of buildup/maintenance approach to P and K recommendations.**

Maintenance. When soil test is at or slightly above the CL, it can be maintained by P or K fertilizer rates that replace P or K crop removal, erosion, and fixation. This approach requires annual soil testing. In some 2-year and double crop rotations, the first crop can be fertilized at sufficient rates for both crops. Again, the removals, losses, and any buildup must be considered in making the recommendations.

With any immobile nutrient management program, the soil must be tested periodically to determine whether the soil fertility level is decreasing or increasing (Fig. 9-68). These data show that soil test P declined below the critical level with $\leq$ 50 lbs P_2O_5/a. In contrast, P soil test was maintained at or slightly above the initial level with annual applications of 100 lbs P_2O_5/a. Notice how soil test level increased with a buildup rate of 150 lbs P_2O_5/a, applied initially and every 3 years, and then subsequently declined with crop removal.

Decisions to maintain, draw down, or build up a soil test level dramatically affect yield potential, nutrient-use efficiency, water quality, and profitability (Fig. 9-69). With medium and high soil test levels, maintenance or starter applications are recommended. If manure is used, fertilizer nutrients are likely not needed at high soil test levels, unless soil, crop, and environmental conditions suggest that a response to starter nutrients is warranted (Chapter 10). When soil tests indicate very high sufficiency levels of P or K, no further additions of these nutrients should be made because of increased risk to water quality. At low soil test levels, buildup or sufficiency programs are recommended, depending on factors such as land ownership, fertilizer costs, and other economic considerations. For example, P or K rates based on sufficiency levels (very low, low, medium) are recommended with short-term (< 2 to 3 years) land rental. If fertilizer costs are high, sufficiency rates might be advisable until costs decrease. Regardless of the management program selected for immobile nutrients, decisions must be based on the information provided from periodic or annual soil testing.

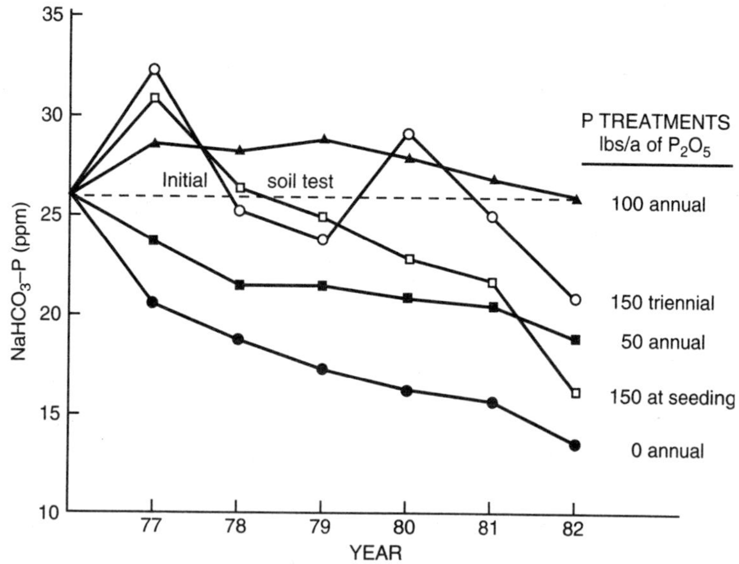

Figure 9-68 **Influence of fertilizer P on the buildup, maintenance, and decline of soil test P in irrigated alfalfa.** *(Havlin et al., 1984,* SSSAJ, *46:331–336.)*

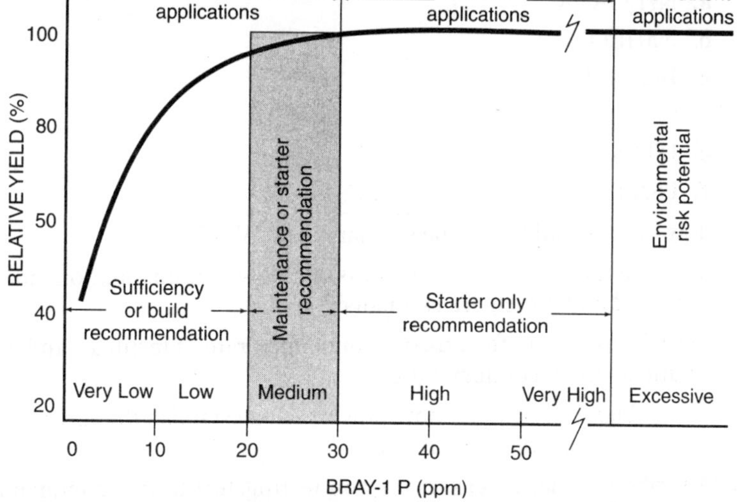

Figure 9-69 Example of buildup and maintenance rates of nutrients based on soil test level. *(Leikam et al., 2003,* Better Crops, *87:6–10.)*

Study Questions

1. What factors must be taken into consideration in interpreting tissue tests?
2. Describe the difference between critical nutrient concentration (CNC) and critical nutrient range (CNR).
3. Identify the potential problems in interpreting plant nutrient ratios in diagnosing nutritional problems.
4. Can any part or growth stage of crops be used in plant analysis? Why or why not?
5. How can plant analysis be useful in soil fertility management? Provide at least 4 examples.
6. Provide several examples of the use of in-season tissue analysis to improve N management.
7. Why must soil tests be calibrated with crop response? How would you set up a series of experiments to determine the calibration of the P soil test in your area?
8. Would you apply a given nutrient if there were a only 50% chance of obtaining a response? A 25% chance? Why or why not?
9. Ten percent of a grower's field is black lowland soil and the remainder is light-colored upland soil. How should the field be sampled? How frequently should it be resampled?
10. What is the primary advantage of point sampling over cell sampling?
11. Explain how selected spatial data can be used to develop a soil sampling plan.
12. When is deep soil sampling appropriate?
13. How does band application of immobile nutrients complicate soil-sampling procedures?
14. Why are N soil tests less reliable in high rainfall areas?
15. Describe the theoretical basis for the following soil tests.
    a. NH_4OAc-K
    b. $NaHCO_3$ – P
    c. Bray 1–P
    d. $Ca(H_2PO_4)_2$ –S
    e. DTPA
    f. PSNT
16. How often should fields be soil sampled? Why?
17. What are the essential components of an N-recommendation model? Which factors are measured and which are estimated?
18. List 5 factors that affect the recommended rate of fertilizer and describe how each factor affects the recommendation.
19. Using diagrams/figures, show how can you establish the "critical level" of a nutrient in the soil and in a plant/plant part.
20. Describe the main steps in the soil testing/fertilizer recommendation process. What are the relative errors involved in each step? What can be done to reduce these errors?
21. Briefly outline how soil tests are developed and how fertilizer recommendations are established.

22. Explain how irrigation, previous fertilizer applications, crop rotation, tillage system, soil test level, yield goal, and intended crop influence a fertilizer recommendation.

23. A grower sampled his okra leaves 8 weeks after emergence and sent them into a lab for analysis. The results showed 0.25% P. The critical level for P in okra is 0.32% (sampled at 4 weeks after emergence). Give two reasons why the grower should not apply P to this crop.

24. Profile NO_3-N is determined prior to planting. The laboratory reported the following data. How many lb N/a−4 ft are present in the profile? If the sample were combined into one 4-ft. sample, calculate the ppm N.

Soil Depth	**ppm NO_3-N**
0–6 inches	3.5
6–12 inches	4.0
1–2 feet	3.0
2–3 feet	1.5
3–4 feet	1.0

Selected References

Brown, J. R. (Ed.). 1987. *Soil testing: Sampling, correlation, calibration, and interpretation.* Special Publication No. 21. Madison, Wis.: Soil Science Society of America.

Havlin, J. L., and Jacobson., J. S. (Eds.). 1994. *New directions in soil testing and nutrient recommendations.* No. 40. Madison, Wis.: Soil Science Society of America.

Walsh, L. M., and Beaton., J. D. 1973. *Soil testing and plant analysis.* Madison, Wis.: Soil Science Society of America.

Westermann, R. L. (Ed.). 1990. *Soil testing and plant analysis.* No. 3. Madison, Wis.: Soil Science Society of America.

Whitney, D. A., Cope, J. T., and Welch., L. F. 1985. Prescribing soil and crop nutrient needs. In O. P. Engelstad (Ed.), *Fertilizer technology and use.* Madison, Wis.: Soil Science Society of America.

CHAPTER 10

Basics of Nutrient Management

Efficient nutrient management programs supply plant nutrients in adequate quantities to sustain maximum crop productivity and profitability while minimizing environmental impacts of nutrient use. Substantial economic and environmental consequences occur when nutrients limit plant productivity. Ensuring optimum nutrient availability through effective nutrient management practices requires knowledge of the interactions between the soil, plant, and environment.

Crop Characteristics

Nutrient Utilization

The quantity of nutrients required by crops (Table 9-1) varies depending on crop characteristics (crop, yield level, and variety or hybrid), environmental conditions (moisture and temperature), soil characteristics (soil type, soil fertility, and landscape position), and soil and crop management. Although these interacting factors affect plant nutrient content and recovery of applied nutrients, nutrient accumulation during the growing season generally follows plant growth (Fig. 10-1). The shape of the curve varies among plants, but nearly all plants exhibit a rapid or exponential increase in growth and nutrient accumulation rate up to a maximum, followed by a period of decline. Some plants exhibit rapid nutrient uptake and growth early in the growing season, while other plants exhibit maximum growth rate much later (Fig. 4-10). Regardless of the shape of the growth curve, nutrients are needed in the greatest quantities during periods of maximum growth rate. Thus, nutrient management plans are designed to ensure adequate nutrient supply before the exponential growth period.

Figure 10-2 illustrates the N-uptake pattern for winter wheat as it relates to the wheat growth stage. In this case, N should be applied preplant or split applied before the stem extension phase. All of the immobile nutrients, including P and K, should be applied before planting. Knowledge of crop-uptake patterns facilitates improved management for maximum productivity and recovery of applied nutrients.

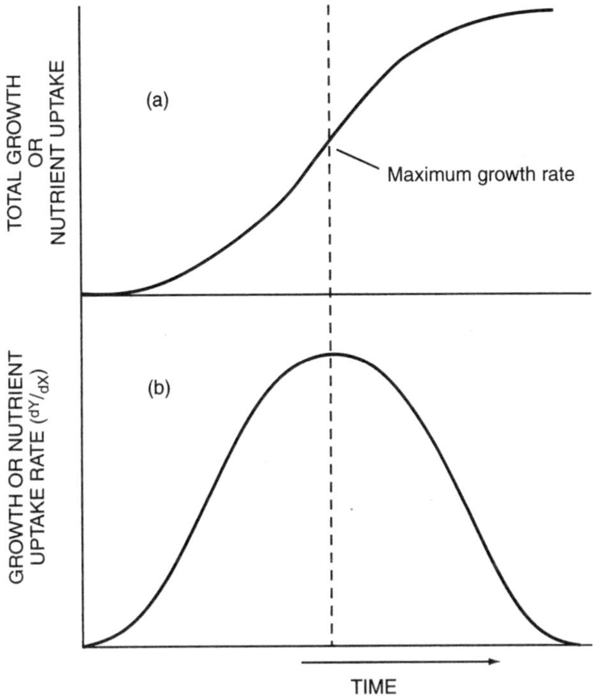

Figure 10-1 **Graphical representation of cumulative plant growth (a) and plant growth rate (b) of a typical annual plant.**

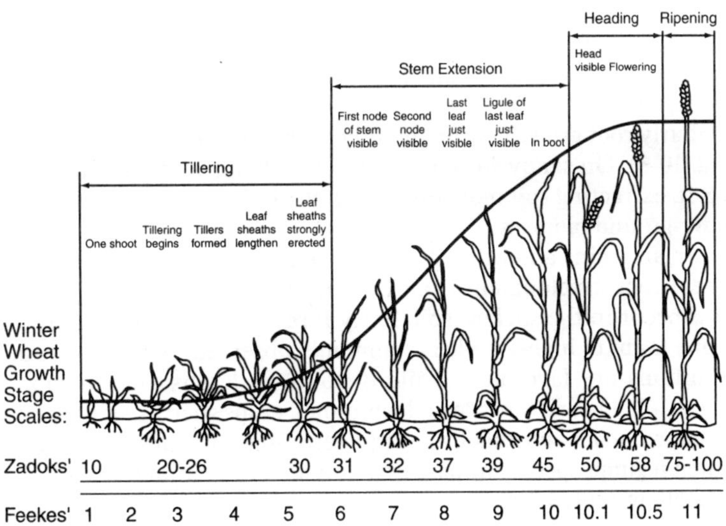

Figure 10-2 **N-uptake pattern of winter wheat throughout the growing season.** ***(Alley et al., 1996, Virginia Coop. Ext., Publ. No. 424-026.)***

Roots

Since most nutrients are absorbed by roots, understanding root characteristics is important in developing efficient nutrient management practices. Root systems are usually either fibrous or tap, and both occur with annuals, biennials, or perennials. The roots' ability to exploit soil

Table 10-1 **Typical Rooting Depths of Selected Crops**

<1.5 ft	*1.6–3.0 ft*	*3.1–6.0 ft*	*>6.0 ft*
Vegetables	Spring small grains	Corn	Alfalfa
Berry crops	Soybean	Sorghum	Sunflower
Lawn grasses	Annual legumes	Biennial clover	Cotton
	Potato	Perennial grasses	Sugar beet
			Safflower

for nutrients and water depends on their morphological and physiological characteristics. Root radius, root length, root surface/shoot weight ratio, and root hair density are the main morphological features (Table 10-1). The presence of mycorrhizae is also important.

Species and Variety Differences Knowledge of early rooting characteristics is helpful in determining efficient nutrient management programs. If a vigorous taproot is produced early, applications should be placed directly under the seed. If many lateral roots are formed early, side placement is recommended. For example, corn and wheat root systems are more extensive than cotton and peanut; thus, nutrients placed under the cotton and peanut rows are important for optimum availability (Fig. 10-3). Soybean also develops extensive root systems, contrasted with those of cotton, potatoes, and other shallow-rooted crops (Fig. 10-4). Carrots show considerable root activity at a 33-in. soil depth (Fig. 10-5), much more than that of onions, peppers, and many other vegetable crops. Reduced root activity at 13 in. indicates a compact subsoil, although activity is increased below the compact layer compared with the peat soil. Potatoes have limited root systems, often confined to only 10 to 20 in. below the soil surface.

Early root growth occurs mainly in the topsoil, increasing with plant age in the subsoil (Fig. 10-6). On sandy soils, roots of corn, alfalfa, and other deep-rooted crops reach depths ≥ 8 ft, extracting soil moisture to 6 ft. With these crops, root biomass can be as great as the above-ground biomass.

Small grains and other grasses also have extensive root systems (Figs. 10-7 and 10-8). Wheat root development from tillering to grain fill shows that, at maturity, most wheat roots occur in the surface soil. Early P response in small grains placed near the seed even on medium- to high-P soils is commonly observed. Alfalfa roots may penetrate 25 ft if soil conditions are favorable, while 8- to 10-ft depths are common even on compact soils (Fig. 10-7). One advantage of deep-rooted crops such as alfalfa and sweet clover is that they loosen compact subsoils by root penetration and subsequent decomposition. Also, deep-rooted legume species in pastures provide more animal feed during drought periods than do shallow-rooted grasses.

Root systems of the same species tend not to interpenetrate, which suggests an antagonistic or toxic effect (Fig. 10-9). Thus, with narrow row spacing and high populations, the characteristic root pattern is altered and there may be deeper rooting if soil conditions permit.

Nutrient Extraction Since roots occupy 1 to 2% of the topsoil volume and much less in the subsoil, nutrient absorption characteristics and root–soil interactions greatly influence nutrient uptake. The CEC of dicotyledonous plant roots is greater than monocotyledonous roots (Table 2-3). Nonlegumes have a lower requirement for divalent cations and take up

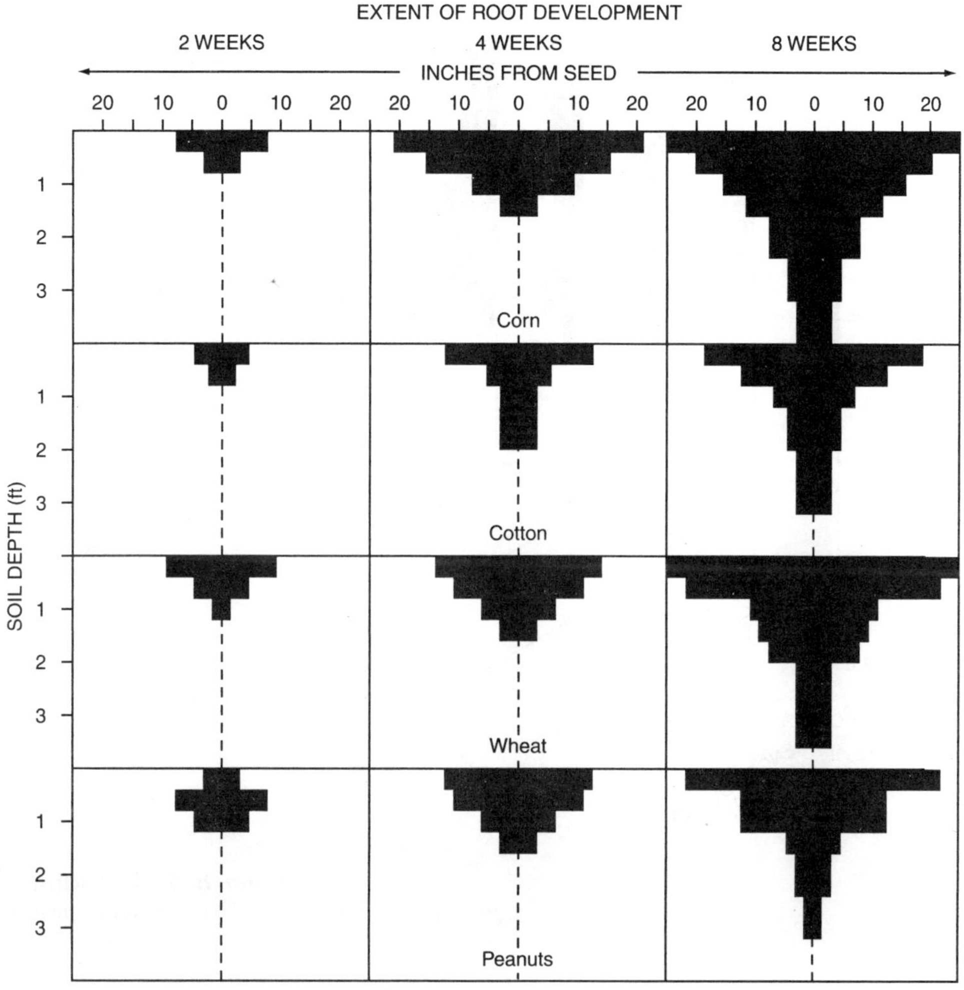

Figure 10-3 **General description of root growth and distribution at 2, 4, and 8 weeks after planting for selected crops.**

more monovalent cations. The relative absorption of cations and anions is related to the release of H^+ or HCO_3^- by the root. Acidity develops from H^+ released in response to absorption of NH_4^+, whereas pH increases with release of HCO_3^- and/or OH^- following NO_3^- uptake. Changes in rhizosphere pH affect the solubility and availability of many plant nutrients.

Mycorrhizal fungi infect roots of most plants and function primarily by enhancing nutrient uptake. Ectomycorrhiza predominately infect tree species, while vesicular-arbuscular mycorrhiza (VAM) infect most other plants, although plants vary in the degree of fungal infection. As new roots develop, mycorrhizal fungi infect or enter the root and develop extensive structures extending into and beyond the rhizosphere influenced by root hairs (Fig. 10-10). Plants with a high dependency on VAM generally exhibit (1) low root surface area due to low root branching, (2) few or short root hairs, (3) slow root

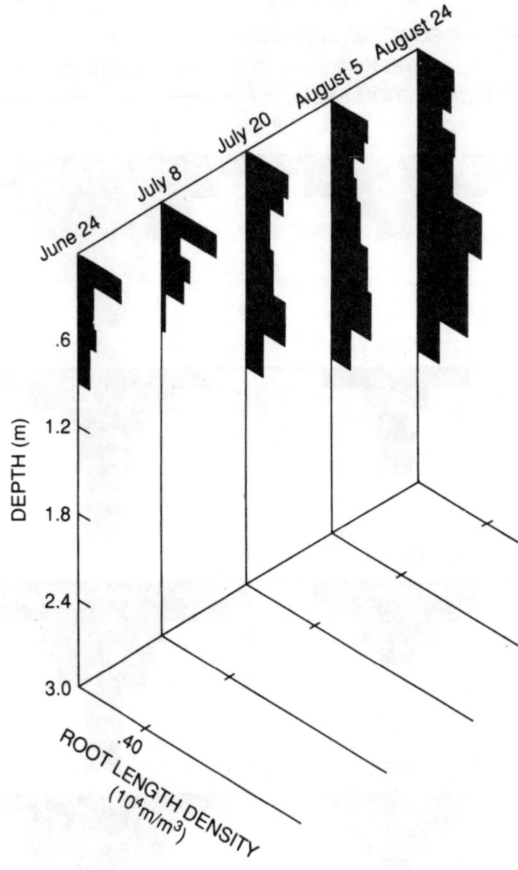

Figure 10-4 Root development in soybean. *(Taylor, 1980,* Agron. J. *72:543.)*

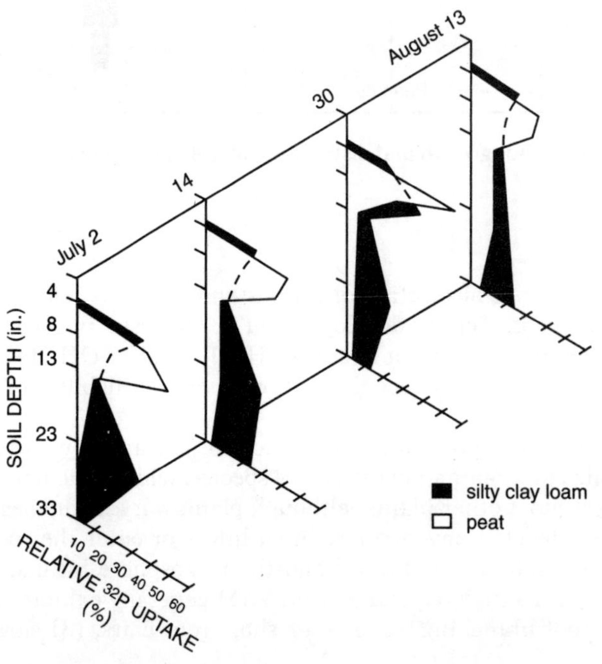

Figure 10-5 Root activity of carrots on a silty clay loam and a peat soil. *(Hammes et al., 1963,* Agron. J., *55:329.)*

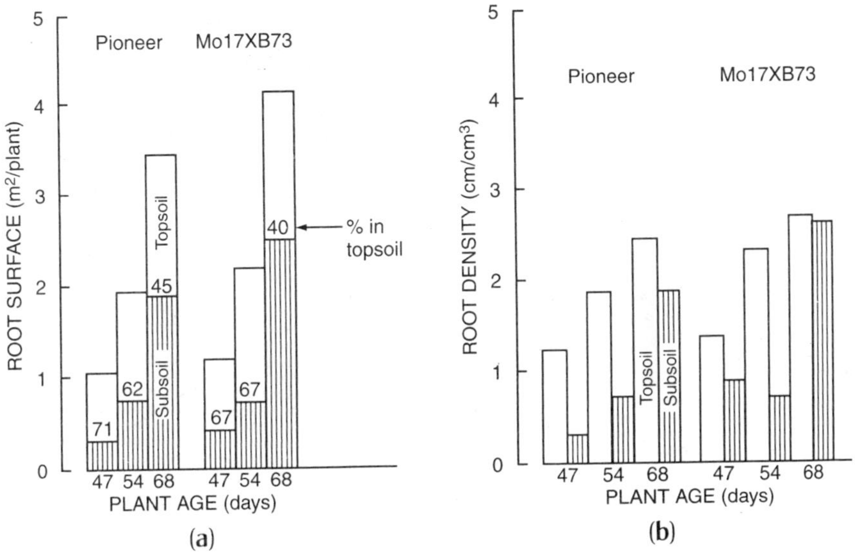

Figure 10-6 Root-surface area per plant (a) and root density (b) in topsoil and subsoil for two corn varieties. *(Schenk and Barber, 1980,* Plant Soil, *54:65.)*

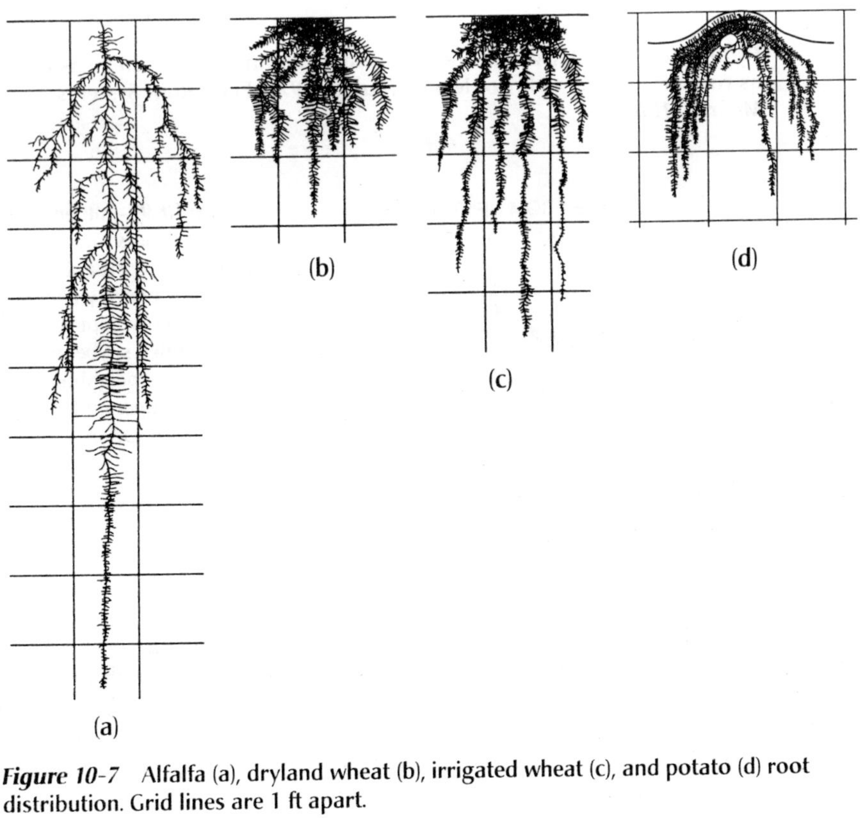

Figure 10-7 Alfalfa (a), dryland wheat (b), irrigated wheat (c), and potato (d) root distribution. Grid lines are 1 ft apart.

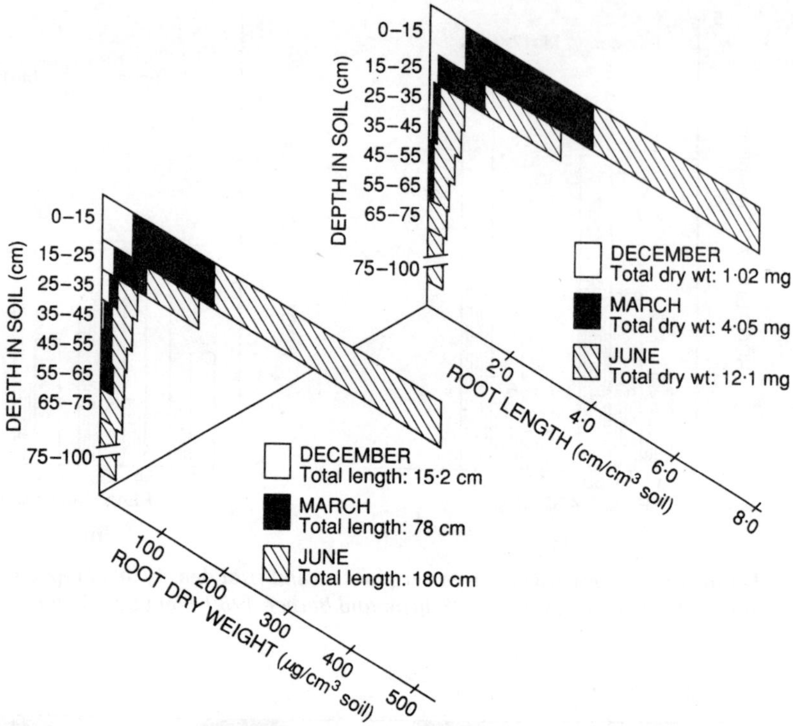

Figure 10-8 **Winter wheat root development and distribution measured as root dry weight and root length.** *(Russel, 1977,* **Plant Root Systems,** *McGraw-Hill, NY.)*

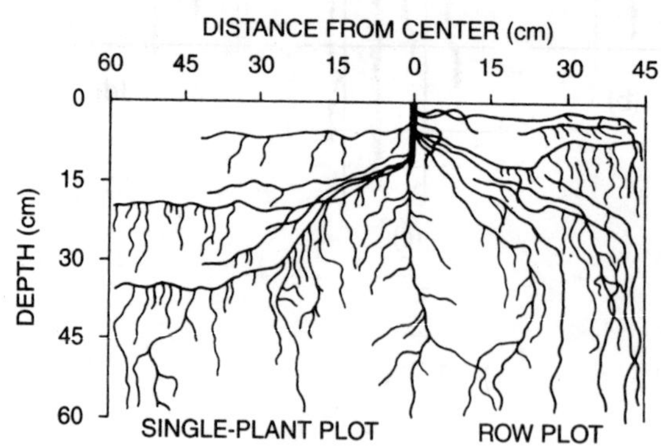

Figure 10-9 **Influence of neighboring soybean roots on root growth. Single-plant plot represents root distribution with only one soybean plant in the plot area, and row plot represents typical row-planted soybean illustrating the influence of neighboring roots on root growth.** *(Raper and Barber, 1970,* **Agron. J.,** *62:581.)*

growth rate, and (4) reduced root exudation. Under low soil-nutrient availability, VAM-infected roots explore a substantially larger soil volume from which to absorb nutrients, primarily P and N (Fig. 10-11). Figure 10-12 illustrates that VAM-dependent plants explore greater soil P extraction volume to satisfy P requirement. In many cases, excessive N and/or P fertilization and soil tillage can reduce the contribution of mycorrhiza-related nutrient uptake.

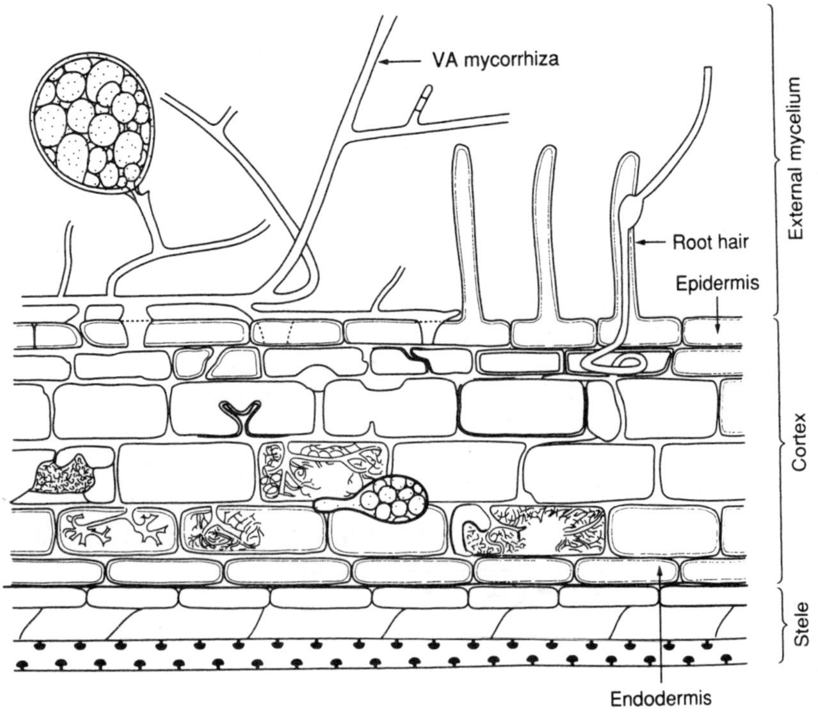

Figure 10-10 Schematic diagram of a root infected with vesicular-arbuscular mycorrhizal fungi. *(Russel, 1977,* Plant Root Systems, *McGraw-Hill, NY.)*

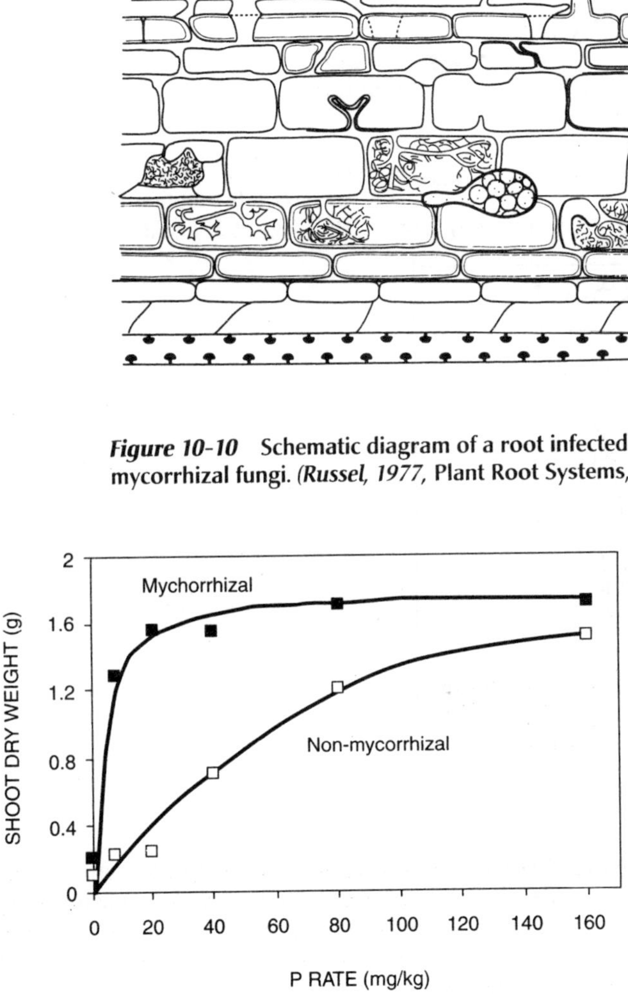

Figure 10-11 Example of increased P uptake by *Cassia pruinosa* infected with VAM. At higher P availability, P uptake is similar between VAM-infected and uninfected plants. *(Jasper et al., 1994, in Pankhurst, C.E. [ed.]* Soil Biota in Sustainable Farming Systems, *CSIRO Publ., East Melbourne. pp. 9–11.)*

Soil Characteristics

Roots must fully exploit soil to obtain nutrients and water for optimum productivity. Since crop yield is directly related to the availability of stored soil water and nutrients, soil physical conditions that restrict root growth will reduce yield potential.

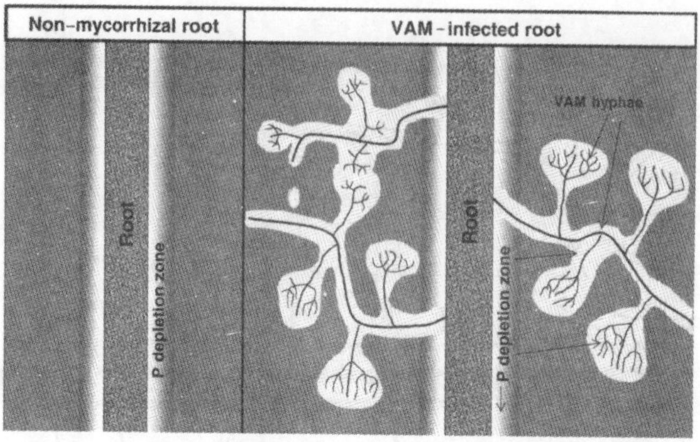

Figure 10-12 Influence of VAM-infected roots on soil volume accessed for P uptake.

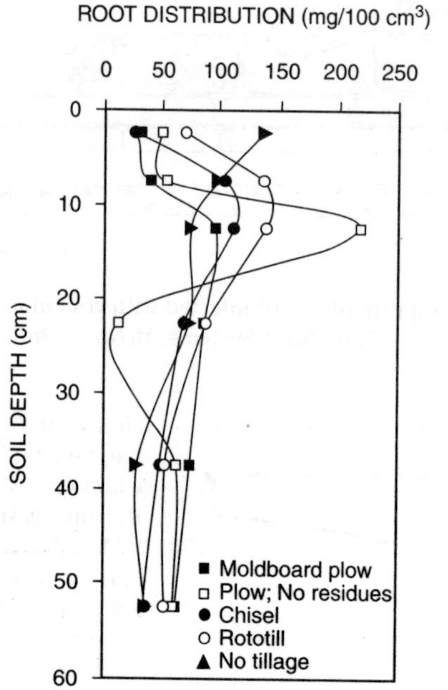

Figure 10-13 Effect of tillage on corn root distribution. *(Barber, 1971,* Agron. J., *63:724.)*

Soil tillage can improve seed placement into moist soil, seed germination, and seedling growth; however, tillage can also influence root growth and distribution (Fig. 10-13). When soil is annually cultivated, roots develop more extensively below 10 cm than with no-till systems, while intermediate root distribution occurs with minimum tillage systems. When residues are removed, there is greater root growth in the 15 cm-soil surface. In some soils, no-tillage can cause some restricted root growth because of increased bulk density compared with full tillage (Fig. 10-13). Attempts to loosen plowpans or heavy subsoils are not always successful. Subsoiling is most effective when the subsoil is dry so that shattering of the soil occurs; however, in most cases, there is a rapid resealing of the subsoil. One cultivation with a disk or similar implement may eliminate any effect of subsoiling. Vertical mulching, in which chopped plant residues are blown into the slit behind the subsoiler, serves to keep the channel open and improve water uptake. In drought-prone areas with root-restrictive soil layers, subsoiling can increase rooting depth and plant-available water, especially in crops such as soybean, cotton, and many vegetable crops that have limited ability to penetrate even moderately compacted soil layers.

Plant Nutrient Effects

Numerous soil physical and chemical factors influence root growth and absorption of water and nutrients in quantities sufficient for optimum productivity. Any management factor that improves the soil environment for healthy root growth will help achieve expected yields (Fig. 10-14). Adequate nutrient supply in the topsoil encourages a vigorous and extensive root system (Fig. 10-15). Stimulation of root development is related to N and P buildup in the cells, which hastens division and elongation.

Plants cannot absorb nutrients from dry soil; thus, shallow applications of nutrients may be less effective under drought. Generally, nutrients should be placed where stimulation of root growth is wanted; therefore, deep placement may be necessary in frequently droughty soils. Root proliferation in locally fertilized soil zones was illustrated earlier (Fig. 5-3). While it is not necessary to fertilize the entire soil volume occupied by roots, fertilized soils exert a strong influence on root growth (Fig. 10-16). The influence of adequate nutrients on winter hardiness is also important, where adequate nutrient availability extends root growth and winter survival (Fig. 10-17).

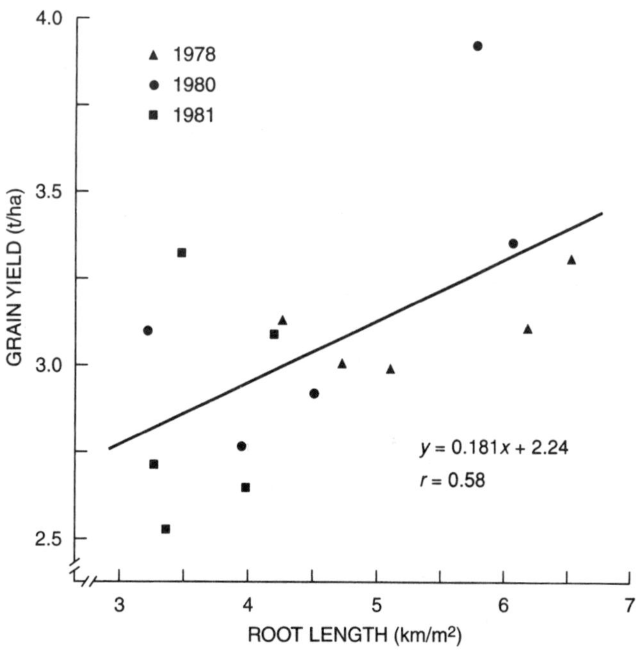

Figure 10-14 **Effect of soybean root length on grain yield.** ***(Barber and Silberbush, 1984, ASA Spec. Publ. No. 49, p. 86, Madison, WI.)***

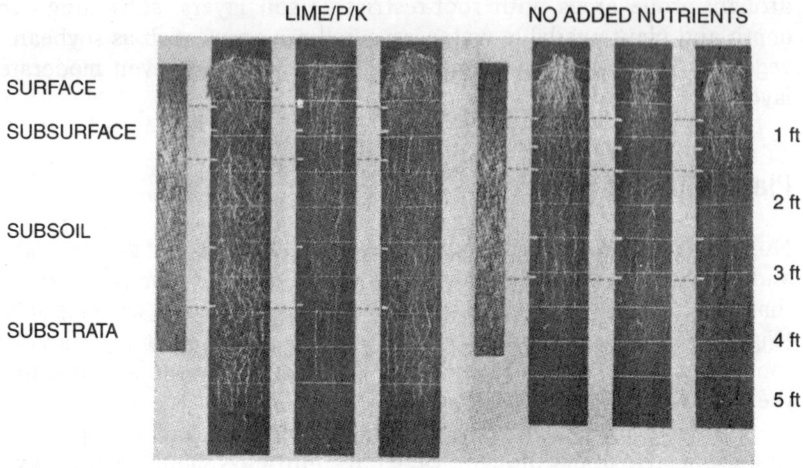

Figure 10-15 **Influence of lime, P, and K on root growth in a low-fertility soil with a claypan at 1-ft. depth.** *(Fehrenbacher et al., 1954,* **Soil Sci.,** *17:281.)*

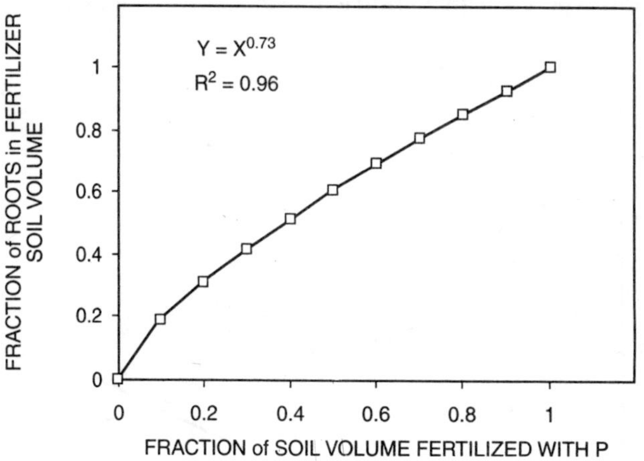

Figure 10-16 **Relationship between fraction of the soil volume fertilized with P and fraction of total roots in fertilized soil volume.** *(Mullins, 1993,* **Fertilizer Res.,** *34:23–26.)*

Nutrient Placement

Determining proper placement of applied nutrients is as important as identifying the correct rate. Placement decisions involve knowledge of crop and soil characteristics, whose interactions determine nutrient availability. Numerous placement methods have been developed, and the following factors should be considered with nutrient placement decisions:

1. *Efficient use of nutrients from plant emergence to maturity.* Vigorous seedling growth (i.e., no early growth stress) is essential for obtaining the desired yield potential and maximizing profitability. Merely applying nutrients does not ensure that they will be absorbed by the plant.

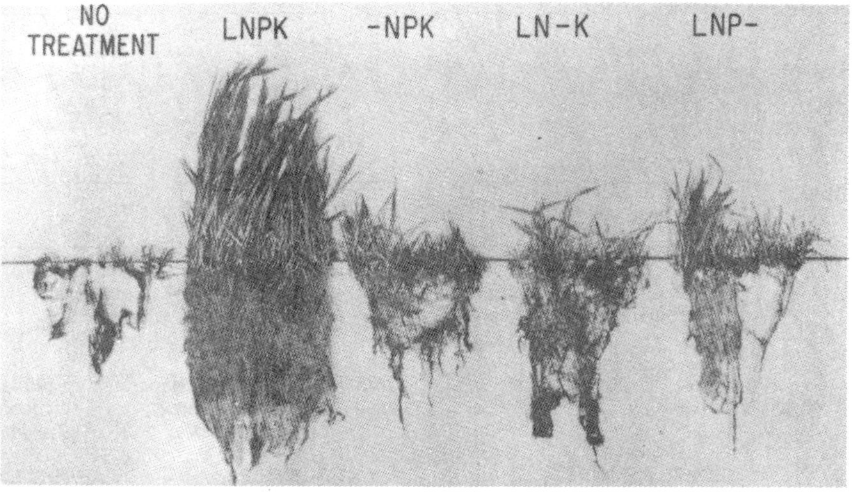

Figure 10-17 **Influence of lime, N, P, and K on root growth and tillering in wheat grown on a low pH and N-, P-, and K-deficient soil.**

2. *Prevention of salt injury to the seedling.* Soluble N, P, K, or other salts close to the seed may be harmful, although the potential for salt injury depends on the source and the crop sensitivity to salts. In general, there should be some fertilizer-free soil between the seed and the fertilizer band, especially for sensitive crops. Urease inhibitors will minimize potential problems with urea placed close to the seed row (Chapter 4).
3. *Convenience to the grower.* Timeliness of all crop management factors is essential for realizing yield potential and maximum profit. In many areas, delay in planting after the optimum date reduces yield potential. Consequently, growers often reject nutrient placement options to avoid delays in planting, even when they may increase yield. Placement decisions influence yield potential; thus, planting date and nutrient placement effects on yield must be carefully evaluated.

Methods of Placement

Fertilizer placement options generally involve surface or subsurface applications before, at, or after planting (Fig. 10-18). Placement practices depend on the crop and crop rotation, degree of deficiency or soil-test level, mobility of the nutrient in the soil, degree of acceptable soil disturbance, and equipment availability.

Preplant

Broadcast. Nutrients are applied uniformly on the soil surface before planting, and can be incorporated by tilling or cultivating (Fig. 10-19). In no-till cropping systems there is no opportunity for incorporation; thus, broadcast N applications will reduce N recovery by the crop due to enhanced immobilization, denitrification, and volatilization losses (Table 4-18).

Subsurface Band. Crop recovery of nutrients can be increased with subsurface banding. Placement depth varies between 2 and 8 in., depending on the crop, nutrient source, and

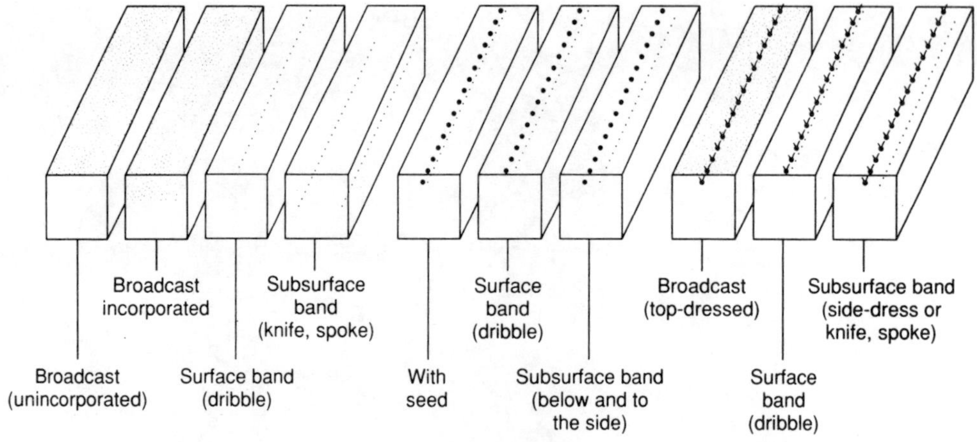

Figure 10-18 **Illustration of various nutrient placement options.**

Figure 10-19 **Broadcast application of solid fertilizers before planting.**

application equipment. In full and reduced tillage systems, a knife applicator is commonly used to apply nutrients below the soil surface (Fig. 10-20). In semiarid regions the commonly used sweep plow tillage implement can also be equipped to apply nutrients (Fig. 10-21). Subsurface point or spoke injection of fluid fertilizers can be effective, especially with application of immobile nutrients (Fig. 10-22). Point injection of N in no-till systems is also more efficient than broadcast N.

Surface Band. Surface-band-applied fertilizers can be effective before planting (Fig. 10-23). However, if not incorporated, dry surface soil conditions can reduce nutrient uptake, especially with immobile nutrients. Surface-band N applications can improve N availability compared with broadcast application in some soils and cropping systems.

(a)

(b)

(c)

(d)

Figure 10-20 Examples of injection knives for subsurface band application of nutrients in conventional and reduced tillage cropping systems. Knife "a" is designed to place anhydrous NH_3 (front tube) and liquid P or 10-34-0 simultaneously. As the NH_3 is converted from a liquid under pressure to a gas, the NH_3 tube freezes. The 1 to 2 cm separation between the tubes behind the knife prevents the liquid P tube from also freezing during application. Knife "b" is similar to "a" except that the backswept design reduces topsoil disturbance during application. Knife "c" is also similar to "a" except that dry P sources (i.e., TSP, MAP, DAP) are delivered through the large hose by forced air. "d" represents a typical application knife mounted on a chisel plow shank. *(Photos (a) and (b) courtesy of L. S. Murphy.)*

At Planting

Subsurface Band. Solid and fluid fertilizer placement can occur at numerous locations near the seed, depending on the equipment and crop. Commonly, fertilizer is applied 1 to 2 in. directly below the seed or 1 to 3 in. to the side and below the seed, depending on the equipment (Fig. 10-24). Single pass or direct seeding, involving application of as much fertilizer as is feasible without harming seed, is practiced in semiarid regions for erosion control and reduced operating costs.

Seed Band. Fertilizer application with the seed is a subsurface band and is commonly referred to as a starter, or pop-up, application. These applications are generally used to enhance early seedling vigor, especially in cold, wet soils. Starter fertilization can also be placed near the seed instead of with the seed. Usually, low nutrient rates are applied to avoid germination or seedling damage. Fluid or solid sources can be used.

(a) (b)

Figure 10-21 The sweep plow is a common tillage implement in semiarid regions (a) that provides weed control with little residue incorporation by operation about 3 to 4 in. below the soil surface. Sweep plows can be equipped to apply anhydrous NH_3 and/or liquid N or P sources through a steel tube placed under the sweep blade (b) with injection orifices spaced every 12 in.

(a) (b)

Figure 10-22 Point or spoke injector (a) for application for fluid fertilizers in no-tillage systems. Inject depth varies from 2 to 6 in. depending on surface soil texture, with little disturbance of surface residues (b).

Surface Band. Fertilizers can be surface-applied at planting in bands directly over the row or several inches to the side of the row (Fig. 10-25). Application over the row can be effective for placement of immobile nutrients with a hoe opener because soil can slough off over time and bury the fertilizer band. Thus, the surface-applied band becomes a subsurface band placed slightly above the seed (Fig. 10-26).

Figure 10-23 Surface-band application of liquid fertilizers before planting. *(Courtesy L. S. Murphy.)*

(a) (b)

Figure 10-24 Band application of fertilizer 2 in. to the side and 2 in. below the seed (a). With some fertilizers, especially at higher rates, separation of fertilizer and seed prevent salt injury to young seedling roots, but still places nutrients in close proximity to (b). *(Courtesy of the Potash & Phosphate Institute, Norcross, GA.)*

After Planting

Topdress. Topdress N applications are common on turf, small grains, and pastures; however, N immobilization in high-surface-residue systems can reduce recovery of topdress N (Fig. 10-27). Topdressed P and K are not as effective as preplant applications. Both solid and liquid sources can be used.

Sidedress. Sidedress N application is very common with corn, sorghum, cotton, and other crops and is done with a standard knife or point injector applicator (Fig. 10-20, Fig. 10-22). Anhydrous NH_3 and fluid N sources are most common. Fluid sources can be surface-band applied beside the row after planting. Sidedress applications increase flexibility since applications can be made almost any time equipment can be operated without damage to the crop.

Figure 10-25 Surface band or dribble application of fluid fertilizer. In this case fertilizer is applied over the row after the press wheel. Application beside the row at planting is also possible.

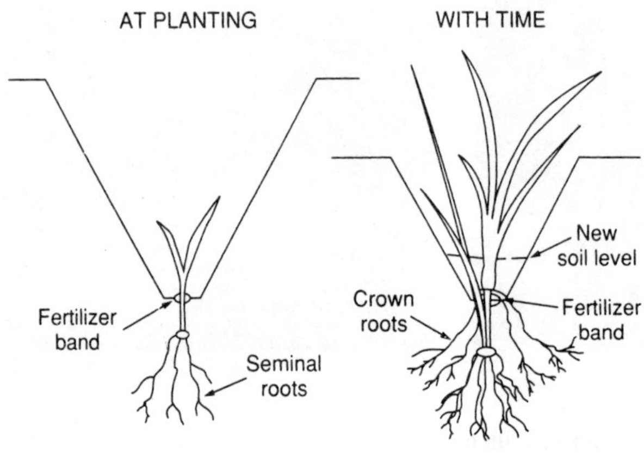

Figure 10-26 With surface-band application of nutrients, soil will slough into the furrow left by the planter press wheel and bury the fertilizer. *(Westfall et al., 1987,* J. Fert. Issues, *4:114–121.)*

(a) (b)

Figure 10-27 Topdress application of nutrients in-season with alfalfa (a) and wheat (b). Either solid or liquid sources can be used. *(Courtesy L. S. Murphy.)*

Subsurface sidedress applications with a knife too close to the plant can cause damage by either root pruning or nutrient toxicity (i.e., anhydrous NH_3). Sidedress application of immobile nutrients (e.g., P and K) is not recommended because most crops need P and K early in the season.

Placement Specific Considerations

Band Applications Vigorous seedling growth is essential to maximum crop productivity. Often a small amount of nutrients near young plants at planting, commonly referred to as "starter" or "pop-up" applications, promotes increased root growth and formation of large, healthy leaves (Fig. 10-28). Starter application represents nutrient placement 2 × 2 in. to the side and below the seed at planting, while pop-up represents nutrients placed in direct seed contact at planting. Starter or pop-up applications include N, but should also include P, K, and S, especially with soil testing low to medium in P and K, and low-OM soils. With cool, wet spring conditions, reduced nutrient availability can be caused by slow mineralization of N, P, S, and micronutrients from soil OM; reduced soil mineral dissolution rates; reduced nutrient diffusion rates; or limited nutrient absorption by the plant. The advantage of early stimulation depends on the crop, variety, soil-test levels, and seasonal conditions. Some factors to consider are:

- *Resistance to pests*—a vigorous young plant is more insect and disease resistant.
- *Competition with weeds*—vigorous early crop growth advances canopy coverage of the soil surface important for reducing light penetration and soil temperature that reduces weed germination. Reduced weed pressure improves herbicide effectiveness and cultivation frequency. Reduced water use by weeds and soil water evaporation enhances water availability to crops.
- *Advanced maturity*—early crop growth vigor, especially with P, can advance crop maturity that enables earlier harvest and lower grain-moisture content at harvest (Fig. 10-29). Early maturity can be important in northern climates, where adverse fall weather may interrupt and delay the harvest. With vegetables, a delay of only 3 to 4 days may result in a producer missing an early, higher value market.

Figure 10-28 **Vigorous early plant growth with application of nutrients with or near the seed at planting often increases yield potential.** ***(Courtesy R. Lamond, Kansas State Univ.)***

Figure 10-29 **Effect of P fertilization on grain sorghum maturity. Application of 12 lbs P_2O_5/a as a starter (7-21-7) on a low-P soil advanced maturity 2 to 3 weeks.** ***(Courtesy R. Lamond, Kansas State Univ.)***

Salt Index. High concentrations of soluble salts in contact with roots or germinating seeds cause injurious effects through plasmolysis or actual toxicity. Plasmolysis occurs when the salt concentration outside root cells exceeds the cellular salt concentration, resulting in cellular H_2O moving out of the cell. As a result, the cell's membrane shrinks away from the cell wall, partially collapsing the cell. Water transport across cell membranes from high water concentration (inside cell) to lower water concentration (outside the cell) causes the plant to exhibit symptoms similar to drought stress.

Fertilizers are categorized for their salt injury potential by the *salt index,* determined by placing the material in the soil and measuring the osmotic pressure of the soil solution. The salt index is the ratio of the increase in osmotic pressure produced by the fertilizer to that produced by the same weight of $NaNO_3$, based on a relative value of 100 (Table 10-2).

N and K salts have much higher salt indices and are much more detrimental to germination than P salts when placed close to or in contact with the seed (Fig. 10-30). Increasing soil clay content decreases salt conductivity; thus, potential problems related to fertilizer salts are greatest in coarse-textured soils.

High initial NH_4^+ concentrations following application of NH_4^+ sources also increases osmotic pressure of the soil solution, and favors temporary accumulation of NO_2^-, which is toxic to plants. Some N sources contribute more to germination and seedling damage than is explained by the osmotic effects. NH_3 is toxic and can move freely through the cell wall, whereas NH_4^+ cannot. Urea, DAP, $(NH_4)_2CO_3$, and NH_4OH will cause more damage than MAP, $(NH_4)_2SO_4$, and NH_4NO_3. Broadcast application or placement to the side and below the seed are effective methods of avoiding salt injury (Fig. 10-31).

Mixed fertilizers of the same grade also vary widely in salt index, depending on sources used. Higher-analysis mixed fertilizers generally have a lower salt index per unit of plant nutrient than lower-analysis fertilizers because they are usually made up of higher-analysis sources. For example, to furnish 50 lbs of N, 250 lbs of $(NH_4)_2SO_4$ would be required, whereas with urea, 110 lbs would be required. Hence, higher-analysis fertilizers are less likely to produce salt injury than equal amounts of lower-analysis fertilizers. In addition,

Table 10-2 **Salt Index for Common Fertilizer Materials**

Material	*Analysis**	*Salt index, relative to $NaNO_3$*	*Partial salt index*†
N Sources			
NH_3	82.2	47.1	0.572
NH_4NO_3	35.0	104.1	3.059
$(NH_4)_2SO_4$	21.2	88.3	3.252
$NH_4H_2PO_4$ - MAP	11.0		2.453
$(NH_4)_2HPO_4$ - DAP	18.0		1.614
Urea	46.0	74.4	1.618
UAN	28.0	63	2.250
UAN	32.0	71.1	2.221
$NaNO_3$	16.5	100	6.080
KNO_3	13.8		5.336
P Sources			
$Ca(H_2PO_4)_2$ - CSP	20.0	7.8	0.390
$Ca(H_2PO_4)_2$ - TSP	48.0	10.1	0.210
MAP	52.0	26.7	0.405
DAP	46.0	29.2	0.456
APP	34.0	20	0.455
K Sources			
KCl	60.0	116.1	1.936
KNO_3	50.0	69.5	1.219
K_2SO_4	54.0	42.6	0.852
Sul-Po-Mag	22.0	43.4	1.971
$K_2S_2O_3$	25.0	68.0	2.720
KH_2PO_4	34.6	8.4	0.097
S Sources			
$(NH_4)_2S_2O_3$	26.0	90.4	7.533
$(NH_4)_2S_x$	40.0	59.2	2.960
$CaSO_4 \cdot 2H_2O$	17.0	8.2	0.247
$MgSO_4 \cdot 7H_2O$	14.0	44.0	2.687
Organic Sources			
Manure salts	20.0	112.7	4.636
Manure salts	30.0	91.9	3.067

* %N in N carriers, % P_2O_5 in P carriers, and % K_2O in K carriers.

†The salt index of a mixed fertilizer is the sum of the partial salt index per unit (20 lbs) of nutrient times the units due to each source in the mixture.

increasing the row width increases the quantity of fertilizer applied in a row, assuming that equal rates are applied. For example, with the same fertilizer rate, fertilizer placed per unit length of row is twice as great in 30-in. rows than in 15-in. rows. In general, total N + K should not exceed 10 to 20 lbs/a applied with the seed.

Broadcast Applications Broadcast applications usually involve large amounts of lime and/or nutrients in buildup or maintenance programs. The advantages of broadcast application of nutrients include:

- Application of large amounts of fertilizer is accomplished without danger of plant injury.

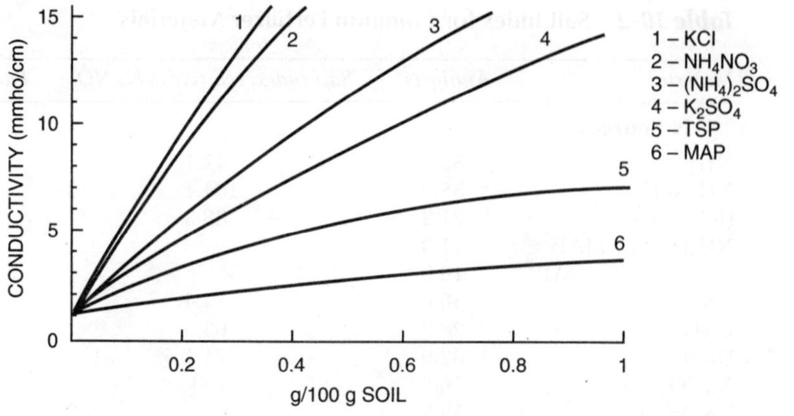

Figure 10-30 **Effect of N, P, and K fertilizers on solution conductivity of a silt loam soil.** ***(Chapin et al., 1964,*** **Soil Sci. Soc. Am. J.,** ***28:90.)***

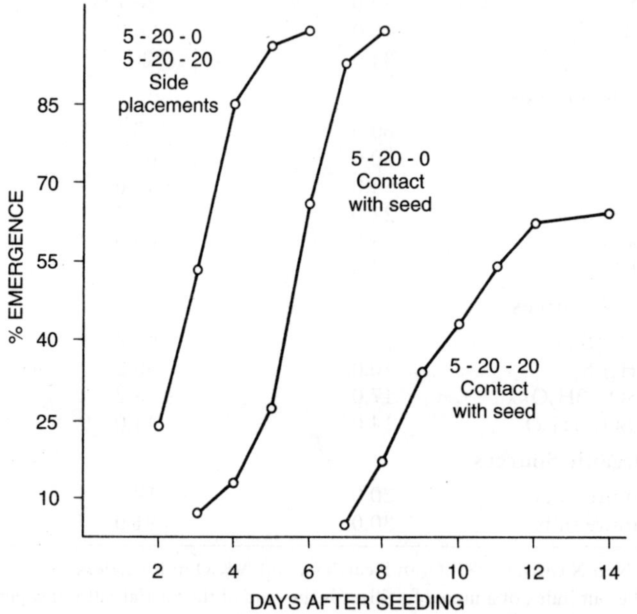

Figure 10-31 **Comparison of fertilizer placed with the seed and 1.5 in. below and 1.5 in. to the side of the seed at planting on seedling emergence.** ***(Lawton et al., 1964,*** **Agron. J.,** ***52:326.)***

- If tilled into the soil, distribution of nutrients throughout the plow layer encourages root exploration of the soil for water and nutrients.
- Labor is saved during planting. The fertilizer application season is spread out through fall, winter, or early spring applications.
- This method can be a practical means of applying maintenance fertilizer, especially in forage and turf crops, and in no-till cropping systems.

Uniform and accurate spreading of fertilizers and lime is essential for effective utilization by the crop (Table 10-3). Some of the disadvantages of broadcast application include:

- In reduced tillage systems, more nutrients remain potentially inaccessible near the surface (Fig. 10-32). In some crops, increasing subsoil nutrient availability can enhance productivity.
- Broadcast N on high-surface-residue systems can increase N immobilization, volatilization, and denitrification.
- Broadcast, incorporated nutrients increase soil erosion potential through loss of protective surface residue cover.

Table 10-3 **Effects of Uneven Application of N-P-K Fertilizer on Crop Yield**

Spread Pattern	*Soybeans*	*Corn*	*Barley*
		Yield (kg/ha)	
No fertilizer	1,278	2,059	592
Uniform	1,345	8,060	2,809
Nonuniform	1,264	7,271	2,540

SOURCE: From Lutz et al., 1975, *Agron. J.*, 67:526.

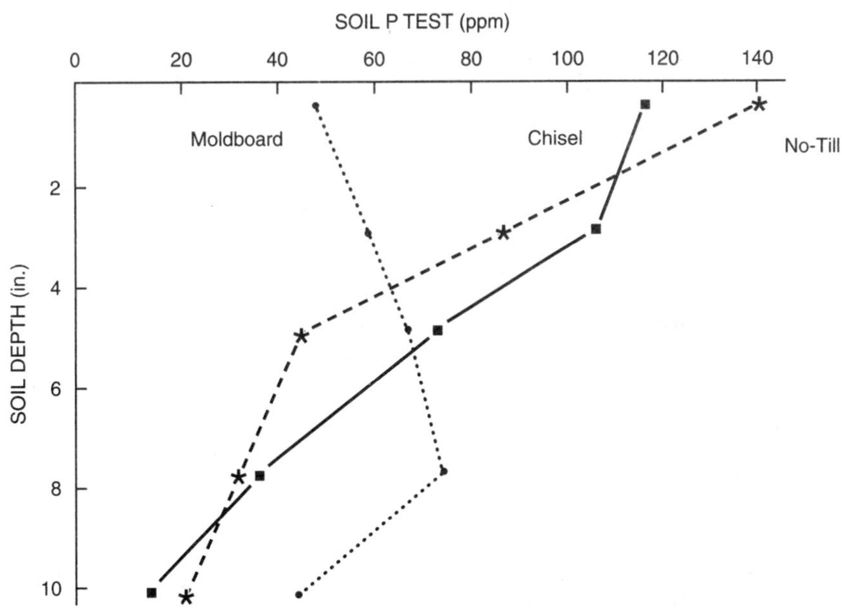

Figure 10-32 **Tillage effect on distribution of soil-test P after three years of P fertilization.** ***(Randell, Univ. of Minnesota.)***

Specific Nutrient Considerations

Nitrogen

It is usually undesirable to apply high N rates near the seed row at planting because of possible injury to the crop, especially on sandy soils. Thus, most N is applied either before planting, or to increase N efficiency part of the N requirement is applied as in-season top- or sidedressing. Prediction of sidedress N rates can be improved by use of the PSNT or with plant analysis (Chapter 9). With broadcast N, H_2O movement carries N down to plant roots. This is particularly applicable on coarse-textured soils but can also be important on medium- and fine-textured soils.

Starter N applications can be important to enhancing early growth and final yield (Table 10-4). Most starter materials contain multiple nutrients, because crop response to mobile and immobile nutrients can occur in high-testing soils in cool, moist conditions. Under conditions conducive to nitrification, the addition of a nitrification inhibitor can improve the crop response to starter N (Table 10-5).

NH_4^+ added to the starter fertilizer has beneficial effects on P absorption. Although dual application of N + P may not increase yield in all soils, positive responses have frequently been observed (Fig. 10-33).

Production of permanent grassland and native range in semiarid regions is limited primarily by moisture and N availability. Low rates of N (i.e., < 150 lbs/a) are generally ineffective, because considerable N is immobilized by the high C/N grass residue (Fig. 10-34).

Table 10-4 **Corn Yield Response to Starter Fertilizer in No-Till Continuous Corn and Corn-Soybean Rotations**

Starter Fertilizer (lbs/a)			*Corn Yield (bu/a)*	
N	*P_2O_5*	*K_2O*	*Corn-Corn*	*Corn-Soybean*
0	0	0	131	131
25	0	0	141	136
25	30	0	147	141
25	30	30	146	143

SOURCE: From Hoeft, 1988, Proc. Illinois Fert. Conf.

Table 10-5 **Corn Response to N and NP Starters With and Without Nitrification Inhibitor**

N	*P*	*N-Serve*	*Yield*	*Grain Moisture*
------------------*lbs/a*	--------------------------		*bu/a*	%
0	0	0.0	91	19.7
16	0	0.0	90	17.8
16	0	0.4	111	22.3
0	54	0.0	85	20.8
16	54	0.0	90	17.7
16	54	0.4	109	21.4

SOURCE: From Anderson, 1988, *Better Crops* vol. 72.

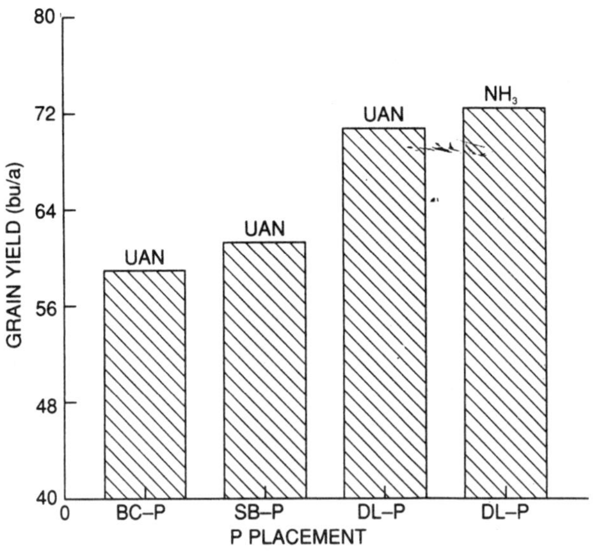

Figure 10-33 **Winter wheat response to dual N-P application compared with N and P applied separately. BC and SB represent broadcast and seed-banded P, respectively, while UAN was knife-applied separately. DL represents dual N-P.** *(Leikam et al., 1983, SSSAJ, 47:530.)*

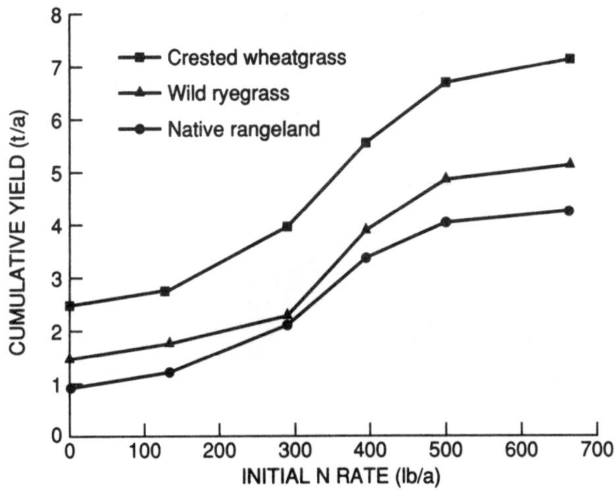

Figure 10-34 **Effect of N fertilization of permanent grassland and native rangeland.** *(Leyshon and Kilcher, 1976, Proc. Soil Fert. Workshop. Publ. 244, Univ. Saskatchewan, Saskatoon.)*

Phosphorus

Since P is immobile in the soil, placement near roots is usually advantageous. Surface applications after the crop is planted will not place P near the root zone and will be of little value to annual crops in the year of application. An exception to the inefficiency of broadcast P is with forage crops and turf crops where broadcast P can be absorbed by plant crowns and very shallow roots. Surface banding can also be effective on low-P or low-K soils.

In establishing forage or turf crops, surface or subsurface band-applied P and/or K is generally superior to broadcast, especially in low-P and/or low-K soils (Fig. 10-35). The question of band versus broadcast application is very important. When all of the P is either banded or broadcast, the relative efficiency is related to both soil-P status and P application rate. In general, differences between seed-placed and broadcast P decline with increasing levels of available soil P (Fig. 10-36).

(a)

(b)

(c)

Figure 10-35 Alfalfa response to P and K placement in the establishment year; P_2O_5 and K_2O were applied at 80 lbs/a by (a) broadcast, (b) surface band or dribble, and subsurface band or knife applications before planting. Early alfalfa growth is enhanced with band-applied P and K compared with broadcast. *(Courtesy of D. Sweeney, 1989, Kansas State University.)*

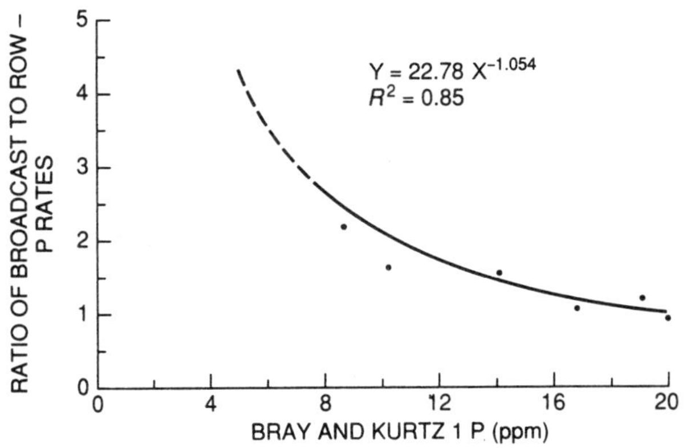

Figure 10-36 **Influence of soil-test P level on the ratio of broadcast- to band-P rates required for equal grain yield.** *(Peterson et al., 1981, Agron. J. 73:13–17.)*

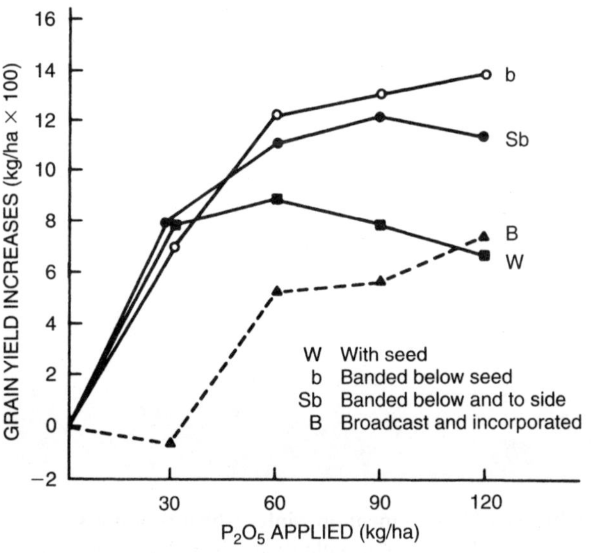

Figure 10-37 **Effect of P placement on barley yield on a low-P soil. Unfertilized yield was 1,700 kg/ha.** *(Bailey et al., 1980, Proc. Western Canada Phosphate Symp., p. 200, Alberta Soil and Feed Testing Laboratory, Edmonton, Aberta.)*

Band-P placement is often more critical for crops with limited root systems caused by shorter growing seasons, cooler temperatures, and grown on low-P soils, which enhances crop response compared to broadcast P. For example, when high P rates are used in dry and/or coarse-textured soils, banding away from the seed at planting may be superior to banding with the seed (Fig. 10-37). Highest yields were obtained when P was banded below the seed rather than with the seed or banded to the side and below the seed at > 60 kg P_2O_5/ha. Yield loss at high rates of seed-placed P supplied as MAP or DAP is probably due to NH_4^+ toxicity.

When properly placed, band-applied P can enhance plant growth and yield potential compared with broadcast P (Table 10-6; Fig. 10-38). In this case, subsurface band P greatly increased wheat tiller number, which is directly related to head number and final grain yield. Increasing broadcast P to 3 times band P did not produce the same growth at late tiller stage. The influence of P management on root growth and head size is evident in Figure 10-38. Similar responses to P placement in corn and soybeans occur (Table 10-7). Notice the decrease in grain moisture content with starter P, which illustrates more advanced maturity with improved P nutrition.

Table 10-6 **No-Till Winter Wheat Response to P Rate and Placement**

P Treatment	*Tillers*	*Dry Matter (lbs/a)*		*Grain Heads*	*Grain Yield*
lbs P_2O_5/a	*#/ft^2*	*Full Tiller*	*Harvest*	*#/ft^2*	*bu/a*
0	11	280	4,978	43	34
BC 15	14	370	5,906	51	40
BC 45	17	475	8,131	65	53
KN 15	29	1,053	7,754	66	49
KN 45	32	1,096	8,641	70	56

*BC=broadcast unincorporated; KN=knifed 2 in. below seed; full tiller=Feekes growth stage 5 (Fig. 10.1).
SOURCE: From Havlin, 1992, Proc. Great Plains Soil Fert. Conf.

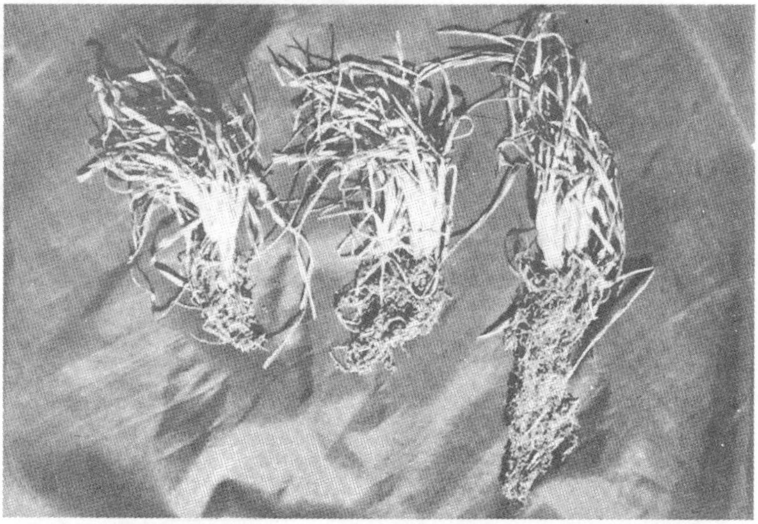

Figure 10-38 **Influence of P placement on winter wheat root growth (a) and grain head size (b). In each photo plants on the left, middle, and right received no P, 15 lbs P_2O_5/a broadcast P, and 15 lbs P_2O_5/a subsurface band (2 in. below the surface) applied P. *(Havlin, 1988, Kansas State Univ.)***

Table 10-7 **Effect of P Rate and Placement on Plant Height, Grain Yield, and Grain Moisture**

		Plant Height, in.		*Grain Yield, bu/a*		
Placement	*P Rate, lbs/a*	*Corn*	*Soybean*	*Corn*	*Soybean*	*Grain Moisture, %*
Broadcast	0	14.6	7.1	115	37	27.0
Broadcast	20	16.5	8.3	124	40	26.1
Broadcast	40	15.4	7.5	119	40	26.6
Broadcast	80	17.3	9.8	123	40	25.6
Starter	0	14.2	7.1	117	35	27.0
Starter	20	27.2	10.2	135	39	24.8
Starter	40	26.8	10.2	132	39	22.5
Starter	80	30.7	10.2	146	45	24.2

SOURCE: From Fixen et al., 1984, *Better Crops* vol. 72.

Table 10-8 **Crop Values from P Fertilization over a 4-Year Cropping Period**

	Gross Crop Value ($/a)						
	1973	*1974*	*1975*	*1976*			
P Applied (lbs/a)	*Sugarbeet*	*Spring Wheat*	*Potato*	*Silage Corn*	*Total*	*P Fertilizer Costs ($/a)*	*4-year Net Return ($/a)*
0	577	240	1,214	232	2,263	0	—
60	661	267	1,204	250	2,382	24	95
150	655	291	1,277	239	2,462	60	139
500	660	306	1,512	252	2,730	200	267

Initial soil test P=5.6 ppm (0–12 in.), P applied fall 1972.
SOURCE: From Westerman, 1977, *Proc. 28th Annu. Northwest Fert. Conf.*, pp. 141–46.

Even with band placement, crops during any one season generally recover < 20% of applied P. In contrast, typical N and K recovery can be 50 to 75%. Band placement of P reduces fertilizer–soil contact, resulting in less fixation than broadcast P. Therefore, band P should increase crop recovery compared with broadcast P. Although generally the most efficient use of limited quantities of P is at planting and the highest return will be obtained by band applications, there may be some advantage in building up soil fertility in a long-term fertilizer program (Table 10-8). When P is applied only once, higher net returns were achieved with high-value crops grown after P fertilization. These results demonstrate that high-P rates may be profitable over several crops. When high-value crops are grown on low-P soils, it may be advisable to increase the soil-test P with a buildup program.

Potassium

K fertilizers applied at ≥ 10 lbs K_2O/a in direct-seed contact commonly causes reduced germination and seedling growth. K placed in a band to the side and below the seed generally avoids salt toxicity effects on plant growth. In contrast, salt-tolerant crops such as barley and other small grains can respond to 15 to 30 lbs K_2O/a placed with the seed. Broadcast K is usually less efficient than banded K; however, as soil-test K increases, there is generally less difference between placement methods. The importance of placement also decreases as higher rates of fertilizer are used. Starter responses from K, similar to those from N and P, occur with many crops planted under cool, wet conditions, even on high-K soils (Fig. 10-39). This response is unlikely to occur in years when warm spring conditions persist.

Micronutrients

As crop yields continue to increase, greater frequency of micronutrient deficiencies can be expected to continue. Specific micronutrients are applied in areas known to be severely deficient or to crops with especially high micronutrient requirements. The micronutrient may be added to a mixed fertilizer, applied separately as a broadcast application or foliar spray, or added as a seed coating (Chapter 8). Micronutrients added to N-P-K fertilizer should be placed in bands 2 in. away from the seed to prevent fertilizer injury. Micronutrients are commonly added to APP and other P sources used in starter applications. B should not be band applied to crops such as beans or small grains.

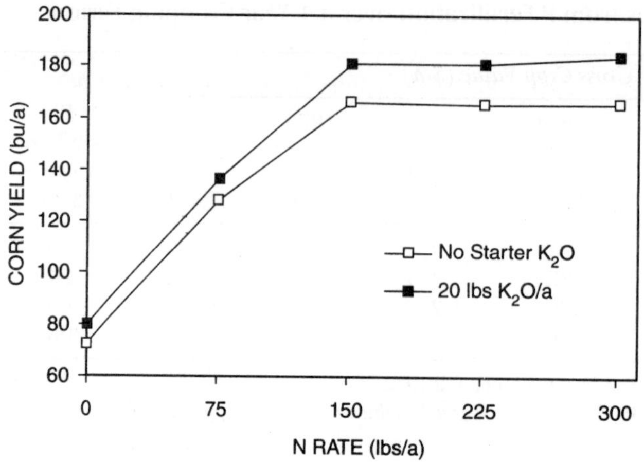

Figure 10-39 **Influence of starter K on grain yield of corn grown on a cold, wet, high-K soil. *(H. Sunderman, 1980, Rep. of Progress No. 382. Colby Branch Exp. Sta. Kansas State Univ.)***

Application Timing

Application timing depends on the soil, climate, nutrients, and crop. However, nutrients are applied during the year when they may not be the most efficient agronomically, but are more favorably priced or better suited to workload or distribution constraints of both the grower and the dealer. Despite these considerations, growers should apply nutrients at a time that will maximize recovery by the crop and reduce potential losses to the environment.

Nitrogen

N-loss mechanisms (Chapter 4) must be considered in selecting the time of application. It is desirable to apply N as close to peak crop N demand as possible; however, this is seldom feasible except with early in-season applications (Chapter 9). Because of N mobility in soils, the amount and distribution of rainfall are important considerations. As annual rainfall increases, N-leaching potential increases, especially if the crop is not growing vigorously or if the land is not protected by plant cover. In addition, conditions conducive to denitrification are likely to occur when soils become waterlogged.

In warmer climates, temperatures are more optimum for nitrification during a greater portion of the year. Thus, N applied before planting would be more subject to nitrification and leaching (Chapter 4). In cooler climates, NH_4^+ application is generally recommended in the fall, after soil temperature drops below 50°F, except on sandy or organic soils. However, compared with fall-applied NH_4^+, spring applications are 5 to 10% more efficient on fine- and medium-textured soils and 10 to 30% more efficient on coarse-textured soils. Nitrification and/or urease inhibitors can be used to improve N efficacy in warm, sandy soils. Many growers apply N in the fall; however, in-season sidedress or topdress N after crop emergence can often be superior to the fall N.

With fall-planted small grains, all or most of the N is applied in late summer or fall. In warm, humid regions, yields will be somewhat below those obtained by topdressing N in late winter because of leaching or gaseous N losses. However, there are several important advantages to fall applications on small grains. In late winter the ground may be too wet for machinery to be operated, and spring N application before jointing is best for small grain response to applied N (Fig. 10-2).

Phosphorus

In general, P should be applied just before or at planting because of the conversion of soluble P to less available forms. The magnitude varies greatly with the P-fixation capacity of the soil (see Chapter 5). On soils low to moderate in P-fixation capacity, broadcast P in the fall for a spring-planted crop is an effective method. On low-P and/or high-P fixing soils, band-applied P as close to planting as possible is the most efficient and should maximize crop recovery of P. On medium- to high-P soils, the time and method are less important and maintenance applications are advised.

Potassium

K is commonly applied and incorporated before or at planting, which is usually more efficient than sidedressing. Because K is relatively immobile, sidedressed K is less likely to move to the root zone to benefit the current crop. Fall-applied K is even more dependable than either P or N applied in the fall because fewer loss mechanisms exist with K. In some cropping systems, K fertilizers may be broadcast once or twice in the rotation. Fall incorporation of K is generally made before planting K-responsive crops, such as corn and legumes. Maintenance application on forage crops can be made almost any time. Fall applications are generally desirable, because the K will have had time to move down into the root zone. On hay crops, application is recommended after the first cutting and/or before the last cutting.

Nutrient Application to Foliage and Through Irrigation

Foliar Applications

Certain fertilizers that are soluble in water may be applied directly to the aerial portion of plants. The nutrients must penetrate the leaf cuticle or the stomata and then enter the cells. This method provides for more rapid nutrient utilization and enables rapid correction of deficiencies compared to soil application, although the response is often temporary due to the small amount of nutrient applied. Various environmental factors (temperature, humidity, light intensity, etc.) affect absorption and translocation of nutrients applied to the foliage. To be most effective, 2 to 3 applications repeated at short intervals may be needed, particularly if the deficiency has caused severe stunting. Care must be taken to identify the nutrient needed.

Foliar application can be an excellent supplement to soil-applied nutrients. Foliar fertilization generally has greater economic value in horticultural than for agronomic crops. Generally, horticultural crops have higher value which encourages more careful monitoring of plant nutrient status.

The greatest difficulty in supplying N, P, and K in foliar sprays is in the application of adequate amounts without severely burning the leaves and without an unduly large volume of solution or number of applications. Nutrient concentrations < 1 to 2% are generally used to avoid injury to foliage. Foliar application of urea has been successful in apples, citrus, pineapple, and other tree crops, because N is absorbed more rapidly than with soil applications. Foliar P application is used less than foliar applied N, largely because most P compounds cause leaf damage when sprayed in quantities large enough to make the application beneficial. The maximum P concentration is < 0.4 to 0.5% for most crops.

The most important use of foliar application has been with micronutrients because of the small requirements. Foliar applications have been found to be many times more efficient than soil applications for fruit trees and other crops. Soil-applied Fe is often not effective on high-pH soil because of precipitation of $Fe(OH)_3$ (Chapter 8). Efforts to correct Fe chlorosis with foliar applied Fe have not always been successful, and more than one application may be needed on some crops.

Fertigation

Fertigation is the application of fertilizer, primarily N, K, and S, in irrigation water (Fig. 10-40). The advantages of fertigation include correction of in-season nutrient deficiencies; application of nutrients, especially N, in synchrony with crop N demand; and the reduction of soil-applied field operations. Corn, for example, has two periods of high N uptake, vegetative growth stages V12 to V18 and reproductive growth or grain fill (R2 to R5). Providing adequate N at these stages is important for maximizing yield. P fertigation is less common because of potential precipitation of P in high-Ca and Mg waters. Application of anhydrous NH_3, UAN, or other N sources containing free NH_3 to irrigation waters high in Ca^{+2}, Mg^{+2}, and HCO_3^- may precipitate $CaCO_3$ and/or $MgCO_3$, causing scaling and plugging problems in irrigation equipment. Their formation can be prevented by the addition of H_2SO_4 or other acid solutions.

Uniform fertigation of nutrients is accomplished with properly designed irrigation systems and skilled irrigation management, since dissolved nutrients are delivered with the water. Poor nutrient distribution can occur with flood or furrow irrigated systems and with low nutrient rates. Under furrow irrigation, a large proportion of the nutrients may be deposited near the inlet.

To prevent nutrients from becoming inaccessible to crops through either leaching below the root zone or accumulating at or near the soil surface, they should not be introduced toward the middle of the irrigation period and application should be terminated shortly before completion of the irrigation.

Figure 10-40 **Center pivot irrigation system equipped to apply nutrients during the growing season.**

Variable Nutrient Management

Site-specific nutrient management can improve nutrient-use efficiency by spatially distributing nutrients based on spatial variation in yield potential, soil-test levels, and other appropriate spatial data. For example, the spatial distribution in soil-test P and associated P-sufficiency levels are used to establish variable P recommendations in the same way field-average P recommendations are developed (Fig. 10-41). The fertilizer P is then applied through a computer-controlled variable rate applicator according to the P recommendation map (Fig. 10-42).

With uniform P application, low soil-test P areas are underfertilized while high soil-test P areas are overfertilized (Fig. 10-43). Similar responses to variable K and lime application are also common. Yield loss due to underfertilization decreases profitability more than overfertilization because the value of lost yield exceeds the cost of the excess fertilizer input. With N, overfertilization may also have negative impacts on environmental quality.

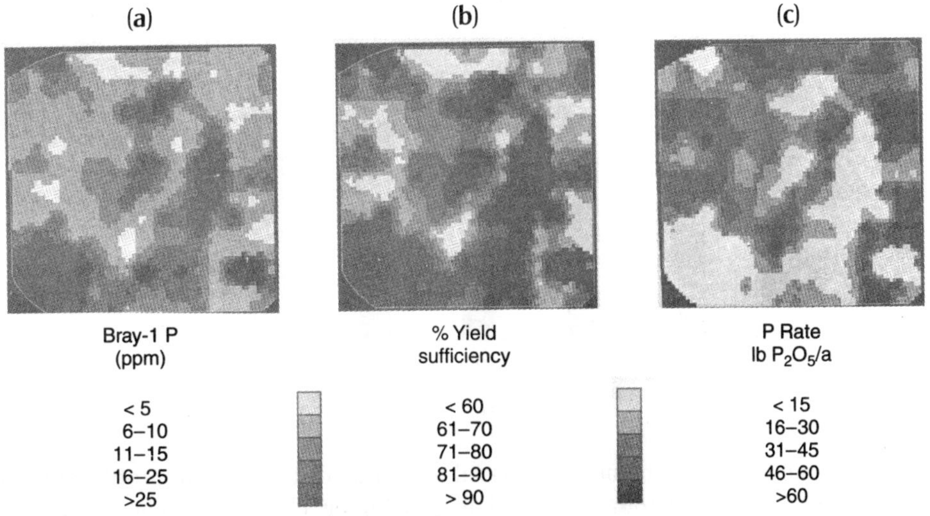

Figure 10-41 **Spatial distribution of soil-test P determined from sampling this 120-acre field on 2-acre square grids (a). These data were used to develop the P sufficiency map (b). Ultimately, a variable P recommendation map is established (c). The white areas represent low-P recommendations and high soil-test P and P sufficiency areas.** *(Courtesy Ferguson, Univ. of Nebraska.)*

Figure 10-42 **Typical variable fertilizer applicator capable of applying several nutrient sources at various rates based on spatially distributed soil-test levels.** *(Courtesy Ag-Chem Equip. Co.)*

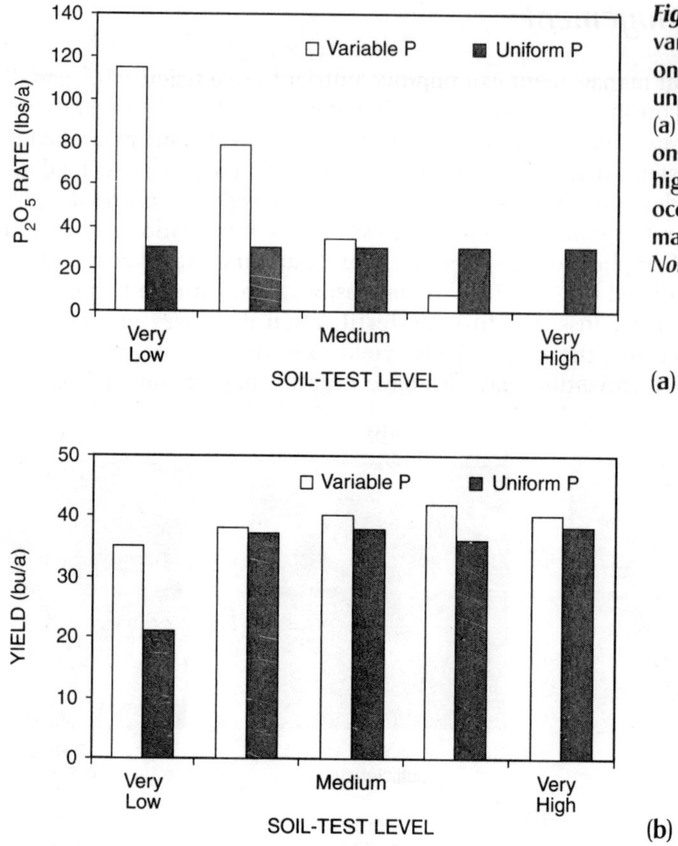

Figure 10-43 **Comparison of variable and uniform P application on soybean yield. Applying a uniform P rate of 30 lbs P_2O_5/a (a) resulted in significant yield loss on very low-P areas (b). On very high-P areas overapplication occurs with uniform P management (a).** *(Heiniger, 2003, North Carolina State Univ.)*

Variable N recommendations based on spatial distribution of profile NO_3^-, yield goal, and other relevant parameters used in developing N recommendations also directs highest N rates to field areas with the highest yield potential. As a result, the total quantity of N fertilizer applied to a field may be reduced, which decreases the amount of fertilizer N left in the profile after harvest (Table 10-9).

Establishing management zones within a field based on specific spatial data can also be used to develop variable nutrient recommendations. These spatial data commonly include aerial photography of soil color (indicates surface-soil OM), previous yield maps, electrical conductivity, slope or elevation, soil type, and other spatial information. These digital data layers can be used to establish management zones related to relative crop productivity (Fig. 10-44). Although variability in climate influences yield potential between years, high-yield areas are generally more productive than low-yield areas (Fig. 10-45). In years when high-yield management zones do not perform as expected, over- and underapplication of nutrients would increase compared to years when management zones perform as expected. In these cases, overapplication of N would contribute to N leaching potential. For this reason, technologies used to establish in-season N recommendations will likely be more efficient than N recommendations determined through technologies to establish management zones (Chapter 9).

Remote sensing techniques can also be used to establish in-season N recommendations. Aerial infrared photography of a growing crop can be used to identify areas in the field exhibiting N stress (Fig. 10-46). The spatial distribution of crop biomass affected by N stress

Table 10-9 Comparison Between Uniform and Variable N Management in a 40 a Field on Average N rate, Total Urea Use, Spring Wheat Yield, and Soil Profile NO_3-N (0–2 ft) After Harvest

N Management	*Average N Rate*	*Urea Applied*	*Yield*	*Soil NO_3-N*
	lbs/a	*lbs*	*bu/a*	*lbs/a*
Uniform	70	6,087	44.0	41.1
Variable	57	4,944	45.6	32.0

SOURCE: From D. Franzen, North Dakota State Univ.

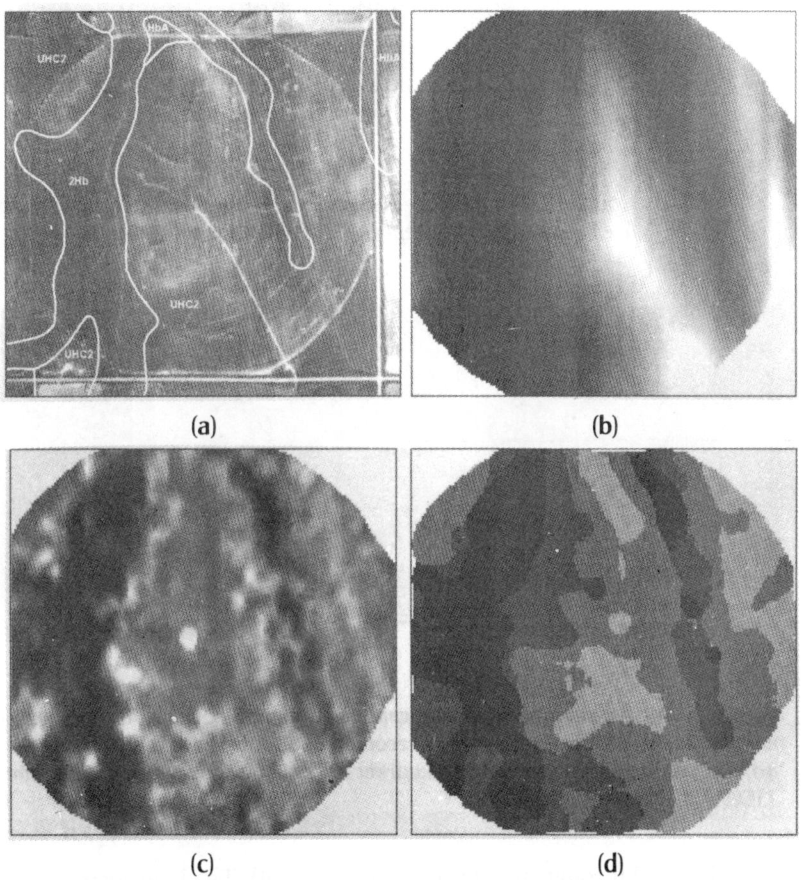

Figure 10-44 Use of remote sensing to determine soil color (a), where dark colors represent areas of higher surface soil OM than lighter color areas; elevation (b), where elevation increases from dark- to light- colored areas; and apparent electrical conductivity (c), where conductivity increases from dark to light. Digitized soil survey data were superimposed over the soil color map (a). These data (a, b, and c) were used to delineate soil management zones (d) that represent areas of similar crop yield potential. The dark-colored zones exhibit higher yield potential (Fig. 10-45) and would require higher nutrient application rates than the light-colored areas. *(Schepers et al., 2004,* Agron. J., *96:195.)*

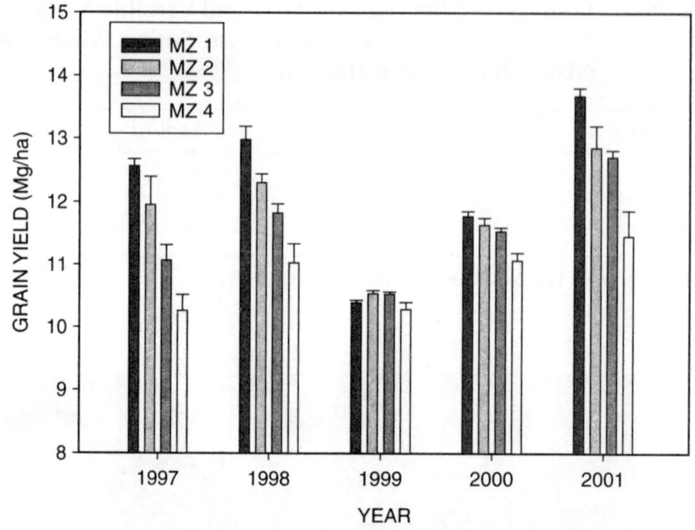

Figure 10-45 Average corn yields of four management zones over five crop seasons. *(Schepers et al., 2004,* Agron. J., *96:195–203.)*

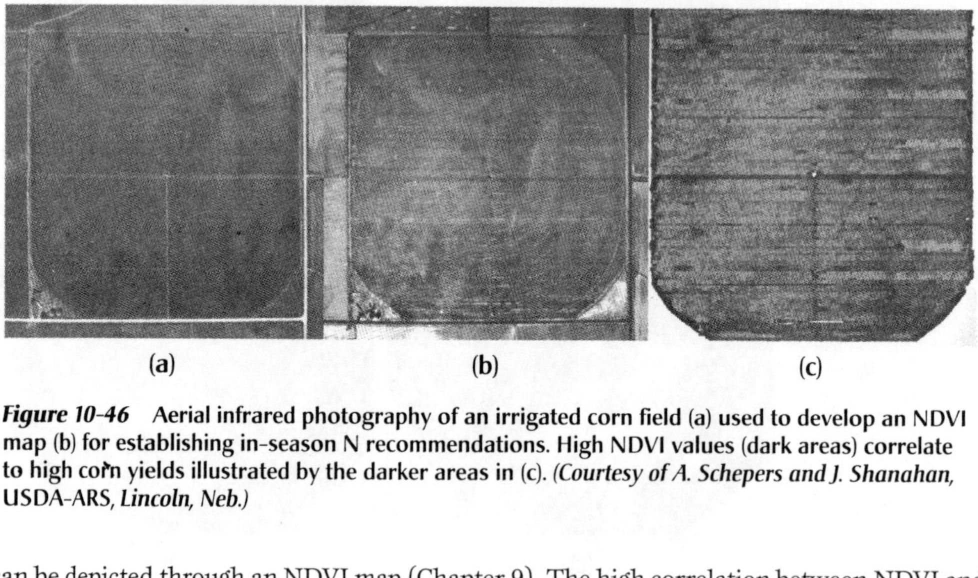

Figure 10-46 Aerial infrared photography of an irrigated corn field (a) used to develop an NDVI map (b) for establishing in-season N recommendations. High NDVI values (dark areas) correlate to high corn yields illustrated by the darker areas in (c). *(Courtesy of A. Schepers and J. Shanahan,* USDA-ARS, *Lincoln, Neb.)*

can be depicted through an NDVI map (Chapter 9). The high correlation between NDVI and grain yield enables use of NDVI in estimating in-season N requirements (Fig. 10-46).

Nutrient Management in Turf

Turfgrass production is a rapidly growing component of agriculture. Regardless of its use in residential or recreational environments, effective nutrient management is essential to turfgrass quality, durability, and aesthetic appeal. A comparison of relative nutrient contents of several turfgrasses with various crops referred to throughout the text is provided in

Table 9-1. The primary difference between most agricultural crops and turfgrass is that most of the nutrients applied to turf systems are not removed. With the exception of fine turf on putting and lawn bowling greens, grass clippings are not removed and thus are allowed to recycle through soil-OM components as the residues are degraded (Fig. 4-1). Most of these nutrients ultimately become plant available in subsequent years. In addition to soil tests, plant tissue can be sampled to assess nutrient status and adequacy of the fertilization program. Samples are collected by clipping leaves slightly above the soil surface two days after regrowth. Nutrient sufficiency ranges are provided in Table 9-3.

Nitrogen

Nitrogen requirements of turfgrass are greater than any other nutrient, which is similar to other agronomic crops (Table 9-1). Adequate N maintains a desirable dark-green leaf color, prolific tillering or shoot density, and some tolerance to other nutrient and pest stresses. Excessive N accumulation in leaf tissue results in increased growth and demand for water, which may cause moisture stress. Too much N enhances susceptibility to certain diseases and reduces tolerance to high-temperature stress. Reduced root, stolon, and rhizome growth with increased heat and water stress results in thin, uneven growth patterns. If these symptoms are misdiagnosed as N stress, additional N applications can severely reduce turf growth and aesthetics and increase the opportunity for fertilizer N runoff into nearby streams. The goal of an efficient N-management program is to provide adequate N to support vigorous growth without overfertilization.

Recommended annual N rates depend on the turfgrass species, desired turfgrass quality, and soil type. N contribution from the irrigation water should also be factored into the N recommendation. Most turfgrass N recommendations range between 2 to 12 lbs/1,000 ft^2 (80 to 520 lbs N/a) annually (Table 10-10). Because N is mobile in the soil, 2 to 4 applications throughout the season are recommended. More frequent applications result in higher quality and longer periods of dark-green color. Because of the midspring to midsummer and mid- to late-fall active growth pattern in cool-season grasses (e.g., bluegrass, ryegrass, and fescue), maintaining high forage quality requires 3 to 4 applications of 1 lb/1,000 ft^2 in late fall and early spring (Table 10-10). Warm-season grasses (e.g., Bermudagrass and zoysia) exhibit active growth from midsummer through midfall. N is applied in midspring (1 lb/1,000 ft^2), followed by monthly applications through early fall.

Table 10-10 **Optimum Annual N Application Rates and Timing for Selected Turfgrass Species***

Turf Species	*Annual N Rate lbs/1,000 ft^2*	*Number of Applications* 1	2	3	4
Fine leaf fescue	1–2	EF	EF, ES	EF, ES, LF	EF, ES, MR, LF
Tall fescue	2–4	EF	EF, ES	EF, ES, LF	EF, ES, MR, LF
Perennial ryegrass	2–4	EF	EF, ES	EF, ES, LF	EF, ES, MR, LF
Kentucky bluegrass	2–4	EF	EF, ES	EF, ES, LF	EF, ES, MR, LF
Bermuda grass	4–8	ES	ES, MR	ES, ER, LR	ES, ER, MR, LR
St. Augustine grass	2–4	ES	ES, MR	ES, ER, LR	ES, ER, MR, LR
Zoysia	2–4	ES	ES, MR	ES, ER, LR	ES, ER, MR, LR

*E, early; M, mid; L, late; S, spring; R, summer; F, fall.

Table 10-11 **Common N Sources Used in Turf and Important Characteristics**

N Source	*Grade*	*N Release Rate*	*Leaf Burn Potential*	*Leaching Potential*	*N Supply with Low Temperatures*
Urea	46-0-0	fast	high	moderate	high
NH_4NO_3	34-0-0	fast	high	high	high
$(NH_4)_2SO_4$	21-0-0-24	fast	high	high	high
KNO_3	13-0-44	fast	high	high	high
MAP	11-52-0	fast	moderate	moderate	high
DAP	18-46-0	fast	moderate	moderate	high
IBDU	31-0-0	moderate	low	low	moderate
SCU	22 to 38-0-0	moderate	low	low	moderate
Resin-coated urea	24 to 35-0-0	moderate/long	low	low	moderate
Methylene ureas & ureaformaldehyde	38-0-0	moderate/long	low	low	low
Liquid manures/ sewage sludge	variable	moderate/long	low	low	low

Low N rates (< 1.5 lbs/1,000 ft^2) should be used with soluble N sources to maximize N recovery by the plant and to minimize N leaching. Higher rates can be used with slow-release N sources such as S-coated urea (Chapter 4). Table 10-11 illustrates N-release rates and other important properties associated with common turfgrass fertilizers (see also Table 4-26).

Phosphorus

Although used in smaller amounts than N, P is important for early seedling vigor and stand establishment (Chapter 5). In low-P soils, increasing P availability improves N utilization and recovery (Fig. 10-47). P deficiencies are uncommon in established turfgrass, where clippings are usually left on the surface and many mixed turf fertilizers contain some P. Soil testing is the best tool to identify low-P soils and the need for P fertilization. With high-P

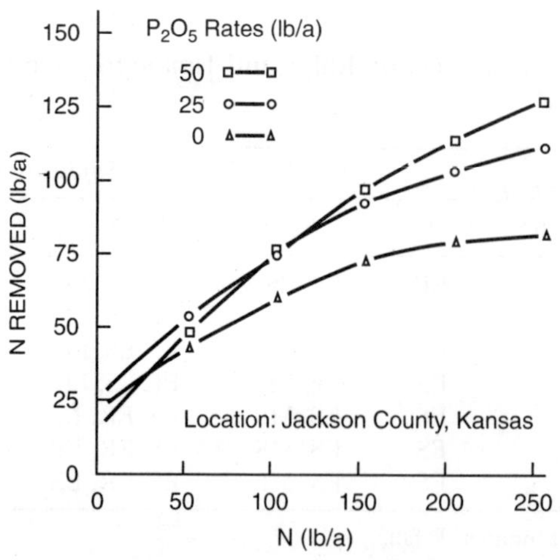

Figure 10-47 **Influence of P nutrition on N recovery in bromegrass.** ***(Courtesy, Kansas State University.)***

soil tests (> 25 ppm Bray-1 P) fertilizers that contain P are not necessary. P is especially important for establishing new turfgrass areas.

Potassium

Turfgrass can require as much K as N, although N is usually the most limiting nutrient. An N:K ratio of 2:1 in leaf tissue is considered normal. Using adequate N without K worsens plant susceptibility to diseases and drought stress. With high N rates, higher K rates are required to maintain turfgrass quality. Balanced N and K nutrition encourages root, stolon, and rhizome growth important for maintaining optimum turf density, water use efficiency, winter hardiness (in northern climates), and tolerance to heavy traffic. K applications preceding heat or water stress periods, as well as an early fall application to improve winter hardiness, are critical. Fertilizers that contain a 1:1 ratio of N:K will supply adequate K in most cases. K fertilizers have higher salt indices than most N and P sources; thus, caution is recommended with applications at germinating and seedling growth stages (Table 10-2). Like N, K is mobile in the soil, and K leaching can occur in sandy soils. The salt index with K_2SO_4 is lower than other K sources.

Sulfur

Turfgrass usually requires more S than P. Adequate S nutrition is important for protein and chlorophyll synthesis that greatly contributes to a healthy, dark-green color. S-deficiency symptoms are often mistaken for N stress. S is also essential for maximizing recovery of N and K, which is important in reducing N-leaching potential. Annual S rates are 0.5 to 2 lbs/1,000 ft^2, either as a single application in early spring or split applied with N in the spring and fall. Split applications of SO_4^- sources reduce the potential for S leaching, especially in sandy soils (Chapter 7).

Micronutrients

Dark-green turf color is also related to Fe and Mg nutrition, since these nutrients function in chlorophyll synthesis. Early-spring and midsummer applications are recommended. Soil testing provides the best guide to identifying soils low in plant-available micronutrients. Foliar applied Fe can enhance turf greenness, even with adequate Fe availability. Soil testing provides accurate information to determine micronutrient requirements.

Other Considerations in Nutrient Management

Conservation Tillage

Wherever feasible, low fertility soils should be brought up to medium or higher fertility before establishing conservation tillage systems. In reduced- and no-tillage systems, nutrients concentrate in the surface 4 in. of soil (Fig. 10-32). Although periodic tillage can partially redistribute nutrients, the original purpose for maintaining surface residue cover would be compromised. Broadcast lime, P, and K is effective, particularly in humid regions. With surface residues there is more moisture near the surface and increased root growth; however, under low fertility and/or in cooler and drier areas, surface P and K

Table 10-12 **Influence of Tillage on K Nutrition and Yield in Corn Grown on a Medium-K Soil**

K_2O *Applied Annually 1973–1976 (lbs/a)*	*Yield Loss (bu/a) with No-Tillage*	*% K in Ear Leaf*	
		Plowed	*No-Tillage*
0	37	0.73	0.59
80	26	1.40	1.04
160	13	1.71	1.42

SOURCE: From Schulte et al., 1978, *Soils, Fertilizer and Agricultural Pesticides Short Course,* Minneapolis, MN.

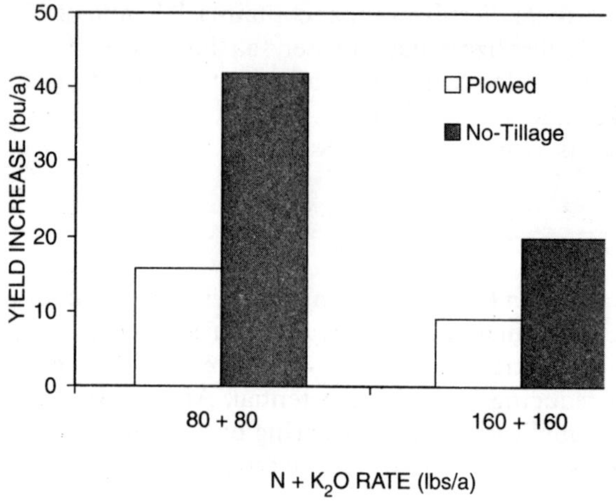

Figure 10-48 **Influence of tillage on broadcast N + K_2O on corn yield response. *(Schulte, 1979,* Better Crops, *63:25.)***

may not be sufficiently available (Table 10-12). These data illustrate reduced K uptake under no-tillage, even with K fertilization. Similar relationships exist with P.

Yield increases from band-applied fertilizer are generally greater under no-till systems than under plowed systems (Fig. 10-48). Conservation tillage maintains greater surface residue cover, resulting in cooler and wetter conditions at planting and lower nutrient availability. A large portion of broadcast N in reduced-tillage systems can be immobilized by surface crop residues (Chapter 4). Therefore, maximizing crop recovery of fertilizer N requires placement below the residue (Fig. 10-49).

Residual Fertilizer Availability

A portion of nutrients applied will remain in the soil after harvest, depending on rate applied, crop yield, portion of the crop harvested, and the soil. Residual N availability is related to buildup of soil OM (Chapter 4 and Chapter 13). With S, residual availability is related to use of S° products and to both S accumulation in soil OM and SO_4^{-2} adsorption to AEC (Fig. 10-50). For immobile nutrients, residual availability can be observed for many years depending on the rate applied and the soil buffer capacity (Fig. 10-51).

Generally, as fertilizer application rate increases, the residual value also increases. In many cases, the cost of fertilization is charged to the crop treated. However, residual fertil-

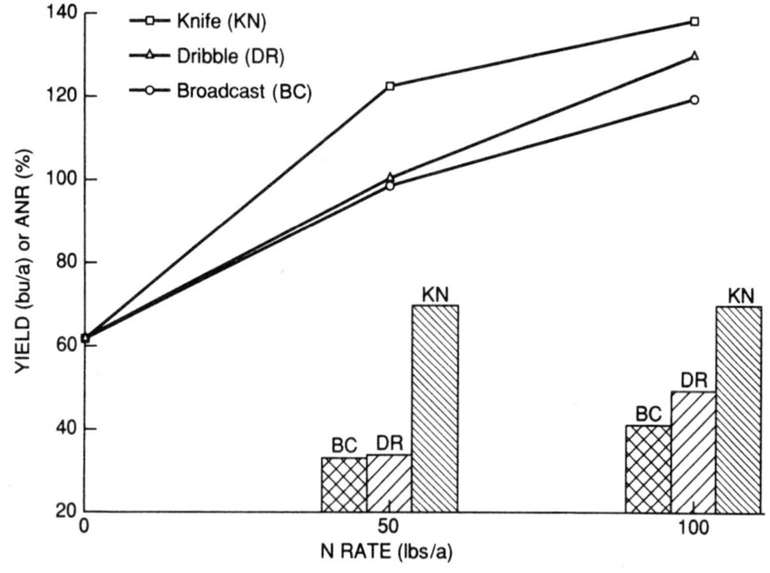

Figure 10-49 Influence of N rate and placement on no-till grain sorghum yield and apparent N recovery in the grain. Placing N below surface crop residue increased yield and % recovery of applied N compared with broadcast and dribble N. *(Lamond et al., 1989, Rep. of Prog., Kansas State Univ.)*

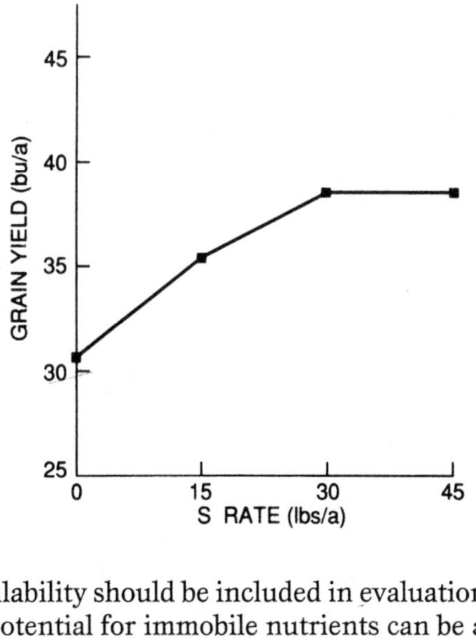

Figure 10-50 Wheat yield response to residual S availability. The S rates shown were initially applied prior to wheat planting in a wheat-pea rotation. The S response is from the 4th wheat crop or 7th crop in the 2-year rotation. *(Ramig and Rasmussen, 1972,* Proc. 23rd Northwest Fert. Conf., *p. 125, Boise ID.)*

izer availability should be included in evaluation of fertilizer economics. The residual availability potential for immobile nutrients can be accurately determined through soil testing.

Utilization of Nutrients from the Subsoil

The utilization of nutrients from the subsoil depends on the ability of roots to explore subsoil, which depends on the crop, soil physical factors that influence drainage and aeration,

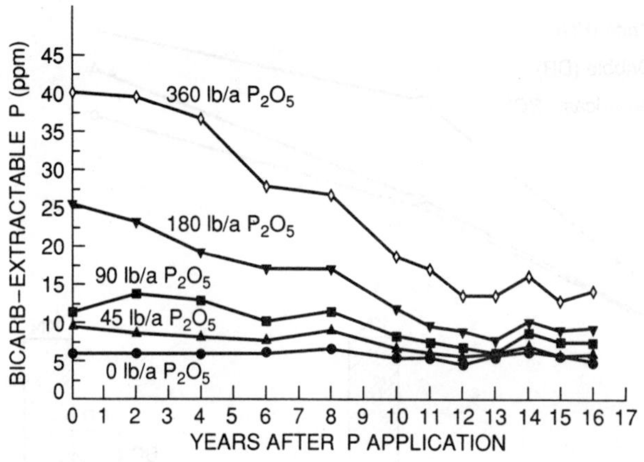

Figure 10-51 Effect of P application rate on residual P availability as measured by the Olsen P soil test. *(Halvorson and Black, 1985,* Soil Sci. Soc. Am. J., *49:928.)*

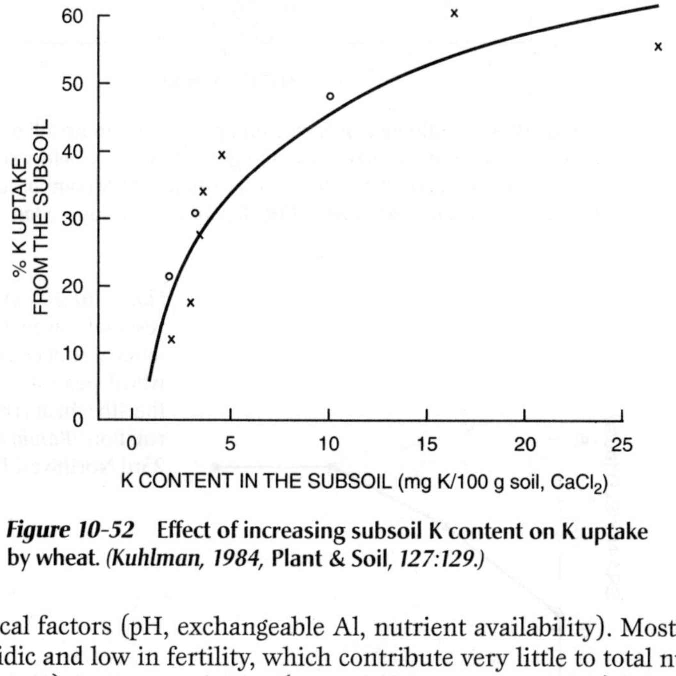

Figure 10-52 Effect of increasing subsoil K content on K uptake by wheat. *(Kuhlman, 1984,* Plant & Soil, *127:129.)*

and soil chemical factors (pH, exchangeable Al, nutrient availability). Most humid-region subsoils are acidic and low in fertility, which contribute very little to total nutrient uptake by crops (Fig. 10-52). Deep-rooted crops (e.g., alfalfa, sweet clover, etc.) increase available P in the surface by upward transfer from the subsoil as the organic residues are returned and decomposed. Surface horizons of forest soils are commonly higher in nutrients than the subsoil horizons because of upward transfer and accumulation.

Loess or alluvial soils can be high in K and P throughout the profile and can be utilized by deep-rooted plants, causing some difficulty in correlating surface-soil test results for P or K. When subsoil P or K content is considered, the relation between extractable P or K and crop response can be improved. Some regions have established relative subsoil nutrient availability for major soil series to improve the accuracy of nutrient recommendations (Fig. 10-53).

In calcareous soils, soil-test K is usually high in both surface soil and subsoil, but most subsoils are low in P and many micronutrients. P and micronutrient fertilization of the surface soil is generally adequate to increase P and micronutrient availability.

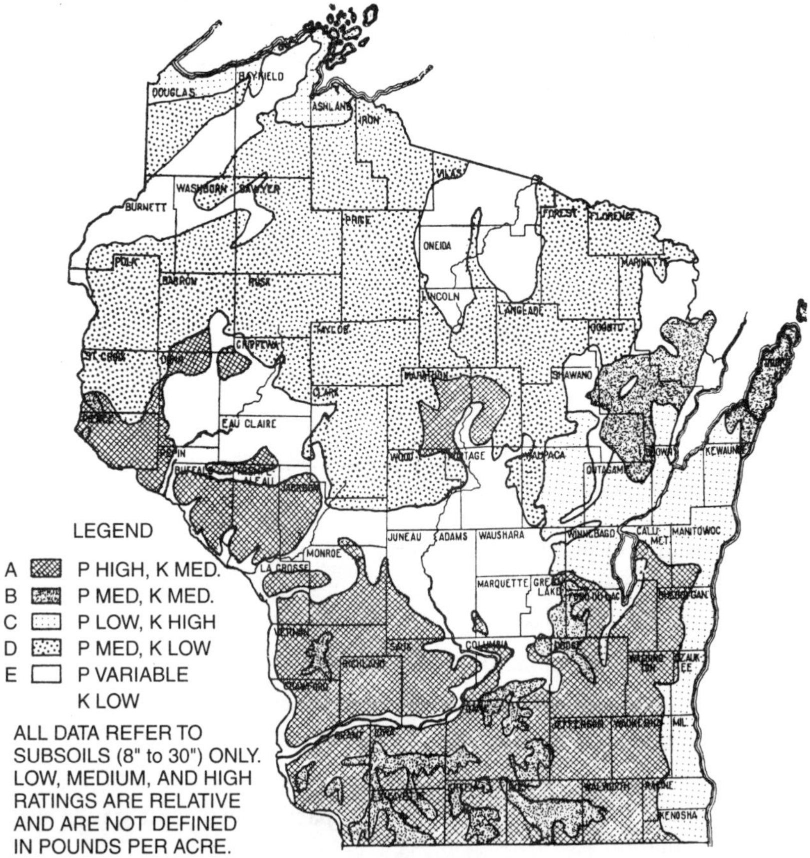

Figure 10-53 **Relative P and K availability in subsoils of major soil series in Wisconsin.** ***(Kelling et al., 1999,*** **Optimum Soil Test Levels for Wisconsin,** ***Univ. of Wisconsin Coop. Ext. A3030.)***

Table 10-13 **Effect of Subsoiling and Deep Incorporation of P and K on Barley Yield**

Tillage / Fertilizer Treatment	*Grain Yield (bu/a)*				
	1974	*1975*	*1976*	*1977*	*Mean*
None	72.8	34.2	51.0	43.2	50.3
Subsoiled alone	77.8	56.4	66.4	52.5	63.2
Subsoiled + P + K	92.4	69.8	67.1	64.6	73.5
P + K to topsoil	67.4	28.3	56.1	47.6	49.9

SOURCE: From McEwan and Johnston, 1979, *J. Agr. Sci.* (Camb.), 92:695.

Subsoil application of nutrients can enhance nutrient availability and root development in the fertilized zone. Lime added to an acid subsoil will not only supply Ca and Mg but will also reduce the Al, Fe, and Mn in solution (Chapter 3). In some cases, subsoiling alone can increase crop yields, although subsoil incorporation of fertilizers can further increase yields (Table 10-13). Subsoiling to a depth of 11 to 22 in. increased the 4-year mean barley yield by 24%, and subsoil incorporation of P and K increased barley yield an additional 20%. In some soils, deep tillage (24 to 36 in.) can improve root growth and crop yield without subsoil fertilization. In this situation, the benefit is related to more efficient use of subsoil water. If the plant is utilizing water from 24 to 36 in. in contrast to only 12-in. deep, the probability of drought stress will be reduced. Under some conditions, turning up heavy clay subsoil material may cause the surface soil to seal off more rapidly and decrease water intake. Deep plowing or chiseling to break up plowpans and improved management practices to encourage deeper rooting are important to enhance productivity.

Management of Organic Waste Nutrients

Animal Manure

Used properly, animal manures are a valuable source of plant nutrients. Some of the beneficial effects of manure use are:

- a source of plant-available NH_4^+;
- increases mobility and availability of P and micronutrients due to OM complexation;
- increased soil OM;
- increased soil moisture retention (Table 10-14);
- improved soil structure, decreased soil bulk density, and increased infiltration rate;
- increased buffer capacity;
- reduced Al^{+3} toxicity in acid soils by complexation with OM; and
- increased CO_2 in the plant canopy, particularly plant stands with restricted air circulation.

Greater attention is being given to effective disposal of animal manures because of (1) increased use of confinement production systems and associated manure-handling problems and (2) increased concern over contamination of ground and surface water by NO_3^- and $H_2PO_4^-$ in the manure. Maximizing crop recovery of soil-applied manure nutrients depends on:

- manure nutrient content,
- application method and time, and
- short- and long-term availability of manure nutrients.

Table 10-14 **Influence of Continuous Manure Application on Soil Water Content**

Soil Water	*No Manure*	*Manure*
	% moisture	
Field capacity	21.6	24.8
Wilting point	7.1	8.2
Available water	14.4	16.6

Manure nutrient content varies, depending on:

- animal type and diet,
- type and amount of bedding,
- manure moisture content, and
- storage method.

Table 10-15 illustrates nutrient contents of typical animal wastes; however, variation exists between regions and local values should be used in estimating the quantity of nutrients applied with a specific manure rate. In most cases, just prior to application, manure samples should be collected and sent to a laboratory for analysis.

Four primary methods used for field application of manure include:

- broadcast solid manure,
- broadcast slurry or liquid manure with a vehicle or irrigation system,
- subsurface band or injection of slurry or liquid, and
- surface band applied preplant or in-season.

Table 10-15 **Approximate Dry Matter and Nutrient Composition of Selected Animal Manure**

Type of Livestock	*Waste Handling System*	*Dry Matter (%)*	*Nutrient (lbs/ton)*			
			N			
			*Available**	*Total†*	P_2O_5	K_2O
		Solid Handling Systems*				
Swine	Without bedding	18	6	10	9	8
	With bedding	18	5	8	7	7
Beef cattle	Without bedding	15	4	11	7	10
	With bedding	50	8	21	18	26
Dairy cattle	Without bedding	18	4	9	4	10
	With bedding	21	5	9	4	10
Poultry	Without litter	45	26	33	48	34
	With litter	75	36	56	45	34
	Deep pit (compost)	76	44	68	64	45
		Liquid Handling Systems*				
Swine	Liquid pit	4	20	36	27	19.0
	Oxidation ditch	2.5	12	24	27	19.0
	Lagoon	1	3	4	2	0.4
Beef cattle	Liquid pit	11	24	40	27	34.0
	Oxidation ditch	3	16	28	18	29.0
	Lagoon	1	2	4	9	5.0
Dairy cattle	Liquid pit	8	12	24	18	29.0
	Lagoon	1	2.5	4	4	5.0
Poultry	Liquid pit	13	64	80	36	96.0

*Primarily NH_4-N, which is plant available during the growing season.

†NH_4-N plus organic N, which is slow releasing.

Application conversion factors: 1,000 gal = about 4 tons; 27,154 gal = 1 acre–inch

SOURCE: From Sutton et al., 1985, Univ. of Minn. Ext. Bull. AG-FO-2613.

Table 10-16 Effect of Animal Waste Handling and Storage Method on N Losses

Handling and Storing Method	*N Loss* (%)*	*Handling and Storing Method*	*N Loss* (%)*
Solid systems		**Liquid systems**	
Daily scrape and haul	15–35	Anaerobic pit	15–30
Manure pack	20–40	Oxidation ditch	15–40
Open lot	40–60	Lagoon	70–80
Deep pit (poultry)	15–35		

*Based on composition of waste applied to the land versus composition of freshly excreted waste, adjusted for dilution effects of the various systems.
SOURCE: Sutton et al., 1985, Univ. of Minn. Ext. Bull. AG-FO-2613.

Table 10-17 Effect of Manure Application Method on N Volatilization Losses

Method of Application	*Type of Waste*	*N Loss* (%)*
Broadcast without cultivation	Solid	15–30
	Liquid	10–25
Broadcast with cultivation†	Solid	1–5
	Liquid	1–5
Subsurface knife	Liquid	0–2
Irrigation	Liquid	30

*Percentage of total N in waste applied that was lost within 4 days after application.
†Cultivation immediately after application.
SOURCE: Sutton et al., 1985, Univ. of Minn. Ext. Bull. AG-FO-2613.

Methods for handling and storing manure will affect its nutrient content. Previously, the common method of disposal was to collect the manure or manure plus bedding and spread it on fields. Liquid waste systems have been developed in which the manure is diluted with water and stored in pits or lagoons. N-volatilization losses in liquid systems can be substantial (Table 10-16). P and K losses are only 5 to 15% under all but the open-lot and lagoon waste systems. In an open lot, about 50% of these nutrients are lost. In a lagoon, much of the P settles out and is lost from the liquid applied on the land.

Manure application methods particularly affect N-volatilization losses that reduce the quantity of plant-available N in the manure (Table 10-17). N losses are greatest with liquid systems and with broadcast solids or liquids. Immediate incorporation will minimize N volatilization (Fig. 10-54). In most cases, little or no N is available if incorporation occurs later than 5 to 8 days after application.

Subsurface application maximizes N availability from manure. The effectiveness of injected liquid manure can be improved by adding nitrification inhibitors to maintain NH_4-N.

In addition to the NH_4^+ present in the manure (Table 10-15), the organic N fraction will slowly mineralize over time providing plant-available N. Depending on the manure source, 20 to 30% of the organic N will mineralize the first year after application, which decreases in subsequent years (Table 10-18). The classic studies in England demonstrated substantial residual N availability of continued applications of high manure rates (Fig. 10-55). Even though maintenance of 100% relative yield required annual manure applications, residual effects were observed nearly 40 years after waste applications were stopped.

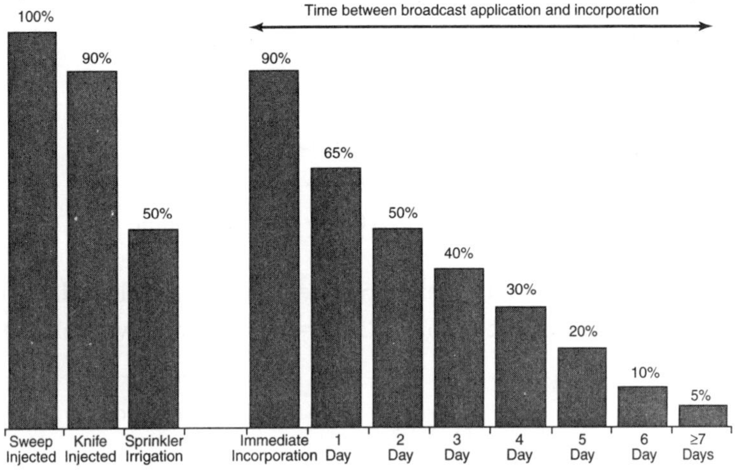

Figure 10-54 **Influence of manure application method and length of time between application and incorporation on % plant-available N of the original manure N. The majority of the decrease in % N availability is due to N volatilization losses.** ***(Leikam and Lamond, 2003, Kansas State Univ. Coop. Ext. MF2562.)***

Table 10-18 **Estimated Quantity of Plant-Available N from the Organic N Applied in Manure over 3 Years**

Manure Source	*Year 1*	*Year 2*	*Year 3*
	% N Mineralized		
Liquid manure	30	12	6
Solid manure	25	12	6
Compost	20	6	3

SOURCE: From Leikam and Lamond, 2003, Kansas State Univ. Coop. Ext. MF2562.

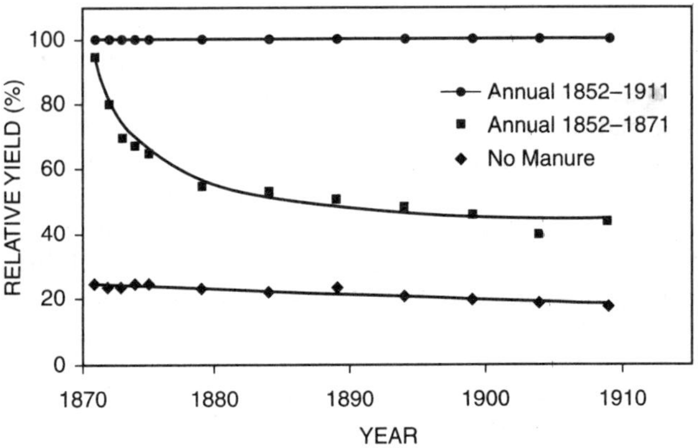

Figure 10-55 **Barley yield influenced by long-term manure application. Annual manure application of 31 Mt ha^{-1} from 1852 to 1911. N availability for mineralizable organic N from manure applied from 1852 to 1871 persisted for 40 years after manure applications were halted in 1871.** ***(Hall, 1917,*** **The Book of the Rothamsted Experiments** ***(2nd ed.), E.P. Dutton and Company, NY.)***

Estimating plant-available N (PAN) in animal waste is provided in the following examples:
Solid beef manure (without bedding)—broadcast and incorporated 2 days after application

$$\begin{aligned} \text{Total N} &= 11 \text{ lbs/ton} \quad \text{(Table 10-15)} \\ \text{Organic N} &= 7 \text{ lbs/ton} \\ NH_4^+ - N &= 4 \text{ lbs/ton} \\ NO_3^- - N &= \text{negligible} \end{aligned}$$

$$\begin{aligned} \text{PAN} = \quad & 4 \text{ lbs } NH_4^+/\text{ton} \times 50\% = 2.0 \text{ lbs available } NH_4^+ - N/\text{ton} \quad \text{(Fig. 10-54)} \\ & + 7 \text{ lbs organic N/ton} \times 25\% = 1.7 \text{ lbs plant-available organic N ton} \quad \text{(Table 10-18)} \\ & \overline{\quad 3.7 \text{ lbs PAN/ton} \quad} \end{aligned}$$

Liquid swine manure (lagoon)—knife injected

$$\begin{aligned} \text{Total N} &= 4 \text{ lbs/1,000 gal} \quad \text{(Table 10-15)} \\ \text{Organic N} &= 1 \text{ lbs/1,000 gal} \\ NH_4^+ - N &= 3 \text{ lbs/1,000 gal} \\ NO_3^- - N &= \text{negligible} \end{aligned}$$

$$\begin{aligned} \text{PAN} = \quad & 3 \text{ lbs } NH_4^+/1{,}000 \text{ gal} \times 90\% = 2.7 \text{ lbs available } NH_4^+ - N/1{,}000 \text{ gal} \quad \text{(Fig. 10-54)} \\ & + 1 \text{ lb organic N}/1{,}000 \text{ gal} \times 30\% = 0.3 \text{ lbs plant-available organic N ton} \quad \text{(Table 10-18)} \\ & \overline{\quad 3.0 \text{ lb PAN}/1{,}000 \text{ gal} \quad} \end{aligned}$$

Many comparisons have been made between the effects of manure on crop production and those obtained from the application of equivalent amounts of N, P, and K in commercial fertilizers. Long-term studies comparing manure and fertilizer use in Missouri (Fig. 10-56) and Oklahoma (Table 10-19) illustrate similar crop productivity with the two nutrient sources.

Distribution of manure by grazing animals presents a problem in the maintenance fertilization of pastures. For N, which does not remain in effective concentrations for more than a year, about 10% of a grazed area is effectively covered annually. In contrast, residual effects of P from animal wastes may last for 5 to 10 years. In general, nearly all of a pasture area will receive deposits of manure in a 10-year period. K is intermediate between N and P in retention in the soil, and manure-deposited K is effective to some degree for ~5 years. During this period, about 60% of a pasture will have been covered. With low stocking rates, animal excreta will essentially have no effect on soil fertility. On highly productive pastures with a high carrying capacity, excreta may have a beneficial effect on soil fertility over a period of time. Grain feeding on pastures will also increase soil fertility.

Producers interested in using manure as the nutrient source in cropping systems should consider:

- high transportation costs potentially result in continued application of manure close to the source, where overapplication is common;

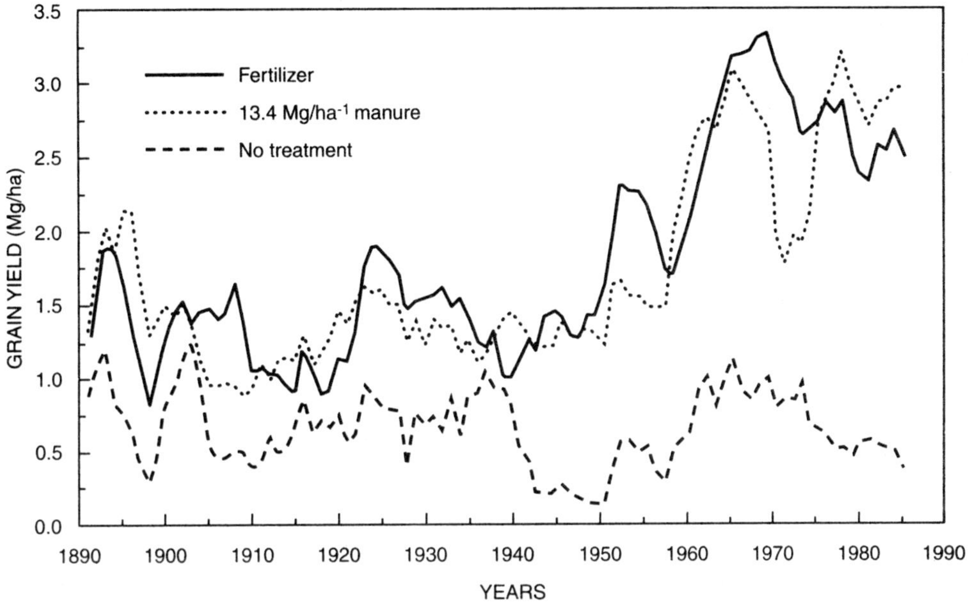

Figure 10-56 Comparison of continuous wheat production between manure and fertilizers (1890–1990). *(Sanborn Plots, University of Missouri.)*

Table 10-19 Comparison of Manure and Fertilizer on Winter Wheat Yield Between 1930 and 2000

Treatments N	P_2O_5	K_2O	1930–1937	1938–1947	1948–1957	1958–1967	1968–1977	1978–1987	1988–1997	1998–2000
			Grain Yield (bu/a)							
0	0	0	16.6	9.5	13.3	18.9	18.0	19.6	15.1	21.1
0	30	0	21.2	15.9	19.1	21.5	18.8	22.4	14.7	20.7
33*	30	0	22.6	17.2	19.8	31.7	36.0	30.5	27.4	39.7
33*	30	30	23.4	17.4	19.9	29.4	33.9	30.9	32.4	42.8
33*	30	30+ lime	22.3	17.3	22.5	33.0	37.6	33.0	32.9	37.2
	Manure†		24.1	17.5	18.0	29.9	30.2	34.1	28.0	36.2

*N rate increased to 60 lbs N/ac in 1968.
†Beef manure applied every 4th year at rates equivalent to 120 lbs N/ac (1930–1967) and 240 lbs N/ac (1967–2000). Lime (L) applied when soil pH ≤ 5.5.
SOURCE: Magruder Plots, Oklahoma State University.

- nutrient content in manure is highly variable, causing considerable uncertainty in quantifying nutrient rates applied;
- high variability in mineralization of the organic N component in manure combined with the year to year environment effects on N mineralization causes uncertainty in estimated N availability to crops;
- increased soil compaction can occur with manure application equipment; and
- possible nutrient imbalances, for example, manure rates based on crop N requirements will result in P applications 3 to 5 times the crop requirement.

Composted Feedlot Manure

Composting is being adopted in some arid and semiarid regions as an alternative means for handling the large volumes of manure produced at confined animal feeding operations. This approach has many benefits, including reduction in mass and volume of material as well as reductions in weed seed viability and fly breeding potential, plus avoiding malodors from land application of manure. N and C losses as high as 33 and 68%, respectively, accompanied by reductions of 21 to 30% in dry matter are recorded in typical windrowing composting. Important changes in bulk handling properties included three- to fourfold increases in bulk density and 83% lower haulage requirements for transporting compost.

Fertilization with Sludge

Disposal of processed sewage materials from treatment plants is of increasing concern because of population pressures, more stringent laws, and increases in energy costs. Use of sludge on agricultural land has both benefits and problems. Sludge is a source of OM containing macro- and micronutrients, and application to crops is an effective alternative to more costly methods of disposal, such as burning or burying.

Land application of sewage sludge is regulated by federal and state governments. Prior to land application, sludge is treated to reduce pathogens, odor, and heavy metal concentration. Two types of pathogen treatment (Class A and Class B) are employed depending on sludge use. Class A is the most rigorous, with no application site restrictions (i.e., all crops, lawns, gardens, and public accessible areas). Class B sludge receives less rigorous treatment, with site restrictions related to crop harvest, animal grazing, and public access. Sludge is also treated with lime, partial composting (aerobic and anaerobic), and reduction in water content to reduce odor and the potential to attract flies and other disease-transmitting organisms (vector attraction reduction).

Like manure, sludge contains both inorganic and organic N (Table 10-20). Sludge application rates to crops are determined by the N requirement of the crop and the N content of the sludge. Most of the inorganic N occurs as plant-available NH_4^+. During and after application, the quantity of NH_3 volatilized depends on the method of application (Table 10-21). Subsurface application or immediate incorporation will minimize NH_3 volatilization losses and increase plant-available N.

The organic N will slowly mineralize to provide plant-available N. Because of variation in the organic-N content in sludge, sludge application rate, and year to year variation in

Table 10-20 **Typical Elemental Analysis of Sewage Sludge on a Dry-Weight Basis**

Component	*Concentration (%)*	*Component*	*Concentration (ppm)*
Organic C	50–60	Fe	40,000
Organic N	3–6	Zn	5,000
Inorganic N (NH_4^+ + NO_3^-)	1–2	Cu	1,000
P_2O_5	6–8	Mn	500
K_2O	0.5	B	100
Ca	3	Cd	150
Mg	1	Pb	1,000
S	0.9	Ni	400

SOURCE: From Univ. of Illinois Soil Manag. Conserv. Ser. Bull. SM-29.

Table 10-21 **Effect of Sludge Application Method on NH_3 Volatilization**

Application Method	*NH_3 Loss (%)*
Broadcast	40–60
Broadcast and incorporation within 3 to 4 days*	10–30
Subsurface band or injection	< 2

*Increasing the time between application and incorporation increases NH_3 loss.

Table 10-22 **N-Mineralization Rates for Various Sludge Materials over Three Cropping Seasons After Application**

Sludge Type	*% N Mineralization**		
	Year 1	*Year 2*	*Year 3*
Unstabilized	0.4	0.2	0.1
Lime stabilized	0.3	0.15	0.07
Aerobic digestion	0.3	0.15	0.07
Anaerobic digestion	0.2	0.1	0.05
Composted	0.1	0.05	0.02

*Represents the proportion of initial organic N applied that is mineralized to inorganic N.

environmental conditions controlling N mineralization rate, it is difficult to assess the annual contribution of organic-N mineralization to plant-available N. First-year N mineralization rates range between 10 to 40% depending on sludge type (Table 10-22). When waste is applied annually, N-mineralization contributions from both current and past applications must be considered in estimating plant-available N. The declining amounts of mineralizable N with time from previous sludge applications are considered in the determination of total plant-available N (PAN) as shown by:

$$
\begin{aligned}
\%\text{PAN} \;=\;& NO_3^- \\
&+ \text{volatilization loss} \times NH_4^+ && \text{(Table 10-21)} \\
&+ \text{mineralization rate (year 1)} \times \text{organic N*} && \text{(Table 10-22)} \\
&+ \text{mineralization rate (past years)} \times \text{organic N*}
\end{aligned}
$$

where *Organic N = Total N − Inorganic N (NO_3^- + NH_4^+)

Like animal waste, sludge applied at agronomic N rates often results in P and micronutrient application in excess of crop requirement. Eventual buildup of these elements can pose environmental and health concerns. It is essential that appropriate application and soil management techniques be used to protect the environment and the health of human beings and animals. Because of the possibility of applying excessive N and subsequent movement of N and P into surface and ground water, careful monitoring of sludge-amended fields is required.

Because of the potential for buildup of toxic levels of selected heavy metals in soils from frequent application of sludge, limits have been established (Table 10-23). For land application of sludge, heavy metal concentrations must meet Level 2 restrictions. Level 1

Table 10-23 **Maximum Allowable Heavy Metal Concentrations in Sewage Sludge and Soil Loading Limits**

	Sludge Concentration Limits		*Soil Loading Limits*	
Metal	*Level 1*	*Level 2*	*Annual*	*Cumulative*
	ppm		lbs/a	
Arsenic	41	75	1.8	37
Cadmium	39	85	1.7	35
Copper	1,500	4,300	67	1,338
Lead	300	840	13	268
Mercury	17	57	0.76	15
Molybdenum	n/a	75	n/a	n/a
Nickel	420	420	19	375
Selenium	36	100	4.5	89
Zinc	2,800	7,500	125	2,497

SOURCE: From U.S. EPA, 1993, *Part 503 Standards for Use or Disposal of Sewage Sludge*, Federal Register Vol. 58, No. 32.

restrictions are imposed on sludge processed for public distribution in small quantities (< 2,200 lbs). If metal concentrations exceed Level 1, then soil-loading limits are used to guide future application rates (Table 10-23). Quantities of heavy metals in bulk additions of sludge must not exceed cumulative limits. With sludge distributed in bags or other small quantities, rates are restricted to annual limits (Table 10-23).

Sewage Effluent

Sewage effluent can be either a valuable water and nutrient resource for crops or a pollutant to land and waters. Large quantities of water are generally involved; thus, it is essential that the soil be (1) internally well drained and medium textured, having a pH of between 6.5 and 8.2, and (2) be supporting a dense stand of trees, shrubs, or grasses. The groundwater should be monitored periodically for NO_3^-. Forage crops are commonly used for effluent application because of their long growing season, high seasonal evapotranspiration, high nutrient uptake, and their capacity to stabilize soil and prevent erosion. Because forages are not eaten directly by human beings, the transfer of human diseases is unlikely. Many crops can receive sewage effluent although restrictions exist on when effluent application should cease relative to harvest and time after application that a field can be accessed. Excellent crop responses to effluent nutrients occur (Table 10-24). In this example, alfalfa was the most suitable forage crop when the system was operated for optimum wastewater utilization. There was sufficient N in the water for high yields of the grasses.

Nutrient Management Planning

Regardless of the source, nutrients are applied to optimize plant productivity, maximize profitability, and minimize potential impacts of nutrient use on water and air quality. Comprehensive nutrient management planning can help ensure efficient nutrient use and protect the environment. A nutrient management plan is developed for each field and includes the following information:

Table 10-24 **Four-Year Annual Dry-Matter Yield of Five Forage Species as a Function of Effluent and Fertilizer Levels**

		Forage Yield					
Wastewater Irrigation	*Fertilizer N-P*	*Alfalfa*	*Reed Canary*	*Brome*	*Altai Wildrye*	*Tall Wheat*	*Mean*
cm/yr	*kg/ha/yr*			*mt/ha*			
	0–0	8.7	5.8	6.0	5.8	5.3	6.3
62.5	56–48	9.4	8.8	8.9	8.4	7.7	8.6
	0–0	10.2	9.4	10.0	9.6	7.9	9.4
125	56–48	10.1	11.5	11.1	11.7	9.8	10.8
Mean		9.6	8.9	9.0	9.0	7.7	8.8

SOURCE: From Bole and Bell, 1978, *J. Environ. Qual.*, 7:222.

Field and soil map. A map of the field with the soil types delineated enables accurate assessment of crop land areas and proximity to water bodies, water wells, residences, and other objects. Knowledge of soil type distribution is essential to the relationship between potential productivity and numerous soil properties that influence nutrient availability and retention.

Soil test. Accurate soil test information depends on a quality soil sampling plan (Chapter 9). This information provides the foundation for assessing the soil's ability to supply plant-available nutrients and establish nutrient recommendations.

Crop and crop rotation. Previous crop and yield level is important information, especially with legumes. Low legume yield in the previous year will provide less legume-derived available N than a high-yielding legume crop. The intended crop will determine the general nutrient requirements.

Yield expectation. Accurate estimates of expected yield are essential to estimating nutrient needs. Historical yield records for each field provide the best record for determining expected yield level. Overestimating yield results in overapplication of nutrients with potential negative impacts on environment, while underestimating yields results in underapplication of nutrients and loss of yield and profitability.

Nutrient sources. Use of organic waste sources requires accurate sampling and analyisis of the waste nutrient content. Fertilizer sources generally behave similarly, although placement and timing can greatly influence potential N losses. If a combination of sources are used, the nutrient-use efficiency for each source is factored into a final recommendation.

Recommended rates. Recommended rates are determined through evaluation of expected yield potential, native soil nutrient supply, and efficiencies of crop recovery of applied nutrients. Most laboratories provide recommended nutrient rates. While these estimates are good guides, adjustments should be made to satisfy requirements for specific field conditions.

Application timing. Nutrient application timing depends on the specific nutrient and the crop growth pattern. Mobile nutrients should be applied just prior to the maximum uptake or growth period. This may require split applications to maximize nutrient-use efficiency. With immobile nutrients, preplant applications are generally recommended.

Placement method. Many placement options exist that greatly influence nutrient availability and crop recovery of applied nutrients. For example, broadcast N with surface residue cover reduces N recovery by the crop. Band-applied P can substantially increase yield in low-P soils compared to broadcast P. Placement decisions are based on specific nutrient and intended crop.

Proximity to nutrient sensitive areas. Assessment of the field and potential nutrient transport will help prevent nutrients from entering unwanted areas (e.g., streams, ponds, groundwater, water wells, etc.). Use of riparian buffers, grassed waterways, conservation tillage, and other management practices reduces potential nutrient transport off the field.

Assessment and revision. After each crop season the nutrient management plan should be evaluated relative to crop productivity and profitability. Adjustments should be made with any nutrient-related influence on decreases in yield or quality.

Study Questions

1. Why is root growth stimulated in response to plant nutrients on an infertile soil? What root characteristics influence the ability of crops to exploit soil for moisture and nutrients?
2. In what part of the root zone does most of the early root growth take place?
3. Are there differences in the extent of root development among crop varieties?
4. What soil conditions might affect depth of crop rooting?
5. What crops in your area are being underfertilized or overfertilized with P or K?
6. Explain specifically why crops are more likely to experience salt injury on a sandy soil than on a silt loam.
7. Why might the nature of the root system of the crop being grown affect the decision to build up the fertility level of the soil versus applying fertilizer in the row? How would the economic status of the farmer affect the decision?
8. Explain how band and broadcast applications complement each other in encouraging efficient crop production.
9. Why can P materials be placed close to the seed or plant? Why is it usually important that P be close to the seed or young plant? How do you account for the marked response of legumes to band seeding?
10. You are planning to apply P broadcast. You have the choice of broadcasting and plowing down, broadcasting and disking in after plowing, or subsurface application in a broad band. Which procedure would be most desirable? Explain fully.
11. What is meant by soil-building and maintenance applications of fertilizer?
12. Under what relative levels of available soil-test P and K would you approve of making broadcast maintenance applications?
13. Under what conditions is surface broadcast P and K taken up by the plant? Explain.
14. Under what specific conditions in your area do you believe that the entire N could be applied before planting? Under what conditions should none be applied before planting?
15. Why does NH_4-N applied with P cause more P to be absorbed by the plant?
16. Under what conditions would you advocate fall fertilization in your area?

17. What are the possibilities for summer, fall, winter, and spring application of fertilizer in your area? Why is there a need to spread the fertilizer season?
18. Explain how mycorrhizas function and their influence on nutrient use.
19. What is meant by *carryover fertilizer?* Why is there an appreciable amount in a properly fertilized rotation?
20. Are there residual benefits from NO_3-N in soils?
21. There are three philosophies of managing immobile nutrients: buildup, maintenance, and drawdown. Describe situations where each would be the most appropriate management.
22. Do crops benefit equally from soil NO_3-N and that derived from fertilizer? Explain any differences if they exist.
23. Give the pros and cons of the two approaches used in applying micronutrients.
24. What is fertigation and what are its advantages and drawbacks?
25. What is foliar fertilization? Discuss any limitations.
26. What is dual deep placement of fertilizers? What are its advantages and disadvantages?
27. Is the distribution of plant nutrients in the root zone modified by tillage?
28. Explain how conservation tillage increases the water available to the crop. Why is the crop better able to withstand periods of moisture shortage?
29. How does the plant-nutrient supply affect the response to increased plant population? Why?
30. Explain why deeper placement of plant nutrients is likely to give a greater response than shallow placement in some areas.
31. Why does planting date affect the response to the fertilizer?
32. Explain why conservation tillage often requires a change in fertilizer management.
33. Why might higher rates of N be required for no tillage compared to conventional tillage?
34. Are soil fertility levels increasing in your area? What are the advantages? Disadvantages?
35. 10 g of NH_4NO_3 (34% N) is added to 3,000 g of greenhouse soil. Calculate the following.
    - **a.** mg NH_4NO_3 added
    - **b.** mg N added
    - **c.** ppm N added
    - **d.** ppm NO_3 added
    - **e.** ppm NH_4 added
    - **f.** % N in soil after adding N
    - **g.** lbs N/ afs
36. A farmer wants to apply 160 lbs N/a. Calculate the following.
    - **a.** lbs NH_3/a
    - **b.** kg NH_3/ha
    - **c.** lbs urea/a
    - **d.** lbs UAN/a
    - **e.** gal UAN/a

37. A homeowner applies 30 N/1,000 ft^2. Calculate the lbs N/a applied.

38. A golf green manager applied N to each green at 75 lbs N/a. Each green is 600 ft^2. Calculate the following.

- **a.** lbs N/green
- **b.** lbs UAN/green
- **c.** gal UAN/green

39. A homeowner applies 10 40-lb bags of fertilizer (10% N content) to a 2,000 ft^2 fescue lawn. Calculate lbs N/a applied and indicate whether this is a normal, high, or low N rate.

40. Broadcast-applied N usually is less efficient than subsurface-applied N in high-surface-residue cropping systems. Using the following data, calculate the percent fertilizer N recovery for each system. What caused the difference?

	Broadcast N	**Subsurface N**	**Unfertilized**
N rate	100 lbs N/a	100 lbs N/a	0 lbs N/a
Grain yield	98 bu/a	110 bu/a	75 bu/a
Test weight	56 lbs/bu	56 lbs/bu	56 lbs/bu
% grain N	2.1%	2.4%	1.8%

41. An aerobically digested sludge has the following analysis: 0.5% NO_3^-, 0.8% NH_4^+, and 6% total N. The material was broadcast and immediately incorporated. Using Tables 10-20 and 10-21, estimate PAN.

Selected References

Follett, R. H., Murphy, L. S., and Donahue, R. L. 1981. *Fertilizers and soil amendments.* Englewood Cliffs, N. J: Prentice Hall, Inc.

Mortvedt, J. J., Murphy, L. S., and Follett, R. H. 1999. *Fertilizer technology and application.* Willoughby, Ohio: Meister Publishing.

Pierce, F. J., and Sadler, E. J. (Eds.). 1997. *The state of site specific management for agriculture.* Madison, Wis.: Amer. Soc. Agronomy.

Randall, G. W., Wells, K. L., and Hanway, J. J. 1985. Modern techniques in fertilizer application. In O. P. Engelstad (Ed.), *Fertilizer technology and use.* Madison, Wis.: Soil Science Society of America.

Rendig, V. V., and Taylor, H. M. 1989. *Principles of soil–plant interrelationships.* New York: McGraw-Hill Publishing Co.

CHAPTER 11

Nutrients, Water Use, and Other Interactions

When two plant growth factors interact, the influence of each factor can be modified by the other. With applied inputs, an interaction takes place when plant response to two or more inputs is different than the sum of their individual responses. Both *positive* and *negative* interactions can occur (Fig. 11-1). A *zero* interaction occurs when the cumulative plant response is the simple addition of the responses to the individual inputs. Negative interactions result when plant response to the combined factors is less than the response to the two inputs applied separately. Positive interactions follow Liebig's Law of the Minimum. If two factors are limiting, or nearly so, the addition of one will have little effect on growth, whereas yield response is greater when applied together. In severe deficiencies of two or more nutrients, all nutrient responses will result in strong positive interactions. Yield increases from an application of one nutrient can reduce the concentration of a second nutrient, but the higher yields result in greater uptake of the second nutrient. This is a dilution effect, which should be distinguished from an antagonistic effect.

Interactions can be between

- two or more nutrients,
- nutrients and cultural practices (e.g., planting date, placement, tillage, plant population, pest control, etc.),
- nutrient rate and hybrid or variety,
- hybrid or variety and row width or plant population, and
- nutrients and the environment (e.g., water and temperature).

Many interactions are not observed with average yields; however, with high yields, increasing stress is being placed on the plant, and interactions between the various factors contributing to those yields are often observed. Future increases in agricultural productivity will likely be related to manipulation of interactions between numerous management inputs and other plant-growth factors. It is essential that growers and consultants recognize and take advantage of these interactions.

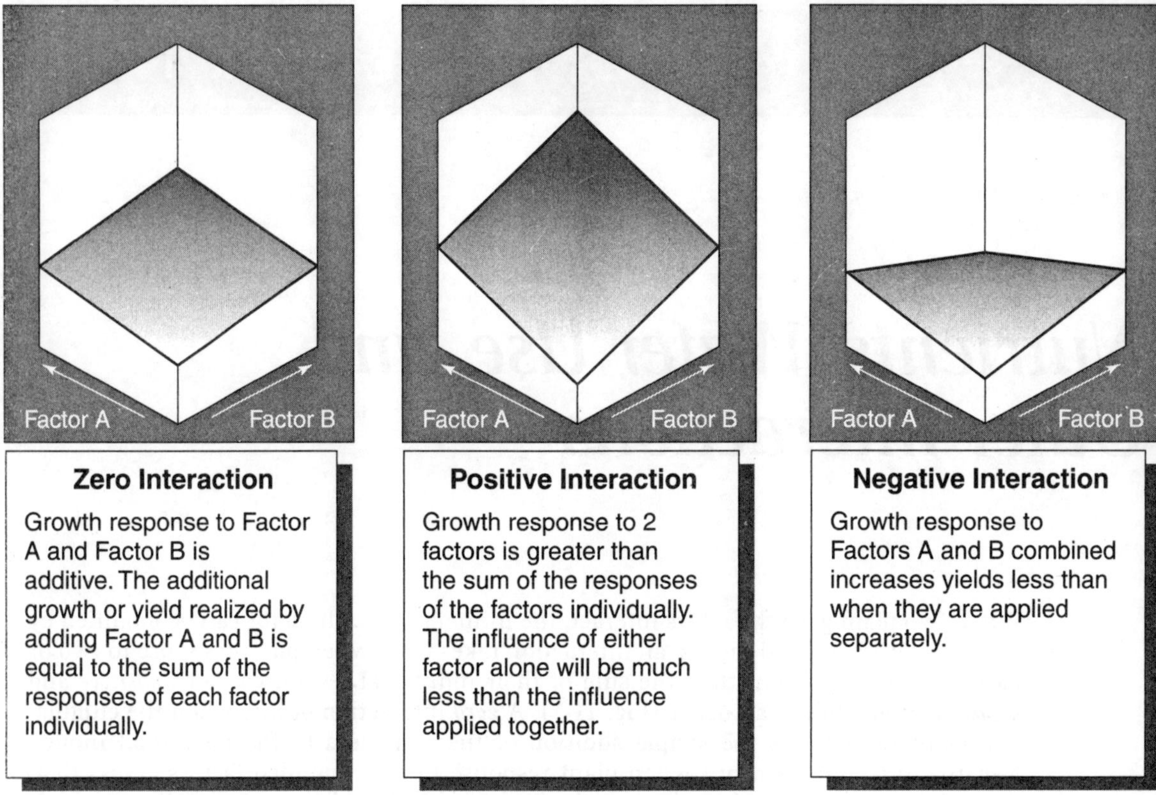

Figure 11-1 **Influence of interactions between two factors on crop growth.**

Nutrient–Water Interactions

Even in regions where annual precipitation exceeds growing-season evapotranspiration, water stress frequently limits crop production. Stresses caused by nutrient deficiencies, pests, and other factors reduce the plants' ability to use water efficiently, which reduces productivity and profit. As pressures grow for increased industrial, recreational, and urban use of water, agriculture will have less access to water for irrigation, increasing reliance on dryland crop production. Increasing water-use efficiency is a major challenge to agriculture. It is estimated that overall efficiency of water in irrigated and dryland farming is 50%. In general, any growth factor that increases yield will improve the efficiency of water use.

Water Use Efficiency

Water use efficiency (WUE) represents the crop yield produced per unit of water used from the soil, rainfall, and irrigation. WUE varies between season and management level (Fig. 11-2). Improved management that increases yield will improve WUE. Crops also vary greatly in WUE (Table 11-1). Because water use is required to produce the first unit of biomass, a minimum quantity of both biomass and water is required to produce the initial unit of grain. Thus, when

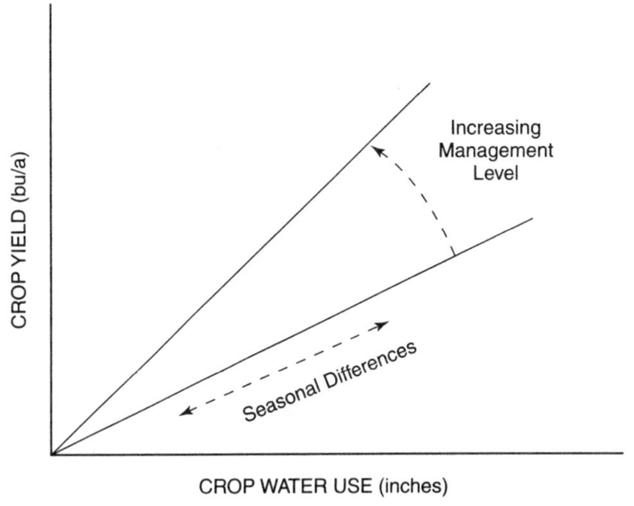

Figure 11-2 Conceptual diagram of growing season and management effects on water-use efficiency (crop yield/water use). *(Adapted from Hatfield et al., 2001,* Agron. J., *93:271.)*

Table 11-1 **Water Use Efficiencies (WUE) for Selected Crops and the Estimated Minimum Quantity of Water Required to Produce First Unit of Grain**

Crop	*WUE, lb Grain / a / inch H_2O*	*H_2O Required to Produce 1st Bushel (Inches)*
Corn	580	9.1
Winter wheat	390	6.8
Proso millet	240	3.5
Safflower	190	9.2
Sunflower	165	5.3

SOURCE: From Neilsen, 1995, *Cons. Tillage Fact Sheet No. 2–95.* USDA-ARS, USDA-NRCS, Colorado Cons.Tillage Assoc.

measuring WUE based only on grain yield, crop yield versus water use lines have a negative Y intercept (Fig. 11-3).

Yields of crops have increased greatly in the past 30 years on essentially the same amount of water, which is directly related to improved soil and crop management practices. For example, tillage systems that leave large amounts of surface residues conserve water by:

- increased water infiltration,
- decreased evaporation from soil surface,
- increased snow collection, and
- reduced runoff.

Although use of irrigation can stabilize production, yields may still be limited by other factors (Fig. 1-10). For example, if yield potential is doubled with irrigation, then nutrient requirement would double. Consequently, the crop must obtain more nutrients from native soil supply, manures, or fertilizers. With optimum nutrient availability, WUE is generally greater under irrigation than under dryland conditions, where water may limit yield potential and crop response to nutrients (Fig. 11-4).

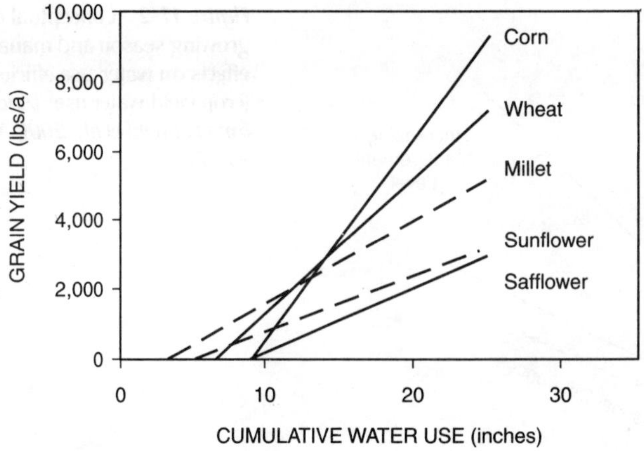

Figure 11-3 **Water use efficiencies for selected dryland crops. The points where lines cross the X intercept represent the minimum quantity of water required to produce the first unit of grain.** *(Adapted from Neilsen, 1995,* Cons. Tillage Fact Sheet No. 2-95. *USDA-ARS, USDA-NRCS, Colorado Cons. Tillage Assoc.)*

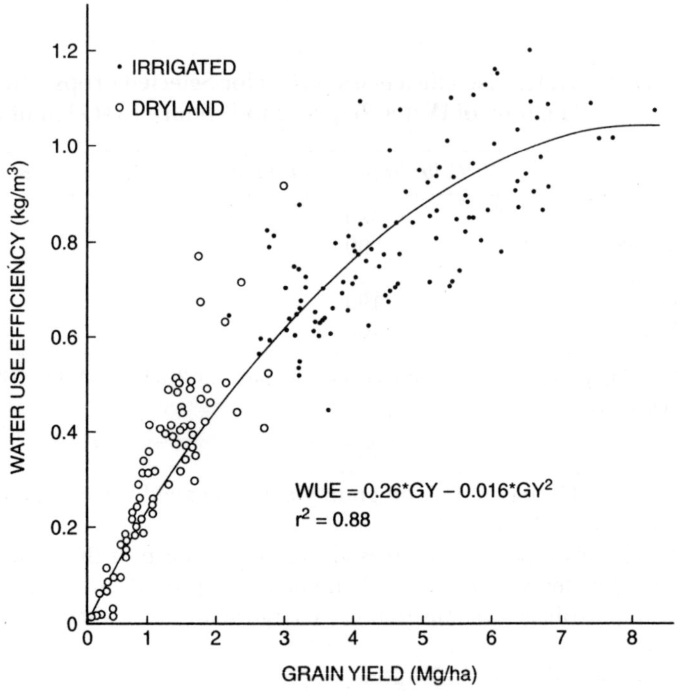

Figure 11-4 **Relationship between irrigated and dryland winter wheat yield and water use efficiency (WUE).** *(Musick et al., 1994,* Agron. J., *86:980.)*

How Water Is Lost from the Soil

Soil water is lost by (1) evaporation from the soil surface, (2) transpiration through the plant, and (3) percolation below the rooting zone. The sum of transpiration and evaporation from soil plus intercepted precipitation is called evapotranspiration. With a sparse stand or growth, more sunlight (radiant energy) will reach the soil surface, increasing soil water evaporation. With a full crop canopy, less evaporative energy reaches the soil due to shading. In addition to reduced soil temperature, the screening effect of the crop canopy restricts air movement and maintains higher humidity at the soil surface. These combined effects reduce soil water evaporation. Even with a heavy canopy, a considerable amount of energy still reaches the soil.

Nutrient availability affects plant size, total leaf area, and often foliage color. Close rows and plant spacing within rows, along with adequate nutrition, provide a full crop canopy. For example, water use would be less with 21-in. rows than 42-in. rows. Differences in evapotranspiration among crops may be small once a complete cover is developed. Daily crop water use varies greatly, depending on soil and environmental conditions (temperature, moisture, and wind); however, daily losses of 0.1 to 0.3 in. water/a are common.

Evaporation from the soil may account for 30 to 60% of total water loss in a crop year in humid areas where the soil is wet. During drought periods or in arid regions, dry soil surface reduces soil water loss, because moisture films between the particles are thin, and little water is transported to the soil surface by capillarity or diffusion of water vapor. Hence, in dry soils most of the water use is by transpiration, although most of the water received in a light shower would be evaporated quickly.

Heat advection, which is turbulent horizontal and vertical air movement, brings in more heat. In a hot, dry area with a strong wind, the hot air may contribute up to 25 to 50% of total evapotranspiration. In arid and semiarid areas advection is great, and thus quite variable evapotranspiration may occur.

Fertilization and Water Extraction by Roots

Most crops use water more slowly from the lower root zone than from the soil surface. As the surface soil is depleted of available water, the plant must then draw water from the lower three-fourths of the root depth (Fig. 11-5). The favorable effects of fertilization on root mass and distribution when soils are nutrient deficient were illustrated in Figures 10-15 and 10-38. Under nutrient stress, the plant may extract water from a depth of only 3 to 4 ft. With fertilization, plant roots may be effective to a depth of 5 to 7 ft or more. If the plant can utilize an extra 4 to 6 in. of subsoil water, the crop may tolerate drought without yield loss. In areas with dry subsoil, increased fertilization will not help crops penetrate subsoil.

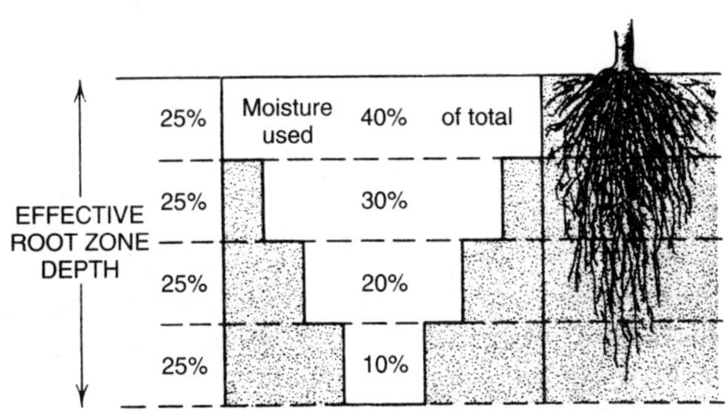

Figure 11-5 **The top 25% of the root zone is the first to be exhausted of available moisture. Certain management practices, including adequate nutrient availability, encourage a deeper root system to extract moisture from the lower root zone.** ***(USDA, SCS. Bull., 1972.)***

The importance of adequate fertility for efficient crop water use and improvement of crop tolerance to low-rainfall conditions can be summarized by:

- Adequate fertility favors expanded root growth and distribution. When roots explore the soil 1-ft deeper, another 1 to 2 in. of water can be obtained.
- P and K moves to roots by diffusion through water films around soil particles. Under moisture stress, water films are thin, increasing diffusion path length, reducing P and K diffusion. Increasing P and K concentration increases diffusion to roots.
- Decreased soil moisture exerts a physiological effect on the roots that reduces nutrient uptake. Elongation, turgidity, and the number of root hairs decrease, mitochondria development slows, and carrier concentration and phosphorylation decreases.
- Adequate K nutrition aids stomate closure during drought, reducing water loss by transpiration.
- Adequate nutrition encourages rapid canopy development that reduces soil water evaporation and increases water availability.
- Adequate nutrient availability advances maturity that may initiate flowering, pollination, and grain fill before summer periods of drought and high temperatures.
- With increased yields, plant and root residues are increased. Increased surface-residue cover increases infiltration, reduces runoff, and lowers wind speeds at the soil surface, all of which increase potential water availability.

Soil Moisture Level and Nutrient Absorption

Water is essential to nutrient uptake by root interception, mass flow, and diffusion. Roots intercept more nutrients, especially Ca^{+2} and Mg^{+2}, in a moist soil than in a dry soil because root growth is more extensive. Mass flow of soil water to supply the transpiration stream transports most of the NO_3^-, SO_4^{-2}, Ca^{+2}, and Mg^{+2} to roots. Nutrients slowly diffuse from areas of high to low concentration but at distances ≤ 5 mm. Diffusion rate depends partly on soil water content; therefore, with thicker water films or with a higher nutrient content, nutrients diffuse more readily.

Nutrient absorption is affected directly by soil moisture content, and indirectly by the effect of water on the metabolic activity, the degree of soil aeration, and salt concentration of the soil solution. Of course, crop yield potential is greater with normal or higher moisture availability (Fig. 11-6). Although Figure 11-6 shows that the response to fertilization was less in dry years, adequate nutrient availability greatly reduced drought-related yield losses.

Dryland Soils Moisture is the most limiting plant growth factor in semiarid and arid regions. In crop-fallow systems, conserving soil water may not always increase grain yield in some crops, but increased soil water conservation will reduce the dependence on fallowing through more intensive cropping (Fig. 11-7). Data illustrate that wheat yields in a wheat-fallow rotation are not greatly increased due to the extra water conserved in a no-till system. Although the additional water conserved in the wheat-fallow rotation under no-till had little influence on wheat yields, it enabled production of wheat-corn-fallow and wheat-corn-millet-fallow rotations (two crops in 3 years and three crops in 4 years, respectively, versus one crop in 2 years). Thus, total WUE increased more than 50% in the 3-year rotation compared with the 2-year rotation.

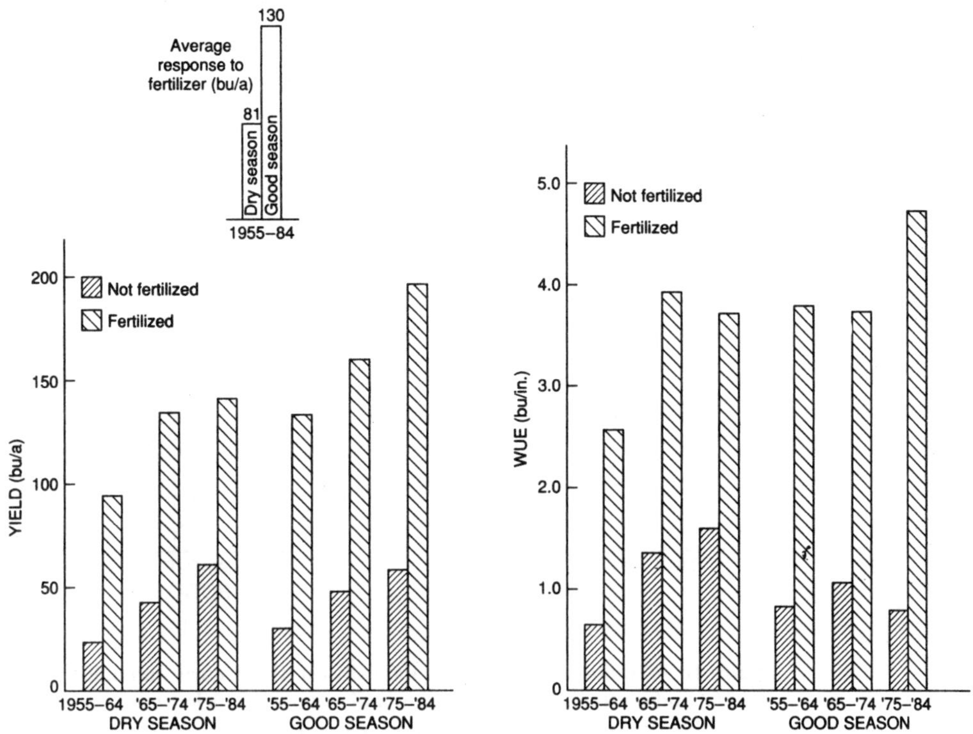

Figure 11-6 **Long-term influence of fertilization on corn grain yield and WUE. (Morrow plots, Univ. of Illinois, 10-year averages).** *(Adapted from Potash & Phosphate Inst., 1990,* **Fert. Improves Water Use.***)*

Although N uptake is reduced in dry soils, it is usually not reduced as much as P and K uptake. Under drought conditions, N mineralization is reduced, in addition to reduced uptake of soluble N. The positive interaction between water and N availability is interpreted by (1) fertilizer N will not increase yield without sufficient plant-available water and (2) increasing stored soil water by conservation practices will not increase production without adequate N (Fig. 11-8). Similarly, Table 11-2 illustrates that increasing N supply increases total water use, but decreases WUE.

Crop yield response to P and other nutrients varies depending on water availability (Fig. 11-9). The lower the rainfall, the greater the response to P. The same relationship is commonly observed with K. In low-P soils the majority of wheat response to N-P fertilization in dry years is due to P. In wet years, wheat yields dramatically increase, with both N and P contributing to the wheat response (Fig. 11-10).

An example of water-K interaction is shown in Table 11-3. On a medium-K soil there was little or no yield response to K in normal rainfall years, while in dry years, good yield responses to K were observed. The inability to take up adequate K probably contributes to lower yields in dry years. Generally, the lower the rainfall, the greater the K response, which is related to the following:

- K moves to roots by diffusion through the water films, and with low water content, K diffusion is reduced. K fertilization increases K content in the water films and increases diffusion.
- In some soils, the subsoil contains less K than the surface. When surface soil is depleted of water in dry periods, roots explore the subsoil, where there is less K.

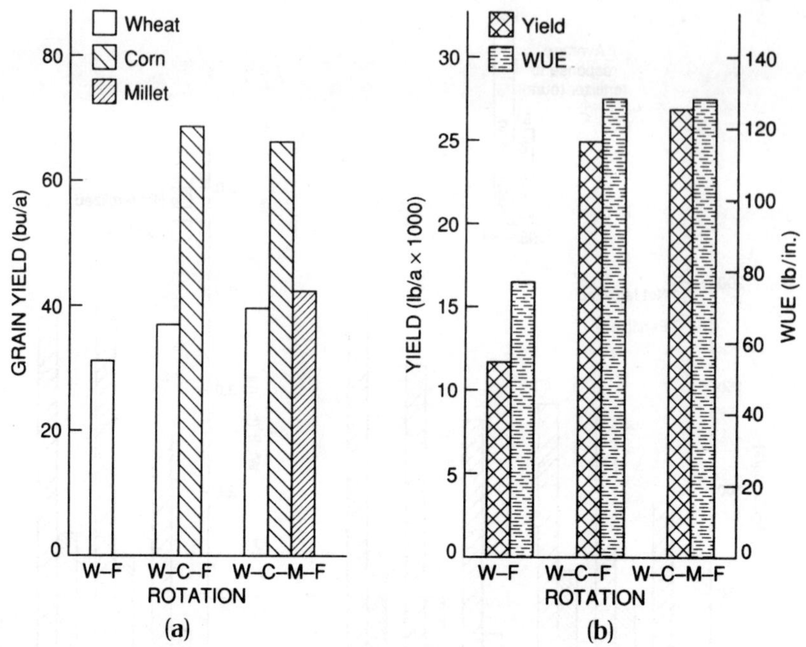

Figure 11-7 **Influence of cropping intensity on wheat, corn, and millet grain yield (a) and on total grain production and water use efficiency in a 12-year cycle (b). W, wheat; C, corn; M, millet; F, fallow.** ***(Peterson et al., 1992,*** **Proc. Great Plains Soil Fert. Conf.,** ***pp. 47–53.)***

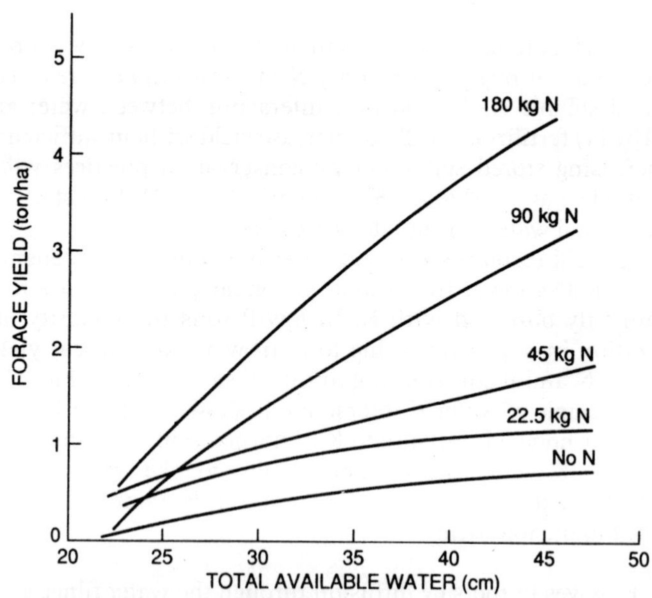

Figure 11-8 **Interaction between soil water content and N fertilization on native grass forage production.**
(Smika, 1965, **Agron. J.,** ***56:483.)***

Table 11-2 **Influence of N Rate on Wheat Yield and Water Use Efficiency**

N Rate (lb/a)	*Total Water Use (in.)*	*Yield (bu/a)*	*WUE (bu/in.)*
0	11.4	27	2.4
20	12.0	36	3.0
40	12.9	45	2.4
60	13.4	50	3.4
80	13.2	54	4.2
100	14.3	64	4.5

SOURCE: From Montana State Univ., 1994.

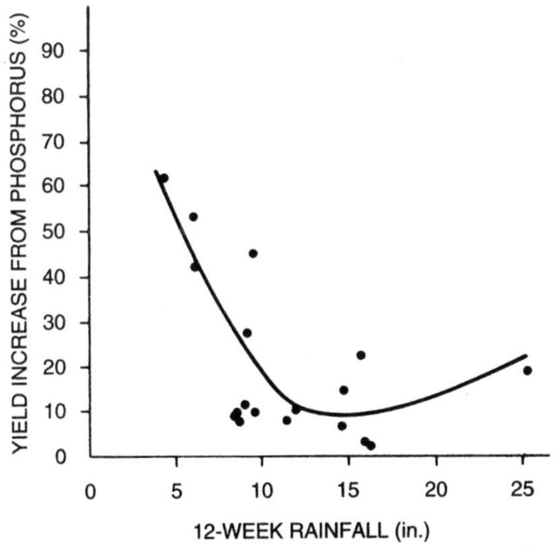

Figure 11-9 **Soybean response to P is greater with low rainfall.** ***(Barber, 1971, Better Crops.)***

Crop response to K in wet soils can be related to the effect of reduced aeration on respiration. Plant roots respire to obtain energy to absorb nutrients and respiration requires O_2. Adequate K enhances respiration.

Since transport of micronutrients to plant roots takes place by diffusion, low soil moisture content will reduce micronutrient uptake in dry weather, as with P uptake. The only difference is that plants require a much smaller quantity of micronutrients than P; thus, drought stress effects are not as great for micronutrients. Temporary B-deficiency common under dry soil conditions is attributed to both restricted release of B from OM and crop uptake in the surface soil and to insufficient removal from subsoil, often low in B. In sandy soils, excessive rainfall may leach some of the plant-available B.

Low soil moisture can also induce deficiencies of Mn and Mo, although Fe- and Zn deficiencies are often associated with high soil-moisture levels. Increased soil moisture results in greater amounts of Mo uptake. Mn becomes more available under moist conditions because of conversion to reduced, more soluble forms.

Irrigated Soils Nutrient and water interactions under irrigated systems are often similar to dryland systems, except the interactions operate at higher yield levels (Fig. 11-4). Fertility is one of the important controllable factors influencing water use in irrigated soils. When N is deficient, increasing N fertilization will increase yield, total water use, and WUE

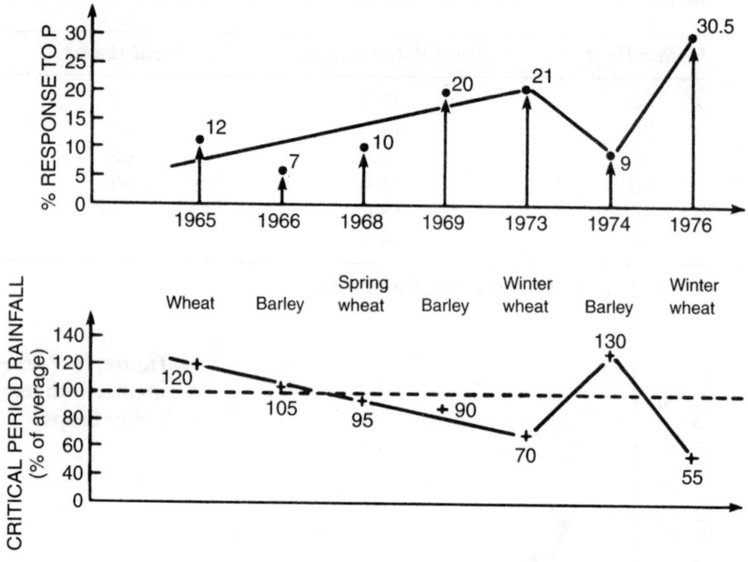

Figure 11-10 **The response of cereals to P is inversely related to the amount of rainfall.** *(Ignaze, 1977,* **Phosphorus Agr.** *70:85.)*

Table 11-3 **Effect of K on Corn and Soybean Yields of Normal and Low Rainfall**

K_2O Rate lbs/a	*Corn (bu/a)*		*Soybean (bu/a)*	
	Normal Rainfall	*Low Rainfall*	*Normal Rainfall*	*Low Rainfall*
0	163	81	56	30
50	163	113	59	42
100	167	121	60	48
200	163	129	58	48

SOURCE: From Johnson and Wallingford, 1983, *Crops and Soils*, 36:15.

(Fig. 11-11). Generally, the crop response to N is much greater under irrigation, where water is nonlimiting (Fig. 11-12). Under both systems, the same N rate was required to optimize yield. This result illustrates the limiting effect of moisture stress on plants' response to applied nutrients. It should also be noted that it is necessary to provide sufficient nutrients to make the greatest use of available water.

Other Interactions

Interactions Between Nutrients

N-K and N-P interactions are commonly observed. For example, under low-yield conditions when other nutrients are limiting or management practices are inadequate, plant growth is slow, and unless K is seriously limiting, release rates of soil K will be adequate to meet crop

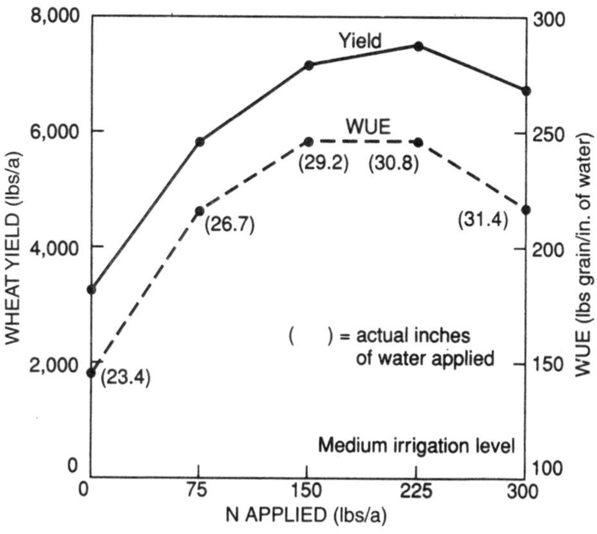

Figure 11-11 Adequate N fertilization increases irrigated wheat yield and WUE. *(PPI, 1990.)*

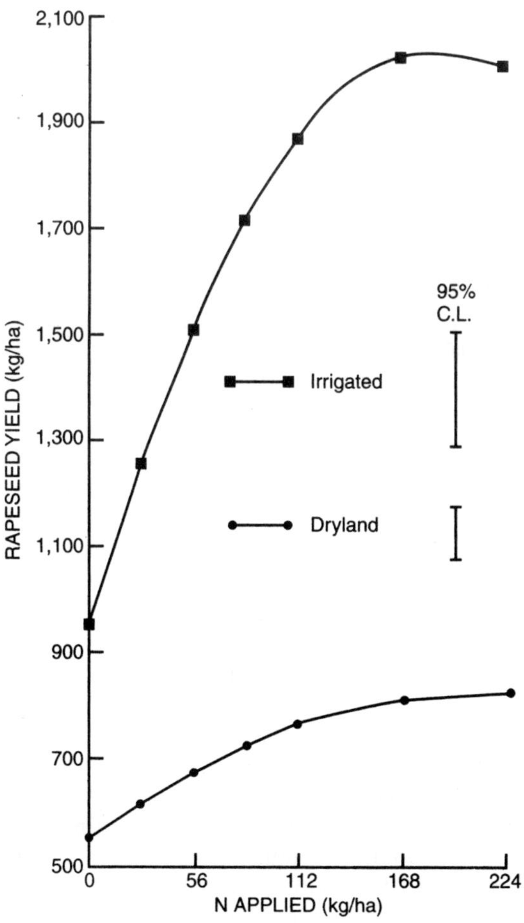

Figure 11-12 Effects of N fertilization on yield of rapeseed under irrigated and dryland conditions. *(Henry and MacDonald, 1978,* Can. J. Soil Sci., *58:305.)*

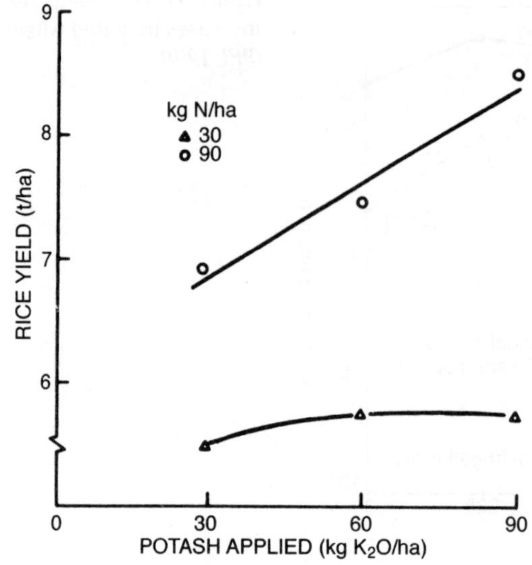

Figure 11-13 N level affects response of rice to K. *(Malavolta,* Nutrição mineral e adubação de arroz irrigado. *Ultrafertil S.A., São Paulo, Brazil, 1978.)*

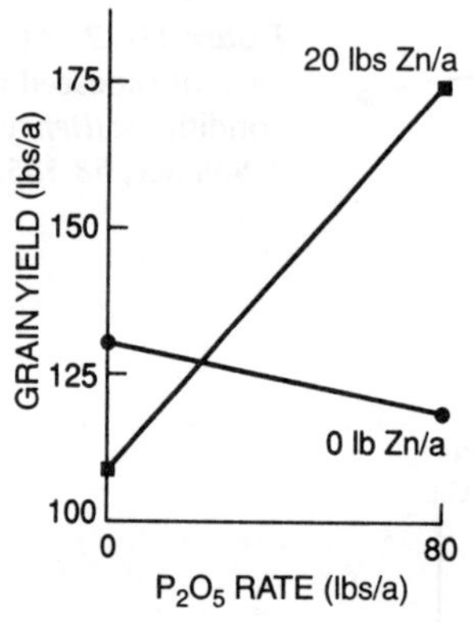

Figure 11-14 Interaction of P and Zn fertilization on corn yield. *(Ellis, 1967,* Kansas Fert. Handbook, *Kansas State Univ., Manhattan, Kans.)*

needs. With adequate N and P and improved management practices, there is more rapid growth, and the potential response to K, S, and other nutrients is greater (Fig. 11-13). With 30 kg/ha of N there was little response to K; however, with 90 kg/ha of N the response to K was linear up to the highest rate applied.

Interactions with micronutrients can be dramatic. On a low-P and low-Zn soil level for irrigation, adding P or Zn separately decreased corn yields (Fig. 11-14). When both nutrients were applied a positive interaction occurred, increasing yield by 44 bu/a.

The effect of soil pH on corn response to P banded beside the row is shown in Figure 11-15. At pH 6.1 there was little response to P, but at pH 5.1, there was an 18 bu/a response to 70 lbs P_2O_5/a. These data also show the effect of liming on P availability (Chapter 5).

Crop response to N is greatly reduced when P is limiting (Fig. 11-16). The N rate required for optimum yield was higher with 40 lbs P_2O_5/a (160 lbs/a of N) compared with no P (80 lbs/a of N). When both N and P were adequate, fertilizer N recovery was approximately 75% compared with 40% without adequate P fertilization. Maximizing crop recovery of fertilizer N reduced profile NO_3^- after harvest (Fig. 11-16). The rooting depth is 5 to 6 ft, and a significant quantity of fertilizer N moved below the root zone and could potentially reach the groundwa-

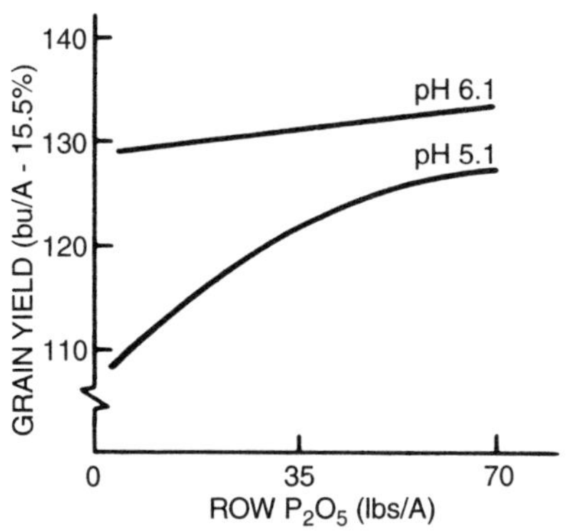

Figure 11-15 Soil pH and row P_2O_5 interact on corn. *(Schulte, 1982,* Better Crops, *66:10.)*

ter. Thus, adequate N and P fertilization will optimize yield and profitability (Fig. 12-7 for an economic analysis of these same data) and maximize the fertilizer N recovered while minimizing the environmental impact of fertilizer N use. Positive interaction of N and P was also shown in wheat with N-P placement (Fig. 10-33).

Many nutrient interactions occur in soils; only a few examples have been provided. The most probable nutrient interactions in a given cropping system involve nutrients that are deficient or marginally deficient. For example, N-P or P-Zn interactions frequently occur on soils marginally deficient in P or Zn, respectively. Therefore, a good soil-testing program will enable the grower or consultant to anticipate potential nutrient interactions.

Interactions Between Nutrients and Plant Population

Increasing plant population may not optimize yield unless there is an adequate quantity of available plant nutrients. Similarly, increasing plant nutrients without a sufficient plant population will not maximize yield. For example, increasing plant population with 80 lbs N/a increased corn yield 46 bu/a; however, with 240 lbs N/a, increasing plant population increased yield 76 bu/a (Fig. 11-17). At 12,000 plants/a, increasing N to 240 lbs/a resulted in a 37 bu/a increase, but with 36,000 plants the increase was 67 bu/a.

Interactions Between Plant Population and Planting Date

Plant population interacts with planting date. Generally, plants are shorter with earlier planting, and a higher population can be utilized (Fig. 11-18). With a later planting date, corn yield is reduced. Plants are taller with the May 30 planting date, and competition for light at this date would be greater with higher populations.

Interactions Between Nutrients and Planting Date

Planting date has a marked effect on nutrient response (Table 11-4). Earlier planting dates for spring-planted crops result in higher yields. Note the greater response of soybeans to increased K soil-test level with earlier planting. Also, the K level had a greater effect on increasing seed size and on decreasing the incidence of seed disease. Similar planting date interactions with both N and P are common. The increased N and P

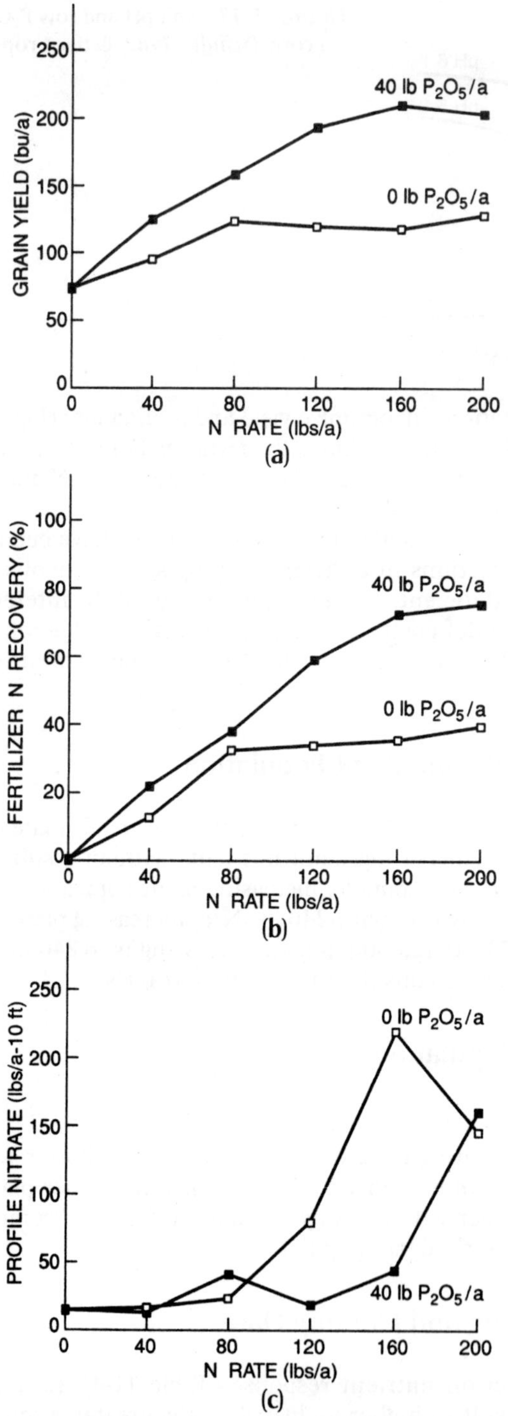

Figure 11-16 **Interaction of N and P fertilization on irrigated corn grain yield (a), fertilizer N recovered in the grain (b), and profile NO_3 after harvest (c).** *(Schlegel et al., 1992,* Proc. Great Plains Soil Fert. Conf., *pp. 177.)*

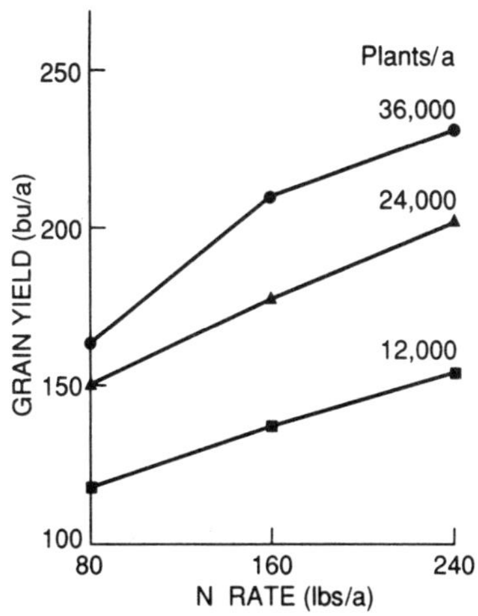

Figure 11-17 Interaction of N and plant population on corn yield. *(Rhoades, 1978, Quincy Res. Rep.)*

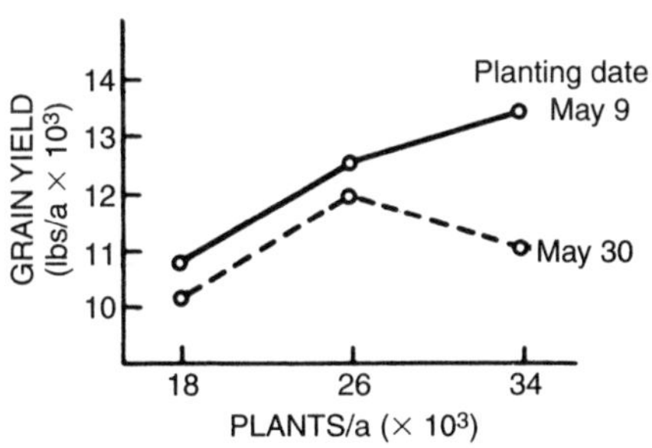

Figure 11-18 Planting date and population interact on corn. *(Arjal et al., 1978, California Agric., Univ. of California.)*

Table 11-4 **Effect of Planting Date on Soybean Response to K**

Planting Date	*Soil-Test K Level*		
	Low	*Medium*	*High*
	Yield (bu/a)		
May 27	40	47	53
June 16	40	44	46
July 8	31	36	37

SOURCE: From R. Peaslee, Univ. of Kentucky, personal communication.

response is related to increased yield potential associated with timely planting and a longer growth period.

Interactions Between Variety and Row Width

Varieties or hybrids can vary in their response to plant spacing. Note in Table 11-5 that soybean variety A gave a 10-bu/a response to 7-in. rows over 30-in. rows, while variety C gave a 20-bu/a response.

Table 11-5 Effect of Row Width and Soybean Varieties on Yield

	Row Width	
Variety	*30 in.*	*7 in.*
	Yield (bu/a)	
A	58	68
B	66	79
C	63	83

SOURCE: From R. L. Cooper, Ohio State Univ., personal communication.

Table 11-6 N Placement Effect on Grain Sorghum Yield and Fertilizer N Recovery

	Riley Co. (1986–88)		Greenwood Co. (1987–89)	
N Placement	*Yield*	*AFNR**	*Yield*	*AFNR**
	bu/a	%	*bu/a*	%
Broadcast	110	64	78	51
Dribble	117	70	81	56
Knife	130	87	89	65

*AFNR, apparent fertilizer N recovery.
SOURCE: From Lamond et al., 1991, *J. Prod. Ag.*, 4:531.

Interactions Between Nutrients and Placement

Crop response to fertilization can be greatly increased if nutrients are applied properly (Chapter 10). Examples are provided in Figures 10-29, 10-35, and 10-38.

Interactions Between Nutrient Placement and Tillage

Under reduced and no-tillage systems, surface accumulation of residue and nutrients combined with cooler temperatures and higher moisture in the spring can influence nutrient use. In some situations, nutrients applied below the soil surface may be needed. In general, higher rates of N and perhaps S are required under no-till systems than under conventional tillage. Under no-till operations, broadcast N is partially immobilized and/or denitrified (Fig. 10-49). To avoid fertilizer N interactions with surface residues, N must be placed below the residue. The data in Table 11-6 show increased grain yield with N placed below the surface (knife) compared with broadcast N. Surface band-applied N (dribble) was only partially effective in minimizing N losses. These data also show that reducing immobilization or denitrification losses by subsurface N placement improved crop recovery of fertilizer N, thus reducing residual profile N after harvest and the potential for N movement to groundwater.

The following points summarize the information on N management in reduced-tillage systems:

- Subsurface N placement can minimize N immobilization and denitrification losses and increase N recovery by the crop.

- After several years of no-tillage, differences in N needs between no-tillage and conventional tillage diminish.
- Under some conditions, yield potential is greater under no-till systems, requiring more N.
- Soil sampling for profile NO_3^- before planting can help predict fertilizer N need.

Interactions Between Nutrients and Hybrid or Variety

Within a given environment, one hybrid or variety may produce a greater response to applied nutrients than another. In Figure 11-19, the Dare soybean variety produced a higher yield and responded more to K than did the Bragg variety on this very-low-K soil. Some corn hybrids are genetically able to produce greater yields than other hybrids from higher rates of applied nutrients (Table 11-7). At the lower fertility level corn hybrids differed by 19 bu/a; at the higher fertility level the difference was 85 bu/a. Selection of hybrids or varieties that respond to a high-yield environment is essential for maximum productivity.

The importance of exploiting interactions in maximizing productivity and profitability cannot be overemphasized. When one practice or group of practices increases yield potential, the nutrient requirement will be increased. Also, as breakthroughs occur in genetic engineering, rhizosphere technology, plant growth regulators, and related areas, they will be successful only if the technology is integrated in a manner that allows the expression of positive interactions.

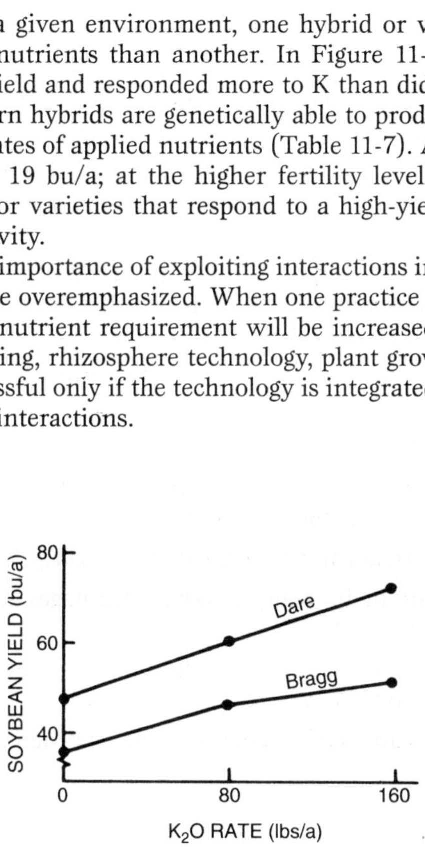

Figure 11-19 **Interaction between soybean varieties and K nutrition.** *(Terman, 1977,* Agron. J., *69:234.)*

Table 11-7 **Interaction of N and Corn Hybrids on Yield**

N	*P_2O_5*	*K_2O*	*Yield (bu/a)*	
lbs/a	*lbs/a*	*lbs/a*	*Hybrid A*	*Hybrid B*
250	125	125	199	218
500	300	300	227	312

SOURCE: From R. L. Flannery, New Jersey Agricultural Experiment Station, personal communication.

Study Questions

1. What is a positive interaction? Illustrate.
2. Why are interactions more critical at higher yield levels?
3. What is meant by a mutually antagonistic interaction? Give an example.
4. Why do higher yields improve fertilizer efficiency?
5. Explain why it is impossible to obtain a full response from an applied nutrient if the level of another nutrient is inadequate.
6. Describe a good or a poor season in an irrigated area and in an unirrigated area.
7. In a given soil volume, why is absorption of many nutrients by plants decreased as soil moisture tension increases?
8. Explain the greater response to K in dry years and in wet years. Why is B generally less available under dry conditions?
9. What is evapotranspiration? How does a heavy crop cover affect the losses in the various components of evapotranspiration? Is there more total water loss with a greater yield?
10. Explain the difference in evaporation losses from a moist soil surface and a dry soil surface. Define water use efficiency (WUE). Why is it so important in agriculture? List factors that affect WUE.
11. What is the effect of adequate plant nutrients on WUE? Why does this effect occur?
12. Explain the effect of adequate nutrients on increasing the extent of the root system. Why is this important in drought periods?
13. On what soils in your area will root penetration be limited by lack of fertility and by the physical condition in the lower soil horizons?
14. How might placement of nutrients affect uptake in a dry year?
15. Why is stored water important in dry regions? What advantages are there in irrigation in the fall after crops are harvested?
16. Are there irrigated farms in your region in which full returns are not being obtained from an investment in irrigation? Why?
17. Average yields of many crops are much higher than 20 years ago with about the same amount of rainfall. Why?

Selected References

Jackson, T. L., Halvorson, A. D, and Tucker, B. B. 1983. Soil fertility in dryland agriculture. In H. E. Dregne and W. O. Willis (Eds.), *Dryland agriculture*. Madison, Wis.: American Society of Agronomy.

Thorne, D. W., and Thorne, M. D. 1979. *Soil, water, and crop production*. Westport, Conn.: AVI Publishing Co.

CHAPTER 12

Economics of Plant-Nutrient Use

Although since 1990 world fertilizer use has stablilized, many developing regions underutilize fertilizers, thus restricting crop productivity and profitability (Fig. 12-1). To meet world food demands in the next 50 years (Chapter 1), increased agricultural productivity will require increased inputs, especially fertilizers. As higher rates of plant nutrients are required, it becomes more important that the nutrients be applied so that they will be utilized most efficiently. Higher crop yields represent the greatest opportunity for reducing per-unit production costs.

To obtain a given level of production, farmers can vary the inputs of land, fertilizer, labor, machinery, and other inputs. Actual input use depends on relative costs and returns. Production costs can vary from year to year, but costs gradually increase over time. The relative costs of many farm inputs have increased more than the costs of fertilizers and chemicals (Fig. 12-2). Although the price of fertilizers and lime will continue to rise, they may not rise as fast as other input prices. Unfortunately, the input prices paid by farmers have increased much more than the output prices received (Fig. 12-3). Therefore, it is imperative that growers achieve optimum productivity through efficient and cost-effective use of only those inputs that will ensure adequate returns on investment.

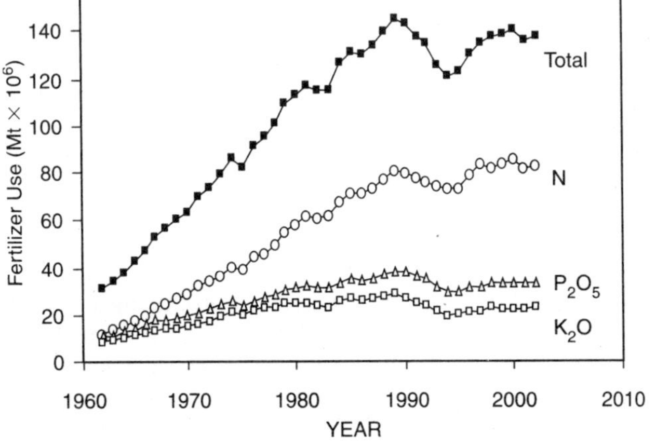

Figure 12-1 Worldwide fertilizer consumption from 1960 to present. *(The Fertilizer Institute, 2002.)*

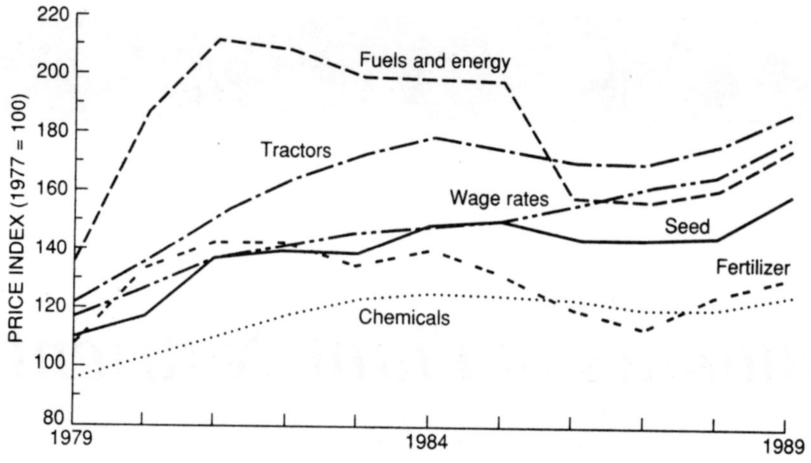

Figure 12-2 **Index of prices paid for selected inputs.** *(ERS-USDA, 1989,* **Costs of Production–Major Field Crops,** *EC1FS 9-5.)*

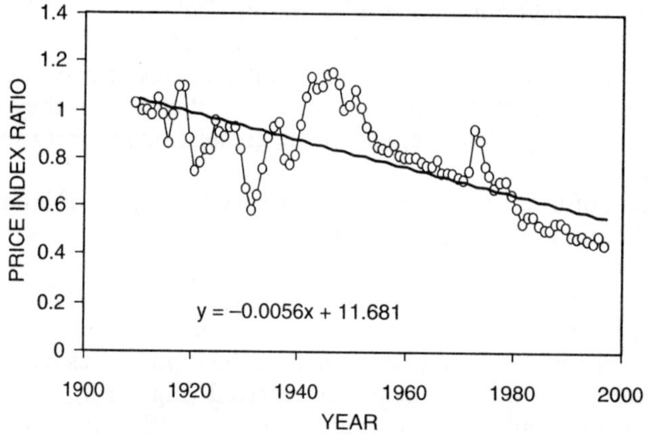

Figure 12-3 **Ratio of prices received to prices paid of all agricultural production in the United States. The trendline illustrates a 0.5% decrease in decline in price ration per year.** *(National Agric. Statistics Ser., 2002.)*

Maximum Economic Yield

Maximum economic yield is somewhat lower than maximum yield and is the point at which the last increment of an input pays for itself (Fig. 12-4). Maximum economic yields vary among soils and management levels, although on most farms they are much higher than those generally achieved, regardless of the soil. To maximize profits higher yields are essential; however, achieving the highest yield will not likely result in the greatest return per unit of investment.

Yield Level and Unit Cost of Production

Practices that increase yield per unit of land lower the cost of producing a unit of crop, since it costs just as much to prepare the land, plant, and cultivate a low-yielding crop as it does a high-yielding crop. Yield improving inputs raise total production costs/a, but decreases costs/bu and increases net profit (Table 12-1). Land, buildings, machinery, labor, and seed will be essentially the same, whether production is high or low. These *fixed* costs occur

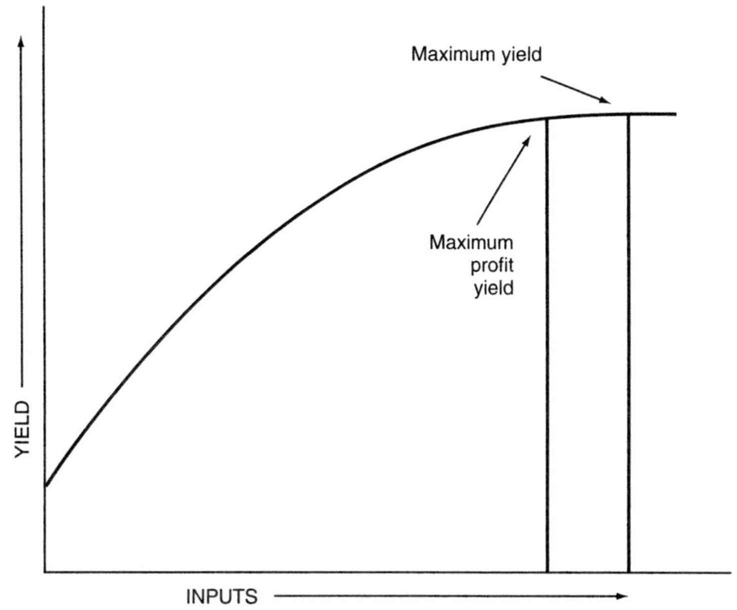

Figure 12-4 **Maximum profit yield is slightly lower than maximum yield.**

Table 12-1 **Effect of Increasing Corn Yield on the Cost/bu and Net Profit/a.**

Grain Yield	*Production Costs*		*Net Profit**
bu/a	*$/a*	*$/bu*	*$/a*
100	331	3.31	−56
125	343	2.74	1
150	359	2.39	54
175	383	2.18	100

*$2.75/bu market price.

SOURCE: Adapted from Hinton, 1982, *Farm Economics Facts and Opinion,* Univ. of Illinois.

regardless of yield level. *Variable* costs are those that vary with yield and include fertilizers, pesticides, harvesting, handling, and so on.

Key factors in obtaining the most efficient use of inputs are weather and the management skill of the farmer. With superior management, higher nutrient rates are generally required (Fig. 12-5). As a grower aims for increased yields, much of the initial increase will come from improved management practices, not just additional nutrients. Many of these practices include:

- *Timeliness.* Timeliness is important in planting, tillage, nutrient application timing, equipment adjustment, pest control, observations, and harvesting.
- *Date of planting.* Delaying crop planting beyond the optimum date reduces yield. For example, corn and soybean yields can be reduced 1 to 2 bu/a for each day of delay in planting.
- *Pest control.* Identifying pest problems early will allow application of effective controls.

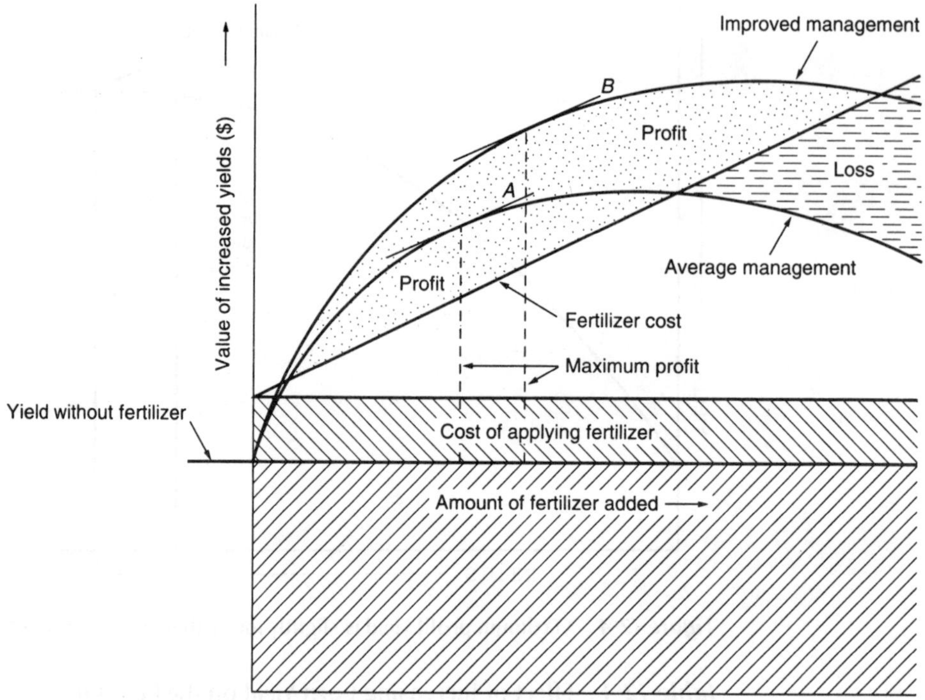

Figure 12-5 **Diagram representing fertilizer economics associated with average management and improved management. The fertilizer rate for maximum yield occurs where the slope of the response curve is equal to 0 or is parallel with the x-axis. The fertilizer rate for maximum profit occurs where the slope of the response curve is parallel to the fertilizer cost line.** *(After Miller, 1990,* Soils, *Englewood Cliffs, N.J.: Prentice Hall.)*

- *Variety selection.* Large differences in productivity, disease resistance, quality, and responsiveness to inputs exist among varieties and hybrids. Proper variety or hybrid selection can substantially affect yield and profitability.
- *Plant population and spacing.* Planting the appropriate population for the productive capacity of the crop, soil, and environment is critical. Row spacing influences yield; for example, narrowing soybean rows from 30 to 7 in. increases yields 10% or more in many areas. In humid regions, reducing wheat row spacing from 8 to 4 in. can increase yields 10 to 20%.
- *Rotation.* Rotating crops is a valuable practice that can increase crop yields and profit. Rotation may not only reduce weed, disease, and insect problems but also improve soil structure.
- *Tillage.* Reduced tillage in many environments increases water availability and yield.

Returns per Unit of Land

Progressive growers recognize the importance of maximizing net return per unit of land. With adequate cash or credit, producers select input levels that earn the greatest net return per acre. In general, as nutrient rate increases, the return/dollar spent decreases as a result of reduced response for each successive incremental input. Eventually, no further response to additional nutrients is realized. This principle is called the *law of diminishing returns.*

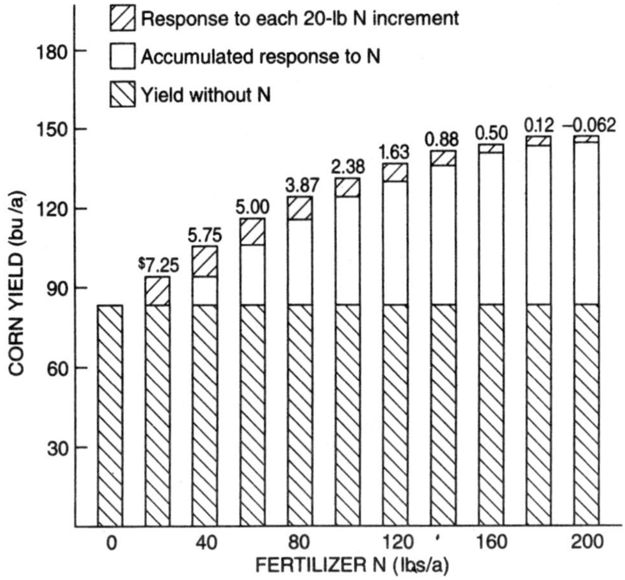

Figure 12-6 **Diminishing returns in yield response of corn to fertilizer N. The dollar values on top of each bar represent the net rate per added dollar invested.**

When a nutrient is deficient, the first nutrient increment results in a large yield increase (Fig. 12-6). The next increment may also give an increase, but not as large proportionately as the first. Consequently, responses to additional increments continue diminishing to the point where the last incremental yield value just equals the input cost, which represents the nutrient rate for maximum profit.

The most profitable nutrient rate can be determined by calculating the maximum net profit or minimum cost/bu of production. Figure 12-7a shows that the N rate for maximum net revenue was about 10 lbs/a less than the N rate for maximum yield, and 10 lbs/a more than the N rate for the least cost/bu. Although these values represent a range of 20 lbs N/a, the most profitable N rate is essentially the same regardless of which parameter is used.

Although yield potential is important in determining the recommended N rate (Chapter 9), the economic N rate usually does not vary greatly, even over a fairly wide range in actual yield potential. In Figure 12-7b, the data were grouped according to yield potential. Using the same costs and prices as before, the economic optimum N rate was 155 to 160 lbs/a for the three yield potentials.

When too much fertilizer is added, the economic loss is not as great as when a crop is underfertilized (Table 12-2). Residual availability of immobile nutrients must also be considered and helps to compensate for the extra fertilizer cost. Over years, it is more profitable to use optimum rates, even if the rate exceeds the optimum in unfavorable years. This guideline does not apply to mobile nutrients that potentially contaminate water resources.

Although the cost per unit of nutrient may fluctuate, these variations are much less than the fluctuation in crop prices. To calculate the nutrient rate required for maximum yield and maximum profit, the equation that describes the yield response is needed. For example, assume the yield response function is (Fig. 12-8):

$$Y = 70 + 1.0X - 0.0025X^2$$

where Y = grain yield (bu/a)

X = N rate (lbs/a)

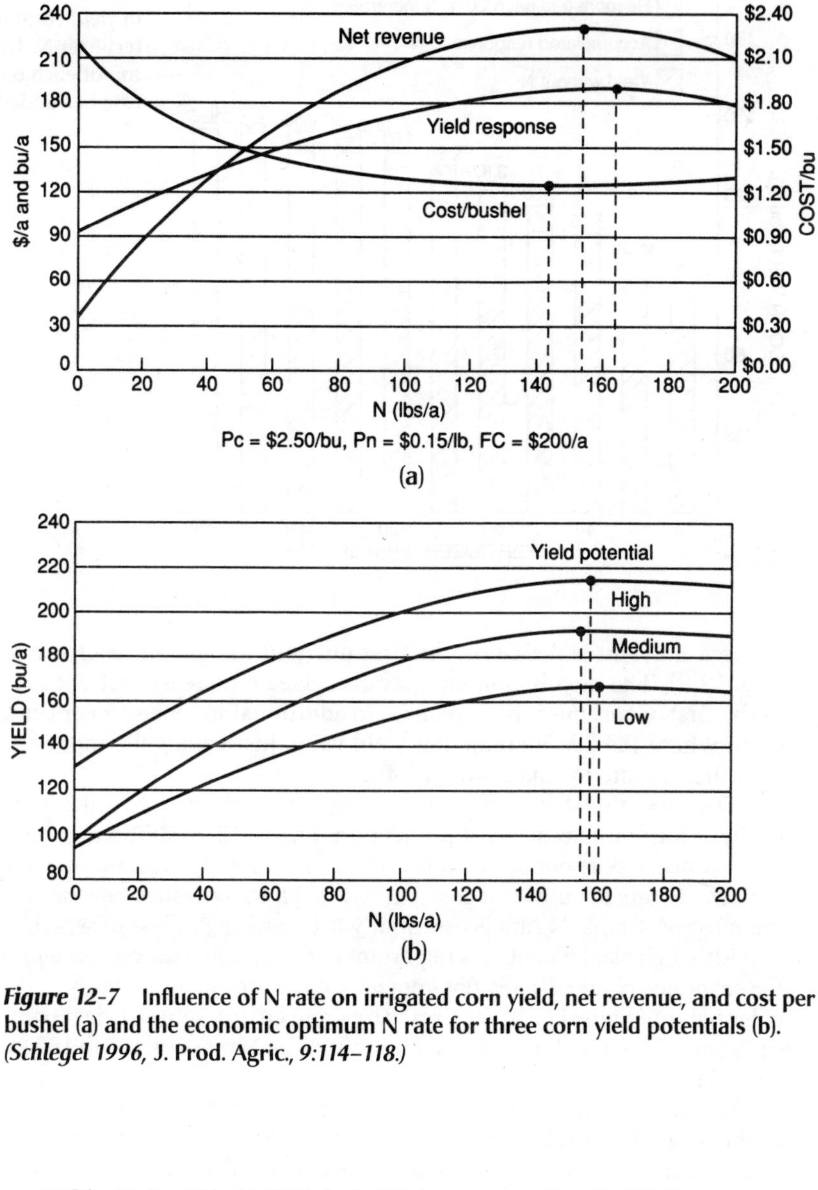

Figure 12-7 **Influence of N rate on irrigated corn yield, net revenue, and cost per bushel (a) and the economic optimum N rate for three corn yield potentials (b).** *(Schlegel 1996,* J. Prod. Agric., *9:114–118.)*

Table 12-2 **Effect of Underfertilizing versus Overfertilizing on Net Return from Fertilizer**

N Rate	*Corn Yield*	*Net Return*	*Difference from Optimum*
	bu/a	*$/a*	
None	79	–	–
1/4 < Optimum	142	50.4	−5.8
Optimum	151	56.2	0
1/4 > Optimum	153	52.0	−4.2

SOURCE: S. A. Barber, 1983, Purdue Univ., personal communication.

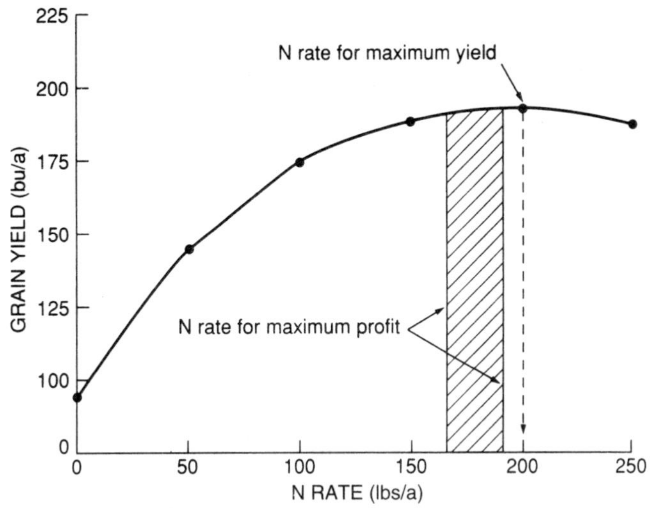

Figure 12-8 Hypothetical response function describing the influence of N rate on grain yield. N rate of maximum yield and maximum profit are shown (see the text for the calculation). The shaded bar represents the range in N rates for maximum profit, which varies with crop price received and fertilizer cost (Table 12-3).

N rate for maximum yield:

- Set the first derivative of the response function equal to zero
- Solve for X

$$\frac{dY}{dX} = 1.0 - 0.005X$$
$$0 = 1 - 0.005X$$
$$X = 1.0/0.005 = 200 \text{ lbs N/a}$$

Thus,

- The N rate for maximum yield (Fig. 12-8) represents that point on the curve where the slope (dY/dX) = 0.

N rate for maximum profit:

- Set the first derivative of the response function equal to the ratio of fertilizer cost (i.e., \$0.20/lbs N) to grain price (i.e., \$2.50/bu).
- Solve for X

$$\frac{dY}{dX} = 1.0 - 0.005X = \frac{\$0.20}{\$2.50}$$
$$1.0 - 0.005X = -0.92$$
$$X = 184 \text{ lbs N/a}$$

- The N rate for maximum profit (Fig. 12-8) represents the point on the curve where the slope is parallel to the fertilizer cost line.

Table 12-3 Effect of Crop Price and Fertilizer Cost on N Rate for Maximum Profit*

Crop Price	N Fertilizer Cost ($/lbs N) 0.15	0.20	0.25	0.30
$/bu	lbs N/a			
4.00	192	190	188	185
3.50	191	189	186	183
3.00	190	187	183	180
2.50	188	184	180	176
2.00	185	180	175	170

*Based on the response function shown in Figure 12-8.

Of course, the nutrient rate required for maximum profit depends on the nutrient cost and crop price (Table 12-3). As the nutrient cost increases at constant crop price, the nutrient rate for maximum profit decreases. Alternatively, as the crop price increases at a constant nutrient cost, the nutrient rate for maximum profit increases. These data also illustrate that although differences exist, changes in crop price and nutrient cost have relatively minor effects on the nutrient rate for maximum profit. The largest differences in optimum N rate occur when the crop price is low and the nutrient cost is high compared with a high crop price and a low nutrient cost. Since it is difficult to predict the crop price at the time of fertilization, it is advisable to fertilize for near-maximum yields and not consider crop price and fertilizer cost factors.

Residual Effects

High crop yields are impossible with low levels of fertility. The soil fertility level is a plant growth factor that is easily controlled; however, the initial cost of building soil fertility from low to high levels may discourage growers if viewed as an annual rather than long-term investment. Residual nutrient availability from past applications should be included in analyses of fertilizer economics. Usually the entire cost of fertilization is charged to the current crop, whereas lime cost can be amortized over 5 to 7 years. With high rates of fertilization, however, residual effects can be substantial, especially with immobile nutrients.

At optimum N rates, about 20 to 30% may be residual for next year's crop, provided that it is not leached below the root zone. The residual value of P and K can vary from 25 to 60%. The lower figure would apply when hay, straw, or stover is removed. Buildup of immobile nutrients is a capital investment to be amortized over years. For example, soil-test P buildup from 45 to 55 lbs/a (Bray-1 P) requires 90 lbs/a, assuming 9 lbs P_2O_5/a to raise Bray-1 P 1 lb/a (Table 12-4). The initial cost is $24.30/a at $0.27/lbs P_2O_5. Using a 15-year payoff and 8% interest rate, the annual payment would be $2.84. A yield increase of 1.2 bu/a of $3/bu corn or 0.6 bu/a of $6/bu soybean would pay for this cost.

Unit Price of Nutrients

Growers are interested in the most economical source but are accustomed to buying on the basis of cost per ton of fertilizer rather than cost per ton of plant nutrients. Wide variations in the cost per unit of nutrient exist, and other factors, such as the cost of application and the

Table 12-4 **Annual Payment Necessary to Amortize \$24.30/a Initial Cost of Buildup P with Various Interest Rates and Amortization Periods**

Payoff Period (yr)	*Annual Payment at Selected Interest Rates*		
	8%	*12%*	*16%*
1	\$26.24	\$27.22	\$28.19
5	6.09	6.74	7.42
10	3.62	4.30	5.03
15	2.84	3.57	4.36
20	2.47	3.25	4.10

SOURCE: Welch, 1982, *Better Crops*, 66:3.

content of secondary nutrients, must be considered. Growers should choose a fertilizer based on the cost per unit of nutrient in mixed fertilizers, mixed and straight materials, or all straight materials. A knowledge of the cost calculation is important. For example, if a farmer has a choice of 12-24-24 (\$350/ton) or 6-24-24 (\$380/ton): Assuming that P and K cost is the same in both mixtures, the additional N in 12-24-24 amounts to \$30, or \$0.25/lbs N. Another example is the cost of high-analysis sources. In a comparison of 5-10-10 and 10-20-20 fertilizers, 2 tons of 5-10-10 are required to furnish the same amount of nutrients contained in 1 ton of 10-20-20. If 5-10-10 costs \$150 and 10-20-20 costs \$280/ton, the 10-20-20 will be \$20 cheaper than 2 tons of 5-10-10.

In addition to the actual fertilizer cost, farmers must consider the cost of transportation, storage, and labor used in fertilizer application. These costs may be difficult to evaluate, but if the nutrient price from one source is the same as another source, growers will purchase the one requiring less labor. The higher analysis sources require less handling and application costs per unit of nutrient.

Liming

Lime applications in accordance with soil and plant requirements are essential for maximum returns from fertilizer. The returns from liming are quite high when it is applied where needed (Table 12-5), although returns vary with lime rate, lime cost, yield response to liming, and crop price. In spite of a high return, lime is often neglected in the fertility program because (1) responses to lime are often not as visual as those obtained with N, P, or K unless the soil is particularly acid and (2) liming effects last for several years and the returns are not all realized in the first year.

Animal Wastes

Soil enriching benefits from manure, in addition to those from macro- and micronutrients, may be related to the organic matter that improves soil structure and moisture relations and increases mobility of P, K, and micronutrients, and stimulates microbial activity. There is considerable variability in manure, depending on methods of storing and handling; however, with current fertilizer, labor, and equipment costs, it is usually profitable for the grower to use livestock manure. Because manure is largely an N-P-K fertilizer, high in water content, the highest returns are obtained on nonleguminous crops. Hauling charges can be

Table 12-5 Effect of Soybean Prices, Limestone Rate, and Yield Response on Net Return to Liming*

Lime Rate	Annual Yield Increase							
	3 bu		6 bu		9 bu		12 bu	
	$6	$8	$6	$8	$6	$8	$6	$8
Ton/a	$/a							
1	14	20	32	44	50	68	68	92
2	10	16	28	40	46	64	64	88
3	6	12	24	36	42	60	60	84
4	2	8	20	32	38	56	56	80

*Limestone cost amortized over 5 years at 10% interest, assuming a total cost of $15/t applied, with net return rounded to the nearest dollar.

SOURCE: Hoeft, 1980, Nat. Conf. Agr. Limestone, Nat. Fert. Development Center, Muscle Shoals, Ala.

reduced by applying it on fields close to the source and using commercial fertilizer on more distant fields. With this strategy, risk of overapplication and N and P loss to surface and ground waters is increased. Composting of manure significantly lowers hauling costs, enabling it to be transported greater distances (Chapter 10).

Soil Fertility Effects on Land Value

When buying land, the farmer may be faced with the possibility of choosing high- or low-priced property. The higher priced land is generally more productive, fertile, and has better improvements. The lower priced land may actually be a good buy, provided the land is not severely eroded or has no other physical limitations to productivity. Low-priced land is usually infertile and may need considerable lime and/or nutrients. Adequate liming and fertilization, as indicated by soil tests and combined with other good practices, can rapidly increase productivity. Expenditures to improve fertility may be included in the land cost, where $100 to $150/a for liming and nutrient buildup may be expected. Thus, with proper management, it is possible to increase land productivity and value, and the cost can be amortized over years.

Additional Benefits from Maximum Economic Yields

Increase in Energy Efficiency Higher yields are an effective means of improving energy efficiency in agriculture. Higher yields require more input energy/a, but energy cost/bu or ton is less. Some costs are the same regardless of yield level. For example, it takes just as much fuel to till a field yielding 40 bu/a of soybean as one yielding 60 bu/a.

Reduction in Soil Erosion Raindrops strike soil with surprising force, dislodging particles and increasing soil erosion. However, crop canopies and residues absorb the raindrop energy, maintaining or increasing infiltration and reducing runoff and soil loss. The damaging effects of wind on erosion and soil moisture depletion are also decreased by the presence of crops and their residues. Highly productive cropping systems are essential to soil conservation and productivity because crop canopy development is advanced and more top and root residues are produced. Conservation tillage practices such as no-till systems and chisel

Table 12-6 Effect of K on Soybean Yield, Disease, and Dockage

K_2O	Yield	Diseased Beans	Dockage	Value at $6/bu
lbs/a	bu/a	%	$/bu	$/a
0	38	31	54	207.48
120	47	12	22	271.66

SOURCE: M. Kroetz, Ohio State Univ., personal communication.

plowing leave more residues on the surface than moldboard plowing (Chapter 13). However, with any given tillage practice, higher amounts of residues will generally decrease soil losses.

Increase in Soil Productivity Increasing soil OM is a long-term process; however, the productivity benefits of raising OM can be substantial (Chapter 13). In areas of higher temperatures and lower moisture, it is more difficult to increase OM; however, larger amounts of decomposing residues improve soil physical conditions and water infiltration that increases water availability to plants, while reducing runoff and erosion.

Reduction in Grain Moisture Advancing crop maturity with adequate nutrient availability decreases grain moisture content at harvest and lowers drying costs (Table 4-4; Table 10-7).

Improvement in Crop Quality Adequate plant nutrition improves grain or forage quality. For example, increasing grain protein of wheat (Fig. 9-7) can increase the market value with protein premiums of $0.10 to 20/bu/% protein. As shown in Table 12-6, supplemental K not only increased soybean yields but also decreased the incidence of disease and mold in the seed.

Study Questions

1. What is maximum economic yield and how is it determined?
2. What are fixed costs? Variable costs? How do they affect the unit cost of production?
3. Using Figure 12-4, describe why fertilizer rate for maximum profit is less than that required for maximum yield. Describe how fertilizer rate for maximum profit might be calculated.
4. Show how the fertilizer rate for maximum profit can be determined graphically.
5. Discuss the factors that determine the most profitable rate of plant nutrients.
6. Why does the level of management affect the return from a given level of fertilization?
7. What are some of the yield improving practices that cost little or nothing? How do they influence returns from high-cost inputs?
8. Why is it desirable to amortize the cost of liming or building P and K levels over years?
9. The function $Y = 90 + 0.6X - 0.0025X^2$ describes the crop response to fertilizer N.
   a. Calculate the N rate for maximum yield.
   b. Calculate the N rate for maximum profit ($2.50/bu; $0.24/lbs N).
   c. Grain price drops 20% and fertilizer cost increases 20%. Calculate N rate for maximum profit. Why is the answer different than in part b?

10. Calculate the cost of the nutrients per lb of N, P_2O_5, or K_2O when the cost of the fertilizer is:

a. TSP (0-46-0) $300/ton

b. KCl (0-0-60) $180/ton

c. NH3 (82-0-0) $180/ton

Selected References

Mortvedt, J. J., Murphy, L. S., and Follett, R. H. 1999. *Fertilizer technology and application.* Willoughby, Ohio: Meister Publishing.

Terman, G. L., and Engelstad, O. P. 1976. *Agronomic evaluation of fertilizers: Principles and practices.* Bull. Y-21. Muscle Shoals, Ala.: Tennessee Valley Authority, National Fertilizer Development Center.

CHAPTER 13

Agricultural Productivity and Environmental Quality

The objective of any soil and crop management program is *sustained* profitable production. The strength and longevity of any civilization depends on the ability to sustain and/or increase the productive capacity of its agriculture. Sustainable agriculture encompasses soil and crop productivity, economics, and environment and can be defined by:

> The integration of agricultural management technologies to produce quality food and fiber while maintaining or increasing soil productivity, farm profitability, and environmental quality.

Achieving agricultural sustainability depends on many agronomic, environmental, and social factors. Common criteria used to assess sustainable farming systems include:

- maintain short-term profitability and sustained economic viability,
- maintain or enhance soil productivity,
- protect environmental quality,
- maximize efficiency in use of resources, and
- ensure food safety, quality of life, and community viability.

Relative to soil productivity, soil conservation is essential for long-term sustainability (Fig. 13-1). Soil management practices that contribute to or encourage soil degradation will reduce soil productivity, place marginal lands at risk, and threaten agricultural sustainability.

Soil erosion represents the greatest threat to sustained soil productivity. Physical removal of nutrient-rich, high-OM topsoil, and oxidation of OM with tillage, reduces soil productivity. Exposed subsoil is often less productive because of:

- poor soil physical condition,
- reduced water availability,

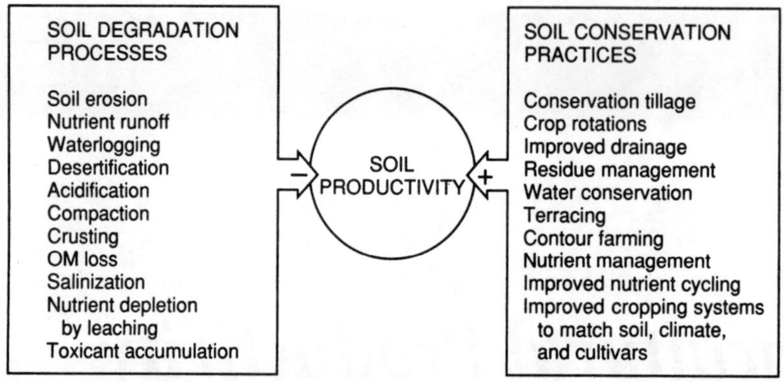

Figure 13-1 **Soil productivity is reduced by soil degradation processes and improved by soil conservation practices.** ***(Parr et al., 1990,*** **Advances in Sci.,** ***13:1.)***

- decreased nutrient supply, and/or
- many other site-specific parameters.

Soil erosion is a symptom of poor soil management. Although growers, consultants, and others recognize or observe soil erosion on the lands they manage, they may not be overly concerned because crop yields have substantially increased since the 1950s. One should not confuse increasing crop yields with increasing soil productivity, because yield increases are primarily due to technological advances in crop breeding and genetics, fertilizers and fertilizer management, pesticides and pest management, and other agronomic technologies (Chapter 1).

Soil and Crop Productivity

The interest and concern for soil productivity has been recognized since the early 1900s. While crop yields remained relatively constant from 1870 to 1930, soil productivity decreased 40% due to decreased soil OM and fertility (Fig. 13-2). Generally, nutrient removal exceeded nutrient addition in manures and fertilizers.

Degradation of native soil fertility by not returning nutrients removed in crops is evident in the first 40 years of dryland production (Fig. 13-3). Technological developments in varieties, water conservation, and P fertilization increased productivity during the next 50 years; however, continued soil erosion and OM loss again limited productivity. After 1950, growers adopted wheat-legume rotations to provide forage for livestock, and the increased N availability from the legume residue dramatically increased wheat yields. ˀoil erosion was reduced, OM increased, and these soils are much more productive now ɿn in 1900.

In the Northern Plains, average wheat yields declined steadily from 1880 to 1935 13-4). While average annual precipitation remained relatively constant, wheat ˀripled from 1940 to 1985. The major technological advances contributing to ɿ productivity were (1) improved varieties, (2) increased water conservation ˀed tillage, (3) increased N and P fertilization, and (4) improved planting and ɿethods.

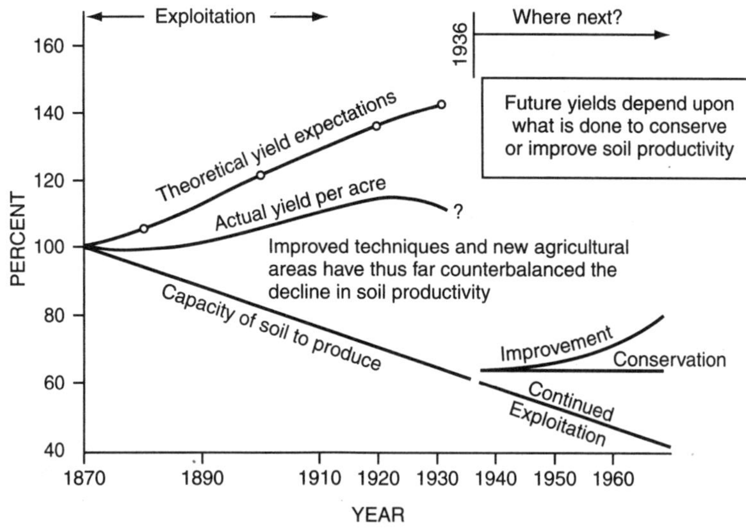

Figure 13-2 **Improved cultural practices should have resulted in 40 to 60% higher yields, but actual yield increased < 15% from 1870 to 1930. Yields can be increased only if proper soil-management programs are adopted.** *(1936, Ohio State Agr. Ext. Serv. Bull. 175.)*

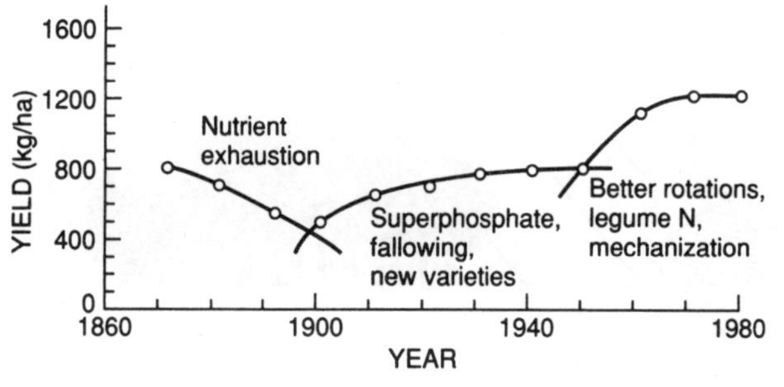

Figure 13-3 Changes in dryland wheat productivity in Australia. *(Donald, 1981,* Agric. in Australian Economy, *Sydney Univ. Press.)*

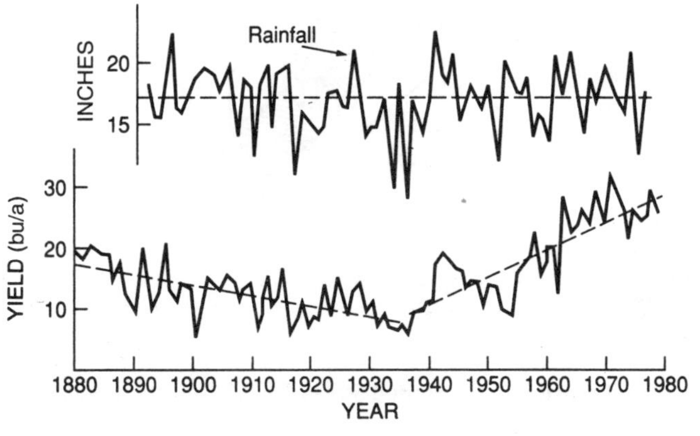

Figure 13-4 Changes in dryland wheat productivity in North Dakota. *(Fanning and Reff, 1981, North Dakota State Univ. Coop. Ext. Ser. Bull. SC-710.)*

Profitable crop production on eroded soils is an important agricultural problem that severely limits our ability to meet world food demand in this century. It is imperative that crop production systems minimize the destructive effects of water and wind erosion. Currently, ~30% of U.S. cropland is subject to erosion severe enough to significantly reduce soil productivity (Fig. 13-5). Despite the extent of soil erosion, losses have been significantly reduced over time as producers adopt technologies that conserve soil and enhance productivity (Table 13-1).

Water and wind erosion of topsoil can reduce productivity by exposing less-productive subsoil (Fig. 13-6). The productive capacity of eroded Ulysses soil is less than that

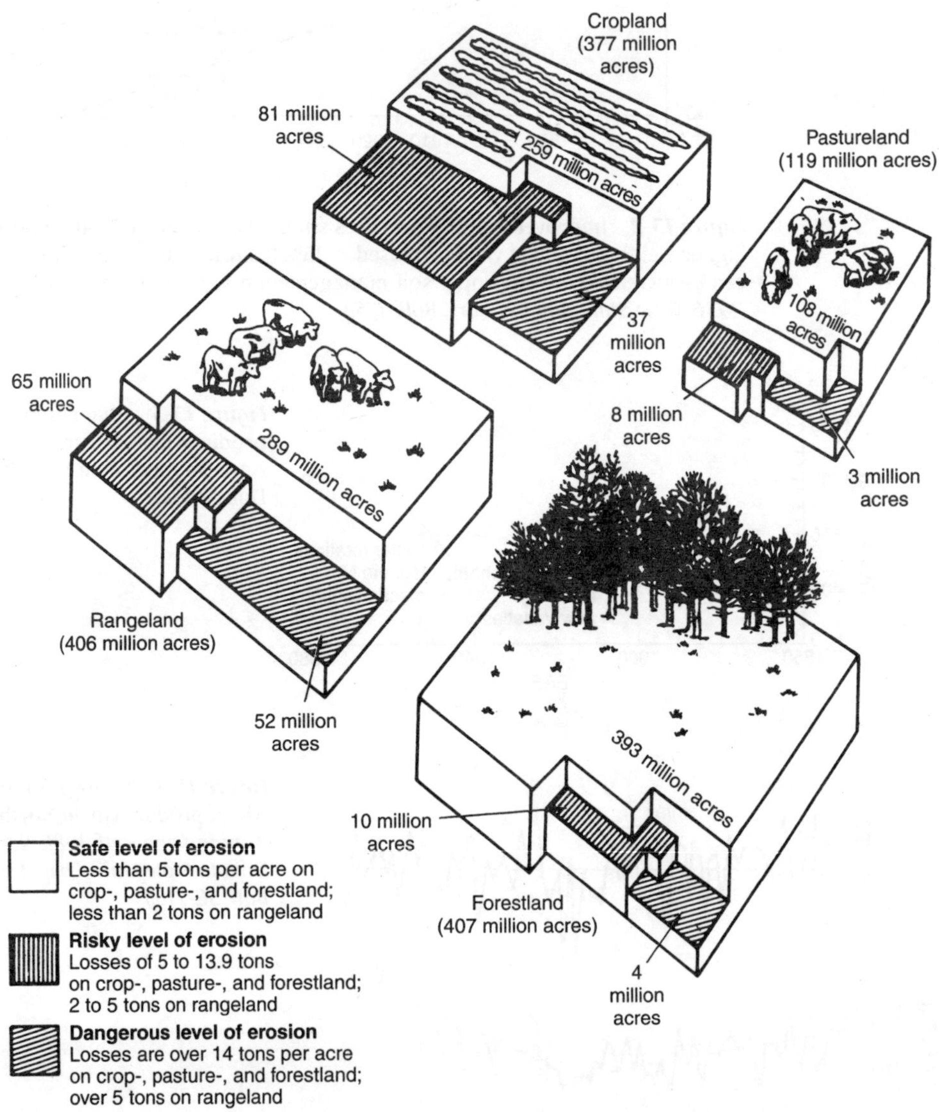

Figure 13-5 **Current estimates of soil erosion in the United States** *(USDA-Natural Resource Cons. Serv., 2002.)*

Table 13-1 Decrease in Soil Erosion on Cropland from 1982 to 1997

	Water Erosion				Wind Erosion			
	1982	*1987*	*1992*	*1997*	*1982*	*1987*	*1992*	*1997*
Total soil loss (billion tons)	1.7	1.5	1.2	1.1	1.4	1.4	1.0	0.8
Annual soil loss (t/a/yr)	4.1	4.4	4.0	3.5	3.6	3.5	2.7	2.5

SOURCE: USDA-NRCS, 2002.

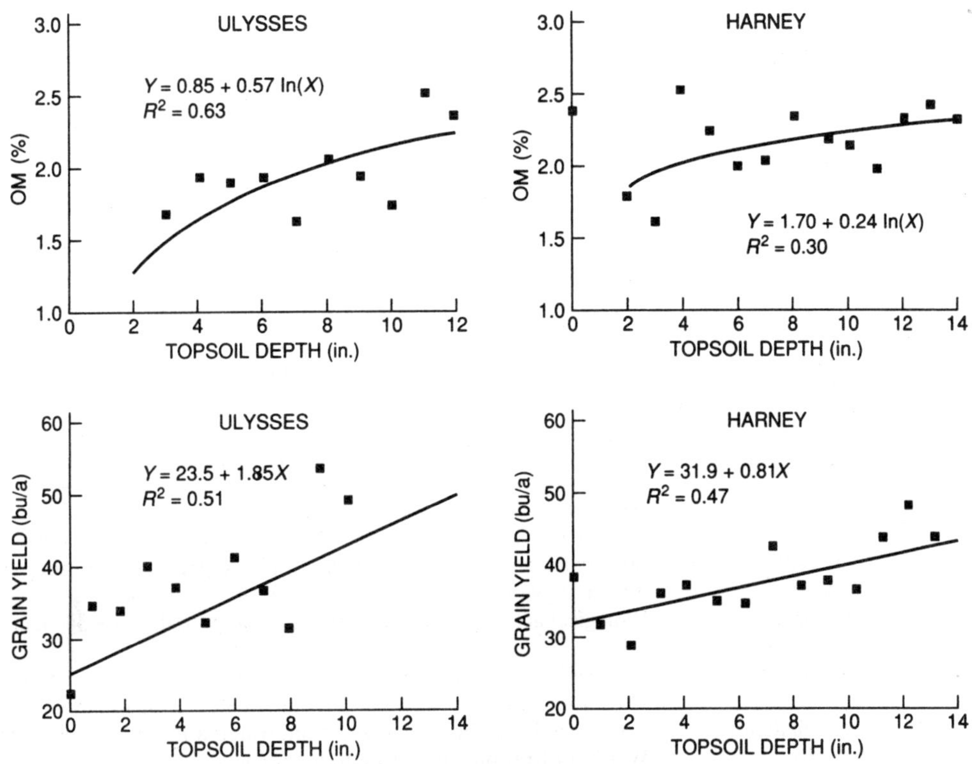

Figure 13-6 **Loss of topsoil by wind and water erosion reduces soil OM, which contributes to wheat-grain yield loss. Loss in productivity varies between soils, depending on initial topsoil depth and productivity of the subsoil. Compared with the Ulysses soil, the Harney soil has a deeper topsoil; thus, productivity is not reduced as much as the Ulysses soil under equivalent topsoil loss.** ***(Havlin et al., 1992, Proc. Great Plains Soil Fert. Conf.)***

of eroded Harney soil because the latter is a deeper soil and has a greater OM content in the subsoil, which improves nutrient availability and water-holding capacity. As a result, the yield loss associated with increasing soil loss is also greater in the Ulysses than in the Harney soil. In the Ulysses soil, 1.8 bu/a yield loss per inch of topsoil occurs compared with 0.8 bu/a yield loss per inch of topsoil in the Harney soil. On many eroded subsoils, reduced soil OM and water availability are common factors limiting productivity (Table 13-2).

Table 13-2 Influence of Soil Erosion on Surface Soil Physical Properties and Corn Grain Yield Loss

Site No.	*Erosion Phase*	*Soil OM (%)*	*Bulk Density (g/cm^3)*	*H_2O Content (cm H_2O)**
3	Noneroded	2.6	1.44	14.1
	Severely eroded	0.7	1.46	12.8
	Depositional	5.5	1.23	18.1
6	Noneroded	3.7	1.37	7.4
	Severely eroded	2.2	1.68	5.1
	Depositional	4.3	1.38	11.1

	1982		*1983*	
	% Yield Loss	*Major Cause*	*% Yield Loss*	*Major Cause*
2	38	N, H_2O	52	H_2O
3	43	H_2O	38	H_2O
5	32	H_2O	35	H_2O
6	66	H_2O, N	59	H_2O

*Plant-available H_2O in 100-cm soil depth.
SOURCE: Battiston et al., 1985, *Erosion and Soil Productivity,* ASAE 8–85, p. 28.

Table 13-3 Selected Soil Properties Related to Soil Quality and Their Impact on Selected Processes

Measurement	*Processes Affected*
Soil OM	Nutrient cycling, pesticide and water retention, soil structure
Infiltration	Runoff and leaching potential, plant water use efficiency, erosion potential
Aggregation	Soil structure, erosion resistance, crop emergence, infiltration
Soil pH	Nutrient availability, pesticide absorption, and mobility
Microbial biomass	Biological activity, nutrient cycling, capacity to degrade pesticides
Forms of N	Availability to crops, leaching potential, mineralization/immobilization rates
Bulk density	Plant root penetration, water- and air-filled pore space, biological activity
Topsoil depth	Rooting volume for crop production, water, and nutrient availability
Salinity	Water infiltration, crop growth, soil structure
Nutrient supply	Capacity to support crop growth, environmental hazard

Soil Quality

Many interrelated factors influence soil productivity. These relationships collectively represent soil quality (Table 13-3). Although all of these properties are important, soil OM content is the most critical, because of its influence on many biological, chemical, and physical characteristics inherent in a productive soil (Table 13-4). For example, increasing soil C increases the stability of soil aggregates, which improves soil resistance to water and wind erosion (Fig. 13-7). Because of increased aggregate stability, bulk density is lower with higher soil C, which improves root proliferation through the soil and ultimately productivity (Fig. 13-8).

The steady-state OM level depends on soil and crop management practices influencing C accumulation and loss. If management practices are changed, a new OM level is attained

Table 13-4 Characteristics of Soil OM and Associated Effects on Soil Properties

Property	*Effect on Soil*	*Effect on Plant*
Color	OM imparts dark color in soils	Can increase surface soil temperature and advance germination and seedling growth
Water retention	OM retains 20 times its weight in H_2O	Increases H_2O availability to plants by improved H_2O holding capacity, especially in sandy soils; also increases infiltration
Interaction with clays	Helps cements soil particles into aggregates	Enhances plant growth by improved soil structure that enhances gas exchange, water infiltration, and root proliferation through soil
Chelation	Forms stable complexes with Fe^{+3}, Mn^{+2}, Zn^{+2}, Cu^{+2}, and other cations	Enhances availability of micronutrients to plants
Solubility in water	Humus is insoluble due to its association with clay; some organic compounds (e.g., chelates) are soluble	Soluble organic compounds complexed with nutrients can leach through the profile, moving nutrients from the soil surface to subsoil areas
Buffer capacity	Exhibits pH and nutrient buffering	Helps buffer changes in pH and nutrients in solution
Cation exchange	Total CEC ranges from 300–1,400 meq/100 g	OM may increase CEC 20 to 70%
Mineralization	OM decomposition yields CO_2 and nutrients	Increases nutrient availability to plants

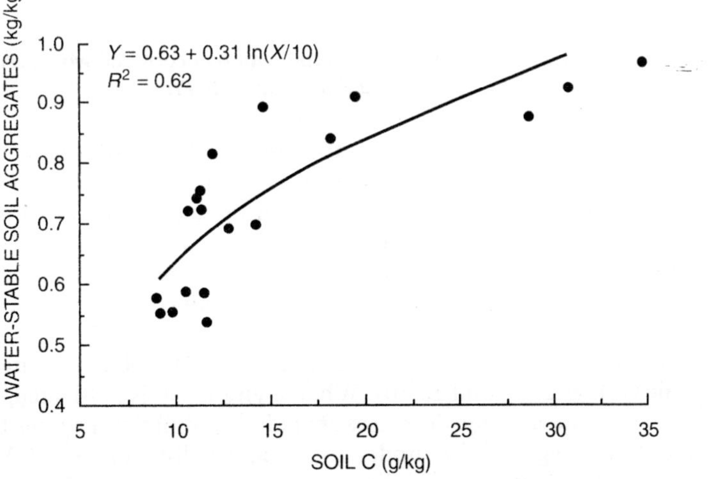

Figure 13-7 Influence of soil C on aggregate stability.

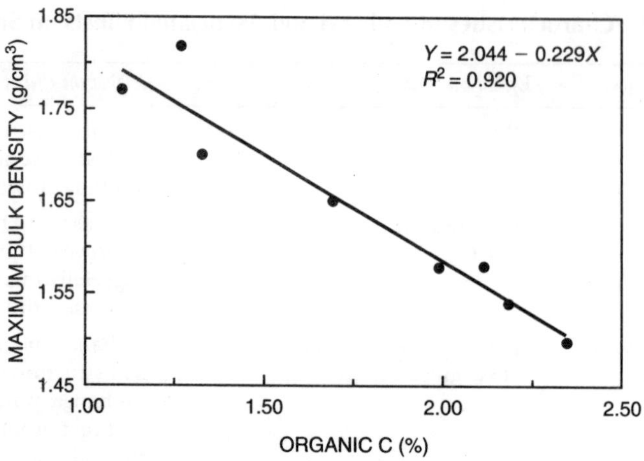

Figure 13-8 **Relationship between maximum bulk density and organic C.**

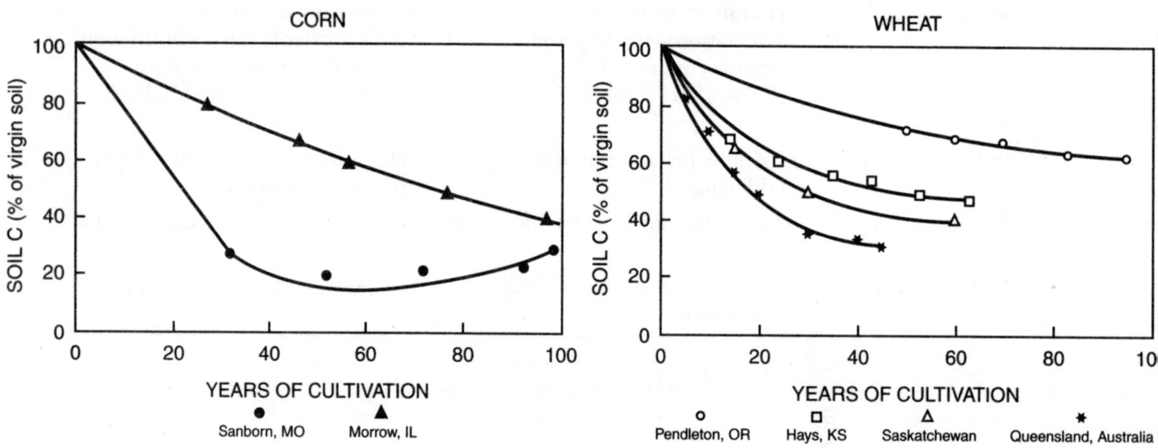

Figure 13-9 **Decline in soil C with time since initial cultivation in corn and wheat cropping systems.** ***(Paustian et al., 1997,*** **Mgmt. Controls on Soil C.,** ***p. 25, Boca Raton, Fla.: CRC Press.)***

that may be lower or higher than the previous level. Maintenance of OM for the sake of maintenance alone is not a practical approach to farming. It is more realistic to use a management system that will give sustained profitable production without degradation of OM and productivity. The greatest source of soil OM is the residue contributed by crops. Consequently, cropping system and method of handling residues are equally important. Proper management and fertilization will produce high yields, which will increase the quantity of residue and organic C sequestered in the soil.

Increased aeration by soil tillage stimulates microbial oxidation or degradation of soil organic C (Figs. 13-9 and 13-10). When a virgin soil is cultivated, OM decline is rapid during the first 10 years then decreases at gradually diminishing rates for several decades. Many studies have suggested that under continuous cultivation, soil OM declines approximately 50% in 40 to 70 years, depending on the environment and quantity of residue returned. Eventually, an apparent equilibrium is reached, where soil OM gains equal losses.

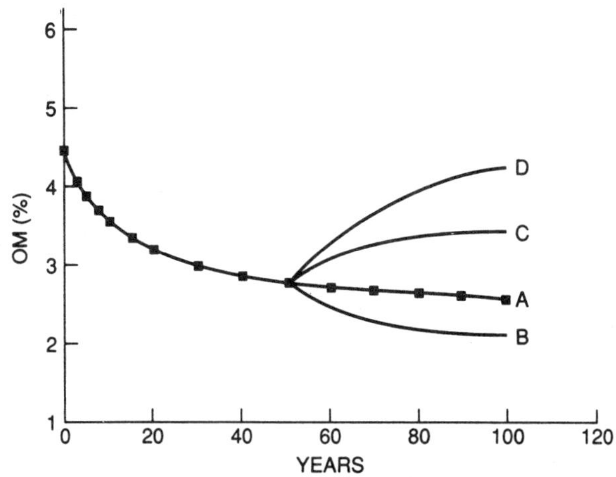

Figure 13-10 **Hypothetical decrease in soil OM with time. At 50 years, changes in soil and crop management system can either continue (A), decrease (B), or increase (C, D) soil OM. (A) represents no change in cropping system, while (B) represents a change that would accelerate OM loss (i.e., more intensive tillage). (C) might represent adoption of reduced tillage or a crop rotation that produces more residue, whereas (D) might reflect the change in OM following adoption of a high-yield no-till system or rotations that return large quantities of residue.**

Several long-term studies demonstrate the exponential decline in soil OM after virgin soils are tilled (Fig. 13-11a). These data show that OM decreased from 3.4 to 2.0% after 45 years in a conventionally tilled wheat-fallow system. Soil OM increased with annual application of 10 t/a manure (C and N added), whereas annual application of 40 lbs N/a had little influence on OM. Reducing the C input by burning the crop residue further decreased soil OM. The influence of C and N balance on grain yield is also evident (Fig. 13-11b). Similarly, the long-term Morrow plots in Illinois show the influence of increasing C and N on soil OM (a) and grain yield (b) through crop rotation compared with continuous corn (Fig. 13-12).

Generally, the quantity of residue returned to the soil will have a much greater effect on increasing soil OM than the residue N content. Figure 13-13 shows that even though N content of alfalfa is much greater than corn, the original organic C content was maintained at 1.8% C by 2 t/a/yr of either corn or alfalfa residue. Increasing residue produced and returned with either crop increased soil organic C. If all of the residue had been left on the soil surface instead of incorporated with tillage, the increase in organic C would have been greater due to reduced C loss with tillage.

Although added N will encourage rapid residue degradation by microorganisms, with little or no immobilization of soil inorganic N (Chapter 4), adequate N use, coupled with the return of crop residues, can maintain or increase soil OM content (Fig. 13-14).

The dryland cropping systems referred to in Figure 11-7 also showed increased soil-OM content with increasing cropping intensity or reduced dependence on fallowing (Fig. 13-15). Soil OM increased as more residue was produced in the wheat-corn-fallow and wheat-corn-millet-fallow systems compared with the wheat-fallow-wheat system.

Soil OM transformations are very dynamic. Intensive tillage systems, fallowing, and low crop productivity, combined with physical soil loss by erosion, decrease soil OM content over time (Fig. 13-10). Increasing soil OM requires reducing tillage intensity and increasing the quantity of CO_2 fixed by plants and returned to the soil. Increasing C input or sequestration depends on the interaction between more productive rotations and reduced tillage.

Many factors determine whether soil OM is increased or decreased by cropping systems. The key is to keep large amounts of crop residues (stover and roots) cycling through the soil. Continued good management, including adequate fertilization, helps to maintain the cycle. Sustaining soil productivity for future generations ultimately depends on maintaining optimum soil-OM levels.

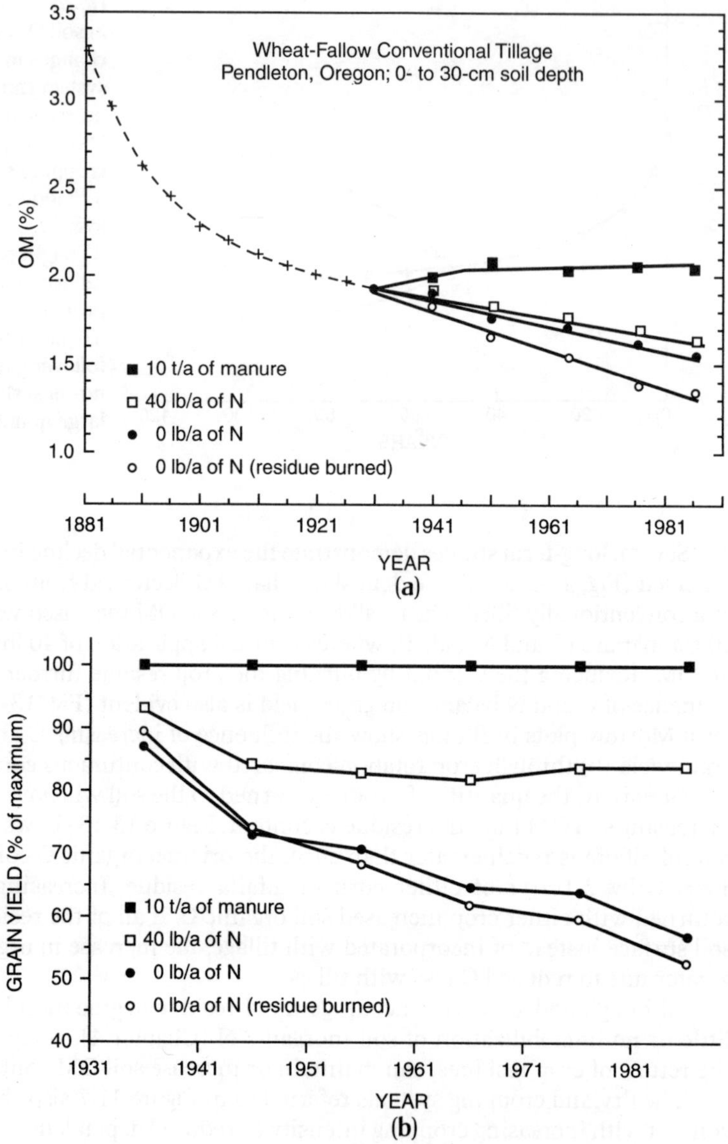

Figure 13-11 **Effects of increasing or decreasing C and N (manure or fertilizer N) inputs on soil OM (a) and grain yield (b) in a wheat-fallow cropping system.** ***(Rasmussen, 1989, USDA-ARS, Bull. 675.)***

Conservation Tillage

Producers have become increasingly interested in reducing tillage to reduce soil erosion and increase plant-available water. The amount of surface residue and surface roughness both have an effect. Crop residue management technologies have been developed to leave more of the harvest residue, leaves, and roots on or near the surface. Conservation tillage represents

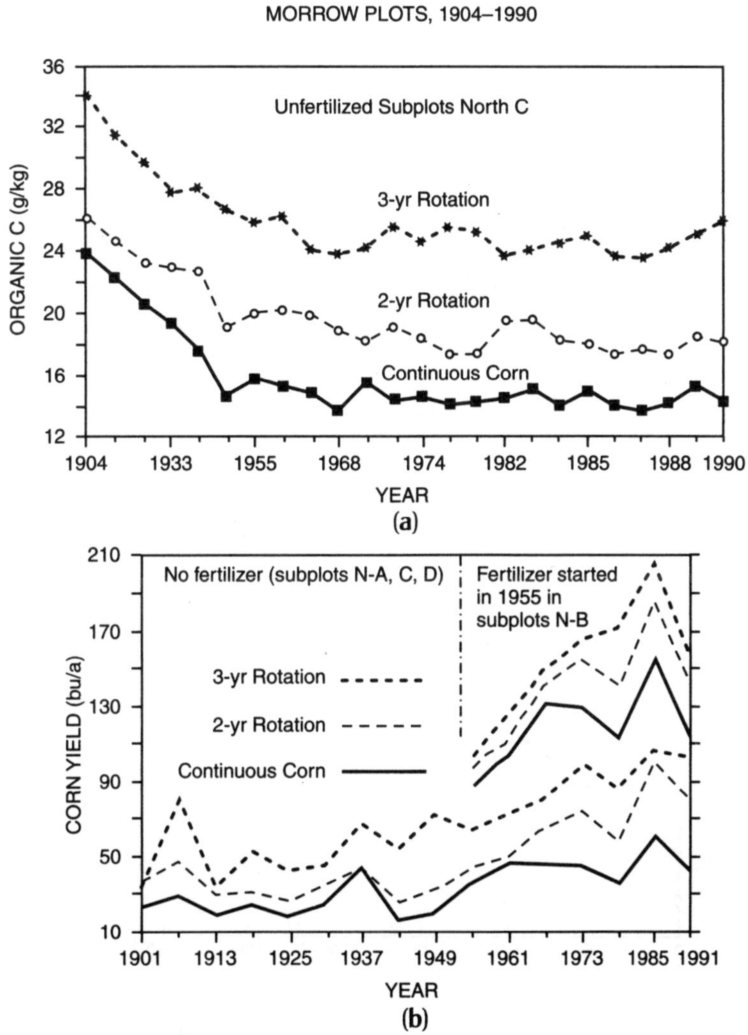

Figure 13-12 **Effects of adding C and N on soil OM (a) and grain yield (b) in corn rotations compared with continuous corn cropping systems.** ***(Darmody and Peck, 1997,*** **Soil Organic C Changes in Morrow Plots,** ***p. 165, Boca Raton, Fla.: CRC Press.)***

any tillage system that reduces soil and/or water loss compared with clean tillage, in which all residues are incorporated into the soil (Table 13-5).

Advantages

- Higher crop yields, except in level, fine-textured, poorly drained soils
- Less soil erosion by water and wind
- Improved infiltration and more efficient use of water
- Increased acreage of sloping land that can safely be used for row crops
- Improved timing of planting and harvesting
- Lower labor, machinery, and fuel costs

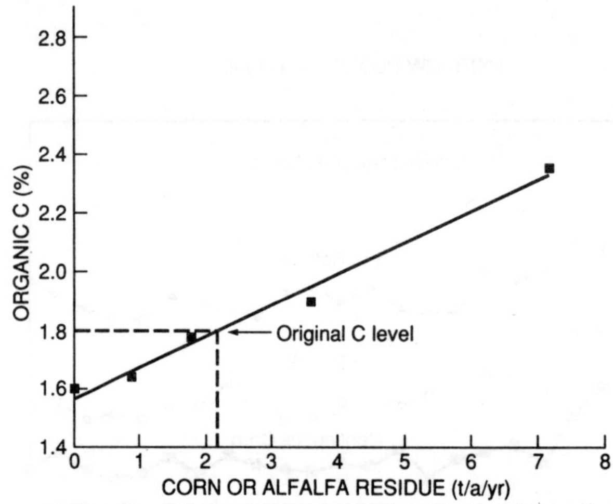

Figure 13-13 Influence of corn or alfalfa residue incorporated into the soil for 11 years. *(Larson et al., 1972,* Agron. J., *64:204.)*

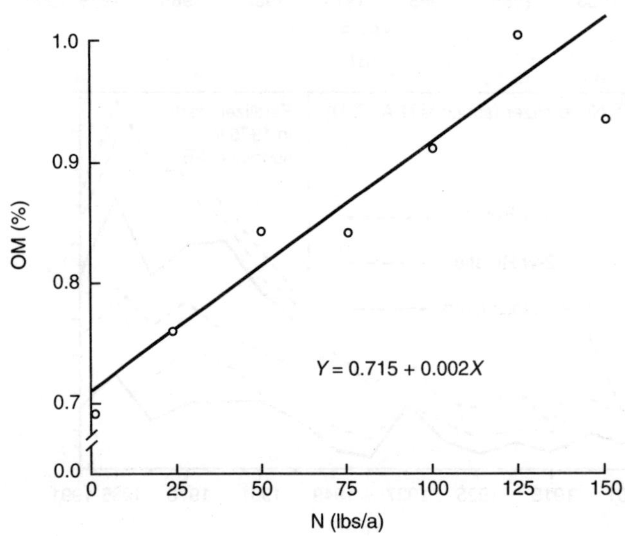

Figure 13-14 Effect of fertilizer N rates applied to cotton on soil-OM content. (Crops and Soils, *1985, 37:34.)*

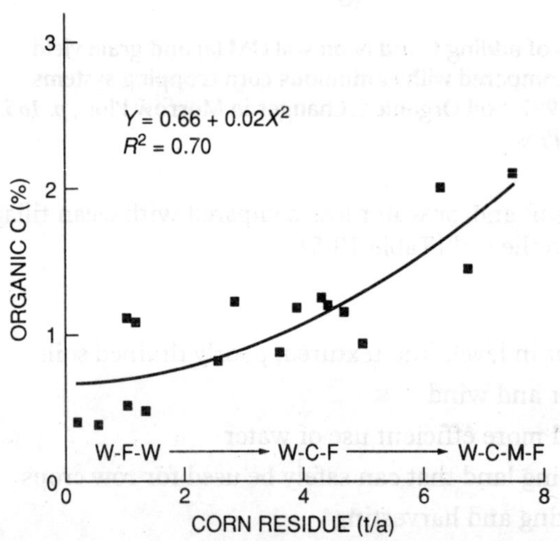

Figure 13-15 Increasing no-till cropping intensity increased OM compared with wheat-fallow-wheat systems. W, wheat; C, corn; M, millet; F, fallow. *(Peterson and Westfall, 1990, Proc. Great Plains Soil Fert. Conf.)*

Table 13-5 General Conservation Tillage Methods

Row Crop Agriculture	*Small Grain Agriculture*
Narrow strip tillage	Stubble mulch farming
No-till, zero-till, slot plant	Stirring or mixing machines
Strip rotary tillage	Disk-type implements
	• One-way disk
Ridge planting	• Offset disk
Till plant	• Tandem disk
Plant conventionally on ridge	Chisel plows
	Field cultivators
Full width—no plow tillage	Mulch treaders
Fall and/or spring disk	
Fall or spring chisel, field cultivate	Subsurface tillage
	Sweep plows
Full width—plow tillage	Rotary rodweeder
Plow plant	Rodweeder with semichisels
Spring plow–wheel–track plant	
	Ecofallow, no-till

SOURCE: Mannering and Fenster, 1983, *J. Soil Water Cons.*, 38:141.

Disadvantages

- More potential for rodents, insects, and diseases in some systems
- Cooler soil temperatures in spring, resulting in slower germination and early growth
- Greater management ability is required

Types of Conservation Tillage

Chiseling A chisel implement may till 8 to 15 in. deep, with points 12 to 15 in. apart. A considerable amount of surface residue is left on the surface, and the surface is rough.

Till Plant and Ridge Till Till plant and ridge till is a single-pass tillage-planting operation. Planter units work on ridges made the previous year during cultivation or after harvesting (Fig. 13-16). The planter pushes old stalks, root clumps, and clods into the area between the rows. This practice is useful on fine-textured, poorly drained soils. Ridges are retained in the same position year after year; hence, wheel tracks are in the same place.

Stubble Mulching Tillage equipment commonly used include disks, chisel plows, and field cultivators that mix crop residues with the surface soil, and sweeps or blades and rod-weeders that cut beneath the soil surface without inverting or mixing the soil. Reduced soil moisture loss and wind erosion are primary goals of stubble mulching.

No-Till No-tillage systems leave all the residue on the soil surface. Consequently, no-till is not well-suited for poorly drained soils. At planting, a seed zone 2 in. wide or less is made by a fluted coulter running ahead of a planter unit with disk or hoe openers. Seeding by this method is successful in residues of many crops. Narrow hoe openers or narrow-angle, double-disk openers are also used for minimum- and zero-tillage seed placement.

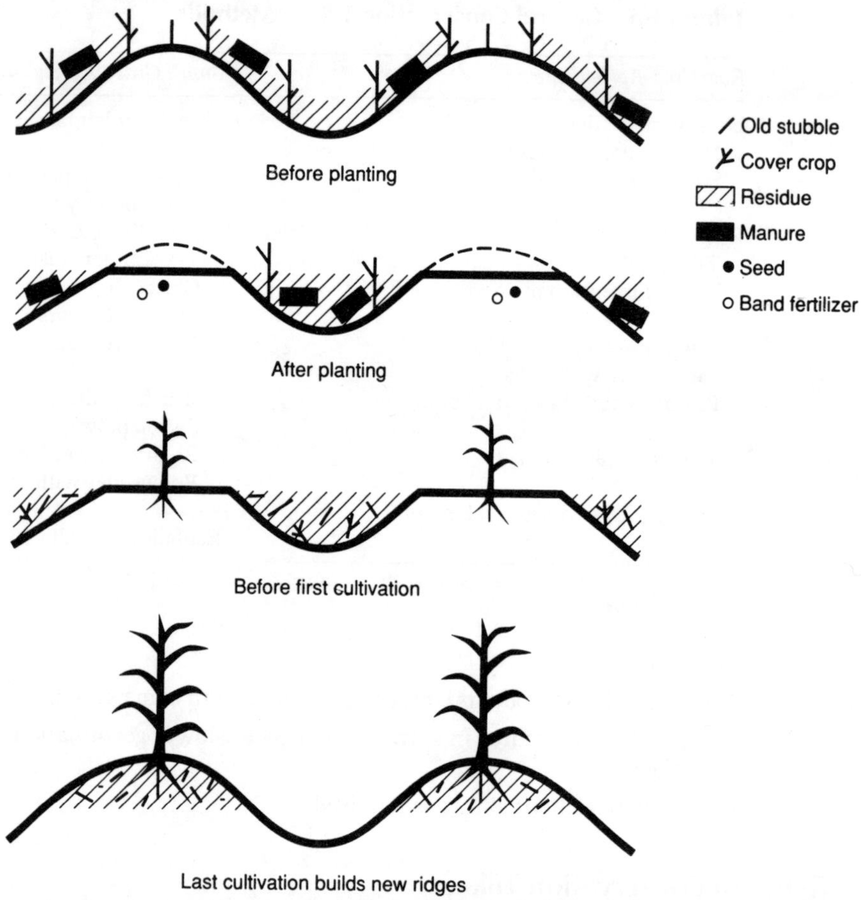

Figure 13-16 **Ridge tillage advantages in production systems. The planter tills 2 to 4 in. of soil in a 6-in. band on top of the ridges. Seeds are planted on top of the ridges, and soil from the ridges is mixed with crop residue between the ridges. Soil on ridges is generally warmer than soil in flat fields or between ridges. Warm soil facilitates crop germination, which slows weed emergence. Crop residue between the ridges also reduces soil erosion and increases moisture retention. Mechanical cultivation during the growing season helps to control weeds, reduces the need for herbicides, and rebuilds the ridges for the next season.**

Effects of Conservation Tillage

Mixing air and plant residues in the surface soil with tillage increases soil aeration and temperature, stimulating aerobic microbial decomposition of plant residue C. These changes depend on tillage intensity.

Surface Residues The approximate quantity of surface residue remaining after one tillage operation varies with the crop residue level and the implement (Table 13-6). Subsurface implements that leave most of the residue on the soil surface help protect the surface against erosion. Figure 13-17 illustrates the relationship between residue cover and residue mass.

Table 13-6 **Effect of Tillage Equipment on Surface Residue Remaining After Each Operation**

Tillage Machine	*Approximate Residue Maintained (%)*
Subsurface cultivators	
Wide-blade cultivator, rodweeder	90–95
Mixing-type cultivators	
Heavy-duty cultivator, chisel, etc.	50–75
Mixing and inverting disk machines	
One-way, flexible disk harrow; one-way disk; tandem disk; offset disk	25–50
Inverting machines	
Moldboard, disk plow	0–10

SOURCE: Anderson, 1968, Great Plains Ag. Council Publ. No. 32.

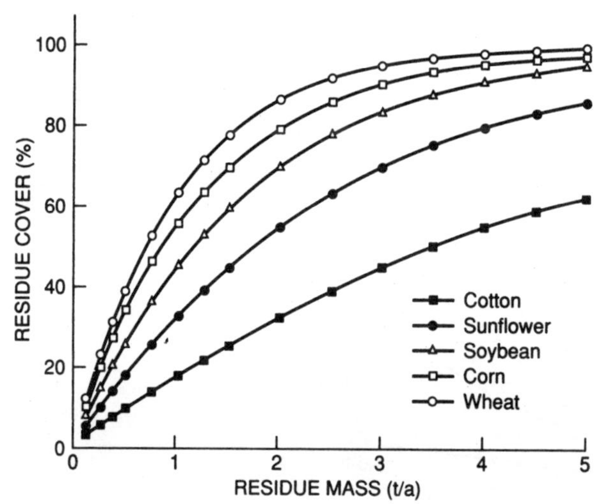

Figure 13-17 **Relationship between residue mass and % surface cover for selected crops.**

Crops such as soybean, sunflower, and cotton provide very little surface cover compared with small- and coarse-grain crops.

Soil Loss The quantity of residue required to prevent or minimize soil erosion depends on:

- soil characteristics (e.g., texture, OM, surface roughness, structure, depth, slope percentages, and slope length);
- residue characteristics (e.g., type, quantity, orientation);
- rainfall characteristics (e.g., quantity, duration, and intensity); and
- wind characteristics (e.g., velocity, direction, gusts, and duration).

In general, as the % surface residue cover increases, the potential for soil loss decreases (Fig. 13-18). In addition, increasing surface residue cover by reducing tillage intensity drastically reduces soil loss (Fig. 13-19). These data also show the value of farming on the contour compared with up and down the slope. The same relationship can be seen in Table 13-7 and Table 13-8. Soil loss was greater with all tillage systems when the crop was planted up and down the slope (Table 13-7) compared with across the slope (Table 13-8).

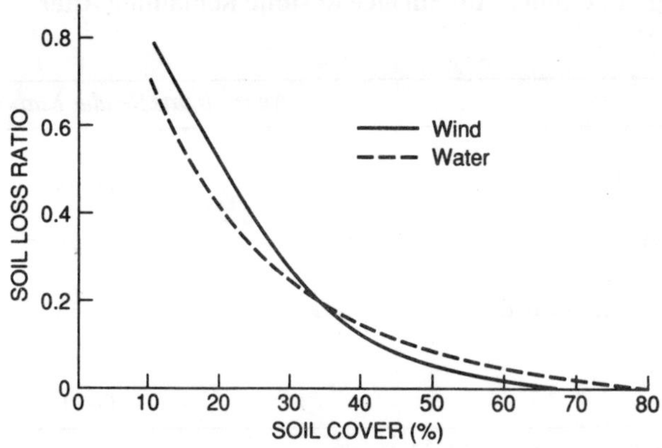

Figure 13-18 **Relationship between soil loss with residue cover divided by soil loss from bare soil (soil loss ratio) and percentage of surface residue cover.** *(Adapted from Laflen et al., 1981, ASAE Publ. 7-81, p. 121; and Fryrear, 1985,* Sci. Reviews, *p. 31, Arizona Res., Scientific Publ.)*

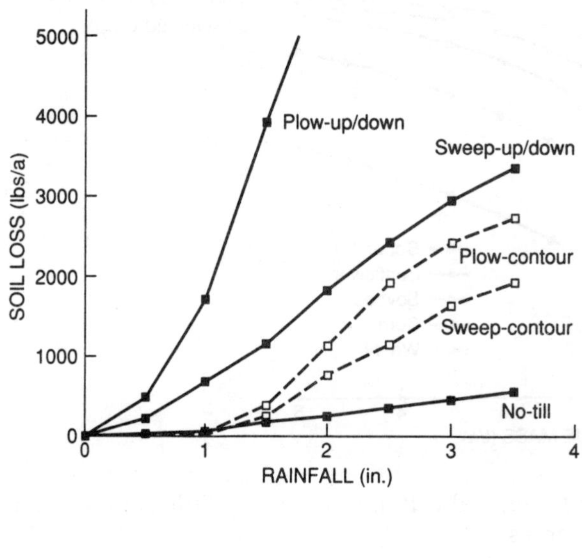

Figure 13-19 **Influence of tillage system and direction (up- or downhill or on the contour) on soil loss for a 4% slope. Initial residue level was 13,500 lbs.** *(Dickey et al., 1981, Neb Guide 181–554 Univ. of Neb.)*

Table 13-7 **Surface Cover and Soil Loss from Various Tillage Systems on a 4% Slope, Tilled up and Down the Slope Following Corn and Soybeans***

	Surface Cover		*Soil Loss*	
Tillage System	*After Corn*	*After Beans*	*After Corn*	*After Beans*
	%		*mt/ha*	
Fall moldboard plow	7	1	22.0	41.0
Fall chisel tillage	25	12	15.0	30.3
No-till	69	26	2.5	13.5

*Morley clay loam with a slope length of 10.7 m. Tests were made after overwinter weathering but before spring tillage. Two storms were applied at 6.25 cm of rainfall each.

SOURCE: Mannering, 1979, Crop. Ext. Serv. Publ. AY-222, Purdue Univ.

Table 13-8 **Surface Cover and Soil Loss from Various Tillage Systems of 5% Slope Land Tilled Across the Slope Following Corn and Soybeans***

	Surface Cover		*Soil Loss*	
Tillage System	*After Corn*	*After Beans*	*After Corn*	*After Beans*
	%		*mt/ha*	
Fall moldboard plow	4	2	12.8	25.6
Fall disk chisel tillage	50	11	1.3	7.4
No-till	85	59	1.1	3.8

*Catlin silt loam with slope length of 10.7 m. Tests were made after overwinter weathering but before any spring tillage; 12.5 cm of simulated rainfall were applied in two storms.
SOURCE: Siemens and Oschwald, 1976, Am. Soc. Agr. Eng. Paper No. 76–2552.

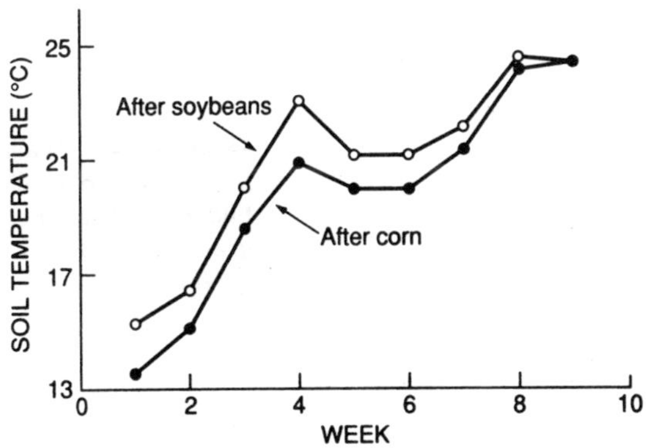

Figure 13-20 **Weekly means for daily maximum soil temperatures in no-till corn.** *(Griffith et al., 1986,* No Tillage and Surface Tillage Agriculture, *p. 34, John Wiley & Sons.)*

In addition, surface cover was much less after planting soybean than corn, resulting in considerably greater soil loss.

Tillage Effects on Soil Temperature, Moisture, and Microbial Activity

Soil temperatures early in the growing season are generally lower under conservation tillage than under conventional tillage due to the insulating effect of the unincorporated surface crop residues. The influence of surface residue cover on soil temperature also depends on the crop. Figure 13-20 shows that surface soil temperature was lower following corn than soybean, which was related to the higher surface cover from corn compared to soybean.

Decomposition of crop residue and soil OM, with subsequent release of plant nutrients, including N, P, and S, is restricted by low soil temperatures. Thus, recycling of essential nutrients may be delayed. Further, low soil temperatures retard root development and activity (Fig. 13-21). In tropical and semitropical regions, the cooling effect of crop residue on soil temperatures may improve productivity by reducing potential evaporation.

Increasing residue on the surface by reducing tillage decreases runoff and soil erosion while increasing infiltration. Soils with tillage pans may require chiseling to gradually create a deeper root zone with greater water intake and water-holding capacity. This deeper root zone may provide an extra inch or two of water at critical stages of growth (Fig. 13-22).

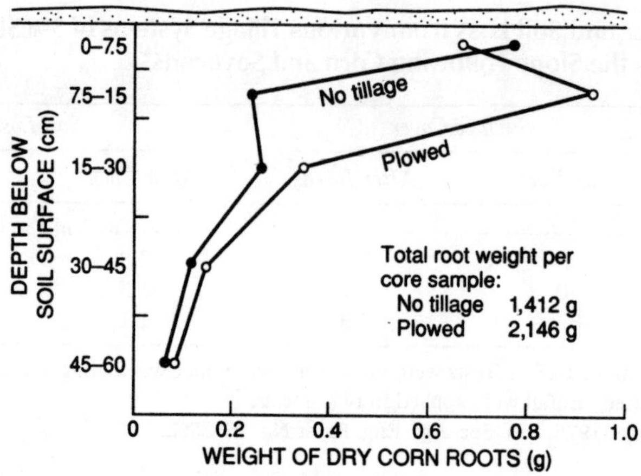

Figure 13-21 **Effect of plowing and no-till planting on amount and distribution of corn roots. *(Griffith et al., 1986,* No Tillage and Surface Tillage Agriculture, *p. 39, John Wiley & Sons.)***

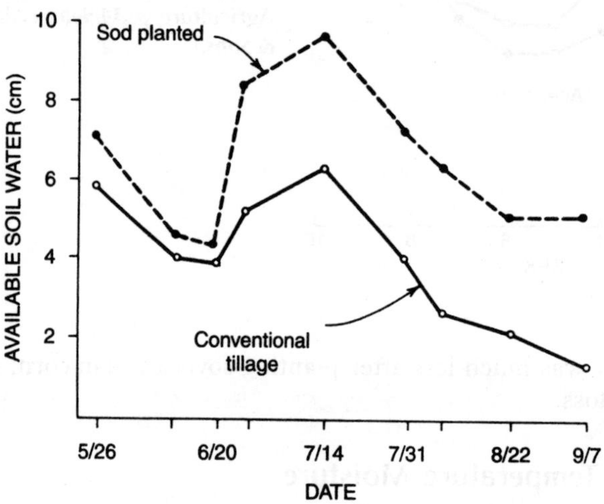

Figure 13-22 **Available soil water in 0- to 60-cm profile as affected by tillage practice for corn with orchard grass. *(Bennett et al., 1973,* Agron. J., *65:488.)***

In semiarid regions, water conservation increases with maintenance of surface residue cover. Increasing residue cover with no-till systems can increase the total water stored, consequently improving yield and water use efficiency (WUE) compared with residue incorporation (Table 13-9).

The interaction of soil temperature and moisture with tillage dramatically influences microbial activity (Fig. 13-23). When the soil is tilled, increased aeration combined with greater mixing of residue C in the soil encourages microbial activity and OM mineralization, which eventually releases N and other nutrients. Microbial activity is lower early in the season because of lower temperature; however, it is slightly higher later in the season because of greater soil moisture.

The net effect of tillage is increased OM mineralization, resulting in gradual OM loss over time (Fig. 13-24). Reducing tillage intensity reduces OM mineralization; thus, soil-OM

Table 13-9 Tillage Effects on Water Storage, Sorghum Grain Yields, and WUE in an Irrigated Winter Wheat–Fallow–Dryland Grain Sorghum Cropping System*

Tillage System	*Precipitation*		*Sorghum Grain Yield*		*Crop Water Use*	*Water Use Efficiency*
	Total	*Storage*				
	mm	*%*	*Mg/ha*	*bu/a*	*mm*	*kg/m^3*
No-till	217	35.2	3.14	47	350	0.89
Sweep	170	22.7	2.50	37	324	0.77
Disk	152	15.2	1.93	29	320	0.66

*Precipitation averaged 347 mm during the fallow period, average 1973–1977.
SOURCE: Unger and Weise, 1979, *Soil Sci. Soc. Am. J.*, 43:582.

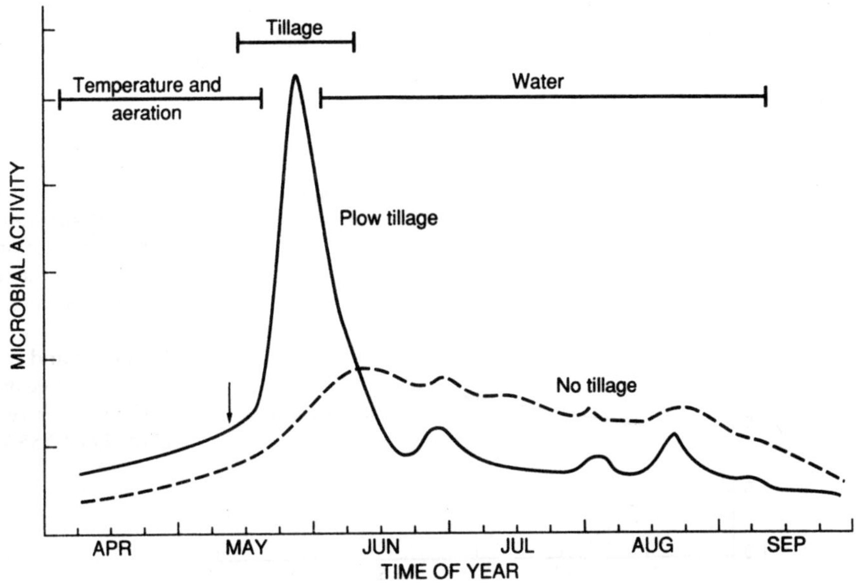

Figure 13-23 Hypothetical relationship between relative microbial activity and time of year in a plowed and a no-till soil; factors controlling activity are shown on top of the graph; the arrow indicates time of plowing. *(J. W. Doran, personal communication.)*

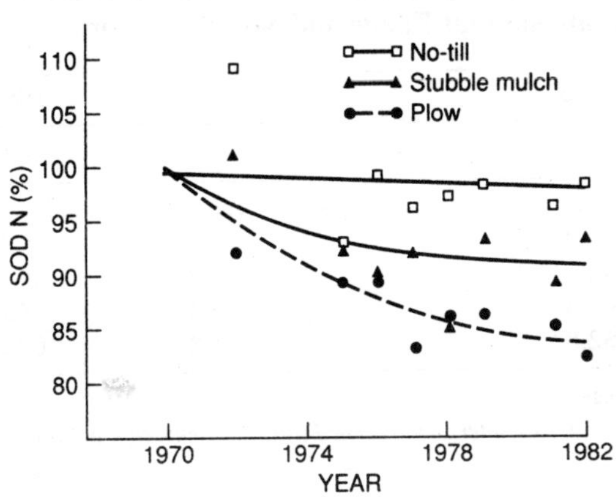

Figure 13-24 Influence of tillage on total-soil-N, measured as a percentage of total N in undisturbed prairie soil. Increasing tillage intensity from no-till to plowing systems increased N mineralization, which reduces soil OM over time. *(Lamb et al., 1985, SSSAJ, 49:352.)*

levels can be sustained. The relationships between tillage and residue on accumulation of OM are well documented (Fig. 13-25). In this study three crop rotations—continuous soybean, continuous sorghum, and sorghum–soybean—were managed for 12 years under conventional and no-tillage systems (0 and 100% surface residue cover, respectively). The total residue returned to the soil increased with increasing frequency of sorghum in the rotation (continuous sorghum > sorghum-soybean > continuous soybean). Under conventional tillage, soil OM increased only slightly compared with no tillage, where all the residue was left on the soil surface. Under no tillage, soil OM increased 45% as the level of residue increased from 1 to 3 t/a/yr. These data illustrate that the quantity of residue returned is important to maintaining or increasing OM; however, reducing oxidation of the organic residue with no tillage had a greater effect on increasing OM. Although soybean residue has a lower C/N ratio (higher N content) than sorghum residue, the quantity of residue added is more important to increasing OM.

As discussed earlier, N applications combined with high-residue-producing cropping systems can increase soil OM, although 5 to 8 years of continuous no-till systems may be needed before effects are measurable (Table 13-10). In the first several years, the increase

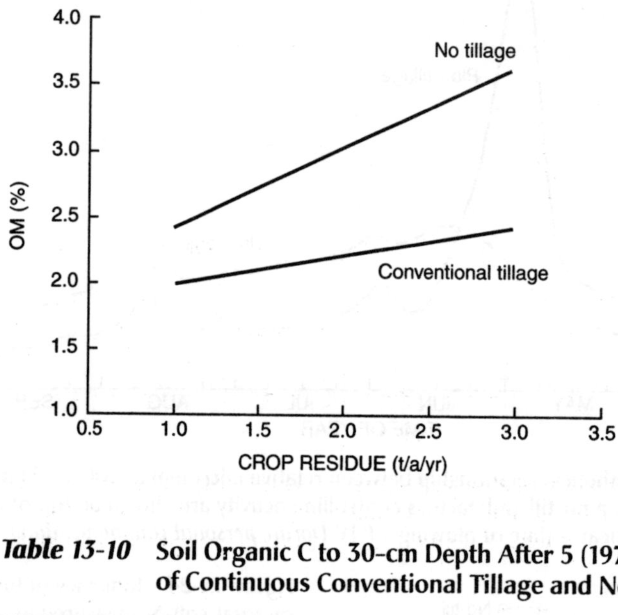

Figure 13-25 **Influence of tillage and rotation on soil-OM content. Crop residue returned per year for the three rotations is about 1, 2, and 3 t/a/yr for continuous soybean, soybean-sorghum, and continuous sorghum, respectively. No tillage and conventional tillage represent 90% and 0% surface residue cover, respectively. *(Havlin et al., 1990, SSSAJ, 54:448.)***

Table 13-10 **Soil Organic C to 30-cm Depth After 5 (1975) and 20 Years (1989) of Continuous Conventional Tillage and No-Tillage Corn**

	1975			*1989*		
N rate	*CT**	*NT**	*Sod*	*CT*	*NT*	*Sod*
kg/ha	*Mg/ha*					
0	39.7	46.8	53.4	48.9	55.3	55.5
84	47.8	48.4		56.2	58.3	
168	47.7	46.3		56.4	58.6	
336	45.9	52.8		61.3	66.2	

*CT, conventional tillage; NT, no tillage.

SOURCE: Frye and Blevins, 1997, *Soil OM Under Long-Term Tillage in Kentucky*, p. 233, Boca Raton, Fla.: CRC Press.

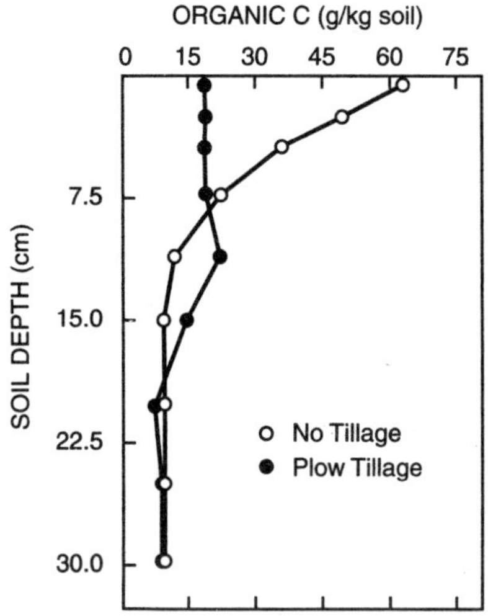

Figure 13-26 **Organic C concentrations in soil profiles after 18 years of continuous plow or no tillage.** ***(Dick et al., 1997,*** **Continuous Application of No-Tillage to Ohio Soils,** ***p. 178, Boca Raton, Fla.: CRC Press.)***

in soil OM occurs predominantly in the surface 2 in., although increased OM can be measured deeper in the profile after decades of continuous no-till cropping (Fig. 13-26).

Crop yields under no tillage systems are often equal to or better than those of conventionally tilled crops. In situations where crop yields are initially reduced with no tillage, yields may improve with time because of reduced erosion; improved weed control; increased levels and/or quality of soil OM; improved availability of N, P, and other nutrients; higher CEC; greater soil water-holding capacity; and better soil structure.

Tillage Effects on N Cycling and Crop N Management

Tillage influences N transformations in soils because OM is the primary source and sink for C and N (Chapter 4). For example, when plant residues with > 25 C:N are incorporated by tillage, much of the inorganic N in the soil solution is initially immobilized by soil microbes in decomposing the residue (Fig. 4-16). Rapidly increasing microbial populations, in response to the large C supply and tillage, greatly increase N required by the microbes. If the period of high microbial activity occurs during early crop growth, then N deficiency could result unless sufficient N is added to meet both crop and microbial N requirements. In many nonlegume cropping systems, 30 to 60% of fertilizer N can be immobilized by microbes degrading previous crop residues. Ultimately, as the residue C supply decreases with time, the C:N ratio decreases to ~10:1, with some of the microbial N mineralized back to plant-available inorganic N. Understanding the N transformations that occur when residue is tilled into soil is important for maximizing crop recovery of added N and minimizing loss of any excess N not used by the crop or the microbes.

In no-tillage systems, greater surface residue cover reduces soil temperature and increases soil moisture, resulting in less aerobic microbial activity than with tilled soils. Although residue decomposition rates may be slower, N mineralization is also reduced, increasing the supplemental N requirement of the crop, despite the higher OM and total N content in no-till soils.

When no-tillage systems are initiated, surface soil OM increases rapidly, increasing the N immobilization potential. During these first years, N management (i.e., rate, placement, and timing) is critical to minimize potential crop-N deficiency. After the soil OM attains a new equilibrium level (Fig. 13-10), N mineralization may increase, resulting in lower N requirements. Often because of increased H_2O availability and other factors that increase productivity, higher yield potential will require greater N requirements. Thus, in many highly productive no-till cropping systems, N rates are equal to or greater than conventionally tilled soils.

N Management in No-Till The challenge with any cropping system regardless of tillage is to synchronize N availability with crop N demand (Fig. 4-10). N applied too far in advance of active crop N uptake may result in decreased plant-available N by immobilization, leaching, denitrification, or volatilization. If N application exceeds crop requirement, residual profile N may also be lost. Therefore, understanding N transformations in soil as influenced by tillage and other management factors is essential to improve N management.

As discussed in Chapter 9, estimated N rate required for optimum yield is especially complicated by uncertainties in N cycling between years. Compared to tillage systems, no-till delays residue decomposition and mineralization, reducing N availability. The contribution of N mineralization to plant-available N varies 2- to 4-fold depending on the environmental conditions that influence microbial activity. These are difficult to predict prior to planting; thus, in-season N adjustments generally will improve N-use efficiency and reduce N losses. In-season N rates can be determined by using soil sampling (e.g., PSNT), traditional plant tissue sampling and analysis, or nondestructive techniques (e.g., chlorophyll meters, leaf color charts, remote sensing) to estimate crop N needs (Chapter 9). These tools enable assessment of N availability from mineralization to better synchronize N availability with crop N uptake.

In no-till, surface or subsurface band placement minimizes immobilization and volatilization of fertilizer N (Fig. 10-49). A starter N application at planting followed by one or more in-season N applications will improve N-use efficiency. Starter N is more important in no-till because of reduced early-season N mineralization in cooler soils compared to warmer tilled soils. In general, single preplant N application reduces labor and time required for N application; however, N application too far ahead of planting increases risks of N loss. Spring preplant is usually more efficient than fall preplant application.

Adoption of No-Till Systems

Currently, about 60% of the cropland in North America is under some form of conservation tillage to reduce wind and water erosion, to increase precipitation efficiency, and to reduce fuel, labor, and equipment costs (Fig. 13-27). No-till cropping is likely to increase, and it is estimated that within the next 20 years, more than 50% of the cropland in the United States will be farmed by no-till systems. The attractive features of no-till systems are:

- Row crop production on sloping lands is more feasible, with less loss of nutrients, soil, and water
- WUE is increased
- No-till corn production can readily follow soybeans
- Double cropping of row crops such as soybeans, sorghum, or corn planted immediately after a wheat harvest is possible in many areas
- Seeding legumes and/or nonlegumes in rundown pastures can be accomplished using the same principle. Fertilizer may be placed beneath the seed or broadcast.

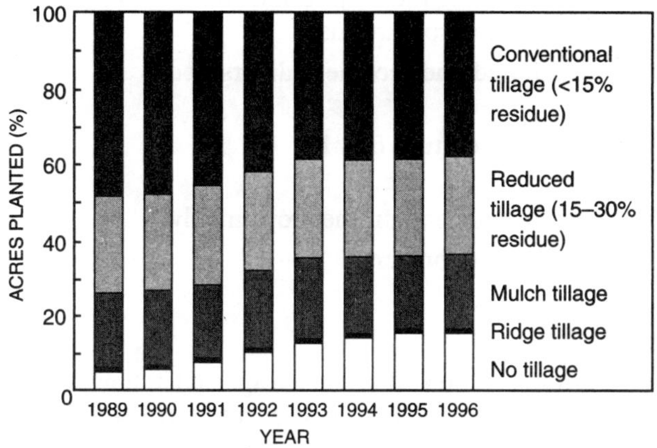

Figure 13-27 **National use of crop residue management, 1989 to 1996.** *(USDA-ERS, 1996.)*

Herbicides are used to kill or retard existing grasses and weeds. Again, this technique is useful on sloping lands that should not otherwise be tilled, as well as on areas that are more level

- Energy, time, labor, and machinery costs are reduced

Rotations versus Continuous Cropping

Although monoculture was once considered a sign of poor farming, the increased supply of fertilizer, especially N in the 1950s, encouraged continuous cropping on soils on which erosion was not a serious problem. Most continuous cropping systems are currently used because of economics. In some regions, crop options may be limited because of climatic constraints or market opportunities; thus, growers continuously produce an adapted crop that maximizes profit potential. Conventionally tilled, continuous dryland wheat, cotton, and irrigated corn are common examples.

Numerous long-term experiments have demonstrated that, in general, rotations increase long-term crop and soil productivity compared with continuous cropping (Fig. 13-12). The reasons for the production advantage with rotation cropping compared with continuous cropping depend on the crops involved, environment, and other interacting factors. In some cases, a crop may have a harmful effect on the subsequent crop, especially if it is the same crop. Allelopathy is the term used to describe the antagonistic action on like or different species. Substances released from roots and foliage or formed during the decomposition of residues can have toxic and inhibitory properties. The comparison of continuous corn versus a corn-soybean rotation is an example. Seeding alfalfa following alfalfa is often unsatisfactory. With time, continuous wheat yields generally decrease in many regions due to allelopathic effects and other factors such as disease and pest pressures. Some specific advantages attributed to crop rotations include:

- Deep-rooted legumes and other crops may improve soil structure, water infiltration, and nutrient redistribution from subsoil to surface soils
- There is more continuous vegetative cover, with less erosion and water loss
- Tilth of the soil may be superior
- Weed and insect control are favored

- Disease control is favored. Changing the crop residue fosters competition among soil organisms and may help reduce pathogens
- Labor is more broadly distributed and income is diversified

Several advantages of continuous monoculture may be:

- Profits may be greater, but they depend on the crops involved
- A soil may be especially adapted to one crop
- The climate may favor one crop
- Machinery costs may be lower
- The grower may prefer a single crop and become a specialist; however, monoculture demands greater skills, including pest, erosion, and fertilization management
- The grower may not wish to be fully occupied with farming year-round

Control of Disease, Weeds, and Insects

In most cases, crop rotation may help control certain diseases, weeds, or insects. For example, reducing root-rot diseases in wheat and other cereals requires crop rotation, together with resistant varieties, clean seed, and field sanitation practices. Legumes, other dicotyledons, and even cereals such as oats, barley, and corn are often suitable alternate crops in place of wheat when take-all disease occurs. However, in some instances, this disease can be severe, even in wheat following other crops. Corn root rots and the severity of several seedling diseases have been reduced in rotations. Susceptible crops should be grown on the same field only once in every 3 to 4 years. For example, due to serious loss in canola yields from at least three widespread diseases, minimum 3- to 4-year rotations are recommended. Cereals and grasses are suitable rotational crops because they are not susceptible to diseases of cruciferous crops.

Crop rotation is important for control of nematodes feeding on the roots of annual crops. Grass crops are commonly used in rotation to control root-knot nematodes. Acceptable yields of irrigated cotton can be obtained following 2 or more years of root-knot–resistant alfalfa. Two years of clean fallow can also effectively control root-knot nematodes. Few important bacterial or viral diseases are controlled by crop rotation.

The role of crop rotation for weed control depends on the particular weed and the ability to control it with available methods. If all of the weeds can be conveniently and economically controlled with herbicides, then crop rotation is not a vital part of a weed control program. However, there are situations in which rotations are necessary for control of a troublesome weed. For example, downy brome and jointed goat grass can severely reduce yields in a wheat-fallow-wheat system. Use of atrazine in a reduced-tillage wheat-sorghum/corn-fallow rotation will eliminate these weed problems. Continuous use of the same herbicides can potentially cause development of weeds resistant to the specific herbicide.

Rotation was once a common practice for insect management, but its use declined with the development of economically effective insecticides. Interest in rotations has increased because of insect resistance to certain chemicals and increased costs. Rotation can be helpful where insects have few generations each year or where more than one season is needed for the development of a generation. For example, northern corn rootworm can be a serious problem in continuous corn. Rotation of soybean and corn replaces the need for insecticide control of this insect. Rotation is only partially successful in reducing damage by cotton bollworm. Sorghum, when planted at the proper time, will protect cotton from worms.

Effect on Soil Tilth

Most recommended crop production practices provide good plant cover and return large amounts of crop residue to the soil. With conservation tillage, the detrimental effects of compaction and deterioration of soil structure are reduced. Rotation can greatly improve soil structure and tilth of many medium- and fine-textured soils. Pasture grasses and legumes in rotation exert significant beneficial effects on physical properties of soil. When soils previously in sod are plowed, they crumble easily and readily shear into a desirably mellow seedbed. Internal drainage can be improved so that ponding and the time needed for drainage of excess water is reduced.

Corn in monoculture is unique, since on many soils it maintains reasonably acceptable physical conditions. The compensating factors are (1) the return of several tons of crop residue to the soil when corn is harvested for grain and (2) the corn crop is well adapted to reduced tillage and decreased damage from traffic on the soil.

Double cropping, such as small-grain–soybeans or small-grain–corn, triple cropping, and even quadruple cropping of rice in areas with long growing seasons and the possibilities of irrigation are becoming more common. With four crops a year, 27 t/ha of rice are possible. This necessitates maximum use of soil, solar, and water resources. If adequate fertility and pest control are provided, soil productivity should gradually increase.

Crop Removal of Nutrients in the Root Zone

Crops vary considerably in their content of macro- and micronutrients. In addition, crops may absorb nutrients from different soil zones, thus making the choice of cropping sequences important to plant nutrition. Deep-rooted crops absorb nutrients from the subsoil. As their residue decomposes in the surface soil, shallow-rooted crops may benefit from the remaining nutrients. On a soil marginal in a particular micronutrient, it is possible that the preceding crop will have a considerable effect on the supply of this nutrient to the current crop. The net effect of cropping practices on P and K levels depends on the removal of nutrients by the harvested portion of the crop, nutrients supplied by the soil, and supplemental fertilization.

Effect of Rotation on Soil Erosion by Water and Wind

Generally, increasing crop yield and residue produced and left on the soil surface will increase water infiltration while reducing runoff and soil loss. Some of the influences of cropping systems on soil erosion are:

- The denseness of the canopy and/or residue cover affects the amount of protection from wind and the impact of rain and evaporation
- Increasing the proportion of time that the soil is in a cultivated crop versus the time in a close-growing crop such as small grains or forage increases erosion potential
- Crop selection to maximize canopy cover in relation to the distribution and intensity of rainfall and wind will reduce soil erosion
- Increasing the amount of residue produced and returned will reduce soil erosion if residues are managed properly

Table 13-11 **Effect of Management Level on Crop Yields, Runoff, and Erosion, 1945 to 1968**

	Prevailing Practices	*Improved Practices*
Corn (t/ha)	5.1	7.3
Wheat (t/ha)	1.5	2.3
Hay (t/ha)	4.3	7.8
Runoff, growing season (cm)	1.9	1.0
Peak runoff rate (cm/hr)	2.3	1.5
Erosion from corn (t/ha/yr)	10.6	3.1

SOURCE: Edwards et al., 1973, *Soil Sci. Soc. Am. Proc.*, 37:27.

Table 13-12 **Hydrologic Data from a 6-a Watershed Comparing Various Cropping and Tillage Systems**

Years	*Cropping System*	*Tillage*	*Annual Rainfall*	*Annual Runoff*	*Annual Soil Loss*
			(in.)	(in.)	(t/a)
1972–74	Fallow/soybean	Conventional	54.0	8.7	11.6
1974–76	Barley/grain sorghum	No-till	52.0	3.5	0.2
1976–79	Barley/soybean	No-till + in-row chisel	46.5	0.8	0.06
1979–83	Crimson clover/ grain sorghum	No-till + in-row chisel	43.7	0.2	0.002

SOURCE: Hargrove and Frye, 1987, *Role of Legumes in Conservation Tillage Systems,* Ankeny, IA: Soil Cons. Soc. Am.

Adoption of improved soil and crop management practices can increase yields and reduce runoff and erosion (Table 13-11). Improved management effects on reducing runoff and erosion are due in part to better surface protection from enhanced canopy cover in the spring, a denser cover throughout the season, and a more extensive root system of the growing crop. The influence of maintaining a surface residue cover and crop rotation on reducing runoff and soil loss is demonstrated in Table 13-12.

Winter Cover-Green Manure Crops

Winter cover crops are planted in the fall and either incorporated with tillage or desiccated with a herbicide in the spring prior to planting. These crops may be a nonlegume, a legume, or a combination grown together. There are several advantages to the combination practice. A greater amount of OM is produced, the nonlegume can benefit from the N fixation, and because the nonlegume is usually more easily established, a stand of at least one of the two crops is ensured.

Decomposition of green manure crops is rapid, but the residual effects can be important. The smallest residual effects generally are expected in areas in which the mean annual temperature is high and the soil is sandy. Small grains or other crops can be grazed in late fall and winter when the amount of growth and soil conditions permit. Adequate fertility, either residual or added, is necessary, and extra N may be needed. Grazing allows additional return from cover crop inputs.

N and OM Added

One important reason for using green manure legume crops is that they supply additional N, depending on yield and N content (Table 13-13). The data show that increasing the quantity of N produced in the legume cover crop increased yield of unfertilized corn. The grain yield after fallowing was greater than following the wheat cover crop because of N mineralization during the fallow period. When a nonlegume is turned under, only the N from the soil or that supplied in fertilizer is returned.

The nutrient content in several legume cover crops is shown in Table 13-14. Increasing the cover crop yield or biomass will subsequently increase N_2 fixation and the N returned to the soil (Fig. 13-28). Legume cover crops can contribute large quantities of N to subsequent nonlegume crops (Table 13-15). One of the benefits attributed to winter cover crops is the OM supplied to the soil (Table 13-16). Green manures will help maintain soil OM and will sometimes even increase it.

Table 13-13 Dry Matter and N Concentration of Various Cover Crops and Their Influence on Corn Grain Yield

				Grain Yield	
Cover Crop	*Dry Matter*	*N Concentration*	*N Content*	*0 lbs N/a*	*200 lbs N/a*
	lbs/a	*%*	*lbs/a*	*bu/a*	
Fallow	—	—	—	63	161
Wheat	1,178	2.01	35	32	121
Winter pea	1,423	4.56	61	132	165
Hairy vetch	2,526	4.62	113	156	168
Crimson clover	2,883	3.67	102	143	172

SOURCE: Neely et al., 1987, *Role of Legumes in Conservation Tillage Systems,* p. 49, Ankeny, IA: Soil Cons. Soc. Am.

Table 13-14 Biomass Yield and Nutrient Accruement by Select Cover Crops

Cover Crop	*Biomass**	*N*	*K*	*Ca*	*P*	*Mg*
	lb/a					
Hairy vetch	3,260	141	133	52	18	11
Crimson clover	4,243	115	143	62	16	11
Austrian winter peas	4,114	144	159	45	19	13
Rye	5,608	89	108	22	17	8

*Dry weight of above ground plant material.

SOURCE: Hoyt, 1987, *Role of Legumes in Conservation Tillage Systems,* p. 96, Ankeny, IA: Soil Cons. Soc. Am.

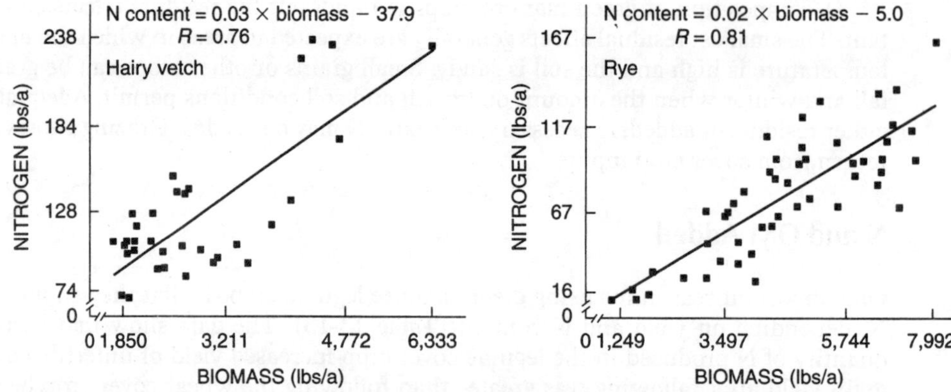

Figure 13-28 **Effect of biomass on N uptake for hairy vetch and rye cover crops.** *(Hoyt, 1987,* Role of Legumes in Conservation Tillage Systems, *Ankeny, IA: Soil Cons. Soc. Am.)*

Table 13-15 **Estimates of the N Contribution of Winter Legumes to the N Requirements of No-Till Corn, Grain Sorghum, and Cotton**

Location	*Crop*	*Cover Crop*	*Fertilizer N Value, lbs/a*
Kentucky	Corn	Hairy vetch	85
		Big flower vetch	45
Georgia	Grain sorghum	Crimson clover	75
		Hairy vetch	81
		Common vetch	53
		Subterranean clover	51
Alabama	Cotton	Hairy vetch	61
		Crimson clover	61

SOURCE: Hargrove and Frye, 1987, *Role of Legumes in Conservation Tillage Systems,* p. 2, Ankeny, IA: Soil Cons. Soc. Am.

Table 13-16 **Influence of 5 Years of Various Cropping Sequences and Tillage on Soil Organic C and N Concentrations in the Surface 7.5 cm of Soil**

Cropping Sequence	*Tillage Treatment*	*N Rate lbs/a/yr*	*Organic C %*	*Organic N %*	*C:N Ratio*
Wheat/soybean	Conventional	70	1.4	0.12	11.7
Wheat/soybean	No-till	70	1.6	0.15	10.7
Clover/sorghum	No-till	0	2.2	0.17	13.0
Clover/sorghum	No-till	120	2.4	0.19	12.6

SOURCE: Hargrove and Frye, 1987, *Role of Legumes in Conservation Tillage Systems,* Ankeny, IA: Soil Cons. Soc. Am.

In rotations where crops return little residue, maintenance of soil productivity may be particularly difficult. The lengthening of the rotation to include green manure crops could be beneficial. The acreage of corn and sorghum silage is increasing in some areas, which leaves the soil with almost no surface residue. Oats or rye seeded immediately after harvesting or seeded by airplane before harvesting will help to protect the soil and increase the residue returned.

Protection of the Soil Against Erosion and Recovery of Plant Nutrients

Protection against erosion is one of the most important benefits of winter cover crops, depending on the distribution of rain and erosion potential during the year. The effect of cover crops on soil loss is generally small when winter cover crops are turned under in early spring.

Surface residue from summer crops, if left undisturbed, may provide more protection than cover crops seeded in the fall. The greater the percentage of soil surface covered by mulch, the less the soil loss. Freshly tilled land is quite susceptible to erosion, and considerable time is required before the cover crop can provide enough protection to have much effect on reducing soil loss. For example, rye cover can be grown after corn, but in comparison to heavy corn residue, it is generally not as effective for erosion control.

For perennial crops such as peaches and apples planted on steep slopes, continuous cover is helpful in reducing erosion. Since the trees and the cover crops occupy the land simultaneously, care must be taken, particularly in young orchards, to prevent competition for water and N. In some of the muck soils suitable for vegetables, a strip of small grain or a row of trees at intervals helps to reduce losses from erosion. In regions of high overwinter rainfall, cover-crop recovery of residual plant nutrients will aid in controlling potential environmental problems.

Environmental Quality

As plant nutrients cycle through the soil-plant-atmosphere continuum, some will be recovered through plant uptake, incorporated into OM, adsorbed to mineral and OM surfaces, and precipitated as solid minerals (Fig. 2-1). The remaining nutrients can be transported from the field through runoff and subsurface lateral flow toward streams and rivers, and by leaching to groundwater (Table 13-17; Fig. 13-29). Volatilization to the atmosphere also occurs with N and S, as discussed in Chapters 4 and 7. Nutrients that are most soluble and mobile in the soil exhibit the greatest potential for movement to groundwater and surface water. This nonpoint source movement is the primary mechanism of nutrient loading into surface- and groundwater in agricultural systems. Figure 13-30 shows that fine soil particles lost through erosion and runoff, and nutrients lost through runoff or subsurface flow, are the most common nonpoint source contaminants. Nutrients and pesticides are the primary contaminants of groundwater. The nutrients of primary environmental concern in agriculture are N and P.

It is important to recognize that nutrient movement to surface- and groundwater occurs in natural ecosystems. Nutrients are found in "background" levels in all waters. For example,

Table 13-17 **Soil Processes Potentially Influencing Surface- and Groundwater Quality**

Soil Process	*Impact on Water Quality*
Soil erosion	Transport of nutrients and other chemicals dissolved in water and adsorbed to sediments in surface water runoff
Leaching	Transport of dissolved nutrients and other chemicals in percolating water
Macropore flow	Rapid transport of water and solutes from soil surface through the profile into a drainage system
OM mineralization	Release of soluble nutrients and other compounds subject to erosion, leaching, or macropore flow

SOURCE: Adapted from Lal and Stewart, 1994, *Soil Processes & Water Quality*, p. 4, Boca Raton, Fla.: CRC Press.

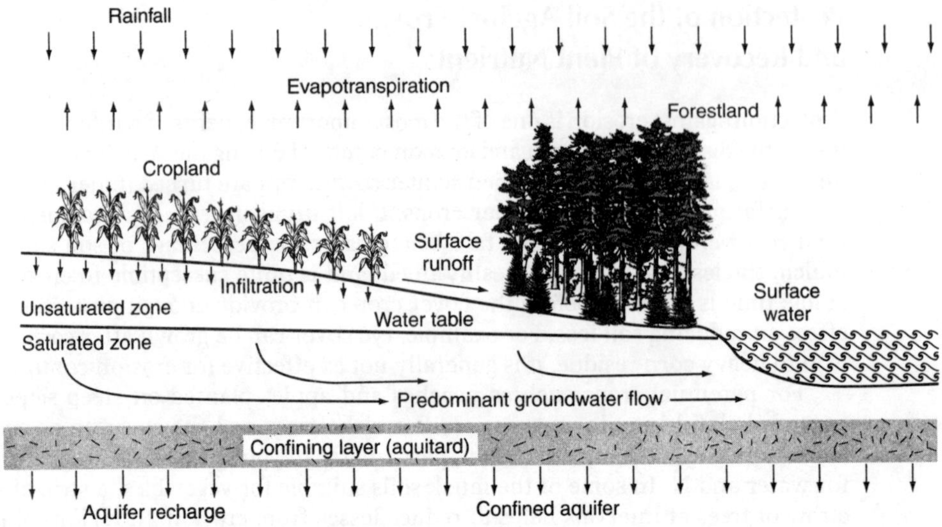

Figure 13-29 **Diagram of the hydrologic cycle showing potential pathways of nutrients to surface- and groundwater. The aquitard, or confining layer to downward movement of water (leaching), is common to the coastal regions of the southeast United States. Aquitards seldom occur in the Midwest and Great Plains regions of the United States.** ***(Evans et al., 1991, NC Agric. Ext. Service, AG-443.)***

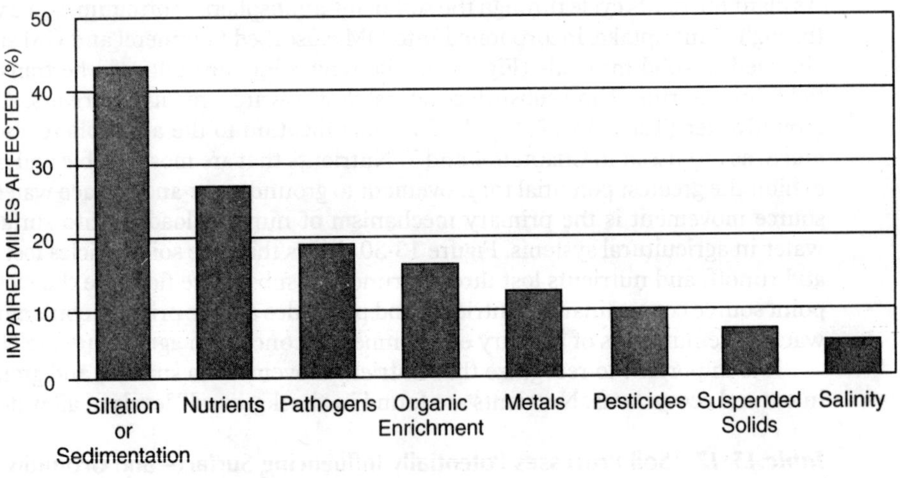

Figure 13-30 **Most common constituents that impact water quality of rivers in the United States.** ***(U.S. EPA, 1996.)***

typical background concentrations of NO_3^- can range between 1 to 10 ppm N. Water quality standards for drinking water have been established for all elements that adversely affect health when present in high concentrations (Table 13-18). Approximately 2% of groundwater wells used for drinking water exceed the primary drinking water standard of 10 ppm N. Several adverse health effects occur when humans or animals consume water high in NO_3^- (Table 13-19). Although rare, the most notable health effect of high NO_3^- water is low blood O_2 in human infants, called methemoglobinemia. Concentrations of $NO_3^- > 40$ ppm N are hazardous to adults and livestock (Table 13-20).

Table 13-18 Water Quality Standards for Human and Livestock Consumption

Element or Compound	Concentration (mg/l)	
	Human	Livestock
Pb	<0.1	0.05
Mo	—	0.01
As	<0.05	0.05
Se	<0.01	0.01
Zn	<15	<20
Cd	<0.01	0.01
Ba	<1.0	—
Ca	<200	<1,000
Hg	<0.01	0.002
NO_3	<45	<200
NH_4	<0.05	—
N	<10	<50
Cl	400	<1,000

SOURCE: Lal and Edwards, 1994, *Soil Processes & Water Quality*, p. 5, Boca Raton, Fla.: CRC Press.

Table 13-19 Potential Adverse Environmental and Health Impacts of N

Impact	Causative Agents
Human health	
Methemoglobinemia in infants	Excess NO_3^- and NO_2^- in water and food
Cancer	Nitrosamines from NO_2^-, secondary amines
Respiratory illness	Peroxyacyl nitrates, alkyl nitrates, NO_3^- aerosols, NO_2^-, HNO_3 vapor in urban atmosphere
Animal health	
Environment	Excess NO_3^- in feed and water
Eutrophication	Inorganic and organic N in surface waters
Materials and ecosystem damage	HNO_3 aerosols in rainfall
Plant toxicity	High levels of NO_2^- in soils
Excessive plant growth	Excess available N
Stratospheric ozone depletion	N_2O from nitrification, denitrification, stack emissions

SOURCE: Owens, 1994, *Soil Processes and Water Quality*, p. 138, Boca Raton, Fla.: CRC Press.

Another impact of nutrient loss from fields is nutrient enrichment or *eutrophication* of surface waters with P and N. Eutrophication is a natural process that typically occurs as a water body ages; however, accelerated eutrophication is usually due to anthropogenic causes. Eutrophication results in several negative impacts on water quality and ecology of the water bodies, including:

- Increased production of phytoplankton and algae
- Reduced light penetration into the water occurs because increased algae growth ultimately decreases productivity of plants living in the deeper waters that are important for producing O_2

Table 13-20 **Guidelines for Use of Water with Known NO_3 Content**

NO_3^-	NO_3–N	*Interpretation**
------------ppm------------		
<45	<10	U.S. Public Health Service standard as safe for humans and livestock
45–90	10–20	Generally safe for human adults and all livestock; should not be used by pregnant women or infants
90–180	20–40	Humans and some livestock at risk, especially young or those in high-risk category; monitor nitrates in livestock feed
>180	>40	Hazardous to humans and livestock; do not use for drinking or cooking without treatment

*Interpretations are primarily based on short-term effects. Chronic, long-term risks are not fully understood.

Table 13-21 **General Guidelines for N and P Loading into Streams and Rivers***

Risk Level	*Total N*	*Total P*
	------------*mg/l*------------	
Low	<0.5	<0.05
Intermediate	0.5-1.0	0.05-0.1
High	>1.0	>0.1

*Total P in streams should not exceed 0.05 mg/L directly entering lakes or reservoirs; total P should not exceed 0.1 mg/L in streams not discharged directly into lakes or reservoirs.
SOURCE: U.S. Evironmental Protection Agency, 2003.

- Depletion of dissolved O_2 by reduced deep-water-zone plant life, use of O_2 by microorganisms decomposing dead algae
- Reduced dissolved O_2 causes death of desirable fish that require high concentrations of dissolved O_2, with a shift to less desirable fish species
- Increasing costs of water purification if used for human consumption
- Reduced esthetics and recreational use of water

Current estimates suggest that 50 to 70% of all P and N reaching surface water are from nonpoint agricultural sources, primarily from land-applied animal wastes and fertilizer. Industrial and municipal point sources also contribute to P and N loading in surfacewater. In general, excess N is particularly a problem in coastal marine regions, where N is often more limiting than P, whereas excess P is more threatening to freshwaters. Although difficult to define, guidelines have been established for loading rate for rivers and streams (Table 13-21).

Nitrogen

N Leaching Although NO_3^- naturally occurs in all waters, NO_3^- loading of surface- and groundwaters can be greatly elevated from N added to agricultural systems. Although fertilizer, legume, and manure N sources are used to meet N requirements of crops, fertilizer N is considered the primary cause of contamination of surface- and groundwater, due to its predominance as an N source (Fig. 4-3). Little fertilizer N is lost directly through runoff, because its solubility and mobility results in immediate movement into the root zone in moist soils. In general, crops recover 40 to 60% of fertilizer N in the first year. The remaining N stays in the soil as NO_3^-, immobilized to organic N, denitrified as N gases, volatilized as NH_3, and leached as NO_3^- below the root zone (Fig. 4-1). High N recovery by the crop (low residual N available for leaching after harvest) will occur with a readily available N source applied to a crop that can utilize it quickly. Slowly available N that is not used during the first crop year can become available and potentially leach during noncrop periods. Thus, applied at appropriate rates, fertilizer N can exhibit a lower potential for leaching than manure, sludge, or legume N because a portion of the organic N in these materials will mineralize during periods of low plant growth and N uptake (Fig. 4-10). Thus, organic N can often contribute more to nonpoint source contamination of surface- and groundwater than fertilizer N at equal application rates.

NO_3^- leaching is normal; excessive NO_3^- loss is unacceptable. For NO_3^- leaching to occur, the soil water must contain NO_3^- and move below the root zone. Water transport below the root zone generally occurs in regions in which rainfall or irrigation exceeds evapotranspiration (Fig. 13-31). In addition, soil profile characteristics are important in determining the quantity of NO_3^- transported below the root zone (Fig. 13-32). In these examples, the time required for NO_3^- to enter the groundwater is very short (3 to 9 months) in a sandy soil with a shallow *vadose zone*, which represents the material below the rooting depth but above the aquifer. With similar vadose zone thickness, time required for transport to groundwater can be two to three times longer in fine-textured soils compared with sands (Fig. 13-32).

Irrigated cropping systems can contribute to nonpoint-source NO_3^- contamination, especially with excessive irrigation combined with high N-application rates. With furrow irrigation systems, more water is applied at the beginning than at the end of the furrow, increasing

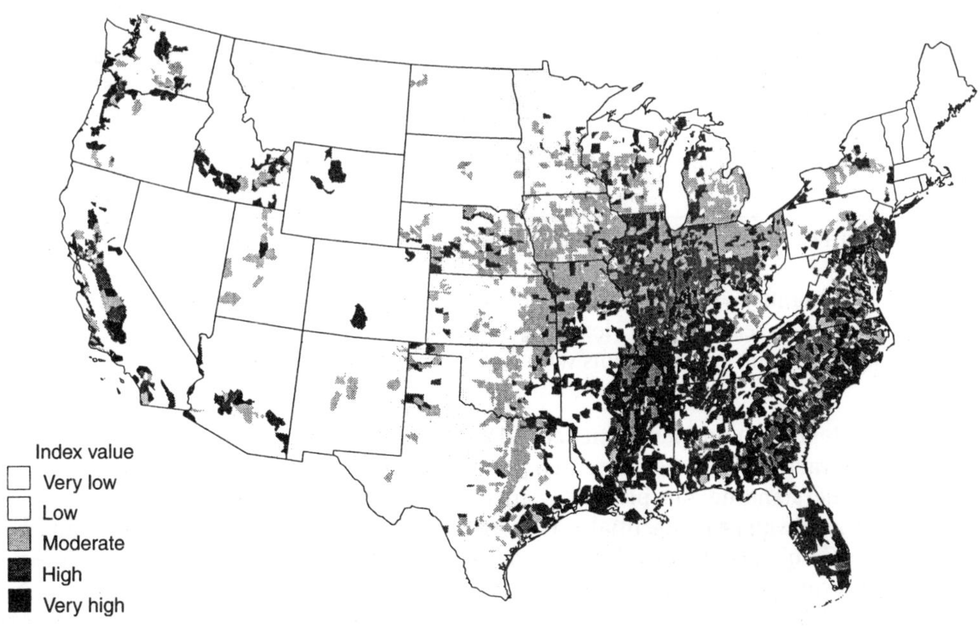

Figure 13-31 Groundwater vulnerability index for N. *(USDA, 1996.)*

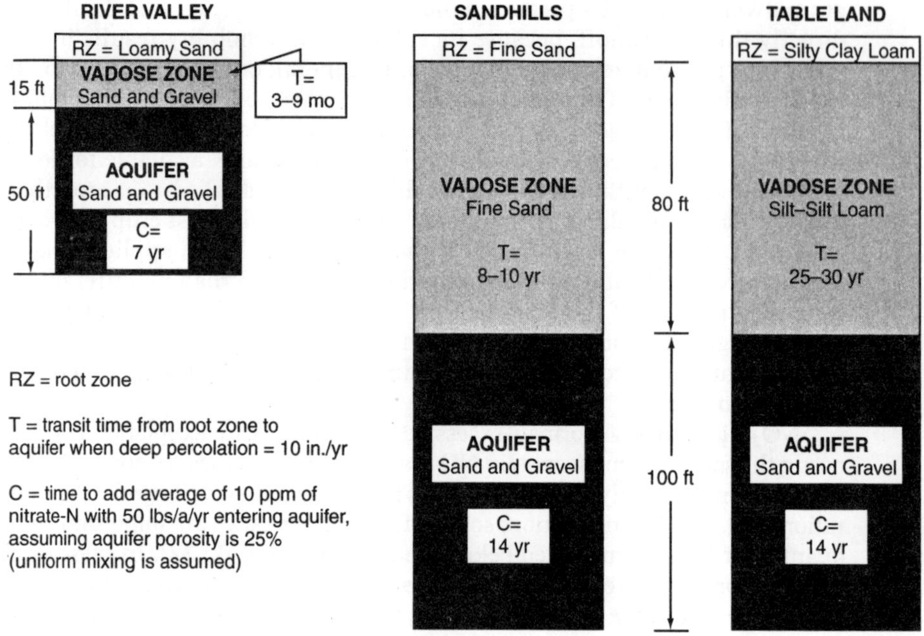

Figure 13-32 **Summary of NO_3-N transit times and aquifer contamination times for three example situations.** ***(Watts, 1992, Univ. of Nebraska.)***

Table 13-22 **Best Management Practices (BMPs) for Controlling N Entry into Surface- and Groundwaters**

Surfacewater Quality	*Groundwater Quality*
Apply appropriate N rate	Apply appropriate N rate
Timely N applications	Timely N applications
Incorporate N	Improved cropping/irrigation management
Proper cropping/residue management	Nitrification and/or urease inhibitors
Control soil erosion	In-season and foliar applications
	Cover crops to scavenge NO_3

SOURCE: Hergert, 1987, Soil Sci. Soc. Amer. Spec. Publ. No. 21.

the quantity of water transport below the root zone during irrigation (Fig. 13-33). After the irrigation season, NO_3^- leaching is greater down field. NO_3^- leaching can be as problematic under center-pivot systems with similar overirrigation and/or overfertilization (Fig. 13-34).

N Best-Management Practices (BMP) Many site, environment, and management factors interact to reduce potential NO_3^- contamination of surface- and groundwaters. Understanding the principles involved in N availability and transport to surface- and groundwaters is essential for identifying the BMPs for reducing the impact of N use on water quality. Figures 13-35 and 13-36 illustrate how these principles direct appropriate best-management strategies.

BMPs for N can be categorized into those essential for groundwater and surfacewater (Table 13-22). Understanding the impact of each N BMP requires knowledge of how

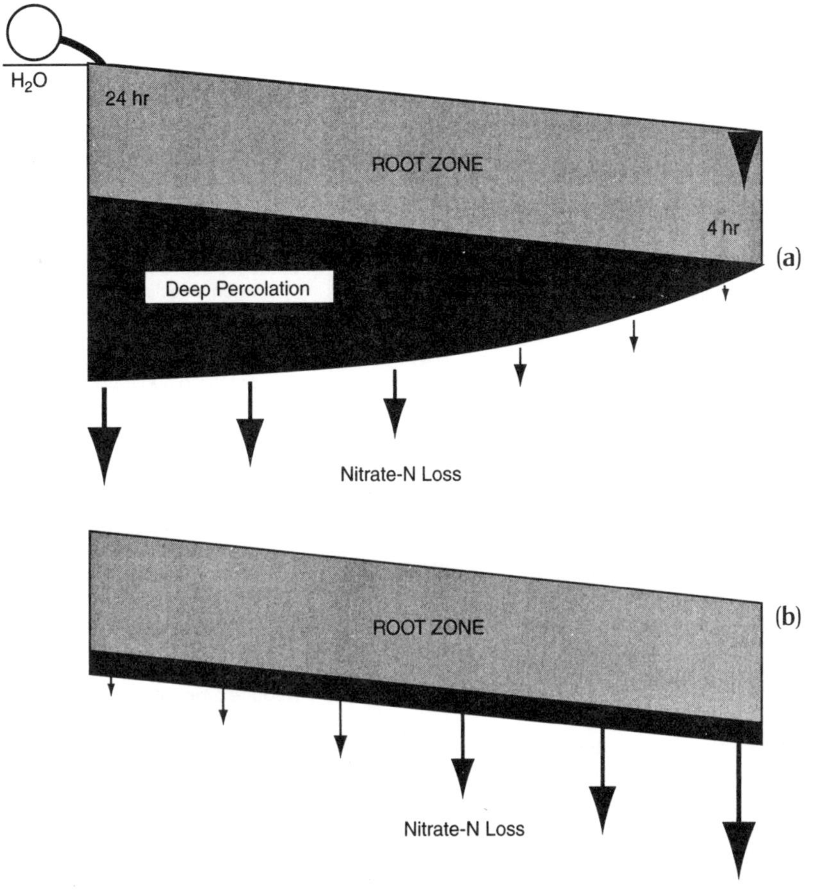

Figure 13-33 **NO_3-leaching pattern during the irrigation season (a) and off-season (b) for long set times and/or long irrigation runs.** *(Watts, 1992, Univ. of Nebraska.)*

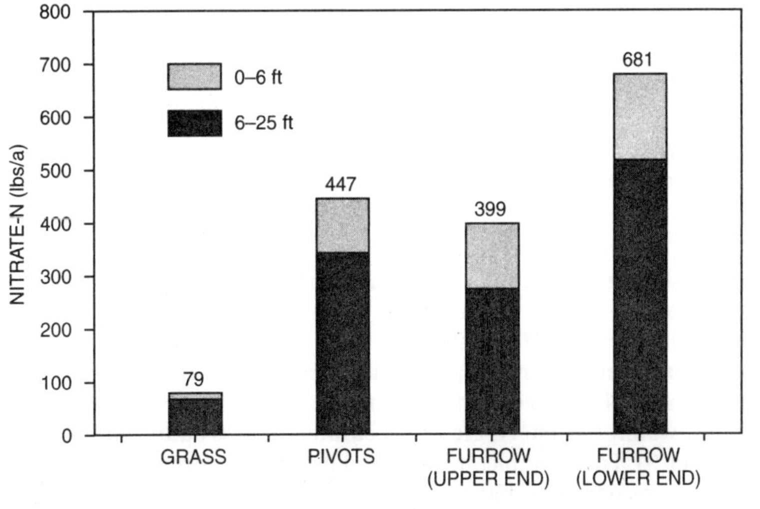

Figure 13-34 **Average lbs/a of nitrate-N in deep-soil samples under 4 center-pivot and 10 furrow-irrigated corn fields.** *(Watts, 1992, Univ. of Nebraska.)*

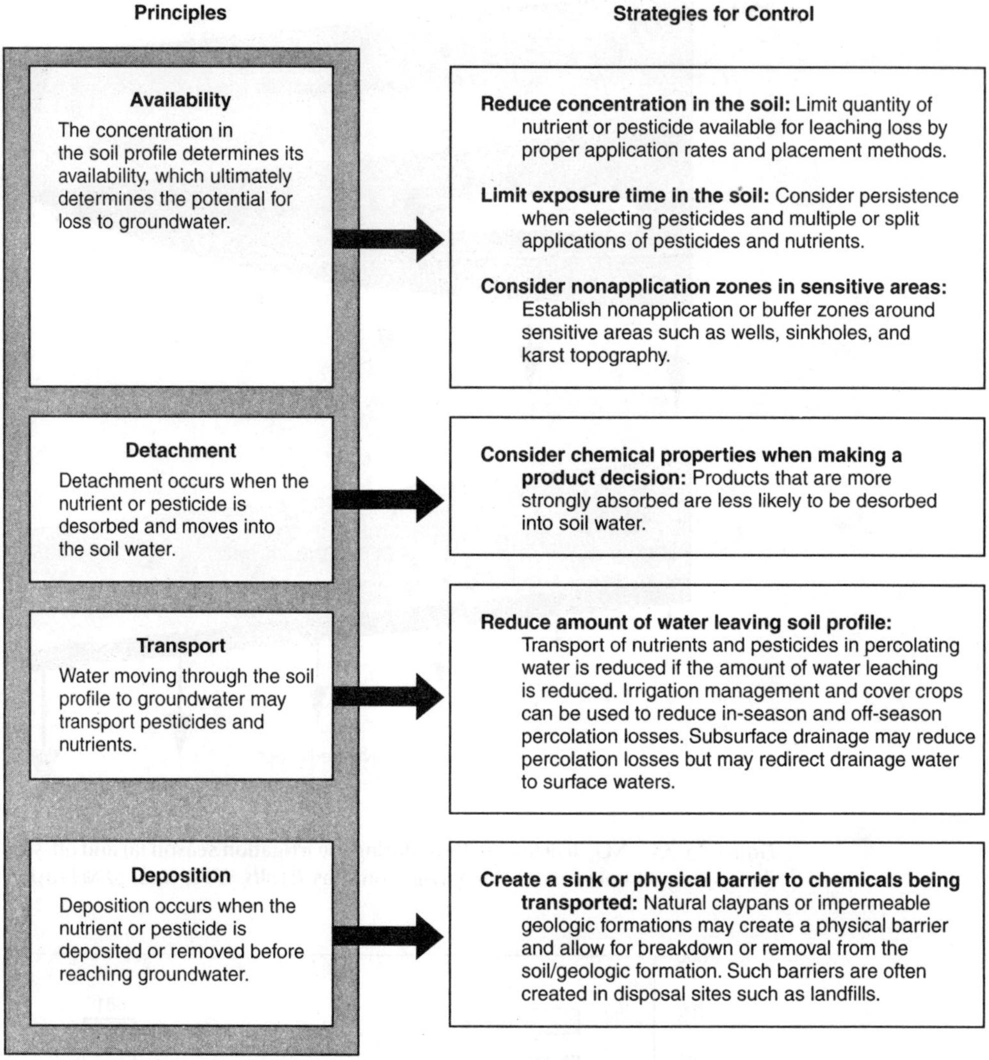

Figure 13-35 **Principles and control strategies of nutrient and pesticide losses to groundwater.** *(*Best Mgmt. Practices for Wheat, *1994, National Assoc. Wheat Growers, Washington, D.C.)*

N transformations in soils influence native N availability (Chapter 4), crop N requirements (Chapter 9), and N management for optimum productivity and maximum recovery by the plant (Chapter 10). The material developed in these chapters provides the foundation for nutrient-management plans that incorporate the appropriate BMPs. An environmentally sound N-management plan involves evaluation of all native N sources (soil OM, irrigation water, legume N, etc.) to accurately assess additional N requirements (Table 13-23; Chapter 9). For example, if estimated crop N requirement is the same under two different systems, recognition that residual NO_3^- is greater under one system than the other results in a lower N recommendation (Table 13-24).

Principles	Strategies for Control
Availability The concentration of a nutrient or pesticide in a shallow zone at the soil surface (often only 1/3 to 1/10 of an inch in thickness) determines its potential to enter surfacewater. Nitrate is soluble in water and can move into surfacewater through lateral subsurface flow or drainage tile.	**Reduce concentration at the soil surface:** Concentration may be lowered by reducing application rates, incorporation, banding, integrated crop management, and foliar application. For nitrate, practices that optimize N-use efficiency and limit the amount of nitrate available for overland flow, subsurface lateral flow, or tile drainage flow. **Limit exposure time at the soil surface:** Consider pesticide persistence and multiple applications of pesticides and nutrients. **Consider nonapplication zones in sensitive areas:** Establish nonapplication or buffer zones around sensitive areas such as delivery points into streams and field borders.
Detachment Situation when nutrients and pesticides are dissolved in runoff water or when soil particles to which nutrients or pesticides are absorbed and detached from the soil are moved off-site.	**Delay the onset of runoff after rainfall begins:** Allow time for nitrate and some pesticides to move below the soil surface, reducing detachment into overland flow. Practices include no tillage, mulch tillage, contour farming, and infiltration enhancement. **Reduce effect of raindrop splash:** Crop residue and green cover can limit the effect of raindrop splash on the detachment of nutrients and pesticides.
Transport Runoff that contains both water and soil particles may transport nutrients and pesticides to surfacewaters. For many pesticides and nitrates, the carrier is overland flow water. For phosphates, ammonium, and a few strongly absorbed pesticides, the carrier in overland flow is sediment.	**Reduce soil erosion losses:** Reduce transport of ammonium, phosphorus, and pesticides attached to sediment. Practices include no tillage, mulch tillage, contour cropping, and terraces. **Reduce overland flow:** Reduce transport of both water and sediment. Practices include increased crop residue levels and contour farming.
Deposition Deposition occurs when the transport of nutrients and pesticides in overland flow or on sediments is stopped before it reaches the receiving water body.	**Create traps for dissolved pollutants and sediment:** Provide a mechanism for nutrients and pesticides to be deposited as they leave the field. Deposition may be difficult to achieve for nitrates or many pesticides, especially when the flow becomes concentrated in small channels. A control practice includes vegetative filter strips. Traps are most effective in reducing sediment and soil-bound pollutants.

Figure 13-36 **Principles and control strategies for nutrient and pesticide entry into surfacewater.** (Best Mgmt. Practices for Wheat, *1994, National Assoc. Wheat Growers, Washington, D.C.*)

Table 13-23 Typical Credits Used for Estimating Crop N Requirements

N Source	*N Credit*
Soil OM	30 lbs N/% OM
Residual soil NO_3	3.6 lbs N/ppm NO_3-N
Manure	10.0 lbs N/t manure
Irrigation water	2.7 lbs N/acre-ft x ppm NO_3-N
Previous alfalfa/sweet clover	50–100 lbs/a of N
Other previous legume crop	30 lbs/a of N

Table 13-24 An Example Data Set from Nebraska to Determine N-Fertilizer Recommendations for Corn with Two Irrigation Systems

Data	*Conventional*	*Center Pivot*
Residual soil N		
0–20 cm (mg/kg NO_3-N)	13.5	12.3
20–90 cm (mg/kg NO_3-N)	7.2	4.5
0–90 cm (mg/kg NO_3-N)	8.8	6.2
% OM (0–20 cm)	1.77	1.9
Irrigation water (mg/l NO_3-N)	30	30
Expected yield (Mg/ha) (21.4) (expected yield) + 39	12.6	12.6
Estimated water application (cm)	25	25
Estimated crop N need (kg/ha)	309	309
N credits		
Residual soil N (kg/ha) = 9 (mg/kg NO_3-N)	79	56
Soil OM (kg/ha) = 2.5 (expected yield) (%OM)	56	60
Irrigation water (kg/ha) = 0.1 (cm depth) (mg/l NO_3-N)	75	75
Others		
Soybean (50 kg ha21)	0	0
Alfalfa (135–170 kg ha21)	0	0
Manure (variable)	0	0
Fertilizer N required (kg/ha)	99	118

SOURCE: Rice et al., 1995, *Fertilizer Research*, 42:89.

The most important factor in reducing NO_3^- leaching potential is to minimize the quantity of soil profile NO_3^- after harvest and before the next crop has established a root system extensive enough to recover residual profile NO_3^-. Important N BMPs include:

N Rate. The most important N BMP is identifying the correct N rate required to maximize yield. When N rate exceeds yield potential, residual NO_3^- may leach if water is sufficient to move below the root zone (Fig. 4-25; Fig. 13-37). Using a linear-plateau model, Figure 13-38 shows that significant NO_3^- accumulation occurred only when N rate exceeded that required for optimum yield. N recommendations should be evaluated for each individual situation.

N Timing. The importance of application timing was discussed in Chapter 10. Figure 13-39 illustrates substantial reduction in total N susceptible to N leaching with four split applications compared with a single application.

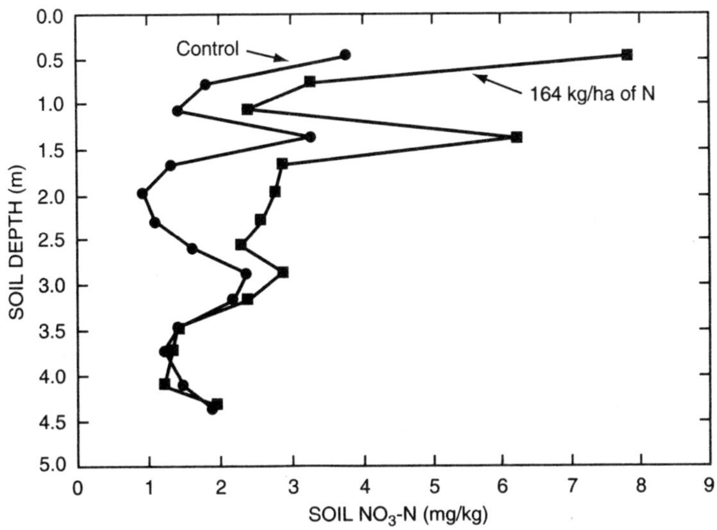

Figure 13-37 **Soil NO_3-N in conventionally tilled corn-wheat rotations when urea was applied at 0 or 164 kg N/ha in April 1990 *(sampled in March 1991).***

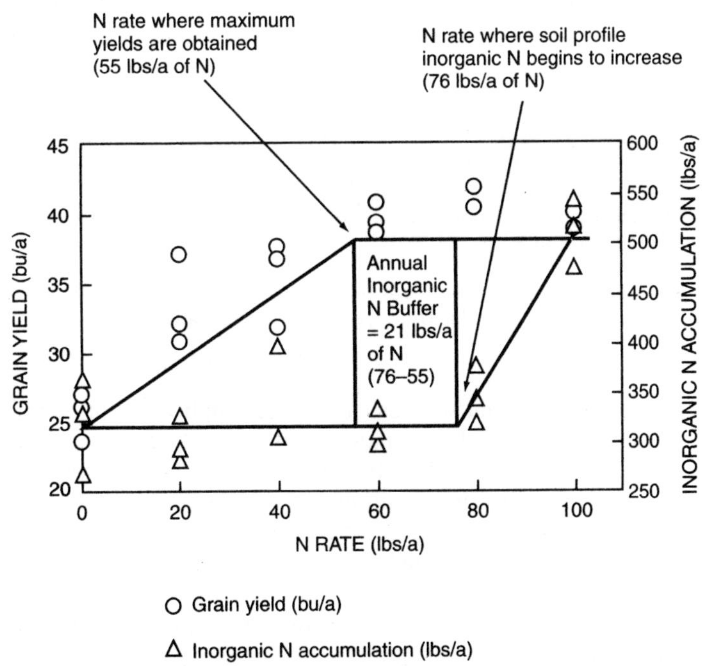

Figure 13-38 **The relationship between inorganic N accumulation and annual N applied and the estimated soil-plant N buffering zone. *(Raun and Johnson, 1995,* Agron. J., *87:827.)***

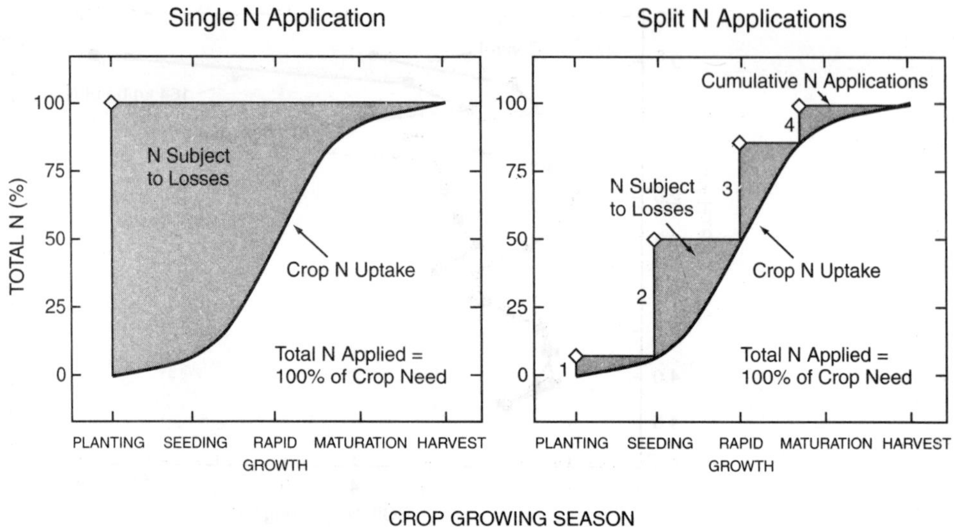

Figure 13-39 **General estimations of potential soil-N losses occurring when N fertilizer is applied in a single or in split applications.** ***(Waskom et al., 1994,*** **BMPs for Irrigated Agric.,** ***Colorado Water Resources Institute Report No. 184.)***

Table 13-25 **Effect of N Source and Placement on Corn Yield, Leaf N Concentration, and Grain N Concentration in Both Plow and No-Till Production Systems**

	Plow			*No-till*		
N Source and Placement	*Yield*	*Ear Leaf*	*Grain*	*Yield*	*Ear Leaf*	*Grain*
	bu/a	*% N*	*% N*	*bu/a*	*% N*	*% N*
UAN broadcast, unincorporated	145	2.48	1.21	128	1.63	1.08
UAN broadcast, incorporated	153	2.34	1.23	—	—	—
UAN injected	149	2.44	1.29	156	2.13	0.94

SOURCE: Mengel, 1989, Purdue Univ., personal communication.

N Placement. In most cases, subsurface application of N will reduce N volatilization losses (Chapter 4). In permanent pasture or turf systems, subsurface applications are less desirable than surface-broadcast-applied N; however, spoke-wheel and other innovative application technologies offer opportunities to maximize recovery of N by the crop (Chapter 10). In reduced-tillage systems, which are critical to ensuring long-term soil and crop productivity, subsurface application of N is essential to maximizing crop recovery of applied N and reducing N immobilization by high-C-containing crop residues. Table 13-25 illustrates the importance of subsurface application of N on yield.

Crop Rotation. There are several issues relative to cropping systems that can influence N-management decisions. Figure 13-40 illustrates that, except for fallow systems that produce the largest amount of leachable N (no N uptake during periods of N mineralization), rotations that include legumes may contribute more leachable N

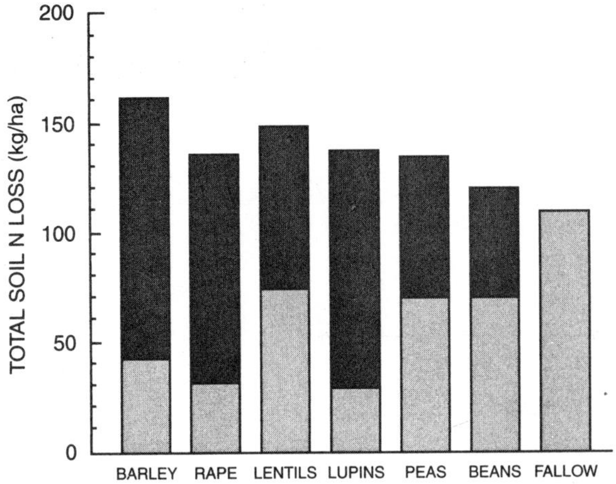

Figure 13-40 **Contribution of net soil-N uptake by grain crop sown in spring 1988 (■) and apparent leaching losses during the following autumn/winter (▒) to the total loss of soil N from spring 1988 to spring 1989.**

Table 13-26 **Comparison of Soil Profile NO_3-N with Soil Solution NO_3-N Below the Root Zone**

	NO_3-N	
Treatment	*Soil Profile (0–0.45m) May, June, July**	*Soil Solution (1.2–1.5m) June, July, August*
	mg/kg (mg/l)	*mg/l*
Corn (1990)		
No-till	14 (56)	9
Tilled	19 (77)	10
Wheat (1991)		
No-till	4 (16)	4
Tilled	6 (24)	10
Beans		
1990	26 (105)	12
1991	33 (133)	27

*Used different times to compensate for the time necessary for the soil solution to flow from the surface to the 1.2- to 1.5-m depth.
SOURCE: Meek et al., 1994, *Soil Sci. Soc. Am. Jour.* 58:1464.

than nonlegume-based systems. Table 13-26 shows that soybean in the rotation increased soil-profile NO_3^- as well as NO_3^- below the root zone.

When soil tests suggest that significant, residual soil-profile NO_3^- is present after harvest, cover crops may recover significant quantities of NO_3^- to reduce N transport to groundwater. Figure 13-41 shows that as N applied to corn increased (with subsequent increase in residual NO_3^-), recovery by the successive oat cover crop was also greater.

N from Organic Wastes. Organic N sources contribute to plant-available N as efficiently as fertilizer N. Unfortunately, if N rates exceed crop N requirement, N mineralization after the peak N uptake period may contribute to leachable N. Figure 13-42 illustrates that increasing poultry manure rate greatly increases soil profile NO_3^-.

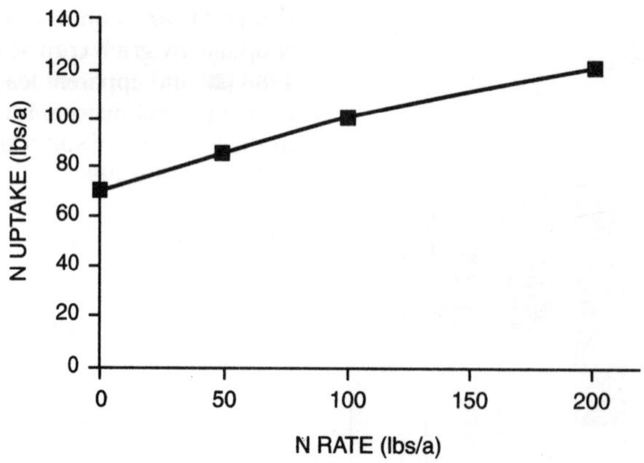

Figure 13-41 **Effect of N rates applied to corn on total N uptake by the succeeding oat crop.**

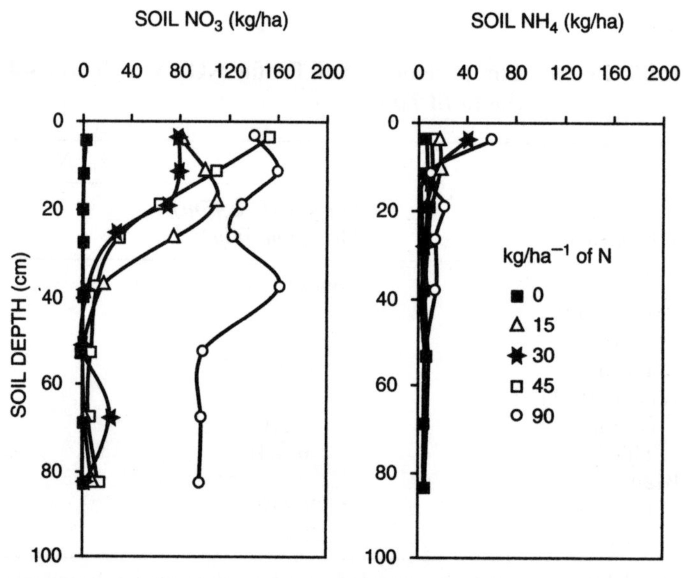

Figure 13-42 **Influence of poultry manure N application on soil NO_3 and NH_4 in the soil profile. NH_4 concentrations are less than NO_3 concentrations because of the significant nitrification that occurs throughout the growing season, regardless of plant N uptake.** ***(Scott et al., 1995, Arkansas Agric. Exp. Bull. 947.)***

Application of sewage sludge materials can produce the same results (Fig. 13-43). Compared with split applications of fertilizer N, manure N can result in greater profile NO_3^- content after harvest (Table 13-27).

Riparian Buffers. Although retaining surface residue cover through conservation tillage systems can substantially reduce soil erosion, riparian buffer zones are effective in reducing NO_3^- in subsurface flow and in filtering sediments and nutrients in surface runoff water (Fig. 13-44). Depending on the width of the grass and/or forest buffer, 60 to 95% reduction in sediment can occur (Table 13-28). Reduction of N and

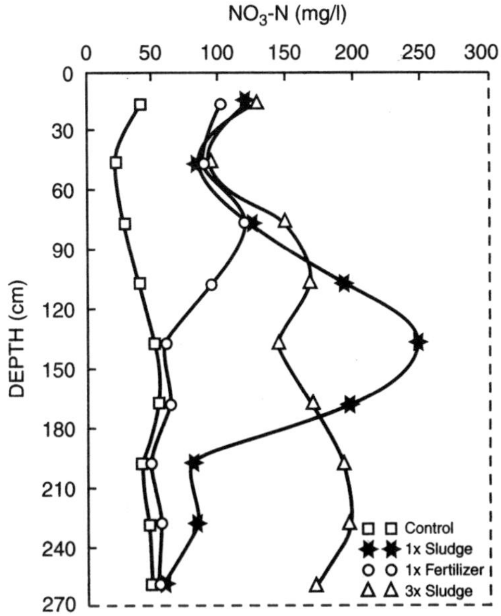

Figure 13-43 **Influence of sludge- or fertilizer-treated soil on profile NO_3-N. 1×, 3× represents one and three annual applications, respectively.** *(Artiola and Pepper, 1992,* **Biology Fertility of Soils,** *14:30.)*

Table 13-27 **N-Management Effects on Corn Yield and NO_3-N Concentration in Soil Water**

N Source	*N Rate*	*N Timing*	*Grain Yield*	*Soil Water NO_3-N†*
	lbs/a		*bu/a*	*ppm*
Anhydrous NH_3	150	Spring	177	12
Anhydrous NH_3	75 + 75	Spring + Sidedress	173	10
Hog manure	196*	Spring	184	41

*Estimated available N. Total N applied was 315 lbs/a, half being inorganic and half organic; 100% availability from inorganic N in year of application.

†Measured at 5-ft depth by suction lysimeters at end of second year.

SOURCE: Griffith, 1989, *Better Crops,* 73:23.

P in surface runoff ranges between 10 and 80%; the wider the buffer area, the greater the deposition of nutrients.

The reduction in NO_3^- concentration in subsurface flow occurs through denitrification (Fig. 13-45). Anaerobic denitrifying microorganisms obtain C from root mass in the buffer zone and convert NO_3^- to N_2 gas. In many crop production fields, the soil solution NO_3^- concentration can range between 15 and 40 ppm N after harvest. Figure 13-46 shows that denitrification reduces NO_3^-concentration to < 10 ppm N, depending on buffer width.

N BMP Summary Although the range of options for BMPs should be evaluated for each site, the decisions on which management practices are utilized depend on the skill of the manager and the particular situation. Table 13-29 compares a conventional production system with one that uses BMPs appropriate for the local environment and cropping system. Although 30% higher N rates were applied, appropriate N management (soil and tissue

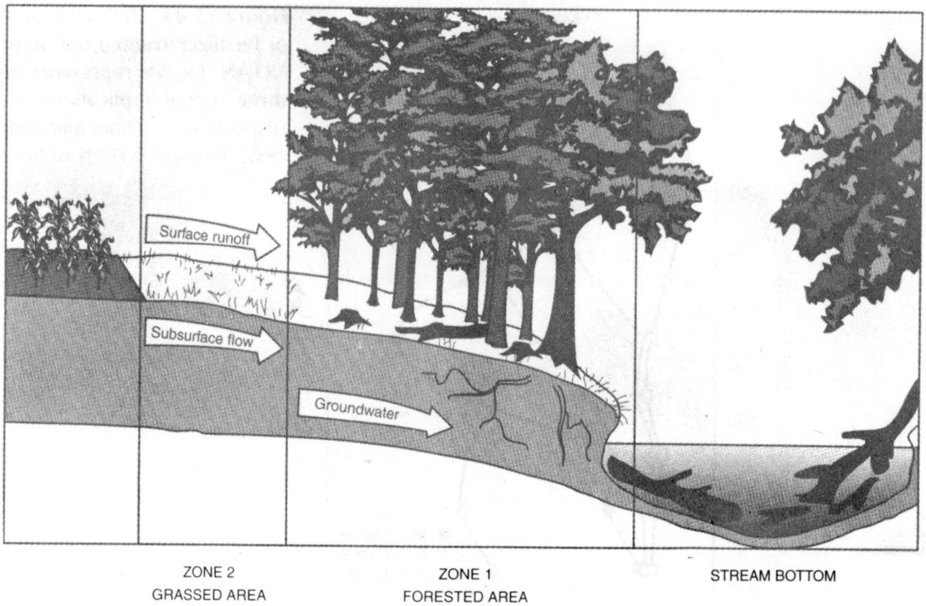

Figure 13-44 **Schematic of the two-zone riparian forest buffer system.** *(Modified from Lowrance et al., 1995, U.S. EPA, Washington, D.C., 903-R-95-004.)*

testing, N timing, reduced tillage, crop rotation, etc.) increased N utilization and decreased the soil profile NO_3^- after harvest. In fact, BMPs substantially increased yield and profit while reducing the quantity of leachable N.

This example illustrates why producer adoption of BMPs is essential to maximizing profit and minimizing the impact of N-use on the environment. It is also important to recognize that substantially less land was required to produce the same yield with the BMPs. Our continued ability to produce sufficient food for an expanding population depends on continued increases in crop yield per unit land area. Under increasing production pressure, conservation of our limited natural resources (quantity and quality) can only occur with full adoption of existing BMPs and continued development of new agricultural technologies that will improve crop N-use efficiency essential to reducing environmental risks associated with N use.

Phosphorus

While industrial wastes, municipal wastes, and urban runoff contribute to P loading in certain watersheds, P applied directly to cropland though fertilizers and animal wastes can be primary contaminant sources in watersheds with predominately agricultural land uses.

In general, 20% of fertilizer P is recovered by crops during the first growing season after application. When P is applied at recommended rates, soil-test P levels generally remain the same or increase slightly with time depending on P rate, soil type, and crop removal. When animal waste application rates are based on crop N requirement, P rates can be 2 to 5 times the crop P requirement. Continued long-term application of P exceeding

Table 13-28 Effects of Riparian Buffers on Reductions of Sediment and Nutrients from Field Surface Runoff

Buffer		*Sediment*			*N**			*P**		
Width	*Type*	*Input*	*Output*	*Reduction*†	*Input*	*Output*	*Reduction*†	*Input*	*Output*	*Reduction*†
m		*mg/l*		%	*mg/l*		%	*mg/l*		%
4.6§	Grass	7,284	2,841	61.0	14.11	13.55	4.0	11.30	8.09	28.5
9.2§	Grass	7,284	1,852	74.6	14.11	10.91	22.7	11.30	8.56	24.2
19.90‡	Forest	6,480	661	89.8	27.59	7.08	74.3	5.03	1.51	70.0
23.6ǀ	Grass/forest	7,284	290	96.0	14.11	3.48	75.3	11.30	2.43	78.5
28.2#	Grass/forest	7,284	188	97.4	14.11	2.80	80.1	11.30	2.57	77.2

*N = NO_3–N + NH_4–N (dissolved + adsorbed) + organic N (soluble + particulate); P = dissolved + particulate.

† % reduction = 100 * (input − output)/input.

§Calculated from masses of total suspended solids, total N, total P, runoff depth, and plot size (22 × 5 m).

‡ Surface runoff concentrations at 19 m into forest.

ǀ4.6-m grass buffer + 19 m of forest.

#9.2-m grass buffer + 19 m of forest.

SOURCE: Lawrence et al., 1995, U.S. EPA, Washington D.C., 903-R-95–004.

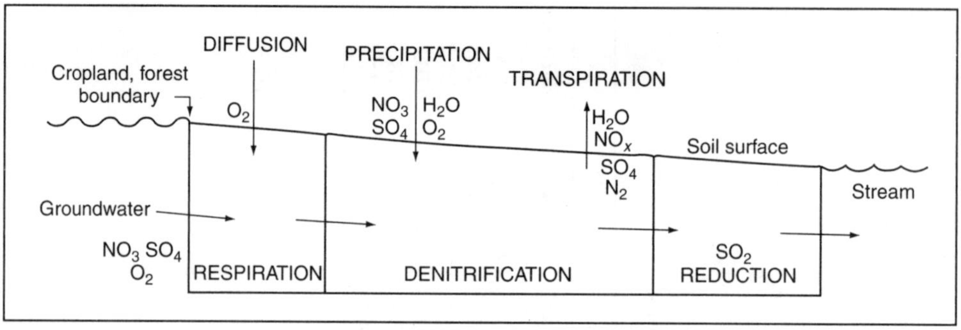

Figure 13-45 Conceptual model of below-ground processes affecting groundwater nutrients in riparian forest. *(From Correll and Weller, 1989,* Freshwater, Wetlands and Wildlife, *p. 9–23, U.S. Dept. Energy.)*

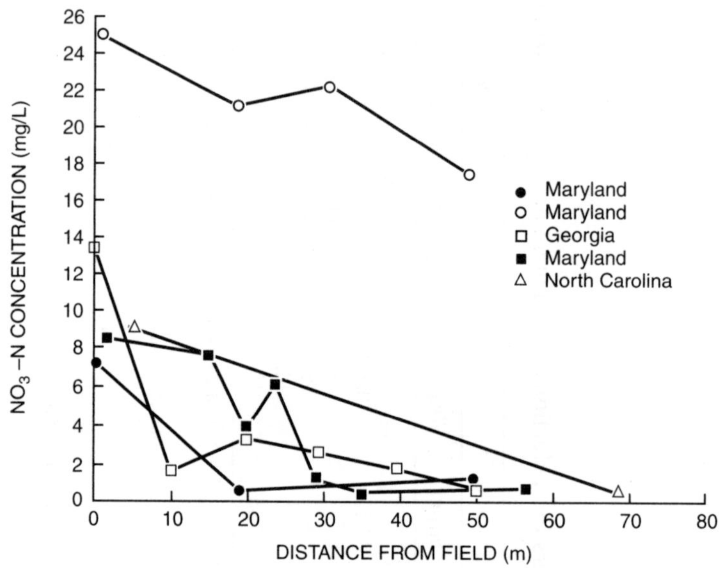

Figure 13-46 Nitrate concentrations in groundwater beneath riparian forests. *(Osmond et al.,* Selected Agric. Best Mgmt. Practices to Control N, *NC Agric. Res. Service Tech. Bull. 311 NC State Univ.)*

crop requirement will increase soil-test P and subsequent risk of P loss to surface- and groundwater (Fig. 13-47).

P transport and loss to surface- and groundwaters involves (1) P adsorbed to eroding sediments, (2) soluble P loss in runoff water, (3) soluble P loss in leaching water, and (4) P losses related to the type of waste P and method of application.

P Adsorbed to Sediments Transported by Water and Wind Although receiving less attention, P can be removed from surface soils in windblown clay and OM sediments containing adsorbed P. With water erosion, P adsorbed to clay and OM leaves the field during

Table 13-29 **N Best-Management Practices for Soft Red Winter Wheat**

Practice	*Previous Management*	*BMP Management*	*Environmental Advantages*
Rotation	Sometimes	Always	Better pest control
Soil test	Unbalanced nutrients	Balanced nutrients	Better N-use efficiency; quicker ground cover; increased crop residue
Seeding rate	1.5 bu/a	22 seeds/ft row	Quicker ground cover
N management	Single application	Use tissue test; split N applications	Increased N efficiency; increased crop residue
Tramlines	None	Establish tramlines at planting	Apply N and other inputs with precision
Pest control	No integrated pest management; no scouting	Use integrated pest management; use scouting	Use pest control only when needed

Expected Results

Parameter	*Previous Management*	*BMP System*
Yield	50 bu/a	85 bu/a
Total production (100 a)	5,000 bu	8,500 bu
Acres to produce 5,000 bu	100	59
N used	100 lbs/a	130 lbs/a
N use efficiency	0.50 bu/lb	0.65 bu/lb
Total N applied (100 a)	10,000 lb	13,000 lb
(59 a)		7,670 lbs
N remaining after harvest	40 lbs/a	34 lbs/a
Production costs, $/a	160	207
Production costs, $/bu	3.20	2.44

SOURCE: D. Brann, 1986, VPI, personal communication to author.

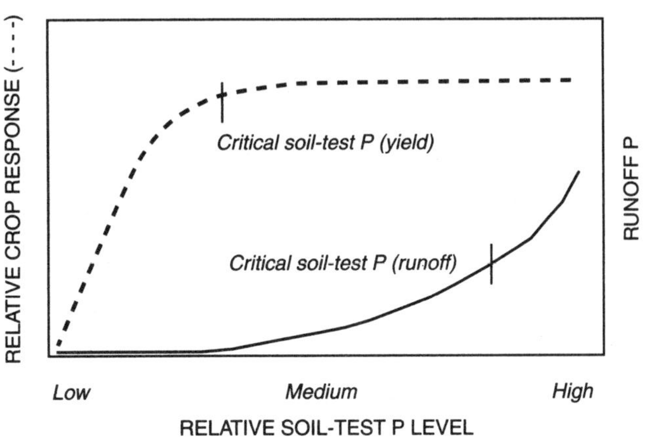

Figure 13-47 **Comparison of an agronomic and environmental interpretation of soil-test P. As the agronomic soil-test P increases above the level where crop response to added P is not expected, dissolved P concentration in runoff increases to levels that could potentially contaminate surfacewater.**

and immediately after storm events through sheet and rill erosion, and may constitute up to 90% of total runoff P from cultivated fields. Sediment P is eventually re-deposited downslope within the field, deposited in a riparian buffer or other sediment-trapping practice, or is delivered to a surfacewater body (Fig. 13-29). The quantity of sediment P delivered to and beyond the field edge is a function of (1) soil erosion rate, (2) amount of sediment deposition within the field, and (3) the quantity of P adsorbed to the eroding soil particles. Beyond the field-edge riparian buffers, sediment basins and water control structures may reduce particulate P delivery to surfacewater. The amount of P adsorbed to soil depends primarily on soil-test P and clay content (Fig. 13-48). As soil-test P and clay content increase, the quantity of adsorbed P and potential sediment-bound P loss increases.

P in Surface Runoff Total soluble P in surface runoff transported to a stream or other water body depends on the quantity of runoff and its P concentration. Dissolved P in runoff is directly related to soil-test P. Since P is adsorbed more strongly in clay soils, higher soil-test P is required for a given runoff P concentration in clay soils compared to sandy soils (Fig. 13-49). This difference is related to P being held less tightly in the sand compared to the clay soil because of differences in P adsorption capacity.

The quantity of runoff water with an individual storm event depends on characteristics of the rainfall (quantity, intensity, and duration), surface soil conditions (residue cover, soil physical properties including water content) that influence infiltration, subsoil properties that influence percolation, and water table depth. During rainfall, water enters

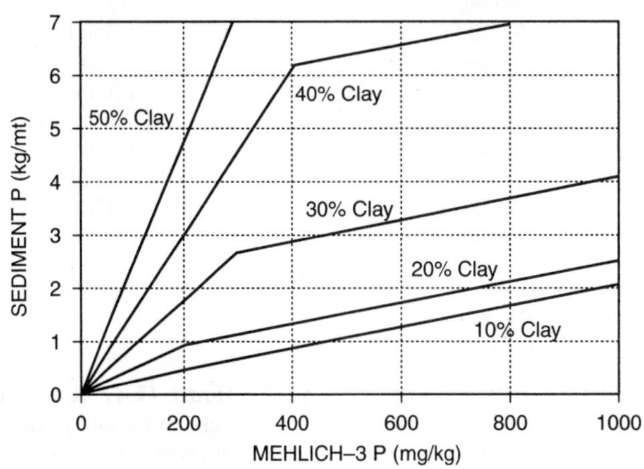

Figure 13-48 **Influence of soil-test P and clay content on quantity of sediment-bound P.** ***(Havlin et al., 2004,*** **J. Animal Sci.** ***82:E277.)***

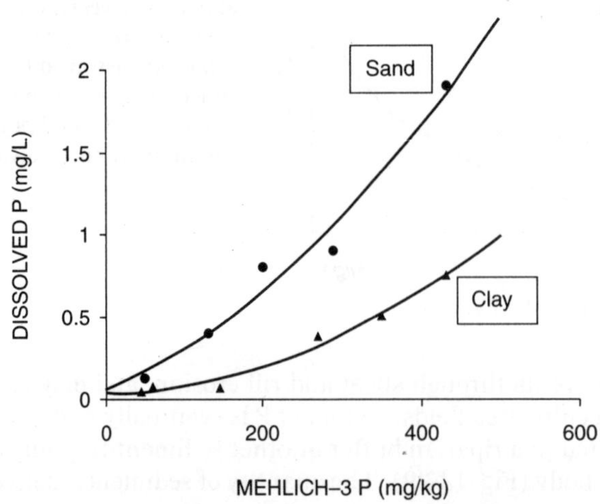

Figure 13-49 **Influence of soil-test P and soil texture on dissolved P in runoff water.** ***(Cox and Hendricks, 2000,*** **J. Environ. Qual.** ***29:1582.)***

the soil through large, surface-connected macropores. Water then diffuses vertically and horizontally into a network of micropores by capillary action or soil moisture tension (SMT). After soil macropores are filled, water moves through micropores toward the highest SMT. Water infiltration or transport rate is governed by the number, size, and continuity of the pore network. The presence of old root channels, earthworm burrows, and natural subsoil structural macropores can substantially increase water infiltration and transport of dissolved P through the profile; however, their presence and influence are difficult to quantify.

P in Leaching Water There is potential for P to leach below the root zone and be transported to surfacewaters through shallow subsurface flow (Fig. 13-29). Since P is strongly adsorbed to clays, P leaching would occur only when % P saturation is increased to very high levels though continued applications of P exceeding crop requirement. Although P leaching is frequently greater in sandy soils (low P adsorption capacity), P leaching can occur in some clay soils through macropore flow.

P leaching commonly occurs in sandy soils where high rates of manure are applied over extended periods (Fig. 13-50). Increasing the manure rate increases potential P transport

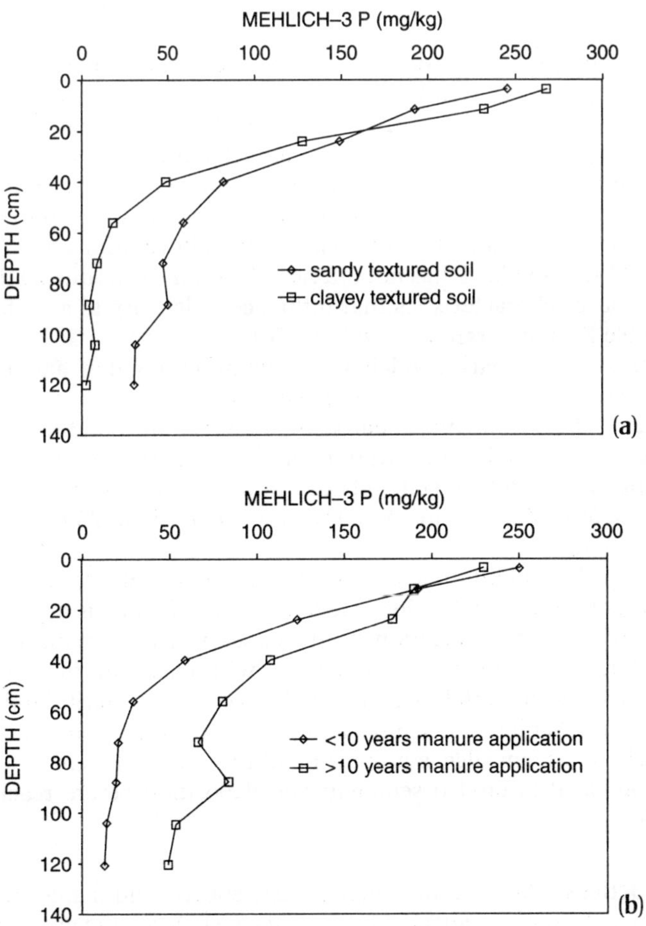

Figure 13-50 **Influence of soil texture (a) and duration after surface waste application (b) on P leaching in a sandy soil.** ***(Ham et al., 2000, Ph.D. Diss., NC State Univ.)***

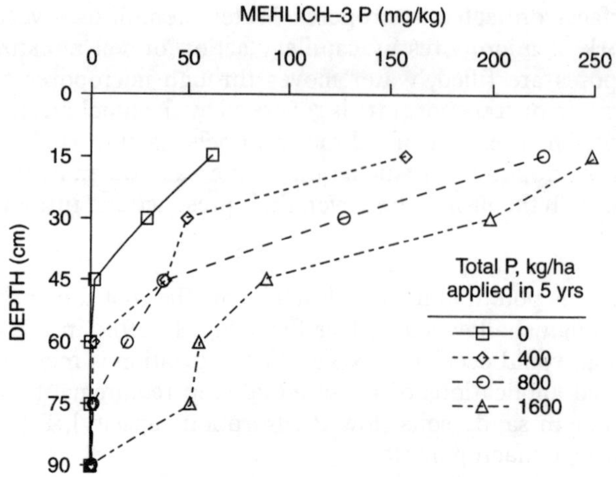

Figure 13-51 Effect of total P applied as swine effluent during a 5-year period on distribution of Mehlich-3 P. *(Reddy et al., 1980,* J. Envir. Qual. *9:86.)*

through the profile (Fig. 13-51). The P leaching potential increases with increasing soil-test P level and sand content.

Waste Source Effects Generally, with fertilizer P applied at recommended rates, P losses are related to sediment transport and to a lesser extent soluble P runoff. With crop N-based applications, animal waste provides 3 to 5 times the crop P requirement, resulting in increased runoff P losses depending on waste source characteristics, application method, soil properties, erosion potential, cropping system, and environmental conditions following P application. During runoff events, soils with low erosion potential have contributed to high soluble P losses. Therefore, consideration of waste source contributions to P transport are important since some of this soluble P has not interacted with the soils during the transport process. The waste source characteristics that influence P delivery to a surfacewater body are total P and soluble P concentrations (Table 13-30).

Total P content of waste sources varies widely with animal species, diet, and method of waste handling and storage. In general, P content in common waste sources follows the order: poultry and turkey > beef > swine > dairy. Increasing P in the animal diet will increase P content in the waste. Total P concentration within a waste source varies depending on the waste handling system, where generally dry litter > liquid > slurry > sludge. Inorganic P comprises 60 to 90% of total P in animal wastes, where about 25 to 80% of total P is water soluble (Table 13-30).

Waste sources with high P solubility result in a high proportion of total P infiltrating into the soil and reducing potential soluble P loss. Generally, runoff P loss is highest during the first runoff event following waste application, with P losses decreasing with subsequent runoff events. Waste materials with high % solid content will remain on the soil surface until decomposed or dissolved with rainfall. Water-soluble P content is a useful indicator of potential P runoff or leaching. While both soluble and particulate P are being transported in runoff water to the field or stream edge, a proportion of this mobile P is retained in the field by adsorption of soluble P to eroded sediment and deposition before reaching the stream or water body edge.

P Best Management Practices Many soil, climate, waste source, and management factors interact to determine potential P transport from fields to surface- and groundwaters.

Table 13-30 **Selected Sources of Animal Wastes and Their P Content**

Waste Source	*Total P*[a]	*Soluble Fraction*[b]	*Soluble P*[c]	*Nonsoluble P*[d]
Beef				
lagoon liquid, kg P · ha-cm^{-1}	15.0	0.80	12.0	3.0
lagoon sludge, g P · l^{-1}	2.7	0.60	1.6	1.1
slurry, g P · l^{-1}	1.2	0.75	0.9	0.3
Dairy				
lagoon liquid, kg P · ha-cm^{-1}	15.0	0.80	12.0	3.0
lagoon sludge, g P · l^{-1}	1.2	0.60	0.7	0.5
scraped, kg P · t^{-1}	1.4	0.60	0.8	0.6
slurry, g P · l^{-1}	0.7	0.75	0.5	0.2
Swine				
lagoon liquid, kg P · ha-cm^{-1}	10.3	0.80	8.2	2.1
lagoon sludge, g P · l^{-1}	2.6	0.40	1.0	1.6
slurry, g P · l^{-1}	1.2	0.60	0.7	0.5
Broiler				
fresh manure, kg P · t^{-1}	3.6	0.25	0.9	2.7
house litter, kg P · t^{-1}	17.3	0.25	4.3	13.0
Stockpiled litter, kg P · t^{-1}	17.5	0.25	4.4	13.1
Layer				
highise manure, kg P · t^{-1}	12.3	0.60	14.8	9.8
lagoon liquid, kg P · ha-cm^{-1}	8.9	0.80	16.2	4.1
lagoon sludge, g P · l^{-1}	4.9	0.50	2.5	2.4
slurry, g P · l^{-1}	3.1	0.60	1.9	1.2
undercage manure, kg P · t^{-1}	6.9	0.50	3.5	3.4
Turkey				
stockpiled litter, kg P · t^{-1}	15.9	0.25	4.0	11.9
house litter, kg P · t^{-1}	11.5	0.25	2.9	8.6

[a]Concentration units vary with waste source.
[b]Wt. basis.
[c]*Soluble P* = Total P × Soluble fraction.
[d]*Nonsoluble P* = Total P − Soluble P.

Reducing potential P loss requires understanding and managing P availability and sediment detachment, transport, and deposition processes (Fig. 13-35; Fig. 13-36). Important P BMPs include:

> *P Rate.* Regardless of the P source, once soil-test P reaches the agronomic optimum level for the specific cropping system and soil, P rates that further increase soil-test P increase potential for P loss (Fig. 9-68; Fig. 13-47).
>
> *P Placement.* Subsurface P placement reduces P susceptible to runoff loss compared to surface applications (Fig. 13-52). Broadcast P applications to pastures or no-till crops results in greater soluble-P loss than in cultivated soils, due to reduced P-soil contact. As the time interval between application and incorporation increases, potential runoff-P loss increases. Incorporation within 2 to 3 days after application is recommended. Subsurface P applications will not reduce potential soluble-P loss by leaching.

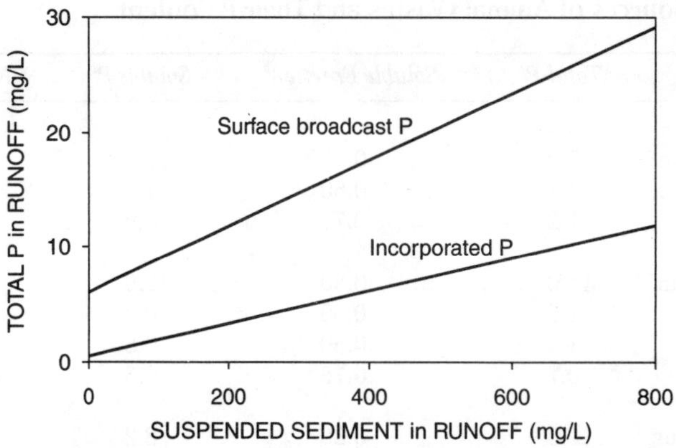

Figure 13-52 **Influence of sediment content in runoff and surface broadcast or incorporated P in manure or fertilizer on total P concentration in runoff.** *(Kleinman et al., 2002,* J. Envir. Qual. *31:2026.)*

P Timimg. Application of animal waste in relation to probability of rainfall is an important factor in managing loss of waste-derived P to surfacewater. Runoff P can be reduced by applying waste during periods of low rainfall probability, with greater reductions occurring on soils with high P-adsorption capacity. Waste application just prior to a rainfall event can lead to significant P losses in runoff.

Soil Conservation Practices. Table 13-31 illustrates the relative effectiveness of selected conservation practices in reducing sediment transport, which would reduce sediment-bound P loss. Generally, increasing surface residue cover will decrease soluble- and sediment-P transport (Fig. 13-53). Because there are many interacting factors that influence soil erosion control, it is difficult to generalize. For example, terracing is one of the most costly conservation practices to implement and consequently is not commonly used unless slopes are > 3 to 5%. However, when properly designed and maintained, terraces can substantially reduce effective slope length, thus reducing the erosive kinetic energy associated with runoff compared to longer slopes. Conservation practices also have cumulative effects. For example, contour cropping and/or contour strip cropping combined with terracing can be more effective than contour cropping or strip cropping alone. If these systems are implemented with no-tillage management, the potential sediment and P loss can be greatly reduced (Fig. 13-19).

Sediment P Trapping Practices. Riparian buffers between the field edge and the surfacewater body can be effective in trapping sediment P, further reducing P loss (Fig. 13-44). Sediments must be evenly distributed within the buffer to maintain long-term effectiveness in reducing sediment P. Vegetative buffers can remove 20 to 80% of sediment P in surface runoff (Table 13-28). Increasing buffer width increases sediment P removed (Fig. 13-54). Although buffers are effective in trapping sediment, they are less effective in trapping soluble P.

Several in-field conservation structures can also help reduce sediment P delivery to the stream edge by 10 to 50%. These include controlled drainage structures, sediment basins, and ponds; ponds will generally maintain standing water throughout the year, while sediment basins do not.

Soluble P Retaining Practices. Unlike sediment P, there are few conservation practices that can reduce soluble P in runoff prior to reaching the stream edge. However, any soil management practice that increases infiltration and decreases runoff (conservation tillage or water control structures) can reduce transfer of soluble P to surfacewater.

Table 13-31 Soil and Crop Management Factors That Reduce Annual Estimated Sediment Loss

RUSLE Factor[a]	*Conservation Practice*	*Relative Reduction*[b]
Slope length (S)	Terraces	high
	Vegetative filter strips[c]	medium
Crop cover (C)[d]	Permanent pasture	high
	No-tillage (standing residue)	high
	No-tillage (residue removed)	medium–low
	50% residue incorporation	medium
	75% residue incorporation	low
Practice factor (P)[e]	Terraces	high
	Contour tillage	low
	Contour conservation tillage	medium–low
	Contour cropping (conventional tillage)	medium–low
	Contour cropping (no-tillage)	medium–high
	Contour strip cropping (conventional tillage)	medium
	Contour strip cropping (no-tillage)	high

[a]Revised Universal Soil Loss Equation. (S) represents the slope length factor, (C) is the crop cover management factor, and (P) represents supporting practice factor.
[b]Relative reduction sediment transport to the field edge as influenced by conservation practices.
[c]Narrow (< 1 m) permanent grass strips planted on the contour. As with terraces, the steeper the slope the smaller the interval between strips.
[d]Crop cover relates the amount of previous crop residue left on the surface and growing crop canopy available to protect the soil surface from raindrop impact. Crop cover factor varies greatly with previous and growing crop. Increasing tillage intensity decreases surface crop residue cover and increases potential sediment loss.
[e]Practice factor reduces estimates of sediment loss with adoption of contour tillage, contour cropping, and contour strip cropping relative to tillage and cropping parallel with the slope direction. Terraces are also included in this factor since terraces are installed on the contour.

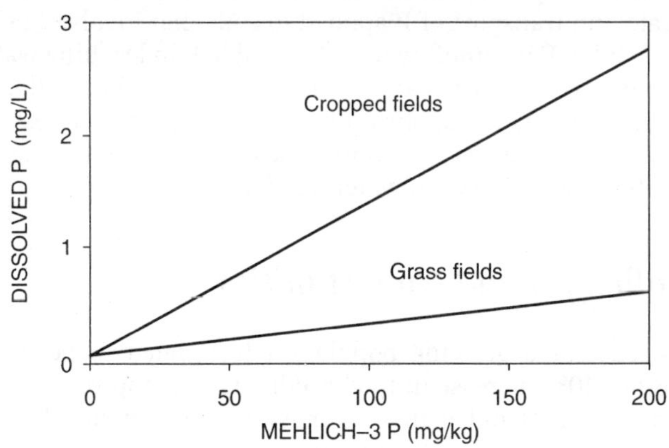

Figure 13-53 **The effect of soil-test P and cropping system on dissolved P in runoff. Cropped fields represent wheat with residue incorporated with a moldboard plow and grassed fields represent native short grass pasture. *(Sharpley et al., 2002,* J. Soil Water Cons, *57:425.)***

P in Animal Feed. About 65% of P in feed grains (corn and soybean) occurs as relatively undigestable phytate-P or phytic acid (Fig. 5-16). Since undigested phytate-P will be excreted by the animal, supplemental P as $CaHPO_4$ is added to the diet to meet P nutritional needs.

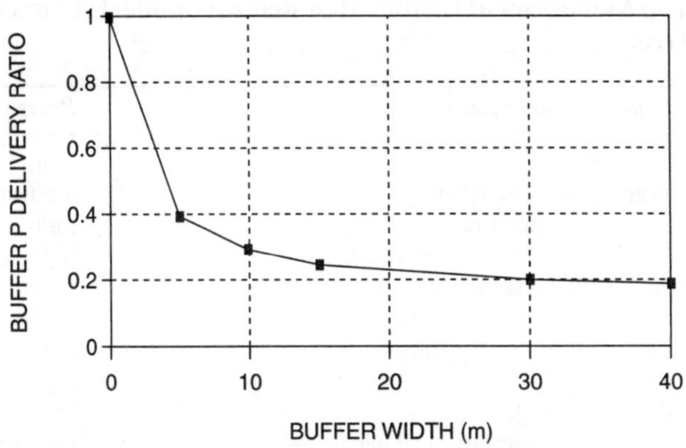

Figure 13-54 **Effect of buffer width on delivery of sediment P.** *(Daniels and Gilliam, 1996,* Soil Sci. Soc. Amer. J., *60:246.)*

Phytase is an enzyme that facilitates hydrolysis of phytate-P into digestible inorganic P ($H_2PO_4^-$). Added to the feed ration, phytase improves grain-P digestibility, reducing the need for supplemental P. Phytase in diets can reduce manure P in poultry 25 to 35% and in swine 25 to 60%, which represents a significant reduction in potential P loss associated with land-applied wastes.

In addition, advances in barley, corn, and soybean genetics have resulted in low-phytate-P hybrids and varieties. Currently, these new genetics have shown reduced yield potential relative to traditional high phytate-P genetics. With continued developments, such as the combination of high-yielding low-phytate genetics and phytase supplemented diets, the manure-P applied to fields can be reduced 30 to 40%, decreasing potential applied-P impact on water quality.

P BMP Summary Recently, changes in nutrient management guidelines suggested by the USDA resulted in development of methods or tools to estimate the quantity of P delivered to surface- and groundwaters. These P-loss assessment tools require a technical service provider to understand fate and transport of P applied to soils that involve (1) P adsorbed to eroding sediments, (2) soluble P in runoff water, (3) soluble P in leaching water, and (4) P losses related to the specific waste sources and management. In addition, the potential P loss associated with fertilizer or waste P applications can be estimated. P-loss assessment tools enable the user to assess the impact of adoption of P BMPs on reducing potential P loss, and thus will reduce the risk of P-use on water quality.

Epilogue–Agricultural Challenges and Opportunities

Meeting food security needs for a growing population (estimated to be 9.5 billion in 50 years) will require a 30 to 40% increase in food production on approximately the same agricultural land area used today. Land managers must adopt economically viable technologies that maintain, enhance, or protect the productive capacity of our soil resources to ensure future food and fiber supplies. While organic nutrient sources are important to meeting the nutritional needs of higher-yielding cropping systems, inorganic fertilizer nutrients will remain the predominant nutrient source. The challenge to the agricultural community is to ensure maximum recovery of applied nutrients, regardless of source, through use of diverse soil, crop, water, nutrient, and other input management technologies to maximize plant productivity. Accomplishing this will significantly reduce nutrient losses to the environment. Protecting water and air quality is essential to the health of diverse ecosystems on Earth, which directly impact our quality of life.

The study of soil fertility and nutrient management is a large and critical component of our agricultural systems. Throughout the text, the relationships between nutrients and other essential inputs and management factors were presented. Sustaining the productivity of agriculture demands a thorough and functional understanding of the interactions between nutrients, water, plant growth, and many other factors that influence plant health and yield. Hopefully you will continue your search for new knowledge and experiences that will help secure a productive agriculture.

Study Questions

1. Why are long-term yield trends likely to be misleading as a measure of soil productivity? What might happen to yield trends if plant breeding studies ceased?
2. What is the aim of a crop and soil management program? How does it relate to agricultural sustainability?
3. Explain why additions of N equal to crop removal help to reduce the loss of OM.
4. Under what soil conditions might a corn small-grain alfalfa rotation be preferable to corn plus commercial N as well as other nutrients each year? Under what condition may the latter cropping system be preferable?
5. What influences how much of its total N a legume will fix?
6. On what soils in your area could OM be increased? Under what soil conditions in your area would additions of OM be beneficial other than for the nutrients supplied?
7. Loss of surface soil varies considerably with the soil. In what soils in your area is the loss likely to be most serious? Explain the statement that a primary cause of erosion is depletion of soil fertility.
8. List the advantages of rotations and monoculture.
9. What cropping systems have depleted P and K in soils in your area? Explain. In what cropping systems have these elements been increased? Explain.
10. In what ways might N, P, and K be lost other than by crop removal? In what ways other than fertilization might the supplies be increased?
11. In what cropping systems might winter cover crops fit? Why?
12. Why will the fertility level of a given farm gradually decrease if manure is the only carrier of plant nutrients used? Explain the fertility distribution problem in a pasture.
13. What is conservation tillage? What are the advantages?
14. Would no-till fit in your area? If so, where? Why?
15. Is planting sometimes more difficult under no-till? Explain.
16. Describe how BMPs protect surface and subsurface water quality.
17. Detail the essential components of N BMPs.
18. How do riparian buffers function to enhance water quality?
19. Nitrate leaching into the groundwater has become an increasingly sensitive issue among both rural and urban constituents. You have been asked to give a short presentation to an urban consumer group on agricultural technologies that reduce the

potential for fertilizer N movement to groundwater. What management technologies would you identify/discuss?

20. A farmer uses conventional tillage on a 2.5% OM soil (0 to 6 in. sample depth). Soil loss by erosion on this soil is 20 tons/ac/yr. How much total soil N does he lose each year?

21. Irrigated fescue has a rooting depth of 6 ft in a sandy loam soil. The fertilizer N requirement is 140 lb N/a and the irrigation requirement is 14 inches/a for the crop year. Assuming all the fertilizer is applied on March 15, calculate the maximum quantity of irrigation water that could be applied at one time which would prevent NO_3 leaching (Volumetric water content = 12%).

22. Fertilizer uptake efficiency by the crop is 45%. If all the water were applied at once, calculate the potential NO_3 loss if 30% of the applied fertilizer N were immobilized.

23. Soil water content of a loam soil is 20% by volume. The grower applied 100 lb N/a preplant to irrigated barley. He will add 12″ of water throughout the growing season. How much NO_3 will be lost by leaching if fertilizer efficiency is 50% and maximum rooting depth is 4 ft.? (Assume uniform leaching and 20% fertilizer N immobilized by OM.)

24. Describe the pathways of P loss in agricultural soils.

25. How does P source and management influence potential P loss?

26. P is strongly adsorbed to soil clays. How is it possible that P can leach in soils?

Selected References

Lal, R., and Stewart, B. A. 1994. *Soil processes and water quality. Advances in soil science.* Boca Raton, Fla.: Lewis Publ.

Paul, E. A., Paustian, K., Elliot, E. T., and Cole, C. V. 1997. *Soil organic matter in temperate agroecosystems.* Boca Raton, Fla.: CRC Press.

Power, J. F. (Ed.). 1987. *The role of legumes in conservation tillage systems.* Madison, Wis.: Soil Conservation Society of America.

Sprague, M. A., and Triplett, G. B. (Eds.). 1986. *No-tillage and surface tillage agriculture: The tillage revolution.* New York: John Wiley & Sons.

Tate, R. L. 1987. *Soil organic matter: Biological and ecological effects.* New York: John Wiley & Sons.

Troeh, F. R., Hobbs, J. A., and Donahue, R. L. 1991. *Soil and water conservation.* Englewood Cliffs, N.J.: Prentice Hall.

Index

A

D

E

F

G

H

I

N

T

U

V

W

Y

Z

N deficiency in grain sorghum. Chlorosis occurs on older, lower leaves first as N is translocated to newer, developing leaves. Yellowing proceeds from the leaf tip down the midrib in a V-shaped pattern. Eventually necrosis or "firing" of the entire lower leaves occurs as the plant matures.

N deficiency in corn. Necrosis of lowest leaf and chlorosis of the 2nd and 3rd leaf (tip only) from the bottom is shown on the N-deficient plant on the left. Plant on the right is N sufficient.

N deficiency in alfalfa. Chlorosis occurs initially on edges of lower leaves. Necrosis of leaf edges and entire leaf occurs as plant matures. Normal plant is on the right.

P deficiency in corn. Stunted plants, delayed maturity, and progression of dark green to purple discoloration of lower leaf edges. Purple discoloration does not occur in all grasses.

P deficiency in wheat. Plants on left exhibit poor tillering, stunted growth, delayed maturity, and yellowing of lower leaves. Normal plants are on the right.

P deficiency in alfalfa. Plant is stunted and older leaves are small and exhibit dark green to purple discoloration. Normal plant is on the right.

K deficiency in corn. Chlorosis and necrosis of edges of lower leaves, as K is translocated to newer, developing leaves. Midrib usually remains green.

K deficiency in soybean. Chlorosis and necrosis of lower leaf edges where tissue along veins and base of leaf remain green.

K deficiency in alfalfa. Small white spots occur along leaf margins, although yellowing of leave edges can also occur. Normal plant is on the right.

S deficiency in corn. Plant is stunted with light green and/or yellow leaves. Although usually occurring on newer leaves, symptoms can be observed on the entire plant. S deficiency symptoms can be confused with N deficiency.

S deficiency in wheat. Chlorotic newer leaves are observed, as S is not translocated from older to newer leaves as readily as N.

S deficiency in soybean. Plant is stunted with light green and/or yellow newer leaves.

Mg deficiency in corn. Interveinal yellowing or white discoloration beginning with lower leaves, as Mg is translocated from older to newer leaves. Can be confused with Fe deficiency.

Fe deficiency in grain sorghum. Severely stunted plant with interveinal chlorosis of entire leaf, occuring in newer leaves first. Leaves turn white under severe Fe stress.

Fe deficiency in strawberry. Interveinal chlorosis of newer leaves.

Zn deficiency in corn. Newer leaves exhibit bleached white or pale yellow discoloration in area between leaf edge and midrib.

Zn deficiency in corn. Severe stunting caused by shortening of internodes. Normal plant is on the right.

Mn deficiency in corn. Pale green to yellow discoloration between veins of newer leaves. Can be confused with Fe deficiency.

Mn deficiency in soybean. Pale green interveinal chlorosis of newer leaves.

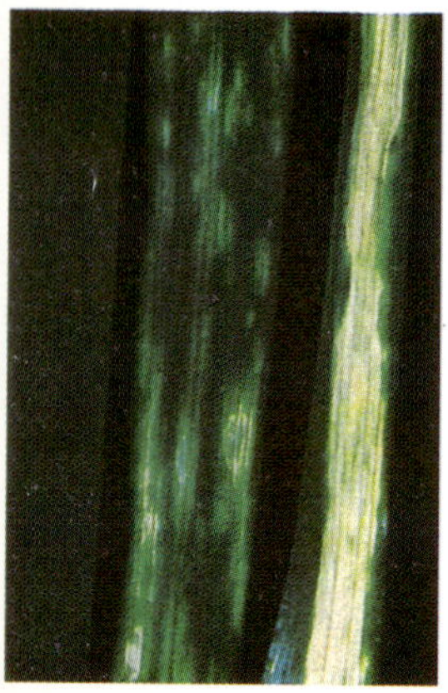

Cu deficiency of wheat. Chlorosis and necrosis of newer leaves. Can be mistaken for leaf diseases.

B deficiency of alfalfa. Stunted plants with chlorosis of newer leaves.

Cu deficiency of corn. Pale yellow to white discoloration of newer leaves that progresses to necrosis of leaf tips and edges.

Mo deficiency of cauliflower. Newer leaves exhibit wilting and necrosis or "die-back" along edges.

Cl deficiency in wheat. Chlorosis and necrosis on leaf edges and tips of older leaves. Can be mistaken for leaf diseases.